Bulgaria

Paul Greenway

LONELY PLANET PUBLICATIONS
Melbourne • Oakland • London • Paris

BULGARIA

VIDIN
Clamber around Bulgaria's best-preserved medieval stone fortress alongside the Danube River

KOPRIVSHTITSA
Soak up the atmosphere and history in this quaint, traditional village

SOFIA
Wander around the numerous museums, art galleries, churches and parks in the bustling capital

RILA MONASTERY
Visit the largest and most revered monastery in Bulgaria, and hike around the nearby mountains

PLOVDIV
Admire the Roman ruins, Turkish mosques and Bulgarian churches in the old town of Bulgaria's second-largest city

ROMANIA

YUGOSLAVIA

MACEDONIA

GREECE

Vidin
Calafat
Lom
Kozlodu
Gara Oreshets
Broussartsi
Belogradchik
Prevala
Chiprovtsi
Kopilovtsi
Montana
Byala Slatina
Borovan
Cherven Bryag
Berkovitsa
Zgorigrad
Vratsa
Roman
Mezdra
Dragoman
Svoge
Botevgrad
Slivnitsa
Novi Iskăr
Breznik
SOFIA
Pirdop
Koprivshtitsa
Anton
Zemen
Pernik
Mt Vitosha (2280m)
Lake Iskăr
Ihtiman
Panagyurishte
Sapareva Banya
Samokov
Kostenets
Kyustendil
Dupnitsa
Govedartsi
Borovets
Septemvri
Pazardzhik
Malovitsa
Rila Mountains
Mt Musala (2925m)
Rila
Velingrad
Peshtera
Plovdiv
Blagoevgrad
Avramovo
Rakitovo
Hrabrino
Asenovgrad
Razlog
Bansko
Batak
Dobrinishte
Pirin Mountains
Mt Vihren (2915m)
Kovachevitsa
Marchevo
Dospat
Boino
Devin
Chepelare
Pamporovo
Sandanski
Melnik
Gotse Delchev
Smolyan
Ardino
Petrovo
Roudozem
Madan
Petrich
Kozlodu
Knezha
Pleven
Levski
Pavlikeni
Lovech
Sevlievo
Troyan
Oreshak
Gabrovo
Chiflik
Apriltsi
Karlovo
Mt Botev (2376m)
Shipka
Kazanlăk
Mt Bogdan (1603m)
Hisarya (Hisar)
Brezovo
Chitpan
Momchilgrad
Kărdzhali
Cherkovitsa
Goulyantsi
Zimnich
Svishtov
Yablanitsa
Teteven
Loukovit
Rodopi Mountains
Sredna Gora
Stara Planina

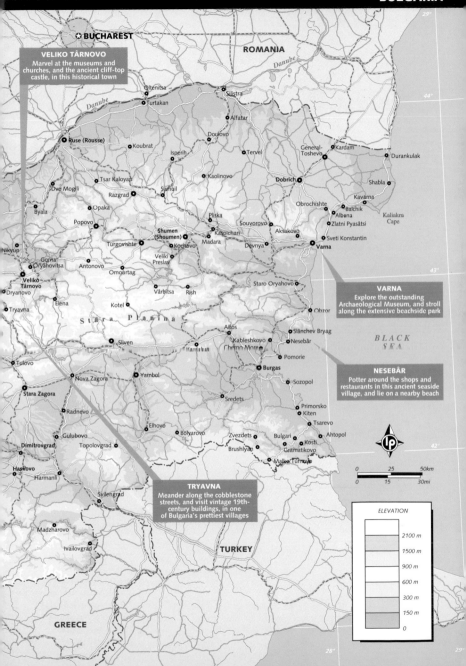

BULGARIA

BUCHAREST

ROMANIA

Danube

VELIKO TÁRNOVO
Marvel at the museums and
churches, and the ancient cliff-top
castle, in this historical town

Oltenitsa

Silistra

Turtakan

Danube

Alfatar

Ruse (Rousse)

Koubrat

Doulovo

Isperih

Tervel

General-
Toshevo

Kardam

Durankulak

Tsar Kaloyan

Kaolinovo

Dobrich

Shabla

Dve Mogili

Razgrad

Samuil

Obrochishte

Kavarna

Byala

Opaka

Pliska

Balchik

Albena

Kaliakra
Cape

Popovo

Shumen
(Shoumen)

Kaspichan

Souvorovo

Aksakovo

Zlatni Pyasâtsi

Turgovishte

Kochovo

Madara

Devnya

Sveti Konstantin

Nikyup

Veliki
Preslav

Varna

Gorna
Oryáhovitsa

Antonovo

Omourtag

Veliko
Tárnovo

Vârbitsa

Rish

Staro Oryahovo

Dryanovo

VARNA
Explore the outstanding
Archaeological Museum, and stroll
along the extensive beachside park

Elena

Kotel

Obzor

Tryavna

Stara   Planina

Altos

Slânchev Bryag

Sliven

Kableshkovo
Cherno More

Nesebâr

B L A C K
S E A

Tulovo

Kamchak

Pomorie

NESEBÂR
Potter around the shops and
restaurants in this ancient seaside
village, and lie on a nearby beach

Nova Zagora

Yambol

Burgas

Stara Zagora

Radnevo

Sozopol

Sredets

Gulubovo

Elhovo

Bolyarovo

Primorsko
Kiten

Dimitrovgrad

Topolovgrad

Zvezdets

Bulgari

Tsarevo

Ahtopol

Haskovo

Harmanli

Brushlyan

Kosti
Gramatikovo

Svilengrad

Malko Târnovo

TRYAVNA
Meander along the cobblestone
streets, and visit vintage 19th-
century buildings, in one
of Bulgaria's prettiest villages

Madzharovo

Ivailovgrad

TURKEY

GREECE

ELEVATION

2100 m

1500 m

900 m

600 m

300 m

150 m

0

0   25   50km
0   15   30mi

Bulgaria
1st edition – June 2002

Published by
Lonely Planet Publications Pty Ltd ABN 36 005 607 983
90 Maribyrnong St, Footscray, Victoria 3011, Australia

Lonely Planet offices
Australia Locked Bag 1, Footscray, Victoria 3011
USA 150 Linden St, Oakland, CA 94607
UK 10a Spring Place, London NW5 3BH
France 1 rue du Dahomey, 75011 Paris

Photographs
Many of the images in this guide are available for licensing from
Lonely Planet Images.
W www.lonelyplanetimages.com

Front cover photograph
Religious artwork in Bachkovo Monastery, Southern Bulgaria
(Paul Almasy, CORBIS)

ISBN 1 86450 148 0

Printed through Colorcraft Ltd, Hong Kong
Printed in China

Contents – Text

2 Contents – Text

Contents – Maps

BULGARIA REGIONAL MAP INDEX

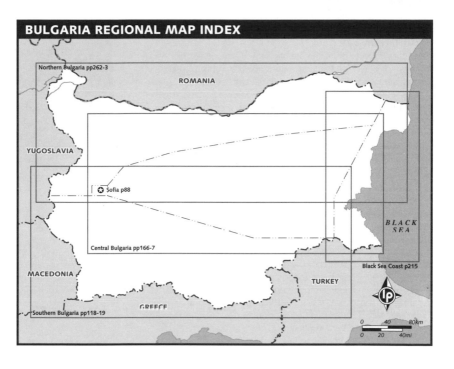

Northern Bulgaria pp262-3

ROMANIA

YUGOSLAVIA

Sofia p88

Central Bulgaria pp166-7

MACEDONIA

BLACK SEA

Black Sea Coast p215

TURKEY

GREECE

Southern Bulgaria pp118-19

0   40   80km
0   20   40mi

The Author

Paul Greenway

Gratefully plucked from the blandness and security of the Australian Public Service, Paul has now worked on about 20 Lonely Planet titles, including *Jordan* and *Botswana*, as well as various guides for India, Indonesia, Africa and the Middle East. During the rare times that he's not travelling – or writing, reading and dreaming about it – Paul relaxes to (and pretends he can play) heavy rock, eats and breathes Australian Rules Football, and will go to any lengths to avoid settling down.

FROM THE AUTHOR

I would like to thank several people who helped me along the way: Daniela Andreeva from the tourist office in Veliko Târnovo; Ivo Marinov, director of the National & International Tourism Policy Dept in Sofia; Petia Koleva-Tzakova from the National Information & Advertising Center in Sofia; Julian Perry; and the gals at *The Sofia Echo*. A special thank you to Kiril, Lili and the gang at Odysseia-In. Thanks also to Delyan Manchev.

Thanks to Stephene Lambert, Yvette Ivanova, Mark Faulkner, Adam Malis & Melissa Swiss for putting up with me one drunken night in Veliko Târnovo; and to my drinking partners in Plovdiv, Mark Johnson and Vera Kurilova.

At Lonely Planet, thanks to Brigitte Ellemor for sending me to Bulgaria, and to all the long-suffering and unsung editors, cartographers and designers who had to battle with my manuscript and maps. I am grateful for all the hard work Christo Stoyanoff put in regarding the Cyrillic. And finally, thanks to all the readers who have written and emailed Lonely Planet with ideas, comments and criticisms.

This Book

This eagerly awaited 1st edition of LP's Bulgaria was written by Paul Greenway.

From the Publisher

Production of this edition of Bulgaria was coordinated by Nina Rousseau (editorial) and Sally Morgan (mapping and design). William Gourlay, Elizabeth Swan, Helen Yeates and Leonie Mugavin assisted with editing and proofing; Liz Filleul and Susie Ashworth were excellent mentors and gave superb editorial support; Darren O'Connell helped with indexing. Amanda Sierp, Csanád Csutoros, Gus Balbontin, Huw Fowles, Leanne Peake and Ray Thomson assisted with mapping; Mark Germanchis provided layout support; Mark Griffiths gave excellent guidance and design support; Celia Wood assisted with map checks; and Rachel Imeson and Kieran Grogan completed the final checks. Thanks to Quentin Frayne and Emma Koch for preparing the language chapter and Dr Angel Pachev for his expertise. Lonely Planet Images provided the wonderful images. Special thanks to Paul Greenway for his enthusiasm and hard work on this project!

Foreword

ABOUT LONELY PLANET GUIDEBOOKS

The story begins with a classic travel adventure: Tony and Maureen Wheeler's 1972 journey across Europe and Asia to Australia. There was no useful information about the overland trail then, so Tony and Maureen published the first Lonely Planet guidebook to meet a growing need.

From a kitchen table, Lonely Planet has grown to become the largest independent travel publisher in the world, with offices in Melbourne (Australia), Oakland (USA), London (UK) and Paris (France).

Today Lonely Planet guidebooks cover the globe. There is an ever-growing list of books and information in a variety of media. Some things haven't changed. The main aim is still to make it possible for adventurous travellers to get out there – to explore and better understand the world.

At Lonely Planet we believe travellers can make a positive contribution to the countries they visit – if they respect their host communities and spend their money wisely. Since 1986 a percentage of the income from each book has been donated to aid projects and human rights campaigns, and, more recently, to wildlife conservation.

> Although inclusion in a guidebook usually implies a recommendation we cannot list every good place. Exclusion does not necessarily imply criticism. In fact there are a number of reasons why we might exclude a place – sometimes it is simply inappropriate to encourage an influx of travellers.

UPDATES & READER FEEDBACK

Things change – prices go up, schedules change, good places go bad and bad places go bankrupt. Nothing stays the same. So, if you find things better or worse, recently opened or long-since closed, please tell us and help make the next edition even more accurate and useful.

Lonely Planet thoroughly updates each guidebook as often as possible – usually every two years, although for some destinations the gap can be longer. Between editions, up-to-date information is available in our free, quarterly *Planet Talk* newsletter and monthly email bulletin *Comet*. The *Upgrades* section of our website (W www.lonelyplanet.com) is also regularly updated by Lonely Planet authors, and the site's *Scoop* section covers news and current affairs relevant to travellers. Lastly, the *Thorn Tree* bulletin board and *Postcards* section carry unverified, but fascinating, reports from travellers.

Tell us about it! We genuinely value your feedback. A well-travelled team at Lonely Planet reads and acknowledges every email and letter we receive and ensures that every morsel of information finds its way to the relevant authors, editors and cartographers.

Everyone who writes to us will find their name listed in the next edition of the appropriate guidebook, and will receive the latest issue of *Comet* or *Planet Talk*. The very best contributions will be rewarded with a free guidebook.

We may edit, reproduce and incorporate your comments in Lonely Planet products such as guidebooks, websites and digital products, so let us know if you don't want your comments reproduced or your name acknowledged.

How to contact Lonely Planet:
Online: e talk2us@lonelyplanet.com.au, W www.lonelyplanet.com
Australia: Locked Bag 1, Footscray, Victoria 3011
UK: 10a Spring Place, London NW5 3BH
USA: 150 Linden St, Oakland, CA 94607

Introduction

At the crossroads of Europe, cresting the Balkan Peninsula and facing the Black Sea, Bulgaria has a long and colourful history. Nomads and merchants, conquerors and settlers have left their footprints in Bulgaria's soil, but sadly it has often been forgotten or ignored by travellers. For over 40 years as a member of the Soviet bloc, Bulgaria remained little-known and difficult to visit. But in 1990, it put paid to its communist past and turned its gaze towards Western Europe.

In the ensuing years, Bulgaria has enthusiastically embraced capitalism and democracy and opened its arms to tourists. It is a country in transition, with countless citizens flocking to the cities. Yet in the countryside rural life goes on at an unhurried pace reminiscent of the 1950s. Crime and corruption have not permeated Bulgaria (as they have in some former Eastern-bloc countries), nor have increasing numbers of tourists meant that cities have become over commercialised. And the strife that has racked other Balkan countries has never affected Bulgaria – it is a safe and hassle-free destination.

The Bulgarian people have also welcomed new freedoms and opportunities, though as in many other former communist states, voters are notoriously unforgiving of political leaders who don't find a quick solution to their post-communist economic woes.

Most tourists come on an all-inclusive package holiday, and stay at one of the developed Black Sea beach resorts such as Albena, the self-proclaimed 'sports capital' of Bulgaria. It is possible to escape the tourist hordes, however, and find a secluded piece of sandy beach even during the peak season in July and August. And budget travellers can stay in small villages or larger cities along the coast and day trip to the beach resorts.

From about mid-December to mid-April, Bulgaria's four major ski resorts usually offer plenty of snow. While facilities may not be world-class, costs are substantially lower than almost anywhere else in Europe.

The scenery is superb along any of the 37,000 kilometres of marked hiking trails across pristine national parks and reserves. There's even great hiking (and skiing in winter) only a 30-minute bus ride from the centre of the capital, Sofia. Other summer activities include mountain biking, horse riding and caving. If the physical activity gets too much, visit one of the plethora of health centres, where mineral-spring pools and mud baths are said to cure rheumatism and relieve stress.

Sofia is a cosmopolitan city with dozens of churches, museums and art galleries to explore. The charming old towns of Plovdiv and Veliko Târnovo just ooze historical ambience. Other picturesque villages, like Koprivshtitsa, Tryavna and Shiroka Lûka, are prime examples of the glorious architectural style typical of the Bulgarian national revival period of the 18th and 19th centuries. Many houses and public buildings throughout the country have been lovingly restored as part of the Beautiful Bulgaria Project.

Bulgarians love festivals, whether it's traditional fire-dancing, family weddings or religious occasions at local churches and regional monasteries. Many special events involve making bread, wearing traditional costumes and drinking copious amounts of palatable, local wine. These days, many festivals cater mainly to tourists and take place between June and September.

Even if you're not religious, you are likely to be impressed by any of the country's 160 monasteries, often large, shrouded in mist and in remote mountains. History enthusiasts are bound to be excited by the remnants of numerous occupying empires such as Roman amphitheatres, Thracian tombs and Turkish fortresses. Culture buffs will enjoy local opera, ballet and theatre, and some of the 200 or more museums and art galleries throughout the country. To relax, do what every Bulgarian seems to do in summer: sit in a cafe, chat, drink, smoke and watch the world go by.

Most travellers visit Bulgaria as part of a jaunt around Eastern Europe and/or the Balkans, but there's enough to justify a visit of at least one month – coincidentally, this is the length of the free visa given to most visitors at borders and airports.

Bulgarians are justifiably proud of their country, and eager to show it off to visitors. Almost everyone in the tourist industry speaks English, French or German. However, it's worth spending an hour or two brushing up on a few Bulgarian words and phrases and, in particular, learning the Cyrillic alphabet.

Bulgaria is easy enough to get around independently, whether by public transport or rented car, but organised tours are also available. And while some of the hotels, roads and buses, for example, may not be up to the standards expected in Western and northern Europe, Bulgaria is excellent value – you could end up spending about 75% less than you would in, say, France, Germany or Switzerland. Foreigners tend to be charged at least twice as much as Bulgarians to stay in hotels and visit tourist attractions but the cost of food, drink and public transport is remarkably cheap. There are few hostels and camp sites worth recommending but one enjoyable way to cut costs and meet a Bulgarian family is to stay in a room at a private home. Hikers can also stay in mountain huts and some monasteries have accommodation in converted monastic 'cells'.

All in all, Bulgaria boasts plenty of things to see and do, from ancient monasteries to world-class beaches. It's a cheap, safe destination, waiting to be discovered. So, hurry up and visit Bulgaria, undoubtedly one of Europe's best-kept secrets.

Farewell to Yugoslavia

In March 2002 representatives of Yugoslavia and its constituent republics Serbia and Montenegro agreed to a new structure and name for the nation. The move, which was designed to counter a push for independence by Montenegro, saw the renaming of the country as Serbia and Montenegro. According to the agreement, a referendum for Montenegrin independence was postponed for three years. At the time of writing Serbia and Montenegro was set to adopt new constitutions that would avoid secession yet give both Serbia and Montenegro more autonomy. For this book the old name of Yugoslavia has been retained.

Facts about Bulgaria

HISTORY

Bulgaria has a fascinating but often bloody history of invasion, occupation and subjugation, punctuated by four comparatively short periods of political and economic independence and stability.

Prehistory

Excavations of caves near Pleven in the Danubian plains in northern Bulgaria, and around Nova Zagora in central Bulgaria, indicate human settlements during the Late (or Second) Palaeolithic Period around 40,000 BC. Archaeologists are now convinced that the earliest permanent settlers, arriving around 6000 BC, were Neolithic people who lived in caves, such as Yagodina cave in the southern Rodopi Mountains. Remains from Tsarevets Hill in Veliko Târnovo, and around Stara Zagora, indicate that more advanced Neolithic tribes lived in both areas between about 5500 BC and 4500 BC in tiny mud homes (examples of which can be seen in a museum in Stara Zagora).

Thracians

An amalgam of tribes, which came to be known as the Thracians, settled around most of modern-day Bulgaria, and later expanded into Anatolia and Greece during the Middle Bronze Age about 2000 BC. In the early stages, the Thracians built settlements in and around caves (for shelter and security) and near springs (for water). Later, they built larger permanent villages around rudimentary fortresses, established on elevated sites for defensive purposes.

Although briefly subjugated by the Macedonians, and engaged in a war with the Greeks, the Thracians were mostly peaceful and stayed intact until the Roman invasion. The Thracians were later absorbed by the Slavs, Macedonians and Greeks. According to legend, the illustrious Orpheus (renowned singer, and writer of hymns) and Spartacus (who led a slave revolt against the Romans) were Thracians born in modern-day Bulgaria.

Remains of Thracian settlements can be found along the Black Sea coast near Burgas and at the town of Mesembria (Nesebâr), which the Thracians settled in about 3000 BC. Other remnants can be found on Nebet Tepe in Plovdiv, where they built the town of Eumolpias in about 5000 BC. Because of the attractive climate and fertile land, the Thracians also built towns in and around modern-day Stara Zagora, Sandanski, Melnik, Bansko, Smolyan, Shumen and Madara. By the 1st millennium BC the Thracians had spread as far north as Cherven, near the Danube River, and as far west as Sofia. One tribe known as the Serdis created Sardonopolis, which was later renamed Serdica, and subsequently became Sofia, the modern-day capital.

The most famous Thracian remains are the tombs dating from about 4000 BC which are displayed in the excellent Archaeological Museum in Varna and the tomb at Kazanlâk built in the 4th century BC. Other Thracian artefacts can be seen in museums in Haskovo, Smolyan, Sofia and Sliven.

The Thracians became relatively advanced in arts, culture and education and wealthy from trading jewellery and metal products, especially copper and gold. Many were prosperous farmers and controlled large parts of the Balkan peninsula. In general, they worshipped several gods, and many tribes practised promiscuity, wore tattoos and inhaled intoxicants. Most neighbouring empires tended to regard these activities as taboo.

The Thracians significantly influenced the religion, architecture and culture of the subsequent Roman and Greek rulers. Some geographical names used today, such as 'rila' (for Rila Monastery) and 'yantra' (the name of the river through Veliko Târnovo) probably originate from Thracian words.

Greeks

From the 7th century BC, seafaring Greeks made their way up the Black Sea coast of

Chronology

before 6000 BC	area permanently settled by Neolithic peoples
6000–2000 BC	settlement by the Thracians
7th century BC	the Greeks inhabit parts of the Black Sea coast
345–46 BC	the Macedonians conquer the Thracians
72 BC	the Romans invade
late 5th century AD	the Slavs settle in the region
late 7th century	the Bulgars arrive
681	establishment of the First Bulgarian Empire
863	Sts Kiril and Metodii create Cyrillic alphabet
865	Christianity becomes the official religion
1018	end of the First Bulgarian Empire after Byzantines invade
1185	establishment of the Second Bulgarian Empire
1396	end of the Second Bulgarian Empire after Ottomans invade
1762	start of the Bulgarian national revival period
1876	April Uprising
1877–78	Russian-Turkish War
3 March 1878	Treaty of San Stefano signed
13 July 1878	Treaty of Berlin signed
16 April 1879	first Bulgarian National Assembly convened
26 June 1879	Alexander Battenberg elected head of state
6 September 1885	Treaty of Berlin reversed, and Bulgaria is reunified
22 September 1908	King Ferdinand declares independence from Turkey
1912–13	the Balkan Wars
14 October 1915	Bulgaria joins Central Powers in WWI
1941	Bulgaria joins the Axis powers in WWII
15 September 1946	The People's Republic of Bulgaria proclaimed by the communists
1954	Todor Zhivkov elected leader of the Bulgarian Communist Party
1962	Zhivkov elected prime minister
10 November 1989	Zhivkov resigns
June 1990	first parliamentary elections won by the Bulgarian Socialist Party
January 1992	first presidential elections
June 2001	former king, Simeon II, elected prime minister
November 2001	leader of Bulgarian Socialist Party elected president

Bulgaria and created settlements they called Apollonia (modern-day Sozopol), Odessos (Varna), Kruni (Balchik) and Pirgos (Burgas). They established large ports for exporting wheat, fish and salt and traded Greek pottery for Thracian metalwork and jewellery.

Despite the proximity to their homeland, the Greeks avoided most of southern and central Bulgaria because the determined Thracians had settled there in large numbers. Only a few towns away from the Black Sea show any evidence of Greek settlement.

These include Pataunia (Kyustendil), southwest of Sofia, and Silistra on the Danube in northern Bulgaria.

Although the Greeks failed to conquer the whole region, they had a profound influence on religion, arts and culture throughout the Balkans for over 900 years. The Greek language was used extensively by non-Greeks for business, administration and education. The Bulgarian language still has many words of Greek origin, and the patriarch of the Bulgarian Orthodox Church was based in Athens for centuries.

Macedonians

By 345–346 BC, the Macedonians, under the leadership of Philip II, had conquered all of Bulgaria and subjugated the Thracians. However their reign lasted only about 50 years. During that short period the Macedonians made their capital at Philipoupolis (Plovdiv), which Philip graciously named after himself, and briefly occupied Odessos (Varna) and modern-day Sofia. But they had little impact on the country and interfered little with the Greeks along the coast.

Romans

During the 1st century BC the Romans started to envy the prosperous Greeks along the Black Sea coast. From about 72 BC the Romans successfully invaded and occupied major Greek ports, such as Mesembria (Nesebâr). They set up a base at Odessos (Varna) where the largest Roman ruins in Bulgaria, and the third-biggest in Europe, can still be seen.

The Romans took over 100 years to control the Thracians and by AD 46 had conquered the entire Balkan peninsula. To shore up vital defensive lines, the Romans built military strongholds and fortified major Thracian and Greek towns along the Danube at Ruse and Bononia (Vidin) and at Debeltus (Burgas) along the Black Sea coast. Although they burned and looted the major Greek settlement of Apollonia, the Romans rebuilt it to become a vital port within the Roman empire.

The capital of the Roman region of Bulgaria (Inner Dacia) became Ulpia Serdica (Sofia). Other towns established by the Romans, or built on existing Thracian, Greek and Macedonian settlements, include Sevtopolis (Kazanlâk), Ulpia Augusta Trayana (Stara Zagora), Nikopolis-ad-Istrum (north of Veliko Târnovo) and Trimontium (Plovdiv), where a magnificent amphitheatre was built, the remains of which still stand. Each Roman city boasted sophisticated cultural buildings, sewerage systems, aqueducts and roads.

Remnants of Roman settlements can be admired in many places, even as far west as Belogradchik. In central Bulgaria, the Romans were the first to build a proper fortress on top of Tsarevets Hill in Veliko Târnovo. They built extensive walls, which partially still stand, at Hisarya to protect prized sources of mineral water.

Through internal strife in Rome, the Roman empire started to crumble about 300 years after it invaded Bulgaria. The Romans' demise in the Balkans was exacerbated by violent but ultimately short-lived invasions by the Goths (238–48), Vandals (378) and Huns (441–47). Collectively known as barbarians, these tribes did nothing but ransack whatever they didn't raze.

The Byzantines

In 330, the city of Byzantium was renamed Constantinople (now called Istanbul) and became capital of the Eastern Roman Empire. By 395, the Byzantines (as they're informally known) had broken away from Rome and had started to conquer parts of the Black Sea coast as far as modern-day Nesebâr. The Byzantines fought the Bulgars and Slavs many times over several centuries in Bulgaria, and ruled most of the country between 1018 (the end of the First Bulgarian Empire) and 1185 (the start of the Second Bulgarian Empire).

In 1453, the Byzantine Empire finally collapsed when the Ottoman Turks conquered Constantinople. In Bulgaria, Byzantine heritage is most prevalent in Veliko Târnovo, where the Byzantine fortress still stands on Tsarevets Hill, and where a Bulgar rebellion against the Byzantines was launched in 1185.

Slavs

Slavic tribes arrived in the late 5th century AD from an area between the Baltic Sea and the Carpathian Mountains (ie, around modern-day Poland and Ukraine). The Slavs were peaceful farmers who established a feudal system of communal land ownership. They later merged with the Bulgars and remaining Thracians and became renowned potters, weavers and metalworkers. They worshipped many gods including Perun, the God of Thunder, after whom the Pirin Mountains are named.

Surprisingly, they didn't have a regular army but all Slavs were obliged to fight during times of war. The number of Slavs sent to war was often immense and usually dissuaded other tribes from invading. Little more is known because they left few reminders: they didn't build extensive military strongholds or large urban settlements for archaeologists to explore and they happily integrated with other tribes.

Bulgars

From the late 5th century the Bulgars, also known as the 'Proto-Bulgarians', migrated from their homelands in Central Asia, arriving in the Balkans in the 7th century. This fierce Turkic tribe settled throughout the region, subjugating and integrating with the Slavs and the last few Thracians.

The Bulgar leader, Khan (Tsar) Asparukh, was responsible for establishing what became known as the First Bulgarian Empire (681–1018). He ruled from 681 to 700 and created a capital at Pliska, near modern-day Shumen. The empire expanded south and west under Khan Tervel, who ruled from 701 to 718 and was revered for repelling an Arab advance. Khan Krum 'The Dreadful' (803–814) later beseiged Constantinople because the Byzantines burnt down Pliska, and the more mild-mannered Khan Omurtag (831–852) further extended the empire. The Bulgars were eventually assimilated by the more numerous Slavs and adopted their language and way of life.

In 865, Tsar Boris I (852–889) attempted to unify the fledgling Bulgar-Slav empire by converting it to Christianity. At about this time, an independent church was established and a Slavonic alphabet devised by two monks, Kiril and Metodii, known in English as Cyril and Methodius (see Religion later in this chapter). The empire reached its zenith under Tsar Simeon (893–927), who moved the capital to Veliki Preslav and ushered in a cultural golden age. The borders of the Bulgarian empire, which stretched from the Adriatic Sea to the Aegean Sea and to the Dneiper River (north-east of Bulgaria) was the largest and most powerful in Europe at that time.

However, Simeon's attempts to gain the Byzantine crown for himself weakened the country, as did internal conflicts after his death. Veliki Preslav was overrun by the Byzantines, and the capital moved to Ohrid (in modern-day Macedonia) under Tsar Samuel (997–1014). At the Battle of Belasitsa in 1014, the Byzantines defeated the Bulgars and, in brutal retaliation, apparently had the eyes of 15,000 Bulgarian soldiers removed. In 1018, Bulgaria officially became part of the Byzantine empire.

In 1185 two aristocratic brothers, Asen and Petâr, led a general uprising against the Byzantines and the Second Bulgarian Empire (1185–1396) was founded, with Veliko Târnovo as the capital. With skilful diplomacy rather than military force, Asen's son, Tsar Ivan Asen II (1218–1241), became the most powerful ruler in south-eastern Europe and established Veliko Târnovo as an influential literary and arts centre. His title, 'King of Bulgarians and Greeks', reflects the extent of his domain, which included newly gained parts of modern-day Yugoslavia and Hungary. His most famous military victory was the crushing defeat of the Byzantines under Comnenus at the Battle of Klokotnitsa in 1230. After the death of Tsar Ivan Asen II, invasions by the Tatars and Arabs sapped the empire's strength, but it was internal fighting among Bulgarian leaders that fatally weakened it.

Ottomans

The Ottoman Turks started to invade the northern Balkan peninsula in 1362. Within the next 30 years they had conquered all of Bulgaria, which officially become part of the Ottoman empire in 1396. Turkish rule resulted in economic growth, but this came at a price: the apparatus of the Bulgarian state was dismantled and many churches and monasteries were destroyed or closed. In one year alone (1657), the Turks burned down 218 churches and 33 monasteries.

Turkish overlords settled in urban areas, forcing Bulgarians to flee into the mountains and rural regions. However, Bulgarian national and cultural identity managed to survive in isolated monasteries (eg, Rila

Monastery) that were allowed to remain open, or were never found or controlled by the Turks. Taxes owed to the Sultan by the Christian Bulgarians were oppressive, but Pomaks (Slavs converted to Islam) were exempt, as were the wealthy citizens of Arbanasi, near Veliko Târnovo.

Bulgarian National Revival Period

The era known as the Bulgarian national revival period was prompted by the work of a monk, Paisii Hilendarski, who wrote the first complete history of the Slav-Bulgarian people in 1762. He travelled across Bulgaria reading the history to illiterate people and igniting a long-forgotten national identity. During the next few decades the Ottoman empire declined, while knowledge about Bulgaria's religious and cultural heritage had slowly moved away from the remote monasteries and villages and into larger Bulgarian communities.

An influential mercantile class of Bulgarians soon emerged, with a wealth and nationalist sentiment shaped by increasing trade in cotton, wine, metals and woodcarvings with Western Europe. These merchants built grand private homes and public buildings, often designed in a unique form (see the Architecture section later in this chapter). They were decorated by woodcarvers from Tryavna and painters from Samokov, who had developed a particular Bulgarian style.

Also at this time, Bulgarian art, music and literature flourished and schools with instruction in the Bulgarian language were opened. *Chitalishtes* (reading rooms) in nearly every town and village provided a communal forum for cultural and social activities – and for political discussions. In 1870, official Turkish recognition of an autonomous Bulgarian Orthodox Church was a crucial step towards independence.

End of Ottoman Rule

Rebel leaders such as Georgi Rakovski, Hristo Botev and Vasil Levski had been preparing a revolution against the Turks for years before the rebellion, known as the 1876 April Uprising, prematurely started at Koprivshtitsa. (See the boxed text 'Vasil Levski' in the Central Bulgaria chapter.)

The Turks suppressed the uprising with unprecedented brutality: an estimated 30,000 Bulgarians were massacred and 58 villages were destroyed. The largest massacre occurred in the town of Batak (see the boxed text 'Massacre at Batak' in the Southern Bulgaria chapter). According to one story, Pazardzhik (near Plovdiv) was saved by a daring clerk who moved one comma in an official order, turning 'burn the town, not spare it' into 'burn the town not, spare it.'

These atrocities caused outrage in Western Europe and led Russia to declare war on the Ottomans in 1877 after the Constantinople Conference failed to resolve anything. Decisive battles were fought at Pleven and Shipka Pass and about 200,000 people, mostly Russian soldiers, were killed throughout Bulgaria during the year-long Russian-Turkish War. As the Russian army, and its Bulgarian volunteers, crushed the Turks and advanced to within 50km of Istanbul, the Ottomans accepted defeat. It ceded 60% of the Balkan peninsula to Bulgaria in the Treaty of San Stefano signed on 3 March 1878.

However, fearing the creation of a powerful Russian ally in the Balkans, the powers of Western Europe reversed these gains at the Treaty of Berlin signed 13 July 1878. They decided that the area between the Stara Planina ranges and the Danube, plus Sofia, would become the independent principality of Bulgaria. The Thracian Plain and Rodopi Mountains to the south would become Eastern Rumelia and, inexplicably, were placed under Ottoman control. The Aegean Thracian plain and Macedonia were returned outright to Turkey. The legacy of the Treaty of Berlin carved up the region irrespective of ethnicity and left every Balkan nation feeling cheated and angry. These redefined borders have haunted the peninsula ever since: between 1878 and WWII, the Balkan countries, including Bulgaria, fought six wars over border issues.

On 16 April 1879, the first Bulgarian National Assembly was convened at Veliko Târnovo in order to adopt a constitution and on 26 June of that year, Alexander Battenberg, a German prince, was elected head of state. On 6 September 1885, the principality of Bulgaria and Eastern Rumelia were reunified after a bloodless coup. This contravention of the Treaty of Berlin greatly angered the Western European powers and Turkish troops advanced to the southern border of the reunified Bulgaria.

However, to the surprise of everyone, Serbia declared war on Bulgaria. Heroic Bulgarian border guards defied the odds and repelled advancing Serbian troops while the Bulgarian army hurriedly moved from the Turkish border to the western front. Eventually, the Bulgarians defeated the Serbs and advanced deep within Serbian territory. The powers of Western Europe intervened, calling a halt to the war and recognising the reunified Bulgaria.

The War Years

Battenberg later abdicated and was replaced by Prince (later King) Ferdinand of the Saxe-Coburg family. Around this time the prime minister, Stefan Stambolov, accelerated the country's economic development and two Bulgarian political parties were founded that would wield enormous influence in the years ahead. These were the Social Democrats, forerunner to the communists, and the Agrarian Union, which represented the peasantry.

King Ferdinand I declared Bulgaria's complete independence from Ottoman control on 22 September 1908. But only four years later, the First Balkan War broke out when Bulgaria, Greece and Serbia declared war on Turkey. Although these states succeeded in largely pushing the Turks out of the Balkans, squabbling among the victors, especially over claims to Macedonia, led to the Second Balkan War (1913), from which Bulgaria emerged a loser.

Bulgaria eventually sided with the Central Powers and entered WWI on 14 October 1915. Facing widespread opposition to his pro-German policies, Ferdinand abdicated three years later in favour of his son, Boris III (father of the current Bulgarian prime minister). The interwar period was marked by political and social unrest, much

The Macedonian Question

The Macedonian region has long been occupied by Romans, Greeks, Bulgarians, Turks and Serbs. During the last 130 years the region has been the primary cause of several wars between Balkan countries, several of whom (including Bulgaria) claim some of Macedonian territory as their own.

The Internal Macedonian Revolutionary Organisation (IMRO), regarded as the world's first terrorist group, was formed in 1893 to fight against occupation by the Turks, and later the Serbs. Within Bulgaria, the modern-day IMRO uses democratic means to further its aim of a greater, independent Macedonia and to support the rights of Macedonians in Bulgaria. Many IMRO leaders, such as Gotse Delchev and Yane Sandanski, are revered in south-western Bulgaria (near Macedonia) and even have towns named after them.

In 1992, most of the region became part of the independent Former Yugoslav Republic of Macedonia, while parts of the region still remain in Yugoslavia, Greece and Bulgaria. (For ease of reference, we have referred to the region and country as Macedonia.)

of it related to what was popularly referred to as the 'Macedonian Question' (see the boxed text).

At the beginning of WWII Bulgaria declared its neutrality. However, by 1941 German troops advancing towards Greece were stationed along the Danube on Bulgaria's northern border with Romania. To avoid a war it could not win, the militarily weak Bulgarian government decided to join the Axis. Bulgaria allowed the Nazis into the country and officially declared war on the UK and France, but it refused to accede to demands that it declare war on Russia. Spurred by public opinion, the Bulgarian government also declined to hand over the country's Jewish population of some 50,000 to the Third Reich. On 28 August 1943, Tsar Boris III died mysteriously one week after meeting Hitler. According to one popular theory, the Führer had Boris III poisoned for refusing to hand over the Jews or declare war on Russia.

During the winter of 1943–44, Allied air raids inflicted heavy damage on Sofia and other major towns in central Bulgaria. Anti-war activity increased, including communist guerrilla actions against the fascist Bulgarian government. A hastily formed coalition government sought a separate peace with the Allies, but to no avail. Then, Russia declared war and invaded Bulgaria. On 9 September 1944 the Fatherland Front, a resistance group coalition that included communists, assumed power. Even before WWII had ended, 'people's courts' were set up around the country at which thousands of members of the wartime 'monarch-fascist' government were sent to prison or executed.

The Rise of Communism

The Fatherland Front swept the November 1945 elections and the communists undermined their coalition partners to gain control of the new National Assembly. Under leader Georgi Dimitrov, a new constitution, created on the Soviet model, proclaimed the People's Republic of Bulgaria on 15 September 1946. The royal family, which included the current prime minister, Simeon II, was forced to flee.

From the late 1940s, industrialisation and the collectivisation of agriculture was imposed. Under Todor Zhivkov, Bulgaria's leader from 1962 to 1989, the country became one of the most prosperous in Eastern Europe. Unlike Dimitrov, Zhivkov was not a cult figure, but a shrewd politician bureaucrat. He juggled government and party leaders among different posts, while managing to keep a balance between the young and old and conservatives and reformists.

Late 20th Century

By 1989, *perestroika* was sending shock waves throughout Eastern Europe and veteran communists became uneasy. On 10 November 1989, an internal Communist Party coup led to the resignation of the ageing Zhivkov, ending his 27-year reign. The Communist Party agreed to relinquish its monopoly on power, and changed its name to the Bulgarian Socialist Party (BSP). In opposition, a coalition of 16 different groups formed the Union of Democratic Forces (UDF). However, the BSP comfortably won the first parliamentary elections in June 1990, so Bulgaria had the dubious honour of being the first country from the former Soviet bloc to elect communists back into power.

But the BSP, hamstrung by ineffective leadership and popular unrest over austerity measures, soon lost favour. Assisted by a disgusted electorate, the UDF managed to eke out a narrow victory in the October 1991 parliamentary elections, but their government collapsed within a year. After a caretaker government of technocrats was similarly unable to deal with the financial disarray, the BSP again captured, in overwhelming fashion, the December 1994 parliamentary elections. Meanwhile, Zhelyu Zhelev of the UDF became the new Bulgarian head of state after the first presidential elections in January 1992.

From 1994 to 1996, the BSP squandered their mandate and led the country into economic chaos. This period was marked by hyperinflation and a sharp drop in living standards, which included the return of bread lines and fuel shortages, while legitimised criminal networks flaunted their new-found wealth. Where hope had burgeoned just a few years before, a culture of desperation took hold.

The election of liberal lawyer Petâr Stoyanov of the UDF as president in November 1996, coupled with the resignation of the unpopular socialist prime minister Zhan Videnov, signalled that the electorate was finally fed up. Nationwide protests and highway blockades eventually forced the discredited BSP to agree to new parliamentary elections.

April 1997 ushered in the seventh change of government in as many years. Ivan Kostov of the United Democratic Forces (UtDF), a coalition which included the UDF, became prime minister and promised to combat corruption and attract foreign investment while adhering to market reforms and strict fiscal policies. But like leaders of all former communist countries, Kostov had

Simeon II

Simeon Borisov Saxe-Coburgotski II became king of Bulgaria at the age of six following the death of his father, Tsar Boris III, in 1943. Three years later, the royal family had to flee Bulgaria after the communists took over. Simeon II lived in Egypt for a while, before moving to Madrid, where he married a Spanish woman and became a successful businessman. Although he did not return to his homeland again until 1996, he remained a popular figure. He is a distant relative of the Queen of England.

to make harsh economic decisions, which pleased the International Monetary Fund (IMF) and European Union (EU), but not the voters.

Bulgaria Today

In June 2001, Bulgaria briefly made headlines across the world when the people voted the National Movement Simeon II (NMSII) party, led by the charismatic and popular former king of Bulgaria, Simeon II, into power during parliamentary elections. What made this result so remarkable was that the party had only formed two months before the election and Simeon II, who did not actually run for a parliamentary seat (but could still become prime minister), had lived most of his life in Spain (see the boxed text 'Simeon II').

The NMSII won exactly half of the parliamentary seats, but did not have a clear majority, so it entered into a coalition with the Turkish Movement for Rights & Freedoms (MRF), the party with the smallest number of elected representatives. Simeon II persuaded some prominent Bulgarian economists to return home in order to, as he promised, turn Bulgaria's fortunes around in '800 days'. He claimed that he was not interested in restoring the monarchy and only accepted the appointment of prime minister grudgingly.

In a stunning reversal five months later, Stoyanov, regarded as one of Bulgaria's most popular politicians, was beaten by Georgi Parvanov in the presidential elections. Parvanov, who had lost two parliamentary elections and one presidential election in the past decade, is leader of the BSP. He stood as the candidate for the new Coalition for Bulgaria, which did not exist three months earlier. Parvanov has stated his support for the economic and political status quo, particularly Bulgaria's hope to join NATO and the EU.

GEOGRAPHY

Bulgaria lies at the crossroads of Europe and Asia in the heart of the Balkan peninsula. An amazing variety of landforms are jammed into its relatively small area of 110,912 sq km, which is a little smaller than Greece, half the size of Victoria (Australia) and about the same extent as Ohio (USA). Bulgaria stretches 520km from the Yugoslavian (Serbian) border to the Black Sea and 330km from Romania to Greece. Although its average elevation is not impressive, about 5% of Bulgaria is over 1600m high and about one-third of its terrain is mountainous.

From the northern border with Romania, a windswept fertile plain gradually slopes south as far as the rounded summits of the Stara Planina mountains, the longest mountain range in the Balkans. The Stara Planina almost stretches from the Yugoslavian border in the west to the Black Sea in the east and, as the geographical backbone of Bulgaria, nearly splits the country into two. The Sredna Gora mountains are separated from the main range by a fault in which lies the Valley of Roses.

Southern Bulgaria is even more mountainous. Mt Musala (2925m) in the Rila Mountains, south of Sofia, is the highest peak between the Alps and Transcaucasia and is almost equalled by Mt Vihren (2914m) in the Pirin Mountains farther south. The Rila Mountains' sharply glaciated massifs, with their bare rocky peaks, steep forested valleys and glacial lakes are the geographical core of the Balkans and a paradise for hikers (and, in parts, skiers). The Rodopi Mountains stretch along the Greek border east of the Rila and Pirin Mountains and spill over into Greece.

The Thracian plain opens onto the Black Sea coast. The 378km-long coast is lined with some of Europe's finest beaches and also features coastal lakes near Burgas, spectacular cliffs near Kaliakra and several huge bays. In addition to the mighty Danube River, which forms much of the border with Romania, the major rivers include the Yantra, which meanders its way through Veliko Târnovo; the Iskâr, which stretches from south of Samokov to the Danube, past Sofia; and the Maritsa, which runs through Plovdiv. Other significant geographical features include about 700 caves, the deepest of which is 415m, and the longest over 15km; and some 1600 sources of mineral water among the mountains and along the Black Sea coast.

CLIMATE

Bulgaria has a temperate climate with cold, damp winters and hot, dry summers. The Rodopi Mountains form a barrier to the moderating Mediterranean influence of the Aegean, while the Danube Plain is open to the extremes of central Europe. Sofia's generally favourable climate is one of its main attributes with average daytime highs of 28°C in July and August and 3°C from December to February. The Black Sea moderates temperatures in the east of the country. Rainfall is highest in the mountains and in winter life throughout Bulgaria is sometimes disrupted by heavy snowfalls.

ECOLOGY & ENVIRONMENT

Like most post-communist countries, the lure of fast cash has outweighed ecologically sustainable development. Logging and animal poaching continue in protected areas and excessive and harmful air and water pollution is infrequently controlled and rarely illegal. Locals often rely on finite fossil fuels, such as coal for heating, and on nuclear power for electricity, and farmers continually (and illegally) burn farmland, which causes many devastating fires each summer.

Tourism Development

Ski resorts are confined to the four major areas of Borovets, Pamporovo, Bansko and

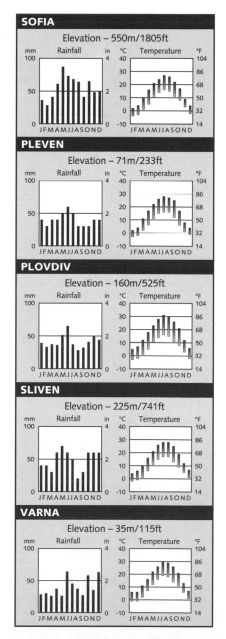

Mt Vitosha. But the incentive of necessary foreign exchange, coupled with a surge in rampant capitalism, has tempted developers to build new ski runs, which by definition disturb precious mountain landscapes. Twenty years ago, construction of new ski runs in the Pirin National Park near Bansko was halted due to international pressure, but it recommenced in 2000. The ski runs, chairlifts and access roads would destroy over 20 hectares of very old conifer trees and create erosion on the mountainside. These changes, by threatening the Park's status as a Unesco World Heritage site, would set a precedent for the development of more ski runs in Pirin National Park and other protected mountain ranges.

Environmental news regarding the Black Sea coast is mixed. On one hand, large German-based tour operators have recently allocated another €23 million to build even more large-scale hotel complexes, no doubt adding further demand on limited freshwater supplies, destroying landscapes and adding to the pollution spewing into the sea. On the other hand, Albena, Zlatni Pyasâtsi (also known as Golden Sands), Nesebâr and Slânchev Bryag (Sunny Beach) continue to receive the prestigious international Blue Flag awards for clean and pollution-free beaches. (See the boxed text 'The Black Sea' in the Black Sea Coast chapter.)

Nuclear Energy
The Kozlodui Nuclear Power Plant (W www .kznpp.org/index-e.htm) near the Danube River, about 200km north of Sofia, was once rated as one of the world's most dangerous nuclear facilities. Since opening in 1974, minor accidents have periodically forced partial shutdowns, leading to power cuts across the country. Massive pressure and financial aid from governments in Western Europe convinced the Bulgarian authorities to close two units of the facility before the end of 2002.

However, because it is a vital source of energy, the Bulgarian government plans to develop and upgrade the rest of the facility and to utilise the remaining units until at least 2010. But the good news is that independent safety checks have confirmed that the plant is now one of the safest in Europe, and it even won an award for 'environmental protection' from the Green Party of Bulgaria.

Pollution
Other than pollution of the Black Sea (see the Black Sea Coast chapter) the main concern is the Danube River, which is often heavily polluted before it even reaches Bulgaria (see the boxed text 'The Danube' in the Northern Bulgaria chapter). In an effort to increase production Bulgarian farmers continue to use pesticides and fertilisers, which often find their way into various rivers and spill into the Danube or Black Sea. Brown coal is used by Bulgaria's iron industry and burned in dirty thermoelectric plants, which causes atmospheric pollution.

Environmental Organisations
Anyone with genuine interest in a specific ecological issue can contact one or more of the following organisations. These groups do not, however, provide tourist information or offer tours. (See Organised Tours in the Getting Around chapter for some companies that offer environmental tours.)

Balkani Wildlife Society (e balkani@bluelink .net) This group hopes to protect the Pirin National Park from being developed as a ski resort (see Tourism Development earlier in this section).

Blue Link (☎/fax 02-217 623, W www.bluelink .net/en) This organisation is involved in many environmental projects throughout Bulgaria.

Bulgarian-Swiss Biodiversity Conservation Programme (BSBCP; ☎/fax 02-980 4131, e bsbcp@inet.bg, W www.bsbcp.inet.bg/ home_en.htm) With support from Swiss NGOs, and the Bulgarian Ministry of the Environment and Waters, the BSBCP aims to maintain and enlarge protected areas and raise public awareness. It's involved in the Burgas Lakes, Kaliakra Nature Reserve, Strandjha Nature Park and Ropotamo Nature Reserve.

Bulgarian Society for the Protection of Birds (BSPB; ☎/fax 02-722 640, e bspb–hq@mb .bia-bg.com) PO Box 50, Sofia 1111. Created in 1988, the BSPB helps to protect birdlife and their habitats and proudly claims to have reintroduced an extinct species, the Cinereous Vulture. It's part of BirdLife International.

Green Balkans (☎ 032-264 516 in Plovdiv, ☎ 056-629 039 in Burgas, ℮ greenbal@ mbox.digsys .bg) This group is involved in numerous projects throughout Bulgaria.

FLORA & FAUNA

Although not a large country, Bulgaria has a significant quantity and diversity of flora and fauna, no doubt helped by the varied climate, topography and relatively small human population. However, all environmental groups believe that the future of Bulgaria's ecology is at a critical stage and that local and international action is urgently needed before the environmental damage already caused becomes irreversible.

Flora

There are about 3500 species of vascular plants, of which 31 are endangered. Of the 6500 or so types of non-vascular plants, about 250 are endemic and many have indigenous names, such as Bulgarian blackberry and Rodopi tulip. About 2650 plants found in Bulgaria have medicinal uses and over 200 types of fungi are edible (but seek local advice before eating anything).

Squeezed between the mighty Stara Planina and Sredna Gora ranges, the Valley of Roses was, until recently, the source of 70% of the world's supply of rose oil. Roses are still grown there extensively, and can be seen and enjoyed most of the year.

Bulgaria can justifiably be proud of the fact that 35% of the country is covered with forests, of which 60% are original. Forests are also protected in the national parks and reserves. The Strandjha Nature Park contains vast areas of oaks and beeches. The Unesco-protected Pirin National Park boasts about 1100 species of flora, and the Vrachanski Balkan National Park is home to 700 species of trees.

The major threats to Bulgaria's plants and trees are not uncommon among most Eastern European countries. These include burning of stubble by farmers (and the occasional subsequent fire), urban sprawl, water and air pollution, logging, government-sanctioned hunting and imprudent farming methods leftover from the communist era.

Fauna

Bulgaria is home to some 56,000 kinds of living creatures, including 383 species of birds (about 75% of all species found in Europe), 36 types of reptiles, 207 species of freshwater and saltwater fish (of which about half are found along the Black Sea coast of Bulgaria) and 27,000 types of insects.

Many larger animals live in the hills and mountains, and understandably far from the urban centres, so most visitors will probably see little wildlife in Bulgaria. If you are keen to see some natural fauna, join an organised tour (see Organised Tours in the Getting Around and Getting There & Away chapters). Alternatively, hike in the Strandjha Nature Park; the Rusenski Lom National Park, home to 67 species of mammals (about two-thirds of those found in Bulgaria); the Rila National Park; or the Pirin National Park, where 42 species of animals such as bears, deers and wild goats thrive.

Bird lovers can admire plenty of our feathered friends at Burgas Lakes, the largest wetland complex in the country, and home to about 60% of all bird species in Bulgaria; the Ropotamo Nature Reserve, with more than 200 species of birds; the Strandjha Nature Park, with almost 70% of all bird species found in Bulgaria; the cliffs of Kaliakra Nature Reserve; the Rusenski Lom National Park, home to 170 species of water birds; and the Srebârna Nature Reserve, where over 160 types of water birds can be seen.

Endangered Species

Included in the official list of the endangered animals of Bulgaria are seals and dolphins, both of which were hunted ruthlessly but can still be seen in limited numbers off the northern coast of the Black Sea. Rusenski Lom National Park is home to several endangered species, including otters and bats.

Bulgaria (and Romania) have among the largest bear populations in Europe. However, they are becoming rarer because of illegal poaching and legitimate hunting. On the other hand, the number of wolves has increased alarmingly (though this is denied by some environmental groups). After being decimated by a deliberate poisoning

Major National Parks & Reserves

national park/reserve	location	accommodation	features
Blue Rocks	Central Bulgaria	Sliven	hiking trails and chairlift
Golden Sands Nature Park	Black Sea coast	Zlatni Pyasâtsi	hiking trails
Kaliakra Nature Reserve	Black Sea coast	Kavarna	watch dolphins and seals; explore ruins
Rila National Park	Southern Bulgaria	mountain huts	vast forests, pastures and wildlife
Ropotamo Nature Reserve	Black Sea coast	Sozopol and Primorsko	walking trails
Rusenski Lom National Park	Northern Bulgaria	private rooms in villages	excellent bird-watching, ancient ruins and a rock monastery
Pirin National Park	Southern Bulgaria	mountain huts	vast landscapes, forests, birds and wildlife
Srebârna Nature Reserve	Northern Bulgaria	Ruse	excellent birdlife
Strandjha Nature Park	Black Sea coast	village hotels	hiking trails
Vitosha National Park	Sofia	mountain huts and hotels in Sofia	hiking and skiing
Vrachanski Balkan National Park	Northern Bulgaria	Vratsa	hiking trails to rocks and caves

campaign in the 1950s, the wolf population has started to recover. They now kill livestock, which farmers keep unfenced because wolves were so infrequent in the past. Authorities have now sanctioned the culling of wolves in contravention of the Bern Convention, which protects native animals. NGOs are desperately hoping that wolves can be listed as a protected species in Bulgaria.

About 16% of all bird species in Bulgaria are rated as rare, 4% are officially endangered and three species are virtually extinct. Rare birds, such as Egyptian vultures, lesser kestrels and great eagle owls, are protected in the Rusenski Lom National Park. And small cormorants, Ferruginous ducks and Dalmatian pelicans thrive in the Srebârna Nature Reserve. One successful, privately run attempt at bird conservation is the Poda Conservation Centre at Burgas Lakes (see Burgas Lakes in the Black Sea Coast chapter). Another is the Nature Information & Conservation Centre 'Eastern Rhodopes' (☎/fax 0372-280), which has established a vulture sanctuary near Madzharovo, about 60km south-east of Haskovo.

About 14% of fish species are officially rare, and three fish are listed as endangered. While fish, such as mullet and carp, are protected in some national parks and reserves, such as Ropotamo Nature Reserve, species in the Black Sea are not. Also, two species of snakes are almost extinct.

National Parks & Reserves

The Bulgarian government has officially established 12 national parks where the flora, fauna and environment are (in theory) protected. These include 89 national reserves, where most of the wildlife and environment is protected, and 2234 vaguely defined conservation areas where strange and unique landscapes (such as caves, mineral springs and mountains) are found. Environmental groups continue to lobby the Bulgarian government to expand areas already under protection, especially the Pirin, Rila and Vitosha mountains, and create new parks and reserves, especially in the unprotected Rodopi Mountains and along the Black Sea coast.

See the boxed text 'Major National Parks & Reserves' for the most accessible and worthwhile parks and reserves (more information is available in the relevant chapters).

GOVERNMENT & POLITICS

Since 1990, Bulgaria has been a multiparty, democratic republic. Elections for the prime minister, who is also leader of the unicameral national assembly (with 240 members), are usually held every four years; the president, as the head of state, is elected every five years. Traditionally, the cabinet consists of 16 ministers – at the time of research, there were three women, six independents (who don't actually represent any party) and two from the BSP. Voting is not compulsory, but an admirable 67% of eligible voters made their choice during the 2001 parliamentary elections; marginally over 50% voted during the subsequent presidential elections.

The major political forces (see History earlier in this chapter) are the former communist party, now known as the BSP; the NMSII, led by the former king, Simeon II; and the UtDF, a disparate coalition of groups with only one thing in common – a

hatred of the BSP. Interestingly, one influential member of the BSP is Evgenia Zhivkova, granddaughter of the reviled former communist dictator, Todor Zhivkov.

Bulgaria is divided into 28 districts (*okrusi*) and 250 municipalities (*obshtina*).

ECONOMY

Prior to WWII, Bulgaria was primarily an agricultural country with over one million small, individually owned holdings, but by 1965 these had been consolidated into 920 collective farms. The farming cooperatives are still being dismantled and the land restored to its former owners but there's much disruption because of conflicting claims.

During the communist era, industry grew from almost nothing until it contributed over half of the gross national product. Some 85% of Bulgaria's foreign trade was conducted with member countries of the Warsaw Pact. Industrial output at the time was concentrated on iron and steel, fertilisers, petrochemicals and machinery.

Then the 1980s witnessed a slowdown, because of technological shortcomings and economic inefficiencies. The quality of many products was low and reorienting Bulgaria's inefficient heavy industries to manufacture for Western markets proved difficult. During the last five years of communism (1985–90), Bulgaria tallied up US$12 billion in foreign debt.

These days, Bulgaria's internal political squabbles continue to retard economic rehabilitation. Tax reform and new banking laws have been enacted, but foreign investment remains meagre and privatisation slow. Bulgaria's strategic location and highly educated and skilled workforce are

Some Economic Statistics

Inflation: 11.4% pa
GDP Per Capita: US$1510
Real GDP Growth: 2.5% pa
Unemployment: officially 18% (but probably higher)
Minimum Wage: 100 lv (US$45) per month
Average Wage: 238 lv (US$108) per month

significant advantages. Vested interests created by the old system, and inexperience from well-intentioned reformers, are hindering economic development.

The fact that 80% of people own their own homes has helped avert widespread destitution, but with an average wage of little more than US$100 per month, and an official unemployment rate of 18% (but probably higher, especially in rural areas), the situation for many is still precarious. According to international development agencies, 80% of the population lives near or below the poverty line. (This statistic is possibly misleading, however – many people in the countryside work on family farms for little or no salary and many barter rather than use money.)

While the past has indeed been bleak, positive steps taken by the recent governments have led to cautious optimism. These steps include pegging the Bulgarian leva to the Deutschmark in 1997 (and to the euro in 2002), which halted the rampant inflation that had ravaged the economy. Also pleading for, and receiving, substantial assistance from the EU, IMF and World Bank has helped. The new Prime Minister, Simeon II, promised to improve conditions for the average Bulgarian, so, immediately after being elected, he raised the minimum wage from 85 lv to 100 lv per month.

Since December 1999, Bulgaria has been frantically lobbying other European countries in an attempt to join the EU (and NATO) by January 2003 – though, privately, Bulgarian authorities admit this is unlikely to happen before 2007. Possible stumbling blocks to membership of the EU and NATO include Bulgaria's treatment of minorities, especially the Roma (gypsies); corruption, which still thrives in many government departments; and drug smuggling from Turkey and across the Black Sea. Bulgaria is listed 57th on the United Nations Development Program's human development report, based on people's wealth, life expectancy and the government's commitment to education. Of the dozen or so European countries striving to join the EU and NATO, only Romania is rated lower (58th).

Major exports include: herbs (Bulgaria is the world's third-largest exporter); wine (see the boxed text 'Bulgarian Wine' in the Facts for the Visitor chapter); machinery, such as tractors and buses; metals, including copper and steel; and chemicals, such as fertilisers, plastics and pharmaceuticals. Bulgaria is also one of the world's largest producers of tobacco but profits have suffered from a worldwide downturn in prices during 2001. Two minor products that Bulgaria creates and exports – and for which the country is renowned – are *lactobacillus bulgaricus* (a micro-organism which helps make yogurt) and rose oil (see the boxed text 'The Valley of Roses' in the Central Bulgaria chapter). Russia, and other countries in the Balkans and Eastern Europe, receive about one-third of Bulgaria's exports; another 40% goes to Western and northern Europe.

Tourism

During 2000, slightly more than two million people visited Bulgaria for 'tourism' purposes and spent nearly US$1 billion. These figures represent a 4% increase in revenue, but a 6% decline in the number of visitors since 1998 – no doubt caused by the civil strife elsewhere in the Balkans, particularly in Kosovo. At the time of writing, tourism contributed about 8% to the country's GDP and employed about 131,000 people.

Significantly more tourists are now visiting in winter, attracted by cheap skiing and generally reliable snow. Most come from neighbouring countries, such as Greece, Macedonia and Turkey, and are not generally big spenders. In summer, most tourists come from Germany, Scandinavia, Belgium, Netherlands, the UK and Russia (in that order). Many arrive on pre-paid package tours, which include accommodation in foreign-owned hotels and transport on foreign airlines, so they don't spend a lot of cash inside Bulgaria. Overall, only Germany (10.1%), the UK (2.5%) and Sweden (1.3%) are in the top 10 countries of origination for tourists to Bulgaria; the rest come from Eastern Europe, the Balkans and Russia. About 70% of all tourists flock to the Black Sea coast between June and September, so if you avoid this area at this time, you'll find that the rest of Bulgaria is remarkably quiet and unaffected by tourism.

Bulgarian officials are hoping that the tens of thousands of foreign tourists expected to travel to Greece for the 2004 Olympic Games in Athens will head north for a side-trip around Bulgaria. By 2020, the tourist representative from the World Trade Organisation (WTO) predicts that Bulgaria will attract 12 million tourists per year.

POPULATION & PEOPLE

In 2000, the official population of Bulgaria was 7,973,671. Nearly 70% now live in urban centres including Sofia, the largest city, and (in order of population size) Plovdiv, Varna, Burgas, Ruse, Stara Zagora and Pleven.

The population has actually fallen by about 503,000 since 1992 because of significant emigration by young educated Bulgarians looking for a better life and the perpetually low birth rates. Even during the communist era, government incentives failed to persuade Bulgarians to have larger families with the exception of Turkish and Pomak minorities. The birth rate continues to be low because of easy access to contraception and abortion. The advent of capitalism also means that people flock to the cities to look for work and those with well-paid jobs often prefer not to have large families.

Bulgarians are actually Slavs and officially constitute 88.3% of the population. The largest minorities are the Turks (8%), the Roma (2.6%), the Armenians (0.3%) and the Russians (0.2%), who came during the communist era and stayed. Unofficially, about 2.5% of the overall population and the majority in some parts of south-western Bulgaria are Macedonians. For almost 100 years, a controversy has raged over whether Macedonians in Bulgaria are 'Bulgarians' or a distinct ethnic group. In 1999, a joint declaration by the Bulgarian and Macedonian governments officially put to rest longstanding disputes over territory, language and other contentious issues. In official statistics, the Macedonians have yet to be accepted as an official minority.

Some Population Statistics

Population: 7.97 million
Under 14 years old: 16%
Over 65 years old: 16%
Gender Ratio: 48.8% (male) and 51.2% (female)
Fertility Rate: 1.13
Population Growth Rate: -4.8% pa
Birth Rate: 0.86% pa
Population Density: 72 per sq km
Living in Urban Areas: 68% .
Life Expectancy: 67 years (male) and 74 years (female)

Most of the 640,000 Turks live in the north-east and in the foothills of the eastern Rodopi Mountains. In 1985, the communists mounted a program to assimilate the country's Turkish inhabitants by forcing them to accept Bulgarian names. At this time mosques were also closed and even wearing Turkish dress and speaking Turkish in public were banned. Mass protests erupted and in early 1989 about 350,000 Turkish Bulgarians left for Turkey (though many subsequently returned to Bulgaria when the repressive policies were overturned). Many Turkish Bulgarians were experienced farmers so their departure significantly affected the agrarian economy at the time.

About 250,000 Pomaks live in the Rodopi Mountains. Pomaks are Slavs who converted to Islam during the Ottoman occupation in the 15th century. In the past, they have been subjected to the same assimilatory pressures as the Turks.

At the outbreak of WWII, about 50,000 Jews lived in Bulgaria. Although forced to assemble in provincial labour camps, none were turned over to the Nazis despite the fact that the Bulgarian government had formed an alliance with Germany. After the war most Jews left for Israel and only about 5000 still remain in Bulgaria.

As a peaceful and comparatively developed country within the troubled Balkans, Bulgaria has some obvious appeal for refugees. In 2001, hundreds of Macedonians

The Roma

The English term for the Roma, the gypsies, reflects an early belief that these nomadic people came from Egypt, though it's now generally accepted that they originated from northern India. Roma (singular Rom) speak Romany, a language that shares common features with Sanskrit and other Indian languages. The Roma began migrating westward towards Persia (modern-day Iran) during the 10th century and reached the Balkans about 400 years later. A second wave of migration began in 1855 after the Roma from Romania were freed from serfdom by the Moldavian prince, Grigore Ghica. About 500,000 Roma were murdered in Nazi death camps during WWII.

According to an international census, about eight million Roma live in Europe; the largest number live in Romania, while Bulgaria is home to about 600,000. (Official Bulgarian statistics, however, indicate that about 207,000 Roma live in Bulgaria.) Many live in the Valley of Roses and Sliven, and three-quarters are Muslims.

Throughout the Balkans, the Roma are despised and remain the convenient scapegoat for everything from minor local crime to major national economic chaos. Largely unrepresented in any government in Europe, the Roma have suffered worsening living conditions, mass unemployment and harassment throughout the region since the fall of communism after 1990.

fled to Bulgaria following strife in Macedonia, but the situation is not (yet) a major concern.

EDUCATION

The first school in Bulgaria to teach in the Bulgarian language was established in Gabrovo in 1835 by the revered Vasil Aprilov. Within 30 or 40 years, more than 2000 Bulgarian schools had been established throughout the country, often built and/or renovated in the style representative of the Bulgarian national revival period. Since 1835, basic education has been compulsory and free to all Bulgarian citizens, regardless of ethnicity. While 100 years ago many children did not, or could not, attend school and illiteracy remained commonplace, an impressive 99% of males and 98% of females can now read and write (according to official figures).

Admirably, the communist government increased education levels to acceptable standards but they also instilled a communist ideology and taught Russian. Education standards have slipped in recent years and low-paid teachers and professors can still be bribed by wealthier students to receive good marks. Students who can afford to further their education in Western and northern Europe do so in droves.

Education is provided by the government from the age of seven to 16 or 17. Primary school is followed by general high school, but those with specific skills and interests may enter high schools that concentrate on languages, arts or sports. Some of the major public universities are in Sofia, Plovdiv, Burgas and Veliko Târnovo. The American University of Bulgaria in Blagoevgrad is privately run and education comes at a comparatively high cost.

ARTS

After centuries of Turkish rule, Bulgarian culture reappeared in the mid-18th century as writers and artists strove to reignite the national consciousness (see Bulgarian National Revival Period earlier in this chapter). But during the communist era, most Bulgarians with artistic, literary, theatrical or musical talents were trained in the former Soviet Union and therefore heavily influenced by the Russians.

Painting & Sculpture

Most of Bulgaria's earliest artists painted on the walls of homes, churches and monasteries. The most famous was unquestionably Zahari Zograf (1810–53), who painted magnificent murals, which can still be admired, in the monasteries at Rila, Troyan and Bachkovo. Many of Zograf's works were inspired by medieval Bulgarian art, but more human than divine. In Orthodox churches, a high partition or wall called an iconostasis separates the public and private areas. Zograf and his contemporaries also painted icons on wooden panels to hang on these intricately carved walls.

Famous Bulgarian artists of the last 150 years include Vladimir Dimitrov, often referred to as 'The Master', and Dimitâr Kazakov, whose works have been shown in the Louvre Museum. Other renowned artists are Iliya Beshkov, Dechko Uzunov, the widely travelled Kiril Tsonev, Tsanko Lavrenov and the Mitov brothers – Georgi, Anton and Boris. These, and other artists, have been immortalised in museums and galleries that are dedicated to their work and lives. For examples, see museums and galleries in Bansko, Sofia, Koprivshtitsa, Kyustendil, Tryavna, Stara Zagora, Pleven and Plovdiv.

Contemporary Bulgarian artists include the renowned sculptor Asen Botev and the abstract painter Kolyo Karamfilov. Young Stefan Todorov is becoming increasingly renowned for his hand-drawn silk paintings and Slav Bakalov has won awards in France for his illustrations. Works by these, and other contemporary artists, hang on the walls in a growing number of private galleries around Bulgaria, particularly in Sofia and Varna, and elsewhere in Europe.

Theatre

Every city and major town has at least one theatre, often built during the communist era, which offers Bulgarian and foreign plays, classical music, puppet shows, choral music and operas. Because local and federal governments can rarely afford to subsidise the arts these days, some theatres are closing down or playing in front of smaller audiences. Despite the revival in Bulgarian arts and culture since the demise of communism, most young people prefer to listen to pop music or hang around nightclubs and Internet centres. Sofia, Plovdiv, Varna, Veliko Târnovo, Blagoevgrad and Ruse are home to renowned opera, ballet and theatre companies and are ideal places for foreigners to enjoy a robust production. (Note: most theatres close during July and August.)

Literature

The first recognised literary work written in Bulgarian was probably *Slav-Bulgarian History* by Paisii Hilendarski. This thin, but detailed, volume was the catalyst for a resurrection of Bulgarian cultural heritage and ethnic identity from the mid-18th century (see Bulgarian National Revival Period earlier in this chapter). Some of Bulgaria's more revered writers, poets and playwrights were also fierce nationalists. Several of them, such as Georgi Rakovski and Hristo Botev, met violent deaths at about 30-years-old fighting the Turks, (see the boxed text 'Hristo Botev' in the Northern Bulgaria chapter).

Other famous literary figures who have been immortalised in museums throughout Bulgaria include Nikola Vaptsarov (in Bansko), Yordan Yovkov (Dobrich), Geo Milev (Stara Zagora), Petko Slaveikov and his son Pencho (Tryavna). Also Ivan Vazov (Sofia), Hristo Danov (Plovdiv) and Dimcho Debelyanov and Lyuben Karavelov (Koprivshtitsa).

Music

Opera & Choral Ancient Greek mythology ascribed a Thracian origin to Orpheus and the Muses and Bulgarians today are still renowned singers. Musical academies continue to churn out world-class opera stars such as a Nikolai Gyuzelev, Gena Dimitrova, Boris Hristov and Anna Tomova-Sintova. All of these stars have performed on international stages.

Bulgarian ecclesiastic music dates back to the 9th century and conveys the mysticism of chronicles, fables and legends. To hear Orthodox chants sung by a choir of up to 100 people is a moving experience. The best place to hear a choral performance is during a service at a large church, such as the Alexander Nevski Church in Sofia.

Traditional Alongside the scholarly Byzantine traditions maintained in Orthodox church music is the Turkish influence evident in the folk songs and dances of the villages. Following are the most common traditional folk instruments:

Daire – similar to a a tambourine.
Gadulka – a small pear-shaped fiddle, also known as a *rebec*.
Gayda – a goatskin bagpipe.
Kaval – a long, open flute.
Tambura – a four-stringed, long-necked lute akin to the Greek *bouzouki,* called a *drunka* in the Pirin Mountains.
Tâppan – a large, cylindrical, double-headed drum.

As in many peasant cultures, Bulgarian women are not given access to musical instruments so they usually perform the vocal parts. They often practise singing while weaving and doing household chores. Bulgarian female singing is polyphonic, ie, featuring many voices and shifting melodies. Characteristic sudden upward leaps of the voice are unearthly in their beauty. Women from villages in the Pirin Mountains are renowned for their unique singing style. Some of the more famous performers include Koyna Stoyanova and Yanka Rupkina.

During the communist era, Bulgarian village music was transformed into a sophisticated art form and communicated worldwide by groups such as the Philip Kutev National Folk Ensemble and albums like 'Le Mystère des Voix Bulgares'. Domestically, traditional folk music has declined in popularity. This is partly because it was prescribed listening under the old regime and also because Bulgarians now have access to as much Western schlock-pop as they can handle.

Modern Most of the modern Bulgarian sounds that you're likely to hear is termed wedding music, a spirited pop-folk idiom often derided as *chalga* (or truck-driver music) by those who dislike it. Nevertheless, it's a standard fixture at festive occasions, and a real treat for foreigners able to witness it. Up to six- or seven-piece bands (often featuring a scantily-clad female lead vocalist) soon get people dancing by playing traditional Balkan tunes on instruments such as the electric guitar, clarinet and synthesiser. Many of the more admired musicians and singers are Roma, such as Velentin Valdez and Gloria.

Popular Bulgarian groups that play other types of modern music include the pop group Atlas, voted by Sofia radio listeners as the most popular band in the early 1990s, and set for a comeback, and D2, voted the most popular group in 2000. Also popular are the long-established heavy rock band BTR and the experimental band Isihia, which incorporates traditional elements into their music. The most innovative music today comes from Teodossi Spassov, an inspired kaval player who is blazing new musical pathways by fusing traditional Bulgarian folk with jazz. Many Bulgarian groups and artists must tour and even live elsewhere in Europe, often Germany and Scandinavia, to further their careers and make decent money.

Costumes
Together with religion, language, music and dance, costumes have been an integral part of the traditional way of life in Bulgaria for centuries. During festivals and special occasions, like weddings and name days, men, women and children like to dress up, particularly in rural areas. General costumes for women include a *soukman* (low-cut dress, usually without sleeves) and *saya* (long dress). Either or both costumes are worn with aprons and a waistband and shirt. Men often wear costumes that are either mainly black *(chernodreshna)* or white *(belodreshna),* with a long shirt, pants and an outer coat. Traditional costumes are usually made from cotton, silk or wool, often weaved at home, and decorated with jewellery and embroidered designs.

Outfits vary from one region to another, and are most diverse among the villages of the Rodopi Mountains, where women often wear dresses of yellow and orange. Wedding costumes sometimes worn in Bulgari village (in the Strandjha Nature Park) feature bright yellows, reds and blacks and occasionally shawls to hide the women's face. Every city and major town has an ethnographic or ethnological museum showcasing various traditional costumes.

Weaving & Embroidery
Bulgarian carpets, rugs, bags and traditional costumes were first made as early as the 9th century but like most arts and crafts,

weaving, and to a lesser degree, embroidery, were most popular and creative during the Bulgarian national revival period. Sadly, weaving is a dying art, only practised in a few remote villages such as Chiprovtsi, Kotel and Koprivshtitsa. Weaving is still done on handmade looms and undertaken almost entirely by women. It's more of a social occasion than a business these days.

Carpets and rugs made in the southern Rodopi Mountains are thick, woollen and practical, while in western Bulgaria, they're often delicate, colourful and more decorative. Items weaved in and around Yambol often feature distinctive short fringes, which has been designated as the *yambolii* style.

Embroidery usually features extensively on traditional costumes, especially female dresses and shirts, but tourists can also buy embroidered coasters, tablecloths and shawls. Most traditional designs are geometric but colours and symbolism vary from one region to another. Examples of weaving and embroidery can be admired at ethnographic or ethnological museums throughout the country.

Woodcarving

This is another traditional craft that started long ago but reached its peak during the Bulgarian national revival period. While weaving was practised mostly by women, woodcarving was almost exclusively a male domain. Men would spend hours designing and creating wooden crosses, chests, cradles, walking sticks, traditional flutes and pipes. More experienced and respected carvers could produce intricately carved ceilings (which can be seen in homes and museums in Koprivshtitsa, Kotel, Tryavna and Plovdiv) and iconostases and altars in churches and monasteries.

The craft is still practised in Koprivshtitsa, Teteven and Lovech but the most famous town in Bulgaria for woodcarving is undoubtedly Tryavna (see the boxed text 'Woodcarving' in the Central Bulgaria chapter). One of the best places to admire woodcarvers at work is the Etâr Ethnographic Village Museum, which you will find near Gabrovo.

Architecture

Probably the most obvious product of the prodigious and creative Bulgarian national revival period is the unique architectural style of homes seen throughout the country. These were either built side-by-side along narrow cobblestone streets, so the homes facing each other almost seem to touch, as in Plovdiv, or surrounded by pretty gardens, as in Arbanasi.

Homes were made of stone, wood and limestone. The ground floor normally consisted of bare stone, while the exterior of the upper floors were often painted brown and white (though some were painted bright blue, crimson or yellow). The upper floors featured several rectangular windows with wooden shutters. There would also be one or two bay windows, often curved with a seat inside offering views. On top, the roof was always tiled.

Inside, ceilings were often intricately carved and/or painted with bright murals and there would be several small fireplaces and low doors. Most were furnished with small tables and chairs because ceilings were normally low. Bright, locally made carpets and rugs were spread across the earthen floor and copper and gold-plated dishes and cups were placed along the mantelpiece.

Architectural designs and styles of furniture differed from one region to another.

Beautiful Bulgaria Project (BBP)

Since 1998, the BBP has been renovating homes and beautifying public buildings in dozens of villages in 42 municipalities including Belogradchik, Elena and Chepelare and the old town of Veliko Târnovo. The BBP ostensibly started as an employment project for the long-term unemployed in rural Bulgaria and is now rated by the EU as the most successful employment initiative in Eastern Europe. The budget for the third (current) phase is US$22 million, jointly funded by the EU, United Nations Development Program and Bulgarian Ministry of Labour & Social Policy. The Swiss Government has also chipped in for specific projects.

The colour, shape and size of the typical home in Melnik contrasts significantly with homes found in Arbanasi. Some of the most stunning examples of Bulgarian national revival period homes can also be appreciated in traditional villages like Koprivshtitsa, Tryavna, Shiroka Lûka, Bansko, Nesebâr and Belogradchik. There are also examples among the old towns of Plovdiv and Veliko Târnovo and at the re-created Etâr Ethnographic Village Museum, near Gabrovo. Many buildings in these and other places have benefited immensely from the excellent work undertaken by the Beautiful Bulgaria Project (BBP).

SOCIETY & CONDUCT
Traditional Culture

Despite, or perhaps because of, Bulgaria's almost permanent occupation and/or control by foreign powers, Bulgarians have clung firmly to their traditions. Besides the religious occasions, public holidays and traditional events (see Public Holidays & Special Events in the Facts for the Visitor chapter) Bulgarians also vigorously celebrate many events. Christenings, 'first steps' (celebrated when a child starts to walk), weddings, house-warmings and birthdays are also cause for celebration. More importantly, name days, the saint's day after which someone is named (for example, Aleksandâr celebrates his name day on 30 November, St Aleksandâr's Day), are also a much-venerated tradition.

For some occasions, particularly Christmas, New Year and Easter, particular types of bread are baked in village homes and bakeries and each is decorated according to tradition. For weddings, kneading of the dough is often accompanied by specific songs. Bulgarian weddings are long and festive occasions, which feature all sorts of complicated symbolic activities that never cease to fascinate tourists. Travel agencies, especially along the Black Sea coast, often arrange outings to witness a (mock) 'Bulgarian Wedding', which includes plenty of dancing, eating and drinking.

Each year, most villages have a fair day. Locals stop work so they can eat, drink and enjoy games such as horse racing and wrestling and practise traditions such as fire-dancing on live coals (still performed at remote villages in the Strandjha Nature Park). Some fair days are listed in the Facts for the Visitor chapter, but generally it's a matter of asking locals and tourist offices about the exact dates and locations.

One of the most fascinating festivals feature *kukeri* (masked dances), part of a pagan tradition that must date back many centuries. Once a year during early spring (March), men from some villages (eg, Shiroka Lûka) dress up in large, colourful and fierce-looking costumes and masks to frighten evil spirits away from the upcoming harvests.

Dos & Don'ts

Bulgarians shake their head in a curved, almost bouncy, motion to indicate 'yes', and less often, nod their head to mean 'no'. To add to the confusion, some well-travelled Bulgarians may do the opposite to 'help' confused foreigners. If there is any doubt, ask *da ili ne* (yes or no)?

Giving flowers is a widely observed practice suitable for any occasion. However, make sure you give the flowers in an odd number, because even numbers are only appropriate for funerals.

When visiting mosques, churches, and especially monasteries, please dress conservatively and act appropriately. While shorts are almost always acceptable, skimpy loose shirts and tight shorts (for both sexes) are frowned upon, although you probably won't be refused entry. Topless sunbathing is permitted at most major beach resorts along the Black Sea coast. Before baring your top half, ladies, check to see if it's an accepted practice along that particular stretch of sand.

RELIGION

Bulgaria is a secular state which allows freedom of religion.

Orthodox Christianity

Orthodox Christianity first appeared in Bulgaria during the 4th century but did not become the official religion until 865. Not long after, all pagan temples and idols were

Icons

One important component of the Orthodox religion is the icon (derived from the Greek word for 'portrait'). Icons normally feature major figures within Christianity, eg, Jesus Christ, the Virgin Mary, the Saints and the Apostles, or significant religious events, such as the baptism of St John. Icons can be made of wood, ceramic, stone, metals or wax and are either individual or form part of complicated murals or mosaics. Icons were probably first created in Bulgaria at the beginning of the 10th century AD but relatively few have survived the sands of time and destruction by the Turks. However, some superb examples were created during (and survived) the Ottoman period than before or after.

Some icons created in Bulgaria during the 18th and 19th centuries were more earthly than heavenly and designed in what became known as the Veliko Târnovo, Samokov, Tryavna or Bansko 'schools'. The most impressive examples can be found in dedicated collections at Bansko and Plovdiv, at museums in Varna and Tryavna, and inside churches at Nesebâr and Veliko Târnovo. Icons held at the Alexander Nevski church in Sofia, and in the Rila, Troyan and Bachkovo monasteries, are particularly stunning.

destroyed and the revered saints Kiril and Metodii (see the boxed text 'Sts Kiril & Metodii' later in this section) visited Pliska, the capital of the First Bulgarian Empire (681–1018). The country's first monasteries were soon built, but poorer followers set up churches and monasteries in caves.

Under Turkish rule, Christianity in Bulgaria was, at best, tolerated, but churches had to be built beneath ground level (ie, lower than the mosques). At worst, churches and monasteries were destroyed and/or looted, however some were spared simply because they were never discovered by the Turks. These isolated churches and monasteries helped preserve the Orthodox religion and Bulgarian culture and were an integral part of the popular uprising against the Turks during the latter half of the 19th century.

Rebels known as *haidouks* were often given sanctuary in monasteries. Many other locals sought refuge in Christian buildings – though the Turks often had no compunction about burning down churches and massacring all those inside.

During the communist era between 1946 and 1989, Bulgaria was officially 'atheist', and only the elderly were left relatively unharassed to pursue their worship.

By Turkish decree, most churches and monasteries had plain exteriors, but they were always richly decorated inside with murals, icons, iconostases and altars. About 160 monasteries are dotted around Bulgaria. The most important monasteries are at Rila, Bachkovo, Troyan and Dryanovo.

About 85% of the Bulgarian population claims to be Orthodox, but nowhere near these numbers regularly visit church. Since the end of communism, young people have failed to return to the church in any numbers, thereby ensuring an erosion of faith in what was once a very religious society. The head of the Bulgarian Orthodox Church is Patriarch Maksim.

Islam
Officially, 13% of the population is Muslim and almost all are Sunni. Most of these are either Turks or Pomaks (see Population & People earlier in this chapter). Over the centuries, the Islam practised in Bulgaria has incorporated various Bulgarian traditions and Christian beliefs and has become known as Balkan Islam. Mosques in Sofia, Shumen, Plovdiv, Samokov and Haskovo are attended by the faithful few.

Other Religions
Bulgaria also has a small Catholic community, mostly immigrants from northern Europe. Judaism was introduced by refugees from Catholic Spain in the 15th century and is still practised at synagogues in Sofia and Vidin. There are also small communities of Armenians, who maintain Armenian Orthodox churches in Sofia, Varna and Plovdiv. One fascinating cult is the White Brotherhood (see the boxed text 'The White Brotherhood' in the Southern Bulgarian chapter).

Sts Kiril & Metodii

The two brothers Kiril (Cyril) and Metodii (Methodius) were born in what was then known as Macedonia in the early 9th century. Both were scholars and monks who had studied and worked throughout the Balkans. They are revered in Bulgaria for developing in 863 the script which became known as the Cyrillic alphabet. But, more importantly, they helped spread Orthodox Christianity throughout the Balkans by seeking and receiving approval from the Vatican for Macedonian (which is similar to Bulgarian) to become the fourth accepted language of the Church (after Latin, Greek and Hebrew).

The Cyrillic alphabet is now used in Bulgaria, Russia, Macedonia, Ukraine, Belarus, Yugoslavia and Mongolia. There are calls from some Bulgarians to change to the Roman alphabet in this modern age of English-language computers; however, this is unlikely to happen: Bulgarians even celebrate Cyrillic Alphabet Day (also known as the Day of Bulgarian Culture) on 24 May.

LANGUAGE

Bulgarian is a South Slavonic language, closely related to Macedonian. It became the official language of Bulgaria in 1879, when the dialect spoken in the capital at the time, Veliko Târnovo, was chosen as the national language. Dialects do exist, as in most other Eastern European countries, but they are more or less mutually comprehensible. Not surprisingly, Bulgarian incorporates words from Greek, Russian and Turkish. More recently, some words from English, for example, *ofis* (office) and *garadj* (garage), Italian (*ciao* for goodbye) and French (*merci* for thank you) have been incorporated into the vernacular.

Students in Bulgaria must learn at least one foreign language – either English, French, German, Spanish or Russian – from an early age and many now opt for English. Older Bulgarians may speak Russian, because it was a required school subject during the communist era, and a few others may also speak French or German. These days, young people, tourism workers and business people are more likely to speak English as a second language.

Almost everything in Bulgaria is written in Cyrillic so it's essential to learn this alphabet, both the standard print and written versions, because some letters are completely different and occasionally used interchangeably.

See the Language chapter at the end of this guidebook for a basic rundown on Bulgarian pronunciation and a list of useful words and phrases. We hope this chapter will be enough for most travellers, but bilingual dictionaries (in Bulgarian, and English, German or French) are available from most bookshops throughout the country. Also, Lonely Planet's *Eastern Europe Phrasebook* contains an extensive list of words and phrases in Bulgarian, and in other languages from nearby countries, such as Romanian.

BULGARIA – SOMETHING FOR EVERYONE

Culture Buffs

Historical Museum Unravel the past at the Historical Museum in Smolyan, in the southern Rodopi Mountains. Tour the many levels of this museum and discover Bulgarian history through architecture and traditional displays of costumes, woodcarving and weaving.

Ethnographical Museum Relive three centuries of Bulgarian culture at Sofia's Ethnographical Museum. Marvel at intricate embroideries used in traditional religious festivals and the wide range of artefacts on display.

National Opera House Catch a performance at the National Opera House in Sofia and be impressed by the best of Bulgaria's international artists.

Archaeological Museum Be awed by the world's oldest gold and copper work at Varna's massive Archaeological Museum on the Black Sea coast. See local sculptures, woodcarvings, ceramics, and religious art.

Veliko Târnovo Stroll along the banks of the Yantra River in the former capital of the Second Bulgarian Empire (1185–1396), see medieval churches and monasteries in the old town or visit the major attraction of Tsarevets Fortress.

Plovdiv old town Stop over in thriving Plovdiv and be amazed by the most spectacular Roman amphitheatre in Bulgaria. Delight in the architecture of the bustling old town, where unique 18th- and 19th-century baroque homes sit alongside museums, galleries and Byzantine ruins.

Gourmands

Wine Sample a glass of dark-red wine in Melnik, Bulgaria's smallest town, in a wine bar cut into the rocks along a cobblestone paths. For over 600 years Melnik has been producing wine and it's definitely a tasty drop.

Plum Brandy Awaken your senses with some local brandy from Oreshak in Central Bulgaria. Made with rich plums by serious brandy lovers, this is not a drink for the faint-hearted but certainly a must-try.

Feta Salt your tastebuds with a slice of Bulgaria's world-famous feta. This delectable cheese is perfect on some schitzel served throughout Central Bulgaria.

Nature Lovers

Rila Mountains Lace up your hiking boots and trek through some of the most spectacular scenery in Bulgaria. Camp in mountain huts along the way, visit waterfalls, look at beautiful flora and do some bird-watching.

Burgas Lakes View our fine feathered friends at Bulgaria's largest wetland complex in Burgas Lakes. Take a guided tour to admire the birdlife up close and spot pelicans, black-winged stilts, ibises and spoonbills in their natural and protected habitat.

Rusenski Lom National Park Marvel at the unique rock churches that are built in and around the 300 caves in Rusenski Lom National Park. Also watch the diverse species of water-birds that live in this gorgeous national park or check out the city ruins built by Thracians and Romans.

Srebârna Nature Reserve Serious bird lovers will swoon at this World Heritage site, established by Unesco in 1983. The Nature Reserve is a popular breeding ground for colonies of Dalmatian pelicans.

Strandjha Nature Park Escape the beaten track and head for the remote Standjha Nature Park, which has some of Bulgaria's most diverse vegetation. Trek for 1km, or 20km, through some of the marked hiking trails.

Hedonists

Mud bath Have a long soak in a bath – full of mud! Never has washing behind your ears been as much fun as in the mud bath at Pomorie, on the Black Sea coast. If taking a bath seems too high-profile maybe a massage is more your style.

Mineral Springs Cure your ailments in the one of the 22 mineral springs at the small town of Hisarya in Central Bulgaria. The springs have been used by people since Roman times and are an excellent way to relax and pamper yourself.

Beach Sloth for hours on one of the many glorius beaches on the Black Sea coast – you've got all day so swim, sunbathe and relax. For the more active there's jet skiing, snorkelling, windsurfing, fishing and water skiing.

Party Throw yourself into the nightlife along the Black Sea coast. Try Zlatni Pyasâtsi for some lively action or if a slower pace is more your style check out Albena with its casual feel and young, fun-loving crowd. Of course, you can always stretch your vocal chords at one of Sofia's many karaoke bars or night clubs.

Festival-Goers

Shiroka Lûka Witness the important Bulgarian ritual of the Kukeri festival at Shiroka Luka, celebrated on the first Sunday of March. Male-only participants don scary masks and perform phallic dances to frighten away the evil spirits of winter and ensure the advent of spring.

1876 April Uprising Revisit history in Koprivshtitsa as locals re-enact the 1876 April Uprising at the tiny Kalachev Bridge and in the main square. Here, Todor Kableshkov first proclaimed the national uprising against the Turks.

Fire-Dancing Experience the traditional ceremony of the fire-dancing festival, which is held in Bulgari in early June. Bulgari was once famous for practicing the ancient art of nestinarstvo (fire-dancing) and it was also thought to have been practiced by the Thracians as part of Dionysian rites.

Festival of the Roses Give your olfactory senses a workout at the Festival of the Roses as Bulgarians celebrate the ancient tradition of rose-gathering. On offer at the festival are rose jam, rose brandy and of course rose oil, which is distilled from the petals. Roses bloom in late May and early June and there are lively parades that mark the festival in Kazanlâk and Karlovo.

Snow Bunnies

Bansko Grab a lift to the peak of Mt Vihren in the Pirin Mountains where skiing is cheap, the snow thick and the local wine free-flowing.

Borovets Escape to Bulgaria's premier ski resort, surrounded by thick pine forests. Snowboard down Mt Musala, the highest peak, or take a gondola to Yastrebets.

Mt Vitosha Leave the bustle of Sofia by taking this easy day trip to Mt Vitosha. Hike through the beautiful national park in summer and swish down the slopes in winter.

Pamporovo Crisscross the 25 kilometres of cross-country trails in the gorgeous Rodopi Mountains. This is a perfect place to surf the slopes on a snowboard.

Village People

Tryavna Step back in time as you wander through historic cobble-stone streets of the old town of picturesque Tryavna and admire the beautifully restored architecture from the national revival period.

Koprivshtitsa Take to the high country of the Sredna Gora Mountains and soak up the historical ambience of the tiny village of Koprivshtitsa. Over 300 buildings at this village are of great historical and architectural importance and are protected by the Bulgarian government.

Arbanasi Wander around the village of Arbanasi and see preserved cultural monuments. Visit the oldest remaining church in the village and admire the lavish murals and wooden iconostases at the 16th-century Nativity Church.

Spiritual Souls

Rila Monastery Take sanctuary in Bulgaria's most significant symbols of national identity. See where artists and writers sheltered and helped keep the culture alive during the 19th-century national revival period.

Dryanovo Monastery Soak up history in this ancient 12th-century monastery. Have the 1876 April Uprising explained and see where revolutionary Vasil Levski hid during the Russian-Turkish War (1877–88).

Bachkovo Monastery Hike from the idyllic village of Bachkovo and see the cover of this book! There are spectacular murals painted by Zahari Zograf, Bulgaria's leading mural artist from the 19th century.

Aleksander Nevski Church Be awed by Sofia's church in memorial to the 200,000 Russian soldiers who lost their lives fighting for Bulgarian independence.

Banya Bashi Mosque Admire Bulgaria's only functioning mosque in Sofia. Built in the 16th century by the Turks the splendid interior is certainly worth a look.

DANI VALENT

Left: The majestic Rila Monastery.

Facts for the Visitor

HIGHLIGHTS
Bulgaria's greatest asset is its diversity of attractions, which appeal equally to those who want to stay off the beaten track and to those who want to stay on it.

History & Culture
As well as the Unesco World Heritage sites listed here, Bulgaria boasts 227 official museums and art galleries. The best are probably the Archaeological Museum in Varna, the Ethnographical Museum in Sofia and the Historical Museum in Smolyan. About 160 monasteries are spread throughout Bulgaria; the big 'four' are the Rila Monastery, Dryanovo Monastery, Bachkovo Monastery and Troyan Monastery.

There are also numerous mosques and churches, none more spectacular than the Alexander Nevski Church in Sofia. The Romans left impressive reminders, such as the Thermae at Varna, the city of Nikopolis-ad-Istrum and the massive Amphitheatre in Plovdiv. Various other empires also built fortresses in Veliko Târnovo, Shumen, Belogradchik and Vidin.

Landscapes
Bulgaria boasts remarkably diverse landscapes including Burgas Lakes and Lake Batak, the four impressive mountain ranges of Rila, Pirin, Stara Planina and Sredna Gora, all of which are great for hiking and skiing, the mighty Shipka Pass, the bizarre Belogradchiski Skali rock formation and the caves near Trigrad and Yagodina.

National Parks & Reserves
Twelve national parks, 89 national reserves and 2234 other areas are protected by the Bulgarian government. These include the Rila National Park, the Srebârna Nature Reserve, the Pirin National Park (Bulgaria's largest), and the Rusenski Lom National Park, which is one of the best places for bird-watching. Smaller reserves include the Ropotamo Nature Reserve, Kaliakra Nature

World Heritage Sites
Unesco has rated nine places in Bulgaria as 'cultural and national treasures of world heritage':
- Boyana Church (near Sofia)
- Ivanovo Rock Monastery (in Rusenski Lom National Park, near Ruse)
- Kazanlâk Thracian Tomb
- Madara Horseman (carved bas-relief near Shumen)
- Nesebâr (ancient city along the Black Sea coast)
- Pirin National Park (in the south-west)
- Rila Monastery (119km south of Sofia)
- Srebârna Nature Reserve (near Silistra)
- Sveshtari Thracian Tomb (between Shumen and Silistra)

Reserve (which protects part of the Black Sea) and Strandjha Nature Park, in the south-east.

Villages & Old Towns
High on the list of 'must-sees' are the traditional villages of Koprivshtitsa, Shiroka Lûka, Arbanasi and, particularly, Tryavna. Nesebâr and Sozopol, both along the Black Sea coast, ooze history and charm, and there are fascinating old towns in the cities of Veliko Târnovo and Plovdiv. Melnik and Bansko to the south, and Belogradchik, in the north-west, are also irresistible.

SUGGESTED ITINERARIES
Your itinerary will largely depend on where you start and/or finish your sojourn, how much money you want to spend, how much time you have, what time of year you want to travel and how you plan to get around (ie, public or private transport).

Try to allow at least two weeks to explore, though one month will give you enough time to experience the best that

Bulgaria has to offer (which is just as well considering that you'll probably only have a 30-day visa anyway). You could stay for three months and still not see everything, but most visitors with that much time will sensibly detour to Greece, Turkey or Romania (or all three).

With one or two weeks, you'll probably only have time to concentrate on outdoor activities or cultural sites. And if you're travelling between Romania, and Greece or Turkey, or vice versa, your itinerary will probably be restricted to a north-south axis. The itineraries here are based on the assumption that you'll mostly use public transport. If you rent or charter a vehicle, you can obviously see more places more quickly, and visit remote villages and monasteries.

One Week
If you want to enjoy sand and sea, base yourself in Varna (four days) and Burgas (three days), and day trip to nearby beaches and villages. If you are a history and culture buff, see the museums, art galleries, villages and monasteries in and around Sofia (two days), Plovdiv (three days) and Veliko Târnovo (two days). If you are on a north-south route, visit Ruse (one day), Veliko Târnovo, Kazanlâk and around, and Plovdiv (two days each).

Two Weeks
The itinerary would be the same for those suggested for one week but with several additions. For beach lovers, spend an extra day in both Varna and Burgas as well as seeing Kiten, Ahtopol and Balchik and the laid-back town of Dobrich. On the history and culture trail, add visits to the traditional villages of Koprivshtitsa, Tryavna and Arbanasi. On the north-south route, add stops in Tryavna, Koprivshtitsa, Sofia and Bansko.

One Month
Most travellers choose a circular route between Sofia and the Black Sea coast (or vice versa). Try staying in Sofia for two or three days, then moving on through Rila Monastery and Bansko, then stopping in and around Plovdiv for four days. Continue through Sliven to spend time in the Black Sea towns of Burgas, Varna and Balchik, followed by stops in Dobrich, Shumen and Ruse in the north. Complete your circuit passing through the centre of the country via Veliko Târnovo, Tryavna, Kazanlâk (and around) and Koprivshtitsa.

Six Weeks
Follow the itinerary for one month, adding trips of two days each to Sandanski and Melnik, Samokov and Borovets, Stara Zagora, Vratsa, Pamporovo and Chepelare, Karlovo and Troyan, and Lovech and Pleven.

Two Months
Follow the itinerary for six weeks, allowing more time to relax at the beach, hike in the mountains, and visit remote monasteries, caves and villages. But bear in mind that you'll probably have to skip over the border into Greece or Turkey to get another 30-day visa.

PLANNING
Before planning your first trip to Bulgaria or Eastern Europe, grab a copy of Lonely Planet's *Read This First: Europe*. It explains the dos and don'ts and outlines the good and bad about travelling in this part of the world.

When to Go
Spring (particularly April to mid-June) is an excellent time to visit. The days are getting longer, the weather is good, the theatres and other cultural venues are in full swing, off-season rates still generally apply, and locals are not yet jaded by waves of summertime visitors. Summer (mid-June to early September) is ideal for hiking and festivals, but is the peak season for travellers from elsewhere in Europe. September can be perfect. The autumn trees are glorious, fruit and vegetables are plentiful, shoulder-season tariffs are in effect, the tourist hordes have returned home, and you can still swim and sunbathe at the Black Sea.

By mid-October, almost all Black Sea resorts close down. As the days get shorter and the weather gets colder over the next two months, a gloom about the impending winter (December to March) permeates Bulgaria. Then, as soon as the first snows fall in around mid-December, Bulgarians start to perk up and flock to the ski resorts, which sometimes stay operating until mid-April.

The peak season along the Black Sea coast is mid-July to late August; at the ski resorts, it's Christmas/New Year and February to mid-March. If you avoid these places at these times, you may be astounded at how few tourists there are in Bulgaria.

What Kind of Trip

Independent travel is really the only way to immerse yourself in the culture and enjoy everything that Bulgaria has to offer. Travelling this way is easy because public transport is cheap and frequent, plenty of restaurants have menus in English (and, sometimes, German), and many hotels have staff who speak English, German or French. However, travelling away from the bigger towns and resorts, and visiting some of the major attractions (which often do not have explanations in any language but Bulgarian), is not always easy.

If learning some Bulgarian words and phrases, and the Cyrillic alphabet, seems too hard, you crave some comfort or your time is short, consider an organised tour (see Organised Tours in the Getting Around and Getting There & Away chapters). The downside is that tours are expensive and inflexible, concentrate solely on a few major attractions, and often only operate during the peak season (July and August). But if you're on a package tour based at a beach or ski resort, it's easy to visit nearby attractions by public bus, hire car or locally organised tours.

Doubtless, many travellers will link their visit to Bulgaria with a jaunt around Eastern Europe and/or the Balkans. If so, it's important to spend some time considering the best places to enter and leave Bulgaria so you can see everything you want without backtracking.

Maps

Good maps are easy to find in Bulgaria, but you might want to buy one or two before you come. For a useful overview of the region, buy Geocenter's *Eastern Europe* map (1:2,000,000). The *Baedeker Bulgaria* map (1:750,000), and *Bulgaria* map (1:750,000) published by Bartholomew, will probably be available in your home country. Both are in English, but the latter annoyingly transliterates from Cyrillic using the 'Croatian' alphabet (eg, 'č' instead of 'ch').

Proper road maps are *essential* if you're driving Bulgaria. One of the best is the *Bulgaria Road Map* (1:500,000), published in English by Kartografia (with a red cover), but place names are also transliterated into the 'Croatian' alphabet. Slightly better is *Bulgaria* (1:530,000), published in English by Datamap (with a blue cover). It's colourful, detailed and has some city maps on the other side. A smaller version (1:760,000), published in Cyrillic, has a red cover (with a prominent ad for Happy Bar & Grill on the front). These maps are readily available in Bulgaria.

The maps in this guidebook will probably be more than sufficient for most visitors, but detailed maps (often in Cyrillic) are available in Bulgaria for most cities, towns and major attractions. Undoubtedly the best publisher is Domino (☎/fax 042-48 104, e press@domino.bg, w www.domino.bg). It offers maps (often with a red cover) of Bansko, Burgas, Blagoevgrad, Gabrovo, Haskovo, Kazanlâk, Koprivshtitsa, Melnik, Pleven, Plovdiv, Ruse, Sandanski, Sofia, Stara Zagora, Varna, Veliko Târnovo and Vidin. Most maps list street names in Cyrillic (which can be handy for linking maps with street signs), provide keys in Bulgarian and English, and include other towns and places in the region. Another respected map publisher is Datamap (☎/fax 02-951 5450, e datamap@mail.techno-link/com).

Also available in Bulgaria are a range of other maps for places along the Black Sea coast (see the Black Sea coast chapter for details), and for hiking (see Activities later in this chapter). Other detailed and useful maps, which are not always easy to find, include *The Monasteries in Bulgaria*, published by Kartografia in Cyrillic, and *Wine Map Bulgaria*, published in English by Bars Agency.

What to Bring

The availability of consumer goods is Bulgaria's most enthusiastic expression of capitalism. It's all there, and relatively cheap. If you're bringing a car or bicycle, it's worth carrying some spare parts, though you'll most likely find those as well.

A backpack is still the most popular method of carrying gear because it's convenient, especially for walking. On the downside, it doesn't offer too much protection for valuables, the straps tend to get caught on things and some airlines may refuse to accept responsibility if the pack is torn or tampered with. Travel-packs (combination backpack/shoulder bags) are increasingly popular. The backpack straps zip away inside the pack when they're not needed, so you almost have the best of both worlds. Another alternative is a large, soft zip bag with a wide shoulder strap so it can be carried with relative ease.

The climate will obviously have a bearing on what clothes you take along. Remember that insulation works on the principle of trapped air, so several layers of thin clothing are warmer than a single thick one (and will be easier to dry). You'll also be much more flexible if the weather suddenly turns warm. Be prepared for rain at any time of year.

A padlock is useful to lock your bag to a luggage rack in a bus or train; it may also be needed to secure your hostel locker. A Swiss Army knife comes in handy for all sorts of things. Toilet paper is provided in almost all hotels, but often not in restaurants or bars, and never in public toilets (where you can often buy a few measly squares), camping grounds, hostels and mountain huts. Tampons and condoms are available at chemists (pharmacies) and supermarkets in all but the most remote places.

A tent is vital if you want to camp and a sleeping bag is required if you're camping or staying at mountain huts. (Blankets and sheets are always provided in hotels, private rooms and larger hostels.) Except at mountain huts, hostels and basic hotels, towels are provided, but they're often threadbare and the size of a pygmy's handkerchief so you may want to bring your own.

Other optional items to bring include a compass, torch (flashlight), alarm clock, pocket calculator for currency conversions and indicating prices, adaptor plug for electrical appliances, universal bath/sink plug, combination knife, fork and spoon, portable short-wave radio and day-pack for city sightseeing. Also useful are clothes pegs, binoculars for viewing detail on churches and other buildings, or when trekking, and pre-moistened towelettes, or a large cotton

handkerchief for soaking in fountains and using to cool off in summer.

RESPONSIBLE TOURISM

Everyone travelling to Bulgaria can minimise the impact of their visit. Try to conserve water and electricity, respect traditions in villages, behave appropriately in religious buildings and leave ruins as they are. In addition, don't litter and don't destroy flora and fauna. Driving is often an ideal way to get around, but please bear in mind that traffic, and air and noise pollution, are increasing problems in Bulgaria.

One local organisation promoting different attractions is the Bulgarian Association for Alternative Tourism (☎ 02-989 0538, ⓔ baat-bg@hotmail.com). Another is the Bulgarian Association for Rural & Ecological Tourism (BARET; ☎/fax 02-971 3485, ⓔ baret@aster.net). According to its literature, BARET hopes to, 'ensure alternative sources of income for the population of rural and semi-mountainous areas, and to support sustainable development through the preservation of natural, cultural and historical heritage.' BARET has already established a number of excellent eco-trails (see Hiking in the Activities section later in this chapter).

For more information about the general problems caused by tourism, contact Tourism Concern (☎ 020-7753 3330, ⓦ www.tourismconcern.org.uk), 277–281 Holloway Rd, London N7 8HN, or contact Rethinking Tourism Project (ⓔ RTProject@aol.com) in the US.

TOURIST OFFICES

Despite large amounts of vital foreign capital obtained through tourism, and constant pleas from travel agencies and tourist operators, Bulgaria still doesn't have a dedicated ministry of tourism. Tourism is the responsibility of the Ministry of Economy, and gets a lower profile than it deserves.

Local Tourist Offices

The National Information & Advertising Center in Sofia (see the Sofia chapter for contact details) is the closest thing to a tourist office in the capital. In a concerted effort to boost regional tourism, the Bulgarian government has opened a number of autonomous, local tourist information centres (TICs) around the country. These TICs, however, are often little more than associations of travel agencies, rather than independent tourist offices dispensing free advice and useful maps. TICs of use to visitors are mentioned throughout this guidebook.

The former government-run tourism monopoly, Balkantourist, has been split up and privatised. The subsequent private agencies now operate under a myriad of different, though slightly ambiguous, names, such as Balkan Tours, Balkan Airtours and Balkan Holidays. These are essentially travel agencies and *not* tourist offices.

Tourist Offices Abroad

Over 40 official 'trade and tourist offices' can be found throughout the world, but most are only representatives. They offer a limited amount of literature and information, so it may be better to access Bulgarian-based Web sites before you arrive (see Digital Resources later in this chapter). Some offices worth contacting in your home country include:

Australia Bulgarian Consulate-General (☎ 02-9362 9838, fax 9362 9756) 4 Carlotta Rd, Double Bay, NSW 2028
Canada (☎ 0613-789 5341, fax 789 3524) 325 Stewart St, Ottawa, Ontario K1N 6K5
France (☎ 01-45 51 05 32, fax 45 51 78 97) 1 Ave Rapp, 75007 Paris
Germany (☎ 069-295 284, fax 295 286) Eckenhemier Landstrasse 101, 60318 Frankfurt am Main
Netherlands (☎ 070-346 8872, fax 363 6704) Alexander Godelweg 22, 2517 JJ, The Hague
UK (☎ 020-7589 8402, fax 7589 4875) 186–88 Queen's Gate, London, SW7 5HL
USA (☎/fax 0202-332 6609) 1621 22nd St NW, Washington DC 20008

VISAS & DOCUMENTS
Visas

Citizens of the following countries can obtain a free, 30-day tourist visa at any Bulgarian border and international airport (ie,

Sofia and Varna): all member countries of the European Union (EU), Australia, Canada, Croatia, the Czech Republic, Hungary, Ireland, Israel, Japan, Macedonia, New Zealand, Poland, Romania, the Slovak Republic, Switzerland, the UK, the US and Yugoslavia. However, it's important to note that at the time of writing tourist visas could not be extended.

If you wish to stay longer than 30 days and don't want to leave Bulgaria to get another 30-day visa, or you come from a country not listed above, apply for a visa before arriving in Bulgaria at one of the embassies or consulates listed (see Embassies & Consulates later in this chapter). Normally, the only option is a 90-day tourist visa which costs from US$30 to US$60 (depending on the country in which you get the visa). You will need to complete a visa application and provide two photos and a copy of your return ticket. The application, a leftover from the communist days, asks for your intended date and place of arrival (though not strictly enforced, it's better to be accurate), details of vehicles (if driving to and around Bulgaria), names of contacts in Bulgaria (if none, list a hotel from this guidebook), names of friends and/or relatives (optional, and not important), and available funds (not checked at the border or airport on arrival or departure). Allow about one week for the visa to be processed.

Strangely, some Bulgarian consulates and embassies, even those in neighbouring countries, are not well informed about current visa requirements. Some, for example, claim that statistical cards are still necessary (they're not) and a border tax is payable (it isn't).

Visa Extensions The 30-day tourist visa available on arrival could not, at the time of writing, be extended within Bulgaria. If you want to stay longer, apply for a 90-day visa (see earlier); better still, simply leave Bulgaria for Greece, Turkey or Romania, and return with another 30-day visa.

Extending a 90-day visa costs the leva equivalent of about US$100. In Sofia, apply at the Passport Office (☎ 02-982 3316) on bulevard Maria Luisa 48. The Passport Office is open Monday to Friday from 8.45am to 12.15pm and 1.30pm to 5.15pm. In Plovdiv, visit the Foreign Citizens Bureau (☎ 032-234 835) on ulitsa Petko D Petkov 9, which is open Monday to Friday from 8.45am to 12.15pm and 1.30pm to 5.15pm.

Registration

One bureaucratic leftover from the communist era, which still prevails for reasons the relevant authorities cannot properly explain, is the requirement that foreigners register with the police. At hotels, hostels, camping grounds, and, often, private homes, staff normally take details from your passport, fill out the registration form (in Cyrillic) and give you a copy. In theory, you must then show all of these forms to immigration officials when you leave. This requirement is almost never enforced, but it pays to keep a few copies of the registration forms with you in case you're asked for them when you leave. If you don't have any forms, or don't have enough, tell the immigration official that you lost the others, weren't given any, went camping, or whatever reasonable excuse comes to mind.

If you're staying with friends and relatives, or, sometimes, in a private home, you're supposed to personally register with the police within 48 hours. Ask someone where you're staying about the current requirements, and, if you need to register, ask them to accompany you to the nearest police station (where no-one is likely to speak anything but Bulgarian and Russian). If you're camping or staying in mountain huts, registration is obviously impossible – a fact which Immigration officials grudgingly accept.

Travel Insurance

A travel insurance policy to cover theft, loss and medical problems is a sensible idea. Some policies offer lower and higher medical-expense options. The higher ones are chiefly for countries, such as the USA, which have extremely high medical costs. There is a wide variety of policies available, so check the small print.

Some policies specifically exclude 'dangerous activities', which can include scuba diving, motorcycling and even trekking. A locally acquired motorcycle licence is not valid under some policies.

You may prefer a policy that pays doctors or hospitals directly rather than you having to pay on the spot and claim later. If you have to claim later make sure you keep all documentation. Some policies ask you to call back (reverse charges) to a centre in your home country where an immediate assessment of your problem is made.

Check that the policy covers ambulances and an emergency flight home.

Driving Licence & Permits

See Car & Motorcycle in the Getting Around and Getting There & Away chapters for information about driving licences, car insurance and other fees and paperwork associated with driving to and around Bulgaria.

Student, Youth & Teacher Cards

The International Student Identity Card (ISIC) is available to full-time students of any age, and the International Youth Travel Card (IYTC) is for anyone under 26 years old. In Bulgaria, holders of either card can obtain discounts of 10% to 20% at museums, some major attractions, hotels and hostels, some medical and dental clinics and

---

Orbita

Any of the cards mentioned in the Student, Youth & Teacher Cards section can be issued to anyone with the correct documentation. They cost the leva equivalent of US$5 each, and are available at the Bulgarian youth agency Orbita (☎ 02-987 9128, [e] orbita@ttm.bg), bulevard Hristo Botev 48, Sofia.

Orbita also has offices, and hostels and hotels available to anyone, at Batak (☎ 03542-3385), Blagoevgrad (☎ 073-25 516), Burgas (☎ 056-841 254), Lovech (☎ 068-21 143), Pleven (☎ 064-33 288), Plovdiv (☎ 032-270 270), Primorsko (☎ 05561-2045), Ruse (☎ 082-234 203), Silistra (☎ 086-27 096), Veliko Târnovo (☎ 062-621 502) and Varna (☎ 052-600 225).

a few restaurants. Selective travel agencies also offer card-holders up to 50% off domestic flights and 10% off train and bus tickets (depending on the agency and time of year). A brochure (in Cyrillic) listing places that offer these discounts is available from Orbita (see the boxed text 'Orbita'). More general information about these cards is available on the Web site W www.isic.org.

Also, an International Teacher Identity Card (ITIC), identifying the holder as a teacher or professor, offers similar discounts. More general information about this card is available on the Web site W www.istc.org.

Many places in Bulgaria that should accept these cards don't advertise the fact, so it's always worth asking at the entrance (as long as you have the right card).

Copies

All important documents (eg, passport data page and visa page, credit cards, travel insurance policy, air/bus/train tickets, driving licence etc) should be photocopied before you leave home. Leave one copy with someone at home and keep another with you, separate from the originals.

It's also a good idea to store details of your vital travel documents in Lonely Planet's free online Travel Vault in case you lose the photocopies or can't be bothered with them. Your password-protected Travel Vault is accessible online anywhere in the world – create it at W www.ekno .lonelyplanet.com.

EMBASSIES & CONSULATES
Bulgarian Embassies & Consulates

Major Bulgarian diplomatic missions around the world include:

Australia
Consulate-General: (☎ 02-9362 9838, fax 9362 9756) 4 Carlotta Rd, Double Bay, NSW 2028
Canada
Embassy: (☎ 0613-789 3215, e mailmn@ storm.ca) 325 Stewart St, Ottawa, K1N 6K5
France
Embassy: (☎ 01-45 51 85 90, fax 45 51 18 68) 1 Ave Rapp, 75007 Paris

Germany
Embassy: (☎ 030-201 0922, fax 208 6838) Mauerstrasse 11, 10117 Berlin
Greece
Embassy: (☎ 01-647 8105) Str Kallari 33, Psyhiko, Athens
Consulate: (☎ 031-829 210) N Manou 12, Thessaloniki
Ireland
Embassy: (☎ 01-660 3229, fax 660 3915) 22 Burlington Rd, Dublin
Macedonia
Embassy: (☎ 02-116 320, fax 116 139) ul HT Karpos 94a, Skopje
Netherlands
Embassy: (☎ 070-350 3051, fax 358 4688) Duinroosweg 9, 2597 KJ The Hague
Romania
Embassy: (☎ 01-211 1106) Str Vasile Lascăr 32, Bucharest
Turkey
Embassy: (☎ 0312-426 7456, fax 427 3178) Atatürk Bulvari 124, Kavaklidere, Ankara
Consulate: (☎ 0212-269 0478, fax 269 2216) Zincirlikuyu Caddesi 44, Ulus, Levent, Istanbul
UK
Embassy: (☎ 020-7584 9400, fax 7584 4948) 186–88 Queen's Gate, London SW7 5HL
USA
Embassy: (☎ 0202-387 0174, fax 234 7973, e consulate@bulgaria-embassy.org) 1621 22nd St NW, Washington DC 20008

Embassies & Consulates in Bulgaria

All embassies listed here are in Sofia (area code ☎ 02). A few consulates are also in Burgas (☎ 056) and Plovdiv (☎ 032). In emergencies, Australians should contact their embassy in Athens, Greece (☎ 30-1-644 7303), or the consulate in Bucharest, Romania (☎ 40-1-320 9802). Irish citizens should ring their consulate in Bucharest (☎ 40-1-302 9600) and New Zealanders should contact their honorary consulate in Athens (☎ 30-1-771 0112).

Albania
Embassy & Consulate: (☎ 946 1222) ul Krakra 10, Sofia. Open Monday to Friday 10am to 1pm; visas are available at the border (US$10).
Croatia
Embassy & Consulate: (☎ 943 3225) ul Krakra 18, Sofia. Open Monday to Friday

10am to 1pm; most visitors can get visas at the border (free).

France
Embassy: (☎ 965 1100, W www.ambafrance .bg) ul Oborishte 27–29, Sofia

Germany
Embassy: (☎ 918 380, e gemb@vilmat.com) ul Frederic Joliot-Curie 25, Sofia

Greece
Consulate: (☎ 946 1562) ul Oborishte 19, Sofia. Open Monday to Friday 9am to noon. *Consulate:* (☎ 632 003) ul Preslav 10, Plovdiv. Visas are available at the border (mostly free).

Macedonia
Embassy & Consulate: (☎ 705 098) ul Frederic Joliot-Curie 17, Sofia. Open Monday to Friday 10am to 1pm; visas must be obtained at the consulate – most are free, but Australians pay US$4.

Netherlands
Embassy: (☎ 962 5785) ul Galichitsa 38, Sofia

Romania
Embassy & Consulate: (☎ 973 3510) bul Sitnyakovo 4, Sofia. Open Tuesday 3pm to 5pm; Wednesday and Thursday 10am to noon; visas for most are available at the border (free), but transit visas (US$25) and tourist visas (US$35) are also available at the consulate.

Turkey
Embassy: (☎ 980 2270) bul Vasil Levski 80, Sofia. Visas are available at the border (mostly free).
Consulate: (☎ 844 2718) bul Demokratsiya 38, Burgas
Consulate: (☎ 239 010) Filip Makedonski 10, Plovdiv

UK
Embassy: (☎ 9339 2222) ul Moskovska 9, Sofia

USA
Embassy: (☎ 963 2022) ul Kapitan Andreev 1, Sofia

Yugoslavia
Consulate: (☎ 943 4590) ul Marin Drimov 17, Sofia. Open Monday to Friday 10am to 1pm; visa requirements change regularly, so contact the consulate for current information.

CUSTOMS

Whether or not you're inspected by customs officers depends on how you enter the country, but, generally, bona fide tourists are left alone. You're allowed to take in and out 'gifts up to a reasonable amount', souvenirs and articles for personal use. Foreigners (over 16 years old) are also permitted to bring in the following duty-free items: 200

Your Own Embassy

It's important to realise what your own embassy – the embassy of the country of which you are a citizen – can and cannot do to help you if you get into trouble. Generally speaking, it won't be much help in emergencies if the trouble you're in is remotely your own fault. Remember that you are bound by the laws of the country you're in. Your embassy will not be sympathetic if you end up in jail after committing a crime locally, even if such actions are legal in your own country.

In genuine emergencies you might get some assistance, but only if other channels have been exhausted. For example, if you need to get home urgently, a free ticket home is exceedingly unlikely – the embassy would expect you to have travel insurance. If you have all your money and documents stolen, it might assist with getting a new passport, but a loan for onward travel is out of the question.

Some embassies used to keep letters for travellers, or have a small reading room with home newspapers, but these days the mail-holding service has usually been stopped and even newspapers tend to be out of date.

cigarettes or 250g of tobacco, 2L of wine or 1L of another alcoholic drink, 500g of coffee and 50ml of perfume.

For information about exporting by plane unusual items like valuable archaeological artefacts and animal skins, contact the Customs authorities at the Sofia airport (☎ 02-0980 4500) or Customs at the Varna airport (☎ 052-225 532).

MONEY

The local currency is called *leva* (singular *lev*), which comprises of 100 *stotinki*. For major purchases such as organised tours, airfares, car rental, mid-range and top-end hotels, prices are almost always quoted by staff in US dollars. (However, in a few years the tendency may be to quote in euros instead.) In these cases, payment is possible in US dollars, leva or any major currency at the current exchange rates, and we have listed these prices throughout this guidebook in US dollars. While budget hotels, and some private rooms, may quote their rates in US dollars, payments should be made in leva (and rates are listed in this book in leva). All other transactions in Bulgaria are in leva (and listed as such in this book).

Currency
Bulgarian banknotes come in denominations of 1, 2, 5, 10, 20 and 50 leva. The word 'leva' is almost always shortened to 'lv', but it's sometimes abbreviated to BGN in official and business documents. Coins come in 1, 2, 5, 10, 20 and 50 stotinki. Prices for smaller items are always quoted in leva, or a fraction of a lev, ie, on a bus ticket, the fare will be listed as '0.40 lv' rather than '40 stotinki'.

In July 1997, a currency board in Bulgaria was established to officially peg the lev to the Deutschmark, ending a nightmarish skid of frequent devaluation and hyperinflation. Two years later, the lev was revalued to bring it into parity with the Deutschmark (ie, DM1 = 1 lev), and old 1000 lv notes, for example, were replaced with shiny new 1 lv notes. This caused temporary confusion, and some unscrupulous characters took advantage of confused foreigners, but happily this is all in the past.

When the euro was introduced in January 2002, the lev was automatically tied to the euro at the rate of exchange at that time. The costs of things in Bulgaria, and prices listed in this book, should not alter as a result of this change in currency policy.

When changing money, make sure that the foreign banknotes you have are not torn or marked (otherwise they may be refused) and if using US dollars always bring the new type of banknotes. Similarly, make sure that any leva given to you are not torn or marked. Foreigners may export and import up to 10,000 lv without restrictions.

Exchange Rates
Here are the official exchange rates for major currencies at the time of printing. Current rates are available on the Web site W www.oanda.com/convert/classic.

country	unit		leva
Australia	A$1	=	1.16 lv
Canada	C$1	=	1.39 lv
euro	€1	=	1.96 lv
Macedonia	1MKD	=	28.50 lv
Netherlands	f1	=	0.89 lv
New Zealand	NZ$1	=	0.92 lv
Japan	Y100	=	1.79 lv
Romania	10,000 lei	=	0.68 lv
Turkey	TL1,000,000	=	0.15 lv
UK	UK£1	=	3.13 lv
USA	US$1	=	2.21 lv
Yugoslavia	10DIN	=	0.33 lv

Exchanging Money
Cash The foreign currencies listed earlier (and several more) can be changed at any of the plethora of foreign-exchange offices at every city, town and major attraction. Most don't charge commission or fees, but some do – despite signs to the contrary on notice boards outside – so always check the final amount that you will be offered before handing over your cash. Lesser-known currencies, such as the Australian dollar, may not be exchangeable at every foreign-exchange office, but you should soon find somewhere in a large town or city that will accept Australian dollars.

The best currencies to take are US dollars but the euro may become the second most convertible currency (after the US dollar) in the future.

Foreign-exchange offices can generally be recognised by the huge 'exchange' signs, almost always written in English. Current rates are always displayed prominently, often on notice boards on the footpath outside. These offices are normally open from Monday to Saturday between about 9am and 6pm, but offices in the centre of cities and larger towns are often open every day. Foreign-exchange offices (and banks) will give you a receipt, but there's no need to keep it.

It's also easy to change cash at most of the larger banks found in cities and major towns; these include the United Bulgarian Bank, Bulbank, Bulgarian Post Bank, Raffeisen Bank and Biochim Commercial Bank. The exchange rates listed on electronic boards in bank windows may offer slightly higher rates than foreign-exchange offices, but many banks charge commission. The other disadvantages with banks are that they're only open between 9am and 4pm from Monday to Friday, and queues can be long.

The leva is freely convertible, so there are no problems changing excess leva back into dollars, or other major foreign currencies.

Travellers Cheques & Eurocheques
Travellers cheques are not as easily convertible as cash, nor as convenient as credit cards, but they are a safe way of carrying money. The downside is that not all foreign-exchange offices and banks will change travellers cheques, and those that do sometimes only accept American Express and Thomas Cook with commission rates of 3% to 5%. So if you need to change travellers cheques always look around for the best exchange rates. Some larger banks, eg, the Bulbank in Sofia, will change travellers cheques in US dollars into cash for a fee of about 2% to 3%.

Guaranteed personal cheques are another way of carrying money or obtaining cash. Eurocheques, available to European bank account holders, are guaranteed up to a certain limit. When cashing them, you'll be asked to show your Eurocheque card bearing your signature and registration number, and perhaps a passport or ID card. Many hotels and merchants in Bulgaria refuse to accept Eurocheques, however, because of the relatively large commissions involved.

ATMs Automatic teller machines (ATMs) which accept major credit cards (ie, Cirrus, Maestro, JCB, Visa, MasterCard and American Express) are an increasingly common sight, and not only in Sofia and along the Black Sea coast. It's best to use credit cards as a back-up for cash in case an ATM swallows your card (more likely if the card is issued outside Europe). Otherwise, bring two or three different cards. Also, before you leave home make absolutely sure your card is hooked up to an ATM network in Bulgaria and check with your bank about exchange rates (which, of course, favour them) and commissions (which can be

about 2%). The total amount you can withdraw depends on how much your bank will allow, and the amount in your account; the maximum allowed per day by most Bulgarian banks is usually 200 lv.

Credit Cards While credit cards for purchases are still not as common or reliable in Bulgaria as in Western or northern Europe, they are gaining ground, especially American Express, Visa and MasterCard. These three cards can usually be used at upmarket restaurants, tourist-oriented souvenir shops, top-end hotels, car-rental firms, travel agencies and some petrol stations, but rarely anywhere else – despite signs indicating acceptance of credit cards. You cannot rely on using a credit card exclusively in Bulgaria; use it to get cash from banks and for major purchases only. Some places, particularly the more expensive hotels, will add a 5% surcharge to your bill if you use a credit card.

If no ATM is available, or you're worried about using one (in case it swallows your card), some larger branches of major banks will provide cash advances in leva over the counter; this service is also sometimes offered by foreign-exchange offices. The fee is usually about 4%, and you'll probably also be charged fees and commissions by your bank. The maximum withdrawal allowed for cash advances depends on what is determined by your bank.

International Transfers Telegraphic transfers are not that expensive but they can be quite slow through a bank. Having money wired through American Express, Money-Gram or Western Union is fairly straightforward, and faster than a bank (funds are sometimes available in less than one day). You should know the sender's full name, the exact amount and the reference number when you're picking up the cash. With a passport or other ID, you can pick up the amount in US dollars or leva. The sender pays the fee, which can range from 5% to 15% depending on all sorts of things.

Black Market With the currency stabilisation, no black market exists in Bulgaria.

Foreigners may still be approached (especially in Varna, Sofia and Plovdiv) to change money, but this is illegal, and there's a high chance you'll be given counterfeit leva, short-changed or robbed.

Security

To keep money, passports etc safe from pickpockets, the best place is out of sight under your clothes. It's easy to make a cloth pouch that hangs around your neck or waist, or is pinned under clothing. Alternatively, buy a moneybelt. Other methods include belts with concealed compartments, and pouches worn around the leg. Try not to keep everything in one place; keep small change and a few banknotes in a shirt pocket to pay for bus tickets and small expenses without having to extract wads of cash from a secret hiding place. It may also help if you distribute valuables about your person and baggage, especially if you must carry all your belongings at once.

Costs

Despite having to pay more than Bulgarians for most hotel rooms and admission fees (see Dual Pricing later), travelling around the country is cheap. All food, drink and forms of transport are surprisingly inexpensive, but imported goods, eg, compact discs of Western music, are prohibitively dear. See Student, Youth & Teacher Cards earlier about discount cards.

As an example, a camp site costs about 10 lv per person and a room in a private home is about 22 lv. In a budget hotel a single room costs from 15 lv, 25 lv for a double. In a midrange hotel a single room is 35 lv, a double 55 lv. A meal of Bulgarian food at a cafe is about 2.50 lv and a feed of non-Bulgarian cuisine at a decent restaurant is around 7 lv, including soup, salad and a beer. A small bottle of local beer is about 1.50 lv and imported beer costs about 2.50 lv. A small bottle of soft drink is 0.60 lv and mineral water is 0.40 lv. Petrol is expensive at 1.50 lv per litre, but public buses are very cheap – about 2 lv per 50km. Taxis are affordable at about 0.30 lv per kilometre. A flight between Sofia and the Black Sea costs from US$50 one-way.

Therefore, if you stay at budget hotels or in private rooms, eat cheap Bulgarian food and catch public buses and 2nd-class trains, allow at least US$16/14 per person per day travelling as a single/double. Budget for about US$17/20 per person per day if you include a beer or two in the evening, an occasional taxi, one decent restaurant meal a day and acceptable budget accommodation. If you want to stay in the cheaper mid-range hotels, eat non-Bulgarian food at nice restaurants, charter occasional taxis, take 1st-class trains and buy souvenirs, allow about US$30/25 per person per day.

Dual Pricing One annoying aspect of travelling around Bulgaria is that tourists are charged considerably more for some things than Bulgarians and foreign residents (those with documents to prove they live and/or work in Bulgaria). Most accommodation costs about two or three times more for foreigners than locals. This can be avoided to some degree by camping, staying in private rooms or looking for hotels that do not discriminate against foreigners.

Also, admission to tourist attractions costs between two and five times more for foreigners – which is even more galling when you consider that most museums don't label exhibits in any language but Bulgarian. While accommodation and admission fees may eat into your daily budget, this is easily offset by remarkably cheap food, drink and public transport.

Before you complain too much about dual pricing, however, it's worth noting that a university professor in Bulgaria may only earn US$150 per month, and a roadworker may take home as little as US$35 each month.

Tipping & Bargaining

Waiters normally round restaurant bills up to the nearest convenient figure and pocket the difference; the same applies to taxi drivers. In some restaurants a 10% service charge is already added. If it's not and the service is good (a rarity) add about 10%. Always leave the tip on the table (but make sure no beggars or street kids are within sight if you're sitting outside); it's sociably unacceptable to give a tip to the waiter by hand.

Unlike in Turkey, haggling is not customary in Bulgaria. An exception is at the seaside resorts where taxi drivers and landlords of private rooms habitually inflate prices for foreigners.

Taxes
The value added tax (VAT) of 20% is included in all prices quoted in Bulgaria – and is included in all prices listed in this guidebook. Some restaurants add service charges of 10%, and some top-end hotels add a 5% surcharge if you use a credit card.

POST & COMMUNICATIONS
Post
The normal cost of sending a postcard anywhere is 0.32 lv, but the 'express service' (which is usually quicker) costs 0.44 lv to all countries in Europe and 0.56 lv to the rest of the world. Normally, letters weighing up to 20g cost 0.65 lv; the 'express service' is 0.77 lv to Europe and 0.89 lv to anywhere else.

If you wish to receive snail mail while travelling, have it sent to a poste restante at the main (central) post office in a major town or city. Tell your correspondents to put the number one (1) after the town/city name to ensure that the letter goes to the main post office, and to underline your last name, because letters are often misfiled under first names. Poste restante offices seldom hold letters longer than one month, and some charge a small fee for each letter picked up. Mail addressed 'c/o Poste Restante, Sofia 1000, Bulgaria' can be picked up at window No 8 in the Central Post Office (see the Sofia chapter for details).

To send a parcel from Bulgaria you usually have to take it unwrapped to a main post office. Anything heavier than 2kg must often be taken to a special customs post office.

Telephone
From Bulgaria, it's easy to telephone anywhere in the world from public telephone booths, telephone centres, private homes, and hotels.

The three operators are the Bulgarian Telecommunications Company (BTC), Mobika and BulFon. Some of the BTC phone booths that accept coins belong in a museum, while others have been upgraded and require a token (0.50 lv) from a nearby shop. The blue booths (Mobika) and the orange booths (BulFon) accept phonecards, while some Mobika booths also accept Visa and MasterCard for long-distance calls (and have instructions in English). Phonecards for either operator, which cost from 5 lv to 25 lv and are available at most newspaper stands and grocery shops, can be used throughout the country. Mobika and BulFon booths can be used to make local calls, and direct long-distance calls to Europe and North America, but to anywhere else you have to use the international operator (see later).

Every major settlement throughout the country has a BTC centre, normally inside or very near to the main post office. BTC centres are normally open from at least 8am to 6pm every day, and often 24 hours a day in larger towns. Making a local or long-distance call at a BTC centre is simple: choose a booth (or take a token indicating which booth to use), call the number and pay the amount displayed on the counter above the telephone.

Calls from a private home are cheapest. As you would expect they are more expensive (often twice as much) from a hotel than a BTC centre. From a BTC centre, a call to the UK and continental Europe costs 1.73 lv per minute; 2.16 lv per minute to North America; and 2.88 lv per minute to Australia and New Zealand. No off-peak rates are available. Local calls are so cheap that most hotels allow guests to use the telephone at the reception desk for no charge.

To ring Bulgaria from abroad, dial the international access code (which varies from country to country), add 359 (the country code for Bulgaria), the area code (minus the first zero) and then the number.

As the telecommunication systems in rural areas are slowly being upgraded some numbers will change – often with the addition of digits to the beginning of the number. If any of the numbers listed in this guidebook do not work, check the telephone directory (mostly written in Bulgarian and English), or ring one of the inquiry numbers listed here. These numbers can be dialled toll-free anywhere within Bulgaria, and there's a good chance one of the operators will speak English.

International directory inquiries	(☎ 124)
International operator	(☎ 0123)
National directory inquiries for businesses	(☎ 144)
National directory inquiries for homes	(☎ 145)
National operator	(☎ 121)

Mobile Phones Bulgarians have taken to mobile (cell) phones like ducks to water, and somehow manage to balance their cigarette and coffee while chatting away on a *handy* (as they are sometimes called). Mobile telephone numbers have different codes (eg, 087 and 088), and are indicated by the abbreviations 'GSM' or 'mob'. Each of the three operators, GloBul, Mobikom and MobilTel, cover most of the country, but contact your own mobile phone company about the usability of your phone in Bulgaria.

Fax
Faxes can be sent from most post offices and BTC centres throughout Bulgaria. One page costs 2.48 lv to the UK and continental Europe, 2.76 lv to North America, and 3.72 lv to Australia and New Zealand. Incoming faxes can be collected for a nominal fee.

Email & Internet Access
Bulgaria is now well and truly 'connected', and even the smallest town has at least one Internet centre. With about 150 Internet service providers throughout the country, competition is fierce and access is remarkably cheap: about 1 lv for 30 minutes, and 1.50 lv to 2 lv per hour. Internet centres are usually open from Monday to Saturday between about 10am and 9pm. Look for places with the word 'cafe' or 'centre' (often in English) rather than anywhere with the word 'games', because these places are usually dingy, smoky bunkers where teenage boys endlessly play violent and deafening computer games.

DIGITAL RESOURCES
The World Wide Web is a rich resource for travellers. You can research your trip, hunt down bargain air fares, book hotels, check on weather conditions or chat with locals and other travellers about the best places to visit (or avoid!).

There's no better place to start your Web explorations than the Lonely Planet Web site (W www.lonelyplanet.com). Here you will find succinct summaries on travelling to most places on earth, postcards from other travellers and the Thorn Tree bulletin board, where you can ask questions before you go or dispense advice when you get back. You can also find travel news and updates to many of our most popular guidebooks, and the subWWWay section links you to the most useful travel resources elsewhere on the Web.

Other useful Web sites (all in English) to access before you travel include:

Bulgarian Business Adviser Best for business news and links W www.bba.bg

Bulgarian Ministry of Foreign Affairs Good for current affairs and links to all government departments W www.mfa.government.bg

Bulgaria Online News, shopping etc, with links to weather and exchange rates, but some information is out of date W www.onlinebg.com

Dir.bg One of the best starting points, with search facilities and excellent links W www.dirbg.com

HotelsCentral.com Offers attractive discounts for hotel rooms (if booked for three or more nights) W www.hotelsbulgaria.com

National Center for Music & Dance The best place for anything musical; also lists cultural events W www.bulgarianspace.com/bmg

News.bg All sorts of information, eg, weather, news and exchange rates W www.news.bg

BOOKS
Be aware that most books are published in different editions by different publishers in different countries. As a result, a book might be a hardcover rarity in one country while it's readily available in paperback in another. Fortunately, bookshops and libraries search by title or author, so your local bookshop or library is best placed to advise you on the availability of the following recommendations of useful titles.

Lonely Planet

Lonely Planet publishes guides to most other Eastern European countries, including *Croatia, Czech & Slovak Republics, Hungary, Poland, Romania & Moldova* and *Slovenia*, as well as the doorstopper *Russia & Belarus*. If you're planning a quick jaunt around a few countries in the region, also pick up Lonely Planet's *Eastern Europe*. If you're heading to this part of the world for the first time, check out *Read This First: Europe*, which is full of predeparture advice, suggested itineraries and route maps.

Guidebooks

We believe you're holding the best guidebook there is to Bulgaria, but for detailed, specific information look out for the colourful but expensive *Bulgarian Monasteries*, the thinner and cheaper *Bulgarian Monasteries Album-Guidebook* by Georgi Chavrakov, the detailed *Traditional Bulgarian Costumes & Folk Arts*, published by the Bulgarian Academy of Sciences, or *Museums in Bulgaria*. Each is translated in English and available at major bookshops in Bulgaria (best in Sofia).

Travel

Most authors of travel books include Bulgaria as part of a journey around Eastern Europe and/or the Balkans.

A Time of Gifts and *Between the Woods and the Water* by Patrick Leigh Fermor are among the most intriguing travel books on Eastern Europe. They detail Fermor's walk in 1933–34 from Holland to Turkey on a budget of UK£1 a week.

Stealing from a Deep Place by Brian Hall details his extensive travels through Hungary, Romania, Bulgaria and parts of former Yugoslavia.

Balkan Ghosts by Robert D Kaplan offers a contemporary traveller's view of a region torn by ethnic strife and economic upheaval.

History & Politics

The Bulgarians from Pagan Times to the Ottoman Conquest by David Marshall Lang has maps, illustrations and lucid text that make this book well worth reading and help bring medieval Bulgaria to life.

Thracian Cult Architecture by Malvina Rousseva is the definitive work about the Thracian history of Bulgaria and is excellent. It has mainly written for history and archaeology buffs.

A Short History of Modern Bulgaria by RJ Crampton gives an incisive and detailed, if somewhat dry, history. It was re-released in 1997 with updated chapters.

Bulgarians: Civilisers of the Slavs is a small and readable, but somewhat biased, account by an unknown author of the country's religious and cultural history. It's also available in German.

The Balkans: A Short History by Mark Mazower is a thin book that covers most of what the average traveller needs to know about the turbulent region.

Eastern Europe and Communist Rule by JF Brown is a readable political history of Eastern Europe's four decades of communism with special attention to the 1970s and 1980s. Also worth reading is Brown's *Surge to Freedom: The End of Communist Rule in Eastern Europe*.

We the People by Timothy Garton Ash offers a clear and insightful interpretation of the collapse of communism throughout the region in 1989. Also recommended is *The Uses of Adversity* and *The Magic Lantern: The Revolution of '89 Witnessed* by the same author.

General

Bulgarian Cuisines by Dimitâr Mantov is the best recipe book (and souvenir) if you want to impress friends with a tasty *kavarma* when you get home. The *Bulgarian Folk Jewellery 18th-20th Century* published by the Bulgarian Academy of Sciences is also worth a look.

If you're going to spend a while in the country, it's a good idea to pick up a bi-lingual dictionary (ie, in Bulgarian Cyrillic, and English, German or French). Gaberoff publishes a number of dictionaries, from ones that can fit into a pocket to others which can double as doorstops. They're all pleasingly cheap: for example, Gaberoff's 800-page Bulgarian-English and English-Bulgarian dictionary costs only 10 lv.

Far more convenient, however, is Lonely Planet's *Eastern Europe Phrasebook*, which also includes languages of neighbouring countries, such as Romanian.

FILMS

The quality and quantity of films produced by Bulgarians is sporadic. Some worthwhile films which have been shown internationally include *Christmas Eve, Blueberry Hill, The Devil's Trail, A Letter to America, The Prize* and *Goat's Horn*. Renowned Bulgarian directors include Stefan Danailov and Ivan Nitchev, who directed the joint German-Bulgarian drama *After the End of the World*.

Foreign films, such as *I Am Here*, are sometimes shot in Bulgaria because of the cheap labour, reliable weather, and beautiful and varied landscapes. Kovachevitsa in the Rodopi Mountains near Gotse Delchev is a particularly picturesque village where scenes from over 100 Bulgarian and foreign films have been shot.

NEWSPAPERS & MAGAZINES

Several hundred newspapers are regularly published throughout Bulgaria. Many are unashamedly politically biased, and others simply aim to, umm, titillate male readers.

Two respected daily newspapers are *Trud* (Work) and *24 Chasa* (24 Hours). If you're visiting Sofia, pick up *The Sofia Echo* (W www.sofiaecho.com), an informative English-language newspaper published on Friday, and the perky *Sofia City Info Guide* (W www.sofiacityguide.com), printed every month in English. Day-old copies of major British and German newspapers are available in central Sofia and at beach resorts along the Black Sea coast.

English-language business magazines of minimal interest to normal tourists include *AmCham Bulgarian Magazine*, published free every month in cooperation with the American Chamber of Commerce, and the bi-monthly *Bulgaria Business*, which is virtually an advertising broadsheet. *Time* and *Newsweek* are available at hotels and bookstalls in central Sofia and at beach resorts along the Black Sea coast.

RADIO & TV

One of the downsides of Bulgaria's embrace of free-market capitalism is the unfettered proliferation of private radio and cable TV stations, most of which put short-term profit above quality broadcasting. The result is bizarre radio playlists (eg, Paul Anka segueing into Black Sabbath), and mundane and technically poor TV programming (eg, fuzzy, dubbed Spanish soap operas), all peppered with rapid-fire ads and listener callins. It's enough to make you wistful for the days of communist censorship.

Some radio stations (usually with announcers speaking in Bulgarian and playing foreign music) worth listening to in Sofia include BG Radio (91.9FM), Radio Contact (106FM), Jazz FM (104FM), also appreciated by jazz fans in most major cities, and Classic FM (89.1FM), for highbrow listeners. Darrik Radio, a nationwide network of stations which usually play contemporary pop music, can be heard in Sofia (98.3FM), Varna (90.7FM), Plovdiv (94.6FM), Ruse (104FM) and Veliko Târnovo (88.9FM).

Several international short-wave services can be found on FM stations in Sofia. These include Voice of America (103.9FM), BBC (91FM), Deutsche Welle (95.7FM) and Radio France Internationale (103.6FM). Elsewhere throughout Bulgaria, the BBC is frustratingly difficult to receive on a short-wave radio.

Bulgarian television is nothing to get excited about, which is why locals with enough money buy satellite dishes. There is one government-run channel (Kanal 1), and three private ones (BTV, Novi Televizyia and Sedemte Dni). Televisions in most – but certainly not all – hotel rooms can pick up a plethora of stations from around the region, so you can enjoy Israeli talent quests, Cypriot game shows and Russian soap operas, as well as CNN, BBC, Eurosport and MTV.

VIDEO SYSTEMS

If you want to record or buy videotapes to play at home, you won't be able to get the picture if the image registration systems are different. Like Australia and most of Europe, Bulgaria uses a PAL system, which is incompatible with the North American and Japanese NTSC system.

PHOTOGRAPHY & VIDEO
Film & Equipment
The people and landscapes of Bulgaria are extremely photogenic so bring (or buy along the way) plenty of film. Photographic and video film and equipment are available everywhere, but, obviously, shops in the larger cities and towns have a wider selection, and everything for sale near tourist sites is overpriced. As an example, a role of 24/36 print film from a photographic shop in Sofia or Plovdiv costs about 4.50/7.50 lv; developing costs are about 0.30 lv per print, more for larger prints or faster service. A roll of 24 slide film (without processing) costs about 9.90 lv, but is not easy to find, so bring your own. Developing slides is also a difficult, lengthy and expensive process, so wait until you get home.

Anyone serious about taking great snaps should pick up *A Guide to Taking Better Pictures* published by Lonely Planet.

Restrictions
Taking pictures of anything in Bulgaria that might be considered of strategic importance – from bridges and tunnels to train stations and border crossings – is not advisable. These days, officials are much less paranoid about photography than they used to be, but use common sense when it comes to this issue. And please ask permission before taking close-up photos of people.

TIME
Bulgaria is on Eastern European Time, ie, GMT/UTC plus two hours, except during daylight saving, when clocks are put forward by one hour between the last Sunday of March and the last Sunday in October. There are no time zones within the country.

Bulgaria is one hour behind Yugoslavia and Macedonia, and the same time as Romania, Greece and Turkey. Therefore, if it's noon in Sofia, it's 2am in Los Angeles, 5am in New York, 10am in London, 11am in Paris and 8pm in Sydney – not taking into account daylight saving (where applicable)

in these countries. The 24-hour clock is commonly used throughout Bulgaria, and always indicated on bus and train timetables.

ELECTRICITY
Bulgaria runs on 220V, 50Hz AC. Most appliances set up for 240V will handle this without modifications. Plugs are the standard round two-pin variety, sometimes called the 'europlug'. If your plugs are of different design, you'll need an adaptor.

WEIGHTS & MEASURES
Bulgaria uses the metric system for everything. To convert between metric and imperial units, refer to the conversion chart on the inside back cover of this book.

LAUNDRY
Coin-operated laundrettes are rare in Bulgaria, but dry cleaners can be found in most cities and major towns. You'll be charged per piece, and they won't accept underwear and socks (so wash your smalls in a hotel sink). Some budget and mid-range hotels, but certainly not all, offer a laundry service to guests. The cost is negotiable and ranges from 5 lv for a large bundle to 3-4 lv for a shirt or skirt.

TOILETS
With the exception of a few Middle Eastern-style squat toilets near the Turkish border, almost all toilets in Bulgaria are the sit-down European variety. All hotels provide toilet paper, but it's rarely offered anywhere else. The small bins near toilets are for used toilet paper; throwing paper down the toilet may block the pipes.

The standard of public toilets, especially at train and bus stations, is generally abominable and staff have the gall to charge at least 0.10 lv per visit (more for a few squares of see-through toilet paper). So, if you can't get back to your hotel, visit a museum, classy bar or restaurant. Western fast-food franchises, such as McDonald's, always have clean toilets with toilet paper. More acceptable privately-run toilets are available for about 0.20 lv a pop in central Sofia and the Black Sea resorts.

HEALTH

While the potential dangers can seem quite frightening, in reality few travellers experience anything more than an upset stomach.

Bulgaria is a fairly healthy place to travel around. Every city and major town has a government hospital of an acceptable – albeit not excellent – standard. Smaller towns and villages may have a clinic, but locals with serious complaints often travel to a larger town with better facilities. There are several high-quality, but comparatively expensive, private hospitals in Sofia.

Although doctors at government hospitals are well-trained and enthusiastic, and most speak English and/or German, equipment can be lacking and outdated. Most clinics have the word 'doctor' (in English) somewhere on or near the door; a red cross is also an obvious and common indicator. However, if you have a really serious problem ask your embassy/consulate to recommend a hospital, clinic, doctor or dentist. In extreme situations you would be advised to go home.

Citizens of Belgium, the Czech Republic, Hungary, Poland and the UK can receive emergency treatment at government hospitals for no charge (but medicines cost extra). All other foreigners must pay for their treatment and medicines in leva, either by cash or by bank transfer.

Dental clinics in Bulgaria are similarly under-equipped, but they are easy to find. Pharmacies (chemists) are common, but are better stocked with more up-to-date medicines in larger towns and cities. Many medicines can be bought at pharmacies without prescriptions from doctors.

Predeparture Planning

Make sure you're healthy before you start travelling. Before a long trip make sure your teeth are OK and if you wear glasses, take a spare pair and your prescription.

If you require a particular medication take an adequate supply, because it may not be available locally. Take part of the packaging showing the generic name rather than the brand, which will make getting replacements easier. To avoid any problems, it's a

Medical Kit Check List

Following is a list of items you should consider including in your medical kit – consult your pharmacist for brands available in your country.

- ☐ **Aspirin or paracetamol (acetaminophen in the USA)** – for pain or fever
- ☐ **Antihistamine** – for allergies, eg, hay fever; to ease the itch from insect bites or stings; and to prevent motion sickness
- ☐ **Cold and flu tablets, throat lozenges and nasal decongestant**
- ☐ **Multivitamins** – consider for long trips, when dietary vitamin intake may be inadequate
- ☐ **Antibiotics** – consider including these if you're travelling well off the beaten track; see your doctor, as they must be prescribed, and carry the prescription with you
- ☐ **Loperamide or diphenoxylate** –'blockers' for diarrhoea
- ☐ **Prochlorperazine or metaclopramide** – for nausea and vomiting
- ☐ **Rehydration mixture** – to prevent dehydration, which may occur, for example, during bouts of diarrhoea; particularly important when travelling with children
- ☐ **Insect repellent, sunscreen, lip balm and eye drops**
- ☐ **Calamine lotion, sting relief spray or aloe vera** – to ease irritation from sunburn and insect bites or stings
- ☐ **Antifungal cream or powder** – for fungal skin infections and thrush
- ☐ **Antiseptic (such as povidone-iodine)** – for cuts and grazes
- ☐ **Bandages, Band-Aids (plasters) and other wound dressings**
- ☐ **Water purification tablets or iodine**
- ☐ **Scissors, tweezers and a thermometer** – note that mercury thermometers are prohibited by airlines

good idea to have a legible prescription, or letter from your doctor, to show that you legally use the medication.

Immunisations Vaccinations are not required for travel to Bulgaria, but there are a few routine immunisations that are

Everyday Health

Normal body temperature is up to 37°C
(98.6°F); more than 2°C (4°F) higher indicates a high fever. The normal adult pulse
rate is 60 to 100 per minute (children 80 to
100, babies 100 to 140). As a general rule the
pulse increases about 20 beats per minute for
each 1°C (2°F) rise in fever.

Respiration (breathing) rate is also an indicator of illness. Count the number of breaths
per minute: Between 12 and 20 is normal for
adults and older children (up to 30 for
younger children, 40 for babies). People with
a high fever or serious respiratory illness
breathe more quickly than normal. More than
40 shallow breaths a minute may indicate
pneumonia.

recommended if you're travelling to, for example, the Middle East, and there are other
jabs that all travellers should have anyway.
However, it is recommended that you have
a vaccination against typhoid as typhoid
fever is common in Bulgaria (especially in
summer). Vaccination is available either as
an injection or capsules taken orally.

Always carry proof of your vaccinations,
especially yellow fever, as this is sometimes
needed to enter some countries. Plan ahead
to get your vaccinations: some require more
than one injection, while others should not
be given together. Note that some vaccinations should not be given during pregnancy,
to children, or to people with allergies. It's
recommended that you seek medical advice
at least six weeks before travel.

Health Insurance Make sure that you
have adequate health insurance. See Travel
Insurance in the Visas & Documents section earlier in this chapter.

Travel Health Guides There are a number
of excellent travel health sites on the Internet. From the Lonely Planet home page,
there are links at w www.lonelyplanet.com/
weblinks/wlheal.htm to the World Health
Organization and the US Center for Disease Control & Prevention.

Basic Rules

Food Vegetables and fruit should be
washed with purified water or peeled where
possible, but most restaurants in Bulgaria
are fairly hygienic. Beware of ice cream
sold on the street, or anywhere it might have
melted and been refrozen. Milk should be
treated with suspicion because it's often un-
pasteurised, though boiled milk is fine if
it's kept hygienically. Tea and coffee will
also be OK, because the water should have
been boiled properly.

Water In all cities and major towns, tap
water is fine to drink – it may not taste
great, but it won't cause you any grief.
However, caution should be taken in
smaller villages, and at remote places like
monasteries where the water pipes may be
as old as the buildings themselves. An ideal
source of drinkable water (and great for refilling water bottles) is the fountains in
town parks and outside monasteries and
churches. Water spouts, known as a
cheshma and often found alongside main
roads, also offer constant supplies of fresh,
delicious and safe water.

If in doubt, boil water thoroughly, or use
a filter. Vigorous boiling should be satis-
factory; however, at higher altitude water
boils at a lower temperature, so germs are
less likely to be killed. Boil it for longer in
these environments. Otherwise, plastic bottles of mineral water can be bought just
about everywhere.

Medical Problems & Treatment

Self-diagnosis and treatment can be risky,
so you should always seek medical help.
Although we do give drug dosages in this
section, they are for emergency use only.
Correct diagnosis is vital. In this section, we
have used the generic names for medications – check with a chemist (pharmacist)
for brands available locally.

Note that antibiotics should ideally be
administered only under medical supervision. Take only the recommended dose at
the prescribed intervals and use the whole
course, even if the illness seems to be cured
earlier. Stop immediately if there are any

serious reactions, and don't use the antibiotic at all if you're unsure that you have the correct one. Some people are allergic to commonly prescribed antibiotics such as penicillin; carry this information (eg, on a bracelet) when travelling.

Environmental Hazards

Heat Exhaustion Dehydration and salt deficiency can cause heat exhaustion. Take time to acclimatise to high temperatures, drink sufficient liquids and do not do anything too physically demanding.

Salt deficiency is characterised by fatigue, lethargy, headaches, giddiness and muscle cramps; salt tablets may help, but adding extra salt to your food is better.

Hypothermia Hypothermia occurs when the body loses heat faster than it can produce it, so the core temperature of the body falls. It's surprisingly easy to progress from very cold to dangerously cold due to a combination of wind, wet clothing, fatigue and hunger, even if the air temperature is above freezing. It's best to dress in layers; silk, wool and some of the new artificial fibres are all good insulating materials. A hat is important, because a lot of heat is lost through the head. A strong, waterproof outer layer (and a 'space' blanket for emergencies) is essential. Carry basic supplies, including food containing simple sugars to generate heat quickly, and fluids to drink.

Symptoms of hypothermia are exhaustion, numb skin (particularly toes and fingers), shivering, slurred speech, irrational or violent behaviour, lethargy, stumbling, dizzy spells, muscle cramps and violent bursts of energy. Irrationality may take the form of sufferers claiming they're warm and trying to take off their clothes.

To treat mild hypothermia, first get the person out of the wind and/or rain, remove their clothing if it's wet and replace it with dry, warm clothing. Give them hot liquids – not alcohol – and some high-kilojoule, easily digestible food. Do not rub victims: instead, allow them to slowly warm themselves. This should be enough to treat the early stages of hypothermia. The early recognition and treatment of mild hypothermia is the only way to prevent severe hypothermia, which is a critical condition.

Diarrhoea Simple things like a change of water, food or climate can all cause a mild bout of diarrhoea, but a few rushed toilet trips with no other symptoms is not indicative of a major problem.

Dehydration is the main danger with any diarrhoea, particularly in children or the elderly as dehydration can occur quite quickly. Under all circumstances *fluid replacement* (at least equal to the volume being lost) is the most important thing to remember. Weak black tea with a little sugar, soda water, or soft drinks allowed to go flat and diluted 50% with clean water, are all good. With severe diarrhoea, a rehydrating solution is preferable to replace minerals and salts lost. Commercially available oral rehydration salts (ORS) are very useful; add them to boiled or bottled water. In an emergency you can make up a solution of six teaspoons of sugar and a half teaspoon of salt to a litre of boiled or bottled water. Urine is the best guide to the adequacy of replacement – if you have small amounts of concentrated urine, you need to drink more. Keep drinking small amounts often. Stick to a bland diet as you recover.

Infectious Diseases

Hepatitis Hepatitis is a general term for inflammation of the liver, and is a common disease worldwide. Several different viruses cause hepatitis, and they differ in the way that they're transmitted. The symptoms are similar in all forms of the illness, and include fever, chills, headache, fatigue, feelings of weakness and aches and pains, followed by loss of appetite, nausea, vomiting, abdominal pain, dark urine, light-coloured faeces, jaundiced (yellow) skin and yellowing of the whites of the eyes. People who have had hepatitis should avoid alcohol for some time after the illness, as the liver needs time to recover.

Hepatitis A is transmitted by contaminated food and drinking water. You should seek medical advice, but there's not much you can do apart from resting, drinking lots of fluids, eating lightly and avoiding fatty foods. Hepatitis E is transmitted in the same way as hepatitis A; it can be particularly serious in pregnant women.

There are almost 300 million chronic carriers of **hepatitis B** in the world. It's spread through contact with infected blood, blood products or body fluids, for example through sexual contact, unsterilised needles and blood transfusions, or contact with blood via small breaks in the skin. Other risk situations include having a shave, tattoo or body piercing with contaminated equipment. The symptoms of hepatitis B may be more severe than type A, and the disease can lead to long-term problems such as chronic liver damage, liver cancer or a long-term carrier state. Hepatitis C and D are spread in the same way as hepatitis B, and can also lead to long-term complications.

There are vaccines against hepatitis A and B, but there are currently no vaccines against the other types of hepatitis. Following the basic rules about food and water (hepatitis A and E) and avoiding risk situations (hepatitis B, C and D) are important preventative measures.

HIV & AIDS Infection with the human immunodeficiency virus (HIV) may lead to acquired immune deficiency syndrome (AIDS), which is a fatal disease. Any exposure to blood, blood products or body fluids may put the individual at risk. The disease is often transmitted through sexual contact or dirty needles – vaccinations, acupuncture, tattooing and body piercing can be potentially as dangerous as intravenous drug use. HIV/AIDS can also be spread through infected blood transfusions; some developing countries cannot afford to screen blood used for transfusions. If you do need an injection, ask to see the syringe unwrapped in front of you, or take a needle and syringe pack with you. Fear of HIV infection should never preclude treatment for serious medical conditions.

Sexually Transmitted Diseases (STDs) HIV/AIDS and hepatitis B can be transmitted through sexual contact – see the relevant sections earlier for more details. Other STDs include gonorrhoea, herpes and syphilis; sores, blisters or rashes around the genitals and discharges or pain when urinating are common symptoms. In some STDs, such as wart virus or chlamydia, symptoms may be less marked or not observed at all, especially in women. Chlamydia infection can cause infertility in men and women before any symptoms have been noticed. Syphilis symptoms eventually disappear completely, but the disease continues and can cause severe problems in later years.

While abstinence from sexual contact is the only 100% effective prevention, using condoms is also effective. The treatment of gonorrhoea and syphilis is with antibiotics. The different sexually transmitted diseases each require specific antibiotics.

Cuts, Bites & Stings
Bedbugs & Lice Bedbugs live in various places, but particularly in dirty mattresses and bedding, evidenced by spots of blood on bedclothes or on the wall. Bedbugs leave itchy bites in neat rows. Calamine lotion or a sting relief spray may help.

All lice cause itching and discomfort. They make themselves at home in your hair (head lice), your clothing (body lice) or in your pubic hair (crabs). You catch lice through direct contact with infected people or by sharing combs, clothing and the like. Powder or shampoo treatment will kill the lice and infected clothing should then be washed in very hot, soapy water and left in the sun to dry.

Bites & Stings Bee and wasp stings are usually painful rather than dangerous. However, in people who are allergic to them severe breathing difficulties may occur and require urgent medical care. Calamine lotion or a sting relief spray will give relief and ice packs will reduce the pain and swelling. Some spiders are poisonous, but antivenins are usually available.

Tick-Borne Encephalitis Between May and September, there is a risk of tick-borne encephalitis in forested areas of Bulgaria.

Encephalitis is the inflammation of the brain tissue. Symptoms include fever, headaches, vomiting, neck stiffness, pain in the eyes when looking at light, alteration in consciousness, seizures and paralysis or muscle weakness. Correct diagnosis and treatment requires hospitalisation. A vaccine is available.

You should always check all over your body if you have been walking through a potentially tick-infested area, because ticks can cause skin infections and other more serious diseases. If a tick is found attached, press down around the tick's head with tweezers, grab the head and gently pull upwards. Avoid pulling the rear of the body as this may squeeze the tick's gut contents through the attached mouth parts into the skin, increasing the risk of infection and disease. Smearing chemicals on the tick will not make it let go and is not recommended.

Rabies This fatal viral infection is found in many countries, including Bulgaria. Many animals can be infected (such as cats, dogs, bats and monkeys), and it's their saliva which is infectious. Any bite, scratch or even lick from an animal should be cleaned immediately and thoroughly. Scrub with soap and running water, and then apply alcohol or iodine solution. Medical help should be sought promptly to receive a course of injections to prevent the onset of symptoms and death.

Women's Health
Gynaecological Problems Antibiotic use, synthetic underwear, sweating and contraceptive pills can lead to fungal vaginal infections, especially when travelling in hot climates. Fungal infections are characterised by a rash, itch and discharge and can be treated with a vinegar or lemon-juice douche, or with yoghurt. Nystatin, miconazole or clotrimazole pessaries or vaginal cream are the usual treatment. Maintaining good personal hygiene and wearing loose-fitting clothes and cotton underwear may help prevent these infections.

Sexually transmitted diseases are a major cause of vaginal problems. Symptoms range from a smelly discharge, painful intercourse and sometimes a burning sensation when urinating. Medical attention should be sought and male sexual partners must also be treated. For more details see the section on Sexually Transmitted Diseases earlier. Besides abstinence, the best thing is to practise safer sex using condoms.

Pregnancy It's not prudent to travel to some places while pregnant, because some vaccinations normally used to prevent serious diseases are not advisable during pregnancy (eg, yellow fever). In addition, some diseases are much more serious for the mother (and may increase the risk of a stillborn child) in pregnancy (eg, malaria).

Most miscarriages occur during the first three months of pregnancy. Miscarriage is not uncommon and can occasionally lead to severe bleeding. The last three months should also be spent within reasonable distance of good medical care. A baby born as early as 24 weeks stands a chance of survival, but only in a good modern hospital. Pregnant women should avoid all unnecessary medication, though vaccinations and malarial prophylactics should still be taken where needed. Additional care should be taken to prevent illness and particular attention should be paid to diet and nutrition. Alcohol and nicotine, for example, should be avoided.

WOMEN TRAVELLERS
In general, travelling around Bulgaria poses no particular difficulties for women travellers. For the most part, sober men are polite and respectful, especially if you're clearly not interested in their advances, and women can usually meet and communicate with local men without their intentions necessarily being misconstrued. That doesn't mean, however, that women can go into a bar or nightclub unaccompanied and expect to be left alone. If you attract unwanted attention, *Omâzhena sâm* means 'I am married', and is a pretty firm message.

Like most places in Eastern Europe, common sense is the best guide to dealing with possibly dangerous situations, such as hitchhiking, sharing hostel rooms, walking alone at night etc. To avoid attracting attention, wear slightly conservative outfits; use dark sunglasses to avoid unwanted eye contact in particularly uncomfortable situations; or a wedding ring (on the left-hand ring finger). For overnight train journeys, choose a sleeper rather than a couchette.

One useful local organisation is the International Women's Club of Sofia (☎ 02-451 967).

GAY & LESBIAN TRAVELLERS

Consensual homosexual sex is legal in Bulgaria from the age of 18 (14 for heterosexuals), but Bulgaria is far from gay friendly. Same-sex couples should refrain from overt displays of affection, and be discreet when booking into hotel rooms.

The *Spartacus International Gay Guide* by Bruno Gmünder is the best male-only international directory of gay entertainment venues in Europe. Lesbians should look out for *Damron's Women's Traveller* by Bob Damron.

The major gay association is the Bulgarian Gay Organization Gemini (☎ 02-987 6872, e bgogemini@eint.bg, W www .bgogemini.org), on bulevard Vasil Levski 3 in Sofia. Contact the group about current gay and gay-friendly bars and nightclubs in Sofia. (There's unlikely to be too many similar groups, bars and clubs elsewhere in Bulgaria.) Another useful resource is the Web site W www.bulgayria.com.

DISABLED TRAVELLERS

Disabled travellers will have a rough time in Bulgaria because few facilities exist for people with special needs. Uneven and broken pavements make wheelchair mobility problematic, and ramps and special toilets for those in a wheelchair are few and far between, except possibly in a handful of five-star hotels in Sofia. In accordance with guidelines established by European authorities, the Bulgarian government plans to upgrade wheelchair access in some existing buildings, and make it compulsory for many new edifices, but this still is a long way from fruition. One Bulgarian organisation involved with disabled locals, and pos-

sibly worth contacting, is The Center for Independent Living in Sofia (☎ 02-989 8857).

Organisations that disseminate information about world travel for the mobility impaired include:

Mobility International USA (☎ 0541-343 1284) PO Box 10767, Eugene, OR 97440, USA
National Information Communication Awareness Network (☎ 02-6285 3713, fax 6285 3714, W www.nican.com.au) PO Box 407, Curtin, ACT 2605, Australia
Royal Association for Disability & Rehabilitation (Radar; ☎ 020-7250 3222, fax 7250 0212) 12 City Forum, 250 City Rd, London EC1V 8AF, UK
Society for the Advancement of Travel for the Handicapped (☎ 0718-858 5483) 26 Court St, Brooklyn, NY 11242, USA

SENIOR TRAVELLERS

Bulgaria shouldn't cause too many obvious problems for able-bodied senior travellers. In all cities and major towns, and at most tourist attractions, there are commodious hotels, restaurants with helpful staff who speak English, French or German, a plethora of taxis, plenty of comfortable inter-city private buses, and car rental agencies. And the resorts along the Black Sea coast are particularly well set up for more senescent tourists.

Of course, joining an organised tour can significantly reduce the hassles you may encounter while travelling independently around Bulgaria – see Organised Tours in the Getting Around and the Getting There & Away chapters.

TRAVEL WITH CHILDREN

Successful travel with young children requires planning and effort. Don't try to overdo things; even for adults, packing too much into the time available can cause problems. Make sure planned activities include the kids as well – balance the morning at a stuffy museum with an afternoon swim at the beach or a walk in the hills. And include children in the trip planning; if they have helped to work out where you'll be going, they'll be much more interested when they get there.

Bulgaria is a safe and healthy country, and medical facilities are generally pretty good. Most of the necessities for travelling with ankle-biters, such as nappies (diapers), baby food, and fresh or powdered milk, are readily available, and there are well-known international fast-food outlets all over the countryside. The kids may like to visit some of the zoo parks (though the animals are forlorn, and the facilities uninspiring); go horse riding (see the Activities section later); or swim in the Black Sea, Danube River or one of the public pools in Sofia. Also, there are plenty of hills, rocks and fortresses to clamber around, and all cities and towns have parks with playground equipment (which is likely to be dated, however). At the beach resorts along the Black Sea coast, children can enjoy water slides, toy trains and paddle pools, and at ski resorts, the young 'uns can learn some basic skills at special creches and 'ski kindergartens'.

The major international car rental firms can provide children's safety seats for an extra nominal cost, but it's essential to book these in advance. It's also worth noting that highchairs are almost unheard of in restaurants, public nappy-changing facilities are rare, and childcare (baby-sitting) agencies are only common among the expatriate community in Sofia.

For further general information and suggestions, see Lonely Planet's *Travel with Children* by Cathy Lanigan.

USEFUL ORGANISATONS

You may wish to contact one or more of the following organisations in Sofia (☎ area code 02) before or during your visit to Bulgaria. Contact details for other useful groups and government departments are listed in the appropriate sections throughout this guidebook.

American Chamber of Commerce (☎ 981 5950, fax 980 4206) ul Patriarh Evtimii 19
Bulgarian Chamber of Commerce & Industry (☎ 981 1632, Ⓦ www.bfia.org/implinks.htm) ul Parchevich 42
Bulgarian International Business Association (☎/fax 981 9169) ul Patriarh Evtimii 36a

Bulgarian Red Cross (☎ 944 1443) ul Dondukov 61
UNICEF (☎ 544 730) bul Pencho Slaveikov 18b
UNHCR (☎ 980 2453) ul Denkoglu 19

DANGERS & ANNOYANCES

Most travellers see that Bulgaria is in the troubled Balkans and feel uneasy, but there's no need to worry. Bulgaria is as peaceful and trouble-free as the neighbouring countries of Greece, Turkey and Romania. If you can handle yourself in the big cities of Western Europe, North America or Australia, you'll certainly have little or no trouble dealing with the less pleasant sides of Bulgaria. You'll be OK if you look purposeful, keep alert, and take the usual safety precautions.

Theft is not as much of a problem as it is in some countries but obviously look after your belongings and watch out for pickpockets in busy markets and crowded buses. Prime targets for thieves are parked cars, especially those with foreign number plates and/or rental agency stickers. Never leave things inside the car; always lock everything in the boot, or take it with you.

Although Bulgarian drivers can be extremely reckless at times, traffic is not too bad. (See the Car & Motorcycle section in the Getting Around chapter.) Undoubtedly, the biggest danger is from cars that speed across pedestrian crossings at traffic lights completely impervious to the rights of pedestrians. Also, watch out for trams and trolley-buses shuttling stealthily along what ostensibly looks like vehicle-free shopping malls.

Beggars ply their trade around some churches and larger squares, but are less common and demanding than in most other countries in the region.

Bulgaria has harsh drug laws. The country is a common route for drugs (and arms) smuggled across the Black Sea from Russian and Armenia, and from Turkey, so always treat the transport, trade and use of drugs with a *great* deal of caution.

Foreigners are sometimes set up for minor monetary rip-offs, but these are fairly obvious and easy to avoid – taxi drivers at the airport and beach resorts normally over-charge outrageously, and moneychangers on the street sometimes offer ridiculously high exchange rates. (Changing money on the street is illegal and unnecessary.) One source of irritation is the policy of dual pricing (see the Money section earlier).

Bulgaria is a major tobacco producer, and smoking seems to be the national pastime. Cafes, bars and restaurants are often poorly ventilated, but this is less of a problem in summer when most patrons sit outside.

EMERGENCIES

We certainly hope you don't need to contact any of the following toll-free numbers:

Fire Brigade	(☎ 160)
Medical Rescue & Ambulance	(☎ 150)
Police	(☎ 166)
Road Assistance (☎ 146 or mobile 048-146) outside Sofia	
Road Assistance in Sofia	(☎ 1286)
Traffic Police & Road Accident	(☎ 165)

These numbers are valid throughout Bulgaria, but operators – even in Sofia – are unlikely to speak English.

LEGAL MATTERS

As the country slowly slides towards membership of the EU, Bulgaria will more or less follow the same legal system as most of the rest of Europe. The days of blatant corruption towards foreign travellers are long gone – traffic police have to abide by a certain code of ethics, but residents do complain bitterly about corruption within some government departments, especially customs. If you do get into serious trouble with the police, it's best to contact your embassy (bear in mind the comments in the boxed text 'Your Own Embassy' earlier in this chapter).

BUSINESS HOURS

Normally, government offices are open on weekdays (ie, Monday to Friday) between 9am and 5pm, but they often close for 45 to 60 minutes any time between noon and 2pm. Private businesses more or less keep the same hours, but rarely have time for a leisurely lunchbreak. Most shops are open on weekdays from about 9am to 7pm, and from about 9am to 1pm on Saturday, but they tend to open and close later in summer. Post offices are open on weekdays from 8am to 6pm, and banks operate from 9am to 4pm on the same days. Some foreign-exchange offices are open 24 hours, but most operate between about 9am and 6pm Monday to Saturday.

Frustratingly, many museums and tourist attractions, even those in major cities, close for one or two days per week, usually between Sunday and Wednesday. (They often also close for lunch.) Opening times do change regularly, so don't be surprised if a museum or art gallery is closed even though it should be open (according to information provided in this guidebook, and the opening hours listed on the window).

PUBLIC HOLIDAYS & SPECIAL EVENTS
Public Holidays

During official public holidays all government offices, banks, post offices and major businesses will be closed. All hotels, restaurants, bars, national parks/reserves and museums (unless it coincides with a normal day off) stay open, as do most shops and petrol stations; border crossings and public transport continue to operate normally.

The official public holidays are:

New Year's Day 1 January – banks and other offices often also close on New Year's Eve

Liberation Day 3 March – celebrates Bulgaria's (short-lived) independence after the Russian-Turkish War (1877–8); also known as National Day

Easter March/April – Orthodox Easter falls one week after Catholic/Protestant Easter.

St George's Day 6 May – celebrates the start of the livestock breeding cycle

Cyrillic Alphabet Day 24 May – also known as Day of Bulgarian Culture

Unification Day 6 September – celebrates the final reunification of Bulgaria in 1885; also called National Day

Bulgarian Independence Day 22 September – celebrates official independence from Turkey in 1908

National Revival Day 1 November

Christmas 25 & 26 December – during the communist era, Christmas Day was outlawed, so it was often celebrated on 26 December instead

Special Events

Bulgaria hosts an inordinate number of religious, folkloric, music and wine festivals. Most have traditions dating back hundreds of years; others are set up mainly to attract tourists, so there's at least one major festival every summer weekend somewhere in the country. The largest event is the mammoth International Folk Festival held in Koprivshtitsa every five years (next in 2005).

More information about the festivals listed here can be found in the relevant sections throughout this guidebook, and current details about some programs and dates can be obtained from the Web sites Ⓦ www.bulgariatravel.org and Ⓦ www .bulgarianspace.com/bmg.

January
St Vasil's Day Folk Concert Sandanski – 1 January

February
Trifon Zarezan Festival Melnik – 14 February

March
Kukeri Shiroka Lûka – first Sunday in March
Songs about Varna Competition Varna – March
Days of Greek Culture Varna – March
March Music Days Festival Ruse – last two weeks of March
Sandanski Celebrations Sandanski – Thursday after Orthodox Easter Sunday

April
Folkloric Festival Melnik – 1 April
Flora Flower Exhibition Burgas – April
Music Festival Shiroka Lûka – one week in mid-April

May
Re-enactment of the April Uprising Koprivshtitsa – 1 & 2 May
Holiday of Amateur Art Activities or Balkan Folk Festival Veliko Târnovo – 10 days in first half of May
Sladkopoyna Chouchouliga Festival Burgas – May
May Festivities of Culture Gabrovo – May (biennial)

Varna Summer International Festival Varna – May to October
International Plovdiv Fair Plovdiv – mid-May for one week
Days of Shumen Cultural Festival Shumen – mid-May
Celebration of Bansko Traditions Bansko – 17–24 May

June
Cultural Month Festival Plovdiv – late May to mid-July
Fire-dancing Festival Bulgari (Strandjha Nature Park) early June
Arts Festival Balchik – early June
Festival of Roses Kazanlâk & Karlovo – first weekend in June
Verdi Festival Plovdiv – early June for two weeks
International Festival of Chamber Music Plovdiv – 10 days in mid-June
Madara Horseman Music Days Festival Madara – mid-June to mid-July.
International Folklore Festival Veliko Târnovo – late June to mid-July for three weeks

July
Burgas Sea Song Festival Burgas – July & August

August
International Folklore Festival Plovdiv – early August
International Jazz Festival Bansko – about 7–15 August
Folklore Days Festival Koprivshtitsa – mid-August
Annual Fair Oreshak – mid-August
Folklore Festival Shumen – August
Sofia International Folklore Festival Sofia – five days in late August
Balkan Youth Festival Gabrovo – August
Pirin Sings Folk Festival Bansko – mid-August (odd-numbered years)
Annual International Film Festival Varna – one week late August & early September
Watermelon Festival Shumen – last Sunday in August
International Folklore Festival Burgas – late August
Rozhen Folk Festival near Pamporovo – late August

September
City Holiday Plovdiv – 6 September
Apollonia Arts Festival Sozopol – 1st half of September

Traditional Events

Every church and monastery has a festival day each year according to its name. Common days for these festivals include Annunciation Day (25 March), St Kiril & Metodii Day (11 May), Transfiguration Day (6 August) and Virgin Mary's Day (15 August). Also, Fool's Day (1 April), Mothers' Day (8 April), Children's Day (1 June) and St Nikolai's Day (6 December) are celebrated throughout the country. (See Society & Conduct in the Facts about Bulgaria chapter.)

While many of the special events listed here are set up for tourists, dozens of other cultural and religious festivals are widely celebrated throughout Bulgaria, and can be enjoyed by visitors. These include:

Sourvakars (1 January) Boys wander around the village wishing everyone a happy new year and lightly touching them with a sprig of leaves.

Trifon Zarezan (14 February) See the boxed text 'Bulgarian Wine' in the Drinks section later.

Baba Marta (1 March) The house is given a spring clean, and Bulgarians give each other *martenitsi*, red and white tasselled threads worn for health and happiness.

Sts Konstantin & Elena Day (21 May) Celebrates the beginning of summer.

Makavei (1 August) Sons-in-law visit their fathers-in-law for a hearty meal (and drink).

Neptune Day (late August) Children along the Black Sea coast commemorate the God of the Sea.

Pirin Folk National Festival Sandanski – early September
Rozhen Fair Rozhen – 8 September
St Sofia's Day Sofia – 17 September
Sofia Fest Sofia – about 14–18 September
Days of Chamber Music Gabrovo – September
Flora Flower Exhibition Burgas – September
International Plovdiv Fair Plovdiv – late September for one week

October
Days of Ruse Ruse – first half of October
Grape Picking Celebrations Melnik – first two weeks of October
Bansko Day Bansko – 5 October
Fair Day Etâr – 14 October

December
Young Red Wine Festival Sandanski – early December
Christmas Festival Ruse – 15–24 December

ACTIVITIES

Through summer and winter, many Bulgarians enjoy a variety of activities in the countryside, and for visitors there is a myriad of things to do throughout the year.

Cycling

One popular summer activity is to take a mountain bike to Aleko on Mt Vitosha (near Sofia) and hurtle down the ski slopes.

More sedate areas for short mountain bike trips can be found around Gabrovo and Troyan. Mountain bikes can be rented through most, if not all, of the tourist offices linked to the Association Stara Planina (see the boxed text 'Hiking in the Stara Planina' in the Central Bulgaria chapter). The Odysseia-In Travel Agency in Sofia, and Pamporovo Sports Services in Pamporovo, also rent mountain bikes; in addition, the former can arrange guided mountain bike trips. See Bicycle in the Getting Around chapter for more information about travelling in Bulgaria on two wheels.

Skiing

The downside of skiing in Bulgaria is that some facilities (eg, ski lifts) may not be world-class, the slopes may not always be immaculately groomed, and artificial snow is never available. But there's usually plenty of *real* snow, the slopes are easily accessible and – best of all – prices are very attractive (though foreigners are charged more than Bulgarians for accommodation, ski lifts and rental of equipment). The ski season runs from about mid-December to mid-April.

The four main ski resorts are listed here. There are other ski slopes, but they are often difficult to reach by public transport, undeveloped and/or poorly maintained, and not well set up with training and equipment rental. See Organised Tours in the Getting There & Away chapter for information about ski holidays to Bulgaria.

Bansko Bulgaria's smallest, least commercialised and most enjoyable ski resort is 157km south of Sofia. Skiing is cheap, but equipment and training are not so easy to arrange. There's plenty of snow, and Bansko town is a charming place to stay.

Borovets The largest and oldest ski resort is 70km south of Sofia. It's compact, caters well to kids and offers reasonable conditions for snowboarders. There's plenty of places to rent gear and organise training, and cheap accommodation can be found nearby.

Mt Vitosha The most accessible resort is on the southern outskirts of Sofia, so it's busy on weekends. Cross-country skiing is ideal here, but, because of rocky slopes, snowboarding is not. Ski equipment and training are limited.

Pamporovo About 83km south of Plovdiv, Pamporovo is ideal for beginners and equipment and training are easy to arrange. Cross-country skiers and snowboarders flock here too. Facilities are comparatively new, and the slopes and lifts are well-maintained, but the resort is extensive, expensive and charmless.

Hiking

Bulgaria boasts about 37,000km of officially marked trails for long-distance trekking (ie, more than two days) and for shorter hiking (one or two days). These trails often begin at towns or villages – you may have to ask directions to the start of the trail – but most trails are easy to follow. Trails are marked on proper maps in yellow, red, green or blue, which correspond to the colours on the signs along the trails. These signs often include the name in Bulgarian of the upcoming mountain hut, so it's imperative that you can read the Cyrillic alphabet.

Most trails mentioned in this guidebook, and detailed on maps and in hiking books, are designed to start and/or finish each day at one of the numerous mountain huts throughout Bulgaria – see Accommodation later. Therefore, there's usually no need to bring a tent, unless you're bypassing the trails (not advisable for safety reasons),

trekking in winter (and get stuck because of bad weather), or hiking to very popular huts in the peak season of mid-July to late August (when beds may be unavailable). Camping in the wild is technically outlawed, but generally OK if you're discreet. Many larger huts have radio-telephones which can be used in emergencies.

The Mountains of Bulgaria, by Julian Perry and available in Bulgaria, is the best book for long-distance trekking, but it is of limited use for short hikes and the maps are inadequate. By far the best hiking/trekking maps available in Bulgaria are published by Kartografia (and most likely found in Sofia at bookshops, the Odysseia-In Travel Agency and the BTC office – see Mountain Huts later in this chapter). These maps cover the Rila Mountains (west and south of Samokov), the Pirin Mountains (with many trails starting at Bansko), the Rodopi Mountains and the mighty Stara Planina Mountains. The most detailed hiking maps are available from Balkan Eden (☎ 01227-373 727, ⓔ balkan–eden@yahoo.com), 31a Canterbury Rd, Herne Bay, Kent, UK, CT6 6AU.

More details about hiking around each of the four major mountain ranges are included in the relevant chapters. Also, refer to the relevant sections for information about hiking around Mt Vitosha (near Sofia), Blue Rocks (near Sliven), Vratsa, Borovets, Malîovitsa, Strandjha Nature Park, and the Rila Monastery.

The Bulgarian Association for Rural & Ecological Tourism (BARET) has established seven 'eco-trails' (also called 'eco-paths') throughout the country. These short hikes cross through some of the prettiest scenery in Bulgaria. Four of the more accessible are the Dryanovo Eco-trail, starting from the Dryanovo Monastery; the Negovanka Eco-trail, around the Emen canyon (near Veliko Târnovo); the Vrachanski Eco-trail, around the Vrachanski Balkan National Park near Vratsa; and the South Rodopi Eco-trail, starting near the village of Yagodina (near Smolyan). Also, see Responsible Tourism earlier for more information about BARET.

Guides for short hikes and long-distance treks can be hired through the offices of the Association Stara Planina in Gabrovo, Tryavna, Troyan and Teteven. You can also try Pamporovo Sports Services in Pamporovo and the Odysseia-In Travel Agency in Sofia.

Rock Climbing & Mountaineering

Mountain climbing is feasible, and major peaks like Mt Musala (2925m) and Mt Vihren (2915m) can be climbed from Malîovitsa and Bansko, respectively. The highest peak in the Stara Planina Mountains, Mt Botev (2376m), is accessible from Troyan or Apriltsi.

Four organisations can arrange rock climbing trips and training: the Bulgarian Alpine Club (☎/fax 02-871 798) on bulevard ·Vasil Levski 54, Sofia; Trapezitsa and Academic VTU, both in Veliko Târnovo; and the Central Mountain School in Malîovitsa. Serious rock climbers should pick up the Climbing Guide (in English) from the tourist information centre in Veliko Târnovo. One popular place for less strenuous rock climbing is near Vratsa.

In Sofia, specialist gear can be bought (but unfortunately not rented) at Stenata, and the Odysseia-In Travel Agency can arrange rock climbing trips.

Caving

About 700 caves throughout Bulgaria have been mapped and listed. The most accessible and developed for tourism are near Trigrad and Yagodina in the southern Rodopi Mountains, and at Ledenika, near Vratsa.

The Bulgarian Federation of Speleology (☎/fax 02-987 8812, ⓔ bfs@nat.bg, ⓦ www .speleo.web.bg) in Sofia is a well-established, but rather sedentary, caving club for local enthusiasts. However, it doesn't offer tours. Serious cave lovers can contact the newer, and more coordinated, Club Extreme (☎/fax 02-952 0633, ⓔ extreme@clubextreme.org, ⓦ www.clubextreme.org) in Sofia.

Water Sports

The beaches along the Black Sea coast are sandy, and long, wide, clean and developed.

It's also possible to swim at places along the Danube River, eg, at Vidin, but nearby tankers and factories would dissuade most visitors from taking a dip. Also, lakes and reservoirs, including Montana Reservoir and Batak Lake, are popular swimming spots with locals, but it's better to wait until you reach the Black Sea before you unpack your swimming gear. Some of these lakes can also be explored by paddle boat and canoe (for a small hourly rate).

Boat trips are possible along the Danube; at the time of writing, these only departed from Silistra. Along the Black Sea coast, visitors can enjoy trips around the Burgas Lakes (great for bird-watching), along Ropotamo River in the Ropotamo Nature Reserve and around tourist spots like Sozopol, Zlatni Pyasâtsi (Golden Sands) and Albena. Other possibilities include kayaking and rafting near Malîovitsa, and scuba diving near Burgas and Sozopol – but for both, equipment is limited and staff rarely speak English.

Despite the extensive beaches and number of tourists, the range of water sports, such as windsurfing and jet skiing, is fairly disappointing. What is available is reasonably cheap compared to beach resorts elsewhere in Europe. Water sports can be arranged at or near Sozopol, Zlatni Pyasâtsi and the self-proclaimed 'sports capital of Bulgaria', Albena.

Other Activities

Horse riding is an enjoyable, quiet and ecologically sound way of seeing some of Bulgaria's glorious scenery. They can be hired for short guided trips (at set rates), and possibly for long-distance journeys (at negotiable rates), at Borovets, Pamporovo, Arbanasi, Zlatni Pyasâtsi, Albena and Ihtiman. Instructions in horse riding are also available at these places (except at Borovets and Pamporovo).

A round of golf is possible at Bulgaria's only course, the Golf Club Air Sofia at Ihtiman, about 55km south-east of Sofia. Other sports, such as tennis, are offered at resorts along the Black Sea coast, particularly Albena, the golf club at Ihtiman, and at Pamporovo.

Over 100 official balneological centres in Bulgaria have access to about 1600 sources of mineral springs. These springs relieve stress and cure all sorts of ailments, such as rheumatism, arthritis and asthma.

Albena boasts the largest number of mineral springs and the country's largest therapy centre, while places like Hisarya, Sandanski and Pomorie are also popular. These centres also offer massages and a confusing range of 'therapy' treatments, such as hydrotherapy and aromatherapy.

COURSES

There are a few courses that are offered to foreigners, but make sure you book these courses before you arrive in Bulgaria.

Language

The Sts Cyril & University of Veliko Târnovo (☎ 062-20 070, e mbox@uni-vt .bg, W www.uni-vt.bg) usually offers a one-month 'International Summer Seminar for Students in Bulgarian Language and Slavic Culture' every August. Contact them for current programs and costs. The Lira Language School (☎ 02-666 568), on ulitsa Midjour 8 in Sofia, also offers Bulgarian language courses for foreigners. Contact them directly for details.

Arts & Crafts

Every summer, Vedafolk (☎ 02-745 540, e radka@vedafolk.com, W www.vedafolk .com) offers an impressive range of one- or two-week residential seminars in traditional Bulgarian folk arts, such as instrumental and vocal music, dance, arts, crafts and languages. These courses often take place in ethnographic enclaves, such as Arbanasi and Momchilovtsi. Contact Vedafolk for current programs and costs.

In an attempt to resurrect the traditions of woodcarving at the gorgeous town of Tryavna, woodcarving courses are offered there. See the boxed text 'Woodcarving' in the Central Bulgaria chapter for details.

WORK

Bulgaria isn't enthusiastic about handing out jobs to foreigners instead of locals, though the government is keen for foreigners to establish businesses as long as most of the staff are Bulgarian. Most foreigners working in Bulgaria are specialists under contracts. These contracts are most often arranged before arriving in the country.

If you do find a temporary job, the pay is likely to be low. Do it for the experience – not to earn a fortune – and you won't be disappointed. Teaching English is one way to make some extra cash, but the market is often saturated. Check the Web sites listed in Digital Resources earlier in this chapter for employment opportunities. Another helpful Web site run by *The Sofia Echo*, Bulgaria's only English-language newspaper is W www.sofiaecho.com.

If you arrange a job before you arrive, your employer should plough through the frightening mass of paperwork from relevant government departments and pay the various fees. If you land a job *after* you arrive, or you're considering setting up a business in Bulgaria, urgently contact some expats for current advice about the plethora of required forms and fees.

Then, apply for the so-called 'blue passport' which entitles you to the same rates for museums, hotels and ski lifts etc as Bulgarians. This is a substantial saving and a great idea if you are planning to do some sightseeing.

Work Your Way Around the World by Susan Griffith provides practical advice on a wide range of issues. Its publisher, Vacation Work, has many other useful titles, including *The Directory of Summer Jobs Abroad*, edited by David Woodworth. *Working Holidays* by Ben Jupp, published by the Central Bureau for Educational Visits & Exchanges in London, is another good source, as is *Now Hiring! Jobs in Eastern Europe* by Clarke Caufield.

ACCOMMODATION

Bulgaria offers a wide range of accommodation options, though standards are often not as high as you might expect in other countries in the region. In Bulgaria, every city, major town, and village with a tourist attraction has at least one decent place to stay. The bad news is that foreigners usually pay considerably more for all types of accommodation than Bulgarians (see Dual Pricing earlier in this chapter).

Camping

These days, camping is not an ideal way of seeing Bulgaria. Camping grounds have struggled since losing government support, and the industry, which once included over 100 locales nationwide (with half that number along the Black Sea coast), is in serious decline. Even privatised camping grounds tend to be rundown, so don't have high expectations.

Camping grounds in Bulgaria are rarely open between November and April, and some along the Black Sea coast only operate from June to early September. These tend to be very crowded in July and August, and while camp sites will normally be available at this time, security, privacy and tranquillity are rarely guaranteed. In addition, camping grounds have a tendency to be placed closer to noisy main roads (to attract passing customers) than to anywhere peaceful or picturesque like a beach or lake.

The cost of setting up a tent at a camping ground is about 7 lv to 10 lv per person per night, but tents are rarely available for hire, so bring your own. Most camping grounds also rent out tiny bungalows for slightly more than the cost of camp sites, but these, too, are often far from inviting.

Camping in the wild (ie, outside a camping ground) is technically prohibited, but normally accepted if you're discreet and, most importantly, do not build wood fires (which attract attention and damage the environment).

Hostels

Few hostels or dormitories in Bulgaria are available to normal tourists; some are only open in summer, and many only cater to Bulgarians on excursions and hiking trips. While foreigners would not normally be excluded from staying at a hostel or dormitory, getting details about locations, opening times and costs is difficult unless you know some well-informed locals and/or speak Bulgarian.

No hostels are part of any international organisation, such as the Youth Hostels Association (YHA) or Hostelling International (HI), and cards from both organisations are *not* accepted at the few hostels in Bulgaria. Most hostels are run by the Bulgarian youth agency, Orbita (see Student, Youth & Teacher Cards earlier in this chapter), but a few private ones are located in the cities.

Mountain Huts

Anyone, especially those enjoying long-distance treks or shorter hikes, can stay at any mountain hut *(hizha)*. Normally, a hizha only offers basic, but clean and comfortable, dormitory beds, with a shared bathroom, which cost from 10 lv to 35 lv per person per night. Most are only open in summer (May-October), but those situated at or near major ski slopes are often also open in winter. In or around a town or village along a popular hiking/trekking route, you can also often find a *turisticheski dom* (tourist home), a fairly comfortable hotel with double rooms, or a *turisticheska spalnya* (tourist bedroom), a more basic dorm-style hostel.

It's often not necessary to book these in advance, but beds at most of the 200 or more mountain huts, hotels and hostels can be reserved at the Bulgarian Tourist Union (BTC; ☎ 02-980 1285, [e] bts@nat.bg), bulevard Vasil Levski 75, Sofia. The office is tucked inside a photo shop in the underpass at the junction of bulevard Vasil Levski and ulitsa General Gurko. The BTC office also sells some hiking maps, and the *Hizhite v Bâlgariya* book (written in Cyrillic) detailing the locations of, and amenities at, most places to stay in the mountains.

Monasteries

About a dozen of the 160 monasteries around Bulgaria offer accommodation to anyone, from pilgrims to foreign tourists. Some rooms are actually inside the monastery, for example, the Rila and Cherepish monasteries, or at guesthouses within metres of the monastery gates, eg, the Troyan, Dryanovo and Lopushanski monasteries. For more information about staying at monasteries, telephone the relevant authority in Sofia (☎ 02-987 56611).

Private Rooms

Some families in certain cities, towns and villages offer individual rooms to visitors. These bedrooms are normally comfortable and clean, but bathroom facilities are often communal. The owners are almost always friendly, but often speak no language except Bulgarian. Rooms cost the leva equivalent of about US$10 per person, but they're normally priced per number of beds so people travelling alone sometimes have to pay for double rooms.

Private rooms can often be arranged through an accommodation agency in a town/city centre, or at a bus/train station. Alternatively, wait to be approached in the street, or look out for relevant signs in Bulgarian, English or German in shop windows or hanging outside the actual home. It's always important to find out where the rooms are before making a decision – in a village like Melnik, all homes are central, but in a city, like Burgas, the home may be in an outlying and dreary suburb.

Hotels

Balkantourist used to enforce its monopoly over foreigners by steering them into one of its 650 hotels. While many of these hotels have now been privatised and renovated, those in less desirable locations may be terribly rundown. Some are abandoned and look as if they're going to fall down at any moment, while others which continue to operate *still* look like they're going to crumble to the ground!

Some hotels offer more expensive 'apartments'. These are usually double rooms, which are more luxurious and feature more amenities (like a fridge and sitting room) than normal rooms. 'Suites' are often family rooms with two double bedrooms.

Hotels (but not private homes, mountains huts or hostels) are rated from one- to five-stars, but one- and two-star places are rarely proud of the fact so they often don't advertise their rating. Some hotels do not offer single rooms or single rates in a double

room. If this is the case, only the rates for doubles are listed.

Although nearly all hotels are overpriced for foreigners (see Dual Pricing earlier), a handful are blazing new trails by adopting a more equitable pricing policy. Most smaller and more remote hotels at the ski resorts are closed in summer (from about mid-April to November), while almost all places along the Black Sea coast do not open between late October and early April.

Whether breakfast is included depends on local competition. In some towns every hotel includes breakfast; in other places, it's never part of the tariff. Sometimes, breakfast costs an extra 2 lv or 3 lv per person (and up to 12 lv in a five-star hotel). This is worth considering for the convenience, but breakfast in a local cafe will probably be tastier and cheaper.

Unless stated otherwise in this guidebook, reserving a room in advance is not normally necessary, except if you're determined to stay at a particular place, or visiting at peak times (eg, Nesebâr in August or Bansko at Christmas) or during a major festival.

FOOD

Refer to the Language chapter at the end of this guidebook for a list of words and phrases relating to food and places to eat.

Restaurants

Firstly, it's important to note that if you order any grilled meats, eg, chicken fillets and pork kebabs, that is *all* you'll get – garnishes, such as chips, salads, rice and vegetables, must be ordered separately and will cost extra. Salads will almost always be served before the main meal, but you can, of course, leave all or some of the salad until the main dish arrives. Bread is almost never provided for free, is rarely fresh, and never comes with butter or margarine.

The waiters/waitresses normally create a bill (tab) by placing tickets from the cash register on your table; you pay the total amount when you leave. Some waiters overcharge foreigners, especially around the beach and ski resorts, so always check the final bill. Most restaurants are rated from one- to five-stars (almost always in a five-star hotel), but only those with three or more stars usually bother advertising their rating.

Some restaurants in the cities and larger towns, at the tourist attractions, and around the ski and beach resorts, offer menus translated in English, and sometimes German and/or French. But beware: prices on any menu written *only* in English, German or French (and not in Bulgarian as well) will usually be considerably higher than those listed on a bilingual menu (written in Bulgarian and another language). In this case, simply insist on seeing the bilingual menu.

Although tiny authentic village taverns may look more appealing than the ubiquitous Happy Bar & Grill, you'll soon realise the futility of staring at a menu written in Cyrillic if you don't understand the alphabet. So, while most of the restaurants (and cafes) in this guidebook are recommended because of their value for money, ambience, convenience and food, we have also listed those places where staff speak English and/or have menus in English. Alternatively, some restaurants offer 'photo-menus', which are great for pointing at photos of dishes you want to order.

Most restaurants are open daily from about 11am to 3pm, and again from about 6pm to 11pm, but fast-food outlets are open all day and evening. All restaurants and cafes are licensed to sell alcohol, and places like KFC even sell beer.

The cheapest place to eat is a cafeteria, where staff place large dollops of pre-cooked Bulgarian food, soups and salads on your plate. These cafeterias are ideal if you want to save money, taste some local food, or avoid deciphering a Bulgarian menu – simply point at what you want, pay the amount shown on the cash register and enjoy. Most cafes (see Drinks later) only serve beverages, but some offer snacks and full meals. A *mehana* is a traditional tavern, often featuring authentic decor, waiters dressed in folk costumes and live music.

Local Food

Popular Bulgarian dishes with a Turkish influence include *kebabche* (grilled spicy

Cooking a Kavarma

To start with you'll need: 800g-1kg of pork; 500g of liver (veal); two tomatoes, five smallish onions, five capsicums (green peppers) and a cup of mushrooms; about one-third of a cup of white wine; dashes of parsley, paprika, pepper and salt; and oil.

Slice the pork and liver into thin pieces, and fry the pork in water and oil. Add onions, then the liver, vegetables, wine, herbs and salt, and some more water. Stir, place in a clay pot (or dish), and heat in an oven. Sprinkle parsley on top.

meat sausages) and *kyufte* (basically the same thing, but round and flat). To try several kinds of meats at one sitting, order a mixed grill *(meshana skara)*. *Musaka* is shaped like the Greek equivalent, but does not contain eggplants (aubergines), and sits in a creamy sauce instead.

As a starter (or main course), try *topcheta supa*, a creamy soup with meatballs, *tarator*, a popular cold dish with cucumbers, walnuts and yoghurt, or *bob*, a hearty bean soup. Most people begin with a salad, such as the ubiquitous *shopska salad*, which is chopped tomatoes, cucumbers and onions covered with grated cheese.

Other traditional dishes include *kavarma* (see the boxed text 'Cooking a Kavarma'), *drob sarma* (chopped liver baked with rice and eggs), *sarmi* (stuffed vine or cabbage leaves), *sardella* (fillets with garlic, onions and black pepper), and *plakiya* and *gyuvech* (rich fish and meat stews). Some tasty regional specialities are *kyopolou*, baked eggplants with garlic and walnuts (from the Varna region), *kapama*, meat, rice and sauerkraut simmered and served in a clay pot (around Bansko), and *midi tzigane*, mussels sauteed with a spicy cheese and mustard sauce (along the Black Sea coast).

Other Food

Franchises of internationally-known fast-food outlets, like McDonald's, KFC and Pizza Hut, can be found all over Bulgaria. Plenty of other places serve tasty, and far cheaper, hamburgers and pizzas, as well as Turkish-style *doner kebabs*.

Bulgarians have taken to Chinese food, but the quality and cost of oriental cuisine varies enormously. Locals tend to spoil their plate of chicken, cashew nuts and mushrooms, for example, by eating it with chips (French fries) rather than rice. Larger cities have Indian and Lebanese restaurants, but these are normally expensive. Italian restaurants are common, popular and often very good value. Also, if you can decipher the Cyrillic letters, it's not hard to understand and pronounce items like 'spageti', 'bolognaiz' and 'carbonara'.

Vegetarian

Vegetarians will not be disappointed with the number of meatless dishes on the menus, but may be disaffected by the lack of imagination. Most restaurants offer a dozen salads, which are usually large enough for a main course if eaten with bread and/or a vegetable soup. Although most Bulgarians love red meat, vegetarian pizzas and pasta dishes are common, and fish meals are frequently on offer along the Black Sea coast and near some rivers (eg, at restaurants around the Rila Monastery).

Other tasty vegetarian meals and snacks include *sirene po shopski* (cheese, eggs and tomatoes baked in an clay pot), *kashkaval pane* (fried breaded cheese), and *banitsa* (a baked cheese pastry), which is so popular for breakfast that lines outside bakeries start at about 7am. Bulgaria is also famous for its yoghurt.

Fruit and vegetables are plentiful in summer, but, in winter, certain dishes and salads may be unavailable. This is less of a problem at tourist spots, such as ski resorts, which can afford to hoard and/or import unavailable items.

Self-Catering

The days of endless lines outside poorly stocked government-owned grocery shops are long gone. Supermarkets have been introduced to the cities, but are tiny compared to those often found in North America and Western Europe. Many larger towns still have a *hali*, an indoor market with a variety of shops, but most locals prefer to visit the market. Because food is so cheap, you probably won't save much money by self-catering. Hotels rarely have cooking facilities, but guests staying at hostels, mountain huts and private rooms can often use the communal kitchen.

DRINKS

Refer to the Language chapter at the end of this guidebook for a list of words and phrases relating to drinks and places to enjoy them.

Nonalcoholic Drinks

The average Bulgarian must be bottle-fed with coffee from an early age; they don't seem to be able to function properly without a serious fix of caffeine (and nicotine) each morning. While instant coffee should be avoided, acceptable espresso coffee is available everywhere, and many places now serve cappuccinos.

Tea is mostly the (unpalatable) *bilkov* (herbal) and *plodov* (fruit) variety. If you simply want European-style *cheren chay* (black tea) ask around the cafes, or bring your own tea bags and request a cup of hot water. Only in the top-end hotels will you be offered milk for your tea.

Major international brands of sugary soft drinks (sodas) are widely available, but comparatively expensive. Mineral water is easy to buy, but to avoid cluttering up the countryside with empty plastic bottles, please consider refilling a bottle with free and safe fountain water (see Water in the Health section earlier). Natural fruit juices are delicious.

Alcoholic Drinks

Thanks to joint ventures with Belgian and Dutch breweries, Bulgaria boasts some fine beers (and a lot of research was done on this subject!). Zagorka produces a decent *special* (500ml), and the more expensive and drinkable *gold* (330ml). Also available throughout the country are bottles of the trendy Astika (330ml) and the unremarkable Kamenitsa (500ml). Some of the better

Bulgarian Wine

The production (and imbibing) of wine in Bulgaria is an ancient tradition dating back to the 6th century BC. It may surprise some wine-lovers to learn that Bulgaria is currently the world's fifth-largest exporter of wine.

The five recognised regions produce palatable red wines, including Cabernet Sauvignon from around Sliven and Melnik, and Merlot from Haskovo and Pazardzhik; and whites, such as Chardonnay from Veliki Preslav, and Sauvignon Blanc from Varna. One of the more charming places to try a drop (or two) is Melnik, where a bottle of plonk (drink at your own peril) is about 2 lv and a far better brand costs from 5 lv.

More information about wines from the Melnik region, and elsewhere in Bulgaria, can be gathered from the *Wine Map Bulgaria* (12 lv), available at the Ethnographic Museum in Varna, and the Web site **w** www.melnikwine .bg. In addition, winery tours are available at Lyaskovets, near Veliko Târnovo, and Damianitza Winery, near Melnik – see the relevant sections for details.

One rather cheerful time to be anywhere near a winery is 14 February, when the Trifon Zarezan festival takes place to honour the patron saint of vineyards, St Trifon. On this day, wine producers start pruning their vines, and pour wine on the vine roots in the hope for a bountiful harvest. Plenty of tasting and drinking is also undertaken (all in the name of tradition of course!).

beers are brewed in provincial towns, but rarely available elsewhere, such as the excellent *Pirinsko Pivo* (from Blagoevgrad) and *Shumensko Pivo* (Shumen).

All Bulgarian-made beers (and other alcoholic drinks) are cheap. A 500ml bottle of beer costs about 1 lv; trendier (and arguably tastier) 330ml bottles cost about 1.50 lv. Most cafes and restaurants offer draught beer for about 1/1.50 lv for 330/500ml.

Whisky and vodka made in Bulgaria, or elsewhere in the region, are cheap, but have a high concentration of alcohol. Other locally produced drinks to be wary of include *slivova rakiya* (plum brandy) and *rosaliika* (rose liqueur).

ENTERTAINMENT

There's always plenty to do, from festivals (see Special Events earlier) to films, nightclubs to operas. Most Bulgarians, however, seem to do little more in summer than sit at a cafe, smoke and watch the world go by.

All cities, and most larger towns, have at least one cinema. Almost all show recent non-Bulgarian films in the original language (usually English), and sub-titled in Bulgarian. Tickets cost from 1.5 lv to 5 lv, depending on the film, session time and comfort of the cinema. And there are always numerous bars in which to enjoy a drink, meet some locals and possibly hear bands play traditional Bulgarian folk music or passable versions of foreign pop (in English and Bulgarian). The Arts section in the Facts about Bulgaria chapter has information about theatre and music.

SPECTATOR SPORTS

Football (soccer) is the main Bulgarian spectator sport, and teams are followed with partisan zeal. The Sofia-based team, Levski, is the current Bulgarian champion, and is reasonably competitive in matches against other European sides. Football games normally take place on Saturday and/or Sunday, from about 4pm, and on Wednesday evening at about 7pm. The football season lasts from late August to late May, with a winter break in January and February. Tickets to matches cost from 3 lv to 8 lv.

Other sports followed throughout Bulgaria, and in which the country has had some international success, include volleyball, basketball, amateur boxing, wrestling, weight-lifting and karate. Recently successful athletes include Theresa Marinova, who won the triple jump at the 2000 Olympics, the 1998 Winter Olympic women's biathlon champion, Ekaterina Dafovska, and highjumper, Venelina Veneza. Magdalena Maleeva is currently ranked 16th in women's tennis. Vesselin Topalov is ranked fourth in the world of chess.

SHOPPING

It's easy to spend lots of money on souvenirs, but, not surprisingly, most of the stuff at popular tourist spots, such as resorts along the Black Sea coast, is tacky and overpriced. For more information about Bulgarian handicrafts, such as woodcarving and weaving, see Arts in the Facts about Bulgaria chapter.

Some of the more exquisite mementos of your trip to Bulgaria may include embroideries from Nesebâr, Varna and Sofia, paintings of traditional village life, or landscapes, from Varna, Nesebâr, Sofia and Plovdiv, woodcarvings from Tryavna or carpets, rugs and bags from Koprivshtitsa, Chiprovtsi and Kotel. The National Fair and Exhibition of Arts & Crafts Complex in Oreshak is a marvellous place to spend up big on embroideries, pottery, ceramics, weavings, woodcarvings and metalwork. As the regional centre for the Valley of Roses, Kazanlâk is the place to buy rose oils, perfumes, shampoos, liqueurs, tea bags and jams. For antiques, head to the old towns in Veliko Târnovo and Plovdiv. The best range of other souvenirs, such as books, traditional costumes, silver-filigree jewellery and dolls, is in Sofia.

Compact discs of foreign music are usually made outside Bulgaria, and prohibitively expensive (eg, 25 lv to 28 lv), but CDs of Bulgarian music often cost about 12 lv. Cassettes and CDs are available throughout the country, but the range is particularly extensive in Sofia and Plovdiv.

Getting There & Away

Many people will visit Bulgaria as part of a jaunt around Eastern Europe and/or the Balkans, though plenty of airlines fly directly to Sofia and Varna, and dozens of buses and trains travel to (and through) the country.

AIR
Airports & Airlines
Before buying a return air ticket to Bulgaria from Western or northern Europe, check the price of package tours to the resorts along the Black Sea coast (in summer) or the ski slopes (in winter). A package tour could be cheaper and you could just throw away some or all of the hotel vouchers and follow your own itinerary.

The Bulgarian national carrier, Balkan Bulgarian Airlines (Balkan Airlines for short), is a shadow of its former self. In recent years, the airline has been struggling to survive and has been taken over several times by international companies.

The major international airport is in Sofia, though in summer a few charter flights also travel to/from Varna.

Major international offices for Balkan Airlines include:

Athens (☎ 01-325 3224) 9B Apollonos St
Berlin (☎ 030-251 4460) 10969, Kochstrasse 74
Frankfurt (☎ 069-284 186) 6000 Frankfurt am Main 1
Istanbul (☎ 0212-245 2456) Gumhuriyet Caddesi, Gezi Dukkanlari 8
London (☎ 020-7637 7637) 322 Regent St
Paris (☎ 01-47 42 66 66) 75009 4 Rue Scribe
Rome (☎ 06-481 4489) Via Barberini 11, 00187

Buying Tickets
It pays to research the options carefully to make sure you get the best deal. The Internet is an increasingly useful resource for checking air fares, because many airlines offer excellent fares to Web surfers. They may sell seats by auction or simply cut prices to reflect the reduced cost of electronic selling. Many travel agencies around the world also have Web sites, which can make the Internet

Warning

The information in this chapter is particularly vulnerable to change: Prices for international travel are volatile, routes are introduced and cancelled, schedules change, special deals come and go, and rules and visa requirements are amended. Airlines and governments seem to take a perverse pleasure in making price structures and regulations as complicated as possible. You should check directly with the airline or a travel agent to make sure you understand how a fare (and ticket you may buy) works. In addition, the travel industry is highly competitive and there are many lurks and perks.

The upshot of this is that you should get opinions, quotes and advice from as many airlines and travel agents as possible before you part with your hard-earned cash. The details given in this chapter should be regarded as pointers and are not a substitute for your own careful, up-to-date research.

a quick and easy way to compare prices. In fact, an increasing number of online agents only operate on the Internet.

However, online fare generators are no substitute for travel agents who know all about special deals, have strategies for avoiding layovers and can offer advice on everything from which airline has the tastiest vegetarian food to the best travel insurance to buy.

Full-time students, and people under 26 years (under 30 in some countries), have access to better deals than other travellers. You have to show a document proving your date of birth, or a valid International Student Identity Card (ISIC), when buying your ticket and boarding the plane.

Travellers with Specific Needs
Airlines can often make special arrangements for travellers, such as wheelchair assistance at airports or vegetarian meals on

flights, if warned in time. 'Skycots', baby food and nappies should also be provided by the airline if requested in advance. Children under two years old travel for 10% of the standard fare (or free on some airlines) as long as they don't occupy a seat, but they don't get a baggage allowance. Children aged between two and 12 can usually occupy a seat for half to two-thirds of the full fare, and do get a baggage allowance.

The disability-friendly Web site W www .everybody.co.uk has an airline directory which details the facilities offered by various airlines.

Departure Tax

The departure tax on all international flights (ie, from Sofia and Varna) is US$8. This tax is included in the price of all tickets bought in and outside of Bulgaria.

The USA & Canada

There are no direct flights between Bulgaria and anywhere in the USA or Canada. Balkan Airlines recently announced a codeshare agreement with Virgin Atlantic. So, Virgin can fly you from one of eight cities in the USA to London, from where Balkan Airlines connects to Sofia on the same day. Expect to pay about US$600/750 one-way/return from New York, Los Angeles or Chicago to Sofia.

Alternatively, fly to any major European city, such as Rome, Frankfurt, Amsterdam or Paris, and catch a regular flight to Sofia, or (in summer) a charter flight to Varna. The cheapest connection to Sofia is probably on LOT Polish Airlines from Chicago or New York, via Warsaw.

Discount travel agents in the USA and Canada are known as consolidators. San Francisco is the ticket consolidator capital of America, though some good deals can also be found in most major cities. Ticket Planet (W www.ticketplanet.com) is a recommended ticket consolidator.

America's largest student travel organisation, with around 60 offices, is Council Travel (☎ toll-free 800-226 8624, W www .counciltravel.com). Call for the office nearest you. STA Travel (☎ toll-free 800-777

0112, W www.statravel.com) has offices in most major cities; ring for office locations.

Fares offered by Canadian discount air ticket sellers are about 10% higher than those sold in the USA. Travel CUTS (☎ toll-free 800-667 2887, W www.travelcuts.com) is Canada's national student travel agency and has offices in all major cities.

Australia & New Zealand

There are no direct flights to Bulgaria from Australia or New Zealand, but most Aussies and Kiwis will probably fly elsewhere to Europe and travel overland to Bulgaria anyway. As an example, a flight to London on Qantas, and a connection to Sofia on British Airways, costs about A$2200 return from Sydney. Flying to Singapore on Singapore Airlines, and then to Frankfurt on Lufthansa, is quicker and slightly cheaper. Travelling on Qantas to Singapore, and then Aeroflot to Sofia, via Moscow, is the cheapest option: about A$1800 return.

Two well-known agents for cheap fares are STA Travel and Flight Centre. STA Travel (☎ 13 17 76 Australia-wide, ☎ 03-9349 2411, W www.statravel.com.au), 224 Faraday St, Carlton, Vic, has offices in all major cities, and on many university campuses. Flight Centre (☎ 13 16 00 Australia-wide, W www.flightcentre.com.au) 82 Elizabeth St, Sydney also has dozens of offices throughout Australia.

In New Zealand, Flight Centre (☎ 09-309 6171), National Bank Towers, on the corner of Queen and Darby Sts, Auckland, has branches throughout the country; and STA Travel (☎ 09-309 0458, W www.statravel .co.nz), 10 High St, Auckland also has offices in the major cities.

The UK

Both British Airways and Balkan Airlines fly between London and Sofia about five times a week for about UK£180/245 one-way/return. Britannia Airways (☎ 0870 607 6757, W www.britanniaairways.com) offers charter flights (in winter) to Sofia for ski trips, and (in summer) to Varna, for the Black Sea resorts, from Gatwick, Manchester and Birmingham. These are mostly for

Brits on package tours, but there's no reason why anyone can't contact them about a possible discounted fare.

STA Travel (☎ 020-7361 6262, W www .statravel.co.uk), 86 Old Brompton Rd, London SW7, has offices across the UK. It sells tickets to all travellers, but caters especially to students and travellers under 26 years.

Continental Europe

France Balkan Airlines and Air France both fly between Sofia and Paris about three times a week for about €277/352 one-way/return. OTU Voyages (☎ 01-40 29 12 12, W www .otu.fr), 39 Ave Georges-Bernanos, 75005 Paris, has branches across France but caters mostly to students and young travellers.

Germany There are more flights to Bulgaria from Germany than from any other European country. Balkan Airlines flies to Sofia from Berlin three times a week for €266/330 one-way/return, and from Frankfurt four times a week for the same price. Lufthansa Airlines flies daily from Frankfurt (€672/511) and Munich (€650/450).

In summer (May-Oct), charter flights to Varna on Hemus Air regularly depart from Leipzig (€246/464); and Air Via and Condor Airlines fly from several German cities most days for about €130 to €150 one-way and €281 to €306 return.

STA Travel (☎ 030-311 0950), Goethesttrasse 73, 10625 Berlin) has branches in major cities across the country.

The Netherlands KLM-Royal Dutch Airlines flies from Amsterdam to Sofia every day for €234/361 one-way/return. Two well-regarded travel agencies are Budget Air (☎ 020-627 1251), 34 Rokin, Amsterdam, and Holland International (☎ 070-307 6307), which has offices in most cities.

Elsewhere in Europe All sorts of flights to Sofia are also available from elsewhere in Europe. From Rome, Balkan Airlines flies twice a week (€277/345 one-way/return); and Alitalia flies regularly from Milan (€297/402) and Rome (€306/416). Both Austrian Airlines and Lauda Air depart from

Vienna three times a week (about €313/416), but Bulgarian Air Charter travels from Vienna to Varna in summer for less.

Also to Sofia, Czech Airlines flies from Prague five days a week; Balkan Airlines travels a few times a week from Barcelona; and LOT Polish Airlines departs daily from Warsaw. In addition, there are regular flights from Brussels on Sabena, from Geneva on Swiss, and from Prague and Budapest on Malev-Hungarian Airlines. From Moscow, Balkan Airlines flies to Sofia, and Aeroflot travels to Sofia and Varna all year.

Rest of the Balkans To Sofia, Tarom flies from Bucharest (€165/338 one way/return) every day. Yugoslav Airlines travels to Sofia from Belgrade (€116/134) most days; and Olympic Airways and Balkan Airlines depart regularly from Athens (€154/239). Also, Turkish Airlines has flights to Sofia on Monday, Wednesday, Friday and Sunday from Ankara (€221/272) and Istanbul (€194/ 216); and Balkan Airlines flies from Istanbul (€188/200) daily. In summer, Hemus Air flies to Sofia from Tirana (Albania) for €229/436, and from Bucharest (€171/342).

LAND

It is vital to check the current state of affairs in the Balkans before travelling overland to Bulgaria from some countries, in particular Macedonia and Yugoslavia. At the time of writing all borders listed were open every day, and nearly all day.

Train

Romania Most visitors travel to/from Romania by train and either start from, or go through, Ruse.

The *Bulgaria Express* (train Nos 26 and 27) runs between Sofia and Moscow, via Bucharest and Kyiv, daily. It leaves Sofia at 7.05pm, Pleven (at 10.29pm) and Ruse (4.15am next day), and arrives in Bucharest at 7am. It arrives in Moscow on the fourth day at 5am. The train leaves Bucharest every day for Sofia at 7.30pm. A 1st/2nd-class sleeper (only sleepers are available) costs 250/158 lv all the way to Moscow from

Border Crossings

Romania
There are several border crossings where you can enter Romania, but if you're driving use the bridge at Ruse (the only one across the Danube River) or a land border further east. If you're using public transport, the quickest border is at Ruse, but the most scenic crossing is probably at Vidin. If you want to take a vehicle on a ferry, allow plenty of time.

For more information about crossing by boat and ferry at Vidin, by ferry and bridge at Ruse, and by ferry at Silistra see the relevant sections in the Northern Bulgaria chapter. You can also cross at Kardam-Negru Vodă (accessible from Dobrich) and at Durankulak-Vama Veche (accessible from Varna). However, there's no public transport to either border from the Bulgarian side, so you need to walk or hitch a ride 5km from Kardam, or 6km from Durankulak.

Greece
The only two border crossings are at Kulata-Promahonas (south of Sandanski) and Svilengrad-Ormenion.

Turkey
Near Burgas the main border crossing point links Malko Târnovo with Derekoy in Turkey. From Kapitan-Andreevo, the border town near Svilengrad, travellers can cross to the Turkish city of Edirne.

Yugoslavia
The main border crossings link Kalotina (near Dragoman) and Dimitrovgrad; Vrâshka Chuka (near Vidin) and Zajc; and Strezimirovtsi (near Pernik) and Klisura. Be careful when travelling overland by train, because crime is not uncommon on services within Yugoslavia.

Macedonia
The main borders are between Gyueshevo (near Kyustendil) and Deve Bair; Zlatarevo (west of Kulata) and Delc; and Stanke Lisichkovo (near Blagoevgrad) and Novo Selo.

Sofia. Between Sofia and Bucharest, this train is called the *Grivitza*.

Every day in summer (15 June-28 Sept), a train from Burgas (leaving at 2.45pm) and another from Varna (at 3.30pm) connect with a train leaving Ruse at 1.15am. Departing Ruse it then stops at Bucharest (at 3.38am), Budapest (8.20pm), Bratislava (11.34pm) and Prague (5.45am the next day). It leaves Prague at 11.22pm, and stops at Bratislava (5.29am the next day), Budapest (8.30am) and Bucharest (1.40am the following day).

Also, every day in summer the *Sofia-Saratov* service travels to Bucharest. It departs from Sofia at 3pm, and stops at Pleven (6.09pm), Gorna Oryahovitsa (7.42pm) and Ruse (10.20pm), before arriving at Bucharest at 3.38am the next day. It departs from Bucharest at 1.40pm.

The daily *Bosfor* (train Nos 40 and 41) between Istanbul (Turkey) and Bucharest also crosses through Bulgaria year-round. To Bucharest, it travels through Stara Zagora at 9.13am, Veliko Târnovo at 11.51am, Gorna Oryahovitsa at 12.18pm and Ruse at 3pm, and arrives in Bucharest at 5.35pm. The same service departs Bucharest at 2.05pm.

The *Trans-Balkan Express* (train Nos 50 and 51) travels daily between Thessaloniki (Greece) and Budapest. To Bucharest, it leaves Sandanski at 3.41am, and travels via Blagoevgrad (5.05am), Sofia (8.25am), Pleven (11.37am), Gorna Oryahovitsa (1pm) and Ruse (3.30pm). It arrives in Bucharest at 7.16pm and then arrives in Budapest at 9.52am the next day. The return service departs Budapest at 8.10pm, and Bucharest at 12.15am.

Fares from Sofia to Bucharest for all trains mentioned here are 37/48 lv for 2nd-class seats/sleeping berths; about 50% more for each in 1st class. Fares for 1st/2nd-class seats (berths are not available) from Ruse to Bucharest are 21.09/20 lv, and from Ruse to Giurgiu, on the other side of the border, they cost 12/4 lv.

Travelling by Train

In Bulgaria, international train tickets can be purchased at any Rila Bureau (most open weekdays only) in the cities and major towns, and at dedicated ticket offices (most open daily) at larger train stations with international connections. Tickets must be paid for in leva.

Travelling around Bulgaria by train is cheap, so it doesn't make a lot of sense to buy a rail pass *just* for Bulgaria. However, if you're travelling between Western Europe and Bulgaria, or visiting Bulgaria as part of a trip around Eastern Europe and the Balkans, you may wish to consider one of the passes listed here. Passes for Bulgaria (where applicable) and for elsewhere around Europe can be bought at Rila Bureaus throughout the country.

Balkan Flexipass
This pass covers Bulgaria, Greece, Macedonia, Romania, Turkey and Yugoslavia. It offers five/10/15 days of unlimited travel in 1st class within one month for about €180/313/376. It's available to anyone, and can be bought inside any of these countries, including Bulgaria.

City Star
'City Star Deutschland' links Sofia with any city in Germany for €300/200 return for 1st/2nd class. More links within the City Star system are being planned with cities in Austria, Hungary and the Czech Republic. It's available to anyone, and can be purchased in Bulgaria.

Euro-Domino
See the Train section in the Getting Around chapter for details.

Inter-Rail
Inter-Rail passes are *only* available to European citizens, and *must* be bought outside Bulgaria. It offers two types of passes, ie, for those under and those over 26, but is only valid for 2nd-class travel. Each country is in one of eight zones; Bulgaria is in Zone H with Romania, Yugoslavia and Macedonia. For those under 26, a one-month pass for one/two/three zones costs €198/264/299, and €351 for all eight zones. For senior travellers, it's €282/370/420, and €496 for all zones. This pass also gives you 50% off rail travel from your home country to your zone(s), and between adjacent zones.

Greece The *Trans-Balkan Express* (see the Romania section earlier) travels south from Ruse at 3.35pm, passing through Gorna Oryahovitsa (5.50pm), Pleven (7.17pm), Sofia (11.05pm), Blagoevgrad (1.10am the next day), Sandanski (2.22am) and arriving in Thessaloniki at 7.13am. The return service departs Thessaloniki at 10.04pm.

The *Sofia-Thessaloniki* service (train Nos 510 and 511) links the two cities every day during summer (15 June-30 Sept). It departs Sofia at 7.10am, Blagoevgrad (9.32am) Sandanski (10.48am) and arrives in Thessaloniki at 4.30pm. It returns from Thessaloniki at midday.

Fares from Sofia to Thessaloniki for both trains are 37/48 lv for 2nd-class seats/sleeping berths. Fares are about 50% more for each in 1st class.

There are also daily trains between Svilengrad and Athens for 125 lv for a 1st class sleeper and 84 lv for a 2nd class sleeper.

Turkey The *Bosfor* (see the Romania section earlier) leaves Ruse for Istanbul at 5.25pm, goes through Gorna Oryahovitsa (7.22pm), Veliko Târnovo (7.45pm) and Stara Zagora (9.32pm), and arrives at Istanbul at 7.20am the next day. It departs from Istanbul at 11.55pm.

The *Balkan Express* (train Nos 492 and 493) travels daily between Istanbul and Belgrade, via Bulgaria. It departs from Sofia at 5.13pm, Plovdiv at 10.05pm, and arrives at Istanbul at 8.27am the next day. The return service departs from Istanbul at 11pm. (These times may have changed, so double-check this information.)

Only sleeper carriages are available to Turkey. From Sofia, fares to Istanbul for 1st/2nd-class sleepers cost 71/49 lv; to Edirne 1st/2nd-class sleepers cost 26/17 lv.

There are also daily trains between Svilengrad and Istanbul for 17 lv (2nd-class seat only).

Yugoslavia The *Balkan Express* (see the Turkey section earlier) leaves Sofia at 1.10pm, travels through Niš, and arrives in Belgrade at 9.06pm. It departs Belgrade at 7am, and travels on to Istanbul, via Sofia and Plovdiv.

The *Sofia-Beograd* service (train Nos 12 and 13) operates daily. It leaves Sofia at 9.50pm, arrives in Niš at 1.16am the next day, and finishes in Belgrade at 6.06am. The return service departs Belgrade at 10pm. From Sofia to Belgrade, 2nd-class seats/ sleepers cost 35/50 lv; 1st-class fares cost 50% more for both seats and sleepers.

Macedonia No trains travel directly between Bulgaria and Macedonia. The only way to Skopje by rail from Sofia is to get a connection in Niš.

Bus

Bordering Countries Buses don't travel directly between Romania and Bulgaria because of the long delays at the border in Ruse. Many buses, however, do travel between Bucharest (Romania) and Istanbul (Turkey), through Ruse and Veliko Târnovo. So, you could simply get off after clearing Bulgarian customs, but you may have to pay the entire Bucharest-Istanbul fare. And you won't be able to get on an Istanbul-Bucharest bus within Bulgaria.

Buses to Greece leave from Plovdiv, Sofia and Stara Zagora and buses for Turkey leave from Burgas, Haskovo, Plovdiv, Sofia and Varna. You can also catch buses to Belgrade that leave regularly from Sofia. Buses to Macedonia leave from Blagoevgrad, Kyustendil and Sofia. See those sections for details.

Elsewhere in Europe If you can stand a long bus trip across Europe, companies at the two main public bus stations in Sofia offer services to Amsterdam (190 lv), Barcelona (320 lv), Berlin (160 lv), Bratislava (90 lv), Brussels (180 lv), Budapest (80 lv), Frankfurt (190 lv), Madrid (340 lv), Milan (170 lv), Munich (150 lv), Prague (100 lv), Rome (170 lv), Vienna (120 lv) and Warsaw (150 lv). Buses to major cities in Europe also leave from Burgas, Plovdiv, Vidin, Veliko Târnovo and Varna (see these sections for details). In summer, buses connect European cities with resorts along the southern Black Sea coast.

Car & Motorcycle

Although driving is a great way to get around, bringing your own vehicle into Bulgaria is expensive, and the paperwork can be daunting. It's probably better to hire a car inside the country (see Car & Motorcycle in the Getting Around chapter). Note that the rates and regulations mentioned here change regularly. Current information should be available from your local automobile association, or the Union of Bulgarian Motorists (☎ 02-883 978), ploshtad Positano, Sofia, but this organisation is of little use.

With the exception of citizens from the Czech Republic, Denmark, France, Germany, Hungary, Italy, the Netherlands, Spain, Sweden, Switzerland and the UK, drivers of normal-sized cars (and motorcycles) are charged an entrance tax of US$10. Also, all drivers from all countries must state which border crossing they plan to use when leaving, and pay a 'highway fee' of US$0.10 cents per kilometre (minimum of US$5) upon leaving Bulgaria. Drivers must also pay a 'disinfection fee' of US$3 when they enter the country. The fees can be paid in US dollars, euros, leva and most other major European currencies.

Drivers of all private and rented cars (and motorcycles) must always carry their registration papers. Your driving licence from home is valid in Bulgaria, so an international driving licence isn't necessary (but it may be useful if you're driving elsewhere in Eastern Europe). Third-party 'liability insurance' is compulsory, and can be purchased at any Bulgarian border. Buying comprehensive insurance in your home country is a better idea (but make sure it's valid in Bulgaria). The Green (or Blue) Card – a routine extension of domestic motor insurance to cover most European countries – is valid in Bulgaria.

SEA

Despite the long, inviting and accessible coastline of the Black Sea, no international passenger boats travelled to or from Bulgaria at the time of writing. The decrepit, abandoned passenger terminals at all Bulgarian ports clearly indicate that there are no plans to resurrect any international service in the future.

ORGANISED TOURS

Most tourists visit Bulgaria on package tours, often for skiing or sunbathing, while others come on tours specialising in birdwatching or hiking. For details about tour operators based in Bulgaria, and for a discussion about the pros and cons of organised tours, see the Organised Tours section in the Getting Around chapter.

Surprisingly few companies offer bus tours, or overland trucks, to and around Bulgaria. A few that specialise in hiking, and other outdoor activities, include Balkan Eden (☎ 01227-373 727, e balkan-eden@yahoo .com), 31a Canterbury Rd, Herne Bay, Kent, UK, CT6 6AU, and Exodus (☎ 020-8673 0859, w www.exodus.co.uk), 9 Weir Rd, London SW12 0LT.

Skiing

Sometimes it's easier to arrange and pay for extras, like lift passes, equipment and training, before you leave home. While it's debatable whether they are cheaper for foreigners at the ski resorts, these add-ons can only be paid for in cash (ie, not credit cards) and will take valuable time to arrange at the resorts. Also, ask your tour company or travel agency about any specials, eg, free lift passes and equipment rental for children.

The peak season is about 20 December to 5 January, and about 9–22 February; the low season is between 5–31 January, and around mid-March. The rates here will be about 40% higher for better and more established hotels closer to the ski slopes, and single supplements are often charged at peak times. These rates do not include air fares.

As an example, expect to pay from UK£315 (low season) to UK£475 (peak) per person twin share for seven nights in a three-star hotel in Borovets, including buffet breakfast and dinner; or UK£395 to UK£549 for 14 nights. In Pamporovo, a three-star

hotel with buffet breakfast and dinner for seven nights will cost from UK£299 to UK£485; UK£385 to UK£499 for 14 nights.

Because the UK is one of the few Western and northern European countries without decent ski slopes, almost all companies offering ski tours to Bulgaria are based in the UK. These include:

Balkan Holidays (☎ 020-754 3555, e res@ balkanholidays.co.uk, w www.balkanholidays .co.uk)
Crystal (☎ 0870-848 7000, e skires@ crystalholidays .co.uk, w www.crystalski.co.uk)
Inghams (☎ 020-8780 4433, e reservations@ inghams.co.uk, w www.inghams.co.uk)
Neilson (☎ 08705-141 414, e sales@neilson .com, w www.neilson.com)

Black Sea Coast

While Brits flock to the ski resorts in winter, most visitors to the Black Sea coast in summer are German. The peak season is about 20 July to 8 August; the low season from about mid-April to 1 June, and 6 September to 3 October. (Note that most places close from late October to early April.) The rates listed here do not include air fares.

A package tour at a three-star hotel (room only) at most resorts will cost from €395 (low season) to €523 (peak) for seven nights, and €427 to €602 for 14 nights, per person twin share. Hotels closer to the beach will cost about 40% more, and some resorts, such as Elenite, are more exclusive and expensive. Because most resorts offer a huge range of restaurants, it makes no sense to pay considerably more for half-board (ie, including breakfast and dinner).

In the UK, the primary operators are Balkan Holidays (see earlier) and Sunquest (☎ 020-7499 9991, fax 7499 9995, w www .sunquestholidays.co.uk). In France, contact Nouvelles Frontiéres (☎ 0825-000 825, w www.nouvelles-frontieres.fr) or try Slav Tours (☎ 02-38 77 07 00, e slavtours@ slavtours.com, w www.slavtours.com) at 6 rue de Jeanne d'Arc, 45000 Orleans. One of the bigger operators in Germany is BG Tours (☎ 030-706 2020, e info@bg -tours.de, w www.bgtours.de), Maiendorfer Damm 147, 12107 Berlin.

Getting Around

Bulgaria is relatively easy to get around and a wide range of trains, buses and minibuses are available. One option worth considering is driving your own vehicle to Bulgaria or hiring one inside the country.

AIR

Bulgaria is reasonably compact, and bus and train services are reliable and cheap, so there's little point flying within Bulgaria unless you're in a real hurry. Anyway, the only internal flights are between Sofia, and Varna and Burgas (see the relevant Getting There & Away sections for specific airlines and prices).

The departure tax for domestic flights is the leva equivalent of US$2. It's included in all tickets purchased in and outside of the country.

BUS

Buses link all cities and major towns and connect villages with the nearest transport hub. In some places, buses are run by the government. These buses are old, uncomfortable (when compared with city buses) and slow. In larger towns and cities, newer, quicker and more commodious private buses often operate and normally cost little more than the fare on a ramshackle public bus.

Tickets for public buses can rarely be booked the day before (or earlier) but seats on private buses can be reserved one or more days in advance. However, except for long-distance services at peak times, eg, between Sofia and Varna in August, there's no need to book any bus more than a few hours ahead. In fact, if you arrive at the bus stop or station about 30 minutes before departure, you'll normally get a ticket for the bus you want. All timetables are listed (in Cyrillic) inside the bus stations and all buses have destination signs (in Cyrillic) in the front window.

For a public bus, buy a ticket from the counter marked *kasa* (каса) inside the station. This way you're guaranteed a seat

(which is never numbered) and you know the correct departure time and сектор (platform) number. Also, timetables normally only indicate direct services from one place to another but you can buy a ticket (if seats are available) for a public or private bus, eg, from Kazanlâk to Sliven on the service from Sofia to Burgas. However, in some cases, the cashier will tell you to buy a ticket on the bus. All public buses – but rarely privately-run services – can be hailed along the road. Look for the destination sign in the front window and wave madly.

Some cities have one or more public bus stations, often simply called the north (*sever*), south (*yug*), east (*iztok*) or west (*zapad*) stations. Most private buses also leave from these public stations, but a few use more convenient spots in the town or-city centre.

MINIBUS

Private and public minibuses ply routes between smaller villages, eg, along the Black Sea coast and between urban centres and ski resorts in winter. Tickets for minibuses cost roughly the same as public buses but are usually bought from the driver (though it's still worth checking this first at the counter inside the bus station). If you can choose between a public bus and minibus, take the latter because it's quicker, normally more comfortable and standing is rarely allowed. Destinations (in Cyrillic) and, often, departure times are indicated on the front window. Most minibuses leave from inside, or very close to, the major public bus station.

TRAIN

Bâlgarski Dârzhavni Zheleznitsi (ЧДЖ), or the Bulgarian State Railways (BDZh) boasts, an impressive 4278km of tracks across the country. While buses are normally quicker and more frequent, especially between cities and major towns, trains are generally more comfortable and offer far nicer views of landscapes, rather than of boring roads. Except for the inter-city express services between Sofia, and Varna and Burgas, standards are not as high as you may expect in Western and northern Europe, but trains are usually comfortable, reasonably quick and astoundingly cheap. While most places of interest in Bulgaria are accessible by train, some are on a spur track and only connected to a major railway line by infrequent and excruciatingly slow trains.

Trains are classified as *ekspresen* (express), *bârz* (fast) or *pâtnicheski* (slow passenger). Unless you absolutely thrive on train travel, you want to visit a smaller village or you're travelling on a tight budget, use a fast or express train.

Two of the most spectacular train trips are along Iskâr Gorge, from Sofia to Mezdra, and on the narrow gauge between Septemvri and Bansko. Railway buffs often go on these trips for no other reason than the journey itself.

Tickets & Fares

All tickets are printed in Cyrillic. Other than the place of departure and destination, tickets also contain other important details:

- клас *klas* – '1' (1st class) or '2' (2nd class)
- категория *kategoriya* – type of train, ie, T (express), 255 (fast) or G (slow passenger)
- влак *vlak* – train number
- час *chas* – departure time
- дата *data* – date of departure
- вагон *vagon* – carriage number
- място *myasto* – seat number

First-class compartments seat six people, eight are crammed into 2nd class, and the inter-city express has individual seats in an open carriage. Sleepers and couchettes are available between Sofia, and Burgas and Varna, for an extra 6 lv to 12 lv per person, but book in advance. Fares during the less-frequented Monday to Friday morning are about 20% less, and fares for 1st class are around 25% higher than for 2nd class.

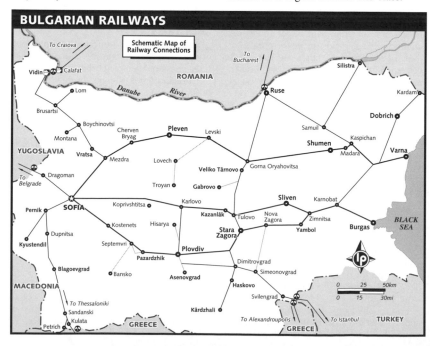

BULGARIAN RAILWAYS

Schematic Map of Railway Connections

Train Passes

Most major European rail passes can be used anywhere in Bulgaria (see the boxed text 'Travelling by Train' in the Getting There & Away chapter). No special individual pass is available within Bulgaria, but the BDZh is part of the Euro-Domino system. This pass allows 1st-class travel on consecutive days, or 2nd-class travel on nonconsecutive days, around specified *individual* countries within Europe, including Bulgaria. A three-day pass for travel around Bulgaria for 1st/2nd class costs about €30/20, plus €5.50/4.50 extra per day, but must be used within a period of 30 days. The pass is only available to Europeans and can only be bought outside Bulgaria. However, unless you plan to travel by train for about 10 hours a day every day, the pass is poor value.

Reservations

For frequent services, for example, between Sofia and Plovdiv, there's rarely a problem if you just turn up at the station and buy a ticket for the next train (but allow enough time, say about 30 minutes, to queue up). Advance tickets are sometimes advisable, for example, to the Black Sea on the inter-city express during a summer weekend. Advance tickets can be bought at specific counters within larger train stations and at Rila Bureaus in cities and major towns. Staff at Rila are normally far more helpful, knowledgeable and likely to speak English than anyone at a train station, so it's best to deal with Rila for advice, schedules and advance tickets.

Often, a 1st-class ticket can only be bought in advance at the point of departure, eg, in Sofia for the Sofia-Varna service. You may be able to buy a 1st-class ticket at a town along the way which is still close to Sofia, in Pleven for example, but any farther away becomes less likely, because the station doesn't know how many 1st-class seats are available. If this is the case, buy a 2nd-class ticket, get on a 1st-class carriage, and pay the difference. Should you come across a particularly surly conductor who won't allow this, then simply return to 2nd class and try again later.

Timetables

Timetables (valid for six months) for all domestic trains within Bulgaria and timetables (valid for 18 months) for all services to/from Sofia are theoretically available at all train stations and Rila Bureaus. These timetables, which are especially useful for smaller towns and villages that are often bypassed by express and fast trains, are very cheap but rarely available. Rila also prints free leaflets in Cyrillic with timetables for major services, eg, Sofia-Varna and Sofia-Burgas.

Timetables are prominently displayed inside every train station, but always in Cyrillic; more current details are often pasted to the window of the ticket counter. Larger stations have computer screens (usually in Cyrillic only) that list upcoming departures and recent arrivals.

CAR & MOTORCYCLE

Probably the best way to travel around Bulgaria, especially when visiting remote villages, monasteries and national parks, is to hire a car (or motorbike) or bring your own. However, there's no point hiring a car and then parking it for three days while you explore Plovdiv or Varna on foot, and it can be difficult driving around any city, particularly Sofia. For information about the relevant paperwork and fees required for travelling to/from Bulgaria see Car & Motorcycle in the Getting There & Away chapter.

Roads

Travelling around Bulgaria by private car or motorcycle is not as relaxing as it may be in Western and northern Europe. Other than a few impressive highways, road conditions

Road Distances (km)

	Blagoevgrad	Burgas	Dobrich	Gabrovo	Haskovo	Kulata	Kyustendil	Lovech	Pleven	Plovdiv	Ruse	Shumen	Silistra	Sliven	Smolyan	Sofia	Stara Zagora	Varna	Veliko Tãrnovo	Vidin	Vratsa
Blagoevgrad	---																				
Burgas	464	---																			
Dobrich	613	185	---																		
Gabrovo	321	234	317	---																	
Haskovo	272	213	388	141	---																
Kulata	82	520	695	403	346	---															
Kyustendil	72	462	602	310	278	154	---														
Lovech	268	299	356	65	206	350	257	---													
Pleven	275	334	347	100	241	357	264	35	---												
Plovdiv	194	270	455	146	78	260	200	159	194	---											
Ruse	421	263	212	152	293	503	410	150	146	298	---										
Shumen	482	148	133	186	302	564	471	225	219	283	115	---									
Silistra	543	262	92	274	374	619	525	272	268	396	122	113	---								
Sliven	353	114	299	130	132	419	359	193	228	159	216	135	248	---							
Smolyan	244	357	541	241	141	207	302	261	296	102	393	356	474	232	---						
Sofia	101	385	512	220	234	183	90	167	174	156	320	381	443	279	258	---					
Stara Zagora	282	182	367	80	61	348	288	145	180	88	232	218	355	71	161	231	---				
Varna	571	134	51	274	371	652	559	313	304	398	203	90	143	248	477	469	316	---			
Veliko Tãrnovo	342	224	271	46	187	424	331	85	120	192	106	140	228	110	287	241	126	228	---		
Vidin	300	538	558	308	433	382	289	243	208	355	356	429	478	429	457	199	388	515	328	---	
Vratsa	217	406	451	172	316	299	206	119	108	237	254	329	376	300	329	116	251	421	193	126	---

are generally taxing. Drivers must cope with potholes, roads under reconstruction, slow-moving vehicles, horses and carts and often erratic driving by other motorists.

You should never rely completely on road signs. They're often frustratingly ambiguous, or nonexistent, and most are written in Cyrillic (except around major cities, along the Black Sea coast and at the borders). It is imperative that you buy an accurate map (see Maps in the Facts for the Visitor chapter) and be able to read Cyrillic. If you're driving at full speed, with a semitrailer metres from your rear, you won't have time to check the Language chapter at the back of this book to work out that Видин means Vidin.

Vehicle security is a concern so take the usual precautions against car theft. If possible, use a guarded parking lot or hotel car park, or park under a streetlight. Never leave any valuables in the car.

And please take care as every month about 100 people die on Bulgarian roads.

The worst time is the holiday season (July to September) and most accidents are caused by drink-driving.

Petrol

Petrol is available in normal (91 octane), unleaded (95 octane) and super (98 octane). Normal petrol has an octane rating that is too low for Western cars but unleaded petrol (Euro 95) is easy to find. Major brands like Shell and OMV are often preferred by local drivers because water has been known to make its way into other brands. Petrol costs about 1.50 lv per litre and the price is remarkably standard throughout the country. Diesel is a little cheaper and costs about 1.40 lv per litre.

Road Rules

Although road signs are rare, the official speed limits for cars are 50km per hour in built-up areas, 90km/h on main roads and 120km/h on highways. Speed limits for motorcycles, trucks and buses are 50km/h in built-up areas, and 50/80/100km/h on highways. Traffic police, who used to routinely flag passing cars at whim for spot checks and fines, are now officially prohibited from doing so without just cause. Drivers and passengers in the front must wear seat belts and motorcyclists must wear helmets. The blood-alcohol limit is 0.05% and these days traffic police are very unforgiving about drink-driving. Fines for the first offence range from 100 lv to 300 lv.

If you have an accident, you *must* wait with your vehicle and arrange for someone to call the local traffic police (see the Emergencies section in the Facts for the Visitor chapter).

Rental

Cars can be rented in Albena, Burgas, Plovdiv, Ruse, Slânchev Bryag (Sunny Beach), Sofia, Sozopol, Sveti Konstantin, Troyan, Varna, Veliko Târnovo and Zlatni Pyasâtsi (Golden Sands), though sometimes it may be cheaper to organise it from Sofia. There is nowhere in Bulgaria to rent a motorbike.

Some agencies don't discriminate against foreigners and will charge you the same rates as for Bulgarians. The cars will be older but will normally be reliable and well-serviced. These agencies should offer you a contract (avoid anywhere that doesn't) but it will be in Bulgarian and staff may not speak your language. Because some agencies are little more than a telephone in a garage in a remote suburb, rental can often be arranged through a travel agent (who may speak your language). A basic Mazda 323 for one to four days costs from US$22 per day and for five to 10 days it's US$18 per day. For 11 to 20 days the cost is US$15 per day. All prices include unlimited kilometres but not petrol or insurance (about US$2 extra per day). A deposit of about US$150 is also required. Credit cards are almost never accepted and cash – in Bulgarian leva, US dollars or euros – is normally required in advance.

Larger and more established Bulgarian-based rental companies offer more or less the same standard of vehicles and service as the international agencies. In the case of mechanical breakdown, they should either fix the vehicle or provide another one promptly. A VW Golf, without air-con but with central locking, costs about US$44 per day (for one day). For two to three days it costs US$32 per day or for four to 11 days it costs US$26 per day. All include unlimited kilometres and accident and theft insurance but not petrol. A deposit of US$150-200 in cash, or a blank signed credit card voucher, is required. Most of these agencies will accept major credit cards.

The rates charged by international rental companies are outrageous. They're only worth considering if you want a new car, you want to drive across a border, or you want to hire extras, such as ski racks, roof racks and snow chains (each of which cost about US$30 for the length of the car rental). The cheapest car offered by Avis, for example, is an Opel Corsa, which costs about US$35 per day, plus US$0.35 per kilometre. For one to three days it costs US$88 per day or US$78 per day for four to six days with unlimited kilometres. Add to this the compulsory 'collision waiver damage' insurance (US$14 per day) and the optional 'theft insurance' (US$7 per day).

Most local and international rental companies insist that you have had a driving licence from your own country for at least one year and be 21-years-old or more (the minimum age required by some international agencies is 25). One-way rental is possible with the more established companies for a negotiable fee, eg, to drop off a car in Varna that has been rented in Sofia costs an extra US$50. Also with the international agencies, nominating another driver costs an additional US$3 to US$15 per day. Watch out for the 20% value-added tax (VAT) which is often not included in the initial rates quoted, but is included in the rates listed previously. Most international firms allow some vehicles to be taken out of the country, but let them know beforehand so they can sort out the paperwork.

BICYCLE

Generally, cycling is not popular in Bulgaria, but it's a viable way of getting around.

The downside is that many roads are windy, steep and in poor condition. Some major roads are always chock-a-block with traffic and bikes aren't allowed on highways. On the other hand, traffic is light along routes between villages and long-distance buses and trains will carry your bike for an extra 5 lv or so. Spare parts are available in cities and major towns, but it's better to bring your own. Mountain bikes are available for rent and there are several specific mountain-bike routes (see Activities in the Facts for the Visitor chapter).

HITCHING

Hitching is never entirely safe in any country in the world and we don't recommend it. Travellers who decide to hitch should understand that they are taking a small but potentially serious risk. People who do choose to hitch will be safer if they travel in pairs and let someone know where they're planning to go.

Despite this general advice, hitching in rural Bulgaria may be preferable to being restricted by infrequent public transport but travel will tend to be in fits and starts because many cars often only travel to the next village. The upsurge in crime over the last few years has dissuaded some Bulgarians from offering lifts to hitchhikers, so you're more likely to be picked up by a filthy Lada than a shiny Mercedes. Bulgaria's borders are not particularly 'user friendly', so hitching across them is not recommended.

Oh, and the pretty ladies standing along the major highways near Sofia waving down male drivers are *not* looking for a lift.

LOCAL TRANSPORT
Public Transport

All cities and major towns have buses, but they're generally not in great condition despite vastly increased fares and they tend to be overcrowded and uncomfortably hot in summer. New minibuses operate in some cities but most visitors will be confused by their ever-changing routes. The few places with useful bus and minibus routes are detailed in the relevant Getting Around sections throughout this book, but you're almost always better off using a taxi (see the following section). Bus tickets are regularly checked by conductors, especially in Sofia, and don't forget to buy an extra ticket for each piece of large luggage (ie, suitcase or backpack). Major cities also have trams and trolley-buses (a cross between a tram and bus) and Sofia boasts a modern metro system.

Taxi

Taxis, which must be painted yellow and equipped with working meters, can be flagged down on most streets in every city and town throughout Bulgaria. They can be very cheap, but rates do vary enormously, so it pays to shop around before jumping in. Taxis can be chartered for longer trips at negotiable rates, which you can approximate by working out the distance and taxi rate per kilometre, plus waiting time.

All drivers must clearly display their rates on the taxi's windows. These rates are divided into three or four lines:

- The first line lists the rate per kilometre from 6am to 10pm (about 0.25 lv to 0.35 lv per kilometre is acceptable); and the night-time rate (sometimes the same, but often about 10% more)
- The second lists, if applicable, the call-out fee of about 0.50 lv if you pre-order a taxi (almost never necessary)
- The third (or second-last) lists the starting fee (0.30 lv to 0.50 lv is acceptable)
- The fourth (last) lists the cost for waiting per minute (0.15 lv to 0.25 lv is acceptable). But remember, the meter will tick over even if you're stuck in traffic.

Taxi drivers in Bulgaria are probably as unscrupulous as their counterparts in many other countries. Some drivers do try to overcharge ignorant and unwary foreigners by rigging the meter (difficult to do), claiming the meter 'doesn't work' (it must work by law) or offering a flat fare (which will always be at least twice the proper metered fare). Dishonest drivers seem to almost exclusively congregate around central Sofia and Varna and the resorts along the Black Sea coast.

ORGANISED TOURS

Most travel agencies in Bulgaria cater to locals. Many will gladly take your money and pack you off to the major attractions, but most agencies require a minimum number of people, unless you're willing to pay hefty surcharges. See Organised Tours in the Getting There & Away chapter for a list of foreign-based companies that offer tours.

If you are pressed for time, crave a bit of comfort or find that getting around is a little difficult, an organised tour is worth considering. Even a one-day tour can be worthwhile, especially to remote monasteries and villages. Travel agencies and tourist offices that offer local tours are listed in the sections for Borovets, Burgas, Kazanlâk, Pleven, Ruse, Sandanski, Sofia, Smolyan, Teteven, Troyan, Varna and Veliko Târnovo. Naturally, plenty of agencies at the Black Sea resorts of Albena, Slânchev Bryag and Zlatni Pyasâtsi offer (expensive) tours.

Enterprising Bulgarian travel agencies that offer interesting tours around Bulgaria are surprisingly few and far between but you could try the following companies:

Balkanfolk Tours (☎ 02-322 010, fax 333 284, ⒺΙ info@balkanfolk.com, Ⓦ www.balkanfolk .com) ul Opalchenska 74, Sofia. Balkanfolk specialises in folk tours such as 7/10 day tours for about US$475/485 to festivals in Bansko or Veliko Târnovo. Tours include transport, accommodation, concert tickets and some entry fees.

Explorer Travel Company (☎/fax 02-430 852, Ⓔ explorer@mail.bol.bg) One of the first ecotourist agencies, it specialises in bird-watching and photography trips, including tours to Burgas Lakes.

Neophron Ltd (☎/fax 056-302 536 in Burgas, ☎/fax 052-302 536 in Varna, Ⓔ bspbvnbr@ mbox.digsys.bg) Associated with the Bulgarian Society for the Protection of Birds, Neophron runs tours of Burgas Lakes and the Vulture Centre near Madzharovo (see Endangered Species in the Facts about Bulgaria chapter).

Odysseia-In Travel Agency (☎ 989 0538, Ⓔ odysseia@omega.bg, Ⓦ www.newtravel .com), bul Stamboliyski 20, enter from ul Lavele. Multilingual staff offer enlightening, tailor-made tours of monasteries, national parks and traditional villages. Tours specialising in hiking, caving, horse riding, mountain biking, rock climbing and paragliding leave regularly in summer. It can also book rooms in over 100 mountain huts, monasteries and village homes.

Sofia София

☎ 02 • pop 1.18 million
Always growing, never ageing
                                    Sofia coat of arms
Sofia, which sits on a 545m-high plateau in western Bulgaria at the foot of the imposing Mt Vitosha, is the highest capital in Europe. Because of its position at the very centre of the Balkan Peninsula, midway between the Adriatic and Black seas, Sofia has always been at the crossroads of trans-European routes. Various empires, such as Roman and Ottoman, have left their marks, but some of the city centre was destroyed during WWII air raids. In recent years, the city has benefited greatly from the European Union's ongoing Beautiful Bulgaria Project, which is gradually sprucing up historic buildings and energising old neighbourhoods.

Almost all international flights start and finish in Sofia, and the capital is also the hub of much of Bulgaria's bus and rail transport. So, most travellers will probably end up here for a few days at least, but there are enough museums, churches and art galleries to keep most visitors happy for that long, and it's only an hour or so to excellent hiking and skiing spots. Sofia is also an ideal base for day trips to the nearby countryside. See the Around Sofia section later in this chapter, and the Southern Bulgaria chapter for information about organised tours to places such as the Rila Monastery.

HISTORY
The Thracian Serdi tribe, who lived in the region during the 7th and 8th centuries BC, called their settlement Sardonopolis, but later renamed it Serdica. Serdica was briefly occupied by the Macedonians, under Philip II, in 339 BC. The Romans, who conquered the region in AD 29, renamed the town Ulpia Serdica, and made it the capital of Inner Dacia. The town became an important staging post along the Roman road from Naisus (modern-day Niš in Yugoslavia) to Constantinople (Istanbul), and reached a zenith in the early 4th century under Emperor Constantine

Highlights

• Amble around Dragalevtsi Monastery, probably Bulgaria's oldest, on the slopes of Mt Vitosha

• Enjoy a spectacular ride on a chairlift to Aleko on Mt Vitosha

• Admire traditional costumes, arts and crafts at the extensive Ethnographical Museum

• Marvel at the huge range of art, carvings and sculptures at the National Gallery for Foreign Art

• Appreciate the grandeur of the magnificent Aleksander Nevski Church, and visit the museum of icons inside

• Sit at one of the plethora of cafes in the city centre and watch the locals stroll by

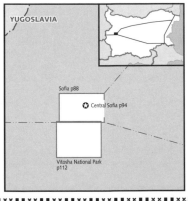

the Great. The Huns invaded in AD 441, but it was soon retaken and rebuilt by the Byzantine rulers after Attila's death.

The Slavs started to settle in the area in the 6th and 7th centuries, and renamed it Sredets, which means 'middle' (ie, of the Balkans). The Bulgar king, Khan Krum, came through in AD 809, and made it a major town (but not the capital) of the First

Bulgarian Empire (681–1018). Then, in 1018 the Byzantine rulers retook the city, and called it Triaditsa (which probably means 'between mountains').

In 1194, the Bulgars replaced the Byzantines in the region, and the city became a major trading centre in the Second Bulgarian Empire (1185–1396). During an unprecedented period of peace, the name of the city was probably changed (for the last time) to Sofia after the Church of St Sofia (which still stands).

The Ottomans captured the city in 1382, and held it for nearly 500 years. Sofia became the regional capital, and regained some prominence as a market town because of its central location. The Ottomans built Turkish baths and mosques, such as the Banya Bashi Mosque (which also still stands), but many churches were destroyed or abandoned.

The city declined during the feudal unrest of the mid-19th century, and it was in Sofia that the famed anti-Turkish rebel Vasil Levski was hanged in 1873. After the liberation of the city from the Turks in early 1878, Sofia officially became the capital of Bulgaria on 4 April 1879. The new roads and railway lines linking Sofia with the rest of Europe and the Balkans soon boosted the city's fortunes. However, Bulgaria picked the wrong side during World War II, so, tragically, a lot of the city's heritage was destroyed during bombing raids.

The border with Yugoslavia is only 55km north-west of Sofia, and the city's western location within Bulgaria is a reminder of the loss of Macedonia to Serbia and Greece after the Second Balkan War (1913).

ORIENTATION

From the central train station, bulevard Maria Luisa heads south past the Princess Hotel, the bus stations, the Lions Bridge, and ends up at the central ploshtad Sveta Nedelya. The city's backbone continues south as bulevard Vitosha, the fashionable avenue of modern Sofia, and passes the NDK National Palace of Culture complex. The narrow ulitsa Graf Ignatiev, Sofia's liveliest shopping precinct, runs south-east from near the start of bulevard Vitosha.

Many travel agencies and airline offices are along bulevard Stamboliyski, which runs west from ploshtad Sveta Nedelya, and ulitsa Sâborna, which runs east. Some attractions and resplendent older buildings are to the north-east of ploshtad Sveta Nedelya, in the triangle between ulitsa Dondukov, ulitsa Tsar Osvoboditel and ulitsa Krakra.

The city centre is full of landmarks, such as the imposing Sheraton hotel and the TsUM shopping centre nearby. Mt Vitosha is (clouds permitting) directly south of the city.

Maps

Unquestionably, the best map is the *Sofia City Map* (1:24,500), published by Domino and printed in English (with a distinctive red cover). All bookshops listed later sell maps of Sofia, and other places in Bulgaria, as do numerous stalls at ploshtad Slaveikov along ulitsa Graf Ignatiev. One of the best sources of maps, especially for hiking, is Odysseia-In (☎ 989 0538, e odysseia@omega.bg, W www.newtravel.com), at bulevard Stamboliyski 20. (Also see Travel Agencies later).

INFORMATION
Tourist Offices

The only place for independent tourist information is the National Information & Advertising Center (☎ 987 9778, e infctr@tir.ttm.bg, W www.bulgariatravel.org) ulitsa Sveta Sofia, across from Goody's restaurant. The office is open Monday to Friday from 9am to 5.30pm. Although not a real tourist office (the centre is run by the Ministry of Economy), staff are happy to help, and they also speak English. It offers a small number of brochures and few details about hotels and tours, but loads of information about the wonderful attractions throughout Bulgaria. It also sells a few books and videos. In summer, the office often stays open (unofficially) until about 8pm or 9pm. Its Web site is also a very useful source of information.

Rumours continue about the establishment of a dedicated tourist office in the future, possibly in the underpass near the President's Building, but if and when this will happen is anyone's guess.

SOFIA

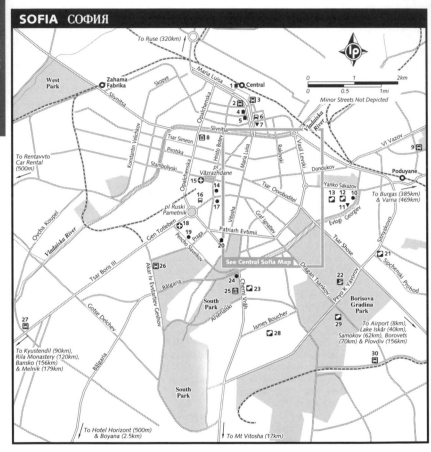

SOFIA СОФИЯ

Odysseia-In Travel Agency (☎ 989 0538, ⓔ odysseia@omega.bg), at bulevard Stamboliyski 20 (enter from ulitsa Lavele), has for many years acted as a de facto tourist office. While staff are more than happy to help visitors, it is a private business aimed at making money, so it charges a reasonable 5 lv for consultation and information. This fee is, however, deducted if you book a tour or accommodation with the agency.

Books, Newspapers & Magazines

Sofia City Info Guide (2.40 lv) is a vital resource for anyone staying in the capital for more than a few days. Printed in English every month, it includes useful practical information, detailed lists of current and future events, and recommended restaurants. It's available at Odysseia-In (☎ 989 0538, ⓔ odysseia@omega.bg) bulevard Stamboliyski 20, and at the front desk of the Sheraton hotel. Also, check its Web site at Ⓦ www.sofiacityguide.com.

The Sofia Echo is an English-language newspaper (1.80 lv), published each Friday and available at most bookstalls. This essential source of information and listings is keenly read by expats and visitors alike.

SOFIA СОФИЯ

	PLACES TO STAY & EAT			
1	Do Kopovza Hotel	9	Poduyane Bus Station	
4	Princess Hotel; Hotel Kom		АВТОГАРА ПОДУЯНЕ	
	ХОТЕЛ PRINCESS.	10	Drenikov Car Rental	
	ХОТЕЛ КОМ		КОЛИ ПОД НАЕМ	
5	Hotel Repos; Tourist Service		ДРЕНИКОВ	
	(Travel Agency)	12	French Embassy; Greek	
	ХОТЕЛ РЕПОС		Consulate	
7	Pizzeria Planeta Italia		ФРЕНСКО ПОСОЛСТВО.	
	ПИЦАРИЯ ПЛАНЕТА ИТАЛИЯ		ГРЪЦКО КОНСУЛСТВО	
11	33 Chairs	13	Yugoslav Consulate	
	33 СТОЛА		КОНСУЛСТВО НА	
20	Tsar Asen Hotel		ЮГОСЛАВИЯ	
	ХОТЕЛ ЦАР АСЕН	14	Orbita (Travel Agency)	
			ОРБИТА	
	OTHER	15	Poliklinika Torax	
2	Princess Hotel Bus Station		ПОЛИКЛИНИКА ТОРАХ	
	West	16	MATPU Bus Office	
3	Princess Hotel Bus Station		МАТРU АВТОБУСНА	
	East		СПИРКА	
6	ATT Bus Office	17	Balkan Airlines	
	АТТ АВТОБУСНА СПИРКА	18	Pirogov Hospital	
8	National Polytechnic Museum		ПИРОГОВ БОЛНИЦА	
	НАЦИОНАЛЕН ПОЛИТЕХН-	19	Malito Car Rental	
	ИЧЕСКИ МУЗЕЙ		КОЛИ ПОД НАЕМ	
			МАЛИТО	

21	Romanian Embassy & Consulate
	РУМЪНСКО ПОСОЛСТВО И КОНСУЛСТВО
22	Maria Luisa Pool
	БАСЕЙН МАРИЯ ЛУИЗА
23	USA Embassy
	АМЕРИКАНСКИ ПОСОЛСТВО
24	Hilton Hotel; Hertz Car Rental
25	Museum of Earth & Man
	МУЗЕЙ НА ЗЕМЯТА И ХОРАТА
26	Hladilnika Bus Terminal
	ХЛАДИЛНИКА АВТОГАРА
27	Ovcha Kupel Bus Station
	АВТОГАРА ОВЧА КУПЕЛ
28	Netherlands Embassy
	ХОЛАНДСКО ПОСОЛСТВО
29	German Embassy; Macedonian Embassy & Consulate
	НЕМСКО ПОСОЛСТВО. МАКЕДОНСКО ПОСОЛСТВО И КОНСУЛСТВО
30	Yug Bus Station
	АВТОГАРА ЮГ

Spot On is a more sophisticated English-language monthly. It's free, and available at some airline offices and top-end hotels.

Sofia Business & Travel Guide, by P Carney and M Anastassova, is indispensable for anyone intending to set up business in the capital. It's available at the bookshop in the basement of the Sheraton hotel.

Money

Foreign-exchange offices are all around the city centre, especially along bulevard Stamboliyski, bulevard Maria Luisa and bulevard Vitosha – look for the word 'change' in English. These offices deal with most major currencies in cash, but only a small number accept travellers cheques. Most are open daily from about 8am to 8pm; some along upper (northern) bulevard Maria Luisa are open 24 hours. For information about commission rates and how to avoid them, see the Money section in the Facts for the Visitor chapter.

Try not to change more than necessary at the handful of foreign-exchange offices at the airport, because their rates are 10% to 15% lower than those in the city centre. The rates offered at the train station are more acceptable, but still marginally lower than the rates in the city.

Bulbank is the best place to change cash and travellers cheques, obtain cash advances over the counter with Visa and MasterCard, or to use an automatic teller machine (ATM). It's at the corner of ulitsa Lavele and ulitsa Todor Alexandrov. Also reliable are the Biochim Commercial Bank on ulitsa Alabin, two doors down from British Airways; and the United Bulgarian Bank on ulitsa Sveta Sofia, just down from Goody's restaurant. Most banks around central Sofia have ATMs that accept all major credit cards.

The American Express (AmEx) representative is MegaTours (☎ 980 8520), on the corner of ulitsa Vasil Levski 21 and ulitsa Graf Ignatiev. It won't change AmEx travellers cheques, but provides the normal services for AmEx customers.

Post & Telephone

The Central Post Office, on ulitsa General Gurko 6, also sells stamps and organises packages, and has a poste restante. Curiously, most signs inside the building are translated into French. It's open daily from 7.30am to 8.30pm.

Nearby, on ulitsa General Gurko, is the new and impressive BTC Centre (open 24 hours), run by the Bulgarian Telecommunications Company. Inside, there are dozens of booths for local, interstate and international calls, an office from where faxes can be sent, and an Internet centre. All services are neatly signposted in English.

Email & Internet Access

Like everywhere else in Bulgaria, Internet access in Sofia is pleasingly cheap: most places charge about 1 lv for 30 minutes, and 1.50 lv to 2 lv per hour. The BTC Centre offers several computers in a classy office-style environment. The Ultima Internet Center is at ulitsa Lavele 16, just down from the entrance to the Odysseia-In Travel Agency. You can surf the Web daily from 9am to 11pm. There's an Internet centre in the Euro-Bulgarian Cultural Centre at bulevard Stamboliyski 17, around the corner from the Happy Bar & Grill. The Internet Centre is open Monday to Friday from 9am to 6pm. Several Internet agencies are also inside, and along the underpass beneath the NDK National Palace of Culture complex.

Travel Agencies

Most travel agencies around Sofia simply book airline tickets and/or offer package tours for Bulgarians; very few actually offer anything of interest to visitors. The places listed here do provide tours for foreigners, have staff who speak English and, often, French and German, and are open Monday to Friday from about 9am to 6pm. More information about the type of tours that some agencies offer is mentioned in the Organised Tours section later in this chapter.

Alma Tours (☎ 986 5691, ℮ almatour@dir.bg) bul Stamboliyski 27. Books tours and hotel rooms along the Black Sea coast and at ski resorts, as well as chartered flights to Turkey and Spain.

Balkan Air Tour (☎ 987 0182, ℮ bat@travel -bulgaria.com, Ⓦ www.travel-bulgaria.com /balkanairtour) ul Al Battenberg 10. This large

and reliable company arranges car rental, and domestic and international flights.

Odysseia-In Travel Agency (☎ 989 0538, ℮ odysseia@omega.bg, Ⓦ www.newtravel .com) bul Stamboliyski 20. Enter from ul Lavele for the best place for maps and advice (see Tourist Offices earlier in this chapter) about skiing, cycling or hiking. The multilingual staff run trips, and book private rooms and hotels in Sofia and throughout Bulgaria (see Places to Stay later).

Orbita (☎ 987 9128, ℮ orbita@ttm.bg) bul Hristo Botev 48. (See the Visas & Documents section in the Facts for the Visitor chapter for more information.)

Camping & Skiing Equipment

Stenata (☎ 980 5491), ulitsa Tsar Samuil 63, is the best place to buy hiking and mountain/rock climbing equipment, as well as tents, mattresses and sleeping bags, but it doesn't hire gear. Odysseia-In (see Travel Agencies earlier) rents mountain bikes for 18 lv per day (plus a deposit of about US$200).

The Orion Ski Shop (☎ 986 4157), inside an arcade along ulitsa Pozitano, sells (but does not rent) all sorts of ski gear. For information about hiring ski equipment, see the boxed text 'Skiing on Mt Vitosha' later in this chapter.

Bookshops

Bookstalls in the city centre, particularly around ploshtad Sveta Nedelya, often sell recent copies of *Time* and *Newsweek*, as well as newspapers from the UK, the USA and Germany.

The bookshop in the basement of the Sheraton hotel sells hard-to-find maps, guidebooks and general-interest tomes about Bulgarian tourism and culture, as well as international magazines and newspapers.

Book World, at ulitsa Graf Ignatiev 15, sells dictionaries and phrasebooks, and local and international maps, and offers one of the better ranges of foreign-language novels. The Euro-Bulgarian Cultural Centre on bulevard Stamboliyski 17, around the corner from the Happy Bar & Grill, has an eclectic range of titles, some in English. The bookshop inside the Fine Arts Gallery, ulitsa Shipka 6, sells books about Bulgaria in French and English, and is the best place for guidebooks about the region. (See the Shopping section later in this chapter.)

Ploshtad Slaveikov along ulitsa Graf Ignatiev is crowded with stalls selling maps, music cassettes, CDs, and books and second-hand novels in English, French and German. Anything in English (or any other foreign language) is generally a little more expensive than its Bulgarian equivalent, but is probably still cheaper than anything in a bookshop. One reader claimed to have 'found a book at ploshtad Slaveikov that I had been looking for for about 10 years'.

Libraries
Built in 1878, the National Library on bulevard Vasil Levski houses seven million books in all sorts of languages. It's open Monday to Saturday from 8.30am to 5.30pm, but mainly caters to Bulgarians studying at the Sofia University down the road. Each cultural centre listed here has a library open to the public, but (paid) membership is required to borrow books.

Cultural Centres
As one of the major cities in the Balkans, Sofia is home to numerous cultural centres, though most cater to Bulgarians wishing to know more about the UK, France etc, rather than to homesick tourists. Other cultural centres not listed here are mentioned in the *Sofia City Info Guide*.

American Cultural Center (☎ 980 4838) ul Kârnigradska 8. Open Monday to Friday 8.30am to 5pm.
British Council (☎ 942 4344, W www.british council.org/bulgaria) ul Krakra 7. Open Monday to Friday 9am to 5pm.
French Cultural Institute (☎ 981 6927, W www .ambafrance.bg) bul Vasil Levski 2. Open Monday to Friday noon to 6pm. This place offers French films and a cafe with decent coffee.
Goethe Institute (☎ 963 0437) ul Lyuben Karavelov 72. Open Monday to Friday 9am to noon and 3pm to 5pm.

Laundry
Some budget and mid-range hotels offer a laundry service for guests. One of the most convenient among a bunch of newly established dry-cleaners is McClean at ulitsa General Gurko 10, virtually behind the Central Post Office. Expect to pay 3 lv to 4 lv for a shirt or skirt, and about 5 lv to 6 lv for trousers or a jumper (sweater).

Toilets
The standard of public toilets in Sofia is certainly better than anywhere else in the country, but it is still nothing to get excited about. The underpasses in the city centre have clean toilets for a standard charge of about 0.20 lv. The best (free) toilets are in the Central Hali Shopping Centre, on bulevard Maria Luisa; and the underpass below the NDK National Palace of Culture complex. Otherwise, use the public conveniences (even if you're not a customer) in a bar, major hotel (for example, the Sheraton) or a fast-food outlet (for example, McDonald's).

Left Luggage
The various bus stations are astoundingly disorganised, so the only place to leave your gear is the left-luggage counter on the lower (underground) level of the central train station. It's open daily from 5.30am to midnight.

Medical Services
The major public hospital for emergencies is the reasonably acceptable Pirogov Hospital (☎ 51 531), bulevard Gen Totleben 21. Poliklinika Torax (☎ 988 5259), bulevard Stamboliyski 57, is a competent, privately run clinic with English-speaking staff. For tooth-related problems, contact Denta (☎ 988 8209), ulitsa Dobrudjha 4. Otherwise, ask your embassy to recommend a hospital, clinic, doctor or dentist.

There are a number of chemists (pharmacies) throughout Sofia. The most convenient one that is open 24 hours is No 7 Pharmacy on ploshtad Sveta Nedelya. Details of other chemists with extended opening hours are available from a special recorded message (in Bulgarian) on ☎ 178. Prescriptions can be delivered through Farmatel (☎ 962 2222).

Emergency

For police matters (between 8am and 6pm daily), there are special contact numbers where operators speak English (☎ 988 5239) and French (☎ 982 3028). Contact Mountain Rescue (☎ 955 5665) if you get into strife on the mountains. Other toll-free emergency numbers are listed in the Emergencies section of the Facts for the Visitor chapter.

Dangers & Annoyances

The major danger is from the traffic: watch out for trams and trolleybuses, which shuttle silently along most major streets, and cars that hurtle through pedestrian crossings regardless.

Beggars ply their trade around some churches and larger squares, but are reasonably harmless, undemanding and infrequent. As always, be careful with bags, wallets and purses in crowded public transport, and, in particular, busy areas such as the Ladies Market.

MUSEUMS

Befitting an ancient capital boasting so much culture and history, Sofia is home to 36 official museums. Many are not worth the effort of visiting, but we have listed the most interesting and accessible museums.

National Museum of History

Probably the most acclaimed (but, perhaps, the most overrated) museum in the country is the National Museum of History (☎ 955 4280, bul Okolovrusten Pat, Boyana; admission 10 lv; open daily 10am-7pm in summer & 9.30am-5.30pm in winter; camera/video permit 20/40 lv).

The first and second floors house various antiquities, including fabulous Thracian gold treasures from the 1st millennium BC to the 1st century BC as well as artefacts from Roman ruins at Varna, Veliki Preslav and Veliko Târnovo. There are also exhibits about Bulgarian history, religion, economics and politics during Ottoman rule between the 15th and 17th centuries and the Bulgarian national revival period (18th and 19th centuries).

It's easy to miss the stairs to the third floor, which contains temporary exhibits (not labelled in English). Currently on show is war memorabilia from the Roman times to WWII and paraphernalia from various Bulgarian political leaders.

Guided tours in English, German, French, Spanish, Italian or Hungarian are available for 10 lv per group of five to six people. The ticket counter also offers a decent range of souvenir books (in English), including four separate titles (5 lv each) about the exhibits at the museum. There's a *cafe* on the ground floor.

While there are, for example, plenty of stunning photographs in the museum, the number of exhibits is surprisingly small. Also discouraging is the hassle of getting to Boyana, the high admission fee and the fact that while all the major exhibits (except on the third floor) are labelled in English, the lengthy explanations about Bulgarian history are not.

In 2000, the museum moved from the city centre to the former presidential residence in the upmarket suburb of Boyana. (In fact, some locals and taxi drivers don't know the museum has moved yet, so, if in doubt, ask for the *residentsia Boyana*.) Take bus No 63 from ploshtad Ruski Pametnik, or bus No 64 from the Hladilnika terminal; or minibus No 21 from along bulevard Vitosha. Bus No 64 and minibus No 21 also connect the museum with Boyana Church (see later). A taxi (about 2.50 lv one-way) from the city centre to the museum is probably easier.

National Museum of Natural History

This well-maintained museum (☎ 988 2894, ul Tsar Osvoboditel; admission 2 lv; open daily 10am-6pm, 4th floor closed noon-2.30pm) houses over one million specimens of animals, minerals and vegetables. The four floors also contain a few creatures in cages and glass tanks – mostly snakes, turtles and mice – which are alive and not stuffed, bottled or pinned to a wall. Most captions are not in English but this rarely distracts too much from the enjoyment.

Ethnographical Museum

This museum (☎ 988 1974, ul Tsar Osvoboditel; admission 3 lv; open Tues-Sun 10am-5.30pm) is housed in the former Royal Palace (built in 1887), which it shares with the National Art Gallery (see later). The museum contains a fascinating series of displays about Bulgarian arts and crafts over the last 300 years, including costumes, embroideries, ceramics, and detailed exhibits about the migration and customs of the traditional Bulgarian way of life.

It's easy to get disoriented along the winding corridors, so make sure you follow the arrow to the ground floor, where more exhibits explain the major religious festivals celebrated throughout Bulgaria.

Everything is fully captioned in English. Tours are available in English for 10 lv per group (up to five people), and an English-language guidebook is for sale (1 lv). Remember to visit the excellent souvenir shop (see Shopping later in this chapter).

Archaeological Museum

The nine lead-covered domes of the Buyuk Djami (Great Mosque), built in 1496, now house the Archaeological Museum (☎ 988 2406, ul Tsar Osvoboditel; admission 3 lv; open Tues-Sun 10am-6pm). The modest collection includes Thracian tablets, Roman statues and Byzantine columns from all over Bulgaria, as well as the largest collection of ancient coins in the country. On the mezzanine level, a private collection features ancient weaponry and mosaics from about 500 BC to AD 600. Everything in the museum is labelled in English.

Other Museums

Arguably, the best of the rest are listed here.

The National Polytechnic Museum (☎ 931 3004, ul Opalchenska 66; admission 1.50 lv; open Mon-Fri 9am-5pm) boasts temporary and permanent exhibits about the early history of TV and photography.

The Ivan Vazov House Museum (☎ 881 270, ul Ivan Vazov 19; admission 3 lv; open Tues & Wed 1pm-7pm, Thurs 1pm-5pm, Fri & Sat 9am-5pm) documents the history and achievements of the renowned poet who lived in this house from 1895 to 1921. Vazov (1850–1921), whose novel Under the Yoke describes the 1876 April Uprising against the Turks, was also a noted travel writer.

The Museum of Earth & Man (☎ 656 639, ul Cherni Vrâh 4; admission 0.80 lv; open Tues-Sat 10am-6pm), also called the Museum of Earth & The People, is mainly for geological buffs.

ART GALLERIES
National Art Gallery

Inside the same building as the Ethnographical Museum is the renovated National Art Gallery (☎ 980 3320, ul Tsar Osvoboditel; admission 2 lv, free on Sun; open Tues-Sun 10.30am-6.30pm). This gallery features several rooms of Bulgarian art, including those by Georgi, Anton and Boris Motev, who between them created hundreds of paintings in the late 19th and early 20th centuries. Displays change from time to time and captions are in English. Tours are available in English, French or German for 10 lv per group of about five people. The English-language guidebook costs 7 lv.

National Gallery for Foreign Art

This huge gallery (☎ 980 7262, W www .ngfa.icb.bg, ul 19 Fevruari; admission 1.50 lv, free on Sun; open Wed-Mon 11am-6pm) was opened in 1985. The 18 halls on the three floors house ancient, traditional and contemporary art, carvings and sculptures from Europe, Asia and Africa – in fact, everywhere but Bulgaria. Some of the more interesting exhibits include 19th-century Japanese woodblock prints, and masks and figures from western and central Africa. Most captions are in English. Guided tours are available in English, Spanish or German for 7 lv per group of about five people.

Other Galleries

Other worthwhile art galleries that hold temporary exhibitions (as advertised in The Sofia Echo) include the Gallery of the Union of Bulgarian Artists (☎ 946 7113, ul Shipka 6; admission free; open Mon-Sat 9am-5pm) and the Sofia Municipal Gallery of Art (☎ 981 2606, ul Al Battenberg; admission free; open

SOFIA

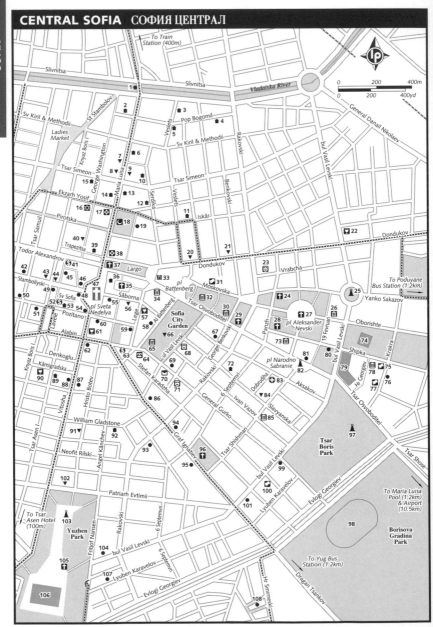

CENTRAL SOFIA СОФИЯ ЦЕНТРАЛ

CENTRAL SOFIA   СОФИЯ ЦЕНТРАЛ

PLACES TO STAY

2 Hotel Enny; Alexander Tour
ХОТЕЛ ЕНИ. АЛЕКСАНДЪР ТУР
3 Hotel Viki
ХОТЕЛ ВИКИ
4 Hotel Pop Bogomil
ХОТЕЛ ПОП БОГОМИЛ
5 Hotel Bolid
ХОТЕЛ БОЛИД
6 Hotel Chance; Passport
Office (Extensions)
ХОТЕЛ ШАНС. ВИЗА ОФИС
10 Hotel Central
ХОТЕЛ ЦЕНТРАЛ
11 Hotel Iskâr
ХОТЕЛ ИСКЪР
12 Markella Accommodation
Agency
АГЕНЦИЯ ЗА НАСТАНЯВАНЕ
МАРКЕЛА
13 Gloria Palace Hotel
ХОТЕЛ ГЛОРИЯ ПАЛАС
14 Hotel Maria Luisa
ХОТЕЛ МАРИЯ ЛУИЗА
15 Hotel Ametist
ХОТЕЛ АМЕТИСТ
36 Sheraton Sofia Hotel Balkan;
Avis Car Rental; Bookshop
39 Hotel Maya
ХОТЕЛ МАЯ
53 Sofia Hostel; China
Restaurant
ОБЩЕЖИТИЕ СОФИЯ.
КИТАЙСКИ РЕСТОРАН
72 Hotel Slavyanska Besseda
ХОТЕЛ СЛАВЯНСКА БЕСЕДА
89 Hotel Baldjieva
ХОТЕЛ БАЛДЖИЕВА
92 Art Hostel
ХУДОЖЕСТВЕНО
ОБЩЕЖИТИЕ

PLACES TO EAT

7 Atlantik
АТЛАНТИК
8 San Valentino
САН ВАЛЕНТИНО
9 Trops Kâshta; Modern Theatre
ТРОПС КЪЩТА. МОДЕРЕН
ТЕАТЪР
20 Pizza Hut
21 Birhale Gambrinus
БИРХАЛЕ ГАМБРИНУС
40 Tsentral
ЦЕНТРАЛ
43 Stateside Americana
ГОСТИЛНИЦА АМЕРИКАНА
44 KFC

56 Trops Kâshta; Lufthansa
ТРОПС КЪЩТА
66 Cafe Theatre
КАФЕ ТЕАТЪР
84 Krim
КРИМ
91 Ramayana
РАМАЯНА
102 Best Burger
НАЙ-ДОБРИЯ БУРГЕР

THINGS TO SEE

16 Sofia Synagogue
СИНАГОГАТА В СОФИЯ
18 Banya Bashi Mosque
ДЖАМИЯТА БАНЯ БАШИ
19 Sofia Town Public Baths
СОФИЙСКАТА ГРАДСКА БАНЯ
24 Church of St Sofia; Tomb of
the Unknown Soldier
ЦЪРКВАТА СВ. СОФИЯ.
ГРОБНИЦА НА НЕЗНАЙНИЯ
ВОЙН
25 Vasil Levski Monument
ПАМЕТНИК НА ВАСИЛ
ЛЕВСКИ
26 National Gallery for Foreign Art
ГАЛЕРИЯ ЗА ЧУЖДЕСТРАННО
ИЗКУСТВО
27 Aleksander Nevski Church;
Aleksander Nevski Crypt
ЦЪРКВАТА АЛЕКСАНДЪР
НЕВСКИ. КРИПТАТА
АЛЕКСАНДЪР НЕВСКИ
28 Holy Synod Church
ЦЪРКВАТА НА СВ. СИНОД
29 St Nikolai Russian Church
РУСКАТА ЦЪРКВА СВ.
НИКОЛАЙ
30 National Museum of Natural
History
ПРИРОДО-ИСТОРИЧЕСКИ
МУЗЕЙ
32 National Art Gallery &
Ethnographical Museum;
Souvenir Shop
НАЦИОНАЛНА ХУДОЖЕСТВ-
ЕНА ГАЛЕРИЯ. ЕТНОГРАФСКИ
МУЗЕЙ
33 President's Building
СГРАДА НА ПРЕЗИДЕНТСТВОТО
34 Archaeological Museum; Art
Club Museum (Cafe)
АРХЕОЛОГИЧЕСКИ МУЗЕЙ
35 Church of St George; Cafe
Rotonda
ЦЪРКВАТА СВ. ГЕОРГИ. КАФЕ
РОТОНДАТА

37 Sveta Petka Samardjiiska
Church; Restorant Perfekt;
Shopping Arcade
ЦЪРКВАТА СВ. ПЕТКА
САМАРДЖИЙСКА. РЕСТОРАНТ
ПЕРФЕКТ
47 Sveta Nedelya Cathedral
КАТЕДРАЛАТА СВ. НЕДЕЛЯ
65 Sofia Municipal Gallery of Art
СОФИЙСКА ГРАДСКИ
ХУДОЖЕСТВЕНА ГАЛЕРИЯ
73 Gallery of the Union of
Bulgarian Artists
СЪЮЗ НА БЪЛГАРСКИТЕ
АРТИСТИ- ГАЛЕРИЯ
74 National Library; The Library
(Nightclub)
НАЦИОНАЛНАТА
БИБЛИОТЕКА
79 Sofia University
СОФИЙСКИ УНИВЕСИТЕТ
81 National Assembly
НАРОДНОТО СЪБРАНИЕ
82 Monument to the Liberators
ПАМЕТНИК НА
ОСВОБОЖДЕНИЕТО
85 Ivan Vazov House Museum
КЪЩА-МУЗЕЙ НА ИВАН
ВАЗОВ
96 Sveti Sedmochislentsi Church;
Fruit & Veg Stalls
ЦЪРКВАТА СВ. СЕДМОЧИСЛ-
ЕНИЦИ
97 Soviet Army Monument
ПАМЕТНИК НА СЪВЕТСКАТА
АРМИЯ
103 1300th Anniversary
Monument
ПАМЕТНИК ПО СЛУЧАЙ 1300
ГОДИЩНИНАТА НА
БЪЛГАРИЯ
105 Memorial & Chapel

ENTERTAINMENT

22 Bourbon Street Nightclub
23 National Opera House
НАЦИОНАЛНА ОПЕРА
57 La Cocaracha Bar; Air France
ЛА КОКАРАЧА
61 Svejk Pub
67 Bulgaria Hall
ЗАЛА БЪЛГАРИЯ
68 Ivan Vazov National Theatre
НАЦИОНАЛЕН ТЕАТЪР ИВАН
ВАЗОВ
71 Puppet Theatre
КУКЛЕН ТЕАТЪР

[Continued on page 96]

SOFIA

CENTRAL SOFIA СОФИЯ ЦЕНТРАЛ

[Continued from page 95]

90 JJ Murphy's
106 NDK National Palace of Culture Complex; Internet Centres; United New Cinema; Balkan Airlines; Rila Bureau
НДК НАЦИОНАЛЕН ДВОРЕЦ НА КУЛТУРАТА КОМПЛЕКС. НОВО КИНО. БЮРО РИЛА

OTHER

1 Lions Bridge
ЛЬВОВ МОСТ
17 Central Hali Shopping Centre
ЦЕНТРАЛИН ХАЛИ
31 British Embassy
ПОСОЛСТВО НА АНГЛИЯ
38 TsUM Retail Centre; Oasis Supermarket
ЦУМ. СУПЕРМАРКЕТ ОАЗИС
41 Bulbank
БУЛБАНК
42 Olympic Airways
45 Odysseia-In Travel Agency; Ultima Internet Center
ПЪТНИЧЕСКА АГЕНЦИЯ ОДИСЕЙА-ИН
46 No 7 Pharmacy
7 АПТЕКА
48 Euro-Bulgarian Cultural Centre (Bookshop, Cinema & Internet Centre); Happy Bar & Grill
ЕВРО-БЪЛГАРСКИ КУЛТУРЕН ЦЕНТЪР
49 Alma Tours
АЛМА ТУРС

50 Stenata Camping Equipment
СТЕНАТА
51 Union of Bulgarian Motorists
СЪЮЗ НА БЪЛГАРСКИТЕ АВТОМОБИЛИСТИ
52 United Bulgarian Bank; The Irish Harp
ОБЕДИНЕНА БЪЛГАРСКА БАНКА
54 National Information & Advertising Centre; Goody's
ИНФОРМАЦИОНЕН И РЕКЛАМЕН ЦЕНТЪР
55 Turkish Airlines
58 Balkan Air Tour
59 Bonjour Supermarket
60 Orion Ski Shop
62 Balkantourist & Budget Car Rental; McDonald's
БАЛКАНТУРИСТ
63 Biochim Commercial Bank; British Airways
ТЪРГОВСКА БАНКА БИОХИМ
64 BTC (Telephone) Centre & Internet Centre
69 Rila Bureau
БЮРО РИЛА
70 Central Post Office; McClean Dry Cleaners
75 Albanian Embassy & Consulate
ПОСОЛСТВО И КОНСУЛСТВО НА АЛБАНИЯ
76 British Council
77 Croatian Embassy & Consulate

ПОСОЛСТВО И КОНСУЛСТВО НА КРОАЦИЯ
78 Fine Arts Gallery & Bookshop
ГАЛЕРИЯ НА ИЗЯЩНИТЕ ИЗКУСТВА
80 Dandy Airlines
83 Denta Dental Clinic
ДЕНТА
86 MegaTours (Amex Representative)
87 Radost Tour Private Lodgings Office; Reks Cinema
ТУРИСТИЧЕСКА АГЕНЦИЯ РАДОСТ. КИНО РЕКС
88 American Cultural Center
АМЕРИКАНСКИ КУЛТУРЕН ЦЕНТЪР
93 Hemus Air
94 Bookworld
СВЯТ НА КНИГИТЕ
95 Alitalia
98 Vasil Levski Stadium
СТАДИОН ВАСИЛ ЛЕВСКИ
99 Bulgarian Tourist Union
БЪЛГАРСКИ ТУРИСТИЧЕСКИ СЪЮЗ
100 Turkish Embassy
ПОСОЛСТВО НА ТУРЦИЯ
101 French Cultural Institute
ФРЕНСКИ КУЛТУРЕН ИНСТИТУТ
104 Yugoslav Airlines
107 Goethe Institute
108 Roman Wall Market
ПАЗАР РИМСКАТА СТЕНА

Tues-Sun 10am-6pm) in the Sofia City Garden. Both galleries also sell paintings.

RELIGIOUS BUILDINGS

Sofia is chock-a-block with churches and to prove that major religions can happily co-exist there's also a mosque and synagogue. Unless stated otherwise, admission to each building is free (but donations are usually welcome), and each is open daily from about 7am to 7pm. None are open to tourists during religious services, though genuine worshippers are welcome.

Aleksander Nevski Church

This church *(pl Aleksander Nevski)* is the largest (3170 sq m) of its kind in the Balkans. It was built between 1892 and 1912 as a memorial to the 200,000 Russian soldiers who died fighting for Bulgaria's independence during the Russian-Turkish War (1877–78).

Designed by the renowned Russian architect, Pomerantsev, the church is obviously influenced by others built in Russia at the time. Note the marble at the main entrance, the domes laden with 8kg of gold, and the dozen very heavy bells. Inside are stained-glass windows, delightful murals and elaborate thrones encrusted with onyx and alabaster. The seemingly permanent scaffolding inside and outside the church does detract from the beauty and ambience, but it's still a majestic place.

A door near the main entrance leads to the **Aleksander Nevski Crypt**, also known as the Museum of Icons (☎ 877 697; admission 7 lv; open Wed-Mon 10.30am-noon & 2pm-6.30pm). It contains one of Bulgaria's best and largest collections (about 300 pieces) of religious icons from the last 1000 years. A **shop** inside the church complex sells religious paintings and icons.

Guided tours are available in English for 6 lv per group of about five people. Otherwise, the guidebook (10 lv) is a worthwhile souvenir, especially as taking photos is not allowed inside the church. Visitors should be discreet at all times.

Church of St Sofia

The capital was named after the Church of St Sofia (ul Panzh). Built in the mid-6th century AD, it is the oldest Orthodox church in Sofia. Minarets were added in the 16th century by the Ottomans who used it as a mosque. Most of the building was destroyed by earthquakes in the 19th century, but it was completely rebuilt in 1900.

St Nikolai Russian Church

This resplendent church (ul Tsar Osvoboditel) was built in 1912 and 1913 by Russian emigres living in Bulgaria. Like the Aleksander Nevski Church, the design is influenced by Russian architecture, and it boasts a golden cross atop. The interior has recently been restored, and features murals painted between the 11th and 14th centuries, contrasting green tiles and various icons. Sitting in a flower-laden park, the church is one of the most photographed sites in the capital, but please be discreet because it's a revered place where supplicants pray for miracles.

Church of St George

Regarded as the oldest preserved building in Sofia is the Church of St George, behind the Sheraton hotel. Originally built as a rotunda by the Romans in the 2nd or 3rd century BC (and still sometimes called the Sveti Georgi Rotunda), it was converted into a church during the Middle Ages. It was destroyed by the Huns, but rebuilt in the 6th century and then again in 1943. The murals inside were painted on three layers between the 10th and 14th centuries.

Inside the entrance, and to the left, there's a small explanation in English about the church. You're also allowed to wander around the extensive, but unexplained, **Roman ruins** next to the church.

Sveta Petka Samardjiiska Church

This church (admission 5 lv; open daily 7am-6pm) is incongruously located under the main road near the TsUM Retail Centre. Named after St Peter of the Saddlers, the church was built during the early years of Ottoman rule (late 14th century), which explains its sunken profile and inconspicuous exterior. Inside there are some remarkable, but faded, murals painted during the 16th century, but little else to justify the admission fee. As nothing is explained or captioned in any language, it's probably best to appreciate it while sipping a coffee at the adjacent *Restorant Perfekt* (see Places to Eat later).

Sveta Nedelya Cathedral

This magnificent building (pl Sveta Nedelya) is one of *the* landmarks in the city centre. Built between 1856 and 1863 on foundations of the Roman city of Ulpia Serdica, the cathedral features an exceptionally ornate interior. A small plaque near the southern entrance explains how the cathedral was rebuilt in 1925 following a bomb attack by a communist group, which unsuccessfully attempted to kill Tsar Boris III (though over 120 people, including most of the cabinet, were killed). It's often full of devout worshippers, so visitors should make sure that they are always discreet.

Boyana Church

The 13th-century Boyana Church (☎ 685 304, ul Boyansko Ezero 3; admission 10 lv; open Tues-Sun 9am-5pm) was listed as a World Heritage site by Unesco in 1979. The 90 murals, which date from 1259, are some of the finest examples of Bulgarian medieval artwork and later, they influenced murals painted in monasteries in Serbia and Russia. Some murals are in poor condition, however, and the scaffolding is evidence of seemingly perpetual restoration. It is not permitted to take photos of the interior.

The (high) entrance fee allows you a quick look at the small number of murals, but nothing is explained inside the church, so the 20-minute tour in English (an extra 5 lv per person) is probably worthwhile. Alternatively, the small brochure (0.50 lv), or larger booklet (3 lv), both in English, provide some explanations and make nice souvenirs. It costs nothing to enter the pretty **gardens** and admire the church from the outside.

It's far cheaper, and almost as revealing, to visit the adjacent **National Church Museum of Boyana** *(admission 2 lv; open Tues-Sun 9am-5pm)*. It houses copies of the murals, as well as other religious icons, but, disappointingly, nothing is captioned in English. The short informative film (an additional 2 lv) in English, French or German helps make sense of it all.

See the National Museum of History section earlier for information about public transport from Sofia to, and between, the museum and church. It's about a 45-minute walk between both sites, so a taxi (not easy to find) may be quicker.

Other Buildings of Interest

The **Banya Bashi Mosque** *(bul Maria Luisa)* was built in 1576 by the Turks. The only functioning mosque left in the capital is worth seeing for its unusual interior, which is so different to mosques found in Turkey. The minaret certainly makes it a convenient landmark.

The nearby **Sofia Synagogue** *(ul Ekzarh Yosif 16)* was consecrated in 1909. It is the largest Sephardic synagogue in Europe, and boasts a 2250kg brass chandelier. However, visitors are only welcome if invited or of the Jewish faith.

The **Sofia Town Public Baths** *(ul Pirotska)* – also called the Turkish Baths or Central Baths – was built between 1911 and 1913. Recently, it laid dormant for several years while authorities debated its purpose and the cost of renovation. At the time of research, it was being restored and will include a museum about Sofia.

PARKS & STATUES

Bulevard Vitosha leads down to the huge **Yuzhen Park** (Southern Park), home to the massive NDK National Palace of Culture complex (see the Entertainment section later). The dodgem cars, swings and toy trains attract local families and children, especially on Sunday. At the northern end is the huge and astoundingly decrepit **1300 Anniversary Monument**, built in 1981 to celebrate the anniversary of the creation of the First Bulgarian Empire. Although only 30 years old, the signs (in Bulgarian) around the monument warn 'caution falling objects'!

Nearby is a poignant contrast: a recently built **memorial** and **chapel** to those 'who died in the communist terror' (according to the sign in Bulgarian). Either side of the memorial is a list of 10,000 names, just some of those who died under the communists, and behind it is a register of towns and places where massacres took place.

The **Borisova Gradina Park** in the southeast is home to the **Vasil Levski Stadium** and **Maria Luisa Pool** *(☎ 963 0054; admission free; open daily 9am-8pm in summer)*, as well as bike tracks and tennis courts.

The **Sofia City Garden** is probably the nicest of the inner-city parks. It's a gorgeous spot with cafes, fountains, swings and plenty of shade and grass. Popular with old men playing chess, it's also an ideal place to relax and watch people watching other people watching…

ACTIVITIES

There's not a lot in the way of activities in Sofia, but there's plenty to do nearby. For details about hiking, skiing and other popular activities, see the Around Sofia section later in this chapter and the Southern Bulgaria chapter. A round of golf is possible at the **Golf Club Air Sofia** *(☎ 0724-3530)*, about 55km south-east of Sofia at Ihtiman. The course may not be exceptional, but expats and wealthy Bulgarians also enjoy the club's swimming pool, **horse riding** and tennis courts. Contact the club for bookings and current costs.

ORGANISED TOURS

There's little point taking an organised tour around Sofia unless you're really pressed for time, crave some comfort or feel uneasy about using local transport. Almost everything to see in Sofia is accessible on foot, and other attractions at Boyana and Mt Vitosha, for example, are easy to reach by public transport or taxi.

The magnificent Rila Monastery (see the Southern Bulgaria chapter) is very difficult to visit in one day by public transport from Sofia, so an organised tour is not a bad idea. However, renting a car, or even chartering a taxi, for the day will probably be cheaper for a group of two to four people and will certainly be more flexible. For details about renting cars and hiring taxis, see the Getting Around section later in this chapter.

The following companies offer tours in and around Sofia for foreigners:

Alma Tours (☎ 986 5691, e almatour@dir.bg) bul Stamboliyski 27. Day trips to Rila cost for two/four people US$35/60 in a car or minibus (depending on the numbers), including lunch; three- to four-hour guided walking tours around Sofia cost US$20 to US$25 per person; and a dinner-dance in a restaurant at the foot of Mt Vitosha is US$30 per person.

Alexander Tour (☎/fax 983 3322, e alextour@ omega.bg, W www.alexandertour.com) ul Pop Bogomil 44. This upmarket outfit, next to Hotel Enny, offers all sorts of tours, from trekking to balneotherapy treatment on the Black Sea coast.

Balkantourist (☎ 980 2324, e sofia.agency@ balkantourist.bg, W www.balkantourist.bg) bul Vitosha 1. The original monolithic government organisation is now privatised, and offers all sorts of mid-priced tours.

Odysseia-In Travel Agency (☎ 989 0538, e odysseia@omega.bg, W www.newtravel.com) bul Stamboliyski 20. Offers all sorts of outdoor activities, including hiking in the Rila, Pirin and Rodopi mountains, rock climbing, mountain biking, horse riding and paragliding for about US$35 per person per day (depending on destination and numbers). It can also arrange day trips to Rila Monastery for about US$45 per person (minimum of two).

Pirin Holidays (mobile ☎ 087-621 984) Offers several fascinating trips on old trains from Sofia to places such as Iskâr Gorge and Sandanski. Half/full-day tours cost about US$40/70 per person, including meals and drinks.

Tourist Service (TUI; ☎ 981 7253, e bg@ tourist-service.com, W www.tourist-service .com, bul Klokotnitsa) Next to Hotel Repos, the TUI runs comfortable three-hour tours by air-conditioned car around Sofia ($18 per person); and 'folkloric evenings' of music, food and dance ($48). Other manageable day trips, which include lunch, are offered to Rila Monastery ($65 per person); and Plovdiv and Bachkovo Monastery ($78).

SPECIAL EVENTS

St Sofia is the Mother of Hope, Love and Faith, and **St Sofia's Day** (17 September) is widely celebrated in the capital. The **Sofia Fest** (about 14 to 18 September) includes cultural events, concerts and exhibits held at various galleries and museums, as well as the Church of St Sofia. The **Sofia International Folklore Festival** takes places in and around the capital for five days in late August.

PLACES TO STAY

Up until about 10 years ago, there were a dozen or more camping grounds in and around Sofia. However, the only place to camp near the capital is at Lake Iskâr or Borovets, but there are also a few hotels, huts and hostels on Mt Vitosha. If the rates charged by the hotels in Sofia are too high, head to Kyustendil (see later in this chapter) or try Borovets, Samokov, Govedartsi or Malîovitsa (see the Southern Bulgaria chapter) where accommodation is far cheaper.

In July and August, it's not a bad idea to book ahead if you're keen to stay in any particular place in Sofia.

Private Rooms At the central train station, the accommodation agency claims to offer rooms for 24 lv to 31 lv per person. The rates are closer to 33 lv, however, so better value can be found elsewhere. The accommodation agency at the airport is almost never staffed, but some readers have been impressed with the service and quality of rooms for 26 lv to 35 lv per person, so it may be worth checking out if you arrive by air.

Odysseia-In Travel Agency (see Travel Agencies earlier) can arrange rooms with a shared bathroom in private homes. Singles are about 26 lv and doubles are around 40 lv.

Shuffling Around Sofia

Happily, most of Sofia's attractions are in the city centre and accessible on foot. Allow most of the day to wander around the attractions and plan to stop at a cafe (as the locals do) every two hours or so. More information about the major sites is mentioned in the relevant sections in this chapter.

The best place to start and finish the tour is **Aleksander Nevski Church**. The surrounding square is the largest in Sofia, and surprisingly devoid of traffic and cafes. Head east and over the road to the **National Gallery for Foreign Art**. Immediately north up bulevard Vasil Levski, in the middle of the roundabout, is the **Vasil Levski Monument**.

Farther down (south) along bulevard Vasil Levski is the **National Library**, with the **Statue of Sts Kiril & Metodii** in front; still farther down, on the corner of ulitsa Tsarigradsko Shose, is the **Sofia University**. Turn right (north-west) along ulitsa Tsar Osvoboditel, and you'll pass the **National Assembly** building, established in 1884, and the **Monument to the Liberators**, built in 1907.

Farther along ulitsa Tsar Osvoboditel (the first street in the capital to be paved) are the **St Nikolai Russian Church**, the **National Museum of Natural History**, and the **National Art Gallery** and **Ethnographical Museum** that are both housed in the former Royal Palace. Head down ulitsa Vasil Levski and admire the eye-catching neoclassical **Ivan Vazov National Theatre**. Walk along ulitsa General Gurko or cut through the **Sofia City Garden** and enjoy a drink or snack at the delightful **Cafe Theatre**. (Go on, you deserve a break!)

Now fully refreshed, head west along trendy ulitsa Sâborna to the **Sveta Nedelya Cathedral**. Then walk northwards along the western side of bulevard Maria Luisa and turn left along one of Sofia's very few pedestrian **malls**, ulitsa Pirotska. At the end of the mall, turn right (north-east) along ulitsa St Stambolov, which soon turns into the chaotic **Ladies Market**. Follow the crowds up to bulevard Slivnitsa, and turn right down bulevard Maria Luisa.

Keeping on the western side of the road, you'll soon see the recently renovated **Central Hali Shopping Centre**, with its striking arched brick and stone facade. Behind it is the resplendent **Sofia Synagogue**. Cross the road (carefully!) to the unmistakable **Banya Bashi Mosque**; between it and the colourful **Sofia Town Public Baths** is a small park full of locals filling bottles with drinking water. Past the revamped **TsUM Retail Centre** is the gorgeous **Sveta Petka Samardjiiska Church**, accessible via an underpass with a cafe (of course) and plenty of shops.

Take this underpass to the Sheraton hotel, which dominates **ploshtad Sveta Nedelya**, and head to the **Church of St George**. Continue east along a footpath to ulitsa Tsar Osvoboditel and the **Archaeological Museum**. Across the street is the former Communist Party Building, now part of the **President's Building** complex. Try to be here on the hour (or wait at the Art Club Museum cafe, next to the Archaeological Museum) for the serious, but rather humorous, **changing of the presidential guards**. Then, head up (north-east) ulitsa Dondukov, turn right at ulitsa Rakovski and left along ulitsa Vrabcha to the **National Opera House**. Down ulitsa Panzh is the **Church of St Sofia** and, nearby, the **Tomb of the Unknown Soldier**. Walk through the park to the **Holy Synod Church** from where it's impossible to miss the Alexander Nevski Church.

Radost Tour Private Lodgings Office (☎/fax 988 2631, e radostur@bol.bg), at bulevard Vitosha 37, offers singles/doubles with shared bathroom for 30/50 lv, and small/large apartments with bathroom for 88/110 lv. This place offers a number of private rooms and apartments with a TV in central Sofia for reasonable prices. Look for the sign (in English) near the Reks Cinema.

The Markella Accommodation Agency (☎/fax 981 1833), at ulitsa Ekzarh Yosif 35,

offers singles/doubles with shared bathroom for 22/31 lv. This agency is run by a helpful English-speaking lady who can show you photos of the rooms on offer.

PLACES TO STAY – BUDGET
Hostels

Surprisingly, there are only two hostels in Sofia. Neither offer many beds, so book ahead in summer. If you're travelling in a group of two or three, a double or triple

Shuffling Around Sofia

1	Aleksander Nevski Church
2	National Gallery for Foreign Art
3	Vasil Levski Monument
4	National Library; Statue of Sts Kiril & Metodii
5	Sofia University
6	National Assembly
7	Monument to the Liberators
8	St Nikolai Russian Church
9	National Museum of Natural History
10	National Art Gallery; Ethnographical Museum
11	Ivan Vazov National Theatre
12	Cafe Theatre
13	Sofia Municipal Gallery of Art
14	Sveta Nedelya Cathedral
15	Central Hali Shopping Centre
16	Sofia Synagogue
17	Banya Bashi Mosque
18	Sofia Town Public Baths
19	TsUM Retail Centre
20	Sveta Petka Samardjiiska Church
21	Sheraton Sofia
22	Church of St George
23	Archaeological Museum; Art Club Museum (Cafe)
24	President's Building
25	National Opera House
26	Church of St Sofia; Tomb of the Unknown Soldier
27	Holy Synod Church

· · · · ·←— Walking Tour

0   150   300m
0   150   300yd

room in a hotel will probably be cheaper than staying at a hostel.

Sofia Hostel (*☎/fax 989 8582, 🇪 hostel -sofia@usa.net, ul Pozitano 16*) Dorm beds with shared bathroom 22 lv per person for the first 1-2 nights,18 lv for each additional night. This hostel offers basic accommodation with breakfast, and a communal kitchen and lounge room with a TV. It's a friendly place and the staff speak English and French. It's above a Chinese restaurant, but is not

well signposted so check with a local if you can't find it.

Art Hostel (*☎ 987 0545, 🇪 art-hostel@ art-hostel.com, ul Angel Kânchev 21a*) Dorm beds with shared bathroom 20 lv per person. This bohemian place doubles as an art gallery and general meeting spot. It's the sort of hostel where you're likely to meet fascinating (English-speaking) locals, but never get any sleep before 3am. It's poorly signed, so look for the graffiti in English on the wall – 'we usually spend our time in the garden' – which is the alternative name for this odd place.

Hotels

The general areas for budget hotels are near the Lions Bridge, around the junction of bulevard Maria Luisa and bulevard Slivnitsa; and the corner of ulitsa Veslets and ulitsa Pop Bogomil, a quieter spot not far from the bus and train stations.

Hotel Viki (☎ *983 9746, ul Veslets 56*) Beds 10 lv per person with a shared bathroom. Although the effusive landlady does not speak a word of English, the rooms are comfortable, but obviously basic at this price. Each room has three beds, so a room to yourself will cost 30 lv.

Hotel Bolid (☎ *983 3002, Cnr of ul Pop Bogomil & ul Veslets*) Singles/doubles with shared bathroom 22/44 lv. Well signposted from bulevard Maria Luisa, the Bolid was, at the time of research, undergoing renovations and will improve. The rooms (which have a TV and sink) are small, the ceilings are low and the floors squeak, but it's good value.

Hotel Kom (☎ *931 9603, bul Maria Luisa 126*) Singles/doubles with bathroom 35/50 lv. This place, about 50m north of the Princess Hotel, is the budget option closest to the bus and train stations. However, there are only two rooms (each with a TV), so it's often full.

Hotel Horizont (☎ *574 217, ul Gen Mihail Kutuzov 23*) Rooms with shared bathroom 22 lv per person. Often recommended by readers, the friendly, family-run Horizont is great value, but inconvenient. Some rooms have a balcony, and there's a convivial TV lounge and kitchen area (or home-cooked meals can be ordered). Contact them about room availability and for free transport from the bus or train stations, or airport. It's linked to the city centre by tram Nos 5 and 19.

Hotel Chance (☎ *983 6411, bul Maria Luisa 50*) Singles/doubles with shared bathroom 15/20 lv. It's always nice to find somewhere that charges foreigners the same rates as Bulgarians. The rooms all have TVs and they are clean, but the walls are thin so it is noisy if other guests are boisterous. Some rooms also face the noisy main road. Look for the sign in English.

Hotel Repos (☎ *317 463,* e *repos@npc .omega.bg, bul Klokotnitsa 1*) Singles/doubles with shared bathroom 40/50 lv, singles with bathroom 50-60 lv, doubles with bathroom 60-65 lv, apartments with private bathroom 100 lv. Very convenient to the bus and train stations, and accessible by tram to the city centre, the Repos offers dozens of rooms on several floors (but with no lifts). The rooms are nicely furnished, bright, airy and reasonably quiet, and the dearer ones have TVs. The apartments, which have sitting rooms and kitchens, are far better value than most mid-range hotels.

Hotel Enny (☎ *983 3002, ul Pop Bogomil 46*) Singles/doubles with shared bathroom 22/44 lv, doubles with TV and shower (no toilet) 66 lv. The Enny is popular, friendly, central and quiet, but a little overpriced, and some rooms (especially the singles) are small. On the other hand, the outdoor courtyard area is a great place to meet other travellers. It's well signposted from bulevard Mara Luisa.

Hotel Maya (☎ *989 4611, ul Trapezitsa 4*) Singles/doubles/triples with private bathroom 44/66/77 lv. This central and friendly guesthouse has cosy rooms either side of a rooftop courtyard, all with TV and fridge. The bathrooms are detached and minuscule. Single rates are possible at quieter times, but staff speak little or no English.

Do Kopovoza Hotel (☎ *932 2763, Central Train Station*) Singles/doubles/triples with shared bathroom 44/88/120 lv. For a late-night arrival or early-morning departure, this place at the central train station is convenient. But the rooms are nothing special, and it's little more than a dorm. It overlooks a noisy platform, and is overpriced for foreigners.

Hotel Central (☎ *983 7332, ul Serdika 19*) Rooms with shared bathroom about 33 lv. This small and friendly guesthouse is clean, central and very good value. The large rooms have a TV, fan and three or four beds, and are ideal for anyone travelling in a small group. However, it can get a bit noisy if there are many guests.

PLACES TO STAY – MID-RANGE
All of the hotels here offer rooms with a private bathroom, unless stated otherwise.

Hotel Iskâr (☎ 986 6750, e hoteliskar@dir.bg, ul Iskâr 11) Doubles with shared bathroom US$25, doubles/apartments with bathroom US$32/49. The sister of the equally appealing and spotless Hotel Pop Bogomil, the Iskâr offers similarly charming rooms, but they're a little smaller. Without breakfast (an extra 4 lv per person), fridge or TV (an extra 11 lv per night) rooms are overpriced, however. The apartments have a fridge, kitchen, spa and fan.

Hotel Pop Bogomil (☎ 983 7065, e hotelpopbogomil@dir.bg, ul Pop Bogomil 5) This hotel has identical rates to Hotel Iskâr. It boasts almost the same decor, standards and service as the associated Iskâr, the Pop Bogomil is a little farther from the city, but closer to the train and bus stations. Like the Iskâr it's not great value.

Tsar Asen Hotel (☎ 547 801, e elena@mbox.infotel.bg, ul Tsar Asen I 68) Singles/doubles/triples US$28/34/45. The Tsar Asen offers clean and comfortable rooms with a TV, on a quiet suburban street, but it's a little inconvenient and pricey. It only has four rooms, so book ahead. Breakfast costs an extra 4 lv per person.

Hotel Baldjieva (☎ 981 2914, ul Tsar Asen I 23) Singles/doubles US$52/64, apartments US$67/79. This pleasant three-star hotel is in an excellent spot. The comfortable, pine-furnished rooms have fans and a TV but are smallish. The apartments contain a sitting room, TV and air-con. Like all other hotels in this range, it's poor value for foreigners. Breakfast is included.

Hotel Ametist (☎ 983 5475, ul Tsar Simeon 67) Singles/doubles US$35/45. This new and friendly place has modern, spotless rooms with a fridge, but it's overpriced (for foreigners) considering TV and breakfast are not included.

Hotel Slavyanska Besseda (☎ 988 0442, fax 875 6383, ul Slavyanska 3) Singles/doubles US$35/50. This decent mid-range option is popular with businessmen from Russia and Eastern Europe. It's close to the city centre, but the air-conditioned rooms, which also offer a balcony, fridge, TV and breakfast, could do with some renovation.

PLACES TO STAY – TOP END
All of the following hotels offer rooms with a private bathroom, and all the mod cons and luxuries, such as satellite TV, air-con and fridge with minibar. Most offer discounted rates (without much haggling) on weekends (Friday, Saturday and Sunday night), and at any other time when business is quiet (which is often).

Princess Hotel (☎ 931 0077, bul Maria Luisa 141) Singles/doubles US$80/100, 'weekend rates' US$60/80. More of a landmark than a hotel because of its proximity to the two bus stations and train station, the Princess is good value, and the rates include a hearty breakfast.

Hotel Maria Luisa (☎ 91 044, e mlisa@mail.bol.bg, bul Maria Luisa 29) Singles/doubles US$80/90. The superb Maria Luisa is central and quiet, and wonderfully decorated with bathrooms fit for royalty. Rates include breakfast.

Gloria Palace Hotel (☎ 980 7895, e gloria@cblink.net, bul Maria Luisa 20) Singles/doubles US$140/160, often discounted to US$84/108. Very new and luxurious, the Gloria Palace is good value if you can get a discounted rate. The hotel is central, the rooms are quiet despite the location, and the rates include breakfast.

Sheraton Sofia Hotel Balkan (☎ 981 6541, e sofia.sheraton@luxurycollection.com, pl Sveta Nedelya) Doubles from US$269, often discounted to US$125. It's perhaps worth inquiring at this imposing landmark in central Sofia about any discounted rates.

PLACES TO EAT
Sofia has so many restaurants, snack bars, fast-food outlets and cafes that it seems a little unfair to mention just a few. The places listed in this section offer some ambience and value, and all restaurants and cafes mentioned have menus in English (unless stated otherwise). Check the ads and reviews in *The Sofia Echo* and *Sofia City Info Guide* to find out what's new and what's recommended.

Bulgarian Restaurants

Trops Kâshta *(branches: ul Sâborna, bul Maria Luisa)* Both open daily 8am-9pm. Salads about 1 lv, main dishes 2.20-3.20 lv. There are several branches of this cheap cafeteria (the one on ulitsa Sâborna is near the Lufthansa office). Although the menu isn't written in English, it's ideal for anyone wanting to try some local nosh without paying through the nose – just point, pay, eat and enjoy. It's packed Monday to Friday from noon to 2pm, but is empty at most other times.

33 Chairs *(ul Asen Zlatarov 14)* Meals from 5-6 lv. This well-established place is a fair walk east from the city centre, but worth the effort. The menu features a vast array of meals, and different specials every day.

Tsentral *(ul George Washington)* Most meals 3-4.50 lv, large beer about 1 lv. This folksy outdoor *mehana* (tavern) has a beer-garden setting with wooden tables. It offers Bulgarian dishes (mainly grilled meats) and a huge range of salads at reasonable prices. The menu has been considerably scrawled into English on a separate piece of paper.

Krim *(ul Slavyanska 17)* Salads about 2.50 lv, main meals 7-8 lv. The Krim offers Russian-Bulgarian fare in several rooms of a restored early 20th-century house, or outdoors in the summer garden. This clubby place is popular with politicos who pull up outside in luxury Western cars.

San Valentino *(bul Maria Luisa)* Meals from 3.50 lv. This classy place, opposite the Modern Theatre cinema, offers Western food (3.50/5 lv for small/large pizzas), as well as a decent range of Bulgarian cuisine (about 5 lv) and schnitzels (about 4 lv). Prices are surprisingly reasonable, and the service is snappy.

Birhale Gambrinus *(ul Dondukov 17)* Soups about 2 lv, meals about 5 lv, grilled dishes 7-8 lv. This is the sort of place where you may want to splurge, though it's easy enough to enjoy a fine meal and excellent service without spending too much.

Other Restaurants

Pizzeria Planeta Italia *(bul Maria Luisa)* Pizzas from 3.20 lv, pasta dishes about 3 lv.

About halfway between Lions Bridge and the bus stations, this simple but homely place offers nothing but pasta, and pizzas lovingly created in large wood-fired ovens. The menu is translated into Italian, which adds to the authenticity, but also to the confusion if you don't speak that language.

Stateside Americana *(bul Stamboliyski 34)* Snacks from 3.50 lv, main meals 4-5 lv. Open Mon-Fri noon-late, Sat 5pm-late. Ideal for homesick Yankees, this cosy underground cafe/bar offers all sorts of American food, such as burgers, as well as Tex-Mex dishes. It has live music on weekends.

Ramayana *(ul Hristo Botev 32)* Soups 2 lv, main meals 7-8 lv. This classy but expensive restaurant gets mixed reviews from expats, but is still the only place in the city to enjoy a curry. The quiet outdoor garden setting is a bonus in summer and the service is usually very good.

China Restaurant *(ul Pozitano 16)* Rice dishes 1.50-3 lv, soups 2.80 lv. Above the Sofia Hostel, this is one of several Chinese restaurants around town. It's always crowded with Bulgarians, especially at lunch time during the working week, because it's excellent value. The large dishes (3.50 lv to 4.50 lv) are normally big enough for two people. It may not be the greatest Chinese food you've ever had, but it's hard to beat the price.

Happy Bar & Grill *(pl Sveta Nedelya)* Salads about 2 lv, snacks about 1.50 lv, meals from 3.50 lv. The Happy Bar & Grill, which has now spread its wings all over Bulgaria, has tasty Western meals, a terrific corner position and friendly staff. It's so popular that by 7.30pm you may need to wait for a table.

Atlantik *(bul Maria Luisa 63)* Pasta dishes 3-4.50 lv, pizzas 3-4.50 lv. Open 24 hours. This triple-fronted place offers almost everything: cheap meals, delicious cakes, alcoholic drinks, and even it's own brand of ice cream. It's very popular, and ideal for breakfast.

Cafes

In summer, it seems that every piece of garden and footpath in Sofia is covered with cafes. Some only offer plastic tables, and self-service drinks in plastic cups (for example, those in front of the mosque), but most are delightfully relaxing places for a meal and/or drink. Most cafes are open from about 8am to midnight.

Cafe Theatre Set in the midst of Sofia City Garden, and facing the imposing Ivan Vazov National Theatre, this cafe is one of the most delightful in the city. It mainly sells drinks and snacks, including 'The Theatre Cake' (2 lv).

Cafe Rotonda Small beers 1.50 lv. This appropriately named cafe shares a superb location next to the Church of St George. The cafe is trendy but quiet, and provides tables outside and a medieval decor inside. It only serves drinks.

Restorant Perfekt Main meals about 3.5 lv. Superbly located overlooking the Sveta Petka Samardjiiska Church along the underpass between the TsUM shopping centre and Sheraton hotel, this place is a little pricey, but worth it for the setting and service. There are tables outside and air-con inside, and the menu is extensive.

Art Club Museum (*ul Tsar Osvoboditel*) Meals 4.50-6 lv. This fashionable place – also called the Art Museum Cafe – boasts a charming and shady location right next to the Archaeological Museum. Most patrons come by at about 6pm for a drink (or three), but it also offers a tempting, albeit limited, range of meals.

Fast Food

Goody's (*pl Sveta Nedelya*) Meals 2-3.50 lv, soft drinks 1.30 lv, beers from 1 lv. This central landmark is more of a fast-food outlet than a restaurant (like Happy Bar & Grill nearby), but offers more interesting meals, such as salads and scrumptious club sandwiches, than the usual junk-food places. It's large, clean and provides plenty of seats. Photos of menu items are displayed behind the counter and labelled in English.

Best Burger (*ul Patriarh Evtimii*) Burgers about 2.50 lv. This is arguably the best place in the city for a cheap, tasty burger, with all sorts of fillings, as well as the usual junk-food extras.

Central Hali Shopping Centre (*bul Maria Luisa 25*) Several places on the top floor of this market complex (see the Shopping section later) sell fast food at reasonable prices. There are also plenty of seats inside.

Colonel Sanders and Ronald McDonald are firmly entrenched, as are most other international fast-food chains. Each is licensed to sell beer. The most central ***KFC*** (*bul Stamboliyski 28*) is a few hundred metres west of ploshtad Sveta Nedelya. One convenient ***McDonald's*** (*bul Vitosha*) is on the corner of bulevard Vitosha and ulitsa Alabin. You could certainly find cheaper pizzas than ***Pizza Hut*** (☎ *981 4575 for free delivery, ul Dondukov 7*), but the service and setting are familiar, and the menu is in English. The pasta dishes at Pizza Hut are also good value.

Vegetarian

Vegetarians won't suffer too much in the capital because every eatery offers a large range of salads and most places can rustle up a vegetable soup. Fresh fruit and vegetables are in abundance at the ***Ladies Market*** (see the Shopping section later in this chapter), the ***Central Hali Shopping Centre*** and the ***fruit and vegetable stalls*** in front of Sveti Sedmochislentsi Church on ulitsa Graf Ignatiev.

Self-Catering

Besides the places listed under Vegetarian earlier, you can stock up on picnic items and other goodies at the ***Bonjour Supermarket*** (*ul Lege*) and ***Oasis Supermarket***, at the northern end of the TsUM shopping centre.

ENTERTAINMENT

The best source of information about what's going on (and where and when) is unquestionably the English-language newspaper *The Sofia Echo*. Its excellent 'Culture Shock' supplement lists just about every current and future activity, concert and children's show. If you speak Bulgarian, or can find someone who does, there are two telephone numbers with recorded messages about cultural shows (☎ 171) and cinema programs (☎ 191).

Bars & Clubs

The explosive growth of live music clubs and trendy bars has put to rest the oft-heard complaint of yore that, culturally speaking, Sofia was dead from the waist down. The *The Sofia Echo* is the best source of information about what's open and what's trendy. Some clubs charge a nominal admission fee, mostly late at night and on weekends.

The Library (bul Vasil Levski) Because it's in the basement of the National Library, this club is also called the Biblioteka. It offers two rooms with live music, one of which features a karaoke bar where Mick Jagger wannabes wail their way into musical infamy.

La Cocaracha (ul Lege 19) A very unassuming door, just around the corner from the Air France office, leads to this laid-back place, currently one of *the* bars in town. It's a bit smoky but features a decent wine list and live music.

Bourbon Street (bul Vasil Levski 114) Live music from jazz to heavy rock is featured in this US-theme bar. Plenty of imported (expensive) liqueurs are available.

Svejk Pub (bul Vitosha 1) Although a bit dark and smoky, this is an ideal place to head for in cold weather. It offers about the widest range of beers in the city as well as meals every day and live music on weekends.

Sofia is home to an inordinate number of Irish pubs, where Bulgarian waiters serve expensive imported European beers (for example, 4 lv for a pint of Heineken). These include *JJ Murphy's (ul Kârnigradska 6)* and, near the United Bulgarian Bank, *The Irish Harp (ul Sveta Sofia 7),* which often features live music.

Cinemas

Sofia boasts 20 cinemas where patrons can enjoy recent English-language films (with Bulgarian subtitles). Tickets cost from 3 lv to 5.50 lv, depending on the comfort of the seats and the times of the sessions. Programs are listed (in Bulgarian) outside the cinemas, but detailed (in English) in *The Sofia Echo* each week.

Some of the more comfortable and convenient cinemas are the *Euro-Bulgarian*

Cultural Centre (☎ 980 4161, bul Stamboliyski 17) just around the corner from the Happy Bar & Grill, the *Modern Theatre (☎ 983 5646, bul Maria Luisa 26)* just near the Trops Kâshta restaurant and the *United New Cinema (☎ 951 5101),* in the underpass below the NDK National Palace of Culture complex.

Theatre & Music

National Opera House (☎ 987 7011, ul Vrabcha; ticket office open daily 8.30am-7.30pm) Performances normally at about 7pm, but only Tues & Sat at 9pm in summer. The best that Bulgaria and the region has to offer is frequently on show inside this impressive building. Bulgarian artists based at the theatre have performed all over Europe and North America.

NDK National Palace of Culture (☎ 916 2300, programs ☎ 174, @ drumev@ndk.bg, Yuzhen Park; ticket office open daily 9am-7pm) The NDK (as it's often called) has 15 halls and 4000 sq m of exhibition area, and is easily the country's largest cultural complex. It maintains a regular program of events in summer (when most other theatres in Sofia are closed) and offers a wide range of shows throughout the year.

Other worthwhile cultural events are held at the *Bulgaria Hall (☎ 987 7656, ul Askakov 1),* the home of the excellent Sofia Philharmonic Orchestra; and the baroque-style, early 20th-century *Ivan Vazov National Theatre (☎ 984 831, ul Vasil Levski 5),* home to the National Theatre Company. The kids may want to see what's on at the *Puppet Theatre (ul General Gurko 14).*

SPECTATOR SPORTS

Football (soccer) is obviously the main sporting passion. The successful Levski side plays at the Vasil Levski Stadium (☎ 930 0666) in the Borisova Gradina Park most weekends.

SHOPPING

Although some towns and villages outside the capital offer a better range and cheaper prices for specific items, Sofia is the best place for general souvenir shopping.

Markets & Shopping Centres

Central Hali Shopping Centre *(bul Maria Luisa 25)* Open daily 7am-midnight. This undercover shopping area, built in 1911 but totally refurbished in May 2000, boasts some 140 shops, as well as some ancient ruins in the basement. Stalls on the ground floor sell baked goodies, coffee, alcohol, dips, fruit, ice cream and cheese. It's sometimes called the Halite.

TsUM Retail Centre *(☎ 953 3133, bul Maria Luisa)* Open Mon-Sat 10am-10pm, Sun 11am-5.30pm. The former all-in-one central department store now has four floors of modern shops selling clothes, souvenirs and music, among other things, but it's nothing to get excited about.

Ladies Market *(ul St Stambolov)* Open daily from 7am. The 'Zhenski Pazar' stretches several blocks along a mall between ulitsa Ekzarh Yosif and bulevard Slivnitsa. It mainly sells grocery items, and fruit and vegetables (including some of the biggest tomatoes and chillies you will ever see). It's great fun to wander around, but it does get very crowded so watch your belongings.

Roman Wall Market *(ul Hr Smirnenski)* Far less chaotic than the Ladies Market is this quaint and aptly named collection of stalls surrounding a huge, unexplained Roman wall.

Souvenirs

Ethnographical Museum *(☎ 988 1974, ul Tsar Osvoboditel)* For good-quality folk art, the best selection and fairest prices can be found on the ground floor at this museum. As well as souvenir-type books in English, French and German, it sells excellent embroidery, woodcarvings, jewellery and carpets. It also offers one of the best selections of traditional and contemporary Bulgarian music (on cassette and compact disc) in the country.

Fine Arts Gallery *(ul Shipka 6)* If you're in the market for an original painting or sculpture by a Bulgarian artist, try this place.

Paintings (mostly with religious themes) are sold at stalls in the park in front of the Holy Synod Church. Also, many artists sell paintings in the park between the Banya Bashi Mosque and Sofia Town Public Baths; these often feature traditional houses and villages, and are reasonably priced. In and around ploshtad Aleksander Nevski, stalls sell bric-a-brac and embroidery most days (best on Sunday).

The underpass that starts and finishes near the President's Building is lined with decent ***souvenir shops*** selling the usual array of postcards, paintings and books, as well as traditional embroidery and costumes at acceptable prices. The shops in the arcade along the underpass between the Sheraton hotel and TsUM shopping centre are generally overpriced.

GETTING THERE & AWAY
Air

For information about international flights to and from Sofia, see the Air section in the Getting There & Away chapter earlier in this book.

The only domestic flights within Bulgaria are between Sofia and the Black Sea coast. Hemus Air flies daily (except Sunday) to Varna ($55/99 one-way/return) between 15 March and 27 October, with extra flights most days between 1 July and 15 September. All year, Balkan Airlines offers between two and four daily flights (depending on the season) to Varna ($52/98).

Dandy Airlines flies to Varna ($52/99) several times a day between 14 July and 30 October, and to Burgas ($50/100) four times a week between 15 April and 30 October.

Airline Offices Except for Aeroflot, Hemus Air, Dandy Airlines and Balkan Airlines, no other airline listed here has an office outside of Sofia. (To keep information simple, we have only included offices for the local, and major European, airlines on the maps of Sofia.)

Aeroflot (☎ 943 4529) ul Oborishte 23
Air France (☎ 980 6150) ul Sâborna 2
Alitalia (☎ 981 6702) ul Graf Ignatiev 40
Austrian Airlines (☎ 981 2424) ul Vitosha 14
Balkan Airlines (☎ 988 3595) ul Alabin 16;
   (☎ 659 517) NDK Underpass

SOFIA

British Airways (☎ 981 7000) ul Alabin 56
Czech Airlines (☎ 981 5408) ul Sâborna 9
Dandy Airlines (☎ 943 3674) ul Shipka 42
Hemus Air (☎ 981 8330) ul Rakovski 157
KLM-Royal Dutch Airlines (☎ 981 9910) ul Uzundjovska 14
LOT Polish Airlines (☎ 987 4562) bul Stamboliyski 27a
Lufthansa Airlines (☎ 980 4141) ul Sâborna 9a
Malev-Hungarian Airlines (☎ 981 5091) ul Patriarh Evtimii 19
Olympic Airways (☎ 980 1040) bul Stamboliyski 46
Swissair & Sabena (☎ 980 4459) ul Angel Kânchev 1
Tarom (☎ 980 2562) ul Hristo Botev 38
Turkish Airlines (☎ 980 3957) ul Sâborna 11a
Yugoslav Airlines (☎ 981 2167) bul Vasil Levski 1

Bus

The bad news is that the two major bus stations (both ☎ 383 191) in Sofia are unquestionably the most disorganised in Bulgaria. The good news is that travelling by bus is far easier everywhere else in the country. These two stations are on either side of bulevard Maria Luisa, just north of Princess Hotel. In lieu of any official names whatsoever, other than, perhaps, the ambiguous Princess Stations or Sever (North) Stations, we have dubbed them the Princess Hotel bus station East and Princess Hotel bus station West.

More buses leave from the western station, but if you can't find a bus at one station, simply cross the road and look around at the other. Because there are so many regular departures on public and private buses each day (especially in summer), it's usually easy enough to simply turn up at the western station and buy a ticket for a bus leaving within the hour or so. But if you are going to a small or more remote town, or travelling on a busy summer weekend, it's worth hanging around one or both of the stations the day before to check departure times, to decide which companies offer the most comfortable buses and, if possible, to buy a ticket in advance.

Departures are less frequent between November and April. The schedules here are for the summer:

destination	frequency	duration	fare
Albena	3-4 daily	8 hours	16-18 lv
Bansko	6-8 daily	3 hours	5 lv
Blagoevgrad	about hourly	2 hours	5 lv
Burgas	about 10 daily	7-8 hours	15 lv
Dobrich	6-8 daily	7-8 hours	16-18 lv
Haskovo	6-7 daily	6 hours	9-10 lv
Kazanlâk	6-8 daily	3½ hours	7 lv
Lovech	5-6 daily	3 hours	9-10 lv
Nesebâr	about 10 daily	7 hours	17 lv
Pleven	8-9 daily	2½ hours	7 lv
Plovdiv	several hourly	2 ½ hours	7 lv
Ruse	hourly	5 hours	10-12 lv
Sandanski	6-8 daily	3½ hours	6 lv
Shumen	10-12 daily	6 hours	11-12 lv
Sliven	hourly	5 hours	10 lv
Smolyan	3-4 daily	3½ hours	10 lv
Stara Zagora	hourly	4 hours	8 lv
Varna	every 45 mins	7-8 hours	about 15 lv
Veliko Târnovo	hourly	4 hours	8-9 lv
Vidin	every 60-90 mins	5 hours	10 lv

From the far smaller Ovcha Kupel bus station (☎ 554 033) on bulevard Tsar Boris III – sometimes called the *Zapad* (West) station – a few buses head south, for eg, to Bansko, Blagoevgrad and Sandanski (although more buses to these places leave from the two major bus stations mentioned earlier). From Ovcha Kupel bus station, there are also regular buses to Dupnitsa (2.80 lv, 1½ hours) and Kyustendil (3.50 lv, two hours). If you're heading to the Rila Monastery in summer, it's worth ringing the station to ask about any direct buses. Tickets for services departing from this station must be bought at counters inside. Ovcha Kupel bus station is linked to the city centre by bus No 60, tram No 5 and taxi (about 3 lv one-way).

From the Yug bus station (☎ 722 345), bulevard Dragan Tsankov, buses and minibuses leave for Samokov (3 lv, 1½ hours) every 30 minutes between 7am and

7.30pm. Despite signs to the contrary, there are no direct services to Borovets, but connections are trouble-free at Samokov. This station also offers an unreliable daily service (at 9am, if at all) direct to Malîovitsa (6 lv, two hours).

From the ramshackle Poduyane bus station (☎ 453 014) on bulevard Vl Vazov – also called the *Iztok* (East) station – buses leave infrequently for the following small towns in central Bulgaria:

destination	departure times	duration	fare
Gabrovo	7.45am	3½ hours	7 lv
Lovech	7.45am	3 hours	6 lv
Teteven	8.30am, 9am & 5pm	2½ hours	5.50 lv
Troyan	9.45am, 2pm & 4.35pm	3 hours	6 lv

International MATPU (☎ 953 2481), ulitsa Damyan Gruev 23, probably offers the best services to Greece. From outside its office, a bus leaves every day at 10.30am for Athens (82.50 lv, 12 hours) via Thessaloniki (49 lv, six hours).

ATT, on bulevard Maria Luisa, also offers daily buses to Athens and Thessaloniki for about the same price. Both companies have several buses a day to Istanbul (50 lv, 18 hours) and Skopje (20 lv, six hours). ATT buses also go to Belgrade (65 lv, nine to 10 hours) via Niš.

Other less comfortable but slightly cheaper buses to Athens, Istanbul, Belgrade and Niš leave from the two Princess Hotel bus stations. From these stations, buses also regularly depart for cities all over Europe (see the Getting There & Away chapter).

Train

Sofia's central train station (☎ 931 1111) can be as overwhelming as most stations in European capitals, but it's a far cry from the old days (not that long ago) when travellers had to deal with destination signs in Cyrillic, platform numbers in Roman numerals and tracks in Arabic numbers. At the time of research, there were grand plans to extensively

upgrade the station and even remodel it on the Olympic Stadium in Munich!

Destinations for all domestic and international services are still listed on timetables in Cyrillic, but departures (for the following two hours) and arrivals (for the previous two hours) are listed in English on a large computer screen on the ground floor. Staff at ticket counters can usually understand a bit of English. (Curiously some signs are translated into French only.)

There isn't an information counter but the 'tourist service' office downstairs is a private company that sells international bus tickets. Other facilities include a post office, cafes and restaurants (especially in the downstairs market-cum-arcade), a hotel and accommodation agency (see the Places to Stay section earlier), bookstalls, and even a cinema. The rates at the foreign-exchange offices vary, so check around; the best rates are probably about 2% lower than in the city centre.

Same-day tickets for any town along the lines to Vidin, Ruse and Varna are sold at counters on the ground floor; same-day tickets to other destinations are sold downstairs. All counters are open 24 hours. Advanced tickets, seat reservations and sleepers for domestic services are available from an office (open Monday to Friday 6am to 7.30pm and Saturday 7am to 2.30pm) downstairs, ie, opposite to, and down the corridor from, the normal ticket counters.

The central train station is easy to reach from ploshtad Sveta Nedelya on tram Nos 1, 2 and 7, by taxi (about 1.50 lv one-way), or on foot (about 30 minutes).

All tickets for international trains, and advance tickets for domestic services, can be bought at one of several Rila Bureaus. They can be found in the city (☎ 987 0777) at ulitsa General Gurko 5 (open Monday to Friday 7am to 7pm and Saturday 7am to 2pm), at the NDK National Palace of Culture complex (☎ 658 402; same hours), and at the central train station (☎ 932 3346; open daily 7am to 10pm). Staff at these offices speak English and are normally helpful.

Major domestic services to and from Sofia are listed in the 'Major Trains from Sofia' table.

Major Trains from Sofia

destination	number of trains (daily)	duration	1st/2nd-class fare
Burgas	5 fast & 2 express	6-7 hours	15/10.50 lv (fast) & 18.50/13.50 lv (express)
Gora Oryahovitsa (for Veliko Târnovo)	6 fast, 4 express & 1 slow	3-6 hours	11.10/7.80 lv (fast) & 12.25/8.90 lv (express)
Plovdiv	8 fast, 3 express & 8 slow	2½-3½ hours	6.50/4.60 lv (fast) & 7.30/5.40 lv (express)
Ruse	4 fast	7 hours	13.80/9.70 lv
Sandanski	3 fast	3½ hours	7.40/5.20 lv
Varna	5 fast & one express	8 hours	16.30/11.70 lv (fast) & 22.05/15.90 lv (express)
Vidin	3 fast & 1 slow	5-7 hours	9.65/6.80 lv (fast)

More information about the schedules and fares for other services to/from Sofia are included in the relevant Getting There & Away sections throughout this book. For information about international services to and from Sofia, see the Getting There & Away chapter.

GETTING AROUND
To/From the Airport
Sofia airport (☎ 720 672) is 12km southeast of the city centre. It can be reached by bus No 84 from opposite the Sofia University; or, better still (especially if you have any luggage), by minibus No 30, which travels along bulevard Maria Luisa and ulitsa Tsar Osvoboditel.

A taxi (using the meter) from the city centre should cost no more than 5 lv. There is no taxi counter at the airport, so taxi drivers in the airport terminal often charge 20 lv to 25 lv into the city centre. Avoid this by walking out of the terminal, finding an official yellow taxi and telling the driver to use the meter.

Some of the car-rental agencies at the airport charge 44 lv for an air-conditioned vehicle heading into the city centre, but this is very poor value: even a dishonest taxi driver will charge half this rate. The Tourist Service travel agency (☎ 981 7253, e bg@tourist-service.com, w www.tourist-service.com) on bulevard Klokotnitsa, offers a shuttle-bus service from your hotel (if it's

central) to the airport for 11 lv per person, but does not offer the same service from the airport.

Public Transport
The various forms of public transport – trams, buses, minibuses and trolleybuses, as well as the underground metro – run from about 5am to midnight every day.

A ticket on any bus, tram, trolleybus or metro within Sofia, and even as far as Boyana (about 8km away), only costs 0.40 lv. Most drivers on public transport sell tickets, but it's far easier and quicker, especially during peak times, to buy one ticket (or more) from any bookstall or cigarette shop along a route before boarding.

If you're going to use public transport frequently, consider buying a pass for one day (2 lv), five days (9 lv) or one month (37 lv), which are valid for all trams, buses and trolleybuses. All tickets must be validated by placing them into a small machine inside the vehicle; once punched, tickets are non-transferable. Mean-looking inspectors are a regular sight, and will issue on-the-spot fines (4 lv) if you don't have a ticket. And don't forget to buy an extra ticket for each piece of oversized luggage.

Probably the most useful trams for visitors are Nos 1 and 7, which link the central train station with Yuzhen Park, via ploshtad Sveta Nedelya. Public transport routes for buses, trams and trolleybuses are indicated on the excellent *Sofia* map, which is published by Domino.

Buses for Boyana, Zlatni Mostove and Aleko depart from the Hladilnika bus terminal. It is near the southern terminus of tram Nos 2, 4, 9 and 12 from ploshtad Sveta Nedelya. (From the final tram stop, walk through the tiny park to the bus stop along the main road.)

Minibuses are an increasingly popular alternative; they're quicker and more comfortable than buses, trams and trolleybuses, but cost a little more (1 lv per trip). Destinations and fares are indicated (in Cyrillic) on the front of the minibus, and tickets are bought from the driver.

The metro only has six stops. It's of little value to visitors because it just shuttles commuters between the far north-western residential districts and the city centre.

Car & Motorcycle

Frequent public transport, cheap taxis and horrible traffic provides little incentive to drive a private or rented car around Sofia. But there are plenty of good reasons to hire a car to places such as the Rila Monastery (and farther afield) – if you can find your way out of Sofia! The Car & Motorcycle section in the Getting Around chapter has details about the approximate costs and the pros and cons of renting a car from foreign and Bulgarian agencies. These include:

Avis (☎ 988 8167) Sheraton Hotel complex, pl Sveta Nedelya; (☎ 738 023) Sofia airport
Budget (☎ 987 1682, bul Vitosha 1, Near McDonald's) Part of the Balkantourist travel agency.
Drenikov (☎/fax 465 551, ul Oborishte 55, W www.service.bg/drenikovrentacar)
Hertz (☎ 980 0461, e office@hertz.autotechnica .bg) Hilton Hotel, ul Cherni Vrâh; (☎ 791 477) Sofia airport
Malito (☎ 547 777, e malito–rent@abv.bg) ul Tsar Petâr 14. Book through Odysseia-In (see the Travel Agencies section earlier)
Rentavvto (☎ 929 5005, W www.rentauto-bg .com) bul Stamboliyski 219; (mobile ☎ 088-1299) Sofia airport
Tourist Service (☎ 981 7253, e bg@tourist -service.com, W www.tourist-service.com, bul Klokotnitsa)

Taxi

Taxis are an affordable and easier alternative to public transport. By law, taxis must use meters, but those that wait around the airport, luxury hotels and within 100m of ploshtad Sveta Nedelya will often try to negotiate an unmetered fare – which, of course, will always be considerably more than the metered fare. All official taxis are yellow, and have obvious taxi signs (in English or Bulgarian) on top. Never accept a lift in a private, unlicensed vehicle, because you will (at best) pay too much or (at worst) be robbed.

Rates per kilometre range enormously from one taxi company to another (see Public Transport in the Getting Around chapter). Taxis can also be chartered for trips per hour (about 12 lv) and per day (about 70 lv).

In the very unlikely event that you can't find a taxi, you can order one by ringing Okay Supertrans (☎ 973 2121) or Taxi-s-Express (☎ 1280).

Around Sofia

The places mentioned here are accessible from Sofia by public transport, but it's worth staying at least one night to avoid excessive travel and to really appreciate the surroundings.

VITOSHA NATIONAL PARK
НАЦИОНАЛЕН ПАРК ВИТОША
☎ 02

Mt Vitosha is the rounded mountain range, 23km long and 13km wide, just south of Sofia. It's known colloquially as the 'lungs of Sofia' for the refreshing breezes it deflects onto the often-polluted capital. The mountain is part of the 22,726-hectare Vitosha National Park, the oldest of its kind in Bulgaria (created in 1934). The highest point (2290m) is Mt Cherni Vrâh (The Black Peak), the fourth-highest peak in Bulgaria and one of 11 in the immediate area over 2000m.

As well as being a popular ski resort in winter (see the boxed text 'Skiing on Mt Vitosha' later), the national park attracts legions of hikers, berry pickers and sightseers on summer weekends. There are dozens of

SOFIA

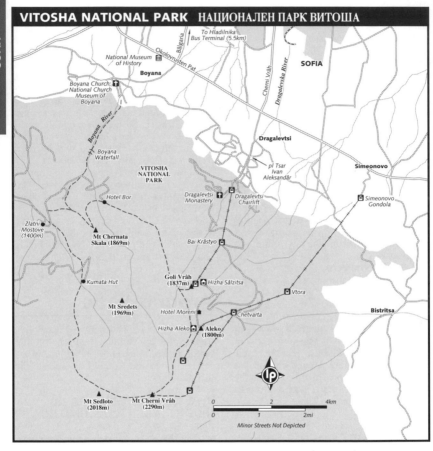

VITOSHA NATIONAL PARK   НАЦИОНАЛЕН ПАРК ВИТОША

To Hladilnika
Bus Terminal (5.5km)

Bulgaria

Okolovrusten Pat

National Museum
of History

Boyana

Cherni Vrăh

Dragalevska River

SOFIA

Boyana Church;
National Church
Museum of
Boyana

Boyana River

Boyana
Waterfall

VITOSHA
NATIONAL
PARK

Dragalevtsi

pl Tsar
Ivan
Aleksandăr

Simeonovo

Hotel Bor

Dragalevtsi
Monastery

Dragalevtsi
Chairlift

Simeonovo
Gondola

Zlatni
Mostove
(1400m)

Mt Chernata
Skala (1869m)

Bai Krăstyo

Kumata Hut

Goli Vrăh
(1837m)   Hizha Sălzitsa

Vtora

Mt Sredets
(1969m)

Hotel Moreni

Chetvarta

Bistritsa

Hizha Aleko   Aleko
(1800m)

Mt Sedloto
(2018m)

Mt Cherni Vrăh
(2290m)

LP

0   2   4km
0   1   2mi

Minor Streets Not Depicted

clearly marked hiking trails, plenty of
hotels, cafes and restaurants and about 80
huts and chalets that can be booked through
the Bulgarian Tourist Union (see Mountain
Huts in the Facts for the Visitor chapter).

Aleko
Алеко
- elevation 1800m

Aleko was named after Aleko Konstantinov,
a Bulgarian writer who first developed the
idea of hiking in the region during the late
19th century. In summer (especially weekends), the area is crammed with picnicking

families, courting couples and hikers. One
popular activity is to take a mountain bike to
Aleko by gondola from Simeonova (see
later), then hurtle down the ski slopes. For
mountain bike hire see Camping & Skiing
Equipment earlier in this chapter.

Zlatni Mostove
Златни Мостове
- elevation 1400m

Zlatni Mostove (Golden Bridges) takes its
name from the extraordinary series of huge
boulders dumped along the stone river by
glaciers many centuries ago. It's another

very popular spot on summer weekends but at other times you may have the place to yourself. It's accessible by bus No 261 from Ovcha Kupel bus station every 20 minutes on Saturday and Sunday, less frequently on weekdays. A taxi from the city centre will cost about 12 lv one-way.

Dragalevtsi
Драгалевци

A two-person **chairlift** (☎ 967 1110) starts about 5km (by road) up from the centre of Dragalevtsi village (though it's about 3km on foot if you take the obvious short cut up the hill). One chairlift (1.50 lv, 20 minutes) goes as far Bai Krâstyo, from where another (1.50 lv, 15 minutes) carries on to Goli Vrâh (1837m). Both lifts operate year-round, but most reliably on Friday to Sunday from about 8.30am to 4.30pm.

This lift is cheaper than the Simeonovo gondola so it's immensely popular, especially on sunny summer weekends. Queues of 200m are common by noon, so start early or simply take the gondola. A pleasant option is to take the chairlift to Goli Vrâh, walk (30 minutes) to Aleko and catch the gondola down to Simeonovo (or vice versa).

From the start of the chairlift, a well-marked trail (about 1km) leads to **Dragalevtsi Monastery**. It was built in about 1345 (and is probably the oldest monastery in Bulgaria), but abandoned only 40 years later. The monastery contains particularly charming murals, and is revered as one of the many hiding places of the ubiquitous anti-Turkish rebel leader Vasil Levski.

Ploshtad Tsar Ivan Aleksandâr in Dragalevtsi village is surrounded by charming *cafes* and traditional but pricey *restaurants*. There are also plenty more places to eat and drink along the road from the village to the chairlift.

Bus Nos 64 and 93 from the Hladilnika terminal go to the village centre; No 93 continues on to the chairlift.

Simeonovo
Симеоново

Take a **gondola** (six-person covered cabin) to the mountains from Simeonovo (2.50/4 lv

one-way/return, 30 minutes). It operates on Friday, Saturday and Sunday from 9am to 4.30pm (1 October to 31 March) and 8.30am to 6pm (1 May to 30 September). It's possible to disembark at one or both of the two junctions – ie, Vtora and Chetvarta, from where hiking trails lead deep into the park – and then continue the trip later at no extra cost. Bus No 123 from the Hladilnika terminal goes directly to the gondola station.

Activities

The best map is probably *Vitosha Turisticheska Karta* (1:50,000), written in Cyrillic and available at bookshops around central Sofia. Also, in summer, an enterprising old man at Aleko sells hiking and skiing maps of Mt Vitosha and other national parks in Bulgaria.

Some of the shorter and more popular hikes around the park include:

Aleko-Goli Vrâh A short trail (30 minutes) between the top of the gondola from Simeonovo and the chairlift from Dragalevtsi.

Aleko-Zlatni Mostove Follow the trail to Goli Vrâh, skirt around Mt Sredets (1969m) and pass Hotel Bor – about three hours.

Aleko-Mt Cherni Vrâh A popular, but steep, 90 minutes on foot. Alternatively, take the chairlift (1/1.50 lv one-way/return, open Friday to Sunday) from Aleko to within 30 minutes' walk of the summit.

Bai Krâstyo-Aleko Another popular hike, which combines the chairlift from Dragalevtsi with a 45-minute uphill trudge.

Boyana Church-Zlatni Mostove At the church, ask for directions to the path which mostly hugs Boyana River and leads to the 15m-high Boyana Waterfall (best in winter). From there, obvious paths lead to Zlatni Mostove – about three hours in total.

Dragalevtsi Chairlift-Goli Vrâh Follow the chairlift from the bottom – a three-hour steep climb.

Zlatni Mostove-Mt Cherni Vrâh A tougher hike, via Kumata Hut and Mt Sedloto (2018m) – about three hours.

Places to Stay & Eat

In Vitosha National Park there are a dozen or more two- and three-star hotels. These cater almost exclusively to middle- and upper-class locals with private transport, so

Skiing on Mt Vitosha

Mt Vitosha is one of the most convenient skiing spots in Europe. The slopes are only 22km or so from Sofia – you can easily check to see if the peak is cloudy or if the weather is lousy, and, if so, do something else in Sofia. (But remember: It could be clear and sunny on the peak while the capital is foggy.) Although Mt Vitosha is Bulgaria's highest ski resort, there is rarely enough snow before mid-December; nonetheless the season can often last until late April.

The 29km of alpine ski runs (the longest is about 5km) range from easy to very difficult, and start as high as Mt Cherni Vrâh (2290m), which is almost always foggy. Cross-country skiing is ideal along the 15km of trails, but snowboarding is not good because of the rocky slopes. As well as the Simeonovo gondola and Dragalevtsi chairlift there are a handful of other chairlifts and draglifts. A lift pass will set you back about 20 lv per day.

While the lift pass is cheap, there are disadvantages. Mt Vitosha is, not surprisingly, impossibly crowded on weekends. A lack of funds means the slopes are not always well maintained and the quantity and quality of ski equipment for hire is not great because so many locals use their own gear. The ski rental shop at the start of the Simeonovo gondola and the Aleko Ski Centre at Aleko (see earlier) both charge about 55 lv per day for a complete set of ski gear.

The ski school at Aleko is small but enjoys a fine reputation. It does cater almost entirely to Bulgarians but instructors are multilingual.

they're difficult and/or expensive to reach otherwise. Hikers can stay at any of the numerous mountain huts.

Hizha Aleko (☎ *967 1113*) Dorm beds 10 lv per person, singles/doubles with shared bathroom 15/25 lv. This hut offers a number of rooms with two to eight beds, and is easy to reach (follow the signs) from Hotel Moreni.

Hizha Sâlzitsa (☎ *967 1054*) Singles/doubles with bathroom 27/54 lv. This refurbished former rest home provides basic rooms and a ***restaurant***. It's accessible by bus along the road to Aleko and not far from the chairlift at Goli Vrâh.

Hotel Moreni (☎/*fax 967 1059*) Doubles with bathroom 44 lv. The best-value hotel at Aleko is about 700m down from the top of the gondola, and accessible by bus. At the time of research the rooms were fairly ordinary, but will improve immeasurably after renovations are completed.

The hiking trails branching out from Aleko are lined with ***cafes*** and ***bars***. Most locals seem happy to bring a picnic, or munch on a *kebabche* (grilled spicy meat sausage) in bread from one of many informal ***stalls*** around Aleko. All prices are pleasingly reasonable.

Getting There & Away

To Aleko, bus No 66 (1.60 lv) departs Sofia's Hladilnika terminal (see Getting Around in Sofia earlier in this chapter) 10 times a day between 8am and 7.45pm on Saturday and Sunday, and four times a day on weekdays. It goes as far as Hotel Moreni. A current timetable for the Hladilnika-Aleko service is pasted on the front window of Hotel Moreni.

KYUSTENDIL
КЮСТЕНДИЛ
☎ 078 • pop 56,500

Kyustendil's strategic position, about 90km south-west of Sofia, and its proximity to Macedonia and Serbia, has provided the town with a colourful history. The sunny climate and mineral springs, which attracted settlers during the Roman, Greek and Thracian periods, are still drawcards for residents of Sofia. For visitors, Kyustendil is a common transit point for travel to and from Macedonia, a day trip from Sofia, and a cheaper place to stay than the capital.

Bulevard Bulgaria is the shady stone pathway that links (15 minutes by foot) the train station (and adjacent bus station) with ploshtad Velbâzhd, the central square.

Things to See

The **City History Museum** (☎ 26 396, bul Bulgaria 55; admission 1 lv; open Mon-Fri 8am-noon & 1pm-5pm) houses an array of Thracian and Roman artefacts, and remnants of Neolithic dwellings transferred from about 40km away. Not far from the museum are the ruins of the 2nd-century Roman **Asclepius Temple** and a large functioning **market**. Also worth a look is the 16th-century **Ahmed Bey Mosque** (ul Stefan Karadzha 2), about 400m north-east of ploshtad Velbâzhd.

On top of the forested **Hisarlâk Hill**, about 2km south of ploshtad Velbâzhd (take a taxi), are ruins of the 2nd-century **ancient fortress** from the Roman city of Pautalia.

The **Vladimir Dimitrov Art Gallery** (☎ 22 503, ul Patriarh Evtimii 20; admission 1.50 lv; open Tues-Sun 9.30am-11.45am & 2pm-5.45pm) is about 200m north of ploshtad Velbâzhd. It houses over 200 works of art, mostly by locally born Dimitrov, also known as 'The Master'.

Places to Stay & Eat

Along ulitsa Arhimand Zinovi, directly behind Hotel Velbâzhd, several homes offer simple and clean *private rooms* for about 10 lv to 15 lv per person. Look for the signs in Bulgarian and English along the road.

Hotel Pautalia (☎ 24 561, pl Velbâzhd) Doubles with bathroom 33 lv. Facing the main square, this two-star hotel is convenient and the rooms (with TV) are comfortable, but the staff were surly and didn't speak English. Rates include breakfast.

Hotel Velbâzhd (☎ 20 246, bul Bulgaria 46) Singles 30-35 lv, doubles 40-53 lv, suites 100 lv. This monstrous place just down the pathway from the train and bus stations has about 250 rooms. The older rooms are dreary, though still clean and reasonably comfortable, but the newer 'luxury' rooms are worth the few extra leva. All accommodation comes with a private bathroom, TV, fridge and balcony, and rates include breakfast. The hotel offers **health-treatment sessions** to the public for 22 lv per person per hour.

Getting There & Away

Buses leave from the Ovcha Kupel bus station in Sofia (3.50 lv, two hours) every 60 to 80 minutes for the Kyustendil bus station (☎ 22 626). From Kyustendil, six daily buses go to Blagoevgrad, eight depart for Dupnitsa and one travels to Plovdiv. Buses also leave everyday for Skopje in Macedonia. From the adjacent train station (☎ 26 041), two fast trains (1st/2nd class, 6.10/4.40 lv) and three slow passenger trains travel every day to Sofia.

LAKE ISKÂR
ЯЗОВИР ИСКЪР

This huge artificial dam serves as the water source for the capital, and is a popular day trip for residents of Sofia. Canoes (5 lv), **sailboards** (7 lv to 8 lv) and **paddle boats** (about 4 lv) can be rented by the hour at several obvious spots along the Sofia-Samokov road.

Shturkelovo Gnezdo Tourist Centre (☎ 07 126-300) Camping 5 lv per person, bungalows 15 lv per person. The well-signed camping ground is along the road to Samokov about 40km from Sofia. Also, unofficial camping is possible anywhere around the lake shore but be discreet. Many locals enjoy picnics by the lake, or stop at one of the innumerable *cafes* and *restaurants* along the Sofia-Samokov road.

Buses to Samokov from the Yug bus station in Sofia stop anywhere alongside the lake if requested.

Southern Bulgaria

Southern Bulgaria is easily defined as the part of the country between the Sredna Gora Mountains and the borders it shares with Greece and Turkey. To the south-east, squeezed between the Sredna Gora Mountains, the Rodopi Mountains and the Black Sea coast, is an area still known by its historical name of Thrace. The Thrace of Greek and Roman antiquity was much larger than modern Thrace, only two-thirds of which lies within Bulgaria. The Maritsa River drains the region and flows south into the Aegean Sea, which forms the border between present-day Greek and Turkish Thrace. Svilengrad is where the three nations meet.

The capital of Bulgarian Thrace, Plovdiv, is a large, modern city with a significant old town crammed with remarkable churches, museums, mosques and some of the best-preserved Roman ruins in the country. The three major mountain ranges, the Rila, Pirin and Rodopi Mountains, offer numerous marked hiking trails in summer and wonderful skiing in winter. These mountains are home to revered monasteries, such as the Rila and Bachkovo monasteries, traditional settlements like Bansko and Melnik and awesome landscapes, such as the caves near Trigrad and Yagodina.

It's easy enough to explore the south-western region from Sofia or Blagoevgrad. The excellent regional tourist association, the Pirin Tourist Forum, is in Blagoevgrad. Plovdiv is the obvious base from which to explore the south-eastern area.

Highlights

- Visit the revered Rila Monastery and hike around the wilderness of the Rila Mountains from Borovets or Malĭovitsa
- Ski the slippery slopes near Bansko in winter or hike in summer around the nearby Pirin National Park
- Explore the extensive Historical Museum in Smolyan
- Enjoy a glass of locally made wine at a cafe in the historic town of Melnik
- Appreciate the Roman ruins, Turkish mosques and Bulgarian churches in the old town of Plovdiv
- Admire the murals and scenic location of the Bachkovo Monastery

Rila Mountains
Рила Планина

The majestic Rila Mountains are the most popular destination for Bulgarians who want to hike and ski. While the mountain range is small (2629 sq km), the area is stunningly beautiful. It boasts a marvellous array of landscapes, including 180 perennial lakes and streams and numerous mineral springs. (In fact, *rila* comes from the Thracian word for 'mountains of water'.) The average height of the mountains is 1500m and roughly 140 peaks are over 2000m high. Mt Musala (2925m), near Borovets, is the highest peak in the country and in the Balkans and is an excellent place to hike.

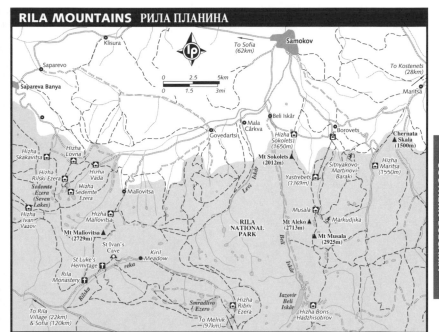

RILA MOUNTAINS РИЛА ПЛАНИНА

The Rila National Park, permanently open with free admission, contains 14,370 hectares of forest and 13,000 hectares of alpine pastures. It protects glorious fir trees and beechwoods (among other conifers), as well as precious wildlife, such as deers, wild goats, eagles and falcons.

As for hiking, the Rila Mountains are steep but the spectacular views, flora and fauna are definitely worth it. Snow can last until mid-June on peaks over 2000m, so hikers need proper boots. Mountain huts, known as a *hizha*, provide basic dormitory accommodation (about 10 lv per person). Many serve meals but sometimes all they have is soup so it's advisable to bring food, or at least inquire first. The larger hostels provide linen so a sleeping bag is unnecessary.

In *The Mountains of Bulgaria*, the author, Julian Perry, details an extensive north-south trek (part of the trans-European 'E-4' trek) across the Rila Mountains. It starts at Klisura and finishes at Hizha Predel, near

Razlog, and takes from seven to 10 days. You'll need more detailed maps than those provided in this guide for the trek and for any other hiking in the Rila Mountains. Buy the *Rila* map (1:55,000), published (in Cyrillic) by Kartografia.

One of the most popular hikes starts at Malîovitsa, visits the magnificent Sedemte Ezera (Seven Lakes) and finishes at Rila Monastery (see the boxed text 'Hiking in the Rila Mountains' later in this chapter). For more information about exploring the mountains from the north, from Malîovitsa or Borovets for eg, see later in this chapter.

BLAGOEVGRAD
БЛАГОЕВГРАД
☎ 073 • pop 77,900
Although Blagoevgrad, about 100km south of Sofia, may not be quaint, historic or loaded with must-see attractions, it boasts the sort of sophistication and cosmopolitan ambience that Sofia can only dream of. This

SOUTHERN BULGARIA

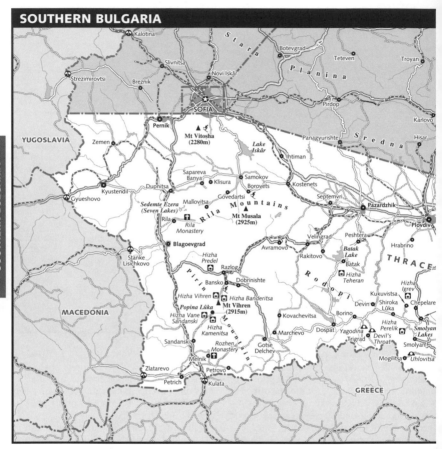

SOUTHERN BULGARIA

is because Blagoevgrad is home to over 16,000 young people who study at the American University of Bulgaria (☎ 25 241), which dominates ploshtad Georgi Izmirliev Makedoncheto, or the Neofit Rilski South-West University (☎ 27 177), about 3km west of the town centre. Blagoevgrad has some of the nicest cafes and trendiest nightclubs in Bulgaria but one definite drawback is the lack of budget hotels.

Orientation & Information

An excellent resource is the Pirin Tourism Forum (☎ 81 458, e ptf@pirin-tourism.bg,

w www.pirin-tourism.bg), which is at ulitsa Komitrov 8. It's open Monday to Friday 9am to 5pm and is next to the laneway leading to the Kristo Hotel. This organisation has helpful English-speaking staff who can assist with general information about attractions and events throughout south-western Bulgaria. It's a regional tourism association but grudgingly acts as a tourist office for Blagoevgrad in lieu of any alternative.

There are foreign-exchange offices along ulitsa Tsar Ivan Shishman and the First East International Bank is along a laneway southwest of ploshtad Makedonia. The combined

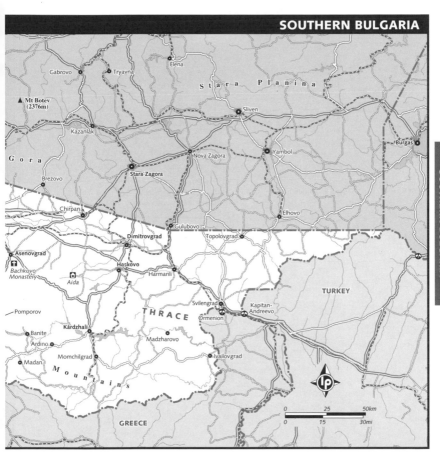

SOUTHERN BULGARIA

Gábrovo • Tryavna
Elena

Stara Planina

▲ Mt Botev
(2376m)

Sliven

Kazanlǎk

Gora

Nova Zagora

Yambol

Burgas

Brezovo

Stara Zagora

Chirpan

Gulubovo

Elhovo

Dimitrovgrad

Topolovgrad

Asenovgrad
Bachkovo
Monastery
Aida

Haskovo

Harmanli

TURKEY

Pomporov

THRACE

Svilengrad
Ormenion

Kapitan-
Andreevo

Banite

Kǎrdzhali

Ardino
Madan

Madzharovo

Momchilgrad

Ivailovgrad

Mountains

GREECE

| 0 | 25 | 50km |
| 0 | 15 | 30mi |

SOUTHERN BULGARIA

post office and telephone centre are along ulitsa Mitropolit Boris. For a university town, there is a surprising lack of Internet centres, but we found one Internet agency on bulevard Aleksandâr Stamboliyski.

History Museum

The History Museum (*☎ 21 170; bul Aleksandâr Stamboliyski; admission 3 lv; open Mon-Fri 9am-noon & 3pm-6pm*) is in a modern building just off the main road, bulevard Stamboliyski. The four floors house over 160,000 exhibits of religious items, archaeological artefacts from the region, information about the military history of Macedonia and plenty of traditional costumes. Try to visit the **natural history** section on the lowest level, which contains the best collection of stuffed animals and birds in Bulgaria. This museum would be one of the best three or four in the country if there were captions in other languages as well as Bulgarian.

Other Attractions

Between bulevard Aleksandâr Stamboliyski and the Forest Park is the old town of **Varosha**. Several renovated Bulgarian national revival period homes, such as the

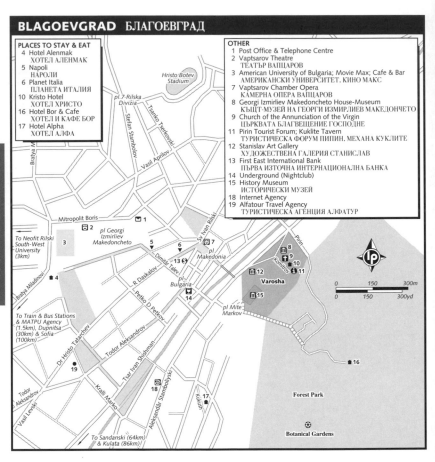

BLAGOEVGRAD БЛАГОЕВГРАД

PLACES TO STAY & EAT
4 Hotel Alenmak
ХОТЕЛ АЛЕНМАК
5 Napoli
НАПОЛИ
6 Planet Italia
ПЛАНЕТА ИТАЛИЯ
10 Kristo Hotel
ХОТЕЛ ХРИСТО
16 Hotel Bor & Cafe
ХОТЕЛ И КАФЕ БОР
17 Hotel Alpha
ХОТЕЛ АЛФА

OTHER
1 Post Office & Telephone Centre
2 Vaptsarov Theatre
ТЕАТЪР ВАПЦАРОВ
3 American University of Bulgaria; Movie Max; Cafe & Bar
АМЕРИКАНСКИ УНИВЕРСИТЕТ. КИНО МАКС
7 Vaptsarov Chamber Opera
КАМЕРНА ОПЕРА ВАПЦАРОВ
8 Georgi Izmirliev Makedoncheto House-Museum
КЪЩТ-МУЗЕЙ НА ГЕОРГИ ИЗМИРЛИЕВ МАКЕДОНЧЕТО
9 Church of the Annunciation of the Virgin
ЦЪРКВАТА БЛАГВЕЩЕНИЕ ГОСПОДНЕ
11 Pirin Tourist Forum; Kuklite Tavern
ТУРИСТИЧЕСКА ФОРУМ ПИПИН. МЕХАНА КУКЛИТЕ
12 Stanislav Art Gallery
ХУДОЖЕСТВЕНА ГАЛЕРИЯ СТАНИСЛАВ
13 First East International Bank
ПЪРВА ИЗТОЧНА ИНТЕРНАЦИОНАЛНА БАНКА
14 Underground (Nightclub)
15 History Museum
ИСТОРИЧЕСКИ МУЗЕЙ
18 Internet Agency
19 Alfatour Travel Agency
ТУРИСТИЧЕСКА АГЕНЦИЯ АЛФАТУР

rarely opened **Georgi Izmirliev Make-doncheto House-Museum** and art galleries, such as the private **Stanislav Art Gallery**, can be found along the cobblestone streets. The area is touristy but worth strolling around.

In a small, serene garden under the Kristo Hotel is the **Church of the Annunciation of the Virgin** (ul Komitrov; admission free; open daily 6am-8pm). It was built in 1844 and contains decorative murals and important religious icons.

A steep road (700m) from Varosha leads to the **Forest Park**, a shady and popular spot with several lookouts offering stunning city

views. If it's open, the *cafe* at Hotel Bor serves hot and cold drinks. The cafe is an ideal place to relax before you head back to the town centre, or walk about 500m farther south to the **Botanical Gardens**.

Places to Stay

The Alfatour Travel Agency (☎ 23 598, fax 62 841) on ulitsa Krali Marko 4 has *rooms* for 22 lv per person. Alfatour is now the only agency in Blagoevgrad that can arrange rooms in private homes. Most rooms have a shared bathroom but are convenient to the town centre.

Hotel Bor (☎ 22 491) Singles/doubles with bathroom 27/54 lv. This large, soulless place is perched on top of the hill in Forest Park, 700m up a steep road from the Varosha district. The lethargy from the staff is infectious but it's comparatively good value.

Hotel Alpha (☎ 31 122, e g.vuchrov@ biz.bg, ul Kukush 7) Doubles 30-40 lv, apartments 50 lv, all with bathroom. Probably the best option in town is the Alpha, which offers sparkling new rooms and apartments, each with a superb bathroom, TV and balcony. It's not well signposted so ask a local if you can't find it.

Hotel Alenmak (☎ 23 031, pl Georgi Izmirliev Makedoncheto) Singles/doubles with bathroom 60/97 lv. This mammoth place faces the American University and acts as a dorm-cum-hotel for university staff, visitors and students. Most of the 100 or so rooms have views of the university and square below, but they're smallish and offer nothing else to justify these rates, which include breakfast.

Kristo Hotel (☎ 80 444, ul Komitrov) Doubles 88 lv. The Kristo is a sparkling new place in a serene setting just up a stone pathway from the main road and overlooking the church. The rooms are cosy, superbly furnished (many with fireplaces) and most have views. Each room is different so check out a few before deciding. Although overpriced for foreigners, it's worth a splurge. Rates include breakfast.

Places to Eat

One place to meet English-speaking university students is the unnamed **cafe and bar** in the eastern side of the American University complex. An inordinate number of **cafes** surround ploshtad Makedonia and ploshtad Georgi Izmirliev Makedoncheto and are dotted along the pedestrian malls between them. The most charming cafes are probably at the eastern end of ploshtad Georgi Izmirliev Makedoncheto.

Locals don't seem to bother much with Bulgarian food, and Italian cuisine is all the rage.

Napoli (ul Dimitâr Talev) Pasta dishes from 2 lv, pizzas 2.20-2.90 lv. With tasty and authentic food, quick and friendly service, an English-language menu, a charming setting and low prices, this is one of the best restaurants in southern Bulgaria.

Planet Italia (ul R Daskalov) Pizzas 2.80-4 lv, pasta dishes from 2.20 lv. The Planet Italia offers tasty food at reasonable prices and a menu in English, but the setting, overlooking the less interesting ploshtad Makedonia, is not quite as appealing as Napoli.

Kuklite Tavern (ul Komitrov) Salads about 2.50 lv, grills from 5.20 lv. Up from the Pirin Tourist Forum, the Kuklite is one of several traditional taverns in authentic Bulgarian national revival period houses around Varosha. Prices are a little high because it caters to tour groups on occasion but the service is excellent and the menu is in English.

Entertainment

As probably expected in a university town there are several cinemas, including a special wide-screen **Movie Max** inside the American University complex. Later, you can join locals at one of the rowdy nightclubs, such as the **Underground** (pl Bulgaria), also called Rock-n-Roll Alley. The respected **Vaptsarov Theatre** (☎ 23 475, pl Georgi Izmirliev Makedoncheto), and the **Vaptsarov Chamber Opera** (☎ 20 703, pl Makedonia), offer something more sedate but are closed during August.

Getting There & Away

The bus and train stations are adjacent on bulevard Sveti Dimitâr Solunski.

Most buses leave from the well-organised bus station (☎ 23 750), about 2.5km southwest of the town centre and next to the train station. A few buses to Sandanski, Sofia and Dupnitsa also leave from the car park in front of the train station. The bus and train stations are both accessible by bus No 2 from outside the History Museum.

Seven daily buses travel directly between Blagoevgrad and Sofia (5 lv, two hours), via Dupnitsa, but many more come through on their way to/from Kulata or Sandanski. Also, there are at least eight daily buses to Sandanski (2.70 lv, 1½ hours), two or three to Gabrovo, Plovdiv and Samokov and four

SOUTHERN BULGARIA

or five to Kyustendil, Bansko and Kulata. To Rila village, buses leave daily at 7am, 11am, 2pm and 4pm.

The MATPU agency on bulevard Sveti Dimitâr Solunski, opposite the bus station, has daily bus services to Bitola (25 lv) in Macedonia.

The train station (☎ 23 695) is on the main line between Sofia and Kulata, via Sandanski. Every day, there are five fast trains (1st/2nd class 6.70/4.80 lv, 2½ hours), and one slow passenger train, from Sofia, via Dupnitsa. Three of these fast trains continue to Sandanski (1st/2nd class 4.40/3.30 lv, two hours) and Kulata (1st/2nd class 5/3.70 lv, 2½ hours).

RILA
РИЛА

Rila village is almost always ignored by the hordes who pass through on their way to the Rila Monastery, 22km to the east. However, if you're relying on public transport, you'll probably need a connection in Rila and the village does offer alternative accommodation and several foreign-exchange offices. (Note: there's nowhere to change money at Rila Monastery.)

Dominating the village square is *Hotel Rila* (☎ 07056-2167). Singles/doubles with a bathroom are 15/30 lv. The rates are good value compared to most places near the monastery. The *restaurant* is popular with occasional tour buses and several *cafes* are nearby.

From Dupnitsa, buses go to Rila village at 10am, 11am, 4pm and 7.20pm. From Rila village, they depart for Dupnitsa at 8.30am, 11.30am, noon and 5pm. There are also four daily buses between Rila village and Blagoevgrad (see Getting There & Away under Blagoevgrad earlier in this chapter).

Buses leave Rila village for the monastery at 7.40am, 12.40pm and 3.50pm and return at 9am, 3pm and 5pm.

RILA MONASTERY
РИЛСКИ МАНАСТИР
☎ 07054 • elevation 1147m

Bulgaria's largest, and definitely most famous, monastery is tucked away in a narrow and forested valley of the Rila Mountains, 119km south of Sofia. It's the most holy place in the country, and probably the major attraction for Bulgarian pilgrims and foreign tourists. It's best to avoid weekends in summer, when the car park is full of cars and tour buses. Try to stay at least one night at a nearby hotel or camping ground (or even at the monastery itself), so you can visit during the more photogenic early mornings and late evenings. If you stay longer, you can also hike in the surrounding mountains (see the boxed text 'Hiking in the Rila Mountains' later in this chapter).

Rila Monastery was founded in AD 927 by Ivan Rilski, a leader of a monastic colony of hermits. It was originally built about 3km to the north-east, but moved to the current site in 1335. By the end of the 14th century, the monastery had become a powerful feudal fiefdom. Plundered early in the 15th century, it was restored in 1469 after the relics of Ivan Rilski were returned from Veliko Târnovo. Under adverse conditions, the monastery helped to keep Bulgarian culture and religion alive during centuries of rule by the Turks, who destroyed the monastery several times.

In 1833, an accidental fire nearly engulfed all of the monastery's buildings. So many donations were received afterwards from various patrons that rebuilding commenced within a year – clearly indicating the monastery's importance and reverence to the Bulgarian people. It was proclaimed as a national museum in 1961 by the Bulgarian government and included on Unesco's list of World Heritage sites in 1983.

Monastery Grounds

The monastery grounds are open daily from about 6am to 10pm, so bear this in mind if you're staying inside the monastery. Admission is free, but there is an entrance fee to the museum of 5 lv. Photos are not permitted inside the main church but are allowed anywhere else in the grounds.

The eastern entrance is the **Samokov gate** but most cars and public buses park near the western **Dupnitsa gate**. A stall sells **souvenirs** and useful English-language **booklets** (5 lv to 10 lv) near the Dupnitsa gate, though

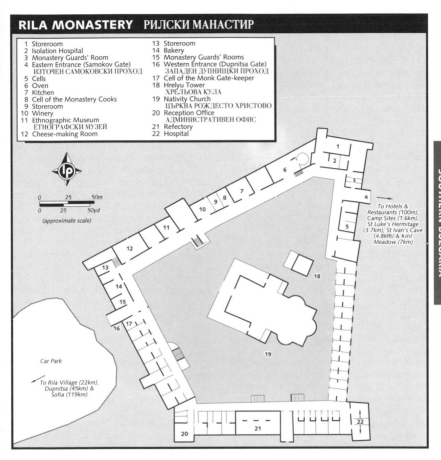

RILA MONASTERY РИЛСКИ МАНАСТИР

1 Storeroom
2 Isolation Hospital
3 Monastery Guards' Room
4 Eastern Entrance (Samokov Gate)
    ИЗТОЧЕН САМОКОВСКИ ПРОХОД
5 Cells
6 Oven
7 Kitchen
8 Cell of the Monastery Cooks
9 Storeroom
10 Winery
11 Ethnographic Museum
    ЕТНОГРАФСКИ МУЗЕЙ
12 Cheese-making Room

13 Storeroom
14 Bakery
15 Monastery Guards' Rooms
16 Western Entrance (Dupnitsa Gate)
    ЗАПАДЕН ДУПНИЦКИ ПРОХОД
17 Cell of the Monk Gate-keeper
18 Hrelyu Tower
    ХРЕЛЬОВА КУЛА
19 Nativity Church
    ЦЬРКВА РОЖДЕСТО ХРИСТОВО
20 Reception Office
    АДМИНИСТРАТИВЕН ОФИС
21 Refectory
22 Hospital

To Hotels &
Restaurants (100m),
Camp Sites (1.6km),
St Luke's Hermitage
(3.7km), St Ivan's Cave
(4.8km) & Kiril
Meadow (7km)

0   25   50m
0   25   50yd
(approximate scale)

Car Park

To Rila Village (22km),
Dupnitsa (45km) &
Sofia (119km)

SOUTHERN BULGARIA

a bit of history in English, French and German, is included on notice boards nailed up at the entrances.

The monastery's forbidding exterior contrasts dramatically with the warmth and cosiness of the striped arcades inside. Four levels of colourful balconies, with some 300 monastic cells, as well as storerooms, a refectory and kitchen, surround the large, irregular courtyard. The top balcony offers outstanding **views** of the surrounding Rila Mountains.

If you enter from the Samokov Gate, you'll soon see the 23m-high stone **Hrelyu**

Tower, named after a significant benefactor. It is the only remaining part of the monastery built in 1335.

The **kitchen**, built in 1816, is at courtyard level in the northern wing. The 22m-high chimney cuts through all storeys by means of 10 rows of arches crowned by a small dome. Food, often cooked for thousands of pilgrims at a time, was prepared here in huge cauldrons (one of which was large enough to fit an entire cow!).

Standing proudly in the middle of the courtyard is the magnificent **Nativity Church**, probably the largest monastery church in Bulgaria. The church, with its three great domes, was built between 1834 and 1837 – the 1200 murals inside were added between 1840 and 1848. These murals, which depict donors, Old Testament kings, apostles, angels, demons and martyrs, were created with an extremely rich ornamentation of flowers, birds and stylised vines. Several artists were involved but only the celebrated Zahari Zograf put his name to his work. The gilded and intricately carved iconostasis were created by artists from Samokov and Bansko. Be sure to dress and behave appropriately when visiting the church.

Ethnographic Museum This two-storey museum *(admission 5 lv; open daily 8.30am-4.30pm)* is in the northern wing of the monastery. It houses an impressive collection, including the monastery's original charter (1378), signed and stamped by Tsar Ivan Shishman. The prized exhibit is the remarkable **Rila Cross**, a double-sided cross which Brother Raphael took over 12 years to create during the late 18th century. It's incised in miniature with 140 biblical scenes and inscriptions and about 650 human figures. Not surprisingly, Raphael eventually ruined his eyesight after staring through a magnifying glass for so long. No items in the museum are labelled in any language except Bulgarian, but the booklet in English (available at the museum) will help. Guided tours (in English or French) are possible for 15 lv per group (maximum of five people).

Places to Stay
Most places to stay are within about 100m of the eastern Samokov Gate but there is also some spartan accommodation available within the monastery.

Camping *Zodiak Camping* (☎ 2291) Camping 10 lv per person, bungalows for singles/doubles with shared bathroom 15/25 lv. This camping ground is not particularly private, and the bungalows are a bit shabby, but the *restaurant* and the riverside setting are superb. It's 1.6km past the monastery along the road to Kiril Meadow.

Bor Camping Camping 3 lv per person, bungalows for doubles with shared bathroom 20 lv. The Bor camping ground offers more privacy, shade and space than the Zodiak, but is not as well established. Guests can pre-order *meals*. The turn-off is 1.2km past the monastery on the road to Kiril Meadow and another 400m along a path.

Hotels Accommodation is also available at Rila village (see earlier in this chapter) and Kiril Meadow (see later in this chapter).
Rila Restaurant Dorm beds 12 lv per person. Only those on *really* tight budgets should consider the dreary and shabby dormitories above the Rila Restaurant. The rooms are not signposted so inquire underneath at the restaurant, which is only metres from the Samokov Gate.
Rila Monastery (☎ 2208) Rooms from 22 to 33 lv per person. The cheaper rooms in the older western wing have three or four beds, and are sparsely furnished, but they are clean enough. The communal facilities for these rooms have toilets, but no showers. For those that would like a shower the newer rooms are far nicer, and have a private bathroom. Arrive early at the reception office (in the southern wing) because the newer rooms are often booked out by midday in summer.
Hotel Tsarev Vrah (☎/fax 2280) Singles/doubles with bathroom 33/66 lv. The Tsarev Vrah has been renovated but is still fairly unexciting and is overpriced for foreigners. Most balconies offer views of the forest and some have glimpses of the monastery. It's signposted about 150m from the Samokov Gate.
Hotel Rilets (☎ 23 031) Singles/doubles with bathroom 38/53 lv. The monolithic Rilets has a huge number of rooms, but it's a typically charmless leftover from the 1960s. It's also a fair walk – the 500m-long access road starts 1.2km past the monastery along the road to Kiril Meadow. Guests without private vehicles will probably have to eat their evening meals at the unexciting *dining room*, or the nearby Zodiak camping ground, to avoid walking in the dark. Rates include breakfast.

Places to Eat

All places listed below are only a few metres from the Samokov Gate. The freshest and tastiest local delicacy is trout but beware: the price may look cheap on the menu, but the cost is per 100g. A decent-sized fish (which can weigh up to 400g) will cost more than 8 lv.

The **bakery** *(open during daylight hours)*, next to the Rila Restaurant, is popular with hikers and anyone looking for a cheap and healthy breakfast. It sells all sorts of crusty bread, donuts and baked goodies, as well as (sheep) yoghurt.

Rila Restaurant Salads about 2 lv, grilled meat and fish dishes 5-7.50 lv. This charming restaurant is in a 120-year-old building with a pleasant outdoor setting. It has an extensive menu (in English) but gets consistently mixed reviews from readers and travellers.

Restaurant Drushlihvitsa Main meals 3-5 lv. One of several unassuming taverns with outdoor tables, the staff here are friendly and can rustle up a menu in English. Most taverns sell bottles of the popular, locally made 'Rilski Monastery' wine.

Getting There & Away

Buses to and from the monastery are frustratingly erratic. At the monastery, check the current schedules with local shopkeepers and restaurant staff (who often rely on the buses). In Sofia, it's worth ringing the Ovcha Kupel bus station (☎ 02-554 033) about direct buses from the capital.

Buses leave Rila village for the monastery at 7.40am, 12.40pm and 3.50pm and return at 9am, 3pm and 5pm. (In summer, the 3pm service may continue to Sofia, but don't count on it.) From Dupnitsa, buses to Rila Monastery leave at 6.40am and 2.15pm and return from the monastery at about 9.40am and 5.15pm. It shouldn't be hard to hitch a ride from the monastery to the village, and even Sofia, if you ask nicely.

To make a really rushed day trip from Sofia to the monastery by public transport, take any bus to Dupnitsa (1½ hours) from the Princess Hotel bus station west or Ovcha Kupel bus station before 8am. Then jump on the 10am (or 11am) bus to Rila village and catch the 12.40pm bus to the monastery. To return to Sofia, take the 5.15pm bus to Dupnitsa, and one of the hourly buses (or trains) back to the capital.

Full-day tours of Rila Monastery from Sofia (or Borovets) cost from US$30 per person. Refer to the Organised Tours section in the Sofia chapter for details.

AROUND RILA MONASTERY
St Luke's Hermitage & St Ivan's Cave

About 3.7km north-east of the monastery, as you drive along the road to Kiril Meadow, there's a trail on the left that leads to St Luke's Hermitage. The trail takes about 15 minutes by foot – look for the picture of St Ivan at the start of the steps. St Luke's Hermitage, built in 1798, features a large courtyard and the **Church of St Luke**. Continue walking along the trail for about 15 minutes to St Ivan's Cave, where Ivan Rilski lived, and is buried. According to local legend, anyone able to pass through the hole in the cave's roof has not sinned, and since it's easy to get through, the legend is very popular!

Kiril Meadow
Кирилова Ливада

The road north-east of Rila Monastery continues for about 7km to Kiril Meadow, another typically gorgeous area with pine trees, picnic spots, *cafes* and stunning **views** of the craggy cliffs. Most of the road from the monastery is flat so it's a pleasant, and mostly shady, walk. There's a place where *rooms* (☎ 076-3268), with four beds and a shared bathroom, cost a very reasonable 25 lv per room. The *bungalows* have five beds and a private bathroom, and cost 50 lv per bungalow. This is an excellent alternative for anyone more interested in the (quiet) scenery than the (busy) monastery.

SAMOKOV
САМОКОВ
☎ 0722 • pop 29,800

Samokov, about 62km south-east of Sofia, is a worthwhile trip from the capital and is a cheaper place to stay than Sofia, or the nearby ski resort of Borovets. Samokov sprang up as an iron-mining centre in the 14th century, and was renowned during the 19th century for the Samokov School of Icon Painting and Woodcarving. Between 1910 and 1912, the local council established the infamous but unsuccessful Samokov Commune. It was Bulgaria's first socialist organisation, and established to improve the safety, health and education of workers. Although the suburbs of Samokov are derelict, the town centre is picturesque and welcoming. Several foreign-exchange offices can be found near the bus station.

Things to See

Easy to spot north of the bus station is the **Bairakli Mosque** *(admission 1.50 lv; open Tues-Fri 9am-6pm)*. It was built in 1840, and designed in a style epitomised by the Bulgarian national revival period.

The **History Museum** *(☎ 22 194, ul Liubcho Baramov 4; admission 1.50 lv; open Mon-Fri 8am-noon & 1pm-5pm)* contains archaeological and ethnographical displays, scale models of iron forges and furnaces, and photos of the old town. It's a few metres west of the town square, at the back of an unkempt garden.

The **Sarafska Kâshta Museum** *(☎ 22 221, ul Knyaz Dondukov 11; admission 1 lv; open Mon-Fri 9am-noon & 1pm-5pm)* is about 200m north of the History Museum. This delightful 1860 national revival period home contains typical period furniture.

Places to Stay & Eat

Hotel Koala (☎ 22 332, ul Hristo Zagrafski 25) Singles/doubles/triples with bathroom 10/20/30 lv. It may have a rather unlikely name, but this charming place is excellent value, and offers large, bright and well-furnished rooms with a TV. It's tucked along a side street about 10 minutes' walk northeast (up) from the bus station – look for the signs in English.

Hotel-Restaurant Nicole (☎ 27 219, ul Tûrgovska 6) Singles/doubles/triples with bathroom 20/30/40 lv. The Nicole is another charming place and also great value. The rooms are attic-style and huge, and decorated with lovely wooden furniture. It's about 10 minutes' walk east of the bus station (ask directions to be sure). The *restaurant/bar* is popular with day trippers from Sofia.

Plenty of *cafes* are dotted around the town centre. One of several decent restaurants near the bus station is *Mehana Golyamata Cheshma (ul Tûrgovska)*, nearly opposite the mosque. Alternatively, both hotels have *restaurants*.

Getting There & Away

Buses and minibuses to Samokov (3 lv, 1½ hours) depart every 30 minutes between 7am and 7.30pm from the Yug bus station in Sofia. From the Samokov bus station (☎ 22 391) on ulitsa Tûrgovska, minibuses head to Borovets, Govedartsi and Malîovitsa. To Dupnitsa (3.50 lv, one hour), buses leave at 7.30am, 2.20pm and 5pm.

BOROVETS
БОРОВЕЦ
☎ 07128 • elevation 1350m

Borovets is the most popular and established ski resort in Bulgaria (see the boxed text 'Skiing at Borovets' later in this section), but is also a lovely place to visit and/or stay in summer. Although touristy and a little expensive, it's easy to escape the crowds – especially on summer weekdays, when you almost feel like you have the place to yourself. Borovets is compact and surrounded by thick pine forests, and offers plenty of things to see and do, and places to eat and drink, year-round.

Orientation & Information

All places listed in this section are along, or just off, the main street (which starts from the road between Samokov and Kostenets), and are open throughout the summer. The staff at the tourist office (☎ 712 8441), open daily 8am to 7pm, in the Hotel Rila complex, seem disinterested in assisting visitors, but locals are always happy to help.

The rates offered by the few foreign-exchange offices vary; the best is about 5% lower than in Sofia. There is a small Internet centre in Hotel Samokov, and a better one along the main street opposite the same hotel. Most souvenir stalls sell tacky stuff but Galerie Borovets, just up from Pension Radenkov, offers excellent artwork for about 15 lv to 25 lv. Gorgeous tapestries at reasonable prices are available at stalls near Hotel Rila.

Activities

Borovets is the best starting point for **hikes** along marked trails around the eastern section of the Rila Mountains. Some hikes simply follow established ski runs, which is just as well because none of the hiking trails around Borovets are included on the *Rila* map, published (in Cyrillic) by Kartografia. The travel agency (☎ 306) inside Hotel Samokov can provide more information about hiking, and can arrange guides.

Some of the shorter and more popular hikes include:

Borovets-Chernata Skala Follow the road towards Kostenets, and look for the signs heading south to Hizha Maritsa – three hours (easy).

Borovets-Hizha Maritsa Use the Borovets to Chernata Skala, and continue along the southern road – 4½ hours (medium).

Borovets-Hizha Sokolets Follow the road through Borovets – 2½ hours (easy). Another

trail (1½ hours) from Hizha Sokolets heads south to Mt Sokolets (2021m).

Yastrebets-Borovets Take the gondola (see the boxed text 'Skiing at Borovets') to Yastrebets (2369m) and walk down – 60 to 90 minutes (easy).

Horse riding is available from outside the main entrance to Hotel Rila, and costs 40 lv (two hours), 66 lv (3½ hours), or 80 lv (full day). The mammoth Hotel Samokov has an **indoor swimming pool** (admission 4 lv), **bowling alley** and **fitness centre**, and offers **saunas** and **massages**. Each is available daily in winter, and from Friday to Sunday in summer. The tourist office (see earlier) offers all-inclusive, good-value **bus trips** to Rila Monastery year-round (37/50 lv half/full-day) and Plovdiv (66 lv full day).

Places to Stay

Book well ahead (three to six months in peak times) if you want mid-range or top-end accommodation during the ski season. The rates listed here are for the summer; expect to pay about 20% more in winter. These places do not have addresses as such, because none of the streets are named.

Skiing at Borovets

Bulgaria's oldest ski resort is built on the slopes of Mt Musala (2925m), one of the highest peaks in the Balkans. Only 70km from Sofia, Borovets is the most developed and compact resort in the country, and has twice hosted World Cup Alpine ski rounds. About 1.5m of snow is almost guaranteed between November and April. The 23 ski runs (including the longest in Bulgaria) are mostly in the main three areas of Markudjika, Yastrebets and Sitnyakovo-Martinovi Baraki. The four cross-country trails total about 19km, and start about 2km on foot from Borovets.

Borovets is reasonably good value, easy to reach from Sofia (but too far to day trip by public transport), and there are cheap places to stay nearby at Samokov, Govedartsi and Maľiovitsa. The downside is that Borovets, like Mt Vitosha, can get very crowded on Friday, Saturday and Sunday. Over a dozen places in Borovets rent ski equipment – just look for signs in English 'ski depot' or 'ski store'. Expect to pay 35 lv to 40 lv per day for complete ski equipment. Plenty of well-qualified and multilingual instructors can provide training for about 250 lv (over six days, including a lift pass and ski gear).

Borovets has three chairlifts, one gondola and 10 draglifts. The gondola (open year-round) from the Borosports complex in Borovets to Yastrebets costs 8/12 lv one-way/return. (The cost of a lift pass for foreigners was not available at the time of research.) A free minibus between the main hotels and ski slopes is available to anyone with a lift pass.

Snowboarding at Borovets is OK, without being exceptional. A snowboard and boots can be hired for about 30 lv per day, and training can be arranged for about 100 lv (six hours).

Cheaper places to stay nearby can be found in Govedartsi (see later) and Samokov (see earlier).

Pension Radenkov (☎ *737*) Camping 3 lv per person, beds in 2-bed or 3-bed rooms 8 lv per person. This rustic place offers basic rooms with few amenities, plus the only camping ground in Borovets. It's a few metres up the second (minor) street that starts along the road from Samokov.

Motel Beds in 2-bed or 3-bed rooms with bathroom 7 lv per person. This unnamed, ramshackle place is on the right-hand side of the street leading to Hotel Rila (look for the 'Motel' sign in English at the back of Boneti House). It's surprisingly good value, but nothing to get excited about.

Siezhno Rano (*mobile* ☎ *087-442 459*) Doubles with private bathroom 44 lv per person (negotiable). Opposite Hotel Flora, this place offers bright and airy rooms with a balcony, TV and fridge. It's remarkable value compared to other places nearby. The rates, which are listed outside the hotel, depend on how busy they are.

Borosports Holiday Village (☎ *517, fax 796*) Singles/doubles with bathroom 40/66 lv, A-frame villas for 4-5 people 127 lv. Right at the gondola to Yastrebets, this place is comparatively good value, though the villas (which have a kitchen, bathroom, TV and sitting room) are not particularly private and are noisy in winter. The rooms at the back of the complex are smallish but secluded and offer views and a TV.

Hotel Rila (☎ *7128*, e *rila@mbox.infotel .bg, Borovets*) Singles/doubles with bathroom 75/105 lv. Of the 10 or so major hotels in Borovets, the largest (with over 250 rooms) and most popular is probably the Rila. It boasts a shopping arcade, three restaurants and an outdoor swimming pool (which must double as a skating rink in winter). Rates include breakfast.

Places to Eat
The main streets of Borovets are lined with masses of cafes, bars and restaurants serving Turkish, Italian, English and Chinese food at higher prices than in Sofia. Menus are almost always in English (and some-times French and German), but if the menu is only in a foreign language, it's likely that the prices are two to three times higher than those on the Bulgarian menu.

The cheapest ***eateries*** are at the turn-off to Borovets along the Samokov-Kostenets road. Some of the cosier and less expensive places in Borovets are along the street between the Borosports complex and Hotel Flora, for example, ***Alpin Restaurant***, one of the few places open early for breakfast.

Just up the street from Hotel Rila, ***Fantasy Restaurant***, also known as Ted's Place, offers inexpensive and tasty food, as does the classier ***Salamander*** next door.

Getting There & Away
There is no direct public transport between Sofia and Borovets. So, take a bus from Sofia to Samokov (3 lv, 1½ hours) and then a minibus to Borovets (3 lv, 20 minutes). Minibuses from Samokov leave about every 30 to 45 minutes between 7am and 7pm. A taxi from Samokov costs a negotiable 5 lv.

Minibuses from Samokov usually drop passengers outside Hotel Samokov in Borovets. To catch a minibus back to Samokov, wait at Jimmi's Supermarket (signposted in English), near the turn-off to Borovets along the Samokov-Kostenets road. Taxis congregate around the turn-off and can be chartered to Sofia for about 50 lv. It's always worth asking about sharing a taxi back to Sofia, or anywhere else in the region.

GOVEDARTSI
ГОВЕДАРЦИ
☎ 07125 • elevation 1200m
Govedartsi is a pretty village 13km southwest of Samokov. It's a cheap and convenient base for visiting Borovets and/or Malîovitsa, and is a starting point for hikes along marked trails in the Rila Mountains (as detailed in the *Rila* map published by Kartografia).

There are two accommodation and eating options.

Number 53 Hotel (*mobile* ☎ *088-57 313*, e *kokojambazki@hotmail.com*) Doubles with shared bathroom 16 lv. The rooms are large, airy, bright and outstanding value,

Just in case you forget where you are!

TOM COCKREM

Sweet treats from a Gabrovo pastry shop.

PHILIP GAME

Woven fabrics from Bansko.

PAUL GREENWAY

Near Yagodina in the Rodopi Mountains, these Muslim women watch the world go by.

DANI VALENT

PHILIP GAME

St Nikolai Russian Church, Sofia.

PHILIP GAME

The Aleksander Nevski Church bell resounds over 30km from Sofia.

PAUL GREENWAY

Changing of the guards outside the Presidential building in Sofia.

PAUL GREENWAY

St George's rotunda is considered the oldest building in Sofia.

PAUL GREENWAY

A splash of green in Sofia.

and the hotel also boasts an outdoor garden, sauna, bar and *restaurant*. It's a three-storey, white building along the Samokov-Maliovitsa road, about 300m east (towards Samokov) of the bus stop.

Kalina Hotel (☎ 2643) Singles/doubles with bathroom 22/44 lv. About 150m up from the town square and bus stop, the Kalina has noisy dogs but friendly owners. The rooms are smallish, but clean, comfortable and nicely furnished (with chandelier and TV). It also has a *restaurant/bar*.

From Samokov, six or seven minibuses go to Govedartsi (1.50 lv, 20 minutes) each day.

MALIOVITSA
МАЛЬОВИЦА
☎ 07125 • elevation 1750m

At the foot of the Rila Mountains 13km south-west of Govedartsi, Maliovitsa is far smaller, less commercial and cheaper than Borovets. It's a charmingly scenic spot with a couple of run-down hotels, so the local name of 'Maliovitsa Resort' is a definite misnomer. In winter, Maliovitsa is a no-frills ski resort, while in summer it's a popular place for rock climbing, mountain climbing, hiking and picnicking. Most visitors are day trippers from Sofia with private vehicles. Those travellers without private transport will probably have to spend at least one night here if travelling from Sofia.

Activities
Skiing here is certainly cheaper than at Borovets, but not nearly as challenging. Ski equipment is available from the Central Mountain School (see Places to Stay & Eat later in this section) for 4 lv to 6 lv per person per day depending on the quality of equipment (pay extra for the better gear!). Elsewhere in Maliovitsa, equipment is about 14 lv per day. The one and only draglift costs a mere 7 lv per person per day.

SOUTHERN BULGARIA

Hiking in the Rila Mountains

As one reader exclaimed: 'Maliovitsa is a fantastic place to walk from; the trails are brilliantly marked and easy to follow'. Still, it's worth buying the *Rila* map, published by Kartografia (with the green cover), though it is in Cyrillic.

Maliovitsa to Rila Monastery
An hour's hike from Maliovitsa is *Hizha Maliovitsa (no telephone; open year-round)* at 2050m above sea level. Some rooms have four beds, but others have 20, so ask for a private room if you're in a small group. *Camping* is allowed for a minimal fee. Basic meals and drinks are available at the cafe but guests can also bring their own food and use the kitchen.

From Hizha Maliovitsa it's about seven hours to *Hizha Sedemte Ezera*, an older hut with simple dormitories. *Hizha Rilski Ezera* (☎ 0701-22524), at 2150m, is a little farther north and is generally regarded as the nicest hut accommodation in the Rila Mountains. It offers dorm beds, as well as rooms with a shared/private bathroom from 28/33 lv per person, including breakfast and dinner. A modest *cafe* is attached. Reservations are not normally necessary for either hut, except during the meeting of the White Brotherhood (see the boxed text later in this chapter) in August.

From the Seven Lakes, it's an easy one-hour hike down to *Hizha Skakavitsa* (1985m), where there's a pretty **waterfall**, or six to seven hours south to the Rila Monastery. You could bypass Hizha Maliovitsa and hike to the Seven Lakes from Maliovitsa, via Hizha Vada and Hizha Lovina.

Sedemte Ezera (Seven Lakes)
It's also possible to visit these sparkling lakes from Sapareva Banya (accessible by bus from Dupnitsa), or from *Hizha Pionerska* (1500m). To reach this hut from Sapareva Banya, walk 13km up the steep road, hire a taxi (more reliably from Dupnitsa) or organise a transfer (for one/two people about 26/30 lv) with Odysseia-In (see Travel Agencies in the Sofia chapter). From the hut, it's about a three-hour hike to Hizha Rilski Ezera.

The White Brotherhood

This Bulgarian-based cult is also known as Dunovism, after the priest who started it in 1918. Adherents practice a curious amalgamation of rituals such as yoga, sun-worshipping and vegetarianism, borrowed from Eastern Orthodox Christianity and Hinduism, among other religions. Followers meet at Sedemte Ezera each August. (Check with the Odysseia-In Travel Agency, or the National Information & Advertising Center in Sofia for the exact dates.) Hikers should note that the Hizha Sedemte Ezera and Hizha Rilski Ezera huts are often booked out for a week or more in August but the public are still welcome at the huts during the day to witness the pilgrimage.

In summer, the Central Mountain School offers **rock climbing** and **mountain climbing** for about 30 lv to 50 lv per person per day, including a guide, but not transport or equipment (which is available at the School). The Sofia-based guide Dobrin Entechev (☎ 02-981 2043, e dobrin–entechev@yahoo.com) charges US$50/80 for one/two people per day, including equipment but not transport.

Between March and June, and in September and October, **kayaking** and **rafting** is possible along local rivers. Kayaks are available from the Central Mining School for 20 lv per day; guides (not necessary) cost 30 lv to 50 lv per day.

Places to Stay & Eat
Hotel Malîovitsa (☎ 2222) Rooms with bathroom in summer/winter 20/25 lv per person. This crumbling monolith above the car park is atmospheric, and the rooms are nicer than the outside of the hotel, and corridors, would suggest. The rates include breakfast and the attached *dining room* is open to the public. The hotel may change money, but it's better to do this before you come.

Central Mountain School (☎ 2270) Doubles with bathroom 27 lv. Near the car park, the school offers basic, untidy rooms, and is not as good as the Hotel Malîovitsa. A basic *restaurant/bar* is attached.

Getting There & Away
In theory, a minibus travels from the Yug bus station in Sofia every day at 9am directly to Malîovitsa (6 lv, two hours). If this doesn't eventuate, simply catch a bus to Samokov and get a minibus to Malîovitsa (3 lv, 45 minutes) at 8.15am or 4.15pm. Minibuses return to Samokov at 9am and 5pm, and (theoretically) to Sofia at about midday.

Pirin Mountains
Пирин Планина

Tucked away in the south-west corner of Bulgaria are the compact Pirin Mountains (2585 sq km), named after Perun, the Slavic God of Thunder. Over the centuries, Greeks, Turks and Slavs have been attracted to these mountains because of the mineral waters (from 230 sources) and 186 pristine lakes, often partially frozen in winter. The average height of the Pirin Mountains is comparatively low at 1033m but over 100 peaks are higher than 2000m (and 12 are more than 2700m). The highest is Mt Vihren (2914m), near Bansko.

Only 1.8km south-west of Bansko is a gate to the Pirin National Park, which is permanently open and free to enter, Bulgaria's largest at 40,447 hectares. It was placed on Unesco's list of World Heritage sites in 1983 to protect the varied and unique landscapes, 1100 species of flora, 102 types of birds and 42 species of mammals, such as bears, deers and wild goats. The Pirin National Park Office (☎/fax 07443-2428) at bulevard Bulgaria 4 in Bansko, is not a tourist office or hiking agency, nor a place to rent equipment, but it can provide help to anyone wishing to undertake a long trek in the mountains.

BANSKO
БАНСКО
☎ 07443 • pop 9740 • elevation 930m
Bansko was founded in the 10th century on the site of an old Thracian settlement. By the mid-18th century, it was a highly prosperous town because of its fortuitous location on

Hiking in the Pirin Mountains

Marked hiking trails, 13 primary and 17 secondary, link 13 huts and shelters throughout the park. The primary trails are best described and mapped in the colourful and detailed map (1:55,000) in the *National Park Pirin* leaflet printed in English by the Ministry of Environment & Waters. The leaflet is available at tourist offices and/or bookstalls in Bansko, Sandanski, Melnik and Blagoevgrad. Also, the free yellow *Bansko* and *Sandanski & Melnik* handouts printed by the Pirin Tourism Forum provide detailed descriptions of short hikes in the mountains. These leaflets are available from Melnik and, most reliably, from the Pirin Tourism Forum in Blagoevgrad (see earlier in this chapter).

The only accurate and detailed hiking map of the whole mountain range is the *Pirin* map (1:55,000), published in Cyrillic by Kartografia, and widely available in Sofia, Sandanski and Bansko. This map indicates numerous marked trails from Bansko and contains enough detail to explore areas around Melnik and Sandanski. Also, the Domino map of *Bansko* includes a small but detailed map in English of 12 hiking trails. These include Bansko to **Hizha Banderitsa** (☎ 07443-2683), 2km south-west of Shiligarnika, and Bansko to **Hizha Vihren** (☎ 07443-2683), 2km farther up. Both offer convenient bases for hikes to nearby **caves** and **lakes**, for example Hizha Vihren to Mt Vihren is about three hours one-way.

From Sandanski, a popular, three-hour hike leads to the glorious **Popina Lûka** region, with lakes, waterfalls and pine forests. Hikers can stay at **Hizha Kamenitsa** (☎ 07443-3198) or **Hizha Yane Sandanski** (☎ 07443-3198).

The Mountains of Bulgaria, by Julian Perry, describes in words (but with poor maps) a trek across the entire Pirin Mountains from Hizha Predel (at the end of the trek across the Rila Mountains) to Petrovo village near the Greek border. It's a tough trek, so allow seven to 10 days – more for delays if the weather is bad.

the overland caravan route between the Aegean Sea and Danubian Europe. At this time, Bansko was home to traders, craftsmen and artists, as well as influential icon-painting and woodcarving schools.

Bansko is one of the shiniest jewels in Bulgaria's tourism crown. It's a base for top-notch skiing (see the boxed text 'Skiing at Bansko' later) and superb hiking in summer. Bansko boasts more than 150 cultural monuments, including many from the Bulgarian national revival period. These buildings were made with stone and timber and built behind fortress-style walls, with hidden escape routes, to shield inhabitants from their Ottoman occupiers. With the help of the Beautiful Bulgaria Project, many of these houses have been transformed into charming *mehanas* (taverns) and cosy pensions.

Orientation & Information

The main square, ploshtad Nikola Vaptsarov, is connected to ploshtad Vûzhrazhdane by ulitsa Pirin. The latter square is dominated by the mammoth Paisii Hilendarski Monument, dedicated to a locally born monk who was one of the instigators of the Bulgarian national revival in the mid-18th century. Most shops and cafes are along the pedestrian mall, ulitsa Tsar Simeon.

The Tourist Information Centre (☎ 5048; open daily 10am-7pm) is inside a small room just to the north-west of ploshtad Nikola Vaptsarov. Whether the office is able or willing to offer anything more than a few brochures depends on who helps you. The office can assist with hotel bookings in Bansko if you're finding it hard to get accommodation, and can provide information about local hiking trails.

There are a few places to change money. Most are along ulitsa Tsar Simeon, such as KSV Ltd, Cafe Nova, the foreign-exchange office next to the supermarket and the DSK Bank, just over the road from the post office and telephone centre. There's an Internet Agency on the corner of ulitsa Pirin and ulitsa Molerov.

SOUTHERN BULGARIA

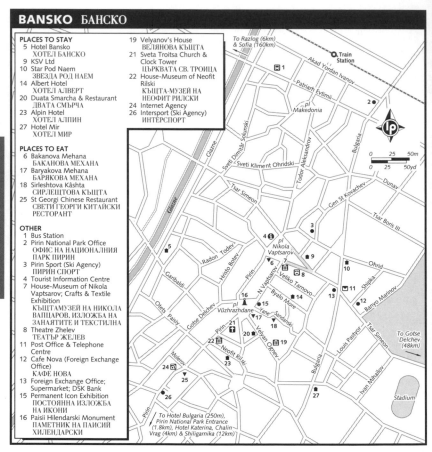

BANSKO БАНСКО

PLACES TO STAY
5 Hotel Bansko
   ХОТЕЛ БАНСКО
9 KSV Ltd
10 Star Pod Naem
   ЗВЕЗДА РОД НАЕМ
14 Albert Hotel
   ХОТЕЛ АЛВЕРТ
20 Duata Smarcha & Restaurant
   ДВАТА СМЪРЧА
23 Alpin Hotel
   ХОТЕЛ АЛПИН
27 Hotel Mir
   ХОТЕЛ МИР

PLACES TO EAT
6 Bakanova Mehana
   БАКАНОВА МЕХАНА
7 Baryakova Mehana
   БАРЯКОВА МЕХАНА
18 Sirleshtova Kâshta
   СИРЛЕЩТОВА КЪЩТА
25 St Georgi Chinese Restaurant
   СВЕТИ ГЕОРГИ КИТАЙСКИ
   РЕСТОРАНТ

OTHER
1 Bus Station
2 Pirin National Park Office
   ОФИС НА НАЦИОНАЛНИЯ
   ПАРК ПИРИН
3 Pirin Sport (Ski Agency)
   ПИРИН СПОРТ
4 Tourist Information Centre
7 House-Museum of Nikola
   Vaptsarov; Crafts & Textile
   Exhibition
   КЪЩТАМУЗЕЙ НА НИКОЛА
   ВАПЦАРОВ, ИЗЛОЖБА НА
   ЗАНАЯТИТЕ И ТЕКСТИЛНА
8 Theatre Zhelev
   ТЕАТЪР ЖЕЛЕВ
11 Post Office & Telephone
   Centre
12 Cafe Nova (Foreign Exchange
   Office)
   КАФЕ НОВА
13 Foreign Exchange Office;
   Supermarket; DSK Bank
15 Permanent Icon Exhibition
   ПОСТОЯННА ИЗЛОЖБА
   НА ИКОНИ
16 Paisii Hilendarski Monument
   ПАМЕТНИК НА ПАИСИЙ
   ХИЛЕНДАРСКИ

19 Velyanov's House
   ВЕЛЯНОВА КЪЩА
21 Sveta Troitsa Church &
   Clock Tower
   ЦЪРКВАТА СВ. ТРОИЦА
22 House-Museum of Neofit
   Rilski
   КЪЩТА-МУЗЕЙ НА
   НЕОФИТ РИЛСКИ
24 Internet Agency
26 Intersport (Ski Agency)
   ИНТЕРСПОРТ

The Pirin National Park office (☎/fax 07443-2428) is at bulevard Bansko 4 for those wishing to find out about long treks in the Pirin Mountains.

Things to See

House Museum of Nikola Vaptsarov (☎ 3038, pl Nikola Vaptsarov; admission 2 lv; open Mon-Sat 9am-noon & 2pm-5.45pm) is in the house where Vaptsarov (1909–42), respected anti-fascist poet and activist, was born. He was a populist writer and labour activist influenced by communist ideology while a student at the Varna Maritime Acad-

emy. Jailed and tortured by the wartime fascist government, Vaptsarov penned his most famous poem while awaiting execution. A small video film, followed by an audio tape in English, French or German provides some details about the exhibits, which are labelled in Bulgarian. The attached **Crafts & Textile Exhibition** features traditional arts, crafts and textiles from Bansko, as well as handmade items from all over the Pirin Mountains. Most items such as small embroidered souvenirs (5 lv to 15 lv) and traditional shirts (from 30 lv) are for sale. The exhibition overlooks the adjacent **Theatre Zhelev** (admission *free; open Mon-Sat 8am-noon & 2pm-5.45pm)*, which houses works of art by the famous local painter Tenio Zhelev.

Velyanov's House *(☎ 4181, ul Velyan Ognev 5; admission 2 lv; open Mon-Fri 9am-noon & 2pm-5pm)* features the sort of elaborately painted scenes and carved woodwork that is representative of the so-called 'Bansko School' of art.

House-Museum of Neofit Rilski *(☎ 2540, ul Pirin 17; admission 2 lv; open daily 9am-noon & 2pm-5pm)* is a converted school room. It contains some manuscripts by, and photos of, Rilski (1793–1881), who is renowned as the father of Bulgarian secular education.

The **Sveta Troitsa Church** *(pl Vûzhrazhdane; admission free, camera permit 5 lv; open daily 7am-7pm)* was built in 1835. Surrounded by a stone wall 1m thick and 4m high, it features magnificent wooden floors, period furniture and faded murals. In the church grounds is Bansko's major landmark: the 30m-high **clock tower**, built in 1850.

The **Permanent Icon Exhibition** *(☎ 4005; ul Yane Sandanski; open Mon-Fri 9am-noon & 2pm-5.30pm)* is in a convent affiliated with the Rila Monastery. A number of exquisite religious icons are displayed here under heavy glass but nothing is labelled in English (this may change when renovations are completed). It's poorly signposted and, at the time of writing, was indicated by a piece of paper nailed to a door. Whether admission (probably no more than 2 lv) is charged depends on the whim – or absence – of staff.

Special Events

The **Pirin Sings Folk Festival**, which takes place near Bansko every second (odd-numbered) year in August, brings together thousands of folk musicians and dancers from throughout the Pirin Mountains. The annual **International Jazz Festival** (about 7 to 15 August) attracts artists from all over Bulgaria, and even as far as Egypt. Most events at this festival are held in a temporary open-air stage at ploshtad Nikola Vaptsarov and in the Theatre Zhelev.

Other special events in Bansko include the **Celebration of Bansko Traditions** (17 to 24 May) and **Bansko Day** (5 October). In nearby Dobrinishte, **St Theodor's Day** (15 March) is celebrated with horse racing.

Places to Stay

It's worth booking ahead during any major festival and in the peak ski season. The rates listed are for summer; in winter add another 20%. All hotels have rooms with a private bathroom. Unofficial, discreet *camping* is possible in the nearby Pirin National Park (see earlier in this chapter).

Star Pod Naem *(☎ 3998)* on bulevard Bulgaria 33 and KSV Ltd *(☎ 3970)* on ulitsa Tsar Simeon 68, can both arrange *rooms* (most with a shared bathroom) in private homes for about 22 lv per person.

Hotel Mir (☎ 2500, [e] bansko@gedimeks .com, ul Neofit Rilski 28) Singles/doubles 30/53 lv. The Mir, in a quiet spot not too far from the town centre, is very good value. The rooms are bright, clean and have a TV and the staff are friendly. Rates include breakfast.

Duata Smarcha (☎ 2632, ul Velyan Ognev 2) Singles/doubles 22/44 lv. Set in a lovely garden, this pension is cosy and the staff speak good English. Traditional home-cooked meals are available, both to guests and the public, at the *restaurant*. The rooms (with TV) are excellent value, which is why it's popular and often full so book ahead. Rates include breakfast.

Albert Hotel (☎ 4264, ul Byalo More 12) Doubles 24 lv. The Albert is clean, comfortable and central, but staff don't speak any English.

Alpin Hotel (☎ 7443, ul Neofit Rilski 6) Singles/doubles 33/44 lv, suites 55/66 lv. The Alpin offers bright, clean and airy rooms. Although rates are high for foreigners, it's good value compared to similar places in this range. TV rental is an extra 7.50 lv per day, and breakfast is an extra 5 lv per person. Guests can also enjoy a sauna for an extra 5 lv.

Hotel Bansko (☎ 4275, [e] bansko@ bg400.bg; ul Glazne 37) Singles/doubles 44/88 lv. The four-star Bansko is good value. If you're looking for an upmarket hotel, but would never consider a four-star

Skiing at Bansko

Nestled at the base of the imposing Mt Vihren (2914m), Bansko enjoys a climate of relatively short summers and long snowy winters. Bansko is not a ski resort in the vein of Borovets or Pamporovo, so it appeals to those who want cheaper skiing without the high costs and apres-ski activities. Although the area's high elevation (1800m to 2500m) ensures Bulgaria's most consistent skiing, it is surprisingly ignored by foreign skiers on package tours.

On the plus side, Bansko is certainly a nicer place to stay than Pamporovo or Borovets and it's not far from Sofia (though too distant to commute without private transport). Also, the snow, which is often 2m thick between mid-December and mid-April, sometimes lasts until mid-May and the lifts and slopes are generally well maintained. On the other hand, the slopes are a hassle to reach with private transport (so take a bus from Bansko), and it can get crowded on weekends.

With regard to skiing, the resort of 'Bansko' really refers to Shiligarnika, at the end of a windy, 12km road south of Bansko. Together with the far smaller Chalin Vrag, 4km south-west of Bansko, there are six ski runs (total of 14km) but only 8km of cross-country trails. There are four chairlifts and four draglifts at Shiligarnika. An all-day lift pass, which includes a free bus ride to/from the slopes, costs about 20 lv.

Equipment (from 20 lv per day) can be hired, and instructors can be arranged at **Pirin Sport** (☎ 537, ul Gen St Kovachev 8), which can also organise snowboard hire and instructors. Equipment and instructors can also be arranged at **Intersport** (☎ 4876, ul Pirin 71) rents out snowboards and **Hotel Bulgaria** (☎ 3005, ul Hristo Matov 2), **Alpin Hotel** (☎ 7443, ul Neofit Rilski 6) and **Hotel Bansko** (☎ 4275, e bankso@bg400.bg; ul Glazne 37) all hire equipment. Hotel Bansko and Intersport also hire out mountain bikes in summer, but don't expect too much in the way of quality and quantity.

place, check the discounted rates that are often available. The rooms have a TV and fridge, and guests have free access to a games room and sauna.

Hotel Katerina (☎/fax 2357, e hotel-katerina@com.bg) Singles/doubles 22/44 lv. The Katerina is great value because it doesn't discriminate against foreigners. The rooms have a TV, balcony and decent heating, and guests can use the gym or sauna for free. It's about 3km inside Pirin National Park and about 4km south-west of Bansko.

Places to Eat

Many of Bansko's 70 or more mehanas offer regional delicacies such as *kapama* (several kinds of meat, rice and sauerkraut simmered and served in a clay pot) and home-made *karvavitsa* (sausage made of, well, possibly anything) – all washed down with a bottle (or two) of locally made wine. Bansko is not frequented by many foreigners, so most restaurants have menus in Bulgarian only.

Baryakova Mehana (ul Velyan Ognev 3) Main dishes 4.50-6 lv. For quality food and

cheery ambience, it's tough to beat the Baryakova. It's an ideal place to try some local plonk (about 5 lv per bottle of red) and is especially popular on cold evenings when everyone seems to fight for seats near the fireplaces.

Sirleshtova Kâshta (ul Yane Sandanski 12) Salads about 2.50 lv, grills about 5 lv. This mehana occupies a building where, in 1890, partisan Gotse Delchev organised the Macedonian Revolutionary Movement. It's a charming place to try some local Bansko cuisine and wine.

Bakanova Mehana (ul Pirin) Salads about 1.50 lv, pizzas 3.50-5.50 lv, grills about 5 lv. Overlooking ploshtad Nikola Vaptsarov, this place offers a huge range of Bulgarian and Italian meals, though most locals flock there for the tasty pizzas. The Bakanova is one of the few places in Bansko with a menu in English.

St Georgi Chinese Restaurant (ul Pirin) Meals about 5 lv. If you're sick of pizzas, and not game enough to try any local food, try Bansko's only oriental restaurant. The food is authentic but it does seem strange tucking into a bowl of noodles in such a traditional Bulgarian town.

Getting There & Away

From Sofia (5 lv, three hours), about six daily buses travel directly to Bansko via Blagoevgrad and several more going to Gotse Delchev also stop at the Bansko bus station (☎ 2420) on ulitsa Patriarh Evtimii. In addition, four or five buses go to Blagoevgrad only and two more depart for Plovdiv (9 lv, 3½ hours) at 7.10am and 8.20am.

The train station (☎ 2215) on Akad Yordan Ivanov, is on the narrow-gauge rail route between Septemvri (on the main Sofia-Plovdiv line) to Dobrinishte. Take this laboriously slow train (about five hours from Septemvri to Bansko) for the scenery and ambience because it's certainly not the quickest way to/from Bansko. Ten daily trains travel along this route and stop at Avramovo, the highest station in the Balkans.

Taxis hanging around the bus station can be chartered for tours around the region.

SANDANSKI
САНДАНСКИ
☎ 0746 • pop 27,600

Sandanski, 65km south of Blagoevgrad, is often ignored and used only as a connection to Melnik. However, it's a pleasant and laid-back town that boasts a long pedestrian mall and huge city park. Sandanski is also an alternative base for anyone wanting a little more nightlife and excitement than Melnik (17km to the south-east) and for hiking (see the boxed text 'Hiking in the Pirin Mountains' earlier in this chapter). Sandanski's constant sunshine and mineral springs, which apparently cure all sorts of ills such as bronchitis and asthma, attract tourists from all over the Balkans.

Sandanski was first settled in about 2000 BC by Thracians and later by the Romans and Slavs. The town is, according to legend, the birthplace of Spartacus, who led a rebellion of slaves in modern-day Sicily against the Romans in 74 BC. The town was almost completely destroyed in the 6th century AD by barbarians but was later rebuilt and became an important town in the First Bulgarian Empire.

Information

The Visitor Centre (☎ 22 549, e bicc@omerga.bg) on ploshtad Bulgaria is supposedly open daily 10am to 7pm but in reality has erratic opening hours. It offers local tours, for example, to Melnik and Rozhen Monastery on Saturday (only) by bus (12 lv per person) and can help with private rooms (see Places to Stay & Eat later in this section). There are foreign-exchange offices along bulevard Makedonia and a bank in the Hotel Sandanski. The post office and telephone centre are at ploshtad Bulgaria.

Things to See & Do

The **Archaeological Museum** (☎ 23 188, *bul Makedonia 55; admission 1.50 lv; open Mon-Fri 9am-12.30pm & 2.30pm-6pm in winter, open daily in summer*) is obviously a labour of love for the curators, but most visitors will see little more than a mass of dishevelled and unlabelled artefacts. Of some interest is the explanation (in Bulgarian) about Sandanski's apparent link to Spartacus and items from the adjacent ruins of the 5th-century **St Joan's Basilica**.

The **Sveti Georgi Church** (*ul Sv Sv Kiril i Metodii 10; admission free; open daily 8am-6pm*) was built in 1861 and is the only church in Sandanski remaining from that period. Visitors are welcome, but please be discreet, because this is a functioning church.

A few art galleries showcase some of the region's better artists, including the **Hudozhestvena Gallery** (*bul Makedonia*).

The huge **Town Park** contains over 200 species of plants from the Mediterranean, as well as **mineral baths** and **swimming pools** (*admission to either about 1.50 lv; open daily in summer about 9am-7pm*), a small **lake** with paddle boats and a **Summer Theatre**.

Special Events

The bigger festivals include **St Vasil's Day Folk Concert** (January 1), the **Sandanski Celebrations** (Thursday after Orthodox

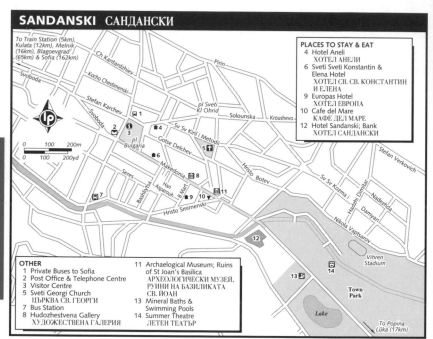

SANDANSKI САНДАНСКИ

To Train Station (5km),
Kulata (12km), Melnik
(16km), Blagoevgrad
(65km) & Sofia (162km)

PLACES TO STAY & EAT
4 Hotel Aneli
  ХОТЕЛ АНЕЛИ
6 Sveti Sveti Konstantin &
  Elena Hotel
  ХОТЕЛ СВ. СВ. КОНСТАНТИН
  И ЕЛЕНА
9 Europas Hotel
  ХОТЕЛ ЕВРОПА
10 Cafe del Mare
  КАФЕ ДЕЛ МАРЕ
12 Hotel Sandanski; Bank
  ХОТЕЛ САНДАНСКИ

OTHER
1 Private Buses to Sofia
2 Post Office & Telephone Centre
3 Visitor Centre
5 Sveti Georgi Church
  ЦЪРКВА СВ. ГЕОРГИ
7 Bus Station
8 Hudozhestvena Gallery
  ХУДОЖЕСТВЕНА ГАЛЕРИЯ
11 Archaeological Museum; Ruins
  of St Joan's Basilica
  АРХЕОЛОГИЧЕСКИ МУЗЕЙ.
  РУИНИ НА БАЗИЛИКАТА
  СВ. ЙОАН
13 Mineral Baths &
  Swimming Pools
14 Summer Theatre
  ЛЕТЕН ТЕАТЪР

Easter Sunday), the **Pirin Folk National Festival** (early September) – which features plenty of dancing and music – and the merry **Young Red Wine Festival** (early December).

Places to Stay & Eat

The tourist office (☎ 22 549, e bicc@ omerga.bg) on ploshtad Bulgaria can organise *rooms* (with a shared bathroom) in private homes for about 22 lv per person. Each hotel listed here offers rooms with a private bathroom.

Hotel Aneli (☎ 28 952, pl Bulgaria) Doubles 20-25 lv, apartments 35 lv. Easy to spot and overlooking the main square, the Aneli offers clean and comfortable accommodation with a TV. It's excellent value and often full so get there early or book ahead.

Sveti Sveti Konstantin & Elena Hotel (☎ 22 423, bul Makedonia) Doubles 20 lv, apartments 30 lv. This place is central, homely and friendly. The rooms are cosy (ie, a little small) and contain a TV.

Europas Hotel (☎ 25 361, e evropas -ml@dir.bg, ul 8 Mart 11) Singles/doubles 24/35 lv. Also popular, central and quiet, Europas offers more amenities (ie, TV, air-con and fridge) than most hotels in this price range. The decor may not be to everyone's taste but it's hard to complain at this price.

Hotel Sandanski (☎ 25 165, fax 25 271, bul Makedonia) Singles/doubles US$72/90. About the only top-end hotel south of Sofia, the Sandanski boasts a pool and the usual amenities (ie, TV and fridge) expected from a four-star hotel, but it's way overpriced for foreigners. Rates include breakfast.

Cafe del Mare (bul Makedonia) Meals from 3.50 lv. This is cafe opposite the Archaeological Museum and is popular with the trendy set. Prices are a little high but it has a menu in English.

Most hotels listed previously also have *restaurants*. Dozens of charming *cafes* can be found along bulevard Makedonia and in the Town Park.

Getting There & Away
Buses to Sofia (6 lv, 3½ hours) leave about every one or two hours and travel via Blagoevgrad and Dupnitsa. Most are run by private companies and leave from offices around the northern section of ploshtad Bulgaria. From the public bus station (☎ 22 130) on ulitsa Hristo Smirnenski, buses go to Melnik, and on to Rozhen, at 5.15am, 7.40am, 11.40am, 3.30pm and 5.30pm. They return to Sandanski about one hour later.

Sandanski is conveniently on the train line between Sofia and Athens (Greece), but the train station (☎ 22 213) is about 5km west of the town centre. From Sofia, three fast trains (1st/2nd class 7.40/5.20 lv, 3½ hours) travel to Sandanski every day, via Blagoevgrad and Dupnitsa, and continue to Kulata (on the Greek border). For details about trains to Greece, see Land in the Getting There & Away chapter.

Any of the plethora of taxis around Sandanski can be chartered as far as Melnik and Rozhen.

MELNIK
МЕЛНИК
☎ 07437 • pop 267
Melnik is wedged into a narrow sandstone valley about 20km north of the Greek border. The village built its reputation on the production, and far-flung trade, of its dark-red wine and tobacco. Almost a century ago, it was a thriving commercial centre with 20,000 inhabitants but today Melnik is officially Bulgaria's smallest town.

Foreigners and locals flock here to walk around the Bulgarian national revival period homes and church ruins, see the strange, so-called 'sand pyramids' that surround the village, and to sample some traditional food and wine. Melnik is also a base from which to explore the southern Pirin Mountains (see the boxed text 'Hiking in the Pirin Mountains' earlier in this chapter). However, it is a little overrated by tourist authorities and travel agencies. While Melnik is certainly worth visiting if you're in the region, traditional villages such as Koprivshtitsa, Arbanasi and Tryavna are larger, more convenient and more attractive.

History
The area around Melnik was first settled by the Thracian Medi tribe, to which the legendary Spartacus belonged. It was later settled by the Romans, then by Slavs between the 7th and 9th centuries AD. The name Melnik probably comes from the Slavic word *mel* for 'sandy chalk', which can be seen in the surrounding cliffs.

Melnik came to prominence in the early 13th century as the regional seat of Alexei Slav (often given the title of Despot). He used the town as the capital of his personal fiefdom and built several monasteries and a large fortress (the remains of which are in evidence today). Melnik became a centre of education and culture, and local artisans produced much sought-after jewellery, wood-carving and ceramics. It also produced large quantities of red wine, which was traded as far as modern-day Croatia and Venice.

Melnik fell into decline during the Ottoman occupation, but regained prosperity through the Bulgarian national revival period in the late 18th and early 19th centuries. During this time, many traditional houses were built, often on the ruins of Roman and Slavic homes. Before the start of the Balkan Wars (1912–13), Melnik was home to up to 20,000 people but the town was largely destroyed by fire in the war. Since then, Melnik has been significantly restored and rebuilt.

Orientation & Information
Melnik's major (unnamed) thoroughfares run east-west along both sides of an often-dry tributary of the Melnishka River. Walking paths and goat tracks run up both sides of the valley to the homes and ruins. If you're driving, please do everyone a favour and park at the western end and walk into the village. And remember, this is really a village: there's nowhere reliable to change money (the nearest bank or foreign-exchange office is in Sandanski) and there is no Internet centre.

Wine Tasting
Melnik has been renowned for producing quality wines for over 600 years. The locally

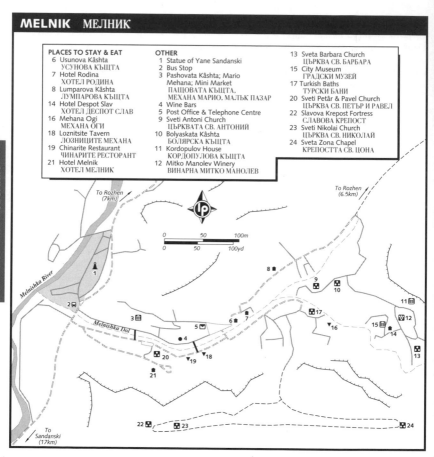

MELNIK МЕЛНИК

PLACES TO STAY & EAT
6 Usunova Kâshta
   УСУНОВА КЪЩТА
7 Hotel Rodina
   ХОТЕЛ РОДИНА
8 Lumparova Kâshta
   ЛУМПАРОВА КЪЩТА
14 Hotel Despot Slav
   ХОТЕЛ ДЕСПОТ СЛАВ
16 Mehana Ogi
   МЕХАНА ОГИ
18 Loznitsite Tavern
   ЛОЗНИЩИТЕ МЕХАНА
19 Chinarite Restaurant
   ЧИНАРИТЕ РЕСТОРАНТ
21 Hotel Melnik
   ХОТЕЛ МЕЛНИК

OTHER
1 Statue of Yane Sandanski
2 Bus Stop
3 Pashovata Kâshta; Mario
   Mehana; Mini Market
   ПАШОВАТА КЪЩТА.
   МЕХАНА МАРИО. МАЛЪК ПАЗАР
4 Wine Bars
5 Post Office & Telephone Centre
9 Sveti Antoni Church
   ЦЪРКВАТА СВ. АНТОНИЙ
10 Bolyaskata Kâshta
   БОЛЯРСКА КЪЩТА
11 Kordopulov House
   КОРДОПУЛОВА КЪЩТА
12 Mitko Manolev Winery
   ВИНАРНА МИТКО МАНОЛЕВ

13 Sveta Barbara Church
   ЦЪРКВА СВ. БАРБАРА
15 City Museum
   ГРАДСКИ МУЗЕЙ
17 Turkish Baths
   ТУРСКИ БАНИ
20 Sveti Petâr & Pavel Church
   ЦЪРКВА СВ. ПЕТЪР И РАВЕЛ
22 Slavova Krepost Fortress
   СЛАВОВА КРЕПОСТ
23 Sveti Nikolai Church
   ЦЪРКВА СВ. НИКОЛАЙ
24 Sveta Zona Chapel
   КРЕПОСТТА СВ. ЦОНА

grown grapes have an unappealing taste but produce a palatable, dark and heavy red wine. Several wine bars can be found along Melnik's cobblestone paths. Bottles of acceptable red and white can be bought for about 5 lv at shops and restaurants.

The **Mitko Manolev Winery** (☎ 234) is basically a cellar dug into the rocks, and an informal hut with tables and chairs, where you can sample, and of course buy, wines from Melnik and elsewhere in the region. It's along the short hillside trail between the Bolyaskata Kâshta ruins and the Kordopulov House.

The nearby **Damianitza Winery** (☎ 0746-24 114, e damianitza@melnik.bg; w www.melnikwine.bg) offers local wine tours. Contact them directly, or through the Hotel Despot Slav, about current programs and costs.

Museums
The houses in Melnik are typically built on the side of cliffs and on top of a basement (made of stone) in which wine is often made and/or stored. The living quarters on the upper floors usually offer glorious views. By decree, all buildings in Melnik

must be built and/or renovated in the Bulgarian national revival period style, and painted brown and white.

Kordopulov House (☎ *291; admission 2 lv, permission to take photos an extra 5 lv; open daily 8am-8pm)*, built in 1754 was the home of one of Melnik's foremost wine merchants. It's now one of the country's largest and more famous revival-period structures. Don't miss the huge warren of a wine cellar with 180m of labyrinthine caves hewn out of rock, and the lovely sitting rooms with murals and stained glass windows. The museum is the four-storey building on the cliff face at the end of the street, south of the creek. It's only 200m along a hillside track from the Bolyaskata Kâshta ruins.

Pashovata Kâshta *(admission 2 lv; open Mon-Fri 9am-noon & 1pm-4pm)* was built in 1815 and became famous as the place where Yane Sandanski proclaimed the liberation of Melnik from the Turks in 1912. It now houses a modest collection about the history of the village.

City Museum *(admission 1 lv; open Mon-Fri 9am-noon & 2pm-6pm)* features some traditional costumes, ceramics and jewellery from the Melnik region. Most interesting are the photos taken in the early 20th century of the bustling town. Look for the sign to the museum just before the Hotel Despot Slav.

Ruins

Bolyaskata Kâshta dates back to the 10th century and is therefore one of the oldest homes in Bulgaria. However, it's now completely ruined and only some walls still stand. Nothing is explained on site in any language but it's worth the short walk for the best **views** of Melnik. In front of the ruins are the remains of the 19th-century **Sveti Antoni Church**, which is closed and not signposted in any language.

Of the 70 or so churches that used to be in Melnik, only 40 have survived, and most of these are now in ruins. A path (signposted in English) starts almost opposite the main (lower) entrance of the Hotel Rodina. It leads to the ruins of the **Sveti Nikolai**

Church, originally built in 1756, and to the remains of the **Slavova Krepost Fortress**, built by Despot Slav. Both can be admired from the Bolyaskata Kâshta ruins, or from near the Lumparova Kâshta hotel (so you can see if the ruins are worth the short, but steep, climb). The trail then heads east along the ridge for about 300m to the ruins of the **Sveta Zona Chapel**.

Other ruins that you can wander about include the **Turkish Baths**, which are easy to miss and difficult to recognise – they're just before the Mehana Ogi tavern so keep an eye out. Also the 1840 **Sveti Petâr & Pavel Church**, down from the car park of the Hotel Melnik, and the 15th-century **Sveta Barbara Church**, not far from the Kordopulov House are worth a look.

Special Events

Not surprisingly, most festivities seem to centre around the local wine-making industry. **Trifon Zarezan Festival** (14 February) is celebrated wildly (see the boxed text 'Bulgarian Wine' in the Facts for the Visitor chapter). Several events take place during the height of the grape-picking season in the first two weeks of October. There's also a **folkloric festival** on 1 April.

Places to Stay

Many private homes in Melnik offer *rooms*. The standard rate is about 22 lv per person, but single travellers will often have to pay for a double room at 44 lv. All rooms have a shared bathroom, but are cosy, clean, central and usually quiet (unless you happen to stay near a particularly noisy mehana). Look for the 'For Rent' signs in English along the main streets.

Lumparova Kâshta (mobile ☎ 0488-92 445) Rooms with shared bathroom 10 lv per person. The cosy rooms contain two or three beds with thick woollen blankets and have balconies with awesome views. The multilingual staff offer traditional food and wine-tasting. It's an ideal place to try some local plonk because you'd never find your way back from here at night after a few glasses. It's up a steepish path that starts behind Usunova Kâshta.

Usunova Kâshta (☎ 270) Singles/doubles with bathroom 20/40 lv. The rooms are quiet, clean and good value so this is one place to head for as soon as you arrive. The rooms surround a quaint courtyard and are painted a dazzling white. Rates include breakfast. It's on the flat side of the river, so no climbing is required to reach it.

Hotel Rodina (☎ 249) Singles/doubles with bathroom 15/20 lv. Although a bit uninspiring compared to other places, it's good value – perhaps it's a last resort if the other places are full. Enter from the lower (southern) door.

Hotel Despot Slav (☎/fax 271) Singles/double/triples 30/40/50 lv, apartments 66 lv, all with bathroom. This is one of the most traditional and authentic places in Melnik and definitely worth a splurge. Although a short walk from most restaurants, it is quiet. The rooms and apartments are large, well-furnished and feature a TV, fridge and kettle. Rates include breakfast. The apartments are worth booking ahead.

Hotel Melnik (☎ 272) Doubles with bathroom 30 lv. This large, comparatively modern hotel has been built (more or less) in the traditional style. It is unobtrusively situated on the hillside with great views of the village. Although some rooms are smallish, they're clean and comfortable and contain a fridge. Officially, there are no singles rates but it's worth asking if business is slow, which it often is.

Places to Eat
Mario Mehana Salads about 1.50 lv, main meals from 3.50 lv. Next to the Mini Market (labelled in English), the poorly signposted Mario is one of several cosy, friendly and traditional taverns along this part of the street.

Mehana Ogi Main meals 3.50-5.50 lv. This tiny tavern is far from the tourist crowds, so you may have the whole place (which is little more than about five tables) to yourself. Service may be slow but the staff are friendly and the food is authentically Bulgarian.

The two largest and most patronised restaurants in Melnik are opposite each other and both offer menus in English (well, sort of). At both, salads cost about 1.70 lv, a plate of grilled meat is about 4.50 lv and a small bottle of beer will set you back about 1 lv. *Chinarite Restaurant* does not offer any Chinese food, despite the name, and is a bit cheerless. The servings are large, however, and each meal comes with a free slice of herb bread. *Loznitsite Tavern* has an inviting, vine-covered outdoor setting, and an extensive menu, but the service could be friendlier.

Getting There & Away
Bus schedules between Melnik and Sofia are erratic and often change, so check with locals in Melnik. At the time of research, one bus leaves Melnik for Sofia (6.80 lv, four hours) at the ungodly hour of 6am and returns to Melnik from the Princess Hotel bus station west in Sofia at about 10am. Buses from Sandanski (see Getting There & Away in the Sandanski section earlier in this chapter) to Melnik continue to Rozhen.

ROZHEN MONASTERY
РОЖЕНСКИ МАНАСТИР
About 7km north-east of Melnik is the Rozhen Monastery (*admission free, but donations of 1-2 lv encouraged; open daily 7am-7pm; photos & video cameras not permitted*), also known as the Birth of Virgin Mary Monastery. It was originally built in 1217, but nothing remains from that era. It was rebuilt in the late 16th century, but destroyed again by the Turks soon after. Most of what remains today was built between 1732 and the end of the 18th century. Much of the monastery has been significantly renovated in the last 30 years.

The **Nativity of the Virgin Church**, originally built in 1600, contains some marvellous stained-glass windows, 200-year-old murals, woodcarvings and iconostases. Unusually, the **refectory** on the second floor also has murals. But it's the proximity to Melnik, the pleasant vine-covered courtyard, and the spectacular setting overlooking the unique sandy cliffs (particularly photogenic in the afternoon), which attract most visitors.

About 200m before the monastery car park is the (closed) **Sts Kiril & Metodii Church**, in front of which is the grave of Yane Sandanski (1872–1915), a Macedonian revolutionary leader. For locals, the year's highlight is the **Rozhen Fair**, which is held on 8 September.

Places to Stay & Eat

Hotel Rozhena (☎ *07437-211)* has comfortable singles/doubles with a TV, bathroom and breakfast for 30/40 lv, more luxurious double apartments are about 100 lv. Sauna and gym are available to hotel guests, and a swimming pool is available to patrons of the *restaurant*. A few *mehanas* are near the bus stop in the village. The *cafe* next to the monastery car park sells drinks and snacks.

Getting There & Away

From Melnik to the monastery by road is 7.2km, including the steep 800m uphill bit from Rozhen village. All buses from Sandanski (see earlier) to Melnik continue to Rozhen village. The popular hiking trail (6.5km) from Melnik starts from near the track up to the Boyaskata Kâshta ruins, and continues along the dry creek-bed – look for the small white, orange and green signs (in English). The trail has no shade, so, in summer, walk early in the morning or late in the afternoon, and take plenty of water.

Rodopi Mountains
Родопи Планина

The 15,000-sq-km Rodopi Mountains stretch from Velingrad to Smolyan and across into Greece (though about 85% of the mountain range is in Bulgaria). Named after the Thracian god, Rhodopa, the mountains are home to spectacular gorges and caves near Trigrad and Yagodina, the Batak and Dospat lakes and the most extensive pine forests in Bulgaria. It's perfect for hiking in summer and skiing in winter at Pamporovo or Chepelare (see later in this chapter). The average height is low (only 785m) but the highest peak, Mt Golyan Perelik, near Smolyan, is 2190m.

BATAK
БАТАК
☎ 03553 • pop 4500

It's hard to imagine that this modest and economically depressed town has had such a bloody history (see the boxed text 'Massacre at Batak'). The major attraction for locals is the nearby **Batak Lake**. It's popular for **fishing** and **swimming** in summer (when it's dry and least attractive) and **boats** are available for rent near the Hotel Panorama. See the boxed text 'Hiking in the Rodopi Mountains' earlier for information about **hiking** around these ranges from Batak.

The Church of Sveti Nedelya, the Ethnological Museum and the History Museum are the three well-signed and adjacent attractions in town. A combined ticket costs 2 lv (admission free on Thursday). Each attraction is open daily from 8am to noon and 1pm to 5pm, but visit the History Museum first to make sure the other two places are unlocked.

The **Church of Sveti Nedelya**, built in 1813, was the final refuge for 2000 locals who fought the Turks in 1876. Inside, there is obvious evidence (captions in English) of the subsequent massacre, such as bullet holes and a macabre, half-covered tomb with dozens of skulls. The nearby **Ethnological Museum**, one of the few Bulgarian national revival period houses in Batak, contains costumes and other incidental items, from the late 19th century.

The Massacre at Batak

During the 1876 April Uprising most of the population of Batak fought against the Turks under the leadership of Peter Goranov. They successfully held the Turks at bay for nine days before the aggressors eventually gained control. In brutal retaliation, the Turks burned down the village and massacred almost every citizen (between 5000 and 6000 people). The massacre was reported in the English press and (eventually) acknowledged and denounced by the British government. It was the catalyst for the Russian-Turkish War that started a year later.

SOUTHERN BULGARIA

Hiking in the Rodopi Mountains

If you want to explore the region around Chepelare, Smolyan and Shiroka Lûka, look for the *West Rhodopean Region* or *Western Rhodope Mountains* maps (1:100,000), available at the tourist offices in Pamporovo, Chepelare and Smolyan. These maps detail (in English) various hiking trails (around three to five hours) and five routes designed for **mountain bikes**. The *Rodopi* map (1:100,000) of the whole mountain range, published by Kartografia, is detailed (in Cyrillic).

The Mountains of Bulgaria by Julian Perry describes (but with poor maps) a trek from Hizha Studenents, near Pamporovo, to Hizha Rodoposki Partizanin, near Hrabrino, about 14km south-west of Plovdiv. Hikers can stay in huts along the way. If you wish to follow the same route allow five to seven days.

The ideal base for shorter hikes is Shiroka Lûka. From there, you can choose one of nine marked trails, including one to Chepelare, via Kukuvitsa (two to three hours one way) and another to Mt Golyam Perelik (five to six hours). Other excellent short hikes along marked trails include:

Batak to Hizha Teheran – about four hours
Chepelare to Hizha Igrev – about three hours. From there, continue to Shiroka Lûka (three hours) or Pamporovo (seven hours)
Haskovo to Hizha Aida – 26km west by road (four to five hours)
Pamporovo to Progled and back across the scenic Rozhen fields – an (easy) five-hour return trip
Smolyan to Hizha Smolyanski Ezera at the Smolyan Lakes – about three hours one-way

On the main square is the **History Museum** (☎ *2339, pl Osvodozhenie*). The downstairs crypt contains names of some locals who fought against the Turks. Predictably, the upper floors contain plenty of graphic displays about the 1876 April Uprising, massacre and Russian-Turkish War. Nothing is captioned in English, but it's hard not to be moved.

There are no hotels in Batak itself but several are dotted along the south-western shore of the lake, such as the ***Hotel Panorama***. The ***International Youth Tourist Centre*** (☎ *3385*), also known as the Orbita Hotel, charges 37/48 lv for singles/doubles including breakfast. These hotels, and several *cafes* and *restaurants*, are strung along the 1.2km access road, which starts about 7km west of Batak along the road to Rakitovo. The larger hotels stay open all year, but some cafes and restaurants only operate on weekends, especially during the winter months.

Four buses leave each day from Batak and go to Plovdiv. The three daily buses between Batak and Velingrad pass the turn-off to the lake.

CHEPELARE
ЧЕПЕЛАРЕ

☎ 03051 • pop 3000 • elevation 1150m

Chepelare is a delightful village and a downmarket ski resort (see the boxed text 'Skiing at Pamporovo & Chepelare'). It's also an alternative base to the expensive and expansive Pamporovo, 6km to the south. In summer, the nearby mountains offer excellent hiking (see the boxed text 'Hiking in the Rodopi Mountains' earlier in this chapter). The town is undergoing some impressive restoration thanks to the Beautiful Bulgaria Project.

The tourist information centre (☎ 2110, e tic@infotel.bg) on ulitsa Murdjovska 23a is open Monday to Friday 8.30am to 12.30pm and 1.30pm to 5.30pm. It's 100m up from the town square, across the park and along the main road. It can provide a few brochures (when staff actually turn up). The Hebros Bank is 300m down the main street, ulitsa Vasil Dechev, from the square. The combined post office and telephone centre is near the square (which is dominated by the abandoned Hotel Zdravets), as is the only Internet agency.

Museum of Speleology & Karst

Also called the Cave Museum, the Museum of Speleology & Karst (☎ 3051, ul Shina Andreeva 9a; admission 2 lv; open Mon-Fri 9am-noon & 1.30pm-5pm), is the only one of its kind in Bulgaria and, possibly, the Balkans. There are of minerals, bats (in bottles) and remnants of previous cave inhabitants (for example, bears and lions) to see, as well as exhibits about the marvellous caves near Trigrad and Yagodina. While only a few captions are in English and/or German, it doesn't matter too much because the manager can play an informative tape over the loudspeaker in either language (though trying to link the narrative with the displays is not easy!). The museum is in the Hotel Pesternika building, about 200m up from the bus station on the hillside overlooking the village.

Places to Stay & Eat

Contact the tourist office in Chepelare or Smolyan (see later) for an updated list of private homes in Chepelare that offer *rooms* for about 20 lv per person with a shared bathroom.

Hotel Phoenix (☎ 3408, ul Murgavets 4) Singles/doubles with bathroom 14/18 lv. About 200m up ulitsa Vasil Dechev from the town square, the Phoenix is centrally located. It offers delightful, spotless rooms with a TV. There's also a *restaurant*.

Hotel Savov (☎ 2036, ul Vasil Dechev 7). Doubles 20 lv, apartments 30 lv, all with bathroom. This homely place, opposite the Hebros Bank, offers large, comfortable and airy rooms with a TV. Apartments have a sitting area, TV, fridge and an extra bed. The *restaurant* is popular, and worth trying even if you're staying elsewhere.

Hotel Gergana (☎ 4201, ul Hristo Botev 75) Doubles with bathroom 33 lv. The Gergana, along the road from Plovdiv, has a handful of rooms with a TV in a cosy, family-run environment. The *restaurant* specialises in home-cooked traditional cuisine, which heavily features potatoes (and nothing much else). Rates include breakfast.

A dozen or more other hotels in Chepelare are signposted from along the Plovdiv road, but they're too far to walk to from the bus station (and there are no taxis in town).

Mehana Chepelare Main meals 4-5 lv. This covered outdoor tavern, near the town square, has a limited menu (in English) and is a great place for a drink.

Getting There & Away

The bus station is across a footbridge, 200m north-east of the town square. Buses leave for Smolyan, via Pamporovo, hourly, and the regular services between Plovdiv and Madan, and Plovdiv and Smolyan, also stop in Chepelare.

MOMCHILOVTSI
МОМЧИЛОВЦИ

☎ 03023 • pop 3000 • elevation 1100m

This charming mountainside village is about 3km up from the main (eastern) road between Chepelare and Smolyan. It's home to a number of Bulgarian painters and writers who appreciate solitude. For travellers, Momchilovtsi is an alternative base to the ski resorts at Chepelare or Pamporovo. It's also a relaxing place to unwind or a great place for hiking in summer.

The **Historical & Ethnographical Museum** (☎ 2272, ul Byalo More), up behind the village square, is rarely open. Ring the museum for opening hours, and if you want to visit (or buy something from) one of the local **artists** or **weavers**.

The village-wide lethargy is suspended during the four-day celebrations either side of **St Konstantin & Elena Day** (21 May).

The tourist office in Smolyan (see later in this chapter) and Chepelare (see earlier in this chapter) can provide a list of private homes in Momchilovtsi that offer *rooms* with a shared bathroom for about 22 lv per person. Several cosy *pensions* are signposted along the road from the south for about 500m before the village square. One is the *Rodopchanka Hotel* (☎ 2863, ul Byalo More 40), which offers singles/ doubles with a bathroom and breakfast for as little as 15/20 lv. *Shadravana Restaurant*, in the park below the square, is a charming place for a meal or drink. A handful of *cafes* surround the village square.

Skiing at Pamporovo & Chepelare

These two ski resorts in the Rodopi Mountains are not nearly as convenient as Vitosha, Borovets and Bansko. But being only 60km north of the Greek border, the resorts boast over 250 days of sunshine a year and with plenty of snow between mid-December and mid-April, skiing conditions are often ideal. More information about the region is available on the Web site [W] www.travel-bulgaria.com/pamporovo.

Pamporovo

Pamporovo has eight major ski runs (total of 17.5km), 25km of cross-country trails and four training slopes. The advantages are that the facilities are comparatively new and the slopes and elevators are well maintained. On the other hand, the resort at Pamporovo is very spread out and charmless, yet so popular that accommodation is hard to come by for independent skiers and travellers. Alternative places to stay are nearby Chepelare, Momchilovtsi and Shiroka Lûka.

There are five chairlifts and nine draglifts. Usually, three of these chairlifts – Nos 1, 2 and 4 – open during the summer. Chairlifts cost 5/7 lv one way/return and a day pass costs about 30 lv. Minibuses from the hotels to the lifts are free to anyone with a lift pass.

Pamporovo caters well to families and provides a ski kindergarten for the kids. The slopes are ideal for beginners and training is easy to arrange. Most instructors speak English and German and charge about 122 lv to 180 lv per person for 12 to 24 hours' training, spread over six to 12 days. Individual instruction costs a lot more: about 31/45 lv for one/two hours.

Equipment can be rented from one of a dozen or more ski shops. As an example, a complete set of alpine ski gear will cost about 25/63/112 for one/three/six days, and full cross-country equipment is about 18 lv per day. **Snowboarding** is ideal; visit the British-run Snow Shack if you want to hire snowboarding gear and/or join a training course.

Chepelare

This quieter and cheaper ski resort, but far less established, is famous as the birthplace of Bulgaria's 1998 Winter Olympic women's biathlon champion, Ekaterina Dafovska. The only ski runs, Mechi Chal I (3200m) and Mechi Chal II (5200m), are two of the best slopes in the Balkans. The chairlift (which doesn't operate in summer) is about 1.5km south of the village centre and is signposted off the road to Pamporovo. The only place to hire gear is *Orion Ski* (☎/fax 03051-2142) at the lift but few instructors are available. Chepelare is a good place to buy some cheap, locally made ski gear.

Buses between Smolyan and Banite, and Plovdiv and Banite, regularly pass through Momchilovtsi, as do the less-frequent services between Sofia and Madan, and Plovdiv and Madan.

PAMPOROVO
ПАМПОРОВО
☎ 3021 • elevation 1650m

Set in the gorgeous eastern Rodopi Mountains, about 83km south of Plovdiv, Pamporovo is one of the four major ski resorts in Bulgaria (see the boxed text 'Skiing at Pamporovo & Chepelare'). It's also an inviting place to visit in summer, though many facilities are closed at this time. The downside is that the resort is both very expensive (in summer and winter) and expansive, and it lacks charm and atmosphere. The highlight of the local social calendar is the **Rozhen Folk Festival** (late August), held in the Rozhen fields between Pamporovo and Progled.

Orientation & Information

The centre of Pamporovo is the T-junction of the roads to Smolyan, Chepelare and Devin, via Shiroka Lûka. From this junction, the resort spreads along several roads for up to 4km. Most hotels, restaurants and shops in more remote parts of the resort are closed from May to October, but everything in and around the central Hotel Perelik is open year-round.

Activities

In summer, a number of activities are on offer. Pamporovo Sports Services, in the Pamporovo Shopping Centre sandwiched between the Perelik and Murgavets hotels, can arrange **mountain bikes** (3 lv per hour), **guides** (15 lv per hour) for hiking, and **tennis** courts and equipment. Some hotels, such as the Murgavets, offer **massages** (about 30 lv per hour). Around the central T-junction, a few motley **horses** can be hired (about 15 lv per hour). For **hiking** see the boxed text 'Hiking in the Rodopi Mountains' earlier in this section.

See the boxed text 'Skiing at Pamporovo & Chepelare' for winter sports.

Places to Stay & Eat

In winter, most foreign visitors will be on package tours (that include accommodation) from overseas, or perhaps Sofia, or be on a day trip from Plovdiv. Consequently, there's little point recommending too many hotels and most hotels in winter don't offer rates that are acceptable to individual travellers.

The following is an example of the sort of rates charged in summer by a few of the larger two- and three-star hotels. Prices in winter will be about 50% higher. Each hotel listed offers rooms with a bathroom, TV and fridge, and rates include a buffet breakfast.

Hotel Perelik (☎ 405, e pamporovo@ bsbg.net) Singles 39 lv & doubles 50-60 lv. This ex-Balkantourist monolith is slowly being upgraded, and offers decent facilities and sensible prices. The more expensive rooms have been nicely renovated and feature spotless bathrooms. The older cheaper rooms are not so welcoming but nevertheless acceptable. The complex also contains a swimming pool, bowling alley, several *restaurants* and a disco.

Hotel Murgavets (☎ 310, fax 366) Singles/doubles 32/65 lv. These rooms are large, new and particularly good value. It's next to Hotel Perelik and fairly convenient.

Hotel Arpha (☎ 322) Singles/doubles 25/55 lv. About 500m farther up from Hotel Perelik, this homely two-star hotel is cheaper and quieter than most places in the centre of the resort.

A plethora of *bars*, *cafes* and *restaurants* also offer all sorts of cuisines. Given the extent of the resort, you'll probably have to eat at, or near, your hotel in the evening if you don't have a car.

The White Deer (Hotel Murgavets complex) Also known as the White Hart, this is one of several bar-cum-restaurants near Hotel Perelik that offer Western food and drinks at typically high prices. For example, a cup of tea is 1 lv, a small bottle of beer is 2 lv, snacks are 3.50 lv and pizzas are from 6 lv to 8 lv. It also features live music most nights year-round.

Barbeque Lime Light Salads 1.50 lv, grills 4.50 lv. Right at the central T-junction, this easy-going place offers grilled fish and meat dishes, as well as tasty pizzas (5 lv for a large 'un), at comparatively reasonable prices.

Getting There & Away

Every hour, buses travelling between Smolyan and Chepelare pass through Pamporovo, as do the regular services between Smolyan and Plovdiv, and Smolyan and Sofia. A couple of buses go daily to Pamporovo directly from Sofia (9 lv to 10 lv, four hours) and up to eight leave Plovdiv (4.50 lv, two hours). The bus stop is at the 'Ski Lift No 1' chairlift at the central T-junction.

SMOLYAN
СМОЛЯН

☎ 0301 • pop 34,300 • elevation 1000m

Smolyan is the administrative centre of the southern Rodopi Mountains, and a bustling town with several worthwhile attractions, including one of the best museums in the country. Although named after a Thracian tribe which settled here in about 700 BC, Smolyan is a modern town with no obvious history. For travellers, it's an alternative place to stay to Pamporovo, a transport hub for connections to villages like Shiroka

SOUTHERN BULGARIA

Lûka (see later in this chapter) and a base for exploring the seven **Smolyan Lakes** (which once numbered 20). For **hiking** see the boxed text 'Hiking in the Rodopi Mountains' earlier in this chapter.

Orientation & Information

Smolyan is undoubtedly the longest (10km) town in Bulgaria and comprises the four villages (from east to west) of Ustovo, Raikovo, Smolyan and Ezerovo. The town centre is based around the Hotel Smolyan along the main road, bulevard Bulgaria. Nearby are the post office, banks and the helpful tourist office (☎ 25 040, W www.rodopi-bg.com), open Monday to Friday 9am to 5.30pm and Saturday 10am to 2pm. An Internet centre is inside the same building as the tourist office. The Regional Association of Rhodope Municipalities (☎/fax 23041, e arm@sm.unacs .bg) on bulevard Bulgaria 14, just down from the tourist office, represents the 20 local districts. It's worth contacting them if you're interested in local arts and crafts or want to organise a tour or guide.

Planetarium

Bulgaria's biggest planetarium (☎ 23 074, e planet@sm.unacs.bg, bul Bulgaria 20; admission 3 lv) is about 200m west of the Hotel Smolyan. It offers shows (35 to 40 minutes) in English, French or German at 2pm from Monday to Saturday; and in Bulgarian at 3pm from Monday to Saturday, and Sunday at 11am and 3pm. But to start the show in either English, French or German, staff need one hour's notice, and a minimum of 10 people or a total payment of at least 30 lv. The show with commentary in Bulgarian is still spectacular, even if you don't understand a word.

Historical Museum

One of the best of its kind in Bulgaria is Smolyan's Historical Museum (☎ 27 028, pl Bulgaria 3; admission 3 lv; open Tues-Sun 9am-noon & 1pm-5pm). The four levels feature over 150,000 exhibits, including archaeological artefacts from the Palaeolithic period and Thracian cemeteries from the late Bronze Age. There are also excavations from nearby caves, fascinating displays about weaving, woodcarving and ironwork and explanations about Bulgarian national revival period architecture. Also covered are musical instruments and frightening masks and costumes from regional festivals. Every item is fully captioned in English and tours in English can also be arranged. The museum is a five-minute walk up the steps beside the Drama Theatre diagonally opposite the Hotel Smolyan.

Smolyan Art Gallery

Directly opposite the museum is the Art Gallery (☎ 23 268; admission 2 lv; open Tues-Sun 9am-noon & 1.30pm-5pm). It houses an overwhelming 1800 paintings, sketches and sculptures by local, national and foreign artists. (You may not have much energy left to wander around the art gallery after visiting the museum.)

Places to Stay & Eat

The tourist offices in Smolyan and Chepelare (see earlier in this chapter) have updated lists of private homes in Smolyan offering *rooms* with a shared bathroom for about 22 lv per person. The tourist office in Smolyan also has a list of the current rates for all 20 or so hotels in town.

Hotel Markelov (☎ 27 442, ul N Filipov 14) Singles/doubles with bathroom 40/57 lv. A short taxi trip from central Raikovo, the Markelov offers three-star amenities and rooms with balconies, views and a TV. Rates include breakfast and a *restaurant* is attached.

Hotel Katerina (☎ 28 805, ul N Filipov 16) Singles/doubles with bathroom 25/35 lv. Not far from the Markelov, the Katerina is a homely, two-star hotel with friendly staff and comfortable rooms.

Hotel Smolyan (☎ 2661, bul Bulgaria 3) Singles/doubles 33/40 lv, apartments 66-154 lv, all with bathroom. This huge, former Balkantourist hotel dominates the town centre. Rooms haven't been updated since the 1970s, but it's OK value. Some rooms have balconies with forest views. Rates include breakfast and the hotel complex has an indoor swimming pool and sauna.

The Hotel Smolyan's outdoor *restaurant* has a menu in English but the prices are double those on the Bulgarian menu. Far cheaper is the *snack bar* between the hotel and tourist office.

Getting There & Away

The bus station in Raikovo (to the east of the town centre) has services to regional villages of little interest to travellers. Most buses to/from Smolyan use the Smolyan Bus Station (☎ 34 251), along bulevard Bulgaria to the west. From there, three or four buses leave each day for Sofia (10 lv, 3½ hours); between six and eight go to Plovdiv (5 lv, 2½ hours); and every hour something goes to Chepelare and Pamporovo. From this station, buses also go to Devin and Teshel for the caves near Trigrad and Yagodina (see later in this chapter). Local bus Nos 3, 8, 9, 11, 14 and 18 travel between both bus stations, via the Hotel Smolyan.

SHIROKA LÛKA
ШИРОКА ЛЬКА
● pop 1500

Shiroka Lûka is a picturesque village with three **Roman bridges** and dozens of 19th-century **homes** renovated in the style typical of the Bulgarian national revival period. Other attractions include the **Church of the Virgin Mary**, which was apparently built in less than 40 days in 1834 and the modest (but rarely open) **Ethnographical Museum**, in the Kalenjievi Kâshta house. For **hiking** see the boxed text 'Hiking in the Rodopi Mountains' earlier in this chapter.

The village is renowned for its traditional music, which is showcased during the week-long **music festival** in mid-April. The major festival is the **kukeri** (first Sunday in March), a classic folk event where locals with frightening masks and costumes chase away evil spirits at the beginning of spring.

The tourist offices in Smolyan and Chepelare (see earlier in this chapter) have updated lists of private homes in Shiroka Lûka that offer *rooms*. The only hotel is the *Hotel Margarita* (☎ 03030-793). Singles/doubles with a bathroom are 22/44 lv. Along the main road on the western side of the creek

this modern, but charming, hotel has rooms with a TV and breakfast is included.

Buses travel between Smolyan and Devin six to eight times daily, and stop anywhere along the road through Shiroka Lûka.

CAVES

Three of the largest and most fascinating of the 700 mapped caves in Bulgaria are in the southern Rodopi Mountains, not far from Smolyan. **Uhlovitsa Cave**, situated about 3km north-east of Mogilitsa, boasts numerous waterfalls (most spectacular in winter), and some bizarre formations, but it's impossible to reach without private transport.

The most accessible and developed caves in this region are near Trigrad and Yagodina. Both are open daily in summer between about 8am and 5pm, but the caretakers sometimes decide not to turn up on Monday. Between mid-October and mid-April, ring first to make sure someone is there to open up and to find out if the cave hasn't been closed (eg, due to a blocked road, or high water levels inside the cave). Admission to both caves includes a guided tour in Bulgarian.

Devin
Девин
☎ 03041

If you want to visit these two caves by bus, it's a good idea to base yourself in Devin, a modest but pleasant town. The **tourist office** (☎ 4161, ul Osvobozhdenie 5) is a good source of information. Several *pensions* are signposted from the bus station, such as *Villa Ismena* (☎ 4872), which has singles/doubles with a bathroom for 20/40 lv. To Devin, there are six to eight daily buses from Smolyan, four or five from Plovdiv and six or seven from Dospat. Between Monday and Friday, buses leave Devin at 7.45am and 6pm and travel through all villages in the region, including Trigrad and Yagodina.

Trigrad
Тпиград
☎ 03040

One of the most visited caves in Bulgaria (☎ 220; admission 4 lv) is near Trigrad. Speleologists revel in the abundant grottoes, while visitors can admire the **Devil's Throat Cave** (Dyavolskoto Gurlo Peshtera) – the name often given to the whole complex. The tour (which leaves when a few people turn up) lasts for about 20 minutes, but you are welcome to stay longer (under supervision of the caretaker). As you descend, you can hear (but unfortunately not see) a 45m-high waterfall. And don't forget to save some energy for the daunting set of steep steps at the exit and to watch out for the (harmless) bats.

Trigrad village is 2.3km south of the road from the cave entrance. All of the hotels in the village were closed at the time of writing, but the caretaker at the cave can arrange a *room* in a private home, or maybe one of the village hotels, such as *Hotel Stanoev* (☎ *225*), will reopen. Otherwise retreat to Devin or Smolyan, or hike to Yagodina (about 2½ hours).

Yagodina
Ягодина
☎ 03419

The Yagodina Cave (☎ *03419-200; admission 4 lv*), at 8km long is the longest known cave in the Rodopi Mountains. It has a number of abysses and labyrinthine tunnels and it is also one of the deepest caves in Bulgaria. The 45-minute tour highlights the remarkable stalagmites and stalactites, which often resemble curtains, and explains some history about Neolithic settlements who lived in the cave during the 6th millennium BC. Tours leave on the hour every hour between 9am and 5pm, except at midday.

Hotel Terzievi (☎ *03419-325*) is the only place in the village, or surrounding area, to stay. It offers singles/doubles with a shared bathroom for 10/20 lv. Rooms are comfortable and spotless, with woollen blankets and rugs and breakfast. It's well signposted about 200m above the village square. This cave is 6.4km south of the turn-off along the Smolyan-Dospat road, and exactly 3km south of Yagodina village.

You can hike to Trigrad (see earlier) or ask directions in Yagodina village to the start of the **South Rodopi Eco-trail**.

KOVACHEVITSA
КОВАЧЕВИЦА
pop 65 • elevation 1050m

One of southern Bulgaria's most picturesque villages is also one of the most difficult to reach. Kovachevitsa has been declared an architectural and historical reservation by the Bulgarian government because of its unique building style, which is influenced by Macedonian designs and uses abundant stone rather than wood. There's little to see or do in the village, except appreciate the fresh air and stunning scenery, but this may change in the future if or when renovations of the village finish and, more importantly, improvements in the road have commenced.

The only official place to stay is *Kapsazov's House* (mobile ☎ *048-902 122*), a gorgeous 19th-century home set in a pretty garden. Bed and breakfast costs 53 lv per person, and 85 lv for full board, which is almost obligatory because there's virtually nowhere else to eat. Several private homes also rent out *rooms* – hang around the village square for a few minutes until someone finds you and leads you to their abode.

At this stage, only two or three daily minibuses make it as far up the shocking road to Kovachevitsa from Gotse Delchev. If you're heading from Gotse Delchev by car, take the first (unsigned) turn-off east of the river and the right-hand (unsigned) road uphill before Marchevo village officially begins.

Bulgarian Thrace

PLOVDIV
ПЛОВДИВ
☎ 032 • **pop 376,500**

Bulgaria's second largest city occupies both banks of the Maritsa River on the Upper Thracian Plain. Like Veliko Târnovo to the north, the small but steep hills of Plovdiv attracted settlers – and invaders – from all regional empires over several millennia. Plovdiv is the second-largest road and railway hub and economic centre in Bulgaria. It's the first or last stop for many travelling between Bulgaria and Greece or Turkey.

Typically, the tourist authorities and travel agencies use cliches like 'you must see Plovdiv to see Bulgaria' and these sorts of phrases are not overstated. This modern thriving city is based around a majestic old town crammed with 18th- and 19th-century homes (often built and/or renovated in a unique baroque style), a dozen or more museums and art galleries, hill top ruins and Byzantine churches. And to top it off, Plovdiv boasts the most remarkable Roman amphitheatre in Bulgaria.

With so much to see in Plovdiv, and even more to explore by bus, train, taxi or private car near the city, most visitors end up staying longer than they originally planned.

History
Plovdiv is where two main transportation corridors converge – one between Asia Minor and Europe and another from Central Asia to Greece, via Ukraine. This strategic position accounts for Plovdiv's pre-eminence among various invaders. From excavations at Nebet Tepe (in the old town), it appears that as early as 5000 BC the Thracians created a settlement here, with several fortresses they called Eumolpias.

In about 341 BC, Philip II of Macedonia conquered the town and renamed it Philipoupolis (after himself). More walls were built around the Thracian fortress and Philipoupolis became an important military centre. The Romans came through in AD 46 and built streets, towers and aqueducts for the town they renamed Trimontium. The area was then plundered, and often destroyed, by the Goths in the mid-3rd century and by the Huns in the mid-5th century. Trimontium was renamed Pupulden when it became part of the First Bulgarian Empire and was still an important centre during the Second Bulgarian Empire.

Pupulden suffered extensive damage during an invasion by the Ottomans in 1371. The Turks eventually rebuilt the town, renamed it Philibe, and used it as a regional seat in the far-flung Ottoman Empire. For the next 200 years, the town grew in economic and military importance, and became a centre of the Eastern Orthodox church.

But it was the Bulgarian national revival period between the late 18th and early 19th centuries that rejuvenated Plovdiv and made the old town so attractive.

Orientation
Most of Plovdiv is south of the Maritsa River. The dreary, modern suburbs are to the north and the old town, with some 5000 residents, is to the east. The city is based around seven hills. The closest hills to the city are Nebet Tepe with the Thracian ruins, Sahat Tepe (Clock Hill) on which a clock tower stands, Bunardjika (also known as the Hill of the Liberators) to the west and Djendem (Hill of the Youth) in the south-west. The main shopping area and pedestrian mall is ulitsa Knyaz Aleksandâr, which links ploshtad Tsentralen with ploshtad Dzhumaya, and continues north to the river as ulitsa Rayko Daskalov.

Decent maps of Plovdiv are hard to find. *The Old Plovdiv Sightseeing Map* (5 lv), with the black cover, is overpriced, but worthwhile if you're planning to spend a lot of time plodding around the old town. Unless you're planning an extended stay, or venturing out into the suburbs, the maps in this guidebook will be sufficient.

Information
Tourist Offices Incredibly, Bulgaria's second-largest city does not have a dedicated tourist office. The Council of Tourism (☎ 55 409, ℮ satellite@euro.net), at ulitsa Tsar Ivaylo 2, open Monday to Friday 9am to 6pm, is an association of travel agencies. It's not a tourist office as such, but may be able to help with specific information.

Money Plenty of foreign-exchange offices can be found along the pedestrian mall and ulitsa Ivan Vazov (ideal if you're walking into town from the train or bus stations). Several exchange offices along the mall will also change travellers cheques, and some even offer cash advances with credit cards (with a 5% commission). Many exchange offices (like most of Plovdiv itself) close on Sunday, except for a few along the mall, and rates vary wildly so check around.

SOUTHERN BULGARIA

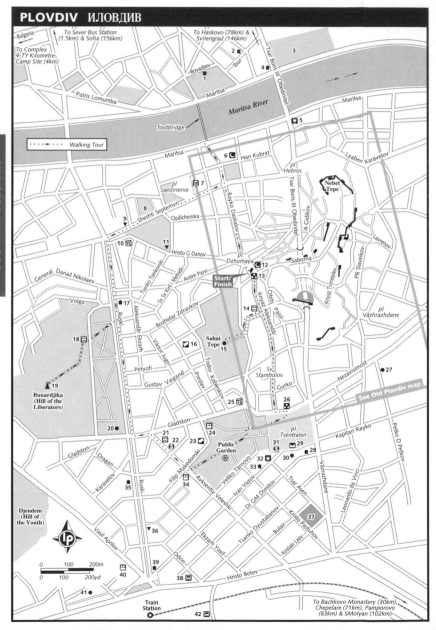

PLOVDIV ИЛОВДИВ

To Sever Bus Station (1.5km) & Sofia (156km)

To Haskovo (78km) & Svilengrad (146km)

To Complex 4-TY Kilometre Camp Site (4km)

Bulgana

Patris Lomumba

Boyadjiev 1

Ibur

Tsar Boris III Obedinitel

2

3

4

Maritsa

Maritsa River

footbridge

5

Maritsa

Maritsa

Lyaben Karavelov

········· Walking Tour

6 Han Kubrat

pl Hebros

Nebet Tepe

pl Saedinenie 7

Sheshti Septemvri

8

9

Opălchenska

Rayko Daskalov

Tsar Boris III Obedinitel

A Gidikov

Lavrenov

10

11

Hristo G Danov

pl Dzhumaya 12

Saborna

Knyaz Tseretelev

PR Slaveikov

General Danail Nikolaev

Tsanko Tserkovski

Sv i Kiril i Metodii

Antim Parvi

Start/ Finish

13

Oets Paisii

Knyaz Aleksandar

pl Văzrazhdane

Volga

17

Aleksandăr Ekzarh

Bozhidar Zdravkov

Viktor Jugo

Preslav

14

Sahat Tepe 15

16

Sv. Stambolov

Gurko

Nezavisimost

27

Petyofi

Gustav Vaigand

Todor Kableshkov

See Old Plovdiv map

Bunardjika (Hill of the Liberators)

18

19

25

26

Gladston

pl Tsentralen

Kapitan Rayko

Petko D Petkov

20

21

22

23

24

Public Garden

31

29

28

30

Dragan

Gladston

Filip Makedonski

Aksentiy Veleshki

Veliko Tănovo

Ivan Vazov

32

33

Tsar Asen

Văzrazhdane

Leonardo da Vinci

Karavelov

Ruski

35

34

Dr GM Dimitov

Tsanko Dyustabanov

Bulair

Kristo Pastuhov

Kostaki Leev

37

Djendem (Hill of the Youth)

Vasil Aprilov

36

Ekzarh Yosif

0   100   200m
0   100   200yd

39

40

38

41

Train Station

42

To Bachkovo Monastery (30km), Chepelare (71km), Pamporovo (83km) & SMolyan (102km)

Odrin

Hristo Botev

PLOVDIV ИЛОВДИВ

PLACES TO STAY
1　Novotel; Avis Car Rental
　　НОВОТЕЛ. АВИС
2　Traikov (Accommodation
　　Agency)
　　ТРАЙКОВ
4　Hotel Maritsa
　　ХОТЕЛ МАРИЦА
17　Noviz Hotel
　　ХОТЕЛ НОВИЦ
28　Trimontium Princess
　　Hotel & Restaurant; Tourist
　　Service Rent-a-Car
　　ХОТЕЛ ТРИМОНЦИУМ
　　ПРИНЦЕС И РЕСТОРАНТ
33　Esperantsa (Accommodation
　　Agency)
　　ЕСПЕРАНЦА
35　Hotel Leipzig 91
　　ХОТЕЛ ЛАЙПЦИГ 91
39　Trakiya Hotel
　　ХОТЕЛ ТРАКИЯ

PLACES TO EAT
9　Ristorante Da Lino
　　РЕСТОРАНТ ДА ЛИНО
11　Cafes
36　The Red Dragon
　　ЧЕРВЕНИЯТ ДРАКОН

OTHER
3　International Plovdiv
　　Fairgrounds
　　ИНТЕРНАЦИОНАЛЕН ПЛОВДИ-
　　ВСКИ ПАНАИР
5　Club Santo
　　КЛУБ САНТО
6　Imaret Mosque
　　ИМАРЕТ ДЖАМИЯ
7　Archaeological Museum
　　АРХЕОЛОГИЧЕСКИ МУЗЕЙ
8　Market; Cafes
10　RNet Internet
12　Dzhumaya Mosque
　　ДЖУМАЯ ДЖАМИЯ
13　Roman Stadium; I Claudius
　　Cafe
　　РИМСКИ СТАДИОН. КАФЕ АЗ
　　КЛАВДИЙ
14　Nikolai Masalitinov Dramatic
　　Theatre
　　ДРАМАТИЧЕН ТЕАТЪР
　　НИКОЛАЙ МАСАЛИТИНОВ
15　Clock Tower
　　ЧАСОВНИКОВА КУЛА
16　Greek Consulate
　　ГРЪЦКА КОНСУЛСТВО
18　Open-Air Theatre; Cafe
　　ЛЕТЕН ТЕАТЪР
19　Monument to the Soviet Army
　　ПАМЕТНИК НА СЪВЕТСКАТА
　　АРМИЯ
20　Gymnasium

21　Plovdiv Opera House;
　　Rondo Dance Club
　　ОПЕРАТА НА ПЛОВДИВ
22　Raffeisen Bank
　　РАФАЙЗЕН БАНКА
23　Turkish Consulate
　　ТУРСКО КОНСУЛСТВО
24　Luki Cinema
　　КИНО ЛЪКИ
25　Net Burger (Internet Agency)
26　Roman Forum
　　РИМСКИ ТЕАТЪР
27　Foreign Citizens Bureau
　　БЮРО ЗА ЧУЖДИ
　　ГРАЖДАНИ
29　Main Post Office &
　　Telephone Centre
30　City Local Transportation Co
　　(Bus Agency)
　　ГРАДСКИ ТРАНСПОРТ СО
31　Bulbank
　　БУЛБАНК
32　Police
34　Cinemax
37　University
38　Yug Bus Station
　　АВТОГАРА ЮГ
40　Cinema Geo Milev
　　КИНО ГЕО МИЛЕВ
41　Rila Bureau
　　БЮРО РИЛА
42　Rodopi Bus Station
　　АВТОГАРА РОДОПИ

SOUTHERN BULGARIA

There are a handful of banks near ploshtad Dzhumaya, such as the United Bulgarian Bank, which has an automatic teller machine (ATM) for all major credit cards. Otherwise, try the Raffeisen Bank on ulitsa Avksentiy Veleshki or the Bulbank, at the end of ulitsa Ivan Vazov.

Post & Communications The telephone centre, inside the main post office, is open daily from 6am to 11pm, and overlooks ploshtad Tsentralen. There are several Internet centres along the mall. Two others worth trying are RNet Internet on ulitsa Aleksandâr Ekzarh, and Net Burger, just down the steps from the overpass along ulitsa Gladston.

Bookshops The bookshops aren't worth recommending. So, for maps of Plovdiv, international magazines and occasional novels

in English, German and French, check out the numerous bookstalls around ploshtad Tsentralen, and at the bus and train stations.

Ruins

Plovdiv boasts several Roman ruins, but the names given to these on maps, tourist brochures and at the sites themselves are ambiguous.

Roman Amphitheatre This magnificent amphitheatre *(ul Hemus; admission 2 lv; open daily 8am-6pm)* was built by the Romans during the reign of Trajanus in early 2nd century AD. Incredibly, it was only uncovered during a freak landslide in 1972. Now lovingly restored, the amphitheatre, which at its peak could seat about 6000 spectators, is once again used for special events (often in late May and early June).

Plodding about Plovdiv

Happily, most attractions are in the city centre and accessible on foot. To help you make the most of your time, and to minimise backtracking, we have suggested a walking tour.

Allow at least half a day to wander around the old town and three hours around the modern city – plus time to climb hills and stop at cafes. More information about major attractions is listed under the relevant headings later in this chapter.

Walking Around the Old Town (Old Plovdiv map)

The best place to start and/or finish is ploshtad Dzhumaya, dominated by the **Dzhumaya Mosque**. From there, head along ulitsa Saborna, and turn right up ulitsa Mitropolit Paisii to the **Danov House**, **St Nikolai Church** and the massive **Church of Sveta Bogoroditsa**. Back on ulitsa Saborna, walk over the incredible overpass and perhaps browse in the quaint **souvenir stalls** and **antique shops**.

Farther up, the **State Gallery of Fine Arts** should not be missed. Continue up ulitsa Saborna and peer through the window of the restored, but often-closed, **Apteka** pharmacy. Not far up is another art gallery known as the **Zlatyo Boyadjiev House**. Before the junction, look for the entrance on the right to the charming **Church of St Konstantin & Elena**.

At the junction, turn left up ulitsa 4 Yanuari and see the abandoned and unexplained **roman columns**. Opposite is the museum known as **Balabanov House**, and just down an unnamed lane is the similar **Hindlian House**. Turn right (north) along the residential street of ulitsa Artin Gidikov, and at the junction walk up the steps to the Armenian **St Kevork Church**. Head back down ulitsa 4 Yanuari and left up ulitsa Dr Chomakov to the dramatic **ruins of Eumolpias** on Nebet Tepe hill. Have a drink at the **Rahat Tepe Bar** – go on, you deserve it! On the way back down, visit the excellent **Ethnographical Museum**.

Turn left along ulitsa Lavrenov and admire the remains of the **Hisar Kapiya** gate. On the left are the mildly interesting **Historical Museum** and **Nedkovich House** and farther down, on ulitsa PR Slaveikov, is the **St Nedelya Church**. Turn back a little and stroll down ulitsa Cyril Nektariev and ulitsa Pulden, at the end of which is **Lamartine House**. From there, follow the signs to the Ancient Theatre up the street, turn right down ulitsa Hemus where the **Roman Amphitheatre** will soon dramatically come into view.

Try to find the short cut that is to the north of the amphitheatre (or backtrack) to Lamartine House, from where a road leads down to the modern city level. As you climb down the steps the ruins of

Visitors can admire the amphitheatre for nothing from one of several lookouts along ulitsa Hemus or from the inevitable *cafes* at the top. But it's certainly worth paying the entrance fee, so you can clamber around the seats and stage. (Ignore requests to pay more than the advertised entrance fee from any unscrupulous character at the main gate.) Although accessible from ulitsa Hemus, there's an unsigned short cut from the back of the Church of Sveta Bogoroditsa along ulitsa T Samodomov.

Roman Stadium Ordinarily, the ruins of this stadium would not get much attention, but the anachronistic juxtaposition with the mall is amazing. Only a dozen rows of the northern section have been unearthed and partially restored. It's not possible to walk around the stadium, but it can be admired from the street level. Even better, enjoy a drink or meal at the aptly named I Claudius Cafe (see Places to Eat later in this section), which almost touches the ruins.

Roman Forum Just down the steps at the overpass near ploshtad Tsentralen are some fairly insignificant ruins, probably of interest to archaeological buffs only. Although not restored, signposted or labelled visitors can see the ruins from over the fence along the main road.

Plodding about Plovdiv

St Petka Church are on the right. You can also climb to the top of the rock for more excellent views of Plovdiv.

From there, take one of two paths to the main street level and turn right. Walk west through the fruit and vegetable **market**, go through the underpass below bul Tsar Boris III Obedinitel and take the steps to the right. Walk north along the bulevard Vâzrazhdane, and turn left along ulitsa Dr Vulkovich just before the tunnel. The **Sveta Marina Church** is on the right. Then turn right up the mall back to the Dzhumaya Mosque. Alternatively, start the walking tour around the modern city.

Strolling around the Modern City (Plovdiv map)
The most convenient place to start/finish is probably ploshtad Dzhumaya, dominated by the **Dzhumaya Mosque**. Stroll north along the mall as far as ulitsa Han Kubrat and have a quick peek at the decrepit **Imaret Mosque**. Return to the mall and, perhaps, look at the **Maritsa River** and the stalls along the **footbridge** farther up. Head back down the mall and turn right along ulitsa Sheshti Septemvri. The unimpressive **Archaeological Museum** is in ploshtad Saedinenie, and there's a busy **market** farther down.

Turn left (south) along bulevard Ruski and head to **Bunardjika**, also known as the Hill of the Liberators. Stroll through the lovely **park** to the **Open-Air Theatre**. If you have the energy, climb the steps to the hill-top **Monument to the Soviet Army**. Take any path back to bulevard Ruski and continue south. Opposite the brightly coloured **gymnasium**, turn left (east) along ulitsa Gladston and, at the **Plovdiv Opera House**, turn right along ulitsa Avksentiy Veleshki. Then stroll through the comparatively unkempt **Public Garden** back to the mammoth ploshtad Tsentralen.

Just down from the overpass at the start of the mall are ruins of the **Roman Forum**. Head up the mall and maybe stop for another drink at one of the plethora of cafes. Turn left at the Lotus Jeans shop, about 100m before the Roman Stadium, and head up the cobblestone street. Take the steps to the right and then turn right again uphill. Look for the sign (in Bulgarian) to the left to **Sahat Tepe**. Stone steps lead through the untidy **park** to the **clock tower** (a misnomer, because there's no clock).

Head back down to the mall, walk north past the **Nikolai Masalitinov Dramatic Theatre** on the left, and stop to admire the incongruous **Roman Stadium** under the street. Then head back to Dzhumaya Mosque and either start the walking tour in the old town (see earlier) or stop (again) for another drink at another cafe.

Nebet Tepe On this hill top *(admission free; always open)* are the **ruins of Eumolpias**, a Thracian settlement from about 5000 BC. The fortress and surrounding town were strategically placed on the 203m-high hill for obvious defensive purposes. The fortress was later invaded, occupied and fortified by Romans, Greeks and Turks. The Turks named it Nebet Tepe (Prayer Hill).

Because everything of importance and value has long since been destroyed and/or looted, there isn't much to see unless you scramble down the hill sides. Nothing is fenced off, so the hill can be climbed from anywhere, but it's easier to reach from along ulitsa Dr Chomakov through the old

town. The hill also offers the same sort of breezy **views** of Plovdiv as the Monument to the Soviet Army, but is easier to climb.

Museums
Some of Plovdiv's dozen or so museums are disappointing and overrated, but the three listed here are worth visiting. If a museum looks closed during what should be opening hours, bang loudly on the front door.

Historical Museum This is also called the Museum of Revival & The National Liberation (☎ 223 350, ul Lavrenov 1; admission 2 lv; open Mon-Sat 8.45am-noon & 2pm-5pm). It generally concentrates on the 1876

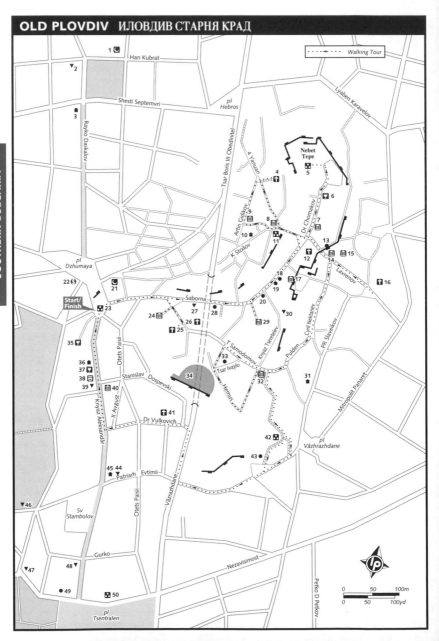

OLD PLOVDIV ИЛОВДИВ СТАРНЯ КРАД

········· Walking Tour

Han Kubrat

Shesti Septemvri

pl Hebros

Lyaben Karavelov

Rayko Daskalov

Tsar Boris III Obedinitel

Nebet Tepe

4 Yanuari

Artin Gidikov

K Stoilov

Dr Chomakov

pl Dzhumaya

Saborna

Start/ Finish

Lavrenov

Cyril Nektariev

Pulden

PR Slaveykov

T Samodomov

Knyaz Tsereletev

Tsar Ivaylo

Hemus

Otets Paisii

Stanislav Dospevski

Mitropolit Panaret

Knyaz Aleksandar

II Avgust

Dr Vulkovich

pl Vāzhrazhdane

Patriarh Evtimii

Vāzhrazhdane

Otets Paisii

Sv Stambolov

Gurko

Nezavisimost

Petko D Petkov

pl Tsentralen

0   50   100m
0   50   100yd

SOUTHERN BULGARIA

OLD PLOVDIV   ИЛОВДИВ СТАРНЯ ГРАД

PLACES TO STAY
3 Hotel Elite
   ХОТЕЛ ЕЛИТЕ
10 Hebros Hotel
   ХОТЕЛ ХЕВРОС
31 Tourist Hotel (Turisticheski
   Dom) & Sportna Sretsha
   (Restaurant)
   ТУРИСТИЧЕСКИ ДОМ И
   СПОРТНА СРЕЩА
36 Prima Vista
   (Accommodation) Agency
   ПРИМА ВИСТА
45 Hotel Bulgaria
   ХОТЕЛ БЪЛГАРИЯ

PLACES TO EAT
2 Totova Hrana
   ТОТОВА ХРАНА
27 Restaurant Kambanata
   РЕСТОРАНТ КАМБАНАТА
30 Pulden Restaurant
   РЕСТОРАНТ ПЪЛДИН
39 McDonald's
44 Happy Bar & Grill
46 Chevermeto Mehana
   МЕХАНА ЧЕВЕРМЕТО
47 Verdi Pizzeria;
   Liverpool Club
   ПИЦАРИЯ ВЕРДИ. КЛУБ
   ЛИВЕРПУЛ
48 KFC

OTHER
1 Imaret Mosque
   ИМАРЕТ ДЖАМИЯ
4 St Kevork Church
   ЦЪРКВАТА СВ. КЕВОРК
5 Ruins of Eumolpias
   РУИНИ НА ЕВМОЛПИЯ

6 Rahat Tepe Bar
   БАР РАХАТ ТЕПЕ
7 Ethnographical
   Museum
   ЕТНОГРАФСКИ МУЗЕЙ
8 Balabanov House
   БАЛАБАНОВА КЪЩА
9 Hindlian House
   ХИНДЛИЯНОВА КЪЩА
11 Roman Columns
   РИМСКА КОЛОНАДА
12 Church of St Konstantin
   & Elena
   ЦЪРКВАТА СВ. КОНСТАНТИН
   И ЕЛЕНА
13 Hisar Kapiya
   ХИСАР КАПИЯ
14 Historical Museum
   ИСТОРИЧЕСКИ МУЗЕЙ
15 Nedkovich House
   КЪЩА НЕДКОВИЧ
16 St Nedelya Church
   ЦЪРКВАТА СВ. НЕДЕЛЯ
17 Zlatyo Boyadjiev House
   КЪЩА НА ЗЛАТЮ
   БОЯДЖИЕВ
18 Souvenir Stalls & Antique
   Shops
19 Apteka (Old Hippocrates
   Pharmacy)
   АПОТЕКА
20 Souvenir Stalls & Antique
   Shops
21 Dzhumaya Mosque
   ДЖУМАЯ ДЖАМИЯ
22 United Bulgarian Bank
   ОБЕДИНЕНА БЪЛГАРСКА
   БАНКА
23 Roman Stadium; I Claudius
   Cafe

   РИМСКИ СТАДИОН. КАФЕ АЗ
   КЛАВДИЙ
24 Danov House
   КЪЩА НА ДАНОВ
25 St Nikolai Church
   ЦЪРКВАТА СВ. НИКОЛАЙ
26 Church of Sveta Bogoroditsa
   ЦЪРКВАТА СВ. БОГОРОДИЦА
28 Souvenir Stalls & Antique
   Shops
29 State Gallery of Fine Arts
   (Old Town)
   ГРАДСКА ГАЛЕРИЯ ЗА
   ИЗЯЩИН ИЗКУСТВА
32 Lamartine House
   КЪЩАТА НА ЛМАРТИН
33 Council of Tourism
   ТУРИСТИЧЕСКА ЦЕНТЪР
34 Roman Amphitheatre
   РИМСКИ АМФИТЕАТЪР
35 Dive Club
37 Sky Bar
38 Nikolai Masalitinov
   Dramatic Theatre
   ДРАМАТИЧЕН ТЕАТЪР
   НИКОЛАЙ МАСАЛИТИНОВ
40 State Gallery of Fine Arts
   (Modern City)
   ГРАДСКА ГАЛЕРИЯ ЗА
   ИЗЯЩИН ИЗКУСТВА
41 Sveta Marina Church
   ЦЪРКВАТА СВ. МАРИНА
42 St Petka Church
   ЦЪРКВАТА СВ. ПЕТКА
43 Fruit & Vegetable Market
49 Plovdiv Airport (Travel
   Agency)
   АЕРОПОРТ ПЛОВДИВ
50 Roman Forum
   РИМСКИ ПЛОЩАД

SOUTHERN BULGARIA

April Uprising against the Turks, and in particular, the massacre at Batak (see the boxed text 'The Massacre at Batak' earlier in this chapter). The three floors also include exhibits of military uniforms and earthenware. The caretaker speaks some English but nothing is labelled in any language but Bulgarian. The museum is in a house built in 1848 by Dimitâr Georgiadi, so it's sometimes also called the Georgiadi Kâshta.

Ethnographical Museum If you only visit one museum or house in Plovdiv, make sure it's the Ethnographical Museum (☎ 225 255,

ul Dr Chomakov 2; admission 3 lv; open daily 9am-5pm). It houses some 40,000 exhibits, including fascinating displays about weaving, pottery and the traditional methods of making tobacco, wine and cheese, among other goodies. The numerous side rooms contain jewellery, costumes, musical instruments, and late-19th-century furniture. The various brochures and booklets (1 lv to 3 lv), in English and French, available at the museum entrance provide more information about the exhibits, and the house itself.

The house, built in 1847 and owned by Agir Koyoumdjioglou, was for decades the most renowned Bulgarian national revival period style home in Plovdiv. It's famous for its niches, carved ceilings and symmetrical design. Before it became the city's pre-eminent museum, the building was also used as a girls' boarding school and a warehouse for tobacco and flour.

Archaeological Museum Given the long history of this great city, the collection is disappointing at the Archaeological Museum (☎ 224 339, pl Saedinenie; admission 2 lv; open Mon-Fri 9am-12.30pm & 3pm-5.30pm; photos not permitted). The small number of exhibits in the two rooms include jewellery, pottery, religious icons and artefacts from Plovdiv and elsewhere in the region. Some items have explanations in English. It's worth noting that the museum department does possess some 60,000 valuable archaeological items. Hopefully, these will be displayed in the future at this museum or elsewhere in Plovdiv.

House-Museums
The 19th-century Plovdiv 'baroque' style house is typified by an overhanging upper storey with jutting eaves, a columned portico and a brightly-painted facade. Inside, the salon, drawing rooms and bedrooms feature finely carved woodwork complemented by painted wall decorations and ornamental niches.

There is now an inordinate number of house-museums in Plovdiv. Unless you're an aficionado of this type of architecture and/or a devotee of mid-19th-century European furniture, you may only want to visit one or two of these houses. Also, entry fees of about 2 lv for each will soon burn a hole in your pocket if you're on a budget. None of the displays at any of the houses have explanations in any language but Bulgarian and staff rarely speak English.

Danov House Probably more interesting than most is the Danov House (☎ 266 804; ul Mitropolit Paisii 2; admission 1 lv; open Mon-Sat 9am-12.30pm & 2pm-4.30pm). It's dedicated to Hristo Danov (a renowned writer and publisher) and several other Bulgarian authors. Before you leave, have a look at the old printing press in the room next to the reception office. From the **gardens** (admission free), there are charming **views** of the old town and new city. The entrance is through a wall up a laneway leading to the Church of Sveta Bogoroditsa.

Balabanov House This house (ul 4 Yanuari; admission 3 lv; open Mon-Fri 9am-12.30pm & 2pm-5pm) was once owned by (and is named after) Luka Balabanov, a rich merchant from the early 19th century. The house was destroyed several decades later, but rebuilt from scratch in 1980 based on the original building plans. The ground floor is a gallery of modern, but curiously unnamed, paintings while the first floor contains some gorgeous antique furniture. The entrance is at the back; follow the white wall around the side.

Hindlian House Once owned by another wealthy merchant, Stephan Hindlian, this house (ul Artin Gidikov 4; admission 2 lv; open Mon-Fri 9am-noon & 1.30pm-4.30pm) was built in 1835. The two floors of this fully restored home contain plenty of period furniture and walls and ceilings with painted landscapes of Venice and Constantinople (Istanbul), which took about six months to complete. Visitors are welcome to enjoy the small **courtyard garden** for free.

Other Houses Built in 1830, **Lamartine House** (ul Pulden) is a baroque-style residence now belonging to the Union of Bulgarian Writers. At the time of writing it wasn't open to the public. With encouragement from the Alliance Francais, the building is named after the French poet, Alphonse de Lamartine, who stayed there for a mere three days in 1833.

Nedkovich House (☎ 626 216, ul Lavrenov; admission 2 lv; open daily 9am-noon & 1pm-6pm Apr-Sept, closed Sat & Sun Oct-Mar) was built in 1863. The exhibits are part of an 'Old Town Life' theme but are musty and uninteresting. It is poorly signposted but is next to the Historical Museum.

Apteka *(ul Saborna)*, also called the Old Hippocrates Pharmacy, is rarely open. It's still worth a look, and a peek through the window, to see how a 19th-century pharmacy must have looked like.

Art Galleries

Confusingly, two places are called the State Gallery of Fine Arts, but only the gallery *(☎ 263 790, ul Saborna 14a; admission 2 lv, free on Tues; open Mon-Fri 9am-12.30pm & 1pm-5.30pm; photos not permitted)* is worth visiting. Housed in a grand and charmingly renovated home built in 1846, this gallery offers an outstanding display of art by various Bulgarian painters from the last 300 years. Although a pleasing amount of explanations are in English, art lovers may prefer a guided tour (10 lv per group, maximum of five people) in English, French or German.

Its counterpart *(☎ 224 220, ul Knyaz Aleksandâr 15; admission 2 lv, admission free on Thur; open Mon-Fri 10am-12.30pm & 1pm-5.30pm)* in the city centre is a disappointment. It offers little more than two rooms of abstract art, though most items are on temporary display.

The **Zlatyo Boyadjiev House** *(☎ 260 706, ul Saborna 18; admission 3 lv; open daily 9am-noon & 1pm-6pm Oct-Mar, closed Sat-Sun Apr-Sept)* contains 76 oil paintings by the local artist, Boyadjiev. Some canvases are so huge they easily fill one side of a wall. The mid-19th-century house was once owned by a local identity, Dr Chomakov, after whom the building is sometimes named.

Religious Buildings

Each place listed below has free admission and is open daily during daylight hours.

The huge, three-nave basilica, **Church of Sveta Bogoroditsa** *(ul Mitropolit Paisii)*, was built in 1844 and is still used as a cathedral. It contains a marvellous array of paintings and murals.

The **Church of St Konstantin & Elena** *(ul Saborna 24; photos not permitted)* is the oldest church in Plovdiv. Excavations reveal that the original church was built in AD 337 for Emperor Konstantin and Elena, his mother. It was destroyed numerous times by the Romans, Greeks and Turks and the current building was mostly rebuilt in 1832. It contains a fine gold-plated iconostasis, carved in 1836, and a collection of icons.

The **Sveta Marina Church** *(ul Dr Vulkovich 7)* was originally built in 1561. It was burnt down fifty years later, rebuilt completely in 1783, and repaired extensively in 1856. Note the 17m-high pagoda-shaped wooden bell tower, built in 1870, and the intricate 170-year-old iconostasis inside the church.

The **St Nedelya Church** *(ul PR Slaveikov 40)* is one of the largest in Plovdiv. Originally built in 1578 and renovated in the 1830s, it contains exquisite iconostases (carved from walnut) and murals from the mid-1800s. The church is rarely open to the public but it's worth a look from the outside.

The **Dzhumaya Mosque** *(pl Dzhumaya)* was built in the mid-15th century and is still used for religious services. It was one of more than 50 mosques built in Plovdiv during the Turkish occupation. The entrance is rather irreverently situated between two cafes. Look for the 23m-high minaret and please remove your shoes before entering.

The Armenian **St Kevork Church** *(ul 4 Yanuari)* was built in 1828 on the ruins of another 12th-century church.

Special Events

Plovdiv hosts the **Cultural Month Festival** (late May to mid-July), which includes the two-week **Verdi Festival** (early June) and the 10-day **International Festival of Chamber Music** (mid-June). Also worth looking out for is the **International Folklore Festival** (early August) and the celebrations during the **city holiday** (6 September).

The week-long **International Plovdiv Fair** (mid-May and late September) is held in the massive **fairgrounds** *(☎ 553 146, bul Tsar Boris III Obedinitel 37)*, north of the river.

PLACES TO STAY
Private Rooms

The three accommodation agencies listed in this section are open Monday to Saturday from about 9am to 5pm, but usually closed on Sunday. Most rooms in private homes have a shared bathroom.

Prima Vista Agency (☎ 272 778) on ulitsa Knyaz Aleksandâr 28 has rooms from 18 lv to 22 lv. Opening hours are occasionally irregular, but staff are helpful, friendly and speak English. The office is at the back of a small arcade – look for the black sign 'accommodation agency' (in English) from along the mall.

Esperantsa (☎ 260 653) on ulitsa Ivan Vazov 14 has rooms for 22 lv per person. This agency can be a bit haphazard and the staff speak little English (but do get by in German and Spanish). However, readers have commented favourably on the quality of rooms on offer. It's easy to reach from the train station, or the Yug or Rodopi bus stations, and is signposted in English.

Traikov (☎ 963 014, fax 766 041) ulitsa Ibur 31 rents singles/doubles for 22/35 lv and apartments for 55 lv to 88 lv. Although reliable, this agency is a fair way from the train and bus stations, so it's worth ringing ahead to avoid a lengthy trip in case no rooms are available. The apartments have a kitchen, bathroom and TV.

Places to Stay – Budget

Although there is a camping ground, staying in a private room or hotel, in or close to the old town, is far better.

Camping *Complex 4-TY Kilometre* (☎ 951 360) Camping 10 lv per person, double bungalows with bathroom 30 lv. Open year-round. This camping ground, also called Gorski Kat Camping, is about 4km west of central Plovdiv on the old Sofia Highway. It provides shade and privacy if you can escape the incessant traffic noise. A *restaurant/bar* is attached. Take bus No 4, 18 or 44 west along bulevard Bulgaria, or bus No 222 from the train station, as far as they go and walk another 200m down the road.

Hotels *Tourist Hotel* (*Turisticheski Dom;* ☎ 633 211, ul PR Slaveikov 5) Rooms with shared bathroom 22 lv per person. No-one staying at this remarkable old place really minds the disadvantages – ie, the noisy

nightclub at the back, musty aroma and saggy beds – because it's so convenient and just oozes atmosphere. The rooms upstairs are huge, and feature high ceilings and old-fashioned (but not antique) furniture. The rates are per person so single travellers can get a double room for 22 lv. It's understandably popular, so arrive early or book ahead.

Hotel Leipzig 91 (☎ 632 250, fax 451096, bul Ruski 70) Singles/doubles with bathroom 40/64 lv. Although the hotel lacks charm, and the rooms need some renovation, this is essentially a mid-range hotel at (almost) a budget price. Rates include breakfast. It's in a tall building (so all rooms offer views), a 20-minute walk from the city centre.

Trakiya Hotel (☎ 624 101, ul Ivan Vazov 84) Singles/doubles/triples with bathroom 40/80/120 lv. This new place is very convenient, about 100m from the train station, but the rooms (with fan and TV) are quiet despite the noisy location and popular bar downstairs. Rates include breakfast.

Places to Stay – Mid-Range

All hotels listed in this section offer rooms with a private bathroom, TV, fridge and air-conditioning.

Hotel Elite (☎ 624 537, ul Rayko Daskalov 53) Doubles US$35. The Elite is new and central and the rooms, thankfully, are insulated from the noisy road below. The original building has some history, but the rooms are fairly unremarkable and expensive for foreigners.

Hotel Maritsa (☎ 952 735, fax 952770, bul Tsar Boris III Obedinitel 42) Singles/doubles US$47/70. The garish decor and ostentatious foyer may not be to everyone's taste, but the Maritsa offers comfortable rooms, and is good value in this range. Rates include breakfast.

Hotel Bulgaria (☎ 633 599, e mng@ hotelbulgaria.net; ul Patriarh Evtimii 13) Singles/doubles US$50/70. Right in the middle of Plovdiv, this is a top-end hotel with mid-range rates, so it's better value than anything else listed in the top-end section. The rooms are modern, if a little charmless, but the location is hard to beat and the price includes breakfast.

Places to Stay – Top End

All hotels listed here offer rooms with a private bathroom, TV, air-conditioning, fridge and breakfast.

Novotel (☎ 934 999, ⓔ reservation@ novotelpdv.bg, ul Boyadjiev 2) Singles/doubles US$125/145. This eyesore north of the river has all the luxuries expected of this international chain such as a swimming pool and tennis courts. For singles/doubles it can be as 'low' as US$65/86 daily on weekends in summer.

Hebros Hotel (☎ 260 180, ⓔ hebros@pl .bia-bg.com; ⓦ www.hebros-hotel.com, ul K Stoilov 51) Doubles US$75, apartments US$75-95. If you want to splurge once during your visit to Bulgaria, do it here – especially if you love antique furniture. This 200-year-old home offers a handful of rooms. Each is crammed with gorgeous beds, chairs, wardrobes etc and each is over 100 years old. The bathroom, however, is sparkling new.

Trimontium Princess Hotel (☎ 605 000, ⓔ trimontium–princess@plovdiv.ttm.bg, pl Tsentralen) Singles/doubles on weekdays US$65/90, on weekends US$55/73. This mammoth place facing the soulless Tsentralen Square is comfortable and central. It's always worth asking about discounted rates, especially on weekends.

Noviz Hotel (☎ 631 281, ⓔ novizinc@ plovdiv.ttm.bg, bul Ruski 55) Singles/doubles US$45/65, apartments US$80-90. Although not as central or convenient as the other top-end places, it's better value. The rooms are large, very comfortable, and offer silly extras – a telephone in the bathroom for example. The hotel also has a gym and sauna for guests.

Places to Eat

Several tiny stalls along the northern section of ulitsa Rayko Daskalov sell tasty *doner kebabs* for about 1 lv to 3 lv (the medium size will satisfy most hunger pangs). Also a popular snack is a slice of *pizza* (1 lv) that is sold all over the city centre. Otherwise, fast-food junkies can always pop into *KFC* or *McDonald's*, both of which are along ulitsa Knyaz Aleksandâr.

Restaurants *Totova Hrana (ul Han Kubrat)* Salads 1 lv, main dishes about 1.50 lv. This is an excellent choice for cheap, cafeteria-style food – just point at what you like and enjoy. There's seating indoors, but between noon and 2pm Monday to Friday it may be standing room only.

Pulden Restaurant (ul Knyaz Tseretelev 8) Soups and salads about 2.50 lv, main meals from 5.50 lv. The Pulden has several unique dining rooms. One occupies a place where dervishes (an Islamic sect from Iran) once whirled themselves into feverish exhaustion. Another is in the cellar where Byzantine-era walls and Roman artefacts make up the decor. Although predictably touristy and expensive, it's worth a visit. The menu is in English.

Restaurant Kambanata (ul Saborna) Starters 2-3 lv, meals 6-7 lv, beer from 1.50 lv. This classy, and rather bizarre, place is virtually under the grounds of the Church of Sveta Bogoroditsa. The tables are set along small terraces so diners can watch the live music being performed most nights. The menu is in English and prices aren't too bad considering the impeccable service and rather unique setting.

Chevermeto Mehana (ul Dondukov 4) Grills about 5.50 lv. The Chevermeto is a unique eatery: it occupies a labyrinthine bomb shelter burrowed deep into the southern side of Sahat Tepe hill. A main course of succulent *chevermeto* (spit-roasted lamb) comes garnished with live Balkan folk music and, for dessert, there's rollicking plate-smashing dancing by local Greek students.

Verdi Pizzeria (ul Gladston) Pizza slices 1 lv, pizzas about 3.50-5 lv. Verdi is probably the best place in town to pig out on pizza. The service is quick and friendly, prices are very reasonable and the covered outdoor garden setting is convivial.

Ristorante Da Lino (ul Sheshti Septemvri 135) Pasta dishes about 5 lv, bottles of wine from 4.50 lv. Set in a converted monastery, this classy place offers authentic Italian cuisine. Prices are understandably high but it's worth a splurge for the tasty food, excellent service and fascinating decor. Waiters can offer a menu in English.

Happy Bar & Grill (ul Patriarh Evtimii 13) Salads 2.20 lv, most meals about 4.50 lv. This popular country-wide chain has a restaurant next to the Hotel Bulgaria. It offers a huge range of meals from burgers to kebabs to noodles. The menu isn't in English, but the handy photo-menu shows large pictures of each dish. Annoyingly, an unannounced 10% 'service charge' is added to the bill.

The Red Dragon (bul Ruski) Meals from 3 lv. The service may not always be snappy, but the portions are massive. For example, one plate of noodles and a starter (such as spring rolls for 3.50 lv) would satisfy two normal appetites. The menu is in English and German.

Trimontium Princess Hotel Restaurant (☎ 605 000, ℮ trimontium–princess@ plovdiv.ttm.bg, pl Tsentralen) Pasta dishes 3.50-3.90 lv, grills 7 lv, fish about 6.50 lv. Although this is a charmless dining room, the service is impeccable, and it's a chance to be treated like royalty. Prices are reasonable considering it's a four-star hotel, and all dishes include garnishes like salads, vegetables and French fries. The menu is written in English.

Cafes The streets around Plovdiv don't seem overcrowded with cafes like other places in Bulgaria. While there are plenty of cafes along the mall, around the old town and anywhere else in between, many are off-the-street, undercover and air-conditioned, so they're not quite as charming. The best places for a leisurely drink and/or light meal are the cafes in the corner of the park on ulitsa Hristo G Danov, around the market on ulitsa Sheshti Septemvri, in the park near the Open-Air Theatre on Bunardjika hill and along ulitsa Saborna – especially near the overpass above bulevard Tsar III Obedinitel.

I Claudius Cafe Salads 2-2.50 lv, meals from 3 lv. Overlooking, and almost touching the Roman Stadium, this cafe boasts one of the best locations in Plovdiv, and is as close as any visitor can get to the ruins. Considering the setting, the prices (for example pancakes for 2 lv) are quite reasonable. The menu is in English.

Sportna Sretsha (ul PR Slaveikov 5) Salads 1.50-2 lv, sandwiches 1.50 lv, main meals about 3.50 lv. Open 8.30am. If you're staying at the Tourist Hotel at the back, or traipsing around the old town, stop here for a drink or meal. It's ideal for breakfast and the menu is in English.

Entertainment

Cultural Opera, ballet and music is often held at the **Roman Amphitheatre** in summer, particularly between late May and early June. Although often performed in Bulgarian, the setting is awesome, so if you're in Plovdiv at this time look for posters around town advertising upcoming events. Also, the **Open-Air Theatre** in the park on Bunardjika hill sometimes has performances of traditional music and dance in summer.

The **Nikolai Masalitinov Dramatic Theatre** (☎ 224 867, ul Knyaz Aleksandâr 38) is one of the most respected theatres in the country and features anything from Shakespeare to Ibsen (performances are mostly in Bulgarian). The *Plovdiv Opera House* (☎ 235 198, ul Avksentiy Veleshki) features performances of international and Bulgarian operas (also in Bulgarian).

Bars For views of the old town, head to *Rahat Tepe Bar (ul Dr Chomakov)*, almost at the top of Nebet Tepe hill. For panoramic views of the modern city, especially at night, visit the *Sky Bar (ul Knyaz Aleksandâr)* on the top floor of one of the tallest buildings along the mall. Prices for drinks are predictably high. The *Liverpool Club (ul Gladston)*, next to Verdi Pizzeria, is a cheap bar with loud music, pool tables and video games.

Discos & Nightclubs One of the trendiest places to head for is the *Dive Club*, at the end of a lane from ploshtad Dzhumaya – look for the distinctive aquamarine murals on the front wall. *Rondo Dance Club (ul Avksentiy Veleshki)*, in the basement of the opera building, is rather sleazy, but popular. *Club Santo (bul Tsar III Obedinitel)*, overlooking the river, is more sedate.

An alpine tarn on Mt Vihren in the spectacularly rugged Pirin Mountains.

hiker faces the northern wall of Mt Vihren.

Common wildflowers bloom in the Pirin ranges.

Canyon near Veliko Târnovo – it's safe, really!

TOM COCKREM

Bansko with a backdrop of the Pirin Mountains.

PAUL GREENWAY

PAUL GREENWAY

Grand 2nd-century Roman Amphitheatre, Plovdiv.

Bachkovo Monastery was built in 1083.

PAUL GREENWAY

Near this fountain on ulitsa Knyaz Aleksânder, numerous cafes line the Plovdiv mall.

Cinemas Several cinemas regularly screen recent foreign films in the original language (with Bulgarian subtitles). Tickets cost from 2.50 lv to 5 lv depending on the session times and the comfort of the seats. Try the *Cinema Geo Milev (ul Vasil Aprilov)*, *Luki Cinema (ul Gladston)* or *Cinemax (ul Avksentiy Veleshki)*.

Shopping

The *State Gallery of Fine Arts (ul Saborna 14a)* in the old town sells cassettes (4.50 lv) and compact discs (10 lv) of traditional Bulgarian music. Along the cobblestone streets of the old town, especially along ulitsa Saborna, there are numerous *souvenir stalls* and *antique shops*. One charming memento of your visit to Plovdiv may be a print of a sketch or painting of the old town.

Getting There & Away

Air There are no commercial flights to or from Plovdiv. The Plovdiv Airport travel agency (☎ 633 081), at ulitsa Gladston 4, is the representative for Balkan Airlines, and can book domestic and international flights for most other airlines.

Bus Plovdiv has three well-organised bus stations. The main Yug bus station (☎ 626 937) is diagonally opposite the train station and is only 10 minutes' walk from the city centre. From this station, public buses (and, where indicated, private buses) go to:

destination	frequency	duration	fare
Bansko	2 daily	3½ hours	9 lv
Blagoevgrad	2-3 daily	3 hours	8.50 lv
Burgas (private)	2 daily	4 hours	12 lv
Haskovo	5 daily	1 hour	3.20 lv
Hisar	8 daily	1 hour	2.90 lv
Karlovo	hourly	1½ hours	2.80 lv
Ruse (private)	1 daily	6 hours	12 lv
Sliven	6 daily	3 hours	10 lv
Sofia (private & public)	hourly	2½ hours	7 lv
Stara Zagora	hourly	1½ hours	3.80 lv
Varna	1-3 daily	6 hours	12.50 lv
Veliko Târnovo (private)	3 daily	4½ hours	9 lv

In summer, one or two daily buses also leave the Yug bus station for the resorts along the Black Sea coast, such as Kiten, Ahtopol, Albena and Nesebâr.

From the Rodopi bus station (☎ 777 607), which is accessible on foot through the underpass by the train station, there are four daily services to Haskovo and Karlovo and between six and eight to Smolyan (5 lv, 2½ hours), via Bachkovo, Chepelare and Pamporovo.

The Sever bus station (☎ 553 705) in the northern suburbs is best accessed by taxi and is of limited use. From this bus station only one daily bus goes directly to Pleven (3pm), Ruse (8am), Troyan (1.30pm), and Koprivshtitsa (4.30pm).

International City Local Transportation Co (☎ 624 274), in the State Philharmonic Building on ploshtad Tsentralen, offers a bus to Athens (102 lv) on Tuesday and Thursday, and between one and three daily buses to Thessaloniki (52.50 lv). Several private companies at the Yug Bus Station also offer daily buses to Istanbul (40 lv) and Izmir (55 lv).

Train Plovdiv is along the most popular railway line in Bulgaria (ie, between Sofia and Burgas), so trains are frequent. The major train services are listed in the boxed text 'Major Trains from Plovdiv' on the following page.

The train station (☎ 622 729) on bulevard Hristo Botev is convenient, and reasonably well organised. Recent arrivals and upcoming departures are listed in Bulgarian on a computer screen at the entrance of the station and in the underpass leading to the platforms. But the platforms, surprisingly, are not numbered and staff at the information office do not speak English.

Advance tickets for domestic services are sold upstairs. For international tickets, go to the Rila Bureau (☎ 446 120). It's open Monday to Saturday 8am to 6.30pm and is along a side street parallel to bulevard Hristo Botev. See Land in the Getting There & Away chapter for information about international trains that pass through Plovdiv.

SOUTHERN BULGARIA

Major Trains from Plovdiv

destination	number of trains (daily)	duration (hours)	1st/2nd class fare
Sofia	8 fast, 3 express & 8 slow	2½ (express)	7.30/5.40 lv (express)
Burgas	4 fast, 1 express	4 (express)	13.60/10 lv (express)
Svilengrad	4 slow	3½	7.50/5.30 lv
Hisar	6 slow	2	4.50/3.50 lv
Karlovo	6 slow	2	4.30/3.30 lv
Veliko Târnovo	5 slow	4	11.95/8.90 lv

Getting Around

Plovdiv is pleasingly compact so it's generally quicker to get around on foot. Little of the old town (except the hotels) is accessible by vehicle, so if you're using a private, rented or chartered vehicle, *please* park it outside the old town and walk. Happily, taxi drivers use their meters with little or no prompting.

There's no point hiring a vehicle to get around Plovdiv, but travelling around the region by car allows you to explore remote monasteries, caves and lakes. Tourist Service Rent-a-Car (☎ 623 496) in the Trimontium Princess Hotel and Avis (☎ 934 481) in the Novotel are expensive, so hire a car through one of the numerous travel agencies along the mall. Prices are more competitive, however, in Sofia, so it's probably even more economical to return to the capital and rent something from a Bulgarian company there.

AROUND PLOVDIV
Bachkovo Monastery
Бачковоски Манастир

About 30km south of Plovdiv, just past the picturesque hill top village of Bachkovo, is the magnificent Bachkovo Monastery *(admission free; open daily 6am-10pm)*. It was founded in 1083 by two aristocrats, the Georgian brothers Gregory and Abasius Bakuriani, who were military officers for the Byzantine rulers. The monastery was a major religious centre during the Second Bulgarian Empire (1185–1396), but was then looted by the nefarious Turks in the 15th and 16th centuries. It underwent major reconstruction in the mid-17th century and

is now Bulgaria's second-largest monastery (after Rila).

In the courtyard, there are two churches: the 12th-century **Archangel Church**, which contains murals painted by Zahari Zograf in the early 1850s and the larger **Church of the Assumption of Our Lady**, built in 1604 on the ruins of the original church. The latter contains 17th-century iconostases, murals painted in about 1850 and a silver icon of the Holy Virgin dating from the early 14th century.

On the northern side of the courtyard, the small **museum** *(admission 1 lv; erratic opening hours)* features some weapons and icons. One corner of the southern side is occupied by the former **refectory**, originally built in 1601. On the ceiling is a marvellous painting of the genealogy of Jesus painted by unknown artists (or artist) between 1623 and 1643. Through the gate beside the refectory is **St Nicholas Chapel**, built in 1836. During the 1840s, Zograf painted the superb *Last Judgment* inside the chapel; note the condemned Turks (without haloes) on the right and Zograf's self-portrait (no beard) in the upper-left corner.

An explanation board at the monastery gate provides a brief history (in English, French and German) about the monastery and a crude map of some short **hiking trails** to nearby villages. *Bachkovo Monastery* (15 lv), available inside the monastery grounds, provides plenty of explanations and photos, but is probably too expensive and detailed for most visitors.

Places to Stay & Eat *Eco Hotel (☎ 048-981 068)* Doubles with bathroom 50 lv.

The only place to stay in the area is on the other side of the road, and river, from the turn-off to the monastery. It offers quiet and comfortable rooms and the rates include breakfast.

Around the turn-off to the monastery, there are several restaurants, many of which serve the local speciality: fresh trout. *Vodolatsa Restaurant* caters to the tourist bus crowds, but the range of meals is extensive, and the service is (usually) snappy.

Dzhamura Restaurant is about 100m south of (and over the river from) the turn-off to the monastery (follow the signs). Dzhamura is worth the short walk, probably more for the riverside setting than the food.

Getting There & Away Take any of the regular buses to Smolyan from the Rodopi bus station in Plovdiv, disembark at the turn-off (obvious from the souvenir stalls and cafes) about 1.2km south of Bachkovo village and walk about 500m up the hill.

HASKOVO
ХАСКОВО
☎ 038 ● pop 90,600

Although often ignored by travellers, Haskovo is the only worthwhile destination in the south-east, and a convenient staging post for anyone travelling to Greece or Turkey, via Svilengrad. The Turkish ambience and heritage of the town is also an ideal introduction if you're heading to Turkey. See the boxed text 'Hiking in the Rodopi Mountains' earlier in this chapter for hiking around these ranges from Haskovo.

You can change money at the Hebros Bank on bulevard Bulgaria, along the river to the west, and not far from the combined post office and telephone centre. Alternatively the Bulgarian Post Bank on ulitsa Otets Paisii also changes money. The Internet Club, ulitsa San Stefano, is open every day, and the bookshop on ploshtad Svoboda sells maps.

SOUTHERN BULGARIA

HASKOVO ХАСКОВО

1 Hotel Oasis ХОТЕЛ ОАЗИС	8 Internet Club
2 Ivan Dinov Dramatic Theatre ДРАМАТИЧЕН ТЕАТЪР ИВАН ДИНОВ	9 Ezhi Dzhumaya Mosque ДЖАМИЯ ЕЖИ ДЖУМАЯ
	10 Cinema Paradiso КИНО ПАРАДИЗО
3 Hebros Bank БАНКА ХЕБРОС	11 Historical Museum ИСТОРИЧЕСКИ МУЗЕЙ
4 Hotel Aida ХОТЕЛ АИДА	12 Art Gallery Kredo ХУДОЖЕСТВЕНА ГАЛЕРИЯ КРЕДО
5 Bookshop КНИЖАРНИЦА	13 Bulgarian Post Bank БЪЛГАРСКА ПОЩЕНСКА БАНКА
6 Bus Station	
7 Restaurant Vesta РЕСТОРАНТ ВЕСТА	14 Post Office & Telephone Centre

To Stara Zagora (61km)
& Plovdiv (78km)

To Hotel Rodopi
(100m)

Rakovski

Saedinenie

Hadzhi Dimitâr

Georgi Kirkov

Rakovski

Otets Paisii

Veliko
Târnovo

pl
Svoboda

Preslav

M Dimov

Ruse

Burgas

Patriarh Evtimii

Veliko Târnovo

Aton

Pirin

Stefan Karadzhi

San Stefano

Bulgaria

Tsar Kaloyan

Saedinenie

To Train
Station (1km)
& Svilengrad
(68km)

To Kârdzhali (54km)

0   150   300m

0   150   300yd

Things to See

Along the south-eastern side of ploshtad Svoboda is the **Historical Museum** *(☎ 24 505)*. The museum houses some unremarkable archaeological and ethnological exhibits, plus some impressive exhibits of Thracian ceramics and earthenware. The **Art Gallery Kredo** *(ul Patriarh Evtimii)* has a reasonable collection of art on display, and for sale.

The **Ezhi Dzhumaya Mosque** *(ul San Stefano)* looks rather lost among the cafes in the mall. It was built in the late 14th century, and is probably the oldest mosque in Bulgaria. Visitors are welcome but remember to be discreet because this is still a place of worship.

Places to Stay & Eat

Each hotel listed here offers rooms with a bathroom and TV.

Hotel Rodopi *(☎ 34 166, bul Bulgaria 39)* Singles/doubles 22/44 lv, apartments 88 lv. The Hotel Rodopi is the cheapest place in town but it's inconvenient and all rooms face the noisy main road.

Hotel Aida *(☎ 25 164)* Doubles 42 lv. The Aida is convenient (just past the end of ulitsa Rakovski) but almost nothing – certainly not the bathrooms – has been renovated or updated in the last 40 years. It's

clean, however, and about the best value in town. A decent *restaurant* is attached.

Hotel Oasis *(☎/fax 63093, ul Rakovski 10)* Doubles 66 lv. The Oasis is a new place about 150m north of the Aida. The rooms are clean and well-appointed but it's overpriced for foreigners.

Dozens of *cafes* are crammed along each pedestrian mall, and, rather irreverently, huddled around the mosque. For pizzas, hamburgers and tasty salads, head straight to **Restaurant Vesta** *(ul San Stefano)*.

Getting There & Away

Most bus services are operated by private companies, all of which have offices inside the chaotic bus station (☎ 24 218) on ulitsa Saedinenie Every day, six or seven buses head to Sofia (9 lv to 10 lv, six hours) and about five go to Plovdiv (3.20 lv, one hour). Also, several public and private buses depart daily for Ahtopol, Varna, Burgas, Gabrovo, Kazanlâk, Stara Zagora and Svilengrad (which shares a border with Greece and Turkey). As the transport hub for south-eastern Bulgaria, numerous companies at the bus station each offer at least one daily service to Istanbul (30 lv).

Haskovo is along an inconvenient spur track so travelling to/from Haskovo by train is futile.

Central Bulgaria

Historically, central Bulgaria was defined as the region between the Rodopi Mountains to the south and the Stara Planina farther north, but these days the centre is determined more by transport routes. So, all places included in this chapter are along, or not far from, the highways (E772 and E70) and the train line which link Sofia with Varna, and the highways (E6 and E773) and train line from Sofia to Burgas.

The backbone of the central region is the mighty Stara Planina range, which starts close to the Yugoslavia border and stretches to the Black Sea coast. Centuries ago, these mountains were ideal locations for secluded monasteries, including those near Troyan and Dryanovo . During the Bulgarian national revival period (18th and 19th centuries), towns such as Karlovo and Lovech were hotbeds of anti-Turkish revolutionary zeal. Soon after, villages such as Koprivshtitsa and Tryavna prospered, and many of the numerous exquisite homes built in the architectural style of the day still survive. The region was also inhabited for centuries by the Romans, Thracians and Turks, all of whom left marvellous hill top fortresses, and by the Bulgars, who established a capital at Veliki Preslav, near Shumen.

KOPRIVSHTITSA
КОПРИВШТИЦА
☎ 07184 • pop 2900
This picturesque village in the highest part of the Sredna Gora Mountains, 113km east of Sofia, has been carefully preserved as an open-air museum from the Bulgarian national revival period. Spread across a lush pasture and pine-clad valley either side of the Topolnitsa River, Koprivshtitsa is crammed with cobblestone streets, restored churches, museums and houses with tiled red roofs, and tiny stone bridges arching across trickling rivulets. The village oozes charm and history, and nearly 400 buildings of architectural and historical importance are registered and preserved by the Bulgar-

Highlights

- Explore the ancient castle, museums and churches in the cliff-side town of Veliko Târnovo

- Meander along the cobblestone streets of Tryavna, one of the prettiest villages in Bulgaria

- Watch artisans working at the picturesque Etâr Ethnographic Village Museum

- Visit the numerous house-museums In the historical village of Koprivshtitsa

- Admire Troyan Monastery, the third-largest monastery in Bulgaria and one of the more accessible

- Clamber around the hill top Shumen Fortress, one of the oldest ruins in the country

ian government. Koprivshtitsa is just the sort of place where you may come for the day and end up staying a week!

History
Koprivshtitsa was first settled at the end of the 14th century by ordinary folk and by nobles from Veliko Târnovo fleeing Turkish conquerors. The local economy prospered

CENTRAL BULGARIA

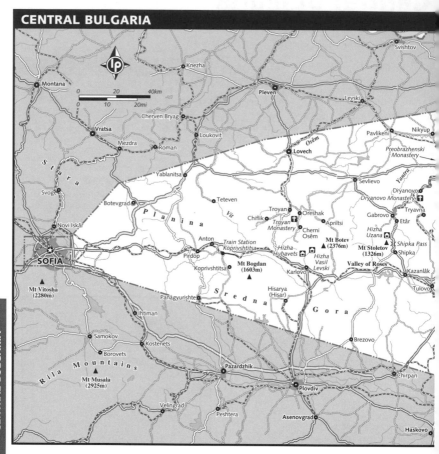

from sheep, cattle and goat herding and a wealthy merchant class was soon created. Sacked by brigands in 1793, 1804 and 1809, Koprivshtitsa was rebuilt during the mid-19th century. Soon after, the population reached about 12,000 (almost as big as Sofia at the time).

Koprivshtitsa is famous as the place where Todor Kableshkov (or Georgi Tihanek, according to some sources) first proclaimed the national uprising against the Turks on 20 April 1876. He did this at the tiny bridge now known as the Kalachev Bridge (also called Kableshkov Bridge)

built in 1813. This great day has lent its name to the main square dominated by the 1876 April Uprising Mausoleum.

After independence from the Turks in 1878, Bulgarian merchants and intellectuals left their mountain retreats for the cities, and Koprivshtitsa has survived largely unchanged to this day. The Bulgarian government declared the village a town museum in 1952, and a historical reserve in 1971.

Information

All visitors – especially those who intend to stay overnight – should first stop by the

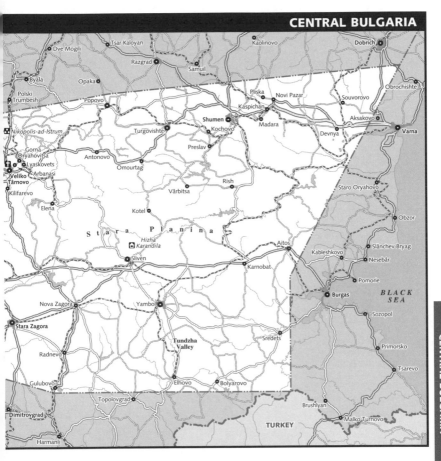

CENTRAL BULGARIA

Tourist Information Centre (☎/fax 2191, e koprivshtitsa@hotmail.com) on the main square, ploshtad 20 April. It's open daily from 9am to 1pm and 1.30pm to 6pm. It gives away brochures, sells books and maps, and arranges rooms in private homes (see Places to Stay later). If you are interested in festivals or cultural events check with the tourist office, or the Hadzhi Nencho Palaveev Cultural Centre (☎ 2034) at ulitsa Hadzhi Nencho Palaveev 78.

The only place to change money is the DSK Bank, behind the bus stop, and the only place to send emails is the Heroes In-

ternet Agency (ulitsa Hadzhi Nencho Palaveev), on the other side of the river.

Karavelov House

Karavelov House (☎ 2176, ul Hadzhi Nencho Palaveev 39) was occupied by the parents of Lyuben Karavelov (1834–79), a journalist and printer who worked for Bulgarian revolutionary groups based in Russia, Serbia and Romania. He was the first chairman of the Bulgarian Central Revolutionary Committee. The three separate buildings were constructed between 1810 and 1835, and include a printing press

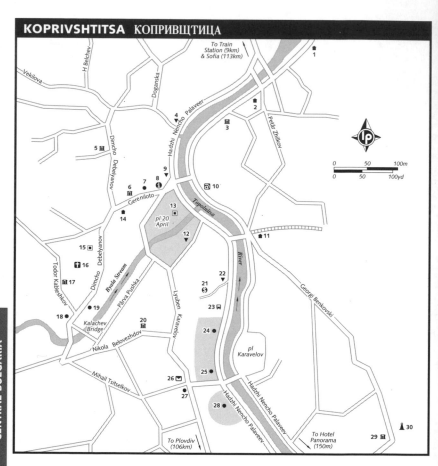

KOPRIVSHTITSA КОПРИВЩТИЦА

where various seditious newspapers were written and distributed.

Oslekov House

This house (☎ 2555, ul Gereniloto 4) was built by Oslekov, a rich merchant who, inevitably, took part in the 1876 April Uprising before being killed by the Turks. Oslekov House was built between 1853 and 1856 and it is possibly the best example of Bulgarian national revival period architecture in the village, evinced by the triple-arched entrance, spacious interior, stylish furniture and brightly coloured walls. Inside, there are carved ceilings, collections of 19th-century costumes, paintings and jewellery, plus several woodcarvings, some of which were bought during Oslekov's extensive travels.

Debelyanov House

Built in 1830, this house (☎ 2077, ul Dimcho Debelyanov 6) is dedicated to Dimcho Debelyanov (1887–1916), a great poet who completed many outstanding works before he died in WWI. The property features a pretty garden and numerous displays about Debelyanov rather than period furniture

KOPRIVSHTITSA КОПРИВЩТИЦА

PLACES TO STAY
1 Hotel Astra
   ХОТЕЛ АСТРА
2 Hotel Kalina
   ХОТЕЛ КАЛИНА
11 Shuleva House Hotel
   ХОТЕЛ ЩУЛЕВА КЪЩТА
14 Hotel Trayanova Kâshta
   & Byaloto Konche
   ХОТЕЛ ТРАЯНОВА
   КЪЩТА И БЯЛОТО
   КОНЧЕ

PLACES TO EAT
4 Lomeva Kâshta Tavern
   ТАВЕРНА ЛОМЕВА КЪЩТА
9 April 20 National
   Restaurant
   НАЦИОНАЛЕН
   РЕСТОРАНТ 20 АПРИЛ
12 Mehana Starite Borove
   МЕХАНА СТАРИТЕ БОРОВЕ
22 Chuchura
   ЧУЧУРА

OTHER
3 Karavelov House
   КАРАВЕЛОВА КЪЩТА
5 Debelyanov House
   ДЕБЕЛЯНОВА КЪЩТА
6 Oslekov House
   ОСЛЕКОВА КЪЩТА
7 Souvenir Shop (Tickets)
8 Tourist Information Centre
   ТУРИСТИЧЕСКИ
   ИНФОРМАЦИОНЕН ЦЕНТЪР
10 Heroes Internet Agency
13 April Uprising Mausoleum
   МАВЗОЛЕЙ НА АПРИЛСКОТО
   ВЪСТАНИЕ
15 Debelyanov's Grave
   ГРОБЪТ НА ДЕБЕЛЯНОВ
16 Assumption Church;
   Kableshkov's Grave
   ЦЪРКВАТА УСПЕНИЕ
   БОГОРОДИЧНО. ГРОБЪТ НА
   КАБЛЕШКОВ
17 Kableshkov House
   КАБЛЕШКОВА КЪЩТА

18 Craft Shop
19 Tepavitsa Valyavitsa Craft
   Complex
   ТЕПАВИЦА ВАЛЯВИЦА
   КОМЛЕКС
20 Lyutov House
   ЛЮТОВА КЪЩТА
21 DSK Bank
23 Bus Stop
24 St Kiril & Metodii School
   УЧИЛИЩЕ СВ. КИРИЛ И
   МЕТОДИЙ
25 Hadzhi Nencho Palaveev
   Cultural Centre
   КУЛТУРЕН ЦЕНТЪР
   ХАДЖИ НЕНЧО
   ПАЛАВЕЕВ
26 Post Office & Telephone
   Centre
27 Town Hall
28 Market & Cafes
29 Benkovski House
   БЕНКОВСКИ КЪЩТА
30 Equestrian Statue

usually found in other house-museums. And watch out for the *very* low ceilings!

Kableshkov House

Todor Kableshkov (1851–76), a well-travelled and astute gentleman, once resided in this glorious building (☎ *2054, ul Todor Kableshkov 8*). Kableshkov is revered as (probably) the person who fired the first shot in anger to start the 1876 uprising against the Turks. Consequently, this house, built in 1845, is basically a museum about the rebellion.

Lyutov House

Also called the Topalov House after the original owner, the Lyutov House (☎ *2138, ul Nikola Belovezhdov 2)* was built in 1854 in a style reminiscent of the baroque houses found in Plovdiv. The best preserved house-museum in Koprivshtitsa, it features a resplendent salon with intricately carved ceilings adorned with landscapes that were hand-painted by Lyutov. The lower floor contains a permanent display (with explanations in English) of locally made felt cloths (see the Shopping section later).

Benkovski House

The least-visited house-museum is probably the Benkovski House (☎ *2811, ul Georgi Benkovski 5)*, built in 1831 on a hillside to the south-east. Georgi Benkovski (1843–76) led the insurgent cavalry on legendary exploits until he died in a Turkish ambush. Above the house, and easy to spot from the village centre, is a huge **equestrian statue** of the man astride a horse. The statue is worth the short climb for the superb **views** of the entire valley.

Other Buildings

On either side of the park along ulitsa Hadzhi Nencho Palaveev are the **Sts Kiril & Metodii School**, built in 1837, and the rather dilapidated **Hadzhi Nencho Palaveev Cultural Centre**, which only comes alive during cultural exhibitions and events.

The **Assumption Church** (*ul Dimcho Debelyanov 26a*), built in 1817, is usually closed, but visitors can peer through the window and wander around the gardens. The church grounds contain **Kableshkov's grave**, and, in the upper section, **Debelyanov's grave**. A poignant statue features

CENTRAL BULGARIA

House-Museums of Koprivshtitsa

Most of the houses in the village are one of two kinds. The early 19th-century wooden houses are characterised by a stone ground floor and a wooden upper floor with two rooms in each. The more richly-decorated houses were built during the second half of the 19th century. The latter type was strongly influenced by the 'baroque' Plovdiv style, epitomised by large salons with intricately carved ceilings, sunny verandas and multicoloured facades.

Some of the houses have been turned into museums. If you have no special interest in or appreciation of Bulgarian national revival period architecture and furniture you may find one much the same as another. The most interesting are probably the extensive Karavelov House, the typical Oslekov House and the well-preserved Lyutov House.

A ticket to each house-museum costs 2 lv. The combined ticket (5 lv) for all six house-museums is better value, and allows you to visit each museum over as many days as you want to spend in the village. Tickets can be bought at the souvenir shop, just up from the tourist information centre; if the shop is closed, simply ask for a combined ticket at one of the house-museums. Photos of the outside of each building are allowed, but you must pay a prohibitive extra fee to take photos inside.

Inside each house-museum there's a detailed explanation in English about the house and its owners but little else is explained in any language but Bulgarian. Each building is open daily from 9.30am to 5.30pm in summer, but most close for one or two days (often Sunday or Monday) in winter.

Debelyanov's mother anxiously awaiting his return, and the words 'I die and am yet born again in light'.

Special Events

The **Folklore Days Festival** (mid-August), and the **Re-enactment of the 1876 April Uprising** (1–2 May) are annual events. Every five years is the mammoth **International Folk Festival** (next in 2005).

Hiking

See the boxed text 'Hiking in the Sredna Gora' later in this chapter for information about local hiking trails.

Places to Stay

The oversupply of rooms in hotels and private homes means the choice is extensive and the prices are often low. The quality of private rooms is similar to those found in most hotels, except the latter (mostly) have private bathrooms. All hotels listed here, and almost all private rooms, include breakfast.

The Tourist Information Centre (☎/fax 2191, e koprivshtitsa@hotmail.com) at ploshtad 20 April can help you with *rooms* in private homes for 18-22 lv per person.

Staff can show photos of many of the rooms on offer.

Shuleva House Hotel (☎ 2122, ul Hadzhi Nencho Palaveev 37) Singles/doubles 18/24 lv, apartments 40 lv. Although the rooms need renovation, this hotel is excellent value. The rooms are large, simple and clean, and readers have commented about the friendly staff. The apartments come with TV. All rooms have bathrooms.

Hotel Trayanova Kâshta & Byaloto Konche (☎ 2250, ul Gereniloto 5) Singles 22-26 lv, doubles 44-53 lv. This hotel/restaurant complex – also called the White Horse – is outstanding value. It offers huge, quiet rooms wonderfully furnished with traditional pieces, and most include a TV. All guests must use shared bathrooms.

Hotel Panorama (☎ 2035, ul Georgi Benkovski 40) Singles/doubles 34/48 lv, 4-bed family rooms 60 lv. Although 400m from the bus stop, it's the only place that offers any views. The rooms are comfortable and well furnished (including TV and bathroom). The French-speaking owners are amiable.

Hotel Astra (☎ 2364, e hotel–astra@ hotmail.com, ul Hadzhi Nencho Palaveev 11) Singles/doubles 40/60 lv. In a gorgeous garden setting, the Astra is popular and homely, and the rooms are large and spotless. It is, however, a little pricey, and not that much better than a private room. All rooms have a bathroom.

Hotel Kalina (☎ *2032, ul Hadzhi Nencho Palaveev 15)* Singles/doubles with bathroom 40/53 lv. The classiest place in town is the three-star Kalina. All rooms have a bathroom, the rates are surprisingly good value, and it gets our 'loveliest garden in town' award.

Places to Eat

Koprivshtitsa is one of Bulgaria's main tourist attractions, so watch out for unscrupulous waiters and menus in English without prices. The cheapest places for a meal – at non-tourist prices, with menus in Bulgarian and prices clearly shown – are the *cafes* behind the market.

April 20 National Restaurant (*pl 20 April*) Salads 2.50 lv, main meals from 4.50 lv. The servings here are large, and the *kavarma* (meat and vegetables in a pot) is particularly delicious. The restaurant is popular with bus groups, so ask for the Bulgarian menu to avoid paying the high tourist prices.

Lomeva Kâshta Tavern (*ul Hadzhi Nencho Palaveev 42*) Salads 1.50 lv, grills from 3.50 lv. Hard to miss with its striking blue exterior, this cosy place offers traditional cuisine at reasonable prices. The low ceilings and fireplace inside are reminiscent of a quaint English pub – perfect for a drink or meal on a cold evening.

Chuchura (*ul Hadzhi Nencho Palaveev 66*) Main meals 3-4.50 lv. This charming place offers an enticing street-side setting near the bus stop. The beer is alarmingly flat and warm, but the meals are tasty and good value.

Mehana Starite Borove (*pl 20 April*) Salads 1.50 lv, most meals 3.50-5 lv. Almost hidden along a laneway near the main square, Starite Borove is nearly jutting into the shady park and is the best place for a drink in summer. It's quieter than places around the main square but the food is fairly unexciting.

Shopping

Predictably, several **souvenir shops** surround the main square, but most of the stuff for sale is tacky. One fine memento of Koprivshtitsa is a carpet or bag made from felt cloth; examples are on display inside the Lyutov House (see earlier). Alongside the Byala Stream, some 19th-century weaving equipment can be seen through the window of the charming **Tepavitsa Valyavitsa Craft Complex** but it's often closed.

At the **Craft Shop** (☎ 2191), on ulitsa Dimcho Debelyanov, visitors can see felt cloth products being made, and buy some items next door. It's open Monday to Saturday from 10am to 4pm.

Getting There & Away

From the Sofia's Princess Hotel bus station West, a bus departs for Koprivshtitsa (4.50 lv, 2½ hours) at 4pm Monday to Saturday, and 5pm on Sunday. From Koprivshtitsa, it leaves for Sofia at about 6.30am Monday to Saturday, and 2pm on Sunday. Another bus departs Koprivshtitsa for Plovdiv at 6.30am, and returns from the *sever* (northern) bus

---

Hiking in the Sredna Gora

The Sredna Gora (Central Range) Mountains are spread over 6000 sq km from Iskâr George (near Sofia) to the Tundzha Valley (south of Yambol). The highest peak is Mt Bogdan (1603m) near Koprivshtitsa.

The Mountains of Bulgaria by Julian Perry provides a detailed description of the popular two- or three-day hike from Hisarya (also known as Hisar) to Koprivshtitsa (or vice versa). No dedicated map of the Sredna Gora Mountains is available, but most of the mountains and hiking routes are included in the map of Stara Planina that is published by Kartografia.

The map of Koprivshtitsa, published by Domino and available in the village, includes a small, but clear, map with five enticing hiking routes around the surrounding hills. One trail (about four hours one-way) leads to Mt Bogdan, and a hut where hikers can stay overnight.

station in Plovdiv at 4.30pm. If the departure times from Koprivshtitsa are not suitable, catch one of the hourly minibuses to Pirdop, via Anton, and get a connection to places like Sofia, Karlovo (the junction for Plovdiv), Kazanlâk and Stara Zagora.

The train station is about 9km north of the village at a place simply called Railway Station Koprivshtitsa. Between the village and train station, about 10 minibuses a day travel in both directions to connect to all train arrivals and departures. From Sofia, five or six slow passenger trains stop at the station each day, but only one fast train (1st/2nd class 4.55/3.20 lv, 1¾ hours) from the capital stops on its way to Burgas, via Karlovo. If you're heading east from Koprivshtitsa, change trains at Karlovo for Plovdiv and at Tulovo for Veliko Târnovo.

There is a train timetable (in Bulgarian), and a bus schedule (in English), that are helpfully placed on the window of the bus stop (☎ 2133) in Koprivshtitsa.

TETEVEN
ТЕТЕВЕН
☎ 0678 • pop 12,400
This picturesque and historic town along the Vit River, 116km north-east of Sofia, is a little remote and often ignored by travellers. The tourist office (☎ 4217, e vita–tur@infotel.bg) on ploshtad Sava Mladenov can provide information about local **hiking trails** and **caves** (which are only accessible by private vehicle or chartered taxi).

The **Teteven Museum of History** (☎ 2005, pl Sava Mladenov; admission 1.50 lv; open daily 9am-noon & 2pm-5pm in summer, Mon-Fri in winter) has over 40,000 archaeological, ethnological and historical displays. Also worth a visit are the **All Saint's Church** (ul Simeon Koumanov 15) and the 14th-century **St Elija's Monastery** in the north-eastern part of town. The monastery boasts beautiful murals.

The best places to stay are *Harmonia Hotel* (☎ 5552, ul Vurshets 30), which has basic doubles with a bathroom for about 30 lv, and *Olimp Hotel* (☎ 3733, ul Treti Mart)*, which has singles/doubles with a bathroom for 22/44 lv.

Buses regularly travel from Teteven to Sofia, Vratsa, Pleven, Lovech and Veliko Târnovo. To get to ploshtad Sava Mladenov from the bus station (☎ 2427), walk (250m) over the river and turn right (east).

LOVECH
ЛОВЕЧ
☎ 068 • pop 49,000
Most travellers tend to bypass Lovech, because it's not on the main east-west highway or railway line from Sofia. This is a shame. Lovech is a likeable and manageable town pleasantly located alongside the Osêm River 35km south of Pleven. It has obviously benefited greatly from the Beautiful Bulgaria Project, especially in Varosha (the old town) where over 150 glorious buildings from the Bulgarian national revival period have been lovingly restored.

During Thracian and Roman eras, and the Second Bulgarian Empire (1185–1396), Lovech was economically and militarily important. The town reached its zenith during the Ottoman occupation, even though it was also the headquarters of the Bulgarian Central Revolutionary Committee during the mid-19th century.

Orientation & Information
From the bus station, and adjacent train station, walk east along ulitsa Zacko Shishkov (as signposted in English), veer to the right and follow the signs (in English) to *centrum* (about 20 minutes). At the end of the road, turn left (north) along ulitsa Bulgaria to the modern town, where the banks, foreign-exchange offices and post office are huddled around the main square, ploshtad Dimitrov. Alternatively, turn right (south) past colourful, renovated buildings, and the Hotel Lovech, to the footbridge and nearby vehicle bridge leading to the old town.

Things to See
Just past the Hotel Lovech is the **Pokrirtya Most** (covered footbridge), which is the only one of its kind in Bulgaria. Built in 1872, and completely restored twice since, the charming wooden interior belies the disappointingly modern shops inside. Walk

across the bridge, and past the Hotel Orbita 2, to the **Art Gallery** (*☎ 23 937, ul Vasil Levski 9; admission free; open Mon-Sat 8am-5pm*). It features works by local and other Bulgarian artists.

From near the art gallery, the cobblestone ulitsa Hristo Ivanov Golemia, heads uphill. About 100m along is the **Ethnographical Museum** (*☎ 27 720; admission 3 lv & photos an extra 3 lv; open Mon-Sat 8am-noon & 2pm-5pm*). The two mid-19th-century buildings contain several fascinating exhibits and period furniture, but the highlight is probably the wine-making equipment in the dark cellar. Ask the caretaker for a (free) leaflet with explanations in English, French or German.

About 50m farther up is the **Vasil Levski Museum** (*☎ 27 990*). Although undergoing renovations at the time of research, the displays about the revered revolutionary will probably be more extensive than those in similar museums around the country. Another 50m uphill is the renovated Byzantine **St Bogoroditsa Church**. If it's not open, visitors can still wander around the grounds and peer through the windows.

From the church, the easy-to-see series of steps pass more renovated **national revival homes** and lead to **Stratesh Hill**, often carpeted with lilac blooms and home to a huge **Levski statue**. Nearby, is a **zoo** (*☎ 22 265*) and the fascinating, and surprisingly extensive, ruins of a **Bulgarian fortress** (*admission free; open daily 8am-6pm*). It was here that a treaty was signed with the Turks, which lead to the creation of the Second Bulgarian Empire.

Places to Stay & Eat

Most hotels in Lovech are overpriced, which is one reason to day trip from Pleven or Troyan. Each hotel listed here offers rooms with a bathroom.

Hotel-Restaurant Varosha (*☎ 25 951*) Singles/doubles 20/40 lv. Just across the footbridge and overlooking the main square in the old town, this hotel is good value. The spacious and basic rooms have balconics, but try to get a room away from the noisy cafes below.

Hotel Orbita 2 (*☎ 23 813,* **e** *tsariana@mbox.digsys.bg*) Singles/doubles/triples 60/80/90 lv. Near the old town square (or follow the signs from the vehicle bridge), this place is a little pricey for foreigners, especially because not all rooms have TVs and fridges. The hotel was being renovated at the time of research, so it will be good value if it doesn't subsequently raise its prices.

Hotel Oasis (*☎ 26 239, ul NV Dracov 17*) Singles/doubles 25/50 lv. Overlooking the river, this quiet and homely guesthouse offers clean and comfortable rooms with TVs and heaps of furniture. Follow the signs (100m) from the vehicle bridge. A decent *restaurant* is attached.

Kafe Varosha Most meals 3.50-5 lv. Almost next door to the Ethnographical Museum (see Things to See), this charming *mehana* (tavern) offers traditional Bulgarian food, and live music if there's enough patrons to get the manager excited.

Kleopatra Bar & Grill Main meals 3-4.50 lv. Opposite the Hotel Orbita 2, the Kleopatra offers Western food at above-average prices with good service and a pleasant outdoor setting.

Getting There & Away

From the bus station (*☎ 23 204*), up to three buses a day head to Burgas, Sliven, Teteven and Veliko Târnovo, and more frequently to Kazanlâk. Buses also leave every hour for Pleven (2.50 lv, one hour) and Troyan (2 lv, 45 minutes). Five or six public and private buses travel to Sofia (9-10 lv, three hours) every day.

Lovech is on an inconvenient spur track from the main Sofia-Varna train line, via Pleven. From the train station (*☎ 24 935*), three slow passenger trains depart daily for Troyan, and another three go to Levski, where connections are possible to Sofia and Gora Oryahovitsa (for Veliko Târnovo).

TROYAN
ТРОЯН
☎ 0670 • pop 26,200

On the Osêm River, which is 36km south of Lovech, Troyan is an unremarkable but pleasant town. It is a good base for day trips

Hiking in the Stara Planina

With an average height of little more than 700m, the Stara Planina (Old Mountain) range is not high, particularly compared to the Rila and Pirin Mountains. Nonetheless it is vast, covering 11,500 sq km (about 10% of Bulgaria) and, at close to 550km long, extending almost the entire length of the country. Nearly 30 peaks are over 2000m high and the mountains feed one-third of Bulgaria's major rivers. The highest point is Mt Botev (2376m), north of Karlovo.

The Mountains of Bulgaria by Julian Perry describes the strenuous 25-day (650-700km) trek across the entire range. This trek, which starts at Berkovitsa, near the Yugoslavian border, and finishes at Emine Cape, about 20km north-east of Nesebâr on the Black Sea coast, is part of the trans-European E3 trek. The text in Perry's book is detailed, but the maps are poor, so buy the *Stara Planina* map, published by Kartografia and available at bookshops in Sofia. The *Troyan Balkan* map, available from the tourist office in Gabrovo, is detailed, but specific to the Troyan and Apriltsi regions.

The best place to get information about hiking, and possibly to arrange guides, is the non-government tourist group, the Association Stara Planina, established in 1996 with help from the Swiss NGO 'Inter Assist'. The association's main office is in Gabrovo, but there are also branches in Tryavna, Troyan and Teteven (see the relevant sections in this chapter for contact details), as well as the smaller towns of Dryanovo and Apriltsi. Many activities promoted by the association focus on the environment, eg, hiking, mountain biking and caving, as well as regional culture and handicrafts.

Some of the more interesting hikes along marked trails include:
Cherni Osêm to Hizha Ambaritsa (four hours)
The Dryanovo Eco-trail (see the Dryanovo Monastery section later)
Etâr to Sokolski Monastery (one hour), and continue to Shipka Pass (extra two-three hours – steep)
Gabrovo to Hizha Uzana (four hours – by road)
Karlovo to Hizha Hubavets (two hours), or continue to Hizha Vasil Levski (another two-three hours) and Mt Botev (further two-three hours)
Shipka Monastery to Shipka Pass (two hours)
Sliven to Hizha Karandila (three hours)

to Oreshak and Troyan Monastery (see the Around Troyan section), as well as Lovech and Karlovo.

Troyan was strategically important in the Thracian period. It later became famous for woodcarving, metalwork and particularly pottery during the Bulgarian national revival period. Examples of these crafts can be admired at the charming museum in Troyan, or bought at Oreshak.

Orientation & Information
From the bus station, or train station, which is a little further to the east, walk (10 minutes) over the footbridge along ulitsa Zahari Stoyanov. From here, turn right and walk along the mall, ulitsa General Kartsov, to Troyan's main square, ploshtad Vûzhrazhdane. The narrow main road, ulitsa Vasil Levski, starts north of the square and hugs the river.

One of the most pleasing aspects about Troyan is the excellent tourist office (☎ 35 064, ℮ info–troyan@tr.bia-bg.com). At ulitsa Vasil Levski 133, it's open daily from 8am to 8pm in summer and Monday to Friday 9am to 5pm in winter. As well as arranging numerous activities and private rooms, it can organise car rental from 35 lv per day, plus insurance and petrol.

Museum of Folk Craft & Applied Arts
At the main square, and excellently signposted in English, is this impressive museum (☎ 22 063, pl Vûzhrazhdane; admission 2 lv; open Mon-Sat 8am-noon & 1pm-5pm). The 10 halls contain displays

about textiles, woodcarving, metalwork, weaving, pottery and ceramics from the region, as well as some archaeological artefacts. Most captions are in English.

Activities

A range of activities can be arranged through the tourist office. Horse riding (15 lv per person per hour) is possible at one of several villages near Troyan. Mountain bikes can be rented (1/8 lv per hour/day) and used along one of five designated mountain bike routes, including to Troyan Monastery and Chiflik. Guides (40 lv per day), who speak French, German or English, are available for local tours and hikes.

Places to Stay & Eat

The tourist office (see earlier) can arrange *rooms* in private homes at villages within 6km of Troyan, such as Oreshak (see the Around Troyan section later). The cost is about 20/35 lv for singles/doubles with breakfast. The tourist office also offers *apartments* in central Troyan with kitchen facilities, sitting room and bathroom for 35 lv to 45 lv per double.

Kupina Hotel I (☎ 23 522, Kupincho Park) Singles/doubles/triples with bathroom 13/19/25 lv . Also called Hotel Kalina I, it is one of two adjacent hotels in the hillside park above the town. No. 1 offers the best value, because foreigners are charged the same as Bulgarians. The decor is typically 1960s, but the rooms are clean and comfortable, and the hotel is quiet. Rates include breakfast. Take a taxi (1 lv) from the bus station or town centre.

Hotel Nunki (☎ 22 160, ul Minko Radkovski) Singles/doubles US$40/50. The rooms here are large, quiet and lovingly decorated with charming national revival style furniture, and the bathrooms sparkle. Rates include breakfast. Attached is a classy *restaurant* with reasonable prices. The Nunki is at the start of the bridge (from where the road leads to Troyan Monastery) about 100m across from the tourist office.

For a snack, try one of the several *pizza joints* where ulitsa Vasil Levski meets ploshtad Vûzhrazhdane.

Getting There & Away

From the Troyan bus station (☎ 22 172), two or three buses a day travel to Veliko Târnovo, Plovdiv (via Karlovo) and Sofia (6 lv, three hours). Every hour, buses also go to Lovech (2 lv, 45 minutes), from where there are immediate connections to Pleven. Troyan is at the end of a spur track south of Lovech, so travelling by train is futile.

AROUND TROYAN
Oreshak
Орешак

About 6km south-east of Troyan is Oreshak, home of the **National Fair and Exhibition of Arts & Crafts Complex** (☎ 06952-2317, *Oreshak; open Tues-Sun 8am-6pm*). This complex displays and sells embroidery, pottery, ceramics, weaving, woodcarving and metalwork. It is the best place in the Stara Planina region to pick up authentic, locally made souvenirs at reasonable prices. The week-long annual fair (usually around mid-August) is held at the complex. Another cheerful time to be in Oreshak is during the **Festival of the Plums and Plum Brandy** (late September).

Oreshak is an alternative place to stay to Troyan, and not far (4km) by bus or on foot from the Troyan Monastery. The tourist office in Troyan (see earlier) can arrange *rooms* in private homes for about 18 lv per person including breakfast. Guests in these private homes can also order large servings of traditional **meals** for an extra cost.

Every hour, a ramshackle bus (1 lv, 20 minutes) leaves the bus station in Troyan for Cherni Osêm, and stops at Oreshak and the Troyan Monastery.

Troyan Monastery
Троянски Манастр

Only 10km south-east of Troyan is Bulgaria's third-largest monastery (*admission free; open daily 6am-10pm*), after Rila (see Rila Monastery in the Southern Bulgaria chapter) and Bachkovo (see Around Plovdiv in the Southern Bulgaria chapter). Troyan is also one of the most accessible monasteries in the country, and consequently is a popular attraction for locals and foreigners.

The Valley of Roses

Rosa Damascena, which probably originated from modern-day India, arrived in Bulgaria from Asia Minor several centuries ago. It flourished in the warm climate of what became known as the Valley of Roses, the narrow plain reaching from Karlovo to Kazanlâk, between the Stara Planina and Sredna Gora mountain ranges. The valley has served perfume industries across Europe, particularly in France, since the early 18th century, and was, until recently, the source of 70% of the world's supply of rose oil.

Roses bloom between about late May and early June (depending on the prevailing weather conditions). Ideally, petals should be plucked while still covered with dew (ie, between 4am and 10am) so the fragrance can be preserved. Petals are then treated with steam to extract the oil. The time, effort and expense required is *staggering*: about 3000kg of rose petals are required to produce 1kg of rose oil. And considering that one rose bush averages about 20 roses per year, and one petal weighs just 2.5g, it's no wonder that 1kg of rose oil can fetch over US$3000.

The Festival of Roses (first weekend in June) features many, umm, 'rosy' events and parades in Kazanlâk and Karlovo.

Some sections of this 16th-century monastery survived numerous attacks by the Turks between the 16th and 18th centuries, but most of what still stands today was built in 1835. The colourful murals inside the **Church of the Holy Virgin** were painted in the 1840s by Zahari Zograf, regarded as the leading mural artist during the Bulgarian national revival period. The monastery is also renowned for its remarkable woodcarvings, including the altar, created in the mid-19th century by experts from Tryavna. The highlight for most, though, is the legendary Three-Handed Holy Virgin, only seen in public during the annual monastery celebrations on **Virgin Mary's Day** (15 August).

The ubiquitous revolutionary Vasil Levski formed and trained insurgents at the monastery and even cajoled the monks to join the fight against the Turks in 1876. This rather irreverent history is highlighted in the small, separate **museum** *(admission 1 lv)* on the third floor. The museum door is usually locked, so ask someone at the reception office inside the gate to open it.

Although not nearly as touristy as the Rila Monastery, several businesses have sprung up in and around the Troyan Monastery, including *cafes*, **souvenirs shops** and **art galleries**. There's even an **Internet centre** in the monastery grounds!

Contact the reception office if you want to stay in one of the basic ***rooms***. These cost 10/20/30 lv for singles/doubles/triples with a shared bathroom.

Every hour, the ramshackle bus between Troyan and Cherni Osêm stops at the monastery gates. A taxi from central Troyan to the monastery costs about 4.50 lv for a one-way trip.

KARLOVO
КАРЛОВО
☎ 0335 • pop 27,700

Karlovo, about halfway between Sofia and Sliven on the E6 highway, is not a bad place to break up a journey. It's also easy to visit on a day trip from the larger and more interesting cities of Kazanlâk and Plovdiv. Karlovo is most famous as the birthplace of Vasil Levski.

Orientation & Information
The main thoroughfare is (of course) called ulitsa Vasil Levski. It stretches for 2km from the train station (on the other side of the park) and passes most places listed here. It turns into a pedestrian mall and finishes at the town square, ploshtad 20 Yuli. (The bus station is about 100m up, and to the left, as you exit the train station.) There are several foreign-exchange offices and Internet centres at the top end of the mall.

Things to See & Do

From the train (or bus) station, walk about 700m up ulitsa Vasil Levski to ploshtad Vasil Levski, where the great man is immortalised (again) in a bold **statue**. Turn right, and right again, to the **St Bogoroditsa Church** *(admission free; open daily 7am-7pm)*, which contains intricate wooden iconostases.

Opposite, in a mustard-coloured building, is the **History Museum** *(☎ 4728, ul Vûzrozhdenska 4; admission 0.50 lv; open Tues-Sun 9am-noon & 1pm-5pm)*. Also known as the Town Museum, it was closed at the time of research, but features a large array of ethnological displays.

Farther up ulitsa Vasil Levski is a small park with the decrepit **Kurshum Dzhamiya mosque**, built in 1485. Continue up the mall to the town square, then head left (west) for about 300m, past the **clock tower**, to the **Vasil Levski Museum** *(☎ 3489, ul Gen Kartzov 57; admission 1 lv; open Mon-Fri 8.30am-1pm & 2pm-5.30pm)*. This quaint collection of rooms around a cobblestone courtyard contains several exhibits about Levski with explanations in English. Ask the caretaker to show you the modern shrine, where you can see a lock of Levski's hair while listening to taped religious chants in Bulgarian. A guided tour in English costs 2.50 lv per person.

For information about **hiking** in the region see the boxed text 'Hiking in the Stara Planina' earlier.

Places to Stay & Eat

The choice of hotels is actually better in nearby Hisarya (see later).

Hemus Hotel *(☎ 4597, ul Vasil Levski 87)* Singles/doubles with shared bathroom 14/28 lv. This small, family home has four basic, but comfortable, rooms. Most were being renovated at the time of research, so the amenities may be better (and the prices higher) by the time you get there.

Sherev Hotel *(☎ 3380, pl 20 Yuli)* Singles/doubles with bathroom cost from US$15/25 to US$40/60. The cheaper standard rooms are nothing to get excited about, but they are reasonable value. The newer 'luxury' rooms, which feature sparkling bathrooms and TV, are overpriced for foreigners. The central location overlooking the main square is an attraction. Rates include breakfast.

Ploshtad 20 Yuli is surrounded by charming *cafes*; the best are either side of the Sherev Hotel.

Getting There & Away

From the bus station *(☎ 3155)*, about eight buses a day go to Hisarya, and several depart for Stara Zagora, Troyan, Kazanlâk, Sofia and Veliko Târnovo. About every hour, a bus travelling to or from Plovdiv (2.80 lv, one hour) stops in Karlovo, not far from the Vasil Levski Museum (see earlier).

The tidy train station *(☎ 4641)* is on the line between Sofia and Burgas, going via Kazanlâk and Sliven. From Sofia, one fast train and one express (1st/2nd class 7.50/5.30 lv, 2¼ hours) stop at Karlovo. The express from Sofia continues to Burgas (9.50/6.90 lv, four hours). Six slow passenger trains a day also go to Plovdiv (4.30/3.30 lv, two hours), but the bus is far quicker and more frequent.

Vasil Levski

The most revered person in recent Bulgarian history may well be Vasil Levski, whose name is lent to numerous streets and squares, and who is immortalised in several statues and museums throughout the country.

Vasil Ivanov Kunchev was born on 6 July 1837 in Karlovo, and given the *nom de guerre* 'levski' (from the Bulgarian word for lion) by his peers. He studied and worked as a monk in Stara Zagora, but in 1862 moved to Belgrade to join the anti-Turkish rebellion led by Georgi Rakovski. Levski later moved to Romania, where he envisaged the creation of an independent and democratic Bulgaria. He then returned to Bulgaria, and travelled extensively establishing revolutionary cells, often based in remote monasteries. In early 1872, he was betrayed by a comrade, and arrested by the Turks in Lovech. In February of the next year, Levski was hanged in Sofia.

HISARYA (HISAR)
ЄИСАРЯ (ЄИСАР)
☎ 0337 • pop 9180

The small town of Hisarya, sometimes called Hisar, is 17km south-west of Karlovo. It's popular with Bulgarian tourists, because of the mineral waters fed by 22 springs, which since Roman times have been used to cure all sorts of ailments. For most others, the main attractions are the remarkable roadside ruins.

From the bus station, and adjacent train station, walk (300m) down to the main road (ulitsa Hristo Botev), turn left to see some of the ruins, and then turn right into ulitsa Ivan Vazov to reach the town centre and the pleasant park.

Ruins
Originally built by the Romans and later fortified by the Byzantines, the walls protected the town and its mineral baths from raiders. The walls escaped damage from the Slavs (who did not come through this part of Bulgaria) and are probably the best preserved in Bulgaria. Still over 5m high and up to 3m thick, the walls once protected an area of 30 hectares. The most visited section (with basic explanations in French) is a short walk from the bus and train stations, while other ruins can be found along unnamed roads heading towards the town centre from the main road. Nothing is fenced, so visitors can wander around any of the ruins at any time.

Archaeological Museum
This museum (☎ 2012, ul Stamboliyski 8; admission 2 lv; open daily 8am-11.30am & 1pm-4.30pm) features a scale model of the city walls, and some photos of early excavations, but is a disappointment. Paradoxically, the displays about traditional regional costumes, and agricultural and weaving equipment, are more interesting. The museum is not well signposted; it's past the post office and accessible from the main road through an arch in one of the walls.

Mineral Baths
Both hotels listed here have **balneological centres**, which offer also sorts of treatments, such as aromatherapy and hydrotherapy.

Consultations with 'head physicians' cost from 25 lv for 30 minutes, depending on the type of treatment required, and the necessary (or unnecessary) extras provided, such as medications and lotions.

Places to Stay & Eat
Both hotels are about 1km down ulitsa General Gurko, which starts about 700m along the main road (ulitsa Hristo Botev) from the bus and train stations – look for the sign (in English) to Hotel Augusta. Both are in an abandoned part of town, but close to the mineral springs.

Hotel Hisar (☎ 2727, fax 3634, ul General Gurko) Singles/doubles with bathroom 35/50 lv. This huge place is truly stuck in the 1950s (eg, the rooms feature few amenities except a wall-mounted radio), but the bathrooms are newish and even contain a bidet.

Hotel Augusta (☎ 3821, e augusta@bse.bg, ul General Gurko) Singles/doubles with bathroom US$31/35. The Augusta is still trapped in the 1970s (which at least makes it more modern than the Hotel Hisar), but the rooms are comfortable and offer a balcony and TV. Rates include breakfast, and there's a swimming pool. The foyer features a decent little collection of **archaeological artefacts**, all nicely labelled in English.

Several classy *restaurants* can be found near both hotels, but the most agreeable place for a drink and/or meal are the *cafes* around the park in the town centre.

Getting There & Away
About eight buses a day travel to Plovdiv and Karlovo, and one or two go to Sofia, Troyan, and Veliko Târnovo, via Kazanlâk and Gabrovo. Regular buses between Karlovo and Panagyurishte also pass through Hisarya. There are no train services to Karlovo, but six slow passenger trains a day depart for Plovdiv.

STARA ZAGORA
СТАРА ЗАГОРА
☎ 042 • pop 155,600

One of Bulgaria's more agreeable cities is Stara Zagora, in the southern foothills of the

Sredna Gora mountain range. Bulgaria's sixth-largest city is also a major transport hub, so many travellers find themselves passing through anyway. It's a modern place with straight, flat, tree-lined streets (signposted in English), one of the nicest central parks in Bulgaria and enough museums and old buildings to keep most visitors happy for a day or two. Stara Zagora is also famous as the home of the much-loved Zagorka Brewery (but tours are not permitted!).

History

The salubrious climate and fertile land around Stara Zagora attracted many invaders and settlers, including the Thracians (from 4th century BC) who called it Beroe. In around AD 100, the Romans came and created a prosperous city they called Ulpia Augusta Trayana. The city was later destroyed many times by the Turks and abandoned in the mid-13th century. It was the centre of fierce fighting during the Russian-Turkish War, and again completely demolished by the Turks in 1877. Most of the Thracian and Roman ruins were also wrecked at this time and the few surviving remnants of those eras are now buried under the modern city. Reconstruction of Stara Zagora commenced in 1879, and the city is now a thriving educational and cultural centre which boasts one of Bulgaria's first opera theatres.

Information

Although Stara Zagora is the headquarters of Domino, which publishes an excellent series of Bulgarian maps, the bookstalls, and the Penguin Bookshop on ulitsa Tsar Simeon Veliki, just down from the Art Gallery, only sell maps of Stara Zagora. The art gallery sells an impressive book of photos entitled *Stara Zagora: An Ancient Town with 8000 Years' History* (5 lv), which makes an ideal memento.

Plenty of foreign-exchange offices can be found along ulitsa Tsar Simeon Veliki, but if you want to change travellers cheques, or use a credit card to obtain cash, go to the Bulbank on ulitsa Tsar Simeon Veliki, or the United Bulgarian Bank, along a tiny mall off ulitsa Rilski. The post office,

ulitsa Sv Knyaz Boris I, is open Monday to Friday from 9am to noon and 2pm to 5pm. The attached telephone centre is open daily from 6am to midnight. In the same building as the Penguin Bookshop is the trendy Cafe Zagora Internet centre.

Old City

Stara Zagora is built on the grid of an ancient Roman city, so some amazing discoveries have been unearthed. For example, the massive **floor mosaic**, dated to the 4th to 5th century AD, is displayed in the eastern entrance of the post office. The room relies on natural light, however, so it's a bit hard to appreciate on an overcast day.

The **Roman Theatre** (*ul Mitropolit Metodii Kusev*), often called the Antique Forum Augusta Trayana, was built in the 3rd century AD. It seems strangely ignored (there's not even a cafe in sight!) and at the time of research no restoration was being undertaken due to a lack of funds. Although visitors cannot wander around, there's plenty to see from the roadside. Alternatively, ask around for information about concerts which are sometimes held at the theatre.

Neolithic Dwellings Museum

The remains of two small one-roomed semidetached homes from the new Stone Age (about 6000 BC) are housed in a secure and airtight environment at the Neolithic Dwellings Museum (*☎ 600 299; admission 3 lv; open Tues-Sat 9am-noon & 2pm-5pm*). The homes were consumed by fire several millennia ago, so they're among the best preserved Neolithic dwellings in the Balkans.

The caretaker can provide a guided **tour** (which may be given whether requested or not) for 5 lv per group (minimum of five people). A tour is really the only way to determine the doors, walls, chimneys, and remains of hand-made pottery, among the rubble. The *Neolithic Dwellings: Stara Zagora* booklet (2 lv), available at the museum, will also help explain it all.

The basement features exhibits of pottery, tools and jewellery from this and other excavations, but nothing is labelled in English, so

STARA ZAGORA СТАРА ЗАГОРА

PLACES TO STAY & EAT
10 Prince Hamburgers
13 Hapkata
     ХАПКАТА
15 Hotel Vereya; Happy Bar & Grill
     ХОТЕЛ ВЕРЕЯ
17 Hotel Ezeroto; Café &
     Restaurant Ezeroto
     ХОТЕЛ ЕЗЕРОТО,
     КАФЕ-РЕСТОРАНТ ЕЗЕРОТО
18 Hotel Zhelezhnik
     ХОТЕЛ ЖЕЛЕЖНИК

OTHER
1 Roman Theatre
    РИМСКИ ТЕАТЪР
2 Hospital
3 Neolithic Dwellings Museum
    МУЗЕЙ НА ПРАЙСТОРИЧЕСКИТЕ ХОРА
4 Geo Milev Drama Theatre
    ДРАМАТИЧЕН ТЕАТЪР ГЕО МИЛЕВ
5 United Bulgarian Bank
    ОБЕДИНЕНА БЪЛГАРСКА БАНКА
6 History Museum
    ИСТОРИЧЕСКИ МУЗЕЙ
7 Post Office; Telephone Centre; Floor Mosaic
8 Market
9 Bulbank
    БУЛБАНК
11 Eski Dzhamiya Mosque
     ДЖАМИЯТА ЕСКИ ДЖУМАЯ
12 District Fine Art Gallery; Penguin Bookshop;
     Cafe Zagora (Internet Centre)
     МУЗЕЙ НА ИЗЯЩНИТЕ ИЗКУСТВА,
     КНИЖАРНИЦА ПИНГВИН, КАФЕ ЗАГОРА
14 Hemus Tours
     ХЕМУС ТУР
16 Geo Milev House-Museum; Café
     КЪЩА-МУЗЕЙ ГЕО МИЛЕВ
19 Bus Station
20 Rila Bureau
     БЮРО РИЛА

the tour or booklet are worthwhile. Perhaps one of the strangest items on display is the 6000-year-old headless hedgehog.

The museum is hard to find: look for the grey-and-brown building surrounded by a wrought iron fence behind the signposted (in Bulgarian) Sudebna Meditsina along ulitsa Dr Todor Stoyanovich.

Other Attractions

The **History Museum** (☎ 600 299, ul Dimitâr Naumov; admission 2 lv; open 8am-noon & 1pm-5pm) was closed, and in disarray, at the time of researching this book. The curators

promise that it will be worth visiting in the future for the Roman and Thracian artefacts, among other things.

The two floors of the **District Fine Art Gallery** (☎ 22 380, ul Tsar Simeon Veliki 110; admission free; open Tues-Sat 9am-noon & 2pm-6pm) contain 4000 works by 19th-century Bulgarian artists, none of whom are particularly famous or talented.

The **Geo Milev House-Museum** (☎ 23 450, ul Geo Milev 35; admission 2 lv; open Mon-Sat 8am-noon & 1pm-6pm) is poorly signposted behind a white wall. The couple of rooms contain some manuscripts and paintings by locally born Milev (1895–1925). Milev lost an eye in WWI, but continued to write poetry dealing with social themes, such as *Septemvri* about the September 1923 agrarian revolution. This work was confiscated by the authorities and Milev was arrested. After the trial, he was kidnapped by the police and murdered. The major attraction of the museum is the charming *cafe* set up in the pretty courtyard. Contemporary artists also sell their work here.

One of the oldest mosques in Bulgaria is the **Eski Dzhamiya Mosque** *(ul Tsar Simeon Veliki)*. Built in the early 15th century, it sits incongruously among banks and department stores along the mall. The mosque has been abandoned, and seems beyond repair.

The **city garden** is one of the most attractive in Bulgaria; it's clean, and offers plenty of shade, grass, (new) seats and (functioning) fountains. At the back is the **Geo Milev Drama Theatre** *(28 Mitropolit Metodii Kusev)*, built in 1914. Almost as enticing is the unnamed **park** along ulitsa Bratya Zhekovi in front of the Hotel Ezeroto (see later). Visitors can hire **paddle boats**, or enjoy a drink alongside the tiny **lake**.

Places to Stay

The good news is that the quality of hotels in Stara Zagora is generally high; the bad news is that nothing is cheap for foreigners. Each hotel listed here offers rooms with a bathroom.

Hotel Zhelezhnik (☎ 22 158, ul Slavyanski) Singles/doubles 44/88 lv, apartments 88 lv. The Zhelezhnik is one of those ex-Balkantourist places still stuck in the 1950s. It probably hasn't been renovated since then – the curtains don't reach across the windows and the showers never work properly. But it is the cheapest place in town.

Hotel Tangra (☎ 600 901, fax 600 903, ul L Karavelov 80) Singles/doubles US$45/65. This quiet new hotel is about 15 minutes' walk east of the city centre, but is way overpriced. Rooms feature air-con, fridge and TV, and the rates include breakfast.

Hotel Ezeroto (☎ 600 103, e stroitel@szeda.bg, ul Bratya Zhekovi 60) Singles/doubles US$50/60, suites US$75. This

hotel boasts the best location in town (overlooking the park). The rooms contain classy furniture, a gorgeous bathroom, air-con, fridge and TV, and the rates include breakfast.

Hotel Vereya (☎ 618 600, e vereya tour@mbox.digsis.bg, ul Gen Gurko) Singles/doubles US$42/46 to US$46/50. The rooms have TV and air-con, but the only redeeming feature of this charmless motel-style place is the central location. Rates include breakfast.

Places to Eat

Prince Hamburgers (ul Tsar Simeon Veliki) Burgers 1.50 lv. This place serves some of the tastiest burgers in Bulgaria and the crunchy bits of onion add enormously to the flavour.

Cafe & Restaurant Ezeroto (ul Bratya Zhekovi) Grills from 3.50 lv. Attached to the hotel of the same name (see earlier), this place is charmingly set alongside a small lake surrounded by willow trees. Happily, it also serves some of the most delicious food in the region.

Dozens of *cafes* are set up along ulitsa Tsar Simeon Veliki; the most agreeable are along the eastern end, ie, opposite the park and near the corner of ulitsa Sv Patriarh. There are a couple of *bakeries* and places selling tasty toasted sandwiches such as *Hapkata* near the corner of ulitsa Rilski and ulitsa Tsar Simeon Veliki.

Getting There & Away

About hourly from the bus station (☎ 22 145) on bulevard Slavyanski, public and private buses leave for Sofia (8 lv, four hours) and Plovdiv (3.80 lv, 1½ hours). There are also regular services each day to Haskovo (3.50 lv, 1½ hours), Sliven (4 lv, 1¼ hours), and Veliko Târnovo (7.50 lv, three hours). There are also a couple of services to Burgas, Ruse and Pleven.

For Kazanlâk (2 lv, 45 minutes), catch a bus towards Veliko Târnovo (which stops at Kazanlâk), or get a direct minibus (which departs when full) from the bus station. Minibuses from Kazanlâk will drop passengers off in the centre of Stara Zagora.

CENTRAL BULGARIA

From outside its office, Hemus Tours (☎ 57 018) ulitsa Tsar Simeon Veliki, offers private buses to Sofia (8 lv), Pleven (11 lv) and Plovdiv (5 lv), and regular services to Athens.

Stara Zagora train station (☎ 50 145) is at the southern end of bulevard Mitropolit Metodii Kusev. Stara Zagora is along the more commonly used train line between Sofia and Burgas, travelling via Plovdiv. For Sofia there are four fast trains and one express (express 1st/2nd class 10.30/7.60 lv, four hours) every day. Heading to Burgas, there are four fast trains and one express (1st/2nd class 10/7.30 lv, two hours) daily. Five trains a day also go to Kazanlâk and Veliko Târnovo.

The Rila Bureau (☎ 22 724), which sells advanced tickets for domestic trains and tickets for all international services, is at the train station.

KAZANLÂK
КАЗАНЛЪК
☎ 0431 • pop 62,750

Kazanlâk is an important transport hub along the train line and highway between Sofia and Burgas. Tucked between the Stara Planina and Sredna Gora mountain ranges, it's at the eastern end of the Valley of Roses (see the boxed text earlier) and is a centre for the production of rose oil. Originally settled as the Roman city of Sevtopolis, Kazanlâk isn't an attractive town, and doesn't boast the history of Veliko Târnovo, or the cafes and parks of Stara Zagora. But, it does offer several worthwhile attractions, and is a useful base for visiting Sliven, Karlovo or Shipka.

Information

There are surprisingly few places to change money; the most reliable is Magic Exchange, on ulitsa Otets Paisii. The combined post office and telephone centre is at ulitsa 23rd Pehoten Shipchenski Polk, and there's an Internet centre just west of the main square, ploshtad Sevtopolis. The travel agency, Agence Pagane (☎/fax 26 900), ulitsa Petko D Petkov, has French- and English-speaking staff who can arrange hotel reservations and local tours.

Thracian Tomb of Kazanlâk & Museum

In the scruffy **Tyulbe Park**, just up from the Kulata Ethnological Complex, is a heavily secured **tomb** (☎ 24 700), built in the 4th century BC for a Thracian ruler. Discovered during the construction of a bomb shelter in 1944, the tomb is now a Unesco World Heritage site, and cannot be visited without official permission.

To satisfy tourists, a full-scale replica has been created in the nearby **museum** (☎ 26 055; admission 2 lv; open daily 8am-6pm). Follow the signs along the obvious path from the tomb. Along the vaulted entry corridor (dromos) of the tomb replica is a double frieze with battle scenes. The burial chamber is 12m in diameter, and covered by a beehive dome which is typical of those built by Thracians between the 3rd and 5th centuries BC. The dome contains several murals which feature events such as a funeral feast and chariot race. The museum is tiny, however, and a little anticlimactic.

Iskra Museum & Art Gallery

Well worth a visit is this combined museum and art gallery (☎ 23 741, ul Sv Sv Kiril i Metodii; admission for both 2 lv; open daily 9am-noon & 2pm-5.30pm in summer & Mon-Fri in winter). The extensive archaeological displays on the ground floor include pottery, jewellery and tools from excavations of several Thracian tombs, including the one in Tyulbe Park (see earlier). All explanations are in Bulgarian, so the brochure (2 lv) in English, French or German is helpful.

Upstairs, a vast number of paintings are on display, including those by renowned local artists such as Ivan Milev and Vasil Barakov. Ask the caretaker for a printed catalogue (in English and French).

Museum of the Roses

The grandly-named Research Institute for Roses, Aromatic & Medicinal Plants houses the tiny Museum of the Roses (☎ 23 741, ul Osvobozhdenie; admission free; open daily 9am-5pm in summer). The photos and displays explain (in Bulgarian only) the 300-year-old method of cultivating the roses,

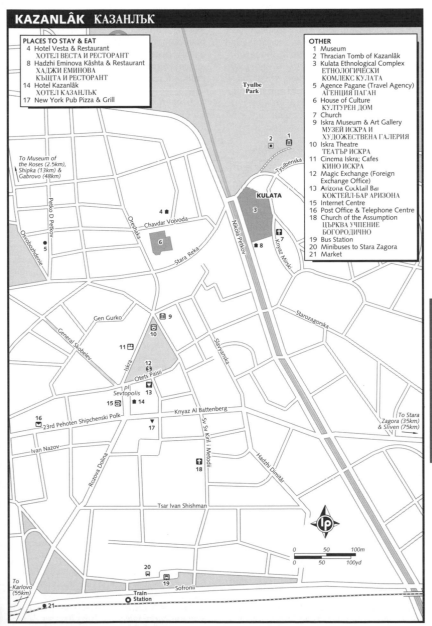

KAZANLÂK КАЗАНЛЪК

PLACES TO STAY & EAT
- 4 Hotel Vesta & Restaurant
  ХОТЕЛ ВЕСТА И РЕСТОРАНТ
- 8 Hadzhi Eminova Kâshta & Restaurant
  ХАДЖИ ЕМИНОВА
  КЪЩТА И РЕСТОРАНТ
- 14 Hotel Kazanlâk
  ХОТЕЛ КАЗАНЛЪК
- 17 New York Pub Pizza & Grill

OTHER
- 1 Museum
- 2 Thracian Tomb of Kazanlâk
- 3 Kulata Ethnological Complex
  ЕТНОЛОГИЧЕСКИ
  КОМЛЕКС КУЛАТА
- 5 Agence Pagane (Travel Agency)
  АГЕНЦИЯ ПАГАН
- 6 House of Culture
  КУЛТУРЕН ДОМ
- 7 Church
- 9 Iskra Museum & Art Gallery
  МУЗЕЙ ИСКРА И
  ХУДОЖЕСТВЕНА ГАЛЕРИЯ
- 10 Iskra Theatre
  ТЕАТЪР ИСКРА
- 11 Cinema Iskra; Cafes
  КИНО ИСКРА
- 12 Magic Exchange (Foreign
  Exchange Office)
- 13 Arizona Cocktail Bar
  КОКТЕЙЛ-БАР АРИЗОНА
- 15 Internet Centre
- 16 Post Office & Telephone Centre
- 18 Church of the Assumption
  ЦЪРКВА УЧПЕНИЕ
  БОГОРОДИЧНО
- 19 Bus Station
- 20 Minibuses to Stara Zagora
- 21 Market

Tyulbe Park

To Museum of the Roses (2.5km), Shipka (13km) & Gabrovo (48km)

KULATA

Tyulbenska

Petko D Petkov

Obvbozhdenie

Orehaka

Chavdar Vojvoda

Stara Reka

Nikola Petkov

Knyaz Mirki

Gen Gurko

General Skobelev

Starozagorska

Slavjanska

Iskra

Otets Paisii

pl Sevtopolis

Knyaz Al Battenberg

Sv Sv Kiril i Metodii

23rd Pehoten Shipchenski Polk

To Stara Zagora (35km) & Sliven (75km)

Ivan Nazov

Rozova Dolina

Hadzhi Dimitâr

Tsar Ivan Shishman

To Karlovo (55km)

Sofronii

Train Station

0   50   100m
0   50   100yd

picking their petals and processing the oil. The attached **shop** sells rose oils, perfumes, shampoos, liqueurs, tea bags and jams, and is popular with the occasional tour group. The museum is 3km north of the town centre up ulitsa Osvobozhdenie; take a taxi (1.5 lv one way), or bus No 3 from the town square. Guided tours (rates negotiable) are available in English and French, but ring first about opening times in winter.

Kulata Ethnological Complex

In the quaint Kulata (Tower) district near Tyulbe Park you will come across the small but interesting Kulata Ethnological Complex (☎ *21 733, ul Knyaz Mirski; admission 2 lv; open daily 8am-noon & 1pm-6pm)*. Inside the grounds there's a replica of a one-storey peasant's home (under renovation at the time of research) and wooden sheds with agricultural implements and carts. A courtyard leads to the two-storey House of Hadzhi Eno, built by a wealthy rose merchant in the style typical of the Bulgarian national revival period.

Some explanations in German and English are nailed to the walls. The caretaker may invite you to try some rose tea, liqueur or jam (for which you'll be expected to pay a small extra amount). The entrance is hard to find: it's along the eastern section opposite the gates to an impressive stone **church**.

Places to Stay

Hadzhi Eminova Kâshta (☎ 42 095, ul Nikola Petkov 22) Rooms 20 lv, apartment 40 lv. This picturesque guesthouse is the best deal in town and one of the nicest places in the region. It's also the only place in Kazanlâk and Stara Zagora that doesn't overcharge foreigners. The handful of big, traditionally furnished rooms (with tiny bathrooms) feature woollen quilts, and overlook an authentic 19th-century walled compound. The (one) apartment is huge, and worth booking ahead. All rooms feature bathrooms.

Hotel Vesta (☎ 20 350, ul Chavdar Vojvoda 3) Singles/doubles/triples US$30/40/60, apartments US$46. This homely and comfortable place is just off the road (so it's quiet) and behind the monolithic House of

Culture. Some rooms are smaller than others, and the rooftop apartment is cramped, but all bathrooms are sparkling new. All accommodation features fan, TV, fridge, bathroom and balcony. Rates include breakfast. Although foreigners pay far more than Bulgarians, it's good value.

Hotel Kazanlâk (☎ 27 210, pl Sevtopolis) Singles/doubles US$30/40 with bathroom. This unexciting hotel is another throwback to the 1960s. The rooms have air-con and a fridge, and the rates include breakfast. It has a central location, an undercover pool and several nightclubs and bars, but little else to recommend it.

Places to Eat

Hadzhi Eminova Kâshta (☎ 42 095, ul Nikola Petkov 22) Salads and soups 2-3 lv, main meals 3.50-5 lv. If you're heading to the Kulata Ethnological Complex, or staying in the attached guesthouse, you must try this superb place. Although prices are a little high, the courtyard setting is charming and the menu is in English.

New York Pub Pizza & Grill (ul Knyaz Al Battenberg) Main meals 3-4.50 lv. Despite the rather incongruous name, the range of meals is impressive and the service is snappy. It offers a helpful 'photo-menu', so anyone who doesn't speak Bulgarian can order by pointing at the meal(s) they want.

Hotel Vesta (☎ 20 350, ul Chavdar Vojvoda 3) Meals 3.50-5 lv. This family-run hotel has a quaint garden-restaurant, which is open to the public.

The best *cafes* are along ulitsa Iskra, near Cinema Iskra. For a drink, try the trendy, outdoor *Arizona Cocktail Bar (ul Otets Paisii)*.

Getting There & Away

From the bus station (☎ 22 383, ulitsa Sofronii), several public and private buses a day go to Lovech (5.50 lv, three hours), Haskovo (5 lv, three hours), Veliko Târnovo (4.5 lv, 2½ hours) and Sofia (7 lv, 3½ hours), but services to Ruse and Plovdiv are less frequent. About every hour, there's also a bus to Gabrovo (3.50 lv, 60-90 minutes), via Shipka. Most buses heading east to Burgas (via Sliven), or west to Sofia (via Karlovo), pick up passengers in Kazanlâk.

To Stara Zagora (2 lv, 45 minutes), catch one of the regular buses from Veliko Târnovo, or a direct minibus from the specific departure point near the bus station.

Kazanlâk is about halfway along the train line that connects Sofia and Burgas, via Karlovo and Sliven. Daily, one fast and one express train stop at the station (☎ 21 448) in Kazanlâk on the way to Burgas (express 1st/2nd class 11.50/8.60 lv, three hours) and Sofia (7.50/6.10 lv, 3½ hours). There are also five daily trains to Stara Zagora.

SHIPKA
ШИПКА
☎ 04324 • pop 2500
Shipka is a quaint village along the steep, windy and often cloudy road between Kazanlâk and Gabrovo. The Freedom Monument and church are worth seeing, especially if you have your own transport.

Shipka Monastery
Шипченски Манастир
Poking through the trees above Shipka village are the unmissable five golden, onion-shaped domes of the **Nativity Memorial Church** *(admission 2 lv & photos an extra 5 lv; open daily 8.30am-5.30pm)*. Part of the Shipka Monastery, and also known as the Church of St Nikolai, this magnificent edifice was built in 1902 as a dedication for those who died at the Shipka Pass during the Russian-Turkish War (1877–78). The design is heavily influenced by Russian architecture of the time, and features 17 church bells which can be heard for several kilometres when rung. Inside the crypt lie the remains of many Russian soldiers who perished. If it's not cloudy, the church offers marvellous **views** of the Valley of Roses. Follow the sign to Hram Pametnik for 1.2km through the village, or walk 300m up from the restaurant along the Kazanlâk-Gabrovo road.

Shipka Pass
Шипченски проход
About 13km of winding road (be careful if driving in foggy conditions) north of Shipka village is the Shipka Pass (1306m). Some 900 steps lead to the top of Mt Stoletov (1326m), dominated by the impressive 32m-high **Freedom Monument** *(admission free; open daily 9am-5pm)*. It was built in 1934 as a memorial to the 7000 Russian troops and Bulgarian volunteers who, in August 1877, died while successfully repelling numerous attacks by some 27,000 Turkish soldiers intent on relieving their besieged comrades in Pleven.

Places to Stay & Eat
Hotel Byalata Rosa *(☎ 2725, Shipka)* Singles/doubles with bathroom 20/25 lv. This modest place in Shipka village is at the start of the 200m road up to the monastery.

Hotel-Restaurant Shipka *(☎ 2730, Shipka Pass)* Singles/doubles with bathroom 10/20 lv. About 50m up from the car park at the top of the pass, this hotel is excellent value because it doesn't discriminate against foreigners. Some rooms are huge and feature separate sitting areas, and all are quiet and well furnished.

Getting There & Away
Bus No 6 runs every hour between the Kazanlâk bus station and Shipka village. Otherwise, the hourly bus between Kazanlâk and Gabrovo stops at the village and Shipka Pass.

GABROVO
ГАБРОВО
☎ 066 • pop 75,000
For reasons that seem lost in time, Gabrovo has been the continual butt of jokes by other Bulgarians. This has been admirably accepted by the citizens of Gabrovo, who have even erected a museum and organise an annual festival dedicated to this unique brand of humour.

To be honest, Gabrovo is not an exciting town. There's nothing particularly wrong with it, but there's little in the way of attractions and only one decent hotel. Gabrovo is useful as a base for visiting Shipka (see earlier) and Etâr (see the Around Gabrovo section later), where there's a better range of accommodation.

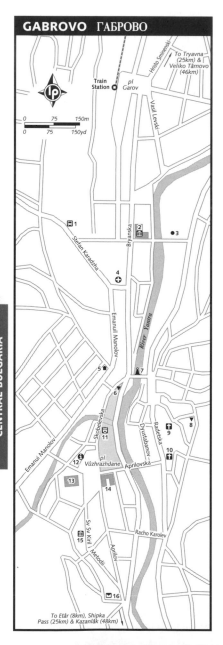

GABROVO ГАБРОВО

1 Bus Station
2 House of Humour & Satire
   ДОМ НА ХУМОРА И САТИРАТА
3 Sports Hall
4 Hospital
5 Hotel Balkan; Gusto Pizza & Grill; Matrix
   Internet Club
   ХОТЕЛ БАЛКАН
6 Cafe Racho Kovacha
   КАФЕ РАЧО КОВАЧА
7 Racho the Blacksmith Statue
8 Stannopriemintsa Inn; Restaurant-Cafe VMRO
   СТАНОПРИЕМНИЦА. РЕСТОРАНТ-КАФЕ ВМРО
9 St Troitsa Church
   ЦЪРКВАТА СВ. ТРОИЦА
10 St Bogoroditsa Church
   ЦЪРКВАТА СВ. БГОРОДИЦА
11 Racho Stoyanov Dramatic Theatre
   ДРАМАТИЧЕН ТЕАТЪР РАЧО СТОЯНОВ
12 Tourist Office
13 House of Culture
   КУЛТУРЕН ДОМ
14 Aprilov School; Museum of Education
   УЧИЛИЩЕ АПРИЛОВ. МУЗЕЙ НА ОБРАЗОБ-
   АНИЕТО
15 Art Gallery
   ХУДОЖЕСТВЕНА ГАЛЕРИЯ
16 Post Office & Telephone Centre

The Gabrovo map, published by Domino and available in town, details 10 mountain bike routes (from 9km to 58km), which pass local villages, monasteries and ancient ruins. These trails are also excellent for hiking. (See also the boxed text 'Hiking in the Stara Planina' earlier in this chapter.)

Information
The tourist office (☎/fax 28 483, e did@ globcom.net), on ploshtad Vûzhrazhdane, claims to be open Monday to Friday from 9am to 5pm but has erratic opening hours. It can rent mountain bikes, advise about mountain bike routes and hiking trails, give away brochures, arrange rooms in private homes and provide information about special events. There are several foreign-exchange offices on ulitsa Radetska, and the Matrix Internet Club is in the Hotel Balkan complex.

Things to See
Certainly one of the more unusual museums in Bulgaria is the **House of Humour & Satire**

(☎ 27 228, W www.humorhouse.org, ul Bryanska 68; admission 4 lv; open daily 9am-6pm). This huge, ugly building has four floors, but ideas relating to humour ran out by the second floor – the upper floors contain unrelated art, as well as fascinating masks from all over the world. Most items are labelled in English, and guided tours are available in English or French (6 lv per group of five people). There's a small number of **national revival period homes** on the eastern side of town, immediately behind the dominant (but rarely open) **St Troitsa Church**. If you want to fill in some time, the quaint **St Bogoroditsa Church** *(ul Dyustabanov)* is mildly interesting. The **Museum of Education** *(☎ 24 071, ul Aprilovska 13)* is accessible through the stunning courtyard in the Aprilov School. Also worth a peek is the **art gallery** *(ul Sv Sv Kiril i Metodii)*.

Special Events
During odd-numbered years, Gabrovo hosts the **Biennial Festival of International Humour & Satire** (May), part of the annual **May Festivities of Culture**. Other festivals include the **Balkan Youth Festival** (August) and the **Days of Chamber Music** (September).

Places to Stay & Eat
There's an alarming lack of hotels in Gabrovo, and the only option doesn't hold a candle to the two choices in nearby Etâr (see later). Ask the tourist office about **rooms** in private homes in Gabrovo, and nearby villages, which cost about 18 lv to 22 lv per person including breakfast.

Hotel Balkan *(☎ 23 474, fax 24 619, ul Emanuil Manolov 14)* Singles/doubles US$45/50, apartments US$60, all with bathroom. The Balkan basically has a monopoly in Gabrovo, and knows it, so foreigners are really overcharged here. It's central, but charmless. All the rooms contain a TV and rates include breakfast.

Gusto Pizza & Grill Grills about 5 lv. If you're craving some decent Western food, head to this trendy place in the Hotel Balkan complex.

A few **restaurants** and **cafes**, including **Restaurant-Cafe VMRO** and the more

touristy and expensive **Stannopriemintsa Inn**, are in the older part of town on the eastern side of the river. In addition, plenty of **cafes** line ulitsa Dyustabanov and the footbridge along ulitsa Aprilovska. One of the most stunning settings for any cafe in central Bulgaria is **Cafe Racho Kovacha**, which has a balcony overlooking the river directly opposite the **Racho the Blacksmith statue**.

Getting There & Away
From the well-organised bus station (☎ 23 277) on ulitsa Stefan Karadzha there are up to three departures a day to Varna, Sliven, Burgas, Stara Zagora and Plovdiv. There are five or six daily buses to Pleven and one directly to Sofia (7 lv, 3½ hours). Buses also leave every hour for Tryavna, for Veliko Târnovo via the Dryanovo Monastery, and for Kazanlâk via Shipka and Shipka Pass.

The train station (☎ 27 127) at ploshtad Garov in Gabrovo is on a spur track off the main line between Veliko Târnovo and Kazanlâk. Services to both towns are infrequent, and of negligible use to travellers.

AROUND GABROVO
Etâr
Етър
☎ 066
One of the more appealing attractions in central Bulgaria is the delightful **Etâr Ethnographic Village Museum** *(☎ 42 023, W www.tourinfo.bg/etar; admission 6 lv; open Mon-Fri 9am-6pm & Sat-Sun 9am-5.30pm)*, about 8km south-east of Gabrovo. First opened in 1964, this open-air museum contains nearly 50 shops and workshops. The village is designed in a style typical of the Bulgarian national revival period (18th and 19th centuries) and spreads over seven hectares of grass and trees. Artisans, such as bakers, cartwrights, cobblers, furriers, glass workers, hatters, jewellers, leather workers, millers, potters and weavers, practise their trades and sell their wares, some in workshops powered by water from a stream running through the complex.

There are entrances at the northern side (near the Hotel Stannopriemintsa) and at the administration building in the middle. There is another entrance at the far southern side, near the major car park. The ticket is valid for one day (you can go in and out of the complex as often as you like on that day). Guided tours (in English, French or German) are available for 7 lv per person (minimum of five people).

A special time to visit is on **Fair Day** (14 October), which features traditional dance and music, including *kavals* (wooden flutes) made in the complex.

The *Gabrovo* map, published by Domino and available in Gabrovo, includes a detailed map of the complex. See the boxed text 'Hiking in the Stara Planina' earlier for information about hiking in the region.

Places to Stay & Eat

Hotel Stannopriemintsa (☎ *42 026, fax 42 023, Etâr*) Singles/doubles/triples with bathroom 44/72/96 lv. At the northern (Gabrovo) end of the complex, this hotel is a little touristy, but not bad value. The doubles have balconies with views (of the less interesting part of the complex), but the singles are tiny and don't have balconies. All rooms have a TV, and rates include breakfast.

Restaurant Stannopriemintsa (*Etâr*) Salads 2 lv, grills 3.50-5 lv, small beer 1.20 lv. Downstairs in the hotel of the same name, this mehana boasts an interesting decor (complete with several deer antlers!) but the food is ordinary and overpriced. The service is good, however, and the outdoor tables overlook the grass and trees.

Hotel Perla (☎ *42 784, Etâr*) Doubles with bathroom 38 lv. Virtually opposite the Stannopriemintsa, the Perla is better value, and one of the best deals in the Stara Planina. The rooms are huge and contain a TV, balcony and a bathroom that cannot be faulted. Breakfast costs an extra 3 lv per person.

Renaissance Tavern (*Etâr*) Salads about 2.50 lv, mains from 5.50 lv. Inside the museum complex, this tourist-oriented place charges twice as much as a normal village restaurant, but the food is tasty and the setting is charming.

The *bakery* inside the complex sells basic take-away food, such as *simit* buns (a local

speciality), which can be enjoyed while sitting on the grass by the stream.

Getting There & Away

From along ulitsa Aprilov in Gabrovo, bus Nos 1, 7 and 8 go directly to the complex. Alternatively, catch one of the hourly buses between Gabrovo and Kazanlâk, get off at the turn-off (signposted in English) and walk (exactly 2km). A taxi from Gabrovo costs about 4 lv one way.

TRYAVNA
ТРЯВНА
☎ 0677 • pop 12,200

Tryavna, about 40km south-west of Veliko Târnovo, is already one of the highlights of central Bulgaria. And when the excellent work undertaken by the Beautiful Bulgaria Project has finished in a few years time, the town will doubtless be one of the top three attractions in the country. The old town is full of tree-lined, cobblestone streets, Bulgarian national revival period homes and quaint stone bridges. It is far less touristy than Arbanasi, costs nothing to wander around (unlike the complex at Etâr) and prices for everything are reasonable. Tryavna was, and to a lesser degree still is, renowned for its handicrafts, especially woodcarving (see the boxed text later).

Orientation & Information

Helpful maps (in English) are at the train station, at the start of ulitsa Angel Kânchev around the corner from the train station, and opposite the (abandoned) Hotel Tryavana. The bus station and train station are 100m apart to the west of ulitsa Angel Kânchev, the main road which runs through the old town and follows the curves of the train line.

The helpful tourist office (☎ 247, 🄴 smile@mbox.digsys.bg), ulitsa Angel Kânchev 22, is in the post office building. The tourist office is open from Monday to Friday from 9am to noon and 2pm to 5pm. It can help with bus and train schedules, and arrange private rooms (see Places to Stay later). The tourist office and museums also sell useful booklets (2 lv to 4 lv) about Tryavna, which make ideal souvenirs.

The only place to change money is the Bulgarian Post Bank, in the post office building, where there's also an ATM. The only Internet centre, ulitsa Angel Kânchev 15, is reliable and cheap.

Things to See

It's easy to see everything in Tryavna on a short walking tour (allow two to three hours). From the bus station, head east (away from the train line), and then turn right along ulitsa Angel Kânchev. The impressive **St Georgi Church** *(ul Angel Kânchev 128; admission free; open daily 7.30am-12.30pm & 2.30pm-5.30pm)* is on the left. It was built between 1848 and 1852, and features some worthwhile icons and carvings. Further down on the right is the **Angel Kânchev House-Museum** *(☎ 2278, ul Angel Kânchev 39; admission 2 lv; open Tues-Sat 8am-noon & 1pm-5pm)*. Built in 1805, it contains exhibits about the revolutionary hero, Kânchev, and the liberation of Tryavna during the Russian-Turkish War (1877–78).

Walk over the bridge, past the shady park and head right (still along ulitsa Angel Kânchev) to ploshtad Kapitan Dyado Nikola. First built in 1814 in the classic Bulgarian national revival period style, this picturesque square is dominated by a **clock tower** (1844) that chimes loudly on the hour. Facing the square is **Staroto Shkolo** *(☎ 3796)*, the school was built in 1836. It was being renovated at the time of research, and will probably house the **Tryavna Museum School of Painting**. Also overlooking the square is the **St Archangel Michael's Church** *(admission free; open daily 8am-4.30pm)*, the oldest church in town. Burnt down by the Turks, but rebuilt in 1819, it boasts some of the intricate woodcarvings for which the town is famous. Inevitably, a couple of private **art galleries** can also be found near the square.

Continue over the stone **Arch Bridge** (1844) to ulitsa PR Slaveikov, one of the nicest, cobblestone streets in Bulgaria. On the left is **Daskalov House** *(☎ 2166, ul PR Slaveikov 27a; admission 2 lv; open daily 8am-noon & 1pm-5pm)*. Built between 1804 and 1808, this home, set behind a large wall and in front of a pretty garden, also contains

Woodcarving

During the Bulgarian national revival period, Tryavna became renowned for the quality and quantity of its woodcarvings, often intricately chiselled from local walnut, birch, poplar and oak trees. Many carvings from Tryavna were used to decorate monasteries in Gabrovo, Veliko Târnovo, Arbanasi and Rila, and carvers were sought after by builders and house owners as far away as Serbia, Turkey and modern-day Iran.

By the early 19th century, over 40 workshops in Tryavna were churning out wooden cradles, frames, icons, friezes, doors and crosses. Each design was individual, but most included the type of ornate and detailed flower motifs which became known as the 'Tryavna School' of woodcarving. Some of the most beautiful exhibits include the 'sun ceiling' inside the Daskalov House in Tryavna, which is also home to the Museum of Woodcarving & Icon Painting.

In an attempt to resurrect the tradition, courses in the 'Tryavna School' of woodcarving are offered to tourists. Courses for one/two/three days (six hours per day) cost 35/60/80 lv, and can be arranged through the tourist office or the Staroto Shkolo school (see Things to See in the Tryavna section). Every even-numbered year, the school also hosts the **International Woodcarving Competition**. Details are available from the tourist office in Tryavna.

the fascinating **Museum of Woodcarving & Icon Painting**. One of a kind in Bulgaria, the museum features some superb examples of the 'Tryavna school' of woodcarving. Ask for the informative leaflet (in English).

Housed in a former chapel, the **Museum of Icons** *(☎ 3753, ul Breza 1; admission 2 lv; open daily 8am-4.30pm)* contains over 160 religious icons from famous local families. The museum is on the other side of the train line; follow the signs to the right from along ulitsa PR Slaveikov.

Back on ulitsa PR Slaveikov is the **Slaveikov House-Museum** *(☎ 2166, ul PR Slaveikov 50; admission 2 lv; open Wed-Sun*

8am-noon & 1pm-6pm). Petko Slaveikov, and his son Pencho, were renowned poets who lived in this house for many years. Farther down on the left is the **Summer Garden Kalinchev House** *(☎ 3694, ul PR Slaveikov 45; admission 1.50 lv; open Mon-Fri 9am-1pm & 2pm-6pm).* This house, built in 1830, features a charming courtyard *cafe (open daily 8am-11pm),* and 500 works by Bulgarian artists, including Kalinchev. More paintings, drawings and sculptures can be found next door in the **Ivan Kolev House** *(☎ 3777, ul PR Slaveikov 47; admission 2 lv; open Mon-Fri 9am-1pm & 2pm-6pm).*

Places to Stay & Eat

Several homes and shops along the first 200m of ulitsa Angel Kânchev from the bus station have signs (in Bulgarian) offering rooms for rent. The tourist office (see Orientation & Information) can also arrange *rooms* in private homes (including in the old town) for about 18 lv to 22 lv per person including breakfast.

Hotel Tigara (☎ 2469, ul D Gorov 7a) Singles/doubles with bathroom 25/40 lv. The Tiger Hotel is a friendly, homely place 200m from the (abandoned) Hotel Tryavna (at ulitsa Angel Kânchev 46) – look for the signs in English. The rooms are clean and comfortable, but ask for the newer ones at the back.

Hotel Family (☎/fax 4691, ul Angel Kânchev 40) Singles/doubles US$25/36, apartments US$50, all with bathroom. This new place is convenient and spotless, but expensive for foreigners, and not good value compared to the Tigara. All rooms have a TV and rates include breakfast. The courtyard *restaurant* and bar are delightful.

Hotel Ralitsa (☎ 2219, **e** *ralica@tr .globcom.net, ul Kaleto)* Singles/doubles US$28/48, apartments US$60, all with bathroom. This three-star place is set in the hills to the south of town. (Take a taxi, because it's a steep walk.) The rooms are large and have a TV, and most doubles feature a balcony with great views. Book ahead on weekends in summer, because it's popular with trendsetters from Gabrovo. Rates include breakfast. A classy *restaurant* is attached.

Starata Loza (ul PR Slaveikov 44) Salads about 1.50 lv, grills about 3 lv. The Old Vine is opposite the entrance to Daskalov House, and probably the most enticing of the several restaurants along this cobblestone street. Although set up for the tourist crowd, prices are pleasingly reasonable. The menu is in English.

Gostilintsa Restaurant Main meals 3.50-6.20 lv. Almost diagonally opposite the Starata Loza, this classy place is uninvitingly located behind a wooden door. The service is excellent, the meals are not too expensive and the menu is in English.

Getting There & Away

From 6am to 6pm, buses travel every hour between Gabrovo (1.50 lv, 30 minutes) and Tryavna. For anywhere else, get a connection in Gabrovo. Tryavna is along a rarely used spur track, and even when passenger trains are running (which is rare) they're infuriatingly slow.

DRYANOVO MONASTERY
ДРЯНОВСКИ МАНАСТИР
☎ 0676

Delightfully located under limestone cliffs only 5.5km from the town of Dryanovo is the charming Dryanovo Monastery *(admission free; open daily 7am-10pm).* Originally built in the 12th century, the monastery was alternately destroyed by Turks and rebuilt by Bulgarians several times in the subsequent 500 years. The **Holy Archangel & Michael Church** was added in 1861.

Like several other monasteries, it provided sanctuary to the revolutionary leader, Vasil Levski, and his insurgents. Later, during the Russian-Turkish War (1877–78), more than one hundred locals hid in the monastery and fought against the Turks for nine days. The Turks eventually invaded the monastery and burnt down everything they could see, so most of what remains has been rebuilt since. This act of bravery is commemorated with a **mausoleum** in the monastery grounds.

Other Attractions

Inside the Komplex Bodopadi (see Places to Stay & Eat later) is a **Historical Museum**

(☎ 2097; admission 2 lv; open Mon-Fri 8.45am-12.30pm & 1pm-4.45pm, Sat-Sun 9.45am-3.45pm). Not surprisingly, most displays feature the 1876 April Uprising and 1877–78 war. In particular note the large and macabre collection of skulls. Downstairs are artefacts from nearby caves, including Bacho Kiro, and some religious icons. All captions are in Bulgarian.

From the bridge near the car park, a 400m path leads through a pretty **forest** to the 1200m-long **Bacho Kiro cave** *(admission 2 lv; open daily 8am-6pm)*, inhabited during the Palaeolithic era. It's reasonably well set up, but not as exciting as other caves in Bulgaria.

The Bulgarian Association for Rural & Ecological Tourism (BARET), with help from the Association Stara Planina tourist office in Dryanovo, has established the **Dryanovo Eco-trail**. This well-marked, circular, four-hour trail starts and finishes near the monastery, and passes through scenic forests. To find the start of the trail, ask at the Mehana Mecha Dupka (see later), or Bacho Kiro cave. Otherwise, contact the tourist office in Dryanovo (☎ 0676-2106), or the Bacho Kiro Tourist Society (☎ 0676-2332), which may be able to arrange local rock-climbing and caving trips.

Places to Stay & Eat

Komplex Bodopadi (☎ 2314) Doubles 22 lv, apartments 44 lv, all with bathroom. Virtually attached to the monastery, this place offers several small but clean rooms. Many have huge balconies (seemingly bigger than the rooms themselves) that overlook the monastery. The apartments are a little larger and have a TV, but are not worth twice as much.

Motini Skali (☎ 2471) Doubles 22 lv, apartments 66 lv, all with bathroom. Anywhere else, this place opposite the monastery gates would be heartily recommended, but the Bodopadi is better value. The apartments here contain a TV, fridge and balcony. All rates include breakfast.

About 100m from the car park along the path to the cave is the delightful riverside *Mehana Mecha Dupka* restaurant.

Getting There & Away

All buses travelling between Veliko Târnovo and Gabrovo will (if requested) stop at the turn-off to the monastery (about 4km south of Dryanovo). From there it's a 1.5km walk to the monastery.

VELIKO TÂRNOVO
ВЕЛИКО ТЪРНОВО
☎ 062 • pop 75,000

One of the most picturesque towns in Bulgaria is Veliko Târnovo (Great Târnovo), also known as the City of Tsars. The Yantra River winds through a gorge partially lined with traditional houses, and above the town the ruined citadel on Tsarevets Hill recalls the time when Târnovgrad (as it was then known) was the capital of the Second Bulgarian Empire (1185–1396).

North-west of Tsarevets Hill, and across the abyss, is the now overgrown Trapezitsa Hill, residence of the nobles and courtiers. In the valley below is Asenova, the artisans' and merchants' quarter dotted with the ruins of medieval churches. Renowned monasteries once stood in Sveta Gora Park, where the prestigious university is now located. And the narrow streets of Varosha, the old town, bear obvious imprints of the Bulgarian national revival period. Veliko Târnovo is one place you should not miss: nowhere is the majesty of medieval Bulgaria more apparent.

History

Between about 5500 and 4500 BC the area was settled by Neolithic people. Tsarevets Hill, on which the fortress stands today, and the nearby Trapezitsa Hill, were inhabited by Thracians in 2000 BC. The Romans built the first fortress walls, and, in the 5th century AD, a Byzantine citadel was established on Tsarevets Hill by Emperor Justinian. Next came the Slavs who captured the town in the 7th century.

Under the able leadership of the brothers Asen and Petâr, Târnovgrad became a major centre of rebellion against the Byzantine rulers. After the subsequent foundation of the Second Bulgarian Empire (1185), Târnovgrad became the second

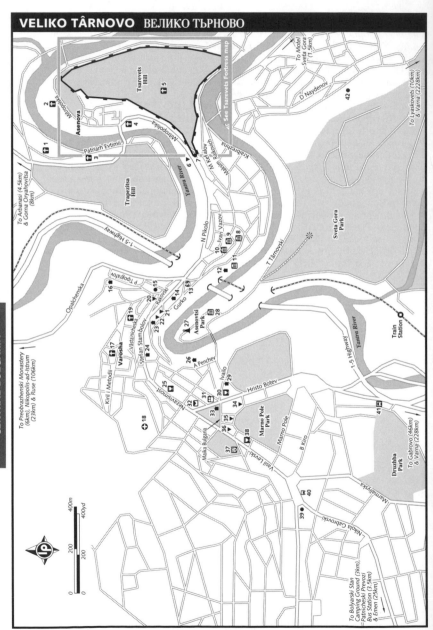

VELIKO TÂRNOVO ВЕЛИКО ТЪРНОВО

VELIKO TÂRNOVO   ВЕЛИКО ТЪРНОВО

PLACES TO STAY
12 Rooms For Rent Gurko 70
14 Hotel Veltted & Restaurant
    ХОТЕЛ ВЕЛТЕД И
    РЕСТОРАНТ
16 Hotel Comfort
    ХОТЕЛ КОМФОРТ
23 Restaurant-Hotel Gurko
    ХОТЕЛ-РЕСТОРАНТ ГУРКО
24 Hotel Trapezitsa; Trapezitsa
    (Adventure Club);
    Ulitsata (Bar)
    ХОТЕЛ ТРАПЕЗИЦА. УЛИЦАТА
26 Interhotel Veliko Târnovo;
    Balkantourist
    ИНТЕРХОТЕЛ ВЕЛИКО
    ТЪРНОВО
29 Hotel Etâr; Intertours; Etap
    Adress (Bus Agency)
    ХОТЕЛ ЕТЪР. ИНТЕРТУРС.
    ЕТАР АДРЕС
33 Hotel Orion
    ХОТЕЛ ОРИОН

PLACES TO EAT
6   Atrion Taverna
    МЕХАНА АТРИОН
20 Stratilat Restaurant
    СТРАТИЛАТ РЕСТОРАНТ
21 Starata Mehana
    СТАРАТА МЕХАНА
22 Restaurant Rich
    РЕСТОРАНТ РИЧ
34 La Scalla
    ЛА СКАЛА
35 Mustang Food; I-Net
    Internet Centre
    МУСТАНГ
36 Barzo Hranene
    БЪРЗО ХРАНЕНЕ

OTHER
1   Church of St Dimitâr
    ЦЪРКВАТА СВ. ДИМИТЪР
2   Sts Peter & Paul Church
    ЦЪРКВАТА СВ. ПЕТЪР И
    ПАВЕЛ
3   Church of St Georgi
    ЦЪРКВАТА СВ. ГЕОРГИ
4   Forty Martyrs Church
    ЦЪРКВАТА 40-ТЕ МЪЧЕНИЦИ
5   Patriarchal Complex
    КОМЛЕКСА НА ПАТРИАРХА
7   Entrance to Tsarevets
    Fortress
8   Museum of Contemporary
    Bulgarian History
    МУЗЕЙ НА СЪВРЕМЕННАТА
    БЪЛГАРСКА ИСТОРИЯ
9   Museum of National Revival
    & Constituent Assembly
    МУЗЕЙ НА ВЪЗРАЖДАНЕТО И
    УЧРЕДИТЕЛНОТО СЪБРАНИЕ
10 Veliko Târnovo
    Archaeological Museum
    ВЕЛИКО ТЪРНОВО
    АРХЕОЛОГИЧЕСКИ МУЗЕЙ
11 Sarafkina Kâshta
    САРАФИНА КЪЩА
13 First East International Bank
    ПЪРВА ИЗТОЧНА
    МЕЖДУНАРОДНА БАНКА
15 Samovodska Charshiya
    Complex
    САМОВОДСКА ЧАРШИЯ
    КОМЛЕКСА
17 Sts Cyril & Methodius
    Church
    ЦЪРКВАТА СВ. СВ. КИРИЛ И
    МЕТОДИЙ
18 Hospital

19 St Nikolai Church
    ЦЪРКВАТА СВ. НИКОЛАЙ
25 Las Vegas Club; Internet
    Millenium; Cafes
27 Monument of the Asens;
    Café
    МОНУМЕНТ НА АСЕНОВЦИ
28 State Art Museum
    ГРАДСКА ХУДОЖЕСТВЕНА
    ГАЛЕРИЯ
30 Tourist Information Centre
    (TIC); Rila Bureau; Balkan
    Airlines; Spyder Nightclub;
    Hotel Orbita; City Pub
    ТУРИСТИЧЕСКИ
    ИНФОРМАЦИОНЕН
    ЦЕНТЪР. БЮРО РИЛА.
    ХОТЕЛ ОРБИТА
31 Cinema Poltava; United
    Bulgarian Bank; Internet
    Club Bezanata; Fashion Club
    КИНО ПОЛТАВА.
    ОБЕДИНЕНА БЪЛГАРСКА
    БАНКА
32 Main Post Office &
    Telephone Centre
37 Konstantin Kisimov
    Dramatic Theatre
    ДРАМАТИЧЕН ТЕАТЪР
    КОНСТАНТИН КИСИМОВ
38 Supermarket
39 Market
40 Minibuses for Gorna
    Oryahovitsa Train Station
41 Yug Bus Station
    АВТОГАРА ЮГ
42 Sts Cyril & Methodius
    University of Veliko Târnovo
    УНИВЕРСИТЕТА СВ. КИРИЛ И
    МЕТОДИЙ

most important town in the region (after Constantinople), and trade and culture flourished for the next 200 years.

On 17 July 1393, Târnovgrad fell again, this time to the Turks after a three-month siege, and the fortress was destroyed. The town remained fairly stagnant until Bulgarian culture and nationalism gradually reasserted itself during the mid-19th century. In 1877, the Russian General Gurko liberated Târnovgrad from the Turks. Because of its importance during the Second Bulgarian Empire, Veliko Târnovo (as it was renamed) was chosen as the place to write the Bulgarian Constitution in 1879, and to officially proclaim the independent State of Bulgaria in 1908. The town is deservedly proud of its history, and educational, religious and linguistic heritage.

Orientation

Veliko Târnovo is based along a ridge above the Yantra River (probably from the Thracian word *yatrus* meaning 'quick flowing'). The river winds in a horseshoe bend between four hills: Tsarevets, on which the fortress is built, Momina Krepost, several kilometres to the east, Trapezitsa, and Sveta Gora (Holy

Forest). The town centre is along ulitsa Nezavisimost and ulitsa Stefan Stambolov between the post office and the huge underpass. The suburbs, which most visitors can happily avoid, spread out to the west and south-west from ulitsa Vasil Levski.

Books & Maps If you're spending more than a few days here, pick up the excellent *Infoguide Veliko Turnovo* booklet (about 7 lv). It provides an abundance of practical and cultural information in English, and is available at the Tourist Information Centre (see later) and most bookstalls. If you're interested in the history of the various monasteries in and around the town, buy *The V.Turnovo Monasteries: A Guide* (5 lv).

The detailed and widely available *Veliko Târnovo* map, published by Domino and (mostly) translated into English, also includes helpful maps of Arbanasi and the Tsarevets Fortress.

Information

Admission fees to the museums and other attractions in Veliko Târnovo are some of the highest in Bulgaria. Students with appropriate identity cards (see the Student, Youth & Teacher Cards section in the Facts for the Visitor chapter) will appreciate discounts of up to 50% at most places.

Tourist Offices The extremely helpful Tourist Information Centre (TIC; ☎ 22 148, ⓔ dtour@vali.bg) at ulitsa Hristo Botev 13A is open Monday to Saturday from 8.30am to 5pm. The English-speaking manager can give away several brochures, sell a few booklets and provide information about activities (see Activities later in this section). At the time of writing, the TIC planned to move to another office about 50m farther (north) along ulitsa Hristo Botev. The new office should be well signposted (in English), and the contact details and opening hours will remain the same.

Money It seems that every third shop in the town centre is a foreign-exchange office, and most provide competitive rates with no commission. To change travellers

cheques, and to obtain cash with a credit card through an ATM or over the counter, try the United Bulgarian Bank, ulitsa Hristo Botev 3, near the Cinema Poltava complex, or the First East International Bank, ulitsa Stefan Stambolov 1.

Post & Communications The telephone centre is in the main post office at ulitsa Hristo Botev 1. It's open daily from 7am to 10pm. There are several Internet centres to choose from. Internet Millennium is on ulitsa Nezavisimost, near the Las Vegas Club. The rather bizarre Internet Club Bezanata is on ulitsa Hristo Botev, in the Cinema Poltava complex. The equally weird I-Net Internet Centre is under the Mustang Food restaurant just off ulitsa Hristo Botev.

Sts Cyril & Methodius University of Veliko Târnovo

One of the most prestigious (and pleasantly located) universities in Bulgaria is the Sts Cyril & Methodius University of Veliko Târnovo, where some 12,000 students can choose from about 50 subjects. Visitors are welcome at the university **library** which houses about 400,000 titles (some of which are in English, French, German, Spanish and Dutch). The university has an activities club (see Activities later in this section) and offers Bulgarian language courses for foreigners (see Courses in the Facts for the Visitor chapter).

Sarafkina Kâshta

Originally built in 1861 by a wealthy Turkish merchant and moneylender, this fine Bulgarian national revival period style house is now a museum (*☎ 358 02, ul Gurko 88; admission 4 lv; open Mon-Fri 8am-noon & 1pm-5pm*). The ground floor contains displays of arts and crafts, such as ceramics, metalwork, woodcarvings and jewellery, and some fascinating exhibits (with helpful explanations in English) about traditional costumes and bread-making. The upper floor is crammed with revival period furniture, and the walls are covered with family photos.

Museum of National Revival & Constituent Assembly

This museum (☎ 29 821, ul Ivan Vazov; admission 4 lv; open Wed-Mon 8am-noon & 1pm-6pm) is in a former Turkish town hall (built in 1872). It was here in 1879 that Bulgaria's first National Assembly was held to write the country's first constitution. The building is probably of more interest to some visitors than the exhibits themselves, especially because almost nothing is labelled in English.

The ground floor contains a vast number of costumes, books and photos about the history of Veliko Târnovo, while upstairs there's a lavish assembly hall with portraits of local VIPs. The basement has photos of the old town (enjoyable without any explanations in English), and some valuable icons (curiously, labelled in English).

Museum of Contemporary Bulgarian History

Poorly signposted (in any language) behind the Museum of National Revival, this not particularly inspiring museum (☎ 23 772; open Mon-Fri 8am-noon & 1pm-5pm) is also called the Regional Historical Museum. It houses old photos, coins, and war memorabilia, such as weapons, uniforms and cannons. It was unclear at the time of research if there would be an admission fee, but if the usual 4 lv is demanded, perhaps give this museum a miss.

Veliko Târnovo Archaeological Museum

This museum (☎ 34 946, ul Ivan Vazov; admission 4 lv; open Tues-Sat 8am-6.30pm & Sat 9am-5.30pm) was closed for renovations at the time of research, but will certainly be open by the time you get there. It contains artefacts from the Roman ruins at Nikopolis-ad-Istrum and a huge collection of Roman pottery and statues from elsewhere. There are exhibits about medieval Bulgaria (including huge murals of the tsars on the second floor) and some ancient gold from regional Neolithic settlements. Frustratingly, like other museums in town, all captions here are in Bulgarian.

Churches

Numerous churches have been built around Veliko Târnovo. The ones that have been restored, and are accessible to the public, are open daily from about 9am to noon and 1pm to 6pm from 1 April to 30 September. To find out about opening hours in winter, telephone the relevant authority (☎ 34 946).

In the old Asenova quarter is the **Forty Martyrs Church** (ul Mitropolska; admission 2 lv), originally built in 1230 to celebrate the victory of the Bulgars under Tsar Asen II against the Byzantines. It was used as a royal mausoleum, and then as a mosque by the Turks. This historic church has been beautifully restored, and contains valuable manuscripts, statues and iconostases.

Two blocks north is the late 13th-century **Sts Peter & Paul Church** (ul Mitropolska; admission 3.50 lv), which features three layers of remarkable murals created between the 14th and 17th centuries. Guided tours in English are available for an extra 4 lv per person (no minimum required).

On the other side of the river, and enclosed by a high stone wall, is the renovated **Church of St Dimitâr** (ul Patriarh Evtimii; admission 4 lv), the town's oldest church. It was built in the so-called 'Târnovo style', and named after St Dimitâr of Thessaloniki. During the church's consecration in 1185, Tsars Asen and Petâr proclaimed an uprising against Byzantine rule, which lead to the eventual creation of the Second Bulgarian Empire (1185–1396).

Nearby is the **Church of St Georgi** (ul Patriarh Evtimii; admission free), probably built in 1612 on the ruins of a medieval church. It was destroyed by the Ottomans, but restored in the early 17th century. Inside, there are some remarkable murals by unknown artists.

In the Varosha district is the **St Nikolai Church** (ul Vâstanicheska; admission free), built in 1879. It was being renovated at the time of research, but visitors are welcome and the garden is particularly pretty. Follow the steps on the left (western) side, and then turn left along ulitsa Kiril i Metodii to the **Sts Cyril & Methodius Church** (admission free), which is distinguished by its elegant tower.

Tsarevets Fortress

Undoubtedly, the highlight of Veliko Târnovo, and one of the major attractions in Bulgaria, is this fortress, part of the **Tsarevets Museum-Reserve** (☎ 38 841; admission 4 lv; open daily 8am-7pm in summer & 9am-5pm in winter).

Tsarevets Hill was settled by Thracians and Romans, but the Byzantines built the first significant fortress on the hill between the 5th and 7th centuries AD. The fortress was rebuilt and fortified by the Slavs and Bulgars between the 8th and 10th centuries, and again by the Byzantines in the early 12th century. The fortress reached its peak when Târnovgrad became the capital of the Second Bulgarian Empire (see the History section earlier), but was again sacked and destroyed by the Turks in 1393.

Archaeologists have so far uncovered remains of over 400 houses, 18 churches and numerous monasteries, dwellings, shops, gates and towers. Other than the patriarch's complex and Baldwin Tower, nothing much has been restored so most of what remains, especially near the walls, is little more than rubble. This shouldn't dissuade you from visiting, however. Sadly, the few explanations on site are in Bulgarian and German, but guided tours (rates negotiable) are possible if they are arranged in advance.

Things to See

From the main entrance, pass through two more gates and then veer to the left (north-east). You'll soon see the remains of **fortress walls**, some of which were once 12m high and 10m thick. It is possible to walk along the adjoining walls – but be careful. Near the **watch tower**, which you can climb for views of the Asenova quarter, is a small separate gateway that was once used as a servants' entrance.

Farther along the wall are the unrecognisable and poorly signposted remains of a 12th-century **monastery**, various dwellings and workshops and a couple of **churches**. At the most northerly point are the remains of a 13th-century **monastery** (with a sign in English), and **Execution Rock**, from which traitors were pushed into the Yantra River. (This has been heavily fortified to stop visitors suffering the same fate!)

The path hugging the eastern edge of the fortress is poorly maintained and passes nothing of interest, so head back to the middle, using the hilltop patriarch's complex as a landmark. Past one of several modern bells (used in the sound & light show – see later) are the ruins of a **nobleman's dwelling** and two **churches** to the left (east).

Just below the patriarch's complex are the foundations of the extensive **Royal Palace**, from where 22 successive kings ruled Bulgaria. It's hard to imagine that this palace once covered 4500 sq metres and housed a stupendous throne (about 30m by 10m) and Romans columns, probably transferred from the nearby city of Nikopolis-ad-Istrum.

State Art Museum

Dramatically situated in a tight bend of the Yantra River, and unmissable from most vantage points in the town centre, is the State Art Museum (☎ 38 961, Asenovtsi Park; admission 2 lv, free on Thurs; open Tues-Sun 10am-6pm). The ground floor of this surprisingly uninspiring looking building contains an array of paintings of Veliko Târnovo and the region by many different artists. The walls of the second floor are full of various other works of art, mostly on permanent loan from galleries in Silistra, Dobrich and Ruse. All labels are in English, and guided tours (in English and French) are available for about 5 lv extra per person (minimum of three).

Nearby, the **Monument of the Asens** is an awe-inspiring commemoration of the establishment of the Second Bulgarian Empire in 1185. From the monument, and the adjacent *cafe*, are glorious **views** of the tiers of rustic houses hanging above the gorge.

Tsarevets Fortress

From the palace, head back down (west) to the main path and walk up the steps to the **patriarch's complex**, which once extended about 3000 sq metres. Also called the Church of the Blessed Saviour, it was probably built in about 1235, but has been extensively restored. The **views** of the city from the front steps are marvellous; disappointingly, the modern murals inside, which outline the history of Bulgaria during in the 14th and 15th centuries, are austere.

From there, walk down the steep steps back towards the main entrance, and take a sharp left along the path hugging the southern wall. At the end of the path is the restored **Baldwin Tower**, where Baldwin I of Flanders, the deposed Latin emperor of the Byzantines, was imprisoned and finally executed after his defeat by the Bulgars in 1205. It's possible to climb to the top of the tower for more wonderful views.

The Sound & Light Show

The sound & light show illuminates the whole of Tsarevets Hill in a stunningly colourful display. However, setting it up is a *massive* effort involving the partial closure of the road to Gorna Oryahovitsa. The show doesn't happen until a minimum of 25 people have paid 12 lv each (or at least 300 lv has been collected). It can take place on any day of the year after dark, and runs for about 40 minutes.

To find out if the show is happening ring the Interhotel Veliko Târnovo (☎ 630 571), or the Balkan-tourist office (☎ 633 975) in the same hotel, at about 7.30pm (in summer); or ring the organisers (☎ 636 828). Alternatively, turn up at the fortress and hope the show is on, or do what most locals and visitors do: listen for the bells, and look for the laser beams. Then find a vantage point anywhere in town and enjoy the show for free!

Map legend:
- ⛪ Church
- 🏛 Monastery
- ▣ Dwellings & Workshops
- ● Bells
-)(Gates
- ·····◄··· Walking Tour

Map labels: Execution Rock, Nobleman's Dwelling, Watch Tower, Royal Palace, Fortress Walls, Patriarchal Complex, Cafe, Main Entrance, Baldwin Tower

0 50 100m
0 50 100yd

Activities

At the time of research, the local tourist authorities were planning to introduce all sorts of adventure and ecotourist activities, so if you are interested in the prospect of hiking, mountain biking, horse riding and caving, contact the TIC (see Information earlier in this section). For information about **horse riding** in Arbanasi and **hiking** in Emen see the Around Veliko Târnovo section later in this chapter.

Trapezitsa (☎/fax 621 593, @ info@trapezica.com), ulitsa Stefan Stambolov 79, can arrange rock climbing trips and training at nearby massifs. It is based in the hotel of the same name and is open Monday to Friday 9am to noon and 1pm to 6pm. Serious rock climbers should pick up the *Climbing Guide* from the TIC.

Academic VTU is operated by adventurous students at the local university (see earlier). Although it is more of a club than a business anyone with a genuine interest in rock climbing and hiking can inquire about tailor-made trips or joining one of its expeditions. It may also have some hiking, rock climbing and caving equipment for hire.

Organised Tours

Seeing the sights of Veliko Târnovo is very easy using a combination of walking, public transport and taxis. Balkantourist (☎/fax 633 975, ⓔ balturvt@mail.vt.techo-link.com), in the Interhotel Veliko Târnovo, offers tours with surprisingly reasonable rates. A two-hour guided walk around town costs 22 lv per person, a half-day bus trip to Arbanasi is 33 lv and a full-day bus tour of nearby monasteries costs 77 lv.

Special Events

The highlight of the cultural calendar is undoubtedly the **International Folklore Festival** (late June to mid-July). Held over three weeks, it features more than 300 acts from all over Bulgaria and the Balkans. More details are available from the TIC, or the organisers (☎ 30 223), from about mid-April. The **Holiday of Amateur Art Activities**, more commonly known as the **Balkan Folk Festival**, takes place over 10 days during the first half of May.

Places to Stay

Don't forget that Arbanasi, only 5km from the town centre, also offers a wide of range of accommodation in a quieter and more traditional setting. See the Around Veliko Târnovo section later in this chapter.

Places to Stay – Budget

Camping There is only one camping option in town, and it's nothing to get excited about.

Bolyarski Stan Camping Ground (☎ 41 859) Camping 10 lv per person, tent hire 10 lv per tent, bungalows 25 lv per double. Open year-round. This camping ground, about 3.5km west of the town centre, is OK if you must camp, but the bungalows are not worth the money, or the effort getting there. Take bus Nos 5 or 110 from along ulitsa Vasil Levski.

Private Rooms Rooms can be booked in private homes through the TIC (☎ 22 148, ⓔ dtour@vali.bg, ulitsa) at Hristo Botev 13A. Rooms in private homes cost around 15 lv to 22 lv per person. Rates depend on the season, location and amenities. Most will have a shared bathroom and rates rarely include breakfast.

Even before you reach the TIC, you may be approached by locals offering private rooms for about the same price. The nicest places to stay are near the Samovodska Charshiya Complex in the Varosha district, and along the lower (south-eastern) end of ulitsa Gurko.

Hotels If possible, choose a hotel in an older part of town, and a room with views of the river and gorge.

Hotel Orion (ul Hristo Botev) Doubles with bathroom 26 lv. This place is a last resort if the TIC (over the road) isn't open and you can't find a private room elsewhere. There may be nocturnal comings and goings, but the rooms are OK and feature enormous bathrooms. It's not as bad as it looks, especially if you can get a room away from the main road.

Hotel Orbita (☎ 621 513, ul Hristo Botev 15) Rooms with shared bathroom 14.50 lv per person (July & Aug), 12 lv (rest of the year). This place is not nearly as inviting as other places run by Orbita elsewhere in Bulgaria. The rooms and reception are on the fourth floor; it shares an entrance with the Spyder Nightclub, just down from the TIC.

Hotel Trapezitsa (☎ 22 061, fax 621 593, ul Stefan Stambolov 79) Singles/doubles/ triples with shared bathroom 14/28/36 lv, with bathroom 18/36/45 lv. This four-storey hostel, right in the centre of town, is outstanding value. Some rooms are a little small and crowded, but they're always clean and cosy. Get a room at the back to avoid the street noise, and to admire the awesome gorge views. This is probably the best choice for budget travellers, especially if you're travelling in a group of three or four (some rooms also have four beds).

Rooms for Rent Gurko 70 (☎ 33 046, ul Gurko 70) Singles/doubles with a shared bathroom 13/26 lv, apartments with bathroom 55 lv. It may have a strange name and be poorly signposted but this place is great value. It's in the old town overlooking the river and most rooms offer appealing vistas. The friendly multilingual owner can arrange tours around the city for guests. He has grand plans to install a swimming pool, so rates will probably rise later. The apartments feature four beds, and a balcony, TV and kitchen.

Hotel Etâr (☎ 621 838, fax 621 890, ul Ivailo 2) Singles/doubles from 26/54 lv to 44/88 lv. The unmissable, 14-storey Etâr has plenty of rooms (so it's never full), and is central. The rooms are unexciting, but clean, and most have decent views (ideal for the 'free' sound and light show at the Tsarevets Fortress!). The cheaper rooms have a shared bathroom, and the dearer ones contain a bathroom and TV. All rates include breakfast. Noise from nearby nightclubs has annoyed some readers.

Hotel Veltted (☎ 29 788, ul Gurko) Singles/doubles with shared bathroom 20/30 lv. It's not be friendliest place in town but the rooms are lovely and it's in a quiet and convenient part of the old town. The hotel, ulitsa Gurko, is accessible by steps that start from near the Starata Mehana restaurant along ulitsa Stefan Stambolov.

Hotel Comfort (☎/fax 23 525, ul P Tipografov 5) Beds in 5-bed dorm with shared bathroom 20 lv per person, singles/doubles/triples with bathroom 30/40/60 lv, apartments 60 lv. This place (still being renovated at the time of research) is in a charming part of Varosha. The rooms are clean and comfortable, and feature huge bathrooms and balconies with awesome views. The effusive manager plans to build more rooms with better views on the upper floors. Breakfast is an extra 2 lv per person. It's well signposted from along ulitsa Stefan Stambolov.

Places to Stay – Mid-Range & Top End

Motel Sveta Gora (☎ 34 810, e dalcomers@ skyboz.com) Doubles with bathroom US$30. This sparkling new place has little to offer in the way of amenities, but the forest setting

and sweeping views of the city are attractive. Rates include breakfast. The motel is 2.5km from the town centre and is really only accessible by taxi.

Restaurant-Hotel Gurko (☎ 627 838, ul Gurko 33) Singles/doubles with bathroom US$50/60. The huge rooms (with air-con and TV) are lovely, and offer views, but the furniture is surprisingly unexciting. Standards vary from one room to another (some have fans, and others have tiny bathrooms), so check out a few before making a decision. Rates include breakfast.

Interhotel Veliko Târnovo (☎ 630 571, e ih-vt@vt.bitex.com, ul A Penchev) Singles/doubles US$72/126. You may stay at this four-star place if you're on an upmarket organised tour, but there's nothing to justify these rates. The Restaurant-Hotel Gurko is just as good at about half the price, and there are far better options in this price range at Arbanasi. Credit cards attract a 5% surcharge. Rates include breakfast.

Places to Eat

Barzo Hranene (ul Vasil Levski) Salads 1.50 lv, meals 2.50-3 lv. Although the choice of meals at this cafeteria is limited, the food is tasty and cheap. Just pick up a plate, point at a dish and enjoy.

Starata Mehana (ul Stefan Stambolov) Main meals about 3-4 lv. The Starata is a friendly little place just down the cliff-side from the main road. The food is delicious, and the prices are reasonable considering the setting and service. The views from the terrace are typically spectacular but are only shared by two tables. The menu has been translated into English.

Restaurant Rich (ul Stefan Stambolov) Salads 1.50-2 lv, main meals 4-4.50 lv. Newer, classier and a little dearer than the Starata, this place has excellent service (with a menu in English), and a larger terrace with several tables and killer views. It's also accessible down some steps from the main road.

Atrion Taverna (ul Mitropolska) Salads and soups about 2 lv & grills about 5 lv. Although prices are a little high because it caters to tour buses visiting the fortress, the views are pleasant, the servings are large and the extensive menu is in English.

Restaurant-Hotel Gurko *(☎ 627 838, ul Gurko 33)* Most meals 3.50-6 lv. The quaint restaurant at the front of this pension doesn't offer the same sort of views as the rooms upstairs, but the service and food are hard to fault.

Stratilat Restaurant *(ul Rakovski 11)* This busy place, just off the main road on the way to the Varosha district, offers drinks and snacks upstairs or at tables outside. The 'Viennese apple pie' is to die for, and the toasted sandwiches seem to hang off the plate. There's a menu in English (if you ask for it).

Mustang Food *(pl Maika Bulgaria)* Grills about 3 lv. Like the Happy Bar & Grill restaurants found elsewhere in Bulgaria, Mustang offers palatable Western-style food in a modern setting at above-average prices. The menu is in English.

La Scalla *(ul Hristo Botev 14)* Small/large pizzas from 3/4.50 lv. La Scalla offers a huge range of tasty pizza and pasta dishes, but little else. The menu isn't in English, but the names of the dishes (eg, carbonara) are easy to understand and order once you've deciphered the Cyrillic.

For a quick, cheap and filling meal, it's hard to walk past any place selling ***doner kebabs*** along ulitsa Nezavisimost. If you wish to self-cater, visit the ***supermarket*** *(ul Vasil Levski)*, or the ***market*** farther along.

Entertainment

Probably because of the number of students in town, Veliko Târnovo's nightlife is second only to Sofia's. Happily, most bars, nightclubs and discos are within easy stumbling distance of one another.

Las Vegas Club *(ul Nezavisimost 17)* It may not be exciting or trendy, and the service is often slow, but the views here are almost unbeatable. If you somehow get sick of the panorama, you can play pool or order a meal.

Ulitsata *(ul Stefan Stambolov)* Arguably the best bar in town is on the cliff-side of the main road next to the Hotel Trapezitsa. The balcony is small, so only a few people

can admire the staggering views, but it's friendly and plays modern (taped) music.

City Pub *(ul Hristo Botev)* Probably the most popular bar in town is this thematic British-style pub just down from the TIC. Despite the unremarkable and pricey meals, it's always busy.

The flashiest nightclub is the ***Spyder Nightclub*** *(ul Hristo Botev 15; closed Sun)*, just near the TIC. Some of the more fashionable locals flock to the ***Fashion Club*** *(ul Hristo Botev)*, which is in the Cinema Poltava complex.

For something more sedate, catch a movie at the ***Cinema Poltava*** *(ul Hristo Botev)*, or ask the TIC about what's on at the ***Konstantin Kisimov Dramatic Theatre*** *(☎ 623 526, ul Vasil Levski)*.

Shopping

From near the Hotel Trapezitsa, ulitsa Rakovski (one of several alternating names) veers upwards from the main road. It leads to an area known as the **Samovodska Charshiya Complex**, which is based around a cobblestone square dominated by a statue of the former prime minister, Stefan Stambolov. The area was once the home of craftsmen, including blacksmiths, potters and gunsmiths; artisans still practice their trades here. Most of the shops selling books, boutiques and art, among other things, have been superbly renovated in the style typical of the Bulgarian national revival period.

Getting There & Away

Air Although there are no flights to Veliko Târnovo, there's a Balkan Airlines agency (☎ 621 545) on ulitsa Hristo Botev in the same office as the Rila Bureau.

Bus The main public Patnicheski Prevozi Bus Station (☎ 40 908) is along ulitsa Nikola Gabrovski, about 4km from the town centre. It's surprisingly quiet and unhurried because most travellers use the more convenient and frequent private buses. This station is linked to the town centre by bus Nos 10, 12, 14, 66, 70 and 110 along ulitsa Vasil Levski. There's a left-luggage office that is open daily from 7.30am to 4.30pm.

Veliko Târnovo is along the main highway between Sofia and Varna, so numerous public buses stop here on the way to Varna (9 lv, four hours), Shumen (5.50 lv, two hours), Pleven (5.20 lv, two hours) and Sofia (8 lv, four hours). Also, there's one bus a day directly to Karlovo (6.50 lv, four hours), five to Kazanlâk (4.50 lv, 2½ hours), two to Lovech (3 lv, 1½ hours), nine to Stara Zagora (7.50 lv, three hours), three to Plovdiv (9 lv, 4½ hours), one to Ruse (3.50 lv, two hours) and two or three to Troyan (3.5 lv, two hours). Buses to Gabrovo (3 lv, 40 minutes), via the Dryanovo Monastery, leave about every hour.

Private buses leave from the Yug bus station at least every 30 minutes to Sofia (9 lv, 3½ hours) and Varna (9.50 lv, 3½ hours). Several companies are based at the Yug Bus station (☎ 2014) on ulitsa Hristo Botev, a 15-minute walk (downhill) from the town centre. Negima has international connections through Sofia; Biomet offers daily buses to Albena, Varna and Sofia. Kasto runs daily services to Burgas, Plovdiv, Ruse, Pleven, Gabrovo and Stara Zagora.

From outside the convenient office under the Hotel Etâr, Etap Adress has 11 departures a day to Sofia, two to Dobrich, eight to Varna, and one to Karvana, via Albena and Balchik. Next door, Intertours runs daily services to Burgas, Sofia and Kiten, as well as international connections through Sofia.

Train Direct services to/from Veliko Târnovo are limited, but plenty of trains travel to/from Gorna Oryahovitsa, one of the largest train stations in Bulgaria, only 8.5km away.

From the Veliko Târnovo train station (☎ 22 130), there are five slow passenger trains a day to Plovdiv (1st/2nd class 11.95/8.90 lv), via Stara Zagora (5.55/4.30 lv). There are six slow trains to Gabrovo (4.05/3.20 lv) and 10 to Gorna Oryahovitsa (2.70/2.30 lv). From the Veliko Târnovo station, bus Nos 10, 12, 14, 66, 70 and 110 (the same ones that end up at the Patnicheski Prevozi bus station) head into town. The left-luggage office is open 24 hours.

Gorna Oryahovitsa train station (☎ 0618-56050) is along the main line between Sofia and Varna. Every day to/from Sofia there are four express trains (12.25/8.90 lv, three hours), six fast trains and one slow passenger train, but of these six leave between midnight and 6am. To Varna, there is one express train (12.10/9.90 lv, three hours) and three fast trains. Eleven trains also head to Ruse each day.

To the Gorna Oryahovitsa train station from Veliko Târnovo, catch a minibus from opposite the market along ulitsa Vasil Levski, take bus No 14 from the Panticheski Prevozi Bus station or jump on bus No 10 from the city centre. Alternatively hire a taxi (about 5 lv).

Tickets for advanced domestic services, and international trains, from Veliko Târnovo and Gorna Oryahovitsa are available from the Rila Bureau (☎ 22 042), ulitsa Hristo Botev 13a. It's open Monday to Friday from 8am to noon and 1pm to 4.30pm.

Getting Around

Plenty of taxis scuttle around the main roads of Veliko Târnovo. Taxis are not ideal for getting around the old districts because of the narrow streets, however, they are worth hiring (at fixed metered rates) to get to places like Arbanasi, or chartering (for negotiable rates) to anywhere further out. If you wish to hire a car, the TIC (see the Information section earlier) can put you in contact with a reliable rental company, which charges a reasonable 30 lv or so per day, including insurance (but not petrol).

AROUND VELIKO TÂRNOVO
Arbanasi
Арбанаси
☎ 062 • pop 1500

Arbanasi, 5km north-east of Veliko Târnovo, is a picturesque settlement and a popular side-trip. Some of Bulgaria's rich and famous live here in large, traditional-style homes behind high walls, and nearly 90 churches, homes and monasteries in the village are protected as cultural monuments by the Bulgarian authorities. Originally founded by Christians from Albania in the 15th century,

ARBANASI АРБАНАСИ

PLACES TO STAY & EAT
4 Hotel Bohemi
   ХОТЕЛ БОХЕМИ
8 Cafes
9 Konstantin & Elena Hotel
   ХОТЕЛ
   КОНСТАНТИН
   И ЕЛЕНА
10 Mehana Izvora
    МЕХАНА ИЗВОРА
11 Pupyaka Restaurant
    РЕСТОРАНТ ПУПЯКА

13 Bolyarska Kâshta & Restaurant
   БОЛЯРСКА КЪЩТА И
   РЕСТОРАНТ
18 Hotel Arbanasi Palace
   ХОТЕЛ АРБАНАСИ
   ДВОРЕЦ

OTHER
1 St Atanassius Church
   ЦЪРКВАТА СВ. АТАНАС
2 Hadjilieva House
   ХАДЖИЛИЕВА КЪЩТА

3 Konstantsalieva House;
   Souvenir Shop
   КОНСТАНЦАЛИЕВАТА
   КЪЩТА
5 St George's Church
   ЦЪРКВАТА СВ. ГЕОРГИ
6 St Bogoroditsa Monastery
   МАНАСТИР СВ.
   БОГОРОДИЦА
7 Nativity Church
   ЦЪРКВАТА РОЖДЕСТО
   ХРИСТОВО

12 St Demetrius Church
   ЦЪРКВАТА СВ. ДИМИТЪР
14 Bus Stop; Kiosk (for Tickets)
15 Arbanasi Horse Base
   ХИПОДУМ АРБАНАСИ
16 St Archangel Michael &
   Gabriel's Church
   ЦЪРКВАТА СВ.
   АРАХАНГЕЛ
   МИХАИЛ И ГАВРАИЛ
17 St Nikola Monastery
   МАНАСТИР СВ. НИКОЛАЙ

Arbanasi grew prosperous after Sultan Süleyman I gave the town to a son-in-law in 1538, thus exempting it from the Ottoman Empire's ruinous taxation. Residents were able to carry on trade as far as Greece, Russia and India, and the town became a favourite summer residence for the fabulously wealthy. All this good fortune came to an abrupt end in 1798 when the town was mostly destroyed by Turkish *kurdjali* gangs.

Things to See At the time of research, only the three places listed here were open to the public in summer. But this may change if

and when renovations of other buildings are completed. One ticket (4 lv) allows you to visit all three places; the ticket is available from the kiosk (not always open) at the bus stop, or from each of the three attractions. Each place is officially open from 9am to noon and 1pm to 8pm every day. In practice, opening hours are erratic, places are rarely open before 9.30am. Most of the attractions are permanently closed between 1 October and 31 March, so check the opening times with the **Museums Department** (☎ 062-349 460) in Veliko Târnovo before visiting Arbanasi in winter.

Cameras (photographic or video) are not allowed at any of the three places. Nothing much is signposted around the village, and the streets have no names. Disappointingly, everything on site is labelled in Bulgarian, and any (brief) explanation on notice boards outside is in German. If you want any more information about the attractions, pick up one of several booklets (2 lv to 3 lv), such as *Arbanasi: A Guide*, in Veliko Târnovo.

The typical house in Arbanasi is in the middle of a large garden, bordered by high brick walls and entered through a large wooden gate. In the older homes, the basement was invariably made of stone, and used to store valuables, make wine, house servants and protect residents during the numerous Turkish raids. The ground floor was more open and featured a drawing room, kitchen, living room, dining room and study. The family lived on the second floor.

The gorgeous **Konstantsalieva House**, built in the 17th century, and rebuilt several times afterwards, most recently in a typical Bulgarian national revival style. The upper floor contains rooms of period furniture (the maternity room, or nursery, is particularly endearing), while the ground floor has a **souvenir shop** with an impressive range of embroidery, among other things, for sale.

The oldest remaining church in the village is known as the **Nativity Church**. During the 16th and 17th centuries, the comparatively benevolent Turkish rulers in Arbanasi allowed several churches to be built. The interior is completely covered with richly and lavishly coloured murals painted between 1632 and 1649; over 3500 figures are depicted in some 2000 scenes. It also contains several lavish wooden iconostases created by carvers from Tryavna.

Built in the 16th century on the ruins of a medieval church is the **St Archangel Michael & Gabriel's Church**. The interior is also covered with marvellous murals, including one from Thessaloniki (Greece) and Bucharest (Romania), but it's rather dark inside and hard to see. The wooden iconostases were also carved by experts from Tryavna.

There are other places which cannot be visited, but can be admired from over the fence or through the window. Wander past the **Hadjilieva House** (closed after a robbery), the unsignposted **St Demetrius Church**, at the back of a scrappy garden, and the pretty **St Atanassius Church**, probably built in 1667, in a cemetery at the top of the lane. If you have the time and inclination, you may also want to visit these three 17th-century buildings: **St George's Church**, the **St Bogoroditsa Monastery** and the **St Nikola Monastery**.

Activities One of the few places in central Bulgaria where visitors can arrange a gallop around the countryside on horseback is the Arbanasi Horse Base (☎ 23 668), on the eastern edge of the village. Phone to ask about current programs and costs. It also hosts a riding tournament each June.

Places to Stay More and more mid-range bed and breakfast pensions are being built in Arbanasi. Although they are all overpriced for foreigners, and at least 50% dearer than the equivalent in Veliko Târnovo, Arbanasi is a marvellous place to relax, and a picturesque alternative to Veliko Târnovo. All places listed here offer rooms with a bathroom (unless stated otherwise), and all rates include breakfast. If you are arriving in winter, ring the hotels to see if they're open.

It may be possible to stay in a *room* in a private home; some readers have reported staying in village accommodation with fan, TV and bathroom for about 44 lv per double. Ask at the shops and kiosk at the bus stop.

Konstantin & Elena Hotel (☎ 600 217) Doubles US$35, apartments US$45. This hotel, opposite the Nativity Church, is an attractive, modern place, and probably the best value in town. The rooms are comfortable, and have a TV, but most don't offer any views. The huge apartments feature charming panoramas, as well as lots of pine cupboards, a sitting room, TV and fridge.

Hotel Bohemi (☎ 33 108) Doubles with shared bathroom US$40, apartments with bathroom US$60. The friendly and homely Bohemi has a handful of small rooms, but some have no amenities such as TVs and all share a bathroom, so it's poor value. The large apartments feature an appealing fireplace and TV, and are worth a splurge.

Bolyarska Kâshta & Restaurant (☎ *20 484*) Singles/doubles US$40/50. Only metres from the main square and bus stop, this hotel is comfortable and the rooms have a TV, but it's overpriced for foreigners. It is popular, however, so book ahead in summer.

Hotel Arbanasi Palace (☎ *630 176,* **e** *ihotels@bis-bg.com*) Singles/doubles US$100/140 to US$135/160. The five-star Arbanasi Palace is a pompous place used mostly for state functions. It's worth visiting the 'palace' for the marvellous views of Veliko Târnovo from the terrace. (The hotel can even be seen from Veliko Târnovo.)

Places to Eat Arbanasi is an ideal place to try some Bulgarian cuisine, but prices in most places are a little high

Pupyaka Restaurant Salads about 2.50 lv, main meals from 4.50 lv. This classy place, close to the village square and bus stop, has outdoor tables which back on to the charming park.

Mehana Izvora Grills from 3.50 lv. The Izvora is a tavern built in a 17th-century home. It's popular with tour groups, who enjoy the extensive menu of traditional food. With a swimming pool and playground, it caters well to families. In the evenings, folk music is provided (at no extra cost) if there are enough customers.

The road around the corner from the Nativity Church is dotted with *cafes*. They offer the same startling views of Veliko Târnovo and the valley for which guests at the nearby Hotel Arbanasi Palace pay dearly.

Getting There & Away From a spot opposite the market along ulitsa Vasil Levski in Veliko Târnovo, minibuses depart for Gorna Oryahovitsa train station when full (about every 30 minutes). If you ask nicely, or other customers are going there too, the driver may detour through Arbanasi. If not, disembark at the turn-off to Arbanasi, along the road between Veliko Târnovo and Gorna Oryahovitsa, and walk (about 700m) to the village. A taxi from Veliko Târnovo costs little more than 2 lv one way.

Preobrazhenski Monastery
Преображенски Манастир

The Monastery of Transfiguration is in a scenic forest about 6.5km north of Veliko Târnovo. Originally built in 1360, it's the largest monastery in the region, and the fourth-largest in Bulgaria. It was destroyed by the Turks in the late 14th century, and rebuilt in 1825 about 500m from the original site, but later damaged by landslides. The three churches feature murals painted between 1849 and 1851 by the renowned Zahari Zograf, but the best selection of older murals are now in the archaeological museum in Veliko Târnovo.

Perhaps, the main reason to visit is the staggering view across the valley. The turn-off is along the road from Veliko Târnovo to Ruse and is accessible by bus No 10. From the turn-off, it's a shady, uphill (but not steep) 3km walk. A taxi from Veliko Târnovo will cost about 3 lv one way.

Emen
Емен

The 3km-long **Emen Canyon**, along the Negovanka River, is the only one of its kind in Bulgaria. The surrounding area (about 25 hectares) has been declared a reserve by the locals authorities to protect species of butterflies, fish, birds and bats, as well as the 10m-high **Momin Skok Waterfall** (not so spectacular in summer).

The Bulgarian Association for Rural & Ecological Tourism (BARET) has established the **Negovanka Eco-trail** in and around the canyon. To find the start of the trail, look for signs in Emen village. Ask at the tourist office in Veliko Târnovo for current details and/or maps. Emen village and the canyon are about 25km west of Veliko Târnovo. Both are accessible by the bus to Pavlikeni, which leaves the Patnicheski Prevozi bus station in Veliko Târnovo at 8.30am and 6pm.

Nikopolis-ad-Istrum
Никополис-ад-Иструм

Worth a visit, especially if you have a private or chartered vehicle, are the ruins of this Roman city (*admission 4 lv; open daily 8am-6pm*). The city was built in AD 102 under Emperor Trayan, but destroyed by, among others, the Slavs in the late 6th century. Tragically, many of the city's treasures have been looted, but some of the greatest artefacts are housed in the archaeological museum in Veliko Târnovo. Excavations have unearthed streets, towers, gates and numerous buildings, but the highlights are the remains of the city square and town hall.

If you are driving from Veliko Târnovo, head north towards Ruse and look for the signposted turn-off to the left (west) after about 20km. But beware: some of the access road is rough. By bus, head towards Ruse, ask the driver to stop at the turn-off to Nikyup and then walk (about 4km) to the ruins following the signs. The site is not always open in the middle of summer (particularly August) because of extensive archaeological work, so check with the tourist office in Veliko Târnovo, or ring the relevant authority (☎ 062-24 474), before heading out there at this time.

Lyaskovets
Лясковец

This quaint town, about 10km east of Veliko Târnovo, has been a centre of viniculture for over 150 years. One of the more established, and accessible, vineyards in the region is **Lyaskovets Wineries** (☎ 0619-23081), renowned makers of fruity sparkling wines and smooth reds. Contact them about wine-tasting tours, which can be arranged from Veliko Târnovo.

ELENA
ЕЛЕНА

☎ 0651 • pop 7500

About 30km south-east of Veliko Târnovo, Elena is trying to spruce itself up with the aid of the Beautiful Bulgaria Project so it can attract a similar number of tourists flocking to other traditional villages such as Etâr, Arbanasi and Tryavna. But there is little to justify a detour to Elena especially because the other three places are easier to reach and offer a better range of accommodation.

The bus station is only metres from the main road through town, ulitsa Sv Neyovski. From the station, turn left and walk (five

minutes) to the main square. Surrounding the square are several banks, cafes, and the tourist information centre (☎ 3732, e elena–hotel@abv.bg), on the first floor of the Hotel Elena. Opposite the square, the **House-Museum of Ilarion Makariopolski** (☎ 2129, Elena) was undergoing some remarkable renovations at the time of writing and should be worth a look when it reopens.

If you walk 300m uphill along the main road, turn left at the (second) park and stroll up ulitsa Yovchev you'll find the **National Revival Museum Complex**. It offers only a few empty, or permanently closed, traditional houses, but there are some fine **churches** in the vicinity.

Overlooking the main square, *Hotel Elena* (☎ 3732, Elena) is the only hotel in town. The unremarkable, but adequate, singles/doubles with bathroom and TV cost 32/45 lv. Each day, five buses go to Veliko Târnovo, four depart for Gorna Oryahovitsa (the nearest major train station), and two travel to Sliven.

SHUMEN (SHOUMEN)
ШУМЕН

☎ 054 • pop 107,650

Shumen (Shoumen) sits at the base of a low flat spur of the Stara Planina ranges, about halfway between the Black Sea coast and the Danube River. It's an industrial and military city with strong ties to the country's communist past, as evidenced by the number of statues and monuments. Shumen doesn't boast the old towns, shady parks and long pedestrian malls of other places in the region, but the hill top Shumen Fortress is one of the highlights of central Bulgaria, and the city is an obvious base for day trips to Veliki Preslav and Madara (see the Around Shumen section later in this chapter).

Shumen hosts the fascinating **Watermelon Festival** (last Sunday in August), as well as the more sedate **Days of Shumen Cultural Festival** (mid-May) and the **Folklore Festival** (August).

History

Both the Thracians and Romans settled in the area over several millennia. During the

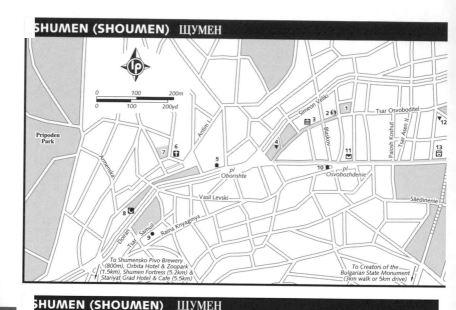

SHUMEN (SHOUMEN) ЩУМЕН

PLACES TO STAY & EAT

4 Mehanas
5 Hotel Shumen &
   Restaurants
   ХОТЕЛ ШУМЕН И
   РЕСТОРАНТ
10 Hotel Madara; Internet
   Club & Café
   ХОТЕЛ МАДАРА
12 Restaurant Yo-Yo
   РЕСТОРАНТ ЙО-ЙО
16 Pizzeria Elit
   ПИЦАРИЯ ЕЛИТ

OTHER

1 Market
2 United Bulgarian Bank
   ОБЕДИНЕНА БЪЛГАРСКА
   БАНКА
3 Museum Complex of Pancho
   Vladigerov
   МУЗЕЕН КОМПЛЕКС НА
   ПАНЧО БЛАДИГЕРОВ
6 Methodist Church
7 Bezisten (Turkish Market)
   БЕЗИСТЕНА
8 Tombul Mosque
   ТОМБУЛ ДЖАМИЯ

9 Clock Tower
11 Post Office & Telephone
   Centre; Cinema Kultura
13 Theatre
14 History Museum; Café
   ИСТОРИЧЕСКИ МУЗЕЙ
15 Bulbank; Cafes
   БУЛБАНК
17 Biochim Commercial Bank
   ТЪРГОВСКА БАНКА
   БИОХИМ
18 Cinema Herson
   КИНО ХЕРСОН
19 Bus Station

early Middle Ages, nearby Veliki Preslav and Pliska became the birthplaces of the medieval Bulgarian kingdom. Shumen was captured by the Turks in 1388 and for the next five centuries Chumla (as it became known) was an important market town. Later, Shumen became part of the Turk's strategic quadrangle (along with Ruse, Silistra and Varna) of towns fortified as a defence against Russian advances. A comparatively large number of Jews, Armenians and Muslims live in Shumen.

Orientation & Information

The bus station, and adjacent train station, are in the eastern part of the city. A pedestrian mall alongside bulevard Slavyanski connects the city park with the main square, ploshtad Osvobozhdenie. Here, Bulgaria's largest, ugliest and unfinished building scars the landscape. Around the city square, you'll find the telephone centre, in the post office, open daily from 7am to 10pm. The Internet Club & Cafe is in the Hotel Madara. To change money, try the United Bulgarian

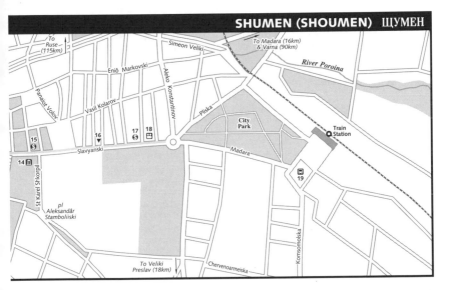

SHUMEN (SHOUMEN) ЩУМЕН

Bank, on ulitsa Tsar Osvoboditel, or the Bulbank or Biochim Commercial Bank, both of which are on bulevard Slavyanski.

Shumen Fortress
Шуменска крепост

On the side of the hill overlooking the city is Shumen Fortress (☎ 58 051; admission 3 lv; open daily 8am-7pm in summer, 8.30am-5pm in winter). It's one of the oldest settlements in Bulgaria, and dates from the early Iron Age. In about the 5th century BC, the Thracians built some walls, and between the 2nd and 4th centuries, the Romans added towers and more walls.

After being ignored for several centuries, the structure was fortified by the Byzantines and became an important military base. During the Second Bulgarian Empire (1185–1396), the fortress was one of the most significant settlements in north-eastern Bulgaria and was renowned as a centre for pottery and metalwork. In the late 14th century, the Ottomans invaded and burnt part of the fortress down and looted the stone.

The fortress is a fascinating place to wander around. There are some basic explanations on notice boards around the site, but the booklet (2 lv), available at the gate, is helpful (even if the photos look about as old as the fortress itself). From the Tombul Mosque, the fortress is about 5.5km uphill, so take a taxi (about 1.50 lv one way). From the entrance to the fortress, a glorious and reasonably flat 3km path leads to the gigantic Creators of the Bulgarian State Monument, from where you can take the steps back down to the city centre.

Creators of the Bulgarian State Monument

This probably gets our award as the ugliest and most conspicuous of many ugly and conspicuous monuments in Bulgaria; it can be easily seen from up to 10km away! This indescribably massive hill top monument was built in 1981 to commemorate the 1300th anniversary of the establishment of the First Bulgarian Empire.

The 5km circuitous road to the monument starts along ulitsa Karel Shkorpil from the History Museum. (Once outside the museum, you can decide whether the monument is too ugly or too far to bother walking.) The best way up there is by taxi (about 3 lv one way), and the best way down is via the steps (about 2.5km) that lead back to the city centre and bulevard Slavyanski. A 3km path goes past the Information Centre and car park and finishes at Shumen Fortress.

The **Information Centre** (☎ 52 598; admission 3 lv; open 8.30am-5pm in winter, 8am-7pm in summer), about 300m from the monument, features some unremarkable displays about the structure and surrounding flora.

Tombul Mosque

The most beautifully decorated mosque in Bulgaria is the Tombul Mosque (☎ 56 823, ul Doiran; admission 2 lv; open daily 9am-6pm). Built in 1744, it is the largest mosque still in use in the country. Also known as the Sherif Halili Pasha Mosque, it was given the Turkish moniker of *tombul* (plump) because of the shape of its 25m-high dome. The 40m-high minaret has 99 steps but is not open to the public. In the courtyard, there's a fountain which some Muslims believe contains sacred water, and a couple of decent **souvenir shops**. Ask at the gate for an informative leaflet (in English and French) about the mosque.

Just down the main road are the ruins of the **Bezisten**, a 16th-century Turkish covered market. It was closed at the time of research, but renovations were under way so it may reopen later in some capacity.

Museums

The **History Museum** (☎ 57 596, bul Slavyanski 17; admission 2 lv; open Mon-Fri 9am-5pm) is a large, ugly brick building along the main road. But inside is a superb collection of Thracian and Roman artefacts, including many from Madara, Veliki Preslav and Pliska. There are also a number of ancient coins and icons and a scale model of the Shumen Fortress as it was in its heyday. A pleasant *cafe* is in the ivy-covered courtyard.

Dotted along the cobblestone western section of ulitsa Tsar Osvoboditel are several houses built, or renovated, in the Bulgarian national revival period, or early-20th-century baroque, style. One of these, the **Museum Complex of Pancho Vladigerov** (☎ 52 123, ul Tsar Osvoboditel 136; admission 1.50 lv; open Mon-Fri 9am-5pm) commemorates Bulgaria's most renowned composer and pianist (ie, Vladigerov). The complex comprises a number of attractive buildings, including a library, arrayed around a shady courtyard garden.

Pripoden Park

This large park (3930 hectares), also known as Kyoshkovete Park, sits on the western edge of the city. The lower parts are spoiled somewhat by the background hum from the Shumensko Pivo Brewery. Near the brewery, there are plenty of **hiking trails**, which lead nowhere in particular but offer plenty of shade. The **zoo park**, next to the Orbita Hotel, features some bored bison, and other caged animals.

Places to Stay

Each hotel listed here offers rooms with a bathroom.

Stariyat Grad Hotel & Cafe (☎ 55 376) Doubles 32 lv. This simple place is ideally located in a serene forest about 300m (and signposted) from the entrance to Shumen Fortress. The rooms are quiet and clean and the owners are friendly.

Orbita Hotel (☎ 52 398, Pripoden Park) Doubles 40 lv, apartments 60 lv. Compared to the other options in Shumen, this is excellent value. The rooms are clean and comfortable, though sparsely furnished, and the apartments feature a sitting room and fridge. It's in a quiet, shady park about a 2km walk (or taxi ride) from the city centre.

Hotel Madara (☎ 57 598, fax 52 591, pl Osvobozhdenie) Singles/doubles/apartments US$55/80/105. The three-star, seven-floor Madara is obscenely overpriced for foreigners, and should be avoided until the management sees some sense. Although central, the rooms (which have a TV and fridge) are barely two-star quality with four-star rates.

Hotel Shumen (☎ 591 416, fax 58 009, pl Oborishte) Singles/doubles US$65/90. For about $10 more, the rooms at this four-star hotel are significantly better than Madara's. However, it's still overpriced for foreigners because guests are paying for amenities they may not need, including an indoor pool and sauna. Rooms contain a fridge and TV, and rates include breakfast.

Places to Eat

A complex of quaint 19th-century wooden buildings at the start of the western end of ulitsa Tsar Osvoboditel contains three traditional *mehanas*. Each offers indoor tables, a courtyard garden setting and almost identical service and prices. You will pay 3 lv to 4 lv for grilled chicken or beef, 1.50 lv for a salad and about 1.50 lv for a small beer. The menus are not in English, but the English-speaking staff can usually help.

Restaurant Yo-Yo (ul Tsar Osvoboditel; not open in the evenings) Chicken meals about 1.50 lv. Distinctive because of the aroma of roasted chicken wafting across the road, this modest but clean eatery also offers *musaka* (about 2 lv) and all sorts of other tasty dishes.

Pizzeria Elit (bul Slavyanski) Pizzas from 2 lv & other meals 2.50-3 lv. Rush here for some of the tastiest pizzas (all topped with a fried egg) in the region. A wide range of other meals is also available. It's also an ideal place to enjoy a cheap drink at a street-side table.

The *Hotel Shumen* (see Places to Stay earlier) has several restaurants, one of which offers a decent buffet breakfast for 5 lv (free to guests). The menus are in English. The best *cafes* are in the mall alongside bulevard Slavyanski, especially those opposite the History Museum.

Getting There & Away

From the bus station (☎ 61 618), there are three or four buses a day to Burgas (6.50 lv, three hours), three to Ruse (5.40 lv, two hours), four to Dobrich (6.80 lv, two hours), three to Silistra (6.80 lv, 2½ hours) and several to Veliko Târnovo (5.50 lv, two hours). Shumen is on the highway between Sofia (11 to 12 lv, six hours) and Varna (4.90 lv, 1½ hours), so numerous buses come through in both directions. Several private buses, such as those operated by Etap Adress, also stop in Shumen on the route between Sofia and Varna.

Shumen is on the main train line between Sofia and Varna. Every day, nine trains (including one express) from Varna (1st/2nd class 7.10/5.40 lv, two hours express), and two fast trains from Sofia (11.95/8.90 lv, four hours), stop at the disorganised train station (☎ 60 155) in Shumen. There's a left-luggage office (open 24 hours) inside the train station.

For information about public transport from Shumen to Madara and Veliki Preslav, refer to the following relevant sections.

AROUND SHUMEN
Madara
Мадара
☎ 05313 • pop 1400

Madara was an important Thracian town around 5000 BC, and, later, during the Roman occupation. These days, this village, 16km east of Shumen, probably only exists because of the famous Madara Horseman.

Madara National Historical & Archaeological Reserve This reserve *(☎ 2095; admission 2 lv; open daily 8am-7pm)* surrounds the so-called Madara Horseman *(Madarski Konnik)*. Carved into a cliff 23m above the ground, the bas-relief features a mounted figure spearing a lion and followed by a dog. It was created in the early 8th century AD to commemorate the victorious Khan Tervel, and, more profoundly, the creation and consolidation of the First Bulgarian Empire. As the only known rock carving in Bulgaria from the Middle Ages, it's protected as a Unesco World Heritage site.

North of the horseman, a 373-step stairway hewn out of the cliff face leads to the top of the cliffs (130m high) and the ruins of the **Madara Fortress**. The fortress was built during the First Bulgarian Empire (1185–1396) as part of a defensive ring intended to protect the capitals of Pliska and Veliki Preslav. The sweeping **views** explain why the fortress was built there.

If you want to explore the area in depth, buy a copy of the *Madara* booklet (2 lv, in English or German) at the entrance gate. It also outlines some of the popular **hiking trails** to the nearby **tombs** and **caves**. Most signs around the reserve are translated into German (not English).

If you're contemplating climbing to the top of the steep steps which lead to the base of the horseman, it's worth noting that the permanent scaffolding hides more of the bas-relief the closer you get, so the whole experience can be an anticlimax up close. The **Madara Horseman Music Days Festival** is held in the reserve on four successive Thursdays from mid-June to mid-July.

Places to Stay & Eat The two places listed here are a short walk from the horseman, and open all year. Watch for the signposts in English. There are plenty of *cafes*, and **souvenir shops**, in the car park area.

Camping Madara (☎ 995 313) Camping 6 lv per person, cabins 20 lv per double with shared bathroom. This shady and peaceful camping spot is 500m from the horseman. It also offers a cosy little *restaurant*.

Hizha Madarski Konnik (☎ 2091) offers dorm beds for about 15 lv per person.

Getting There & Away Public transport to Madara is limited, and the horseman is 3km up a steep road from the village. Several slow passenger trains travel each day between Shumen and Varna, stopping at Madara. Buses to Madara from Shumen are infrequent, so get a bus (five times a day) to Kaspichan, then a minibus to Madara from there. A taxi from Shumen costs a negotiable 12 to 15 lv return, including waiting time. There are no taxis in Madara.

Veliki Preslav
Велики Преслав
☎ 0538 • pop 10,600

Veliki Preslav (sometimes known as just Preslav) is an unremarkable town about 18km south-west of Shumen. It's worth visiting for the ruins of the ancient capital but there's no need to stay because it's an easy day trip from Shumen. The main square is about 300m up the main road west of the bus station.

History Veliki Preslav was founded in the early 9th century AD by the Bulgar king,

Khan Omurtag, but it was Tsar Simeon who moved the capital of the First Bulgarian Empire (681–1018) from Pliska to Veliki Preslav in 893. In the new capital, Tsar Simeon decreed Orthodox Christianity as the religion, and Bulgarian as the language, of the empire. Veliki Preslav soon became one of the most glorious cities in the Balkans.

The city was captured and burnt down by the Byzantines in 972. However, it was later rebuilt and flourished as a cultural and religious centre. During the Second Bulgarian Empire, the capital was moved to modern-day Veliko Târnovo, so Veliki Preslav fell into decline. In 1388, it was again sacked by the Turks, who hauled away much of the stone to construct mosques elsewhere.

Ruins & Museum Protected by a high stone wall, the outer city spread over 5 sq km and contained churches, monasteries and residences of nobles. An inner wall encircled the 1.5-sq-km citadel with the royal palace at its centre. The most famous building was the **Round Golden Church**, built in 908 and partially restored in the last few years. It derived its name from the dome, which was gilded on the outside and covered with mosaics inside.

Visitors should first stop at the **archaeological museum** *(☎ 2630; admission 3 lv; open daily 9am-6pm in summer & 9am-5pm in winter)*. The numerous artefacts from the ruins, and other items, are well displayed and labelled in English. A cutaway model of the palace helps you visualise the grandeur of the ancient city (though explanations for this are in Bulgarian only). The prize exhibits, such as seals, jewellery and the exquisite regal gold necklace, are displayed in a walkthrough safe. If you ask, staff will show a film (in English) about the ancient city.

Guided tours (in English) by an archaeologist cost 10 lv per group (maximum of five people). They are worthwhile because the ruins are spread over a large area, and nothing much is signposted. If you want to explore the site independently, ask for directions at the museum, or just head down the road (away from the modern town) towards the **southern gate**, and wander about.

From the bus station, walk (2km) along ulitsa Boris I, cross the road over to ulitsa Ivanlo, turn right into ulitsa Tsar Asen and look for the sign (in English) at the ruins of the **northern gate**. From there, the museum is another 300m down the road, with the (modern) cemetery on your left.

Places to Stay & Eat There is only one hotel in town.

Hotel Preslav (☎ *3305*) Singles/doubles with bathroom 10/20 lv. This fairly unexciting place is at the back of the main square. It's a bit drab, but clean enough, and the rates are low. Eat at the basic hotel *restaurant*, or one of *cafes* near the bus station.

Getting There & Away Every day, 11 buses travel directly between Shumen and Veliki Preslav (1.60 lv, 30 to 60 minutes), often via Kochovo. Another option is to take a bus from Shumen to Vârbitsa (six daily) – but not the ones via Rish – and jump out at Veliki Preslav.

SLIVEN
СЛИВЕН
☎ 044 • pop 109,600

The Thracians, Romans and Greeks all settled in the area around Sliven, but little evidence remains. The history of Sliven is inextricably linked to the *haidouks*, the anti-Turkish rebels who lived in the rocky hills nearby from the early 18th to the mid-19th century. These insurgents eventually united under the leadership of Hadzhi Dimitâr and the revered Vasil Levski and defeated the Turkish overlords. Sliven is a modest, yet appealing, city, under several peaks that are over 1000m high.

Orientation & Information
The city centre is the typically massive and permanently empty main square, ploshtad Hadzhi Dimitâr. To the east of the square is a modern clock tower, to the north is the Stefan Kirov Dramatic Theatre, and to the south is the quaint Deboya Church. The post office and telephone centre are also on the square.

Over the river is a surprisingly expansive (and mostly undercover) market, one of the most vibrant in Bulgaria. Several foreign-exchange offices can be found along the upper (south-eastern) section of ulitsa Hadzhi Dimitâr and the pedestrian mall, ulitsa Tsar Osvoboditel. The Internet Club is just off the mall.

Hadzhi Dimitâr Museum
A delightful building, which sits incompatibly among concrete apartment blocks and shops, is the Hadzhi Dimitâr Museum (☎ *22 496, ul Asenova 2; admission 2 lv; open Mon-Fri 9am-noon & 2pm-5pm),* dedicated to the leader of the anti-Turkish rebels. It is well worth a visit, but nothing is labelled in English. It features several rooms of furniture – including antique weaving equipment – set around a cobblestone courtyard.

History Museum
In a grand old building, seemingly lost among the modern shops and cafes along the mall, is the History Museum (☎ *22 495, ul Tsar Osvoboditel 18; admission 2 lv; open Mon-Fri 9am-noon & 2pm-5pm).* The three floors house a large array of exhibits, including archaeological and ethnological items such as coins, weapons and books. Most interesting are the displays about the anti-Turkish rebels. Nothing is captioned in English, however.

Blue Rocks
Сините скали
It's easy to understand how the *haidouks* (rebels) were able to hide from the Turks for so long among these hills, commonly called the Blue Rocks. Beware: According to a brochure published by the local tourist authority, anyone can become a haidouk just by looking at the cliffs in the hills!

Take the **chairlift** *(5/10 lv one way/return, 20 minutes)* or walk (60 to 90 minutes) up the hill following the chairlift – however, it's not always easy going because of the occasional inexplicable sections of barbed wire you must detour around. From the top of the chairlift, take the obvious path (300m), cross the main road, and walk down (another 500m) through the woods to *Hizha Poveda*, which serves drinks and basic meals.

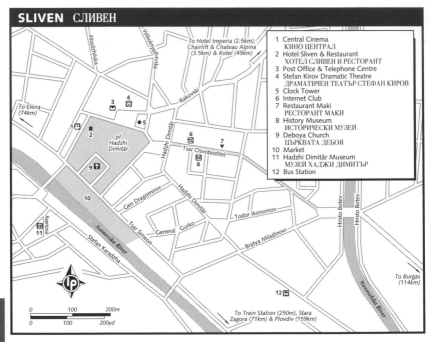

SLIVEN СЛИВЕН

1　Central Cinema
　КИНО ЦЕНТРАЛ
2　Hotel Sliven & Restaurant
　ХОТЕЛ СЛИВЕН И РЕСТОРАНТ
3　Post Office & Telephone Centre
4　Stefan Kirov Dramatic Theatre
　ДРАМАТИЧЕН ТЕАТЪР СТЕФАН КИРОВ
5　Clock Tower
6　Internet Club
7　Restaurant Maki
　РЕСТОРАНТ МАКИ
8　History Museum
　ИСТОРИЧЕСКИ МУЗЕЙ
9　Deboya Church
　ЦЪРКВАТА ДЕБОЯ
10　Market
11　Hadzhi Dimitâr Museum
　МУЗЕЙ ХАДЖИ ДИМИТЪР
12　Bus Station

To reach the chairlift from Sliven, catch minibus No 13 outside the train station or Hotel Sliven. You can also walk about 1km uphill (following the signs) from the end of the route for trolleybus Nos 18 or 20 from the city centre. Taxi are about 3 lv one way.

Hiking

From both the information centre (usually closed) along the road to the chairlift, and the Chateau Alpina (see Places to Stay later), marked trails head through the hills to the (signposted) caves used by the haidouks. Information (in English) about the trails is included in a leaflet (1.5 lv), available at the chairlift, but the leaflet has no maps.

More general information about hiking in the area is available from the local national park authority (☎/fax 22 926, ⓔ dpp .skamani@sl.bia-bg.com). For details about hiking in the region see the boxed text 'Hiking in the Stara Planina' earlier in this chapter.

Places to Stay

Each hotel listed here offers rooms with a bathroom.

Hotel Sliven (☎ 27 065, fax 25 112, pl Hadzhi Dimitâr) Singles/doubles 44/66 lv. This unmissable high-rise dominates the main square. It offers the sort of standards expected at an ex-Balkantourist hotel, ie, a couple of beds and little else. It's overpriced for foreigners, but is the only option in the city centre. Rates include breakfast.

Hotel Imperia (☎ 85 071, fax 80 741, ul Panaiot Hitov) Doubles 135 lv, suites 180 lv, apartments 224 lv. This classy place offers a range of rooms, each painted a different colour, and each with a sparkling bathroom. All rooms feature air-con, balcony, fridge and TV. It's inconvenient (about 3km from the city centre and about 1km from the chairlift), but boasts a swimming pool and tennis courts.

Chateau Alpina (☎ 89 215, fax 73 016) Singles/doubles 57/114 lv. Rooms here have air-con, and a TV, and rates include breakfast. The Alpina is only 100m from the start of the chairlift, and far from the city centre, but is deservedly popular so book ahead.

Places to Eat

The best places to enjoy a drink or meal are the *cafes* along the mall.

Restaurant Maki (ul Tsar Osvoboditel) Salads about 2 lv, meals from 3.50 lv. The Maki has a useful 'photo-menu', which makes it easy for non-Bulgarian speakers to point at the meal they want. The other attraction is the huge outdoor seating area.

An alternative is the dining room at the *Hotel Sliven* (see Places to Stay). It's typically charmless, but the menu (in English) is extensive, and it offers a decent cooked breakfast (free to guests).

Getting There & Away

From the unimpressive bus station (☎ 26 629), on ulitsa Hadzhi Dimitâr just past the massive Bila Supermarket, buses regularly go to Veliko Târnovo, Plovdiv, Stara Zagora (also minibuses) and Karlovo. Sliven is just off the main highway, so most buses travelling between Burgas and Kazanlâk, Stara Zagora and Sofia (10 lv, 5 hours) pass through here.

Sliven is also along the train line between Sofia and Burgas, via Kazanlâk. One fast train and one express stop at the train station (☎ 36 614) in Sliven every day. The express to Sofia (1st/2nd-class 13.60/10 lv) takes 5½ hours; and to Burgas (7.40/5.60 lv) takes 1½ hours.

KOTEL
КОТЕЛ

☎ 0453 • pop 7500

A small town 49km north-east of Sliven, Kotel has a proud history of anti-Turkish rebellion. It's also the birthplace of a remarkable number of scholars, writers and revolutionaries including Safronii Vrachanski, Georgi Rakovski and Petâr Beron.

Kotel is also renowned for its **carpets** and **rugs**, which are made from wool in homes on wooden looms. The 'Kotel style' predominantly features four colours: red, black, green and blue. Examples can be admired, and bought, at the **Exhibition Hall of Carpets & Woodcarving** (☎ 2613, ul Izvorska 17), 500m north-west of the bus station. Also worth a look are the **Museum of National Revival** (☎ 2549, pl Vûzhrazhdane), at the main square (500m north of the bus station); and the **Ethnographic Museum** (☎ 2315, ul Altûnlû Stoyan 5), about 200m west of the Exhibition Hall. Admission to each place is 1.50 lv, and they're open Monday to Friday 8am to noon and 1.30pm to 6pm.

The best place to stay is *Hotel Kotel* (☎ 2885, ul Izvorska 59), about 600m west of the bus station. Also known as the Mel Invest Hotel, it's inconvenient, but adequate, and singles/doubles with bathroom cost 25/35 lv. A *restaurant* is attached. The cosy *Vetrila Hotel* (☎ 2711, ul Vetrila 1) is also inconvenient (about 200m east of the bus station), and costs about the same. The bar serves limited *meals*.

Every day eight buses travel between Sliven and Kotel; they all leave Sliven between 6.30am and 2.30pm.

CENTRAL BULGARIA

Black Sea Coast

Foreigners have been visiting the Black Sea coast of Bulgaria since the 5th millennium BC. Initially, it was marauders from the Thracian, Roman and Greek empires lured by the attractive coastline and opportunities for trade; these days, it's masses of tourists from Germany, Poland, Russia and the UK (among others) attracted by the quality of sandy beaches, seemingly perpetual summer sunshine and the variety of water sports. (Bulgaria has a coastline of 378km, of which about 30% is sandy beaches.)

In summer, the main cities of Burgas and Varna take on a carnival atmosphere, and small towns such as Nesebâr and Sozopol become jammed with tourists. Fortunately, the hotel mega-developments are concentrated in a few flashy resorts, including Albena, Zlatni Pyasâtsi (also known as Golden Sands), Sveti Konstantin and Slânchev Bryag (Sunny Beach), so it is possible to avoid the larger crowds by visiting the beaches at southern villages such as Kiten and Ahtopol. Even if you have no interest in sun, sea and sand, there are plenty of excellent museums to enjoy, and nature lovers can hike around the Strandjha Nature Park and spot birdlife at the Burgas Lakes.

Information

Every day during summer, life guards work – or at least *should* work – between 8am and 6pm; they usually rescue a few tourists who ignore the warnings and don't swim between the flags. Topless bathing is acceptable at the major resorts, but less so elsewhere. For hire at most beaches are large umbrellas (about 2 lv per day), lounge chairs (about 3 lv per day) and tables with two chairs (about 6 lv per day).

Various maps of the Black Sea coast, and the cities, towns and resorts along it, are readily available at bookstalls throughout the region. The *Southern Black Sea Coast* and *Northern Black Sea Coast* maps, published by Kartografia, are the best for hiking. They have been translated into English, but in-

Highlights

- Wander around the magnificent Archaeological Museum in Varna
- Sunbathe, jet ski or windsurf at one of the many glorious beaches
- Potter around the cobblestone streets in the ancient villages of Sozopol and Nesebâr
- Amble along the extensive Maritime Park in Burgas on a summer evening
- Visit the marvellous Summer Palace of Queen Marie and Botanical Gardens in Balchik
- Admire the array of birdlife at one of the four Burgas Lakes

clude some rather useless details, for example, road directions at major roundabouts. If you're visiting the northern beaches and can read Cyrillic, the Domino map of *Varna* (1:11,300) has a detailed plan of the city, and includes useful maps of Albena, Zlatni Pyasâtsi and Sveti Konstantin. For the southern coast, Domino's *Southern Black Sea Coast* (in English) includes small maps of Ahtopol, Burgas, Kiten, Nesebâr, Pomorie, Primorsko, Slânchev Bryag and Sozopol.

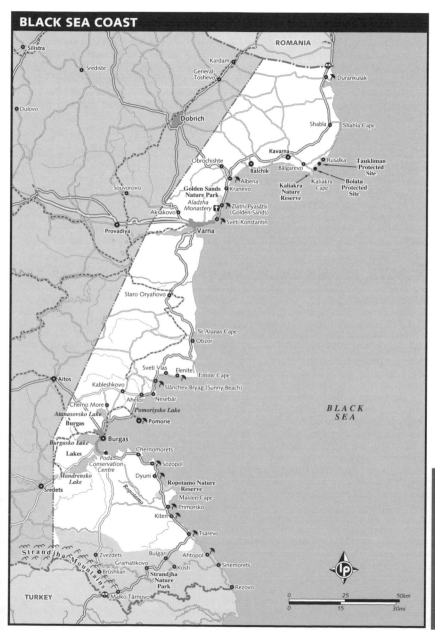

The Black Sea

Turkish, Greek and Roman invaders gave the sea various names, including the 'dark sea' and 'dangerous sea', which obviously indicate that the seas were rough (or sailing vessels were not seaworthy) and the people were unfriendly (or averse to being invaded).

The 413,500-sq-km Black Sea has a coastline of 4090km, of which Bulgaria claims less than 10%. In about 6000 BC, the sea was completely full of freshwater until the Bosphorus (in Turkey) was formed, which now links the Black Sea with the Mediterranean. The water in the Black Sea still contains comparatively low levels of salt because of the significant inflow from major rivers such as the Danube, which acts as a partial border between Bulgaria and Romania, and the Dnieper from Ukraine.

Inevitably, the environment in and around the Black Sea has suffered for many decades from industry, and, more recently, from excessive tourism. For instance, pollution is spewed straight into the sea from all six major rivers which flow into it. This affects the quality of water and the number of fish and mammal species (such as seals and dolphins which were once abundant, but are now rare).

The six bordering countries of Georgia, Romania, Russia, Turkey, Ukraine and Bulgaria have adopted the Black Sea Action Plan, one of several fairly lacklustre projects aimed at halting uncontrolled pollution from rivers, boats and tourist developments. But in lieu of any apparent action from any government, the Black Sea NGO Network, with help from the Peace Corps in Bulgaria, has taken up the cause.

When to Go

In summer, the climate is warm and mild, so it's obviously the best – and the busiest – time to visit. The average temperature is a warm 23°C, but sea breezes keep it cool. During winter the temperature rarely drops below freezing, but at least once a season a storm (or three) howls in from the Black Sea and buries the coast in snow.

All accommodation prices listed in this chapter (unless stated otherwise) are what you should expect to pay during the high season (July and August). During the shoulder season (May, June, September and October), room prices drop by up to 50%, so along with the continually good weather and greatly reduced crowds, this is the best time to visit.

Almost all hotels, restaurants and cafes in the resorts of Albena, Zlatni Pyasâtsi, Sveti Konstantin and Slânchev Bryag close in the 'off-season' (between mid-October and early April), while some places in the cities and larger towns stay open year-round.

If for some crazy reason you wish to visit the Black Sea coast in winter, ring your choice of hotel before you arrive – not to see if there's a vacancy (there will be plenty), but to find out if the hotel is actually open. Of the few camping grounds along the coast, all close between early October and early May (see Accommodation in the Facts for the Visitor chapter).

Southern Coast

BURGAS
БУРГАС
☎ 056 • pop 210,000

Burgas (often incorrectly spelt as Bourgas in English) is smaller and less crowded than Varna. Varna is the other major city along the coast. Burgas is Bulgaria's largest port and this is the primary focus of the city. Because of this focus Burgas has less to offer in the way of attractions such as museums, beaches and parks, than its rival tourist town to the north.

While Burgas is a fairly relaxed place with good shopping and an abundance of restaurants and outdoor cafes, for most travellers the city is used mainly as a convenient base for exploring the southern coast as far as Ahtopol, and the northern coast as far as Slânchev Bryag. Burgas is hemmed in by four lakes which are havens for abundant birdlife (see Around Burgas later in this section).

History
Recent excavations reveal that the area was inhabited for centuries by the Thracians before the Greeks came in the 2nd century AD and built the city of Pirgos (Greek for 'tower'), from which the name Burgas originated. Later, the Romans invaded, fortified existing walls and expanded the city which they renamed Debeltus. Most of what remains in present-day Burgas dates from the 17th century, when fisher folk from Pomorie and Sozopol settled in the area and called the city Burgas. The city grew quickly after the completion of the railway from Plovdiv in 1890 and the development of the port in 1903.

Orientation
The backbone of the city is the lively pedestrian mall, ulitsa Aleksandrovska, which links the Burgas University in the north to the convenient Yug bus station and the adjacent train station to the south. About halfway up ulitsa Aleksandrovska, another mall, ulitsa Aleko Bogoridi, heads eastwards towards Maritime Park. Burgas is pleasingly compact, so almost everything, except a few hotels, is within walking distance.

The *Burgas* map (1:10,500), published by Domino, is detailed but is in Cyrillic only. Less thorough, but still adequate for most visitors, is the *Bourgas City Guide*, published by Makros in English and German, and distinguishable by its blue and yellow cover. Both of these maps are available at any bookstall in the city.

Information
Tourist Offices Remarkably, there's still no official tourist office in Burgas, but specific questions (or complaints) may be directed to the Burgas Chamber of Tourism (☎ 843 641, fax 848 541).

Money Numerous foreign-exchange offices can be found along ulitsa Aleksandrovska and ulitsa Aleko Bogoridi. Bulbank, on ulitsa Aleksandrovska, has an automatic teller machine (ATM) which accepts all major credit cards. Banks that change cash and travellers cheques, and have ATMs, are United Bulgarian Bank, with branches on ulitsa Ferdinandov and ulitsa Aleksandrovska, and Raffeisen Bank on ulitsa Ferdinandov.

Post & Communications The most convenient post office is along ulitsa Tsar Petâr. Long-distance telephone calls can be made from any number of booths and telephone centres along the two malls. Most Internet centres can be found near the university, including ENet Internet Agency, on ulitsa Tsar Boris, which charges about 1.50 lv per hour. The dark and dingy Internet Club, ulitsa Georgi Kirkov, is in the Cinema Septembri building.

Travel Agencies Most travel agencies in Burgas cater to Bulgarian tourists, but there's no reason why foreigners can't join an organised tour. For example, many agencies offer all-inclusive two-day trips to Istanbul for US$60 per person (but only in summer). Tourist Services Bulgaria (☎ 840 601), in the foyer of Hotel Bulgaria, has knowledgeable and helpful English-speaking staff. It can arrange tours, car rental and long-distance (but not international) bus tickets.

Bookshops The Helikon Bookshop, ulitsa Aleksandrovska, near the university, is one of the best in Bulgaria, and sells a wide range of books, and local, regional and international maps. Velkaimo Bookshop, ulitsa Knyaz Al Battenberg, also offers an excellent variety of books, as well as postcards and souvenirs.

Archaeological Museum
Located incongruously along the modern mall is the Archaeological Museum *(☎ 843 541, ul Aleko Bogoridi 21; admission 2 lv; open daily 9am-5pm, closed Sun in winter)*. It houses a small collection of antiquities, such as Neolithic and Thracian artefacts from the 6th century BC, and various bits and pieces from the Roman period (1st to 3rd century AD). The staircase is lined with

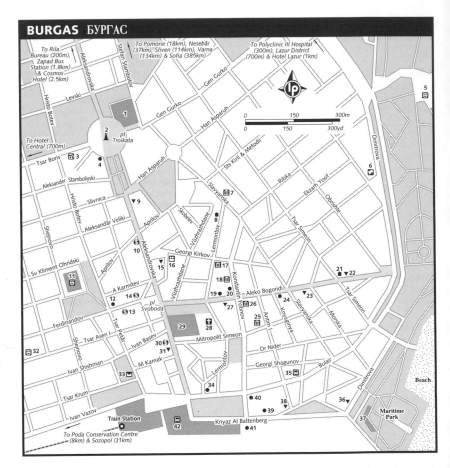

glass tanks of live reptiles, no doubt to boost sagging interest in antiquities. The highlight of the museum is probably the wooden tomb of a Thracian king, the only one found so far in the region. A leaflet provided by staff, and printed in English, French or German, makes the collection more interesting and is ideal for a self-guided tour.

Ethnographical Museum

The Ethnographical Museum (☎ 842 586, ul Slavyanska 69; admission 2 lv; open Mon-Sat 9am-5pm, closed Sat in winter) is pretty much the same as most other ethnographical

and ethnological museums throughout Bulgaria. Housed in the Brakalov House (which is an alternative name for the museum), the collection includes some period furniture, plenty of regional costumes and exquisite jewellery, as well as displays about weaving, fishing, boating and traditional fire-dancing. Everything is labelled in Bulgarian, however.

Other Museums

The National Science Museum (☎ 843 239, ul Konstantin Fotinov 20; admission 2 lv; open Mon-Sat 9am-5pm, closed Sat in

BURGAS БУРГАС

PLACES TO STAY
8 Hotel Mirazh
ХОТЕЛ МИРАЖ
21 Dim-ant (Accommodation Agency)
ДИМ-АНТ
29 Hotel Bulgaria, Tourist Services Bulgaria & Panorama Restaurant
ХОТЕЛ БЪЛГАРИЯ, ТУРИСТИЧЕСКИ СЕРВИЗ БЪЛГАРИЯ, РЕСТОРАНТ ПАНОРАМА
37 Hotel Primorets
ХОТЕЛ ПРИМОРЕЦ

PLACES TO EAT
9 McDonald's
15 Pub Bar & Grill
22 Restaurant Porto Rico
РЕСТОРАНТ ПОРТО РИКО
23 Fast Food Beit
27 Restaurant Memphis; Doner & Pizza Stalls
РЕСТОРАНТ МЕМФИС
31 BMS
36 Burgaska Sreshta Restaurant
РЕСТОРАНТ БЪЛГАРСКА СРЕЩА
38 National Restaurant & Tavern
НАЦИОНАЛЕН РЕСТОРАНТ И МЕХАНА

OTHER
1 Burgas University
БУРГАСКИ УНИВЕРСИТЕТ
2 Soviet Soldier Monument
3 ENet Internet Agency
4 Helikon Bookshop
КНИЖАРНИЦА ХЕЛИКОН
5 Summer Theatre
6 Turkish Consulate
7 Ethnographical Museum
ЕТНОГРАФСКИ МУЗЕЙ
10 United Bulgarian Bank
ОБЕДИНЕНА БЪЛГАРСКА БАНКА
11 Opera & Ballet Theatre
ОПЕРЕН И БАЛЕТЕН ТЕАТЪР
12 Bourgas Airport Travel Agency
АЕРОПОРТ БУРГАС ТУРИСТИЧЕСКА АГЕНЦИЯ
13 United Bulgarian Bank
ОБЕДИНЕНА БЪЛГАРСКА БАНКА
14 Raffeisen Bank
РАЙФАЙЗЕН БАНКА
16 Cinema Septembri; Internet Club
КИНО СЕПТЕМВРИ
17 City History Museum
ГРАДСКИ ИСТОРИЧЕСКИ МУЗЕЙ
18 Natural Science Museum
ПРИРОДНО-НАУЧЕН МУЗЕЙ

19 Balkanov Tourist Bureau (Accommodation Agency)
ТУРИСТИЧЕСКО БЮРО БАЛКАНОВ
20 Safari Hunting & Fishing Shop
САФАРИ ЛОВНО И РИБАРСКИ МАГАЗИН
24 Triton Diving
ТРИТОН ГМУРКАНЕ
25 Art Gallery
ХУДОЖЕСТВЕНА ГАЛЕРИЯ
26 Archaeological Museum
АРХЕОЛОГИЧЕСКИ МУЗЕЙ
28 St Hach Armenian Church
АРМЕНСКА ЦЪРКВА СВ. ХАЧ
30 Bulbank
БУЛБАНК
32 Adriana Boudevska Drama Theatre
33 Post Office
34 Primorets Travel (Accommodation Agency)
ТУРИСТИЧЕСКО БЮРО ПРИМОРЕЦ
35 Enturtrans (Bus Agency)
ЕВРОТРАНС
39 Velkaimo Bookshop
КНИЖАРНИЦА ВЕЛКАЙМО
40 TS Travel
41 Maritime Passenger Terminal (Disused)
42 Yug Bus Station
АВТОГАРА ЮГ

winter) offers informative displays about regional flora and fauna, and is of specific interest to anyone planning to visit the Strandjha Nature Park (see that section later in this chapter).

The **City History Museum** (☎ 841 815, ul Lermontov 31; admission 1.50 lv; open Mon-Fri 9am-6pm) explains the history of Burgas. It contains 100-year-old photos of the city and beach, but is fairly uninteresting: cans of tuna even fill up the display cabinets on the top floor.

Art Gallery

The small Art Gallery (☎ 842 169, ul Mitropolit Simeon 24; admission 2 lv; open Mon-Fri 9am-noon & 2pm-6pm) is within a synagogue that was built in 1909. It contains an eclectic collection of contemporary Bulgarian art and sculpture, as well as religious icons. Some of the gallery's art and tapestries are for sale, but they cost between US$600 and US$1500!

St Hach Armenian Church

This quaint church (ul Lermontov; admission free; open daily 6am-10pm), built in 1855, appears to almost touch the ugly Hotel Bulgaria. The interior of the church is charming, and it's open to visitors.

Maritime Park

Burgas' showpiece is this swathe of greenery running alongside the Black Sea coast. Within walking distance of the city centre, the park features manicured flower beds, spouting fountains, Soviet-era war memorials, modern sculptures and plenty of cafes.

BLACK SEA COAST

The park is full of bench-warming pensioners, boisterous kiddies in playgrounds, rollerblading teenagers and cuddling young lovers, and is particularly enjoyable and photogenic on a summer evening.

Beach
Burgas' beach is a disappointment, so do your swimming and sunbathing at nearby Sozopol or Pomorie, or wait until you visit a resort such as Slânchev Bryag. Next to the port and overlooked by several rusting oil tankers, the beach has greyish sand (which contains iron, so it retains heat longer in summer), and scrappy facilities. **Paddle boats** (*about 3 lv per hour*) are available for hire, but are really hard work if the waves are high, which is often. A charge down the **water slide** costs about 1 lv.

Activities
The **Safari Hunting & Fishing Shop** (☎ *841 432, ul Konstantin Fotinov*) rents and sells fishing and snorkelling equipment, and **Triton Diving** (☎ *956 984*, e *baracuda@abv .bg, ul Knyaginya*) rents and sells scuba-diving gear. Sadly, the latter agency is not interested in arranging any diving tours for foreigners, and its staff speak no English. No fishing or diving trips along the Black Sea coast are available from Burgas, so you'll have to find a boat, and then negotiate a price with the boat owner; your best chance is at one of the smaller villages along the southern coast.

Special Events
The main event in Burgas is the **International Folklore Festival** in late August. The program for this festival is well advertised, and shows take place during the evening at places along ulitsa Aleksandrovska and ulitsa Alex Bogoridi, inside the Ethnographical Museum and around ploshtad Troikata.

Other special events include the **Burgas Sea Song Festival** (July and August); the **Sladkopoyna Chouchouliga Festival** (May), with children's choirs; the **Emil Chakarov Music Festival** (early July); and the **Flora Flower Exhibition** (April and September).

The patron saint of Burgas is St Nikolai, whose **saint's day** is celebrated with gusto on 6 December.

Places to Stay
Private Rooms Burgas has a few accommodation agencies that can arrange rooms with local families. However, these rooms are often in the dreary Lazur residential district, which is not too far from the northern section of the Maritime Park and beach, but is a fair walk from the malls and cafes. If you arrive in Burgas during normal working hours, try one of the following agencies, listed in order of reliability. Otherwise, book a room in advance, or contact Dim-ant.

Primorets Travel (☎ 842 727) on ulitsa Ivan Vazov, is open Monday to Friday 9.30am to 5.30pm and has rooms for 11 lv per person. It's in a bright blue-green building opposite the train station – look for the 'accommodation agency' sign (in Bulgarian). Its staff speak no English.

The Balkanov Tourist Bureau (☎ 844 597), ulitsa Aleko Bogoridi 14, is open Monday to Friday 10am to 7pm, though the hours are irregular. Doubles are 20 lv and the staff speak some English.

TS Travel (☎/fax 845 060, e tstravel@ ns.comnet.bg) is on the corner of ulitsa Konstantin Fotinov and ulitsa Bulair and rooms cost 7 lv per person. Convenient to the train station, this agency offers a few private rooms and the staff speak English. The standards and amenities of the rooms are nothing to get excited about, however.

Dim-ant (☎ 840 779, fax 843 748), ulitsa Tsar Simeon 15, is open daily from 8am to 10pm. Singles/doubles cost 7.50/15 lv. Although a fair way from the bus and train stations, it's the only agency that is open on weekends. Not all staff speak English.

Hotels There's a dire lack of hotels in Burgas, with nothing in the budget range and only one mid-range option in the city centre. The first three places listed here are owned by the same company, so if one hotel is full ask the staff to check with another. Unless stated otherwise, all hotels offer rooms with a private bathroom and TV.

Hotel Mirazh (☎ *838 177, ul Lermontov 48*) Doubles with shared bathroom 44-49 lv. The Mirazh is central and clean, and its rooms are large (only the dearer ones have a TV). Most rooms have a balcony, plenty of seats and even a sofa, but those facing the street are noisy during the day.

Hotel Lazur (☎ *838 196, ul Kalofer 1*) Doubles 48 lv. Lost among the ugly apartment blocks about 2km north-east of town, the Lazur offers smallish and unremarkable rooms. The hotel is in a quiet area, but the downside is that it's a fair walk to any decent bar or restaurant. Catch bus No 12 or 15 from the bus or train stations or, better, take a taxi.

Hotel Central (☎ *815 468, ul Ivailo 60*) Doubles 55 lv. Although this hotel is not particularly central, it is in a pleasant suburb. The rooms are large and well furnished, and the bathrooms are huge. To get here, take a taxi.

Hotel Primorets (☎ *843 137, fax 842 934, ul Knyaz Al Battenberg*) Singles/doubles 80/120 lv. Although it has a good location fronting Maritime Park, the Primorets is a little overpriced. All rooms have balconies (some with reasonable sea views), and most have sparkling new bathrooms. Rates include breakfast.

Hotel Bulgaria (☎ *842 820,* e *hotelbulgaria@2plus.bg, ul Aleksandrovska 21*) Singles/doubles US$38/50, 'luxury' rooms US$62/72. This huge place dominates the city centre and is very convenient. However, it's *way* overpriced considering the rooms probably haven't been updated for 50 years. Rates include breakfast.

Cosmos Hotel (☎ *813 399,* w *www.hotelcosmos.com, ul Stefan Stambolov 2*) 'Standard' doubles US$50, 'luxury' rooms US$60/70, suites US$80. This place is about 3km north of the city centre so it's a bit inconvenient but good value. Cosmos is not just another 1960s Balkantourist-style white elephant: the rooms are large and smartly furnished with enormous beds, and the suites feature a spa. Rates include breakfast.

Places to Eat
Restaurants Each place listed here offers a menu in English.

National Restaurant & Tavern (*ul Filip Kutev 6*) Soups 1.50 lv, meals 3-6 lv. The chefs inside this authentically decorated Bulgarian national revival period building offer a huge array of national dishes, and cuisine from all around Europe. For those with late-night munchies it's open 24 hours, but service can be a bit slow at any time.

Burgaska Sreshta Restaurant (*ul Dimitrova*) Meals 5-7 lv. For atmospheric dining, the trellised patio of this lovely late 19th-century restaurant, opposite Hotel Primorets, is tough to beat. Prices are predictably high, however.

Panorama Restaurant (*ul Aleksandrovska 21*) Salads 2.50 lv, meals 8-12 lv. On the 17th floor of Hotel Bulgaria, this aptly named restaurant offers the best views along the Black Sea coast especially at sunset. Not to be confused with the restaurant of the same name in Cosmos Hotel, the Panorama has impeccable service but surprisingly ordinary food.

Pub Bar & Grill (*ul Georgi Kirkov*) Grills 3.50-5 lv. This is obviously a clone of the popular nationwide chain of Happy Bar & Grills, but the meals here are not quite as delicious. It offers a handy 'photo menu', which features pictures of all available meals, but adds an annoying, unannounced 6% 'service charge' to the bill.

Restaurant Porto Rico (*ul Aleko Bogoridi*) Meals about 3.50 lv. In a nicer section of the extensive mall on Aleko Bogoridi, the Porto Rico has a pleasant setting, cheap and tasty food, and a menu also in German.

Restaurant Memphis (*ul Aleko Bogoridi*) Meals from 2.50 lv. Recognisable by the small keg of beer hanging at the entrance, the Memphis provides huge servings of Bulgarian, Italian and other Western food. Prices are a little high (eg, pasta about 3 lv and a large pizza from 5 lv), but a breakfast (eg, omelette for 2.50 lv) or lunch could fill you up for the rest of the day.

Fast Food A couple of stalls near the Restaurant Memphis (see restaurants earlier) sell tasty takeaway *doner kebabs* and *pizzas*, ideal for munching on while enjoying the sea breezes in Maritime Park. Of course, there is

BLACK SEA COAST

a *McDonald's* *(ul Aleksandrovska)*, strategically located near the university.

BMS *(ul Aleksandrovska)* Meals about 2.50 lv. The popular BMS offers cafeteria-style service and huge dollops of Bulgarian food. It's one of those cheap and cheerful places where you can simply point at what you want, pay, eat and enjoy.

Fast Food Beit *(ul Aleko Bogoridi)* Meals from 2 lv. The signs (in English) on the notice board and window list a decent range of continental and oriental food at reasonable prices. This casual outdoor eatery is ideal for vegetarians who don't want to resort to yet another salad.

Entertainment

In summer, *nightclubs* and *bars* materialise among the trees of Maritime Park. The centre of activity is often the *Summer Theatre* (☎ 842 814). The Hotel Bulgaria (see Places to Stay earlier in this section) has a *casino* which offers 'free food and drinks' to patrons – but probably only to those losing money. The *Art Gallery* (see that section earlier) sometimes features piano recitals.

Cinema Septembri *(ul Georgi Kirkov; tickets about 3 lv)* shows recent films every evening. For something a bit more sophisticated, find out what's on offer at the *Adriana Boudevska Drama Theatre* (☎ 841 524, ul Tsar Asen 1 35) or the *Opera & Ballet Theatre* (☎ 843 057, ul Sv Kliment Ohridski 4).

The best *cafes* are in Maritime Park, particularly those overlooking the Black Sea. Other inviting places for a drink and/or snack are along ulitsa Aleko Bogoridi, particularly along the upper (eastern) end; and along ulitsa Aleksandrovska, especially near the corner of ulitsa Georgi Kirkov.

Getting There & Away

Air Balkan Airlines no longer flies to/from Burgas airport (☎ 683 181). The quaintly named Dandy Airlines links Burgas with Sofia (US$50/100 one way/return) four times a week, but only between 15 April and 30 October. The Bourgas Airport Travel Agency (☎ 842 631), on the corner of ulitsa Hristo Botev and ulitsa Ferdinandov, is the agency for Balkan and Dandy airlines, and its staff can book and confirm (for a small fee) other international flights.

Bus Most buses and minibuses leave from the Yug bus station (☎ 840 841) at the southern end of ulitsa Aleksandrovska. Fortunately, all destination signs are in English.

Buses and minibuses leave every 30 to 40 minutes throughout the day to popular places along the Black Sea coast, including Sozopol (1.90 lv, 40 minutes), Nesebâr (2 lv, 40 minutes) and Slânchev Bryag (2 lv, 45 minutes). Buses also go to Primorsko (3.20 lv, one hour) every 30 minutes between 6am and 7pm, and to Kiten (3.40, one hour) every 60 to 90 minutes between 6am and 8pm, but only four times a day as far as Ahtopol (4.90 lv, 1½ hours). Minibuses travelling directly to 'Pomorie Central' (1.50 lv, 25 minutes) leave every 60 to 90 minutes.

Each day, buses also travel to Plovdiv (12 lv, four hours) at 7.30am and 9.15am; to Varna (6 lv, two hours) about every 30 to 40 minutes; to Haskovo (9 lv, three hours) four times, mostly between 2pm and 5pm; to Sofia (15 lv, seven to eight hours) about 10 times; to Stara Zagora (5.50 lv, 2½ hours) at 10.30am; and to Sliven (5 lv, two hours) about every two hours.

Enturtrans (☎ 844 708), ulitsa Bulair, is one of several private bus companies with services to various destinations in Europe via Sofia. It also has bus services to Sliven, Pleven, Veliko Târnovo, Haskovo, Kazanlâk and Varna for slightly more than the fares on public buses. Enturtrans has the monopoly on services to Turkey; buses leave four times daily to Istanbul (40 lv) from outside its office.

From the Zapad bus station (☎ 821 094), about 1.8km north-west of ploshtad Troikata, buses leave for Malko Târnovo (6.20 lv, three hours), in the Strandjha Nature Park, near the Turkish border four or five times daily.

Train The historic train station (☎ 843 337) on ulitsa Ivan Vazov, built in 1902, has been overhauled, and is now the most attractive and cleanest in Bulgaria. Through the windows on the right (open daily 8am to 6pm) you can buy advance tickets for domestic and international services, while same-day tickets can be bought at the windows on the left (open 24 hours). At the time of writing, timetables were badly signposted but this may improve. The left-luggage office, open daily 6am to 10.45pm, is outside the station.

Seven trains travel daily between Burgas and Sofia (18.50/13.50 lv 1st/2nd class for the express, six to seven hours). Of these seven, four fast trains and one express (13.60/10 lv 1st/2nd class) travel via Plovdiv (four to five hours); and one fast and one express (13/9.60 lv 1st/2nd class) travel via Karlovo (four to five hours).

Fares on the express from Burgas to Kazanlâk are 11.50/8.60 lv (three hours); 10/7.30 lv (two hours) to Stara Zagora; and 7.40/5.60 lv (1½ hours) to Sliven.

International tickets are also available at the Rila Bureau (☎ 820 523), at ulitsa Aleksandrovska 106, about 200m north of ploshtad Troikata. The office is open Monday to Friday 8am to 6.30pm, Saturday 8am to 1.30pm and Sunday 8am to 2pm.

Getting Around

Many travel agencies offer car rentals, but most seem to be representatives for TS Travel (☎/fax 845 060, e tstravel@ns.comnet.bg, w www.tstravel.org). It's better to approach TS Travel directly, at the corner of ulitsa Konstantin Fotinov and ulitsa Bulair. The cheapest car it can offer costs US$39 per day (one to two days), or US$245 per week, including unlimited kilometres and insurance, plus petrol. A deposit of US$100 to US$200 is required, and the vehicle can be dropped off at Sofia, Plovdiv or Varna for a supplementary charge of US$0.20 lv per kilometre from Burgas.

Any of the inordinate number of taxis around Burgas can be chartered for negotiable rates to nearby beach resorts and villages.

BURGAS LAKES
БУРГАСКИ ЕЗЕРА

The four lakes surrounding Burgas are Pomoriysko (or Pomorie), Atanasovsko, Mandrensko (Mandra) and Burgasko (Burgas).

These are collectively known as the Burgas Lakes. Comprising over 9500 hectares, it's the largest wetland complex in Bulgaria, and is home to about 60% of the country's bird species.

The **Poda Conservation Centre** (☎ 056-850 540; admission 1 lv; open daily 8am-6pm) was opened in 1998 under the auspices of the Bulgarian Society for the Protection of Birds (BSPB). The centre ostensibly provides education about conservation issues to local people, but is also open to foreign visitors. It's worth a visit, especially if you're interested in this genuine and admirable effort at conservation and bird protection at a place so close to the urban sprawl of Burgas.

In the **Poda Protected Area** which surrounds the centre, bird-lovers will delight in spotting pelicans, black-winged stilts, ibises and spoonbills. Most birds can be seen at any time of the year, and hundreds of cormorants are always nesting on the disused electricity poles. Some of the 15 mammals – unlikely to be seen in the tall grass and reeds, however – include pygmy white-toothed shrews.

From the roof of the conservation centre, it is possible to observe some birds with binoculars (free of charge) and telescopes (if you ask nicely).

But to really admire the birdlife up close, go on a **nature walk** along the signposted 2.5km-trail. It will take you about three hours to complete, and there's an explanatory leaflet in English available from the centre. Access to the trail costs 10 lv per group with a maximum of six people. It's recommended that you get a guide (English- or German-speaking), which will cost an extra 15 lv per group.

East of Burgas, the 28-sq-km **Burgasko Lake** (or Lake Vaya) is the largest sea lake in Bulgaria. It is home to pelicans throughout the year but the best time to see them is between April and October. A 90-minute **boat trip** around this lake costs about 5 lv per person, but a minimum of six passengers is required. A guide is recommended and costs extra. For details, contact the conservation office (☎ 056-849 255) in Burgas, or the Poda Conservation Centre.

The centre also offers other day trips and overnight **excursions** around the other lakes, and elsewhere in the region, with an emphasis on flora, fauna and birdlife. The costs of these tours depend on your requirements and the numbers in the group. Tours of the lakes are also offered by Neophron Ltd (☎/fax 056-302 536, [e] bspbvnbr@mbox.digsys.bg) in Burgas. At the time of writing, another information centre was being built along the shore of Atanasovsko Lake, along the road to Pomorie.

The Bourgas Lakes map (4 lv), available from the Helikon Bookshop in Burgas, is excellent. It provides maps (in Bulgarian and English) of each lake, as well as the locations of lookouts, walking trails, access roads and nesting areas of major bird species.

The Poda Conservation Centre offers a few basic **bunk beds** for 5 lv per person. Bring your own food to cook in the kitchen and book all accommodation in advance.

The centre is poorly signposted on the left, about 8km south of Burgas on the road to Sozopol. It's accessible by taxi (about 5 lv one-way), or catch bus No 5, 17 or 18 from opposite the Polyclinic III hospital along bulevard Demokratsiya.

SOZOPOL
СОЗОРОЛ
☎ 05514 • pop 5000

This picturesque little town, 31km southeast of Burgas, compares well with historic Nesebâr, its rival to the north. Although the archaeological remains at Nesebâr are far more significant, Sozopol is more relaxed, has a vibrant artistic community, and boasts two long, wide beaches. Sozopol is still as touristy as Nesebâr, but not as tacky, and the old town of Sozopol is also charming. Importantly, prices for food and accommodation are far lower than in Nesebâr.

Sozopol is divided into two areas. The old town to the north is a collection of narrow cobblestone streets lined with sturdy wooden dwellings built on lower floors made of stone; 180 of these buildings are listed by the Ministry of Culture for their historical and cultural significance. To the

south of the bus station is the new town, often called Harmanite. On the western side of the peninsula is a Bulgarian naval base.

History
Until about 2000 years ago, Sozopol was, in fact, an island. The original inhabitants were Thracians who lived there from about 4000 BC. In 611 BC, Greek colonists from Miletus settled in the area and lived (more or less) peacefully with the Thracians. The Greeks called their home Apollonia, after the Greek god of healing, Apollo.

Despite a short-lived invasion by the Persians in 532 BC, Apollonia flourished by trading meat, salt, leather and weapons, among other things, with neighbouring states. Eventually the Romans realised the potential of the region and, under Marcus Lucullus, attacked Apollonia in 72 BC. Most of the town was destroyed and the famous 13m-high bronze statue of Apollo was taken to Rome as booty, but Apollonia later regained some importance as an economic centre in the far-flung Roman Empire.

In AD 330, the town was renamed Sozopol ('Town of Salvation') and was later settled by the Slavs. It became part of the First Bulgarian Empire (681–1018) in 969. For centuries, Sozopol remained a tiny fishing village occupied by Genoan and Turkish invaders. Early in the 19th century a revival of fortunes saw about 200 houses built in the traditional Black Sea style, with stone foundations, roofs of Turkish style tiles and walls of wood and stone.

At the end of the Russian-Turkish War (1877–78), most citizens of Sozopol fled to Russia to avoid potential retaliation by the Turks. The town remained empty for several decades before being resettled by Turks, Bulgars and Greeks.

Orientation & Information
Sozopol is popular with Bulgarian rather than foreign tourists, so unlike Nesebâr, signs and menus are less often translated into English or German. The booklet *Sozopol: The Eternal City* (6 lv), written in English, German and French, is a worthwhile souvenir, and is available at the Archaeological

Rila Monastery, Bulgaria's largest, was founded by Ivan Rilski in 927 and was originally a hermits' colony.

Samokov Gate (Eastern Gate) at Rila Monastery.

Peaceful Kiril Meadows in the Rila Mountains.

Medieval Bulgaria stands still on the banks of the the Yantra River in picturesque Veliko Târnovo.

The Patriarchal Complex at Tsarevets Fortress.

One of the 90 churches in Arbanasi.

National revival period architecture in Tryavna.

Remains of Tsarevets Fortress in Veliko Târnovo.

Farming life in the Veliko Târnovo countryside.

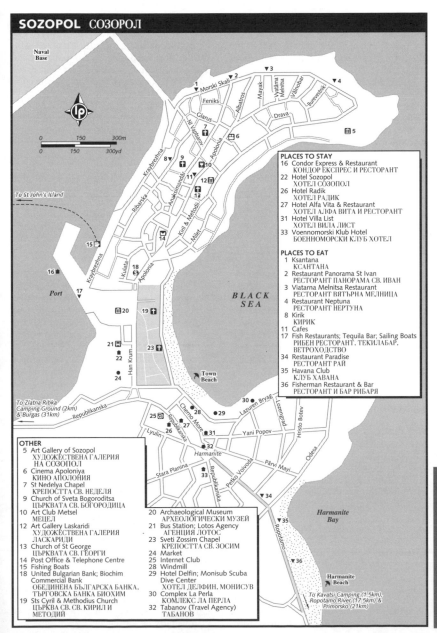

SOZOPOL СОЗОРОЛ

PLACES TO STAY
16 Condor Express & Restaurant
   КОНДОР ЕКСПРЕС И РЕСТОРАНТ
22 Hotel Sozopol
   ХОТЕЛ СОЗОПОЛ
26 Hotel Radik
   ХОТЕЛ РАДИК
27 Hotel Alfa Vita & Restaurant
   ХОТЕЛ АЛФА ВИТА И РЕСТОРАНТ
31 Hotel Villa List
   ХОТЕЛ ВИЛА ЛИСТ
33 Voennomorski Klub Hotel
   БОЕННОМОРСКИ КЛУБ ХОТЕЛ

PLACES TO EAT
1 Ksantana
   КСАНТАНА
2 Restaurant Panorama St Ivan
   РЕСТОРАНТ ПАНОРАМА СВ. ИВАН
3 Viatarna Melnitsa Restaurant
   РЕСТОРАНТ ВЯТЪРНА МЕЛНИЦА
4 Restaurant Neptuna
   РЕСТОРАНТ НЕРТУНА
8 Kirik
   КИРИК
11 Cafes
17 Fish Restaurants; Tequila Bar; Sailing Boats
   РИБЕН РЕСТОРАНТ, ТЕКИЛАБАР,
   ВЕТРОХОДСТВО
34 Restaurant Paradise
   РЕСТОРАНТ РАЙ
35 Havana Club
   КЛУБ ХАВАНА
36 Fisherman Restaurant & Bar
   РЕСТОРАНТ И БАР РИБАРЯ

OTHER
5 Art Gallery of Sozopol
   ХУДОЖЕСТВЕНА ГАЛЕРИЯ
   НА СОЗОПОЛ
6 Cinema Apoloniya
   КИНО АПОЛОНИЯ
7 St Nedelya Chapel
   КРЕПОСТТА СВ. НЕДЕЛЯ
9 Church of Sveta Bogoroditsa
   ЦЪРКВАТА СВ. БОГОРОДИЦА
10 Art Club Metsel
   МЕЦЕЛ
12 Art Gallery Laskaridi
   ХУДОЖЕСТВЕНА ГАЛЕРИЯ
   ЛАСКАРИДИ
13 Church of St George
   ЦЪРКВАТА СВ. ГЕОРГИ
14 Post Office & Telephone Centre
15 Fishing Boats
18 United Bulgarian Bank; Biochim
   Commercial Bank
   ОБЕДИНЕНА БЪЛГАРСКА БАНКА,
   ТЪРГОВСКА БАНКА БИОХИМ
19 Sts Cyril & Methodius Church
   ЦЪРКВА СВ. СВ. КИРИЛ И
   МЕТОДИЙ
20 Archaeological Museum
   АРХЕОЛОГИЧЕСКИ МУЗЕЙ
21 Bus Station; Lotos Agency
   АГЕНЦИЯ ЛОТОС
23 Sveti Zossim Chapel
   КРЕПОСТТА СВ. ЗОСИМ
24 Market
28 Internet Club
28 Windmill
29 Hotel Delfin; Monisub Scuba
   Dive Center
   ХОТЕЛ ДЕЛФИН, МОНИСУВ
30 Complex La Perla
   КОМЛЕКС ЛА ПЕРЛА
32 Tabanov (Travel Agency)
   ТАБАНОВ

BLACK SEA COAST

Museum. Also very informative, and a great memento, is *Apolonia & Sozopol: The Eternal City* (7 lv), available at bookstalls in the old town. Surprisingly, few maps of Sozopol are available.

Many foreign-exchange offices can be found along the main streets in the old town, and around the main square in the new town. Cash and travellers cheques can be changed at the United Bulgarian Bank at ulitsa Apolonia 4, which has an ATM; and the Biochim Commercial Bank at ulitsa Apolonia 17, about 50m up the road. The post office on ulitsa Apolonia has a telephone centre, which is open daily 7am to 8.30pm. The Internet Club, ulitsa Republikanska, is small but it's open all day every day.

Archaeological Museum

This unimpressive museum *(☎ 2226, ul Han Krum 2; admission 1.50 lv; open daily 9am-5pm & Mon-Fri only in winter)* is along an unnamed laneway leading to the port. It contains a limited array of artefacts, such as coins, pottery and ceramics from settlements along the Black Sea coast which have since been submerged. All of the better items are, however, in national museums in France and Germany. The few exhibits in the foyer, such as the anchors dated to the 4th century BC, have explanations in English, but nothing else in the museum is labelled in any language but Bulgarian.

Art Gallery of Sozopol

This art gallery *(☎ 2202, ul Kiril & Metodii 70; admission 1 lv; open Mon-Sat 10am-7pm)* is perched on a bluff with marvellous views of the sea. It offers a collection of sea-motif paintings and sculptures, some donated by art galleries in Sofia. The opening hours are fairly erratic: staff seem to enjoy a long lunch (and who can blame them!).

Churches

Each church listed here is open daily between about 6am and 10pm, and admission is free.

The 15th-century **Church of Sveta Bogoroditsa** *(ul Anaksimandâr 13)* is on the ruins of another church dating from the Mid-

dle Ages, and as required by the Ottoman rulers it was built below street level. The church contains exquisite wooden iconostases inspired by carvers from Macedonia. The gates are mostly closed, however, so get the keys from the Archaeological Museum. Otherwise, just peek over the fence.

Sveti Zossim Chapel is a small working church in the shady gardens opposite the bus station. It was built in the 13th century, on the foundations of another church from the Middle Ages, to honour the patron saint of sailors.

Also worth a quick look are the **Church of St George** *(ul Apolonia)*; the **St Nedelya Chapel** *(ul Anaksimandâr)*; and the **Sts Cyril & Methodius Church** *(ul Han Krum)*, which is comparatively new (built in 1899) and not open to the public.

St John's Island

The 660-hectare St John's (Ivan) Island is the largest along the Bulgarian coast. Although it's now uninhabited, the ruins of a 13th-century monastery and temple, and the lighthouse built in 1884, clearly indicate previous habitation. The island is now a nature reserve and protects about 70 species of birds. It can be visited by boat, or admired from the window of any restaurant along the north-western side of the old town.

Activities

Sailing boats moored near the fish restaurants in the port area take passengers on trips along the coast and to St John's Island for about 15 lv per person per hour (depending on the distance and number of passengers). During sunset is a particularly grand time to be on board. The **fishing boats**, docked farther north along ulitsa Kraybrezhna, can also be rented for a negotiable fee (about 7 lv to 8 lv per person per hour, with a boatman) for trips to the island.

Zlatna Ribka (see Places to Stay later in this section) is the only spot offering water sports. **Wind surfing** *(10 lv per hour)* is available here for experts, and lessons (for a negotiable fee) are possible for beginners. Other water sports such as **jet skiing** can also usually be arranged.

Monisub Scuba Dive Center *(Hotel Delfin Complex)* is not set up particularly well and it's not advisable for divers to just turn up at the office and expect to immediately join a diving tour or sign up for any training without organising it beforehand. The best time for scuba diving is between June and October; at other times, the sea is too cold and the waves are too rough.

Beaches

The town's two beaches are pleasant, but on most days the waves can be reasonably high. The 1km-long **Harmanite Beach** is wide and clean, and offers a water slide and paddle boats. The **Town Beach** (or Northern Beach) is also long, but not as wide, and doesn't offer the same number of beachside cafes, restaurants and bars as Harmanite.

Along the beaches there are the camping grounds of Zlatna Ribka and Kavatsi, about 2km north-west of Sozopol and 2km to the south, respectively (see Places to Stay). These two **beaches** *(admission 0.50 lv per person & 3 lv per car; open daily 7am-11pm)* are open to the public, and offer a couple of cafes and bars.

Special Events

The **Apollonia Arts Festival**, held in the first half of September, is undoubtedly *the* highlight of Sozopol's social calendar, and is one of the most popular events along the Black Sea coast. It features all sorts of jazz, pop and alternative music at various venues in the old and new town.

Places to Stay

Private Rooms Lotos Agency (☎/fax 2429, e k–bobtchev@dir.bg) is open daily 8am to noon and 1pm to 8.30pm. Private rooms cost 13 lv to 44 lv per person. Rates depend on whether you want a shared bathroom (13 lv per person), private bathroom (22 lv), bathroom, TV and breakfast (33 lv), or all of the amenities plus an evening meal (44 lv). The helpful manager speaks English, and he can show you photos of the rooms on offer. The agency is conveniently located close to the bus station.

If the Lotos Agency is closed (and it does keep fairly erratic hours), go to the main square in the new town, look lost and someone will soon offer you a private room in a local home. Otherwise, at the main square ask at one of the cafes or shops with the words 'accommodation' in English or Bulgarian on the window.

Camping The two camping grounds mentioned in this section are large complexes along thin, clean and uncrowded stretches of beach not far from Sozopol.

Zlatna Ribka (☎ 2427) Camping 7 lv per person, bungalows with bathroom 23 lv. About 2km north-west of Sozopol along the road to Burgas, this huge complex offers all sorts of accommodation. It's one of the few camping grounds in the region away from the main road, so there's not much noise from passing traffic. On the downside, the bungalows are minuscule and are built too close together, so peace and privacy are not guaranteed in the high season. Water sports (see Activities earlier) are available.

Kavatsi Camping (☎ 2261) Camping 9.50 lv per person, bungalows with toilet & shared bathroom 42 lv, double hotel rooms with bathroom 60 lv, cottages 100 lv. Kavatsi is the best-equipped complex in the area, but the bungalows are tiny and crammed together. The cottages (with four beds, a TV, kitchen and terrace) and hotel rooms (with TV) are overpriced. It's about 2km south of the main square in the new town, along the coastal road to Primorsko.

Hotels If the places listed in this section are full, or not suitable, there are several others of very similar standard and price nearby. Rooms overlooking the main roads are obviously noisy, but most of the others offer great views. Disappointingly, there's nowhere to actually stay in the old town.

Hotel Radik (☎ 3706, ul Republikanska 4) Singles/doubles 26/52 lv June-Aug, 22/44 lv (rest of year), apartments 55 lv (year-round). These bright and immaculately clean rooms and apartments feature a balcony, TV, fridge and private bathroom, and are tremendous value.

Hotel Alfa Vita (☎ *4477, ul Republikanska 6)* Doubles with bathroom 40 lv. The Alfa Vita offers similar amenities (eg, a TV, fridge and balcony) to Hotel Radik, but is not great value for single travellers. The views from some rooms are superb, and the bathrooms are large. The *restaurant* underneath is recommended, and has a menu in English.

Voennomorski Klub Hotel (☎ *4362, ul Republikanska 17)* Doubles with bathroom 50 lv. This large complex overlooks the main square in the new town. The quiet, air-conditioned rooms are smallish, but are reasonably comfortable, and nicely furnished with pinewood. It's not signposted or particularly obvious, so look for the word 'Hotel' in Bulgarian.

Condor Express (mobile ☎ *088-007)* Beds in 4-person cabins 5 lv per person, singles/doubles in 2-person cabins 6/12 lv, all with shared bathroom; 'captains' apartments' with bathroom 40 lv per double. Probably the most unusual place to stay in Bulgaria is *Condor Express*, a massive sailing boat moored here between early April and late September. The cabins are tiny and claustrophobic (how could a sailor live in one for months?), but they're clean and the bathrooms are new. The apartments are also small and poorly furnished but some have a fridge. Stay here for the novelty value.

Hotel Sozopol (☎ *2362, ul Han Krum)* Singles/doubles with bathroom 44/48 lv. Convenient to (and easy to spot from) the bus station, this remodelled three-storey hotel is unexceptional. It lacks the sort of amenities you'd expect for this price, though some rooms have a fridge and all have a balcony. Breakfast costs an extra 4 lv per person.

Hotel Villa List (☎/fax *2235, ul Cherno More 5)* Singles/doubles 39/56 lv, apartments 89 lv, all with bathroom. The Villa List is understandably popular with tour groups and is often full in July and August. The hotel is still worth trying (especially in the off-season) because it's close to the beaches, has competent and friendly staff, the rooms have air-con, TV and balcony, and the rates include breakfast. The hotel also boasts a swimming pool with sea views.

Places to Eat

Of course, fish meals are tasty and fresh, but usually expensive. The cheapest *fish restaurants* are strung along the port area. These include the *Tequila Bar*, bobbing up and down on a pontoon off the harbour wall; and the breezy *Condor Express* (see Places to Stay earlier), which offers salads for about 1.50 lv and fish meals from 2.50 lv.

Ksantana (ul Morski Skali) Fish meals 5-7.50 lv. The split-level terraces of this folksy establishment afford a bird's-eye view of St John's Island from the courtyard balcony. The restaurant is at the top of the steps and can be easy to miss.

Restaurant Panorama St Ivan (ul Morski Skali 21) Fish meals from 4.50 lv. Similar to the Ksantana, this small and homely restaurant features a small courtyard with glorious views and breezes. Meals are reasonably priced, and the menu is in English.

Viatarna Melnitsa Restaurant (☎ *2844, ul Morski Skali 27)* Salads 2 lv, fish meals 4-6 lv. Immediately obvious from the small windmill at the entrance, and the larger one in the grounds, the Viatarna Melnitsa caters mostly to tour groups. It's not as quaint or homely as other taverns, nor does it offer the same sea breezes. Prices are not too bad, and the menu is in English and German.

Restaurant Neptuna (ul Morski Skali) Meals from 5 lv. One of four or five similar places in the vicinity, the Neptuna offers delicious fish meals, superb views and welcome breezes in a family-run tavern. The menu is in English.

Kirik (ul Ribarska 77) Meals from 3.50 lv. For fresh fish, it's tough to beat Kirik. The *midi tzigane*, locally raised mussels sauteed with a spicy cheese and mustard sauce, will make your tongue curl with delight.

The mall on ulitsa Ropotamo, alongside Harmanite Beach is absolutely packed with *cafes*, *restaurants* and *bars*. All of them are pretty much the same, but three places do stand out. *Restaurant Paradise* has a quiet, raised and off-street eating area, and reasonable prices. Most of the *Fisherman Restaurant & Bar* is on the beach. The menu is extensive, but surprisingly it doesn't offer a great number of fish meals (about 3.50 lv). *Havana Club* distinguishes itself from the others with a small swimming pool for guests (more suitable for the kiddies).

Some of the best *cafes* are in the shady park opposite the bus station. The *cafes* along ulitsa Apolonia offer no views, but the ones along the middle stretch of the street are trendy and ideal for people-watching.

Entertainment

After a hard day of swimming, eating and shopping, most visitors relax with a drink at one of the numerous bars or cafes. Any of the fish restaurants (mentioned in Places to Eat earlier), or any cafe or bar along the north-western coast, is ideal for a late afternoon or evening drink. For views of the northern beach and old town, it's hard to beat the *Complex La Perla (ul Lazuren Bryag)*.

Art Club Metsel (ul Apolonia) has live music most evenings, and *Viatarna Melnitsa Restaurant* (see Places to Eat earlier) features folkloric music and dancing. The marvellous *Cinema Apoloniya (ul Apolonia; tickets about 5 lv)* shows modern English-language films on an outdoor screen, so obviously it's only open in summer.

Shopping

Naturally, the streets in the old town are lined with souvenir stalls. **Art Gallery Laskaridi** *(ul Kiril & Metodii)* sells contemporary art, as well as books about Sozopol.

Getting There & Away

The small public bus station is along ulitsa Han Krum between the old and new town. Buses leave for Burgas (1.90 lv, 40 minutes) about every 30 minutes between 6am and 9pm in the summer, and about once an hour in the off-season. Quicker and more comfortable minibuses also service this route for about the same price.

Only one public bus a day goes directly to Ahtopol (2 lv, one hour), currently at 7am via Primorsko (1.20 lv, 20 minutes) and Kiten (1.60 lv, 30 minutes); while another leaves for Kiten via Primorsko at 7.30am. Public buses leave up to three times a day for Shumen, Stara Zagora, Sofia and Haskovo.

South to the Turkish Border

South of Sozopol, the crowds start to thin out and the roads become gradually worse. Public transport is less frequent, but you'll always find something heading your way every hour or two. Towns and villages along the southern coast offer none of the ambience and history of Sozopol and Nesebâr, but they attract far less tourists. So, while prices for accommodation and food are cheaper, English and German are not widely understood by hotel and restaurant staff. Some beaches, particularly those closer to the Turkish border, are empty and undeveloped (so far), but only accessible by private or chartered vehicle.

Larger and more comfortable private buses arrive and depart from spots around the main square in the new town. Daily, three or four private buses go to Sofia, one or two depart for Plovdiv, and another one or two travel up and down the southern coast as part of the overnight Haskovo-Ahtopol service.

Also, almost all private and public buses from Burgas, Sofia, Sliven, Plovdiv and Stara Zagora to anywhere along the southern coast normally stop in Sozopol and pick up passengers.

Getting Around

Sozopol is easy to get around on foot, but there's also plenty of taxis. Infrequent public transport along the southern coast means it's a good idea to hire a car. There are several travel agencies around the main square in the new town, which can arrange car rental from about US$40 per day, including unlimited kilometres and insurance, plus petrol. One agency to look out for is Tabanov (☎/fax 388 725, e tabanov@abv.bg).

ROPOTAMO NATURE RESERVE
НАЦИОНАЛЕН РЕЗЕРВАТ
РОПОТАМО

This reserve was established in 1940 to protect fragile landscapes of extensive marshes and the largest sand dunes in Bulgaria, as well as rare flora such as the endemic sand lily. The reserve also protects more than

200 species of birds (seven of which are endangered); reptiles such as snakes and turtles; and mullet and carp, which cannot be caught here because fishing is illegal. This pristine reserve, which has always been surprisingly unpopulated with people, is now run by the Bulgarian-Swiss Biodiversity Conservation Programme (BSBCP).

At several well-signposted places along the road between Burgas and Primorsko, visitors can stop and admire some of the reserve, and wander along short **walking trails**. Explanations (in English) about the local flora, fauna and natural landscapes are provided along the trails.

Where the main road crosses the Ropotamo River between Sozopol and Primorsko is the major entrance to a **parkland** *(admission free, parking 3 lv)*, favoured by day-trippers and bus groups. There are a couple of *cafes* and *picnic spots*, and some short **hiking trails**, but most visitors come for a **boat ride** *(7/8 lv per person for 40/70-minute trip, boats carry up to 25 people)* along the murky, green-and-brown river. To get to the parkland entrance by public transport, take any bus or minibus south of Sozopol, and get off at the prominent, well-signposted bridge.

PRIMORSKO
ПРИМОРСКО
☎ 05561 • pop 2500

Primorsko, 52km south of Burgas, is less commercial and hectic than other resorts to the north, and the town centre is pleasant and far less crowded than Nesebâr and Sozopol. The **beach** is long, curved and sheltered, so it's ideal for swimming and boating, but it's a bit scrappy and the water is often shallow at low tide.

In summer, **microlights** *(40 lv for 20 minutes)* can be heard buzzing overhead; inquire about flights at one of the travel agencies around the main square. Most of these agencies also offer good-value but rushed **day trips** by bus to Sozopol (6 lv per person), Varna (25 lv) and Nesebâr (15 lv).

From the town square, along bulevard 3 Mart (the main road into town), it's a short walk down (south) to the beach. The best shops are along ulitsa Cherno More, which heads south-east from the square.

Places to Stay

See Desi Travel has rooms for 6 lv to 15 lv per person. At the bus stop, this is the only agency in Primorsko offering *rooms* in private homes. Rates vary according to the proximity of the home to the town centre and beach, and whether the room has a private bathroom.

Hotel Rusalka (☎ *2090, ul Nadezhda 12)* Rooms with shared bathroom 7 lv per person. This cosy and friendly home offers a few basic rooms to tourists. The Rusalka is signposted, just off the main road, so it's quiet, and is only a short walk to the town centre and beach.

International Youth Centre (☎ *2045)* Rooms with shared bathroom from 20 lv per person June & Sept, 24 lv July & Aug. The massive communist-era complex with 3000 beds (!) is well signposted (in English) along the road about halfway between Primorsko and Kiten. Although it's not close to any shops or cafes, it has a *restaurant* and is within walking distance of a decent beach. Rates include breakfast.

Hotel Koral (☎ *2230, fax 3730, ul Strandjha 17)* Singles/doubles with shared bathroom 25/50 lv (July & Aug), 18/36 lv (rest of year). Along a quiet street that heads east from the main square, the Koral is convenient to the town centre and bus station, and is good value. Rates include breakfast.

Hotel Moni (☎ *2245, bul 3 Mart)* Singles/doubles with bathroom 35/45 lv. The Moni is one of several unremarkable hotels along the noisy main road, which offers comfortable rooms with TV. Any hotel farther west along bulevard 3 Mart is too far from the town centre and beach.

Places to Eat

Most locals and visitors seem to be more than happy to buy a doner kebab, pizza or toasted sandwich from one of many *stalls* along the main road. Hotel Moni is the only hotel listed earlier with a *restaurant*, but a dozen other hotels in the town centre and near the beach have *eateries* of some sort.

Plenty of other *cafes*, bars and *restaurants* can be found around the town square and along the main road.

Getting There & Away
From the makeshift bus stop at the town square, buses go to Ahtopol (2.20 lv, 45 minutes) via Kiten (1.20 lv, 10 minutes), daily at 9.30am. Also, buses regularly stop at Primorsko on the way between Burgas, Sofia or Haskovo and Ahtopol or Kiten, but many of these services pass through, in either direction, late in the evening. In addition, buses travel daily to Burgas (3.20 lv, one hour) every 30 minutes between 6am and 7pm. About six private buses a day also go to Sofia, and one or two travel to Stara Zagora, Plovdiv and Sliven via Sozopol and Burgas.

KITEN
КИТЕН
☎ 05561 • pop 550
Kiten, about 5km farther south of Primorsko, was first permanently settled as recently as the 1930s, but nearby excavations indicate evidence of settlement in the 6th century BC. Kiten is pleasantly situated around pockets of forest, but there's no town centre as such, so all shops, restaurants and hotels are dotted along the roads between the two beaches.

The northern **Atliman Beach** is along a horseshoe-shaped bay, one of the cleanest and prettiest along the Black Sea coast, and the hills in the background thankfully hinder all possible future development. **Morski Beach** to the south is sheltered and ideal for swimming, and has plenty of beachside *cafes*.

Hotel Atliman (see Places to Stay & Eat) offers **day trips** by bus to Nesebâr (22 lv per person), Sozopol (10 lv) and Varna (45 lv), and all-inclusive **boat trips** (13 lv) in the Ropotamo Nature Reserve.

Places to Stay & Eat
Yug Camping Camping 5 lv per person, single/double bungalows with shared bathroom 5/9 lv, apartments with private bathroom 45 lv. This place doesn't suffer from the must-overcharge-foreigners-syndrome,

so it's remarkably cheap, but then the quality of accommodation is very ordinary indeed. The well-signed (500m) access road is about 1.5km south of the turn-off to Kiten from Burgas.

Hotel Bohem (mobile ☎ 088-512 481, [e] bohem@c4.comtel, ul Strandjha 14a) Singles/doubles 20/40 lv (July & Aug), 15/30 lv (rest of year), apartments 100 lv (July & Aug) & 80 lv (rest of year). This small but homely place is along the main street just down from the bus station, and is well positioned between the two beaches. All rooms have a TV, fridge and private bathroom, and those away from the main street offer views and breezes.

Hotel Assarel Medet (☎ 2445, ul Strandjha) Doubles/triples 55/77 lv, apartments 99 lv, all with bathroom. Considerably better than the outside suggests, this hotel is not just another boring Balkantourist-style throwback to the 1960s. The rooms are clean and bright, and have a TV and balcony with lovely views. Rates include breakfast. It's about 200m north of Morski Beach.

Hotel Atliman (☎ 2349, fax 2823) Singles/doubles with bathroom 37/44 lv. This is the only place within walking distance of Atliman Beach. It offers large, clean rooms with a balcony and views, but check a few of the rooms first because some are better than others. At the time of research, all bathrooms appeared to have been recently renovated.

All three hotels listed earlier have *restaurants*; the pick of the bunch is the one at Hotel Bohem. Also, try *Restorant Smokinya* (ul Urdoviza 20) about halfway between the two beaches, for tasty fish meals.

Getting There & Away
The bus station is at the top end of ulitsa Strandjha at the junction of the roads to Primorsko and Ahtopol. Daily buses to Burgas (3.40 lv, one hour) leave every 60 to 90 minutes between 6am and 8pm, and travel via Primorsko and Sozopol. Also from Kiten, one or two buses a day go to Stara Zagora via Haskovo, and three or four depart for Sofia. All buses and minibuses travelling to or from Ahtopol will also stop in Kiten to pick up passengers.

AHTOPOL
АБТОРОЛ
☎ 5563 • pop 1350

Ahtopol, about 30km farther down the coast, is a strange little place: the beach is between 500m and 1500m from the town centre, and there are very few hotels because most visitors stay in bungalows owned by their employers. The attraction here is the unhurried pace, cheaper prices and village-like atmosphere. Many locals work as fishermen, so the town doesn't rely entirely on tourism. The **beach** is long, curved and a little crowded in spots, but it's easy to get some sand and space to yourself. The beach is below some hills, so few cafes (and no hotels) blot the landscape.

If there is a town centre, it's based around the park where the bus stops, though the post office and administration buildings are about 500m to the east of this. To find the beach, walk back (south-west) from the park and bus stop along ulitsa Sveti Nikola towards the main coastal road for about 300m, and then head down (north-west) along any laneway. The rocky coastline east of the town's park is also begging to be explored.

Hotel Neptun (☎ *2164, Cnr ul Sveti Nikola & ul Georgi Kondolov)* Singles/doubles with bathroom 10/20 lv. Pleasingly, the Neptun doesn't overcharge foreigners, but it has seen better days. Most rooms are adequately comfortable and, as it's only metres from the sea, some have balconies with great views.

Of the several pleasant *mehanas* (taverns) along the main streets, the best is probably *Cafe Varna*, which has a shady courtyard. It's at the north-eastern end of the town park.

Public transport to Ahtopol is not regular, and no buses or minibuses go any further along the barren and remote stretch of coastal road that extends as far as the Turkish border. Four buses a day depart for Burgas (4.90 lv, 1½ hours), two or three a day go to Sofia, and one or two leave for Haskovo and Stara Zagora. Almost all transport to and from Ahtopol stops in Primorsko, Kiten, Sozopol and, usually, in Burgas.

STRANDJHA NATURE PARK
НАЦИОНАЛЕН ПАРК СТРАНДЖА
☎ 05952

In the south-eastern corner of Bulgaria is the infrequently visited Strandjha Nature Park, which was established in 1995. The 1161 sq km of rolling hills protect the country's most diverse vegetation, including vast forests of oak and beech trees, as well as 40 species of fish, 261 types of birds (almost 70% of those found in Bulgaria), 65 species of mammals (six of which are endangered), and various unexcavated Byzantine fortresses.

The park's ecotourism potential is slowly being developed with the aid of the Bulgarian-Swiss Biodiversity Conservation Programme and the US Peace Corps in Sofia. But the park is not – and probably never will be – set up for major tourism, if only because it's so remote and visiting is not easy without private transport. And don't stray too close to the Turkish border: this is an area of smugglers and trigger-happy border-patrol guards.

The park is ideal for **hiking**, because it's sparsely populated and relatively flat. Several short hikes between 1km and 8km long, and longer treks of about 20km between the coast and the centre of the park, are detailed in the colourful *Nature Park Strandjha* map (1:70,000), available at the Helikon Bookshop in Burgas (4 lv). The park also contains what are probably the most undeveloped stretches of sandy **beaches** along the Bulgarian coast of the Black Sea. If you visit in early June, make sure you witness the **fire-dancing festival** in Bulgari.

The administration centre is Malko Târnovo, an economically depressed town in the south-west of the park. The **History Museum** (☎ *2998*) complex, and the **Ethnographical Museum** (☎ *2126*), contain some displays about the park, and staff at both museums are good sources of information. For more details about the park, contact the **park office** (☎/fax 2963, [e] strandjapark@yahoo.com, ul Janko Maslinov 1) in Malko Târnovo.

There are a couple of *guesthouses* and *homes* that offer cheap rooms in Malko

Târnovo and Brûshlian. *Malko Turnovo Hotel* (☎ *2182*) in Malko Târnovo has basic singles/doubles with a private bathroom for 15/25 lv. Free *camping* is permitted inside the nature park.

From the Zapad bus station in Burgas, four or five buses a day leave for Malko Târnovo (6.20 lv, three hours) via Bulgari, but transport to other villages in the park is infrequent. If you have a private vehicle, Ahtopol and Kiten are convenient bases for day trips to the park.

Central Coast

POMORIE
ПОМОРИЕ
☎ 0596 • pop 14,500
Pomorie, 18km north-west of Burgas, is probably the least attractive seaside town along the Black Sea coast. The **beach** is badly littered and marred by breakwaters every 100m to 200m, and the water is full of seaweed. The town centre is pleasant enough, but is far from the beach, which seems to be full of people who wished they could afford to stay somewhere nicer like Slânchev Bryag. It's not all bad news, however: Pomorie is a comparatively cheap base from which to visit Burgas and Nesebâr, and some water sports are available.

Pomorie once rivalled Nesebâr in beauty and antiquity, but was mostly destroyed by fire in 1906. There are still a few things to see in town, however, including the quaint **Sveti Bogoroditsa Church** in the shady park in the town centre, and the ruins of **St George Monastery** (*ul Knyaz Boris 1*), about 700m from the main bus station towards the beach. In the older, nicer part of town, with its occasional cobblestone streets and wooden houses, is the **Preobrazhenie Hristovo Church** (*ul Han Kubrat 1*). Many Bulgarian tourists ignore the beach and wallow in a **mud bath** (*20 lv per hour*), or enjoy a **therapeutic massage** (*25 lv to 30 lv per hour*), both at Hotel Pomorie.

It's often windy at the beach, making it ideal for **windsurfing** (*8 lv per hour*) and **paragliding** (*30/50 lv per person for 20/30*

minutes). Pomorie is one of the few places along the coast where you can hire **motorbikes** (*5/9 lv for 30/60 minutes*). They are available from stalls at the south-eastern end of the beach.

There are two bus stations in Pomorie – the main bus station is about 3km before the town centre (and accessible by local bus No 1 or taxi), and the central station is outside the town hall. From the latter station, it's about 200m north-east to the beach and 100m south to the town centre.

Places to Stay & Eat
None of the hotels listed here have single rates, and all offer rooms with a bathroom.

Hotel Horizon (☎ *6172, ul General Skobelev*) Doubles 35 lv. Looking rather abandoned at the end of the road from the *central* bus station, the Horizon boasts a good position and sea views, but the rooms probably haven't been updated or even maintained for about 30 years.

Hotel Byal Dom (*White House;* ☎ *7651, ul Raina Kniaginia 15*) Doubles 30 lv. This is a far better option than Horizon. Although the hotel doesn't overlook the beach, it's a modern, clean and friendly place, and some rooms have ocean views. The popular *restaurant* is recommended.

Hotel Pomorie (☎ *2440, fax 2280, ul Yavorov 3*) Doubles 60 lv. On a rocky outcrop equidistant from the town centre and beach, the Pomorie is not great value. While some rooms have views, and all have a TV and fridge, most bathrooms haven't been renovated since the 1950s. The distance from the beach is offset by the indoor swimming pool with sea views. Rates include breakfast.

The best *restaurants* and *cafes* overlook the nicer part of the beach to the south-east.

Getting There & Away
The regular buses and minibuses between Burgas and Nesebâr and/or Slânchev Bryag invariably stop at the main bus station. From this station, seven or eight daily buses go to Sofia each day, and several travel to Plovdiv, Sliven, Varna and Stara Zagora.

Every 60 to 90 minutes, daily minibuses marked 'Pomorie Central' (in Bulgarian) leave from Burgas (1.50 lv, 25 minutes) and Slânchev Bryag (1.30 lv, 30 minutes) and stop at Pomorie's small central bus station.

NESEBÂR
НЕСЕБЪР

☎ 0554 • pop 9500

Nesebâr, 37km north-east of Burgas, sits on a small rocky island connected to the mainland by a narrow man-made isthmus. Designated by Unesco as a World Heritage site, Nesebâr is a glorious town with many church ruins along cobblestone streets and a couple of worthwhile museums. Unlike Sozopol, Nesebâr offers plenty of great hotels in the old town, but its beach is nowhere near as good.

If you have been wandering around Bulgaria, and wondering where all the tourists are – well, they seem to be in Nesebâr. By 10am each day in summer, dozens of tour buses start unloading hundreds of visitors from the nearby beach resorts. However, the crowds are nonexistent before about 10am and after 5pm, and always thin out in the eastern part of town. As one reader said: 'Nesebâr is a tourist trap with some beautiful sights...best explored at dawn'.

History

The first inhabitants were the Thracians who settled in what became known as Mesembria in about 3000 BC. In 512 BC, the Greeks came to live with the Thracians, and built and/or fortified fortresses, temples, gates and towers – most of which are now submerged after the level of the Black Sea rose around 2000 years ago.

To avoid the same sort of looting and fires which destroyed Apollonia (Sozopol), the populace of Mesembria accepted the Roman invaders in 72 BC. But the city fell into decline as the Romans concentrated on other ports and ignored this part of the coast.

Under Byzantine rule from AD 395, Mesembria regained its former glory as a centre of commercial and strategic importance. During the 5th and 6th centuries, a number of walls, towers and imposing churches were erected, including the basilica (see Churches later in this section).

After the Bulgar invasion in 812, the town was renamed Nesebâr for reasons unknown to historians. Many times over the next few centuries, Nesebâr passed back and forth between the Byzantine rulers and the First Bulgarian Empire (681–1018), but the town remained unscathed.

Even the Turks left Nesebâr alone, and decided to strengthen existing fortifications to defend it against Cossack pirates. The town reached some heights between the 13th and 15th centuries, but again fell to the Byzantines and then to the Ottomans in 1453. During the Bulgarian national revival period of the 18th and 19th centuries, Nesebâr prospered and many merchants constructed numerous typical buildings, some of which remain today. Overshadowed by Varna and later by Burgas, Nesebâr ceased to be an active trading town from the early 20th century, and these days survives almost entirely on tourism.

Orientation

Every second or third shop seems to be a foreign-exchange office. Many of these change travellers cheques but charge different commissions, so shop around. The only bank is the Biochim Commercial Bank on ulitsa Mesembria, which is open Monday to Friday 8.30am to 7.45pm and Saturday and Sunday in summer from 11am to 7.45pm in summer. It changes travellers cheques, and has an ATM which accepts major credit cards. The post office also on ulitsa Mesembria has a telephone centre, which is open Tuesday to Saturday 8am to 8pm. To use the Internet, head to the Internet Club in the Hotel The White House (see Places to Stay later in this section).

Information

The old town is on a rocky outcrop, 850m long and 300m wide. It's connected to the new town on the 'mainland' by a narrow causeway that goes through the 3000-year-old fortress walls, built by the Thracians and later fortified by the Greeks and Byzantines. There's no reason to visit the new town: all hotels, restaurants, shops and other attractions listed in this section are in the old town.

NESEBÂR НЕСЕБЬР

PLACES TO STAY
1 Hotel Victoria
   ХОТЕЛ ВИКТОРИЯ
2 Hotel Toni
   ХОТЕЛ ТОНИ
3 St Georgi Hotel
   ХОТЕЛ СВ. ГЕОРГИ
6 Prince Cyril Hotel
   ХОТЕЛ ПРИНЦ КИРИЛ
28 Rony Hotel
   ХОТЕЛ РОНИ
31 Hotel Mesembria
   ХОТЕЛ МЕСЕМБРИЯ
32 Hotel The White House;
   Internet Club
   ХОТЕЛ БЯЛАТА КЬЩТА
34 St Stefan Hotel
   ХОТЕЛ СВ. СТЕФАН

PLACES TO EAT
5 Neptun Restaurant
   РЕСТОРАНТ НЕПТУН
11 Restaurant Chaika
   РЕСТОРАНТ ЧАЙКА
12 Regatta Restaurant
   РЕСТОРАНТ РЕГАТА
13 Vega Restaurant
   РЕСТОРАНТ ВЕГА
21 Restaurant Chaika Pizzeria
   РЕСТОРАНТ ЧАЙКА ПИЦАРИЯ
26 Cheap Eateries

OTHER
4 St Todor Church
   ЦЬРКВА СВ. ТОДОР
7 Nesebâr Orthodox Church
   РЕСЕБЬР ПРАВОСЛАВНА
   ЦЬРКВА
8 St Paraskera Church
   ЦЬРКВАТА СВ. ПАРАСКЕВА
9 Archangels, Michael &
   Gabriel's Church
   ЦЬРКВАТА АРАХАНГЕЛ
   МИХАИЛ И ГАВРИИЛ
10 Basilica
   БАЗИЛИКА
14 Ethnographical Museum
   ЕТНОГРАФСКИ МУЗЕЙ
15 Nesebâr Theatre
   РЕСЕБЬРСКИ ТЕАТЬР
16 Bul Ins Tourist Service
   (Accommodation Agency)
   БУЛ ИНС АГЕНЦИЯ ЗА
   НАСТАНИВАНЕ
17 St Spa's Church
   ЦЬРКВАТА СВ. СПАС
18 Church of St John the Baptist
   ЦЬРКВА СВ. ЙОАН КРЬСТИТЕЛ
19 Biochim Commercial Bank
   ТЬРГОВСКА БАНКА БИОХИМ
20 Pantokrator Church
   ПАНТОКРАТОРСКА ЦЬРКВА
22 Water Taxis to Slânchev Bryag
   (Sunny Beach)
23 Tequila Bar
   ТЕКИЛА БАР
24 Fortress Walls
25 Bus Station
27 Archaeological Museum
   АРХЕОЛОГИЧЕСКИ МУЗЕЙ
29 Post Office & Telephone Centre
30 Kentavor 45 Travel Agency
   КЕНТАВЬР 45
33 St Stefan Church
   ЦЬРКВА СВ. СТЕФАН
35 St John Alturgetos Church
   ЦЬРКВА СВ. ЙОАН
   КРЬСТИТЕЛ
36 National Disco; Maritime
   Passenger Terminal (Disused)

The best map is the *Sunny Beach & Nessebur City Guide*, published by Makros and distinguishable by its yellow-and-blue cover. For a detailed history of Nesebâr, look for *The Ancient City of Nessebur* (9 lv), which contains plenty of photos and makes a decent souvenir. Also worthwhile is *Nessebur: A Town with History*, a booklet (10 lv) with gorgeous photos and some historical details. Maps and books are available at any of the town's plethora of bookstalls.

Churches

Incredibly, Nesebâr was once home to about 80 churches and chapels, but most are now in ruins. Characteristic of the Nesebâr style of church design are the horizontal strips of white stone and red brick, which are offset by striped blind arches resting on the vertical pilasters, the facades highlighted by ceramic discs and rosettes. Except where indicated, each church is open daily during daylight hours and admission is free.

No visitor can help but be impressed by the dominant ruins of the **Basilica**, also known as the Metropolitan Church and Old Bishopric. Originally built in the early 6th century and then rebuilt in the late 9th century, it served as the bishopric until about 1257 when the churched was ransacked by Venetians. It contained three naves, and boasted a spacious interior with high walls and wide windows. The unmissable ruins are accessible from along the main street, ulitsa Mitropolitska.

Typical of the characteristic Nesebâr construction mentioned earlier is the well-preserved **Pantokrator Church** *(ul Mesembria)*. Built in the mid-14th century, it's renowned among religious historians for its bell tower and unusually deliberate and conspicuous urban location. It now contains a classy art gallery.

Probably the most beautiful church in old Nesebâr was the **St John Aliturgetos Church**, accessible down some steps from the end of ulitsa Ribarska. Built in about the mid-14th century and dedicated to St John the Unbeliever, the church was mostly destroyed by an earthquake in 1913. Concerts are sometimes held here in summer.

The **Church of St John the Baptist** *(ul Mitropolitska)* was built in the 10th century, and features some of the best-preserved murals from the 14th and 17th centuries. It's also now occupied by an art gallery. The **St Spa's Church** *(ul Aheloi; admission 1.70 lv; open Mon-Fri 10am-1pm & 2pm-5.30pm, Sat-Sun 10am-1.30pm)* was built in 1609. Like all churches established during Ottoman rule, it had to be built below street level. It features some comparatively well-preserved murals, but nothing much else.

St Stefan Church *(ul Ribarska; admission 1.70 lv, permission to take photos 3 lv extra; open daily 9am-noon & 2pm-6pm)* was built in three stages between the 10th and 12th centuries. It became the new bishopric (which is an alternative name for the church) after the basilica was looted. The interior of St Stefan's is almost completely covered with murals dating from the 15th and 16th centuries, and was one of the first churches in Bulgaria to be decorated with ceramics.

The **Archangels Michael & Gabriel's Church** *(ul Hemus)* was built over a few decades during the 13th and 14th centuries. It remains in relatively good condition, but entry is usually forbidden. Very little is known about the origins of **St Todor Church** *(ul Neptun)*, which has been partially restored but is also usually closed. A fine example of 13th-century architecture is **St Paraskera Church** *(ul Hemus)*, which had only one nave. The building is now occupied by a restaurant. **Nesebâr Orthodox Church** *(ul Slavyanska)* is the only functioning church in town and visitors are welcome.

Archaeological Museum

Although the number of exhibits is limited, it's still worth visiting the Archaeological Museum *(☎ 26 018, ul Mesembria 2; admission 2.10 lv, photos 3 lv; open Mon-Sat 9am-1.30pm & 2pm-9pm, & Sun 9am-1pm & 2pm-7pm in summer only)*. The ground floor houses earthenware pots from between the 5th and 2nd centuries BC, as well as other artefacts such as anchors detailing the naval history of previous civilisations. Other highlights include Thracian tombs, Roman tablets and gold jewellery. The basement has a token collection of unre-markable religious icons recovered from Nesebâr's numerous churches.

All items are labelled in English, except, disappointingly, those detailing any history and explaining the model of the ancient city. The museum can get very busy at times, with tour group leaders shouting at their flocks, so come before 10am or after 5pm.

Ethnographical Museum

Ignored by the shopaholics and forgotten by the tour groups is this small museum (ul Mesembria 32; admission 1.20 lv, free Sat; open daily 10am-2pm & 3pm-6pm). Inside a typical, wooden Bulgarian national re-vival period building (constructed in about 1840), it features regional costumes and displays about weaving. All labels are in Bulgarian and German.

Beach

The beaches are popular with some locals and visitors, but they're small and rocky, and the water is often choked with seaweed. The best place for a dip is either side of the two jetties to the north-east. Alternatively, head to the far superior beach at Slânchev Bryag, only a few kilometres away.

Places to Stay

If you come in the off-season (October to May), and/or stay for more than two or three nights, it's worth asking for a dis-count; the town has so many hotels that bar-gaining is common.

Private Rooms Kentavor 45 Travel Agency (☎ 45 880, fax 44 050, ⓔ tfs94@ hotmail.com) offer *rooms* in a hotel for 20 lv or in a private home for 12 lv per person. This agency is along a tiny laneway off ulitsa Ribarska. Staff were not entirely clear about which hotels they could offer for 20 lv per person, but it's worth contacting them anyway.

Bul Ins Tourist Service (☎ 42 199) on ulitsa Mitropolitska has *rooms* in private home for about 15 lv per person. If the Ken-tavor 45 can't help, try Bul Ins. Opening hours are erratic, however.

Hotels All hotels listed here offer rooms with a private bathroom, and rates include breakfast unless stated otherwise.

Hotel Toni (☎ 42 403, ul Kraybrezhna) Doubles 40 lv (July & Aug) & 30 lv (May, June & Sept), closed in the off-season. Poorly signposted next to St Georgi Hotel, this guesthouse caters to independent trav-ellers, but features the same sort of setting and views as adjacent hotels costing far more. Breakfast costs an extra 5 lv.

Hotel Mesembria (☎ 43 255, ul Rib-arska) Singles/doubles 41/54 lv. The Mesembria is a throwback to the 1960s, though the bathrooms have been updated sometime in the last 40 years. It's musty, charmless and poor value, but central. Breakfast is not included.

Hotel The White House (☎ 333 103, ul Tsar Simeon 2) Doubles 70 lv & apartments 150 lv. The US president probably would not stay here, but it's sparkling new and cen-tral, and the staff are friendly. Some rooms are so dazzlingly white and neat, that they look exactly like a hospital room – albeit a very nice one. The air-conditioned rooms have a TV and fridge, and the massive apartments contain two bedrooms and a dining room, sitting room and kitchen.

St Georgi Hotel (☎/fax 44 045, ⓔ gsk@ dir.bg, ul Sadala 10) Singles/doubles/apart-ments 40/60/80 lv June-early July & Sept-Oct, 50/75/90 mid-July–Aug. This spotlessly clean hotel is good value, though a bit charmless. The rooms are small but com-fortable, and feature a lovely bathroom and balcony. A TV and fridge can be rented for an extra 5 lv per item per day. It's about the only hotel along the esplanade where inde-pendent travellers are likely to get a room in the high season without booking. Rates do not include breakfast.

Rony Hotel (☎ 44 002, fax 44 001) Doubles/triples 43/53 lv (May & Oct), 52/65 lv (June & Sept), 72/95 lv (July & Aug). Rony's central location at the back of the Archaeological Museum is hard to beat. The smallish rooms are modern, and con-tain a TV and fridge, and the air-con *really* works. Some rooms also have balconies with excellent views. Independent travellers will probably be able to walk off the bus and straight into a room during the high season. It offers attractive discounts for longer stays.

St Stefan Hotel (☎ 43 604, ul Ribarska 11) Singles/doubles 70/90 lv. Opposite the picturesque St Stefan Church, this modern hotel is far better value than others in this price range. The modern rooms contain a TV, fridge and air-con, and those on the upper floors have balconies with views. The hotel also has a gym, sauna and jacuzzi.

Hotel Victoria (☎ 46 000, [e] seamex@ spnet.net, ul Kraybrezhna 22) Rooms per person US$28 July & Aug, US$23 June & Sept, US$15 May & Oct & US$10 rest of year, apartments US$67/60/50/35. Many rooms in this recommended three-star hotel have wonderful views, and all have a TV, fridge and air-con. The hotel is usually full in the high season, but the rates are remarkably cheap in the off-season.

Prince Cyril Hotel (☎ 42 215, ul Slavyanska 9) Double/family rooms US$40/50. Like the Victoria, this place is almost always filled with tour groups in July and August, but prices can be negotiated to about US$30/40 at other times. It's certainly worth inquiring about off-season discounts considering the excellent location and amenities, including TV and air-con.

Places to Eat

Fish is the local delicacy. If you look around, a plateful of tasty grilled trout with the trimmings should cost no more than 6 lv. If you've been to Slânchev Bryag, you won't be shocked by the restaurant prices in Nesebâr, but you will be horrified if you've arrived from anywhere else in Bulgaria.

Numerous tourist-oriented ***cafes*** and ***restaurants*** are along the north-eastern end of ulitsa Mitropolitska. If possible, escape the crowds and find a quiet place with views and breezes in the eastern part of town. The cheapest places for a meal are the harbourside ***eateries*** near the bus station.

Neptun Restaurant (ul Neptun 1) Fish meals from 5.50 lv. For truly fresh seafood, such as *lefer* (bluefish), the Neptun is recommended. It's one of several decent

restaurants at the end of the main drag, blissfully distant from the noise and crowds.

Vega Restaurant (Off ul Mesembria) Fish meals 5-6 lv. This waterside bar and restaurant is so close to the sea that you can almost dangle your feet in the briny depths while sipping a beer or espresso. It offers the best location and layout of the restaurants along the eastern edge of town, and the private balconies are a delightful attraction.

Regatta Restaurant (Off ul Mesembria) Meals 2.50-7 lv. This unmissable place along the unnamed road to the east is charmingly located inside and around a huge old sailing boat. It's ideal for breakfast, which starts at 4 lv.

Restaurant Chaika (ul Ivan Asen II) Salads about 3 lv, main meals 5-6 lv. Although set up squarely for the tourist crowds, Chaika is an ideal place to try fresh fish at reasonable prices. It has a quiet, vine-covered courtyard.

Restaurant Chaika Pizzeria (ul Kraybrezhna) Small pizzas 2.50-4, large pizzas 4-6.50 lv. If you're sick of fish, visit this popular pizzeria – though the *pièce de résistance* is the seafood pizza. *Fruits de mare* is French for seafood.

Entertainment

Follow the strobes to the ***National Disco*** on the 2nd floor of the defunct maritime passenger terminal. The ***Nesebâr Theatre*** (ul Mesembria) was being renovated at the time of research, but is bound to offer something more cultured. Most locals and visitors do nothing more in the evening than sit at a *cafe* and sip on a beer or coffee. For something a little different, try ***Tequila Bar***, set up on a pontoon. Prices are high, but it's an ideal place to watch the sun set and to throw scraps to the seagulls on the nearby rocks.

Shopping

Among all the tacky stuff for sale, some authentic and delicate embroidery can be found; prices range from about 5 lv for a small coaster, to 80 lv to 150 lv for an intricate tablecloth. Several aspiring and inspiring artists line the central streets painting scenes of Nesebâr (minus all the tourists!).

Their results are priced from only 10 lv and make wonderful mementoes.

Getting There & Away

If you're driving, *please* do everyone a favour and park in the new town and walk over the causeway.

At the bus station near the harbour, tour buses regularly disgorge flocks of tourists, and taxis linger nearby like eager birds of prey. From Nesebâr, buses and minibuses go to Burgas (2 lv, 40 minutes) every 30 to 40 minutes between 6.30am and 9pm; to Varna (4.50 lv, 1½ hours) about six times a day; and to Sofia (17 lv, seven hours) about 10 times a day, mostly early in the morning and late at night.

There are several ways to reach Slânchev Bryag: catch a taxi (about 3 lv), but make sure the driver uses the meter; take a bus (1.50 lv), which leaves every 15 minutes between 6am and midnight; or jump into a water taxi (6 lv), which leaves from an obvious spot north of the bus station about every 30 minutes between 9am and 9pm.

SLÂNCHEV BRYAG (SUNNY BEACH)
СЛЬНЧЕВ БРЯГ
☎ 0554

Slânchev Bryag is one of the two major resorts along the Black Sea coast. Called Sonderstand by German tourist agencies and Sunny Beach by their English counterparts, it's a purpose-built resort along a perfect stretch of beach about 8km long and up to 100m wide. The resort is home to over 100 hotels (with nearly 30,000 beds) and about 600 cafes, restaurants, bars, shops etc. Because the hotels are spread out among shady parks, Slânchev Bryag doesn't feel nearly as overcrowded or hectic as other resorts along the coast, so it's popular with families. Prices for everything are high, naturally.

Orientation & Information

If there is a town centre, it's along a 300m stretch of the main road between the Cuban and Svejest hotels, and along the mall from the Hotel Cuban to the beach. Along the former road, the United Bulgarian Bank and First East International Bank have ATMs, and there are also market stalls, a post office, a telephone centre with an Internet agency, and a laundry. Dozens of foreign-exchange offices are set up here and elsewhere around the resort. Day-old copies of English and German newspapers can be bought at hotel reception desks and book-stalls for about 3 lv each.

Activities

Slânchev Bryag caters mainly to families, so there's plenty of activities for the kids, but surprisingly few places to organise any water sports. Unfortunately, you can't just walk onto the beach and expect to go wind-surfing, paragliding or jet skiing. The most exciting thing to do on the water is splash about on a two-person **paddleboat** *(about 8 lv per hour)*. So, if you're keen on water sports, it's best to head to Pomorie.

Organised Tours

Most visitors end up joining one or more tours. The shopping tours to Burgas are fairly pointless, because it's just as easy (and far cheaper) to get there by public transport. More interesting trips include two-day tours to Istanbul (US$80 per person), and day trips to the Rila Monastery (by plane, via Burgas and Sofia) for about US$100 per person. More affordable are the folkloric evenings (30 lv) of traditional dance and music, and boat trips along the Ropotamo River (22 lv per person).

Places to Stay

Almost everyone who stays in Slânchev Bryag is on a package tour which includes accommodation (and, often, meals and all sorts of activities), so there's little point recommending any particular hotel. Also, most independent travellers will almost certainly choose to do a day trip by bus from Burgas or Nesebâr; the latter offers the best range of budget and mid-range accommodation in the region, and is linked very frequently to Slânchev Bryag by public transport. No agencies in the resort offer rooms in private homes, because so few people really live here.

There are about 120 hotels to chose from, but try to avoid any place too close to the main road. The two hotels listed below (like almost every other hotel in the resort) offer rooms with a bathroom, TV and air-con. No hotel has an address as such because the streets are not named.

Hotel Globus (☎ *22 018*) Doubles 45 lv May & Oct, 60 lv June & Sept, 85 lv July & Aug. The Globus is a large three-star hotel only metres from the beach, and not far from the Hotel Cuban. It offers an indoor pool and health centre, and is surprisingly good value.

Venus Hotel (☎ *22 460*) Singles/doubles 66/88 lv. This small and comparatively cosy place is quiet, charming and convenient to the beach. It's one of few places that offers single rates.

Places to Eat

The cost of a meal at a major hotel is two or three times more than at a simple cafe nearby. In major hotels and restaurants, expect to pay 10-12 lv for a decent meal, 4 lv for a toasted sandwich and even 2 lv for a simple cup of tea.

Homesick Brits may want to visit the Tudor-style ***Red Lion*** pub for some tasty nosh, though (ironically) some staff don't speak English. Among the various pizzerias, Indian takeaways and hamburger stalls, it is still possible to find a restaurant serving authentic Bulgarian cuisine. One of the best is ***Chuchura*** (just behind Hotel Trakia), which has folkloric music most evenings and food at reasonable prices.

Getting There & Away

About every 40 minutes, minibuses and buses travel between Slânchev Bryag and Burgas (2 lv, 45 minutes) via the scenic road through Pomorie and Nesebâr or, occasionally, through Kableshkovo and Aheloi. From Slânchev Bryag, minibuses also go to Pomorie Central (1.30 lv, 30 minutes) every 60 to 90 minutes, and another six depart daily for Varna (4.50 lv, 1¼ hours).

Most buses and minibuses use the station just off the main road about 100m up from the Hotel Svejest. Minibuses from Burgas

stop anywhere along the main road (and within walking distance of your hotel) as far north as Hotel Cuban. From the bus station, several daily buses go to Sliven, Plovdiv and Stara Zagora, and eight or nine depart for Sofia. From anywhere along the main road, buses head to Sveti Vlas (about every 90 minutes) and Elenite (five times a day).

For information about travelling between Slânchev Bryag and Nesebâr, see Getting There & Away in the Nesebâr section earlier.

Getting Around

Trolleybuses (1.50 lv) shuttle along three numbered routes every 15 to 20 minutes between 9am and 11pm. The streets around the resort are uncrowded and flat, so bicycles are an ideal way of getting around. These can be rented from outside Hotel Svejest for about 3/8 lv for one/three hours, or 15 lv for the whole day. Cars can be hired through several travel agencies and at hotel reception desks, and rental costs start at US$45 per day, including unlimited kilometres and insurance, plus petrol.

Northern Coast

VARNA
BAPHA
☎ 052 • pop 350,000

In recent years, Varna, Bulgaria's third-largest city, has developed into a kind of urban resort along the Black Sea coast. It's an atmospheric city on a bay hemmed in by hills that offer scenic views, and the Beautiful Bulgaria Project has renovated more than 100 historic buildings and other sites. Varna boasts the largest and most impressive museum in Bulgaria (as well as several other worthwhile museums), a marvellous seaside park, about 20 art galleries, seemingly endless summer festivals, and the most extensive archaeological ruins in the country.

Varna is also an ideal base for day trips to nearby beach resorts such as Sveti Konstantin and Zlatni Pyasâtsi (Golden Sands), and the charming towns of Balchik (see that section later in this chapter) and Dobrich (see the Northern Bulgaria chapter).

History

Remnants of an ancient Thracian civilisation dated to about 4000 BC have been found at Varna Necropolis, an area of some 100 tombs found near Varna. In 585 BC, the Greeks from Miletus settled in the area, and created the city of Odessos. The Greeks only lived there for about 150 years before it again came under the control of the Thracians. Odessos withstood initial attacks from the Macedonians in 342 BC, but was eventually annexed by Alexander the Great. The city didn't really regain any regional importance until the Romans conquered the area and set up a base in Odessos during the 2nd century AD.

During the First Bulgarian Empire (681–1018), the city was renamed Varna but its fortunes declined. The city alternated between Byzantine and Bulgarian rule during the Middle Ages, and eventually re-emerged as a prosperous settlement. Next came the Turks, who captured Varna in 1393, and turned it into a northern bastion of their empire. After the Crimean War (1853–56), Turkey allowed its allies, Britain and France, to sell their products throughout the Ottoman Empire, so Varna became a great trading centre once more.

In 1866, a railway between Ruse and Varna was built. This provided a direct route from the Danube River to the Black Sea coast and proved a catalyst for an economic resurgence. Varna became a major shipbuilding centre and port, and resorts based on mineral springs and beaches were later established nearby.

Orientation

Varna is pleasingly compact, so most hotels, restaurants and attractions are within walking distance of the city centre. From the train station, ulitsa Tsar Simeon leads into ploshtad Nezavisimost, which acts as the city centre. From the square, a short thoroughfare heads north-west, passes the domineering cathedral towering over the market and several theatres, and turns into bulevard Vladislav Varenchik which leads to the main bus station and airport. Also from ploshtad Nezavisimost, another broad pedestrian mall, ulitsa Knyaz Boris I, runs east and then north-east towards Primorski Park and the sea.

Maps If you're going to stay in Varna for a while, or want to explore the northern beach resorts in depth, pick up the detailed *Varna City Map*, published in English by Slavena (with a blue cover). Maps are readily available from any of the plethora of bookstalls around the city and at the bus and train stations.

Information

Tourist Offices Incredibly, for a huge city and administrative centre, at times buckling under the weight of tourists, there is still no dedicated tourist office. The best sources of information are staff at your hotel or one of the town's travel agencies. Otherwise, for specific information or complaints, contact the Varna Chamber of Tourism (☎ 602 672, fax 236 155).

Money Bulbank, on ulitsa Slivnitsa, will change travellers cheques and provide cash advances over the counter, and has an ATM which accepts major credit cards. (At the time of research, the bank was soon to move about 150m further down ulitsa Slivnitsa.) The United Bulgarian Bank on ulitsa Knyaz Boris I, and the Biochim Commercial Bank, on bulevard Vladislav Varenchik, near the main post office, both provide the same services as Bulbank. Oodles of foreign-exchange offices around the city centre offer competitive rates of exchange.

Post & Communications The telephone centre, open daily 7am to 11pm, is inside the main post office at ulitsa Sâborni 36. There is a surprising lack of Internet centres in Varna, and only two came to our attention: Cyber X Internet Club on ulitsa Knyaz Boris I, just around the corner from McDonald's; and Skylark Internet Bar & Cafe, downstairs on the corner of ulitsa Tsar Simeon and ulitsa Asen Zlatarov.

Travel Agencies ETAP Adress and Megatours, both on the ground floor of the Cherno More Hotel complex, are the best

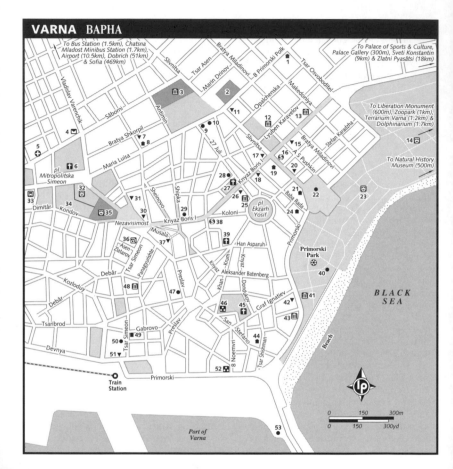

VARNA BAPHA

To Bus Station (1.5km), Chatsna Mladost Minibus Station (1.7km), Airport (10.5km), Dobrich (51km) & Sofia (469km)

To Palace of Sports & Culture, Palace Gallery (300m), Sveti Konstantin (9km) & Zlatni Pyasätsi (18km)

To Liberation Monument (600m), Zoopark (1km), Terrarium Varna (1:2km) & Dolphinarium (1.7km)

To Natural History Museum (500m)

BLACK SEA

Primorski Park

Train Station

Port of Varna

0   150   300m
0   150   300yd

places to book organised tours, buy tickets on private long-distance buses, and ask general questions in the absence of a proper tourist office.

Bookshops Several bookstalls around the cathedral and along ulitsa Knyaz Boris I sell recent copies of newspapers from the UK and Germany for a reasonable 3 lv each; they also sell international magazines. The two-storey Penguin Bookshop on ulitsa 27 Juli, just behind St Nikolai Church, sells English-language novels. The PS Bookshop, on ulitsa Maria Luisa, offers an im-

pressive array of books, including many about Bulgaria, in English and German.

Dangers & Annoyances Probably more than any other Bulgarian city or town, Varna attracts lowlifes, pickpockets, beggars, and unscrupulous taxi drivers (see Getting Around later in this section). At the bus and train stations, moneychangers offer outrageously high exchange rates, trying to set up new arrivals for a rip-off or robbery. Do *not* change money on the street. Also, watch out for large buses and silent trolleybuses speeding along pedestrian malls.

VARNA ВАРНА

PLACES TO STAY
1 Orbita Hotel
   ХОТЕЛ ОРБИТА
8 Voennomorski Club
   БОЕННОМОРСКИ КЛУБ
19 Cherno More Hotel;
   Mustang Food; ETAP Adress;
   Megatours; Vendor
   (Car Rental)
   ХОТЕЛ ЧЕРНО МОРЕ,
   МУСТАНГ, ЕТАР, МЕГАТУР,
   БЕНДОР
21 Hotel Odessa;
   Tourist Service
   (Accommodation Agency)
   ХОТЕЛ ОДЕСА
24 Hotel Santa Marina
   ХОТЕЛ САНТА МАРИНА
44 Hotel Akropolis
   ХОТЕЛ АКРОПОЛИС
49 Three Dolphins Hotel
   ХОТЕЛ ТРИТЕ ДЕЛФИНА

PLACES TO EAT
7 Mustang Food; Mustang
   Cinema
   МУСТАНГ, КИНО МУСТАНГ
11 Komplex Hâshove
   КОМПЛЕКС ХЪЩОВЕ
15 Pizza Hut
17 McDonald's; Cyber X
   Internet Club
18 Trops Kâshta
   ТРОПС КЪЩТА
20 Birariya
   БИРАРИЯ
26 BMS
30 Happy Bar & Grill
31 El Taco; McDonald's;
   Restaurant Chuchura
   РЕСТОРАНТ ЧУЧУРА
37 Restaurant Arkitekta
   РЕСТОРАНТ АРХИТЕКТА

42 Paraklisa
   ПАРАКЛИСА
51 BMS

OTHER
2 City Hall
3 Archaeological Museum
   АРХЕОЛОГИЧЕСКИ МУЗЕЙ
4 Main Post Office &
   Telephone Centre; Biochim
   Commercial Bank
5 City Hospital
6 Cathedral of the Assumption
   of the Virgin
   КАТЕДРАЛАТА УСПЕНИЕ
   БОГОРОДИЧНО
9 PS Bookshop
   КНИЖАРНИЦА ОЫ
10 Aeroflot
12 Varna Art Gallery
   ХУДОЖЕСТВЕНА ГАЛЕРИЯ
   ВАРНА
13 Center of Contemporary Art
   ЦЕНТЪР ЗА СЪВРЕМЕННО
   ИЗКУСТВО
14 Open-Air Theatre
16 Bulbank
   БУЛБАНК
22 Festival Hall
   ЗАЛА ФЕСТИВАЛНА
23 Summer Theatre; Cafes
25 Museum of National Revival
   МУЗЕЙ НА ВЪЗРАЖДАНЕТО
27 St Nikolai Church
   ЦЪРКВА СВ. НИКОЛАЙ
28 Penguin Bookshop
   КНИЖАРНИЦА ПИНГВИН
29 Varna International Airport
   Travel Agency
32 Storya Bachvarov Dramatic
   Theatre; Clock Tower; KFC
   ДРАМАТИЧЕН ТЕАТЪР СТОЯН
   БЪЧВАРОВ

33 Makedonia Dom
   (Minibuses to Albena)
   МАКЕДОНИЯ ДОМ
34 Market
35 Varna Opera House; Night
   Club Danvi
   ОПЕРАТА ВАРНА
36 Skylark Internet Bar &
   Cafe
38 United Bulgarian Bank
   ОБЕДИНЕНА БЪЛГАРСКА
   БАНКА
39 St Sarkis Armenian
   Apostolic Church
   АРМЕНСКА ЦЪРКВА СВ.
   САРКИС
40 Aquarium; Cafes
   АКВАРИУМА
41 National Naval Museum
   ВОЕННОМОРСКИ
   МУЗЕЙ
43 Museum of Medical
   History
   МУЗЕЙ НА ИСТОРИЯ НА
   МЕДИЦИНАТА
45 St Anastasios Orthodox
   Church
   ОРТОДОКСАЛНА ЦЪРКВА
   СВ. АНАСТАС
46 Roman Thermae
   РИМСКИ ТЕРМИ
47 Rila Bureau
   БЮРО РИЛА
48 Ethnographic Museum
   ЕТНОГРАФСКИ МУЗЕЙ
50 Tourist Agency George
   (Accommodation Agency)
   ТУРИСТИЧЕСКА АГЕНЦИЯ
   GEORGE
52 Roman Baths
   РИМСКИ БАНИ
53 Maritime Passenger
   Terminal (Disused)

Roman Thermae

One definite highlight of Varna is the well-preserved ruins of the Roman Thermae (☎ 456 476, ul Khan Krum; admission 2 lv; open Tues-Sun 10am-5pm in summer & Mon-Fri 10am-5pm in winter). The ruins are the largest in Bulgaria, (the third biggest in Europe). Only a small part of the original complex (estimated to be 7000 sq metres) still stands. The baths were built in the late 2nd century AD as part of the re-

construction of the city of Odessos by the Romans. Probably abandoned only 100 years later when the Roman Empire started to collapse, the complex was only occupied again once more – by artisans in the 14th century.

Some boards around the complex contain basic explanations (in English) about the use of the rooms, for example, the frigidarium (where guests bathed in freezing cold water) and the tepidarium (where they luxuriated in tepid water) before jumping into the caldarium (with scaldingly hot water).

The ruins can be admired for free from the grounds of St Anastasios Orthodox Church (see Other Churches later). However, it's far better to pay the entrance fee and explore the ruins from within – but allow enough time to enjoy it all. The booklet (2 lv), available at the entrance gate on the south-western corner, is a bit ancient itself, but provides a useful summary about the baths' history and purpose.

Roman Baths

The ruins described earlier are called Roman *thermae* (Latin for 'baths') to differentiate it from the Roman Baths *(bul Primorski)*. The baths were built in around the 4th century AD, so they're not as old as the Roman Thermae, nor are they as impressive. There's nothing much to see here, and a lamentable lack of explanations on site doesn't help either. The grounds are closed, but it's worth peering over the fence if you're walking past.

Cathedral of the Assumption of the Virgin

This mammoth cathedral *(☎ 225 435, pl Mitropolitska Simeon; admission 2 lv; open daily 6am-10pm)* was built between 1880 and 1886. Although the location and size are impressive, the design and interior are fairly unremarkable. It features three altars – one dedicated to St Nicholas of Myra, one to the Russian martyr, Aleksander Nevski, and one to the Assumption of the Virgin. Note the murals (painted in the late 1940s), the stained glass windows, and the icons and thrones delicately carved from wood.

A priest stands by the door and demands that foreigners pay the admission fee. (Locals buy candles at the door, look at ease and pay nothing.) A leaflet (1 lv), translated into French or English, and available inside the cathedral, includes photos of some murals, but is of limited use otherwise.

Other Churches

Two other churches are worth exploring; admission to both is free, and they're open daily from about 6am to 10pm. The beautiful **St Anastasios Orthodox Church** *(ul Graf Ignatiev)* overlooks the Roman Thermae. Built in 1602, it's one of the oldest churches in the city, and features an intricately carved throne. The quaint **St Nikolai Church** *(ul Knyaz Boris I; photo/video cameras 5/15 lv)*, which looks out of place along the modern mall, is worth a visit for its murals.

The elegant **St Sarkis Armenian Apostolic Church** *(ul Han Asparuh 15)* was built in 1842. It's not normally open, but its exterior can be admired from over the fence or from within the church grounds.

Archaeological Museum

If you only visit one museum in Bulgaria, make sure it's the Archaeological Museum *(☎ 237 057, ul Maria Luisa 41; admission 2 lv; open Tues-Sun 10am-5pm in summer & 10pm-5pm Tues-Sat in winter)*. The 100,000 objects are housed in 39 rooms along two massive floors, so allow plenty of time to take it all in. All exhibits originate from the Varna area, and are placed in chronological order, from the Old Stone Age to the Late Medieval Period.

The highlights are perhaps the 6000-year-old gold and copper objects. Unearthed by chance in 1972 from the Varna Necropolis (closed to the public), about 4km west of central Varna, these items are reputedly the oldest of their kind in the world. Other rooms contain religious icons from the 16th to 18th centuries, Bulgaria's largest collection of ceramics, sculptures and bas-reliefs, and fine examples of woodcarving from Tryavna. Two other rooms contain temporary exhibits, and a huge library caters to students of archaeology.

All exhibits have detailed captions in English, and it's easy to work through the displays chronologically by following the arrows. It is not permitted to take photographs in the museum. If you want any further information, buy the informative *Varna Archaeological Museum Guide* (6 lv). The entrance to this massive building (a former girls' high school) faces the south-east, and is accessible through the park.

Ethnographic Museum

One of the largest of its kind in Bulgaria is Varna's Ethnographic Museum (*☎ 630 588, ul Panagyurishte 22; admission 2 lv; open Tues-Sun 10am-5pm in summer & 10am-5pm Tues-Sat in winter*). The ground floor contains a large and varied collection of agricultural implements, and displays about weaving, wine-making, iron-smelting and fishing from the late 19th and early 20th centuries. The second floor has an impressive range of costumes and jewellery, and the four rooms on the third floor feature the sort of furniture that would have filled this Bulgarian national revival period house (1860).

Some of the museum's captions are in English, and a few are also in French and German. The booklet (2 lv), written in French, English or German, and available at the museum, provides further explanations. The museum also sells some unexciting and overpriced souvenirs and maps.

Museum of National Revival

This is also called the National Bulgarian Renaissance Museum (*☎ 223 585, ul 27 Juli 9; admission 1.50 lv; open Tues-Sun 10am-5pm in summer & 10am-5pm Mon-Fri in winter*). It mainly features displays about the local involvement in the Russian-Turkish War (1877–78), but it also contains one of the largest collections of wooden icons in Bulgaria, and some old photos of Varna. The building (constructed in 1861) was the first school in Varna, and was also used as the St Michael Archangel Church; remnants of these former purposes are also featured in the museum. The lovely **garden courtyard** is worth a visit in itself.

A useful (free) hand-out in French or English explains the history of the building, and some displays and photos are labelled in English.

National Naval Museum

Unmissable from the city beach is the National Naval Museum (*☎ 633 015, bul Primorski 2; admission 2 lv; open Mon-Fri 10am-6pm*). Also called the Maritime Museum, it houses various exhibits outlining the history of the Bulgarian Navy from the Russian-Turkish War (1877–78) to the present day, and features anchors, artillery, uniforms and models of ships. The museum is certainly more interesting than the typical archaeological and ethnological museums found all over Bulgaria, and the only one of its kind in the country.

Even if the museum is not open, or you don't want to pay to go in, you can see still many exhibits in the grounds, such as the incongruous lighthouse, and wander around the adjacent warship *Druzki*, which torpedoed a Turkish boat and turned around the Balkan Wars of 1912–13.

Other Museums

Anyone with specific interests may also wish to visit one of Varna's other museums. All of their captions are in Bulgarian, and admission to each costs 2 lv.

The **Museum of Medical History** (*☎ 241 015, bul Primorski; open Mon-Fri 10am-4pm*) details the use of medicines throughout Bulgaria.

In the grounds of the Institute of Fisheries & Aquaculture, within Primorski Park, is the **Aquarium** (*☎ 222 586; open daily 9am-7pm*). Disappointingly, it's little more than a motley and outdated collection of live and bottled marine life. The entrance is on the north-western side near all the cafes.

A missable collection of pinned insects and bottled molluscs resides in the **Natural History Museum** (*☎ 228 194; open Tues-Sun 10am-5pm in summer & 10am-5pm Mon-Fri in winter*). It's in Primorski Park near the bizarre gorilla sculpture!

Art Galleries

Art lovers will thrive among some of Varna's 20 public and private art galleries. Devotees should pick up the *Varna Art Galleries* (2 lv) brochure from the Varna Art Gallery. The brochure describes the exhibits at each gallery, details the opening hours, and contains a useful map with locations of each gallery.

There are three galleries probably worth visiting. The **Varna Art Gallery** (*☎ 243 123, ul Lyuben Karavelov 1; admission 2 lv; open Tues-Sun 10am-5pm*), also known as the Boris Georgiev Art Gallery, features two floors of mostly Bulgarian contemporary art. The **Center of Contemporary Art** *(☎ 603 238, ul Knyaz Boris I 65; admission free; open Tues-Sun 10am-6pm)* is another gallery with a collection of rather bizarre modern art. Also mildly interesting is the **Palace Gallery** *(☎ 234 421, admission free; open Tues-Sun 10am-6pm)*, in the Palace of Sport & Culture.

Primorski Park

This 80-hectare, wooded seaside park stretches for about 8km, and is apparently the largest of its kind in Europe. Easily accessible from the city centre, it's bursting with people and festivals in summer, and is a wonderful place for an evening promenade.

In the northern section, the **Zoopark** *(☎ 302 528; admission 1 lv; open daily 8am-8pm)* features a ragged collection of deers, jaguars, emus and lions. About 200m farther north, the **Terrarium Varna** *(admission 1.20 lv; open daily 9am-6pm)* offers a collection of creepy crawlies such as spiders and scorpions.

Another 500m farther up is the **Dolphinarium** *(☎ 302 199; admission 10 lv; open Tues-Sun)*. Although the only one of its kind in the Balkans, it offers little more than what you would expect, ie, dolphins jumping in and out of water. Forty-minute shows are held at 11am and 3pm (January to May), 11am, 2pm and 3.30pm (June to August), and 11am and 3pm (September to December). You can also watch the dolphins at play before or after the show for the price of a drink at the cafe.

Beach

Varna certainly boasts the best suburban beach in the country. The beach is long, seedy in a charming English-seaside-resort way, and lined with cafes and bars. There's a water slide not far from the Aquarium, and paddle boats for rent further north. Parts of the beach can get impossibly crowded on Saturday and Sunday; if so, simply move farther up the beach to avoid the masses. However, serious worshippers of sun, sand and sea would be better off going to Sveti

Konstantin, Zlatni Pyasâtsi or Albena (all of which are detailed later in this chapter).

Special Events

Between May and October, Varna hosts the renowned **Varna Summer International Festival**. First established in 1926, the festival features outstanding events, including opera, the biennial International Ballet Competition (held in even-numbered years), and choral, jazz and folkloric music. Events are held at the **Open-Air Theatre** *(☎ 228 385)* in Primorski Park and in some of the nine halls in the massive **Festival Hall** *(☎ 621 331)* on ulitsa Slivnitsa. Programs and information about buying tickets are well advertised beforehand in Varna and Sofia. The Festival Hall also hosts the Annual International Film Festival for one week or so in late August and early September.

Other special events around the city include the **Songs about Varna Competition** and the **Days of Greek Culture** festival, both held in March.

Places to Stay

Private Rooms Two agencies at the train station offer *rooms* in private homes for a fairly pricey 20 lv for singles and 30 lv for doubles. Both agencies are open daily from about 9am to 5pm, but the Isak is less reliably open on Sunday. Astra Tour *(☎ 605 861, ⓔ astratur@mail.vega.bg)* is at the end of platform 6, and Isak Accommodation Bureau is signposted at the eastern entrance.

Tourist Agency George *(☎/fax 607 474, ⓔ georgesm@revolta.com)* on ulitsa Tsar Simeon 36B offers singles for 18 lv and doubles for 26 lv, all with a shared bathroom. It's open daily 8am to 8pm and is closed Sunday in winter. This is one of several accommodation agencies at the southern end of ulitsa Tsar Simeon.

Tourist Service *(☎ 225 313)* has singles from 22 lv to 26 lv and doubles for 31 lv, most with shared bathroom. It's open Monday to Friday 9am to 6pm and is in the foyer of the Hotel Odessa. The prices of rooms offered by this agency are comparatively high, but the quality of accommodation is better than most.

The accommodation agency (☎ 601 136) at the airport is rarely staffed.

The agency at the bus station offers rooms for 10 lv per person, but the rooms are normally quite basic and inconveniently located.

Hotels The choice of hotels in Varna is not great, possibly because most visitors stay at one of the nearby beach resorts. All hotels listed here offer rooms with a bathroom, unless stated otherwise.

Voennomorski Club (☎ 238 312, ul Maria Luisa 1) Doubles with shared bathroom 22 lv, singles/doubles with bathroom 22/36 lv, apartments with bathroom 55 lv. This bright-blue building opposite the cathedral offers small, sparsely furnished but clean rooms in an unbeatable location. It's a musty old place, and most rooms and apartments can be noisy, but it's excellent value.

Three Dolphins Hotel (☎ 600 911, ul Gabrovo 27) Singles 44-55 lv, doubles 55-66 lv. In a quiet area near the train station, this small, homely guesthouse is great value. All rooms have a TV, and the newer rooms are worth the extra few leva. It's a good idea to book ahead in high season. Rates include breakfast.

Hotel Santa Marina (☎ 603 826, fax 603 825, ul Baba Rada 28) Singles/doubles US$30/40, apartments US$50. This tiny, cosy place is centrally located, and good value in the mid-priced range. Rooms and apartments have a TV, fridge and air-con, and rates include breakfast. It's often full especially on summer weekends, so book ahead.

Orbita Hotel (☎ 225 162, [e] orbita@abv.com, ul Tsar Osvoboditel 25) Singles/doubles/triples US$20/32/39, newer doubles/triples US$28/40, apartments from US$40. The more expensive rooms, which have been remodelled and contain a TV and fridge, are good value. The standard rooms are large and clean, but unremarkable and overpriced. The whole place is noisy, however, and a little distant from the city centre. Rates include breakfast.

Hotel Akropolis (☎ 603 107, [e] hacropolis@abv.bg, ul Tsar Shishman 13) Singles/doubles US$27/36. This brash place looks like it has been transplanted from Sozopol beach. The modern rooms feature a TV, fridge and air-con, and it is close to many attractions, but ultimately devoid of any character and overpriced. Still, it's popular, so bookings are advisable in summer.

Hotel Odessa (☎ 228 381, fax 253 083, ul Slivnitsa 1) Singles/doubles US$36/44 with park view, US$47/54 with sea view. This three-star, four-storey hotel overlooking Primorski Park has modern, clean and comfortable rooms. Not all rooms have balconies with views, and those that do, overlook the crowded square. It's overpriced thanks to the wonderful location, but it's always popular, so book ahead in summer. Rates include breakfast.

Cherno More Hotel (☎ 223 925, fax 236 311, ul Slivnitsa 33) Singles US$20-42, doubles US$33-64. The three-star Cherno More is housed in Varna's tallest building, and has so many rooms that it has probably never been full. Compared to other places in the city centre, it's remarkably good value. The smallish rooms contain classic Balkantourist-style furniture from the 1970s, but it's quiet and all rooms offer superb views from the tiny balconies. Rates include a buffet breakfast, which is served on the top floor.

Places to Eat

Some of the best Bulgarian restaurants along the Black Sea coast can be found in Varna.

Bulgarian Restaurants *Paraklisa (☎ 223 495, bul Primorski 47)* Starters about 3.50 lv & main meals 6-9 lv. Closed Sun. In the grounds of the quaint St Prorok Iliya Church, Paraklisa is Varna's most distinctive restaurant due to its location and cuisine. The menu features old Bulgarian recipes from throughout the country, such as marvellous cheeses stewed in cognac and wine. Reservations are a must; otherwise, dine here during off-peak hours. The menu is in English.

Komplex Hâshove Soups 2-3 lv, main meals 3.50-7 lv. This complex features a cafe, bar, mehana and restaurant, and a fountain in the courtyard. It is atmospheric, and is always buzzing with well-heeled locals.

Restaurant Arkitekta (ul Musala) Salads about 1.50 lv, grills from 2.90 lv. This restaurant is based in a delightful, wooden Bulgarian national revival period house, once occupied by an architect. Although the servings are not huge, it's worth visiting for the service, and the shady, quiet setting. It offers a menu in English.

Restaurant Chuchura (pl Nezavisimost) Salads & soups about 2 lv, grills from 3.50 lv. Almost lost and forgotten behind El Taco, this restaurant, based in a national revival house, is heartily recommended. It features a menu in English, and the service is impeccable. The daily specials, costing around about 2 lv, often include the delicious Bulgarian *musaka*.

Birariya (ul Slivnitsa) Salads from 1.50 lv, grills from 3 lv. This eatery is one of the few places along this mall with sensible prices. It doesn't seem to have a name, so we've called it 'Birariya', taken from the sign (in Bulgarian) outside. The food is cheap, the beer is cold and the menu is in English and German. Look for the words 'barbeque' and 'beer' in English (two words that grabbed our attention!).

Other Restaurants *El Taco (pl Nezavisimost)* Meals from 4 lv. Next door to McDonald's, El Taco is a bit 'el tacky', but offers decent Tex-Mex fare. It's an ideal place to buy a beer during the late afternoon and watch the masses strolling aimlessly around the massive square.

Happy Bar & Grill (pl Nezavisimost) Grills about 5 lv. The Varna-based but country-wide Happy Bar & Grill chain has several restaurants in town, including at this central location. It's a cheerful place which serves tasty salads and grilled meat dishes at comparatively higher prices.

Mustang Food (two outlets: bul Vladislav Varenchik & ul Slivnitsa) Salads 2-3 lv, breakfast 3 lv, grills from 3.50 lv. Similar in style and popularity to Happy's, Mustang offers large servings of Western style meals, but at more competitive prices. There are several branches around the city: the most convenient are under the Cherno More Hotel and opposite the cathedral.

Fast Food Junk-food addicts won't suffer withdrawal symptoms while in Varna. *KFC* is near the clock tower opposite the cathedral; there's a convenient *Pizza Hut (ul Knyaz Boris I)* along the mall; and the golden arches of *McDonald's* can be found in several places – most conveniently on the corner of ulitsa Slivnitsa and ulitsa Knyaz Boris I, and at ploshtad Nezavisimost.

Trops Kâshta (ul Knyaz Boris I) Salads 1.50 lv, meals 2.50-4 lv. This chain of nationwide cafeterias is just as busy during the working week as those in Sofia and Plovdiv. It's an ideal place to enjoy a cheap, simple meal without needing to speak Bulgarian or plough through a menu in Cyrillic. Just point and pay.

BMS (ul Knyaz Boris I & ul Devnya) Salads 1.50-2 lv, meals 2.50-4 lv. The BMS offers similar choices, prices and service to Trops Kâshta. It has two convenient locations: opposite the train station, and across from St Nikolai Church.

Entertainment

Varna Opera House (☎ 602 086, pl Nezavisimost) Bulgaria's second most important opera house (after Sofia) hosts performances by the Varna Opera and Philharmonic Orchestra all year except July and August.

Storya Bachvarov Dramatic Theatre (☎ 600 779, pl Mitropolitska Simeon) Near the clock tower and at the back of KFC, this theatre hosts various cultural programs. Prices for events in Varna are, generally, considerably less than in Sofia, but the quality of performances is usually commensurately lower.

Open-Air Theatre (☎ 228 385, Primorski Park) Complete with mock, ivy-covered Roman arches, this theatre hosts anything from ballet to rock concerts. Details are available at the adjoining ticket office. Live music is also played most evenings in summer at the temporary *Summer Theatre (Primorski Park)*.

Night Club Danvi (pl Nezavisimost) One of the better late-night haunts in town is the Danvi, incongruously located under the Varna Opera House.

Mustang Cinema (bul Vladislav Varenchik) Tickets about 4 lv. Next to the Mustang Food restaurant, this is probably the most comfortable and most expensive cinema in town. Recent European and American films are also shown all year at *Festival Hall*.

Some of the best *cafes* are in Primorski Park, eg, near the entrance to the Aquarium, and around the Summer Theatre. In the city centre, try the cafes along the north-eastern end of ulitsa Knyaz Boris I and the south-eastern section of ulitsa Slivnitsa. Along the esplanade just down from the park, competition is fierce among cafes and bars, so prices of drinks (eg, 0.70 lv for a large cold 'un) and fish meals (from about 2.50 lv) are excellent value.

Shopping
The best selection of embroideries in Varna, if not all of Bulgaria, is available at stalls in the small park at the back of the cathedral. The quality is outstanding, and some genuine bargains can be found from coasters (about 3 lv) to exquisite tablecloths (about 50 lv). Quality paintings are sold outside St Nikolai Church along ulitsa Knyaz Boris I.

Getting There & Away
Air Note that all domestic and international flights to and from Varna – except those offered by Aeroflot (from Moscow) and Balkan Airlines (from Sofia) – *only* operate between about mid-April and late October.

Domestic Balkan Airlines flies up to four times a day (depending on the season) between Sofia and Varna ($52/98 one way/return). The local agency for bookings is the Varna International Airport travel agency (☎ 622 948) at ulitsa Knyaz Boris I 15.

Hemus Air (☎ 501 039) flies between Varna and Sofia every day but Sunday between mid-March and late October, and once or twice a day between 1 July and mid-September. The fare is US$55/99 one-way/return. Dandy Airlines (☎ 501 338) flies between Varna and Sofia several times a day for US$52/99 one-way/return. Bookings for

Hemus and Dandy flights can be made at the relevant offices at the airport, or at the Varna International Airport agency.

International Varna is the international gateway to the Black Sea coast in Bulgaria, so hundreds of foreigners arrive and depart each day in summer on chartered flights from all over Europe. The international section of Varna airport (☎ 650 835) is often hopelessly inadequate during peak times, so allow plenty of time to process your baggage and get through immigration.

Details of international flights to and from Varna are listed in the Getting There & Away chapter. Most international airlines have offices at the airport, including Air Via (☎ 500 274, e airvia@techno-link.com) and Bulgarian Air Charter (☎ 505 092). Aeroflot (☎ 231 082) has an office in town on ulitsa Maria Luisa.

Bus – Domestic The bus station(☎ 448 349) is on bulevard Vladislav Varenchik, about 2km north-west of the city centre. From there, public buses to Sofia (about 15 lv, seven to eight hours) leave about every 45 minutes, and travel via Shumen (4.90 lv, 1½ hours) and Veliko Târnovo (9 lv, four hours).

Most long-distance services are operated by private buses. Tickets for these can be bought at agencies in town (as well as at the bus station), but all departures are from the public bus station. Two travel agencies, ETAP Adress and Megatours, both on the ground floor of the Cherno More Hotel complex, offer several private buses to Sofia each day.

From the bus station, there are public and private buses every day to Burgas (6 lv, two hours) every 30 to 40 minutes, nine to Kavarna (3.60 lv, 1¼ hours), and eight or nine to Dobrich (3 lv, 40 minutes). Between one and three buses a day head directly to Plovdiv (12.50 lv, six hours), Gabrovo (8 lv, 4½ hours), Sliven (9 lv, three hours), Silistra (4.20 lv, 1½ hours), Stara Zagora (10 lv, five hours), Haskovo (11 lv, six hours) and Ruse (11 lv, four hours). There's also one daily bus (currently at 4pm) to Durankulak (5.50 lv, 1½ hours) on the Romanian border.

From the tiny Chatsna Mladost Station, minibuses go to smaller places along the Black Sea coast, including Dobrich (2.50 lv) every 30 minutes; Balchik (2.50 lv, one hour) every hour; Kavarna (3.50 lv) at 7am, 10am and 5pm; Burgas (6 lv) every 40 to 60 minutes; and Nesebâr (4.50 lv, 1½ hours), via Slânchev Bryag (4.50 lv, 1¼ hours) six times daily. This minibus station is about 200m along a road that starts almost opposite the public bus station; look for the sign in English opposite the bus station.

Buses from the south (eg, those from Burgas) usually drop off passengers at a convenient spot opposite the main post office on bulevard Vladislav Varenchik.

For details about buses and minibuses between Varna and the beach resorts along the northern coast, see the Getting Around section, and the relevant Getting There & Away sections later in this chapter.

Bus – International Zlatni Piasaci Travel (☎ 355 419), based at the public bus station, seems to have the monopoly on services to Turkey. It offers buses to Istanbul every day but Sunday at 10am (19 lv) and 5pm (25 lv). Inter (☎ 505 160), also based at the public bus station, has services all over Europe via Sofia.

Train The train station (☎ 630 444), along bulevard Primorski, looks impressive but is smaller than the station at Burgas and can get crowded. A computer screen in the foyer lists departures and arrivals in Bulgarian. The left-luggage office is open daily from 6am to 10pm.

Fares listed here are for 1st/2nd class. Six daily trains travel between Varna and Sofia (22.05/15.90 lv, eight to nine hours express). Of these, three fast trains and one express travel via Gorna Oryahovitsa (12.10/9.90 lv, three hours express), the main junction for Veliko Târnovo, and Pleven (15.70/11.40 lv, five hours for the fast train); one fast train travels via Plovdiv (17.70/13.00 lv, 5½ hours); and another fast train goes through Karlovo (15.90/12.10 lv, five hours).

Daily from Varna, there are also nine trains (including one express) to Shumen (7.10/5.40 lv, about two hours express); two

fast trains to Ruse (11.95/8.90 lv, four hours) via Shumen; and two slow passenger trains to Dobrich (5.85/4.50 lv, two hours).

The Rila Bureau (☎ 226 273), at ulitsa Preslav 13, sells tickets for international services and advance tickets for domestic trains. Its opening hours are Monday to Friday 8am to 6.30pm and Saturday and Sunday 8am to 3pm. For details about international trains to and from Varna, see Land in the Getting There & Away chapter.

Getting Around

The bus and train stations are on opposite sides of the city, and linked by bus Nos 1, 22 and 41. The most useful bus for visitors is No 409, which connects the airport with Zlatni Pyasâtsi (Golden Sands) every 15 minutes between 6am and 11pm. This bus passes the public bus station in Varna and Primorski Park (including the Dolphinarium), and stops near Sveti Konstantin. It can be caught at designated spots near the main post office on bulevard Vladislav Varenchik, and along ulitsa Slivnitsa.

To tee up a rental car, Hertz (☎ 500 210) and Avis (☎ 500 832) have offices at the international section of the airport. Vendor (☎ 605 111), in the foyer of Cherno More Hotel, is cheaper: it charges US$60/50/45 per day for one/two/three days, including insurance and unlimited kilometres (but not petrol). Cheaper still is the car-rental agency at Sveti Konstantin (see that section later).

The taxi drivers who congregate around the cathedral are probably the most dishonest bunch of ratbags in Bulgaria, so if they refuse to use their meter, simply get out and try another taxi. Varna is also one of the few places in the country where you should carefully check the taxi rates listed on the windows before climbing in. Newer models of taxis, and those with air-con, charge about three times more than others.

SVETI KONSTANTIN
СВЕТИ КОНСТАНТИН
☎ 052

Sveti Konstantin is a small beach resort about 9km north-east of Varna. Established in 1946 and called Druzhba (Friendship), it was later renamed Sv Konstantin & Sv Elena, but is now simply known as Sveti Konstantin. The hotels at the resort are attractively spaced out among oak, beech and pine trees. Also, Sveti Konstantin is less commercial than other resorts, and quieter because of the lack of roads and, therefore, vehicles. The downside is that the beaches are not as spectacular, but many visitors prefer to soak in the mineral baths anyway.

Orientation & Information
The centre of Sveti Konstantin is the road between the bus stop and beach which passes the post office; and the unnamed laneway (which we've called Post Office Lane) between the post office and the Grand Hotel Varna. Hotels are astoundingly badly signposted, and many signposts (in English) are ambiguous, so you may need to invest in a map (2 lv to 3 lv), available at any bookstall at the resort.

Of course, there are dozens of foreign-exchange offices, as well as the Biochim Commercial Bank along Post Office Lane. An Internet centre is on the ground floor of the International Home for Scientists (see Places to Stay later in this section).

Sv Konstantin & Sv Elena Monastery
Манастир Св. Константин и Св. Елена
This tiny church (admission free; open daylight hours except Sun morning) is just off Post Office Lane. It was built below street level in the style demanded by the Ottoman rulers during the early 18th century. The church was destroyed not long after but was rebuilt in 1912. More information about the church and the general development of Sveti Konstantin is featured in a small but fascinating display (with photos and explanations in English) on the ground floor of the International Home for Scientists.

Mineral Baths
Sveti Konstantin is popular with Bulgarians (but less so among foreigners) for the mineral springs, which apparently offer relief from various ailments and stress. Several

'health' complexes are signposted around the resort. The admission fee to a swimming pool is 2 lv, a sauna costs from 4 lv for 30 minutes, and a 30-minute massage will set you back about 10 lv. The most developed but expensive place for these activities, and other medical treatments, is the Balneocentre in Grand Hotel Varna.

Beach
The beach is serviceable without being attractive; it's more like a series of small stretches of sand bordered by jetties, breakwaters and rocky outcrops. Because of this, and the fact that the resort often attracts guests who are retired and on package tours, no water sports are available. If you want to windsurf or jet ski, head for Albena farther up the coast.

Places to Stay
The only option for anyone on a budget is a room in a private home – look for an 'accommodation office' sign (in English) around the resort. *Tourist Service Kapka 94* (☎ 361 003), near the post office, charges 18 lv per person for private rooms, and 26 lv per person for a room in a two-star hotel (most probably a fair way from the beach).

If you normally stay at hotels in the mid-priced range, it's better to do a day trip from Varna. If you want to stay here in a top-end hotel, then it's far cheaper to inquire about a package tour from your home country, or at a travel agency in Sofia. Examples of the sort of hotels on offer at the resort are listed here. There are no roads, so none of the hotels have addresses.

International Home for Scientists F Jolet Curie Singles/doubles 73/101 lv, apartments 132 lv, all with bathroom. With a name like this we had to mention it, and the complex certainly dominates the centre of the resort. It is, however, a typical leftover from the 1960s, complete with barely functioning TVs, fridges and wall-mounted clocks. The prices charged for foreigners are far too high.

Estreya Hotel (☎ 361 135, fax 361 316) Singles/doubles with bathroom 86/150 lv. This is a sparkling new place and features an immaculate garden and swimming pool in a central but secluded location, only metres up from the monastery. The comfortable rooms have a TV and fridge, and the rates include breakfast. It's open all year.

Hotel Dolphin (*☎ 361 171*) Singles/doubles US$102/170 lv June-Sept, US$93/141 Oct-May. Rates include all meals, drinks and some sports and activities. The Dolphin is a massive, new place on the waterfront, which caters almost exclusively to people on package tours. The pool is attractive, and the rooms are air-conditioned.

Grand Hotel Varna (*☎ 361 491,* e *ghv –res@mail.techno-link.com)* Singles/doubles US$138/188. The Grand Hotel is so big it has a bowling alley, casino and three swimming pools, and seems to have thousands of rooms and a couple of hundred bars. In fact, you name it, and it's probably here.

Places to Eat
The cheapest eateries are the small cafes such as **Texaco** at the bus stop, which offers half a grilled chicken for under 3 lv. Also worth trying is **Amforia**, along Post Office Lane, which charges 4.50 lv for a plate of tasty fish and vegetables.

There are masses of restaurants featuring all sorts of cuisines, from the **Delhi Restaurant** (near Grand Hotel Varna), which offers set-price four-course meals for 7 lv, to the **Ukrainian Restaurant** (in Hotel Bor). All menus at all restaurants are in English and German, and restaurant staff are likely to speak both languages.

Restaurant Zaliva Fish meals 5.20-7.50 lv. Despite the rather unfortunate name, the grilled fish is delicious and reasonably priced. The views and breezes are also an attraction. It's at the end of the road that passes Grand Hotel Varna towards the beach.

Bulgarska Svatba Meals about 5 lv. One of the few places that actually offers Bulgarian cuisine is the Bulgarska Svatba, housed in a traditional building just over the road from Hotel Plaza.

Getting There & Away
Bus No 409 travels from Varna airport to Zlatni Pyasâtsi every 15 minutes between 6am and 11pm. It stops outside the Hotel Panorama at Sveti Konstantin, along the road between Varna and Zlatni Pyasâtsi, from where it's a short walk down to the hotels and beach. From along the laneway down from the Panorama, turn right at the first road towards the bus stop and then left down to the beach. Also, every 15 to 20 minutes between 6am and 11pm, bus No 8 goes directly to Sveti Konstantin, via ulitsa Maria Luisa, ulitsa Slivnitsa and the north-eastern end of ulitsa Knyaz Boris I in Varna. One convenient bus stop in Varna is near Mustang Food along bulevard Vladislav Varenchik (see Varna earlier in this chapter).

Getting Around
Budget (*☎ 361 491)* car rental has a counter in the foyer of Grand Hotel Varna. Tourist Service Kapka 94 (see Places to Stay earlier in this section) offers cars for an all-inclusive fee of US$35 per day (plus petrol), which is cheaper than anywhere in or near Varna.

ZLATNI PYASÂTSI (GOLDEN SANDS)
ЗЛАТНИ ПЯСЬЦИ
☎ 052
Zlatni Pyasâtsi (also called Golden Sands) is 18km north-east of Varna, and is Bulgaria's second-largest coastal resort. Some 60 hotels and villas, with nearly 15,000 beds, are clustered along the 4km stretch of sandy beach, or hidden among the trees. Most hotels don't actually offer genuine sea frontage, unlike those in Slânchev Bryag, but the resort is so narrow that most hotels are less than 300m from the beach anyway. Golden Sands may be a corny name, but it's certainly apt. In fact, the area has been given similar names for centuries because of the quality of the beach.

Orientation & Information
Driving a private car into the resort costs 3 lv per vehicle, but visitors arriving by private/public bus or taxi do not have to pay any entrance fees. The resort is long, thin and easy to get around, but there's plenty of helpful signs in English. Several maps are available at bookstalls; the best is *Nessebur*

& *Sunny Beach City Guide*, published by Makros, and printed in English and German (with a distinctive yellow-and-blue cover). The post office and telephone centre are near Hotel Yavor, about halfway along the resort, and there is an Internet centre a few metres up from the post office.

Aladzha Monastery
Аладжа Манастир

Understandably, a major local attraction is the Aladzha Monastery (☎ *355 460; admission 2 lv & use of video camera 15 lv; open Tues-Sun 9am-6pm in summer & 9am-4pm Tues-Sat in winter*). Very little is known about this bizarre rock monastery, and reports about its history vary considerably. The cave was probably inhabited during the 5th century BC, but what remains today was probably created during the height of the Ottoman occupation (13th and 14th centuries), when normal churches and monasteries could not be built. The monastery was used by monks from the Hesychast order until the 18th century, but was not discovered again until 1928.

Several sets of stairs and walkways lead to and around these astonishing caves, which were carved up to 40m above ground. Erosion has undoubtedly caused a lot of damage to the caves, including to the extensive murals inside the monastery, but it's still quite a remarkable place. A signposted path (600m) leads to the **Catacombs**, a set of tri-level caves that were probably created in the 13th century. The second level was probably used for burials, but the exact purpose of the other two caves is unknown.

Everything at the monastery is signposted and labelled in English, but the small booklet, written in English and French and available inside the grounds, contains more explanations and makes a nice souvenir. The **museum** also provides some detailed explanations (in English, French and German) about the use and excavations of the monastery. Apparently to fill up space, some unrelated art is displayed on the second floor of the museum.

To walk to the monastery from the resort, head up the road past the post office, cross the main Varna-Albena road outside the Economic & Investment Bank, and follow the signs to 'Kloster Aladja' and the markings along the obvious trail. The walk takes 50 to 60 minutes one way, and wends its way through a wonderful, shady forest, part of the 1320-hectare **Golden Sands Nature Park**, which hinders any expansion of the resort into the hills.

The road (3km) is steepish in parts, and starts about 500m south along the Varna-Albena road from the start of the walking trail. A good idea is to take a taxi to the monastery (about 2 lv) and walk back down to the resort through the forest. Bus No 33 from the public bus station in Varna to Kranevo drops passengers outside the front entrance of the monastery, but only runs in both directions four or five times a day.

Activities

Most of the agencies in Zlatni Pyasâtsi that once offered water sports have moved to Albena, the self-titled 'sports centre of Bulgaria'. If any outfit decides to set up a water sports centre in Zlatni Pyasâtsi in the future, it will almost certainly do so along the beach near the unmissable International Grand Hotel. This part of the beach is the location of the **Water Sports Centre**, which offers **jet skiing** (*40 lv for 15 minutes*) and **parasailing** (*40 lv for 15 minutes*).

The **Equestrian Picnic Riding School** offers all sorts of equine activities, such as 'advanced' **riding** (*40/50 lv per one/two hours*) and shorter rides (in distance) for beginners (*about 30/45 lv per two/three hours*). The school is signposted about 1km up the Varna-Albena road from the southern entrance to the resort.

Water from the **mineral springs** in the area apparently cures stress, rheumatism, arthritis and various respiratory ailments. Most major hotels offer all sorts of **massages** (*from 12/20 lv per 20/40 minutes*), as well as **mineral baths** (*25 lv per 30 minutes*), and a confusing array of 'health treatments'. The main centre of activity is the Balneocentre at Ambassador Hotel.

Kiddies will delight in the children's **entertainment centre**, with paddle pools, toy trains and water slides, which is just near Hotel Sirena.

Organised Tours

Dozens of agencies and stalls along the esplanade sell tours such as three-hour yacht rides (30 lv per person including lunch), and bus trips to Nesebâr (25 lv), Balchik (12 lv), and Kaliakra Cape (20 lv), including a stop in Balchik.

Places to Stay

Almost every visitor to Zlatni Pyasâtsi will be on a package tour (with prebooked accommodation) from overseas or, perhaps, Sofia; or be on a day trip from Varna or elsewhere along the Black Sea coast. Consequently, there's little point recommending any particular hotel, and most places simply don't offer rates that are acceptable to individual travellers anyway.

If you want to stay here, but have not prebooked any accommodation, visit the accommodation office (☎ 355 683), which is open daily 9am to 6pm, next to the Economic & Investment Bank along the Varna-Albena road. It offers *rooms* in two-star hotels (no doubt, a reasonable walk from the beach) for 33/26 lv per person in high/low season, including breakfast.

Hotel Rodina (☎ 355 252, fax 355 587) Singles/doubles with bathroom 70/85 lv. The Rodina is a modern, three-star place. It's convenient to the beach and the resort's better restaurants and shops. It has good service, and the rates (which include breakfast) are comparatively reasonable.

International Grand Hotel (☎ 357 182, fax 357 190) Singles/doubles US$155/180. At the other end of the spectrum, this monstrous glass edifice in the centre of the resort offers the sort of five-star luxuries you would expect – and certainly hope for – at these staggering prices.

Places to Eat

Food and drink in Zlatni Pyasâtsi costs about twice as much as in Varna, but prices are not quite as outrageous as in Albena. Naturally, the plethora of restaurants, cafes, bars and fast-food joints offer the usual array of Western food as well as Chinese and Indian cuisine. For something different, try the *Georgian Restaurant*, opposite the Hotel Rodina.

Vodenitsata Starters 2.50-3.50 lv, main meals from 5.50 lv. This charming place serves traditional Bulgarian meals in a shady courtyard setting, and features live folkloric music most evenings. It's along the road between the post office and the accommodation office (see Places to Stay earlier).

Tsiganski Tabor Most meals 5.20-6.50 lv. Although catering more to the tourists hurtling along the Varna-Albena road, this inviting place, with classic Bulgarian fare, is nevertheless worth the short walk up from Hotel Trapezitsa.

Getting There & Away

There are many entrances to the resort, but the most frequently used ones are in the far south, near the Riviera Hotel complex; at the start of the road to Aladzha Monastery; at the accommodation office and Economic & Investment Bank 500m farther north; and outside the Hotel Zora in the far north.

Bus Nos 109, 209, 309 and 409 leave Varna every 10 or 15 minutes between 6am and 11pm. The buses stop along the main Varna-Albena road at each main entrance to Zlatni Pyasâtsi, from where it's no more than a 10-minute walk to any major hotel or the beach. Bus No 9 from Varna stops at the southern entrance only, while No 409 goes all the way to the Varna airport. These buses can be caught along ulitsa Maria Luisa, ulitsa Slivnitsa and the north-eastern end of ulitsa Knyaz Boris I in Varna; one convenient bus stop is near the Mustang Food restaurant along bulevard Vladislav Varenchik (see Varna earlier in this chapter).

Getting Around

If you're not keen on walking, there are several options: hire a bicycle from outside Hotel Rodina for 5/9 lv (one/two hours) or 25 lv (all day); take a trolleybus (1.50 lv) along the esplanade; or jump into one of the (few) cute 'solar taxis', which charge about 5 lv for a trip anywhere within the resort. Avis car rental (☎ 500 832, Hotel Rodina) charges from US$70 per day, including 200 free kilometres and insurance, plus petrol.

ALBENA
АЛБЕНА
☎ 0579

While Zlatni Pyasâtsi probably has a livelier nightlife, Albena's more casual feel makes it appealing to a younger fun-loving crowd. The beach is about 4km long, up to 100m wide, and stunning. The water is shallow up to 150m offshore, and ideal for the abundance of water sports on offer. The downside is the horrendous prices charged for just about everything – this is certainly the most expensive place in Bulgaria. Opened in 1969, Albena is named after the beautiful heroine from the play of the same name written by Bulgarian playwright and author, Yordan Yovkov.

Orientation & Information

Albena is the most organised resort in Bulgaria, so there's plenty of maps along the streets and multilingual staff at tourist booths. The accommodation office (see Places to Stay later in this section) at the bus station is not a tourist office, but the helpful multilingual staff can answer basic questions. Of course, dozens of foreign-exchange offices all over Albena will be able to change money, and most offer competitive rates. Along the main road, both the Biochim Commercial Bank, and the SC Express Bank at the administration building opposite the post office, change travellers cheques and offer cash advances on major credit cards. The post office has an Internet centre and plenty of telephones for long-distance calls. Most of the better shops are lined along the unnamed laneway between the Dobrudja and Dorostol hotels.

Entry to the resort by private car costs 2 lv; admission is free for anyone travelling by taxi or private/public bus or minibus.

Cultural Centre

The Cultural Centre in the middle of the resort is a token effort at offering something that isn't so hedonistic. The centre hosts regular **concerts** *(tickets about 15 lv)* of Bulgarian music and dance. Posters on the front door of the centre, and elsewhere around the resort, advertise upcoming programs. The centre also houses an **Archaeological Museum** *(admission 3 lv; open daily 9am-8pm)* which is, frankly, pathetic, and set up entirely for oblivious tourists. Don't forget that the best archaeological museum in the country is a short trip down the road in Varna.

Activities

Albena promotes itself as a 'sports resort' and the 'sports capital of Bulgaria'. It certainly does offer the best range of activities in the country, and adventurous and sporty types will find enough to satisfy their needs – and to empty their wallets. Prices are probably lower than most places in Europe, but *very* expensive compared to the cost of almost everything else in Bulgaria.

The **Borian Yacht Club** in the northern part of the resort offers **windsurfing** and **waterskiing** courses over six days for 150 lv and 180 lv, respectively. Also available at the club are **jet skiing** *(35 lv per 15 minutes)*, **yacht rides** *(30/50 lv per one/four hours)* and **fishing trips** *(30/50 lv per three/five hours)*.

Tennis is a popular pastime and is offered at a dozen or more courts all over the resort. Court hire is about 15/18 lv per hour (daytime/evening), and coaching costs from 20 lv per hour. Equipment costs extra, and the tennis complexes can even find you a partner to play with (for a supplementary fee).

The more adventurous can enjoy a **microlight rides** *(45 lv for eight to 10 minutes)* at a runway just past the Arabela restaurant in the far north. **Parasailing** is available at several places along the beach (look for the parachutes in the air) for about the same price. The best place for all types of water sports is along the beach opposite the signposted (in English) 'bazar' in front of Hotel Kardam. Several stalls here offer **jet skiing** *(40 lv per 15 minutes)*, **parasailing** *(40 lv per 10 minutes)*, **surfing** *(board hire 15/50 lv per hour/day)*, **water skiing** *(20 lv per 10 minutes)* and **windsurfing** *(12 lv per hour)*.

Konna Baza Riding Club *(mobile ☎ 048-776 056)*, along the main road, offers equestrian activities, including 50-minute walks

(18 lv per person), advanced rides for 40/50/70 lv (one/two/three hours), training for 150 lv (12 hours) and basic rides for 30/45/60/75 lv (two/three/four/five hours).

Albena boasts the largest number of mineral springs in Bulgaria. The **medical centre** *(☎ 62 305,* e *mcalbena@mbox.digsys .bg, Hotel Dobrudja)* is the country's largest therapy centre. It offers all sorts of **massages** *(45 lv for the 'works')* and **therapies** (eg, aromatherapy and hydrotherapy) for about 50 lv per hour.

Organised Tours
Most hotels and travel agencies around Albena can organise all sort of tacky tours, such as seeing a 'Bulgarian wedding' (not a real one!) for 120 lv per person, including food and drinks. Perhaps more enlightening are the bus trips to Varna (29 lv, or 35 lv including the Dolphinarium), and both Balchik and Kaliakra Cape (40 lv).

Places to Stay
The Accommodation Office (☎ 62 920) is an agency that can organise singles from 54 lv to 135 lv and doubles from 70 lv to 210 lv. It is open daily from 8am to noon and is at the bus station. It only offers *hotel rooms* (ie, not rooms in private homes), but the cheaper rooms are likely to be far closer to the main road than the beach. All rates include breakfast. If you want a private room, look for the relevant signs in English, German and Bulgarian outside homes along the main Varna-Balchik road.

Camping *Gorska Fey (☎ 62 961)* Camping 8 lv per site, bungalows with bathroom 80 lv, A-frame bungalows 220 lv. Also known as Albena Camping, this camping ground is spread out through the forest just behind the bus station. It's a lovely, shady place; a little remote, perhaps, but regularly connected to the beach and restaurants by trolleybus. The A-frame bungalows are large, luxurious, and feature four beds and a TV, fridge and veranda. The other type of bungalows (also with four beds) are not cheap compared to those in the rest of Bulgaria, but they're bargains for Albena.

Hotels Almost everyone visiting Albena will be on an organised tour (with accommodation included) or on a day trip from Varna or elsewhere. Consequently, there's little need to recommend any particular hotel, and most decent places do not offer rates which are acceptable to individual travellers anyway. Rates for the two hotels mentioned here will give you some idea of what to expect.

Hotel Dobrudja (☎ 62 501, e *dobrudja@ al.bia-bg.com)* Singles/doubles 130/190 lv. This four-star hotel offers all the usual amenities (including breakfast) in a central location. It's the only place in Albena likely to stay open in winter.

Hotel Kardam (☎ 62 368) Singles/doubles 80/120 lv July-Aug, 65/100 lv May-June & Sept-Oct. One of several three-star places close to the beach and shops, the Kardam is cheaper and cosier than most others. Rates include breakfast.

Places to Eat
At last count, Albena had over 120 places to eat. Food and drink in the resort costs about two or three times more than in Varna. If money does matter, check the menu (always with English and German translations) before sitting down. Typically, an omelette will cost 4-5 lv; small/large pizzas 7/10 lv; grills with garnishes 10-12 lv; a small bottle of local/imported beer 2/4 lv; and a cup of tea 2 lv.

Slavyanski Kut Meals about 12 lv. This large complex in the southern section of the resort is one of the few places that offers Bulgarian cuisine, as well as folkloric performances most evenings.

Starobulgarski Stan Meals 10-12.50 lv. Along the road between the bus station and the Cultural Centre, this classy place also offers tasty traditional dishes.

Arabela Starters 6-7 lv, main meals from 9.50 lv. For something different, try this unmissable restaurant, which is inside an old sailing ship along the far northern beach.

Kafe Kiz (Cultural Centre) Snacks from 3 lv. This is one of the few places that we can recommend for snacks (eg, pizzas and sandwiches) and drinks at acceptable prices.

On the Black Sea coast, fishing boats line the western port in the tourist town of Sozopol.

The imposing 19th-century Cathedral of the Assumption of the Virgin in Varna.

Sozopol's long Town Beach is a very popular spot in the summer months.

Ruse Theatre on Svoboda square, Ruse.

Monument to freedom at Svoboda square.

The ancient Stambul Kapiya Turkish gate on the main Bdintsi square of Vidin.

PAUL GREENWAY

PAUL GREENWAY

PAUL GREENWAY

Getting There & Away
The well-organised bus station (☎ 62 860) in Albena is about 800m from the beach, and connected to the hotels and beach by trolleybus. Minibuses from Varna (2.50 lv, 45 minutes) via Zlatni Pyasâtsi (2 lv, 20 minutes) depart every 30 minutes between 8am and 7.30pm from a spot known as Makedonia Dom (see the Varna map earlier in this section). Also between about 8am and 7.30pm, minibuses leave from Albena for Balchik (1.20 lv, 20 minutes) every 15 minutes, and to Dobrich (3 lv, 45 minutes) every 30 to 60 minutes. Three or four buses a day travel between Sofia (16/18 lv, eight hours) and Albena.

Getting Around
Trolleybuses (1.50 lv) putter along two set routes every 20 minutes between 9am and midnight. Other ways to get around include horse and cart at *very* negotiable rates; bicycles, which are available for rent outside the 'bazar' and Slavyanska Hotel for 5/9 lv (one/two hours) and 20 lv (all day); motor scooters, which cost 15/25 lv (one/two hours) and 50 lv (all day); and, even, rollerblades for 5/9 lv (one/two hours).

Albena Rent a Car (☎/fax 62 010) at Hotel Dobrudja charges 65 lv per day (one to three days), or 45 lv per day for more than one week, including unlimited kilometres and insurance, but excluding petrol.

Plenty of predatory taxi drivers line the main roads, and need plenty of persuasion to use their meters.

BALCHIK
БАЛЧИК
☎ 0579 • pop 13,760
Balchik is a picturesque old town huddled below weathered white chalk bluffs. Steep cobblestone streets and whitewashed, red-tile roofed houses hug the terraces and ravines that lend the town its distinctive skyline. The locals are refreshingly open and friendly, a relief after the contrived atmosphere of the purpose-built resorts. The major attraction is unquestionably the magnificent palace. The downside is that Balchik has no beach at all, only a bit of

token transplanted sand below the palace complex; the rest of the waterfront consists of rocks and breakwaters.

Although it's an easy day trip from Varna, Balchik is ideally suited as a cheap base from which to explore attractions in the countryside, such as Dobrich (see the Northern Bulgarian chapter) and Kaliakra Cape (see that section later in this chapter), as well as the beach resorts to the south.

History
Greek traders who settled here in the 6th century BC initially called the place Kruni (which sort of means 'town of 100 springs'), but later changed the name to Dionissopolis in honour of the God of Wine. Centuries later, the Romans used the town to defend their northern empire. The poet Ovidius, exiled here by Augustus Caesar, wrote of Balchik: 'Hail, whitestone city and thy unique beauty'. The town was rebuilt on higher ground in the 6th century AD after being destroyed by a tidal wave. In medieval times, Balchik (from the name of a local ruler, Balik) thrived on the export of grain from the hinterlands. In 1913, Balchik (and the rest of the region) was annexed by Romania, before it was literally sold back to Bulgaria in 1940 for 7000 'golden leva'.

Information
The quaint and colourful *Sea Telegraph* newsletter (2 lv), available at Balchik Hotel, provides a potted history of the town in English, French and German. Balchik is not set up for tourism, so there are few places to change money, (try some larger shops and hotels) and there's no Internet centre. The post office and telephone centre are at the main square on ploshtad Nezavisimost.

Summer Palace of Queen Marie & Botanical Gardens
The main reason to visit Balchik is this magnificent palace (☎ 72 559; admission 4 lv; open daily 8am-6pm). It was built in 1924–26 by King Ferdinand of Romania because his wife, the UK-born Queen Marie, requested a place of solitude. (Balchik was then part of Romania.) She understandably

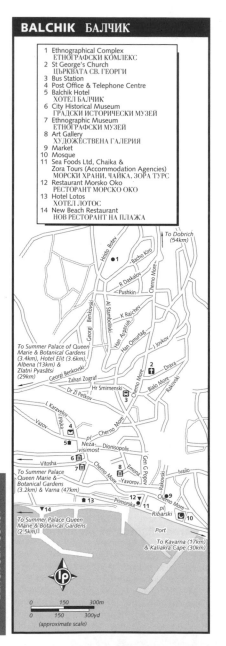

BALCHIK БАЛЧИК

1 Ethnographical Complex
ЕТНОГРАФСКИ КОМПЛЕКС
2 St George's Church
ЦЪРКВАТА СВ. ГЕОРГИ
3 Bus Station
4 Post Office & Telephone Centre
5 Balchik Hotel
ХОТЕЛ БАЛЧИК
6 City Historical Museum
ГРАДСКИ ИСТОРИЧЕСКИ МУЗЕЙ
7 Ethnographic Museum
ЕТНОГРАФСКИ МУЗЕЙ
8 Art Gallery
ХУДОЖЕСТВЕНА ГАЛЕРИЯ
9 Market
10 Mosque
11 Sea Foods Ltd, Chaika &
Zora Tours (Accommodation Agencies)
МОРСКИ ХРАНИ, ЧАЙКА, ЗОРА ТУРС
12 Restaurant Morsko Oko
РЕСТОРАНТ МОРСКО ОКО
13 Hotel Lotos
ХОТЕЛ ЛОТОС
14 New Beach Restaurant
НОВ РЕСТОРАНТ НА ПЛАЖА

called it 'The Quiet Nest', though the regular bus loads of visitors these days ensure that it's not so tranquil.

The 35-hectare complex is a glorious collection of laneways, many lined with water mills. One laneway leads over the Venetian-styled **Bridge of Sighs** and down to the elegant palace, often called the **Quiet Nest Villa**. The palace, which overlooks the sea, is deliberately designed in styles reminiscent of the Islamic architecture (note the minaret) and the Bulgarian national revival period.

The surrounding **botanical gardens** took over five years to complete during the 1950s and, in summer, they are a riot of colour with rose beds and Mediterranean plants. In all, about 600 different species of flora are featured, including the second-largest collection of cacti in Europe at Allah's Garden. An **arts festival** takes place in the gardens each year in early June.

The palace and gardens can get crowded at times, but if you visit before 10am or after 4.30pm you may have much of the complex to yourself. At the main entrance, it's worth buying a booklet (3 lv; in French, German and English), which provides a more helpful map and list of explanations than any of the captions and signs inside the complex.

If you're travelling to the complex by bus from the southern coast, get off at the obvious bus stop opposite the palace – either look for the hotels and tour buses, or ask the driver to drop you off at the *dvorets* (palace). Then walk down the access road, enter the palace at the main entrance, visit the complex, exit at the beach (where there's another entrance), and stroll 3km into town along the waterfront.

Art Galleries & Museums

Each place listed in this section is open Monday to Friday from 8am to noon and about 1pm to 5pm, though the hours at the Ethnographical Complex are less reliable. Admission to each is 2 lv.

The **Art Gallery** (☎ 74 130) is in the white building, on the right off ulitsa Cherno More if you're heading uphill from the port. There are two floors of modern local and foreign art, but the primary attraction is the statue of Dionis after whom the town was once named.

Farther up ulitsa Cherno More is the **City Historical Museum** (☎ 72 177, pl Nezavisimost). It contains a small but diverse collection ranging from fossilised mammoth bones to WWII memorabilia. Check the Thracian carriage and the model of the Roman tomb discovered nearby in 1907.

Opposite the Historical Museum is the **Ethnographic Museum** (☎ 72 177, ul Vitosha 3). In an old wooden house built in 1860, it features a limited but varied number of authentic costumes, and displays about traditional trades and crafts such as fishing and woodcarving.

The **Ethnographical Complex** (☎ 72 177, ul Hristo Botev 4), also known as the Bulgarian National Revival Complex, houses a few unremarkable displays about local folklore and education. From the bus station, walk up ulitsa Cherno More for 20 minutes and look out for the clock tower in the grounds. If you're near the port, take a taxi (about 1.50 lv), because it's a steepish walk.

Places to Stay
Three accommodation agencies, all in the same building opposite the port, offer *rooms* in private homes for about 11 lv to 13 lv per person in summer, and 9 lv to 11 lv per person in the off-season: Sea Foods Ltd (☎ 72 531, e sea-foods@hotmail.com); Chaika (☎ 73 775, e chaika@mail.bg); and Zora Tours (☎ 72 732, e zora–tour@abv.bg).

Balchik Hotel (☎ 72 809, fax 72 862) Singles/doubles with bathroom 22/27 lv May-Sept, 15/18 lv in Oct-Apr. The Balchik fronts a quiet park near the main square. Although a Balkantourist style leftover from the 1960s, the big, clean rooms feature a balcony, and are excellent value. Rates include breakfast. Look for signs (in English) opposite the post office at ploshtad Nezavisimost.

Hotel Elit (☎ 75 006, fax 74 197) Doubles with bathroom 20 lv May-Sept, 11 lv Oct-Apr. The Elit is a well-maintained, former government residence in a wooded area about 200m from the main entrance to the palace. It offers clean, comfortable rooms with a TV, fridge and balcony, and is good

value. Rates include breakfast, and guests can pre-order lunch and dinner for an extra 7 lv per person. The cheap *restaurant* is also open to the public.

Hotel Lotos (☎/fax 72 195) Singles/doubles with bathroom 62/77 lv. The Lotos is one of several unremarkable three-star hotels with TV, fridge, air-con and breakfast along the 'beach' – well, at least it has some breezes and views.

Places to Eat
The western waterfront between the port and palace is lined with humble *eateries* serving fish fillets and kebabs with chips. In the same area are new but mostly empty hotel-cum-restaurants replete with fancy outdoor swimming pools and waterslides, such as the *New Beach Restaurant*. Popular among locals is *Restaurant Morsko Oko*, just up from the port area.

Getting There & Away
In summer, minibuses travel from Balchik to Albena (1.20 lv, 20 minutes) about every 15 minutes; to Varna (2.50 lv, one hour) about every hour; and to Dobrich (2.40 lv, 45 minutes) every 30 minutes. There are also four buses a day to Kavarna (1.70 lv, 30 minutes), and three or four to Sofia (19 to 20 lv, 10 hours). The bus station (☎ 74 069) is a steep walk of about 1km up ulitsa Cherno More from the port.

KAVARNA
КАВАРНА
☎ 0570 • pop 15,000
Kavarna, 17km east of Balchik, is an unappealing administrative town with a small nearby port, but it may be useful for anyone wishing to explore the Kaliakra Cape (see that section later in this chapter).

The town has several places to visit, including the small **History Museum** (☎ 82 150, ul Chirakman 1), which is in an old mosque and includes several Thracian artefacts from the region; the rarely open **Ethnographical Revival Complex** (☎ 85 017, ul Sava Ganchev 18); and the **Art Gallery** (☎ 84 235, ul Aheloi 1), where most works have been inspired by the Black Sea coast.

The Legend of Kaliakra

According to a local myth, a group of 40 beautiful young women tied their long hair together and, holding hands, threw themselves off a cliff along the Kaliakra Cape in the 14th century. They did this to avoid a life of slavery, dishonour or worse under the Turks who were advancing to Kavarna. Some displays about this legend are in Kavarna's History Museum, and a monument along the Kaliakra Cape is dedicated to the women.

Camping is possible at *Morska Zvezda*, where tiny bungalows cost about 15 lv per person, and overpriced singles/doubles with a bathroom cost 40/45 lv, including breakfast. The best of a poor choice of hotels is *Hotel Dobrotitsa (ul Chernomorska 22)*, which charges 55/77 lv for singles/doubles with a bathroom.

Every day, there are four buses to Balchik (1.70 lv, 30 minutes), one bus every 30 to 60 minutes to Dobrich (3.50 lv, one hour), and a dozen buses to Varna (about 3.60 lv, 1¼ hours). Minibuses regularly travel to Bâlgarevo, Rusalka and Shabla, but public transport is infrequent anywhere else farther north.

KALIAKRA CAPE
НОС КАЛУАКРА

Kaliakra (Beautiful) Cape is a pronounced 2km-long headland (the longest along the Bulgarian coastline), about 13km south-east of Kavarna. Together with Balchik, it is a popular day trip by boat and/or bus for folks staying at the southern beach resorts.

Most of the cape is part of the 687-hectare **Kaliakra Nature Reserve** *(admission 3 lv; open 24 hours)*, the only reserve in Bulgaria that partially protects the Black Sea (up to 500m offshore). The reserve also protects fragile wetlands at **Bolata** and **Taukliman** (Bay of Birds); about 100 remote **caves**; and over 300 species of **birds**. Most of the year, the official lookouts along the cape and near Rusalka are ideal spots to watch numbers of increasingly rare dolphins and seals.

Also in the reserve are the ruins of an 8th-century **citadel**, with remnants of baths, churches and various tombs. The history of the area is explained in some detail at the **Archaeological Museum** *(admission free; open daily 10am-6pm)*, wonderfully located inside a cave (look for signs to the museum).

Anyone visiting the reserve must firstly go to the **Nature Information Centre** *(☎ 05744-424)* in Bâlgarevo village, about halfway between Kavarna and Kaliakra Cape. Set up with the aid of the Bulgarian-Swiss Biodiversity Conservation Programme, the centre features a modest but well-intentioned display (in English) about the flora, fauna and marine life of the Black Sea. Kartografia's *Northern Black Sea Coast* map provides essential details about the reserve and its attractions.

Public transport from Kavarna does not reliably go any further than Bâlgarevo. So, the best way to visit is by private car, rented vehicle (from Varna or one of the beach resorts), or taxi from Kavarna.

Northern Bulgaria

Probably the most ignored region of Bulgaria is between the central Stara Planina ranges and the Danube River. Even those travelling overland between Romania and Bulgaria often rush through the region without exploring it. Though public transport is less frequent in some of the northern areas it's worth the effort of visiting. If you want to admire the Danube in its glory from a riverside cafe, you may be disappointed, however. Few major towns are actually built along the Bulgarian side of the Danube because of perpetual flooding hundreds of years ago. The river is also polluted and unattractively shallow in summer. Only Vidin and Silistra can boast any scenic riverside settings and only Silistra offers boat tours.

Northern Bulgaria can be divided into four areas for the purposes of exploration. The region between Vratsa and Vidin includes several remote monasteries that are best explored by private car. Historical Pleven is home to several war memorials and museums. Ruse is the major gateway to Romania and a base for trips to the cave monasteries and ruins in the nearby Rusenski Lom National Park. The charming town of Dobrich is ideal for visiting the northern coast of the Black Sea.

CHEREPISH MONASTERY
ЧЕРЕПИШСКИ МАНАСТИР

The Cherepish Monastery *(admission free; always open)* was originally built in the 14th century. It has been razed and rebuilt several times since and is considerably smaller than it used to be. Like many other monasteries in the area, it was used by rebels as a hiding place before and during the Russian-Turkish War (1877–78).

The attached **museum** offers little more than a few religious icons and books (in Bulgarian) for sale. At the time of research, a block of basic *guest rooms* (with shared bathroom) was being built. According to the monks, accommodation will cost as little as 3 lv per person.

Highlights

- Potter around the cobblestone streets at the Stariyat Dobrich Ethnological Museum Complex and watch artisans at work
- Watch locals stroll by while sipping a drink alongside the magnificent ploshtad Svoboda in Ruse
- Admire the serene Lopushanski Monastery and eat or stay at the guesthouse in the grounds
- Visit the remarkable cave monastery and ancient ruins in the Rusenski Lom National Park
- Stroll around the majestic Belogradchik Fortress overlooking the pretty village and unique rock formations
- Clamber around the riverside Baba Vida Museum-Fortress in Vidin, the best preserved medieval stone fortress in Bulgaria

The poorly signposted monastery is about 600m down from the roadside restaurant of the same name along the road from Mezdra to Zverino. If driving from Sofia, consider taking the scenic, but slower, road through the stunning **Iskâr**

NORTHERN BULGARIA

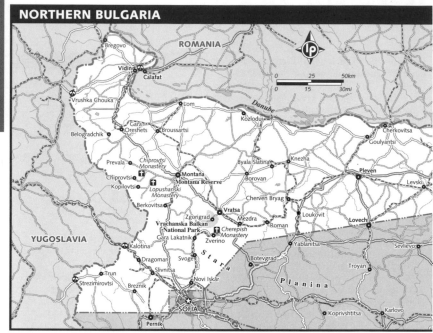

Gorge, via Novi Iskâr. By bus from Sofia, catch anything heading towards Mezdra, Vratsa, Montana or Vidin. Disembark at the turn-off to Zverino and wait for a connecting minibus or head west for about 6km.

VRATSA
ВРАЦА

☎ 092 • pop 78,900

Vratsa is a likeable, mid-sized town 116km north of Sofia. It's worth visiting for the spectacular setting under the nearby Vrachanska Mountains, which are part of the Vrachanska Balkan National Park (see that section later in this chapter) and for the couple of decent museums in the town centre. Vratsa is also a more pleasant and useful base than Montana for visiting nearby villages and monasteries.

Orientation & Information

The town centre is typical: the large, and mostly empty, ploshtad Hristo Botev is dominated by a grotesque statue of Botev (see the boxed text 'Hristo Botev') and surrounded by ugly concrete buildings. Most locals prefer to congregate around the cafes and shops lining the main pedestrian mall called (you guessed it) ulitsa Hristo Botev. This thoroughfare heads east from the square and finishes at the market near the train station. The banks along ulitsa Hristo Botev will change money, as will a few foreign-exchange offices at the market.

Historical Museum

The museum (☎ 20 373, pl Hristo Botev; admission 5 lv; open Tues-Sun 8am-noon & 2pm-6pm) is sometimes known as the 'Archaeological Museum'. It houses impressive displays of coins and jewellery from the Thracian periods, artefacts from nearby Neolithic dwellings and historical items relating to Macedonia. Like most museums, however, the complete lack of captions in any language other than Bulgarian is

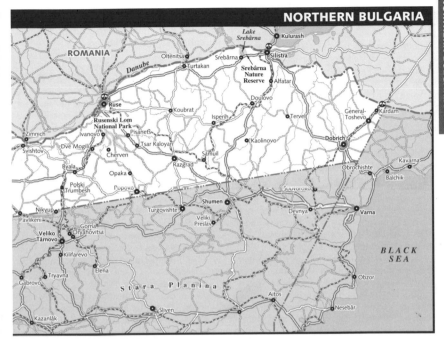

NORTHERN BULGARIA

frustrating, especially given the high admission fee for foreigners. The antiquated guidebook for 2 lv, written in French, may help explain some of the displays. The museum is behind the 16th-century **tower** to the left (west) of Hotel Bolid (see Places to Stay & Eat later in this section) as you face it.

Ethnographic Complex

Confusingly, this place is also called the Regional Historical Museum with Art Gallery (☎ 20 209, ul Gen Leonov; admission 5 lv; open Tues-Sun 8am-noon & 2pm-6pm). Several structures are built in the styles reminiscent of the Bulgarian national revival and British Tudor periods. They contain the usual array of traditional costumes, as well as displays, among other things, about the author and musician, Diko Iliev. Don't forget to pop into the **Museum of Carriages** at the back of the complex, where several fascinating buggies and carts lie idle. Your ticket is valid for entrance here as well.

It costs nothing to wander around the museum **gardens** and the adjacent **St Sofronni Vrachanski Church** (ul Gen Leonov; open daily 8am-7pm). From ploshtad Hristo Botev, head down the mall to ulitsa Hristo Botev and turn right along the cobblestone lane of ulitsa Gen Leonov.

Hiking

The charming hills to the south-west of the main square are ideal for short hikes, eg, the obvious tiny **church** perched on the hill top is easily accessible along stone steps through the forest. Only about 1km from the Tourist Hotel (see Places to Stay & Eat) along the road to the Ledenika Cave is a scenic area where locals enjoy **picnicking**, **hiking** (trails marked in Cyrillic) and watching suicidal amateur **rock climbers**.

Places to Stay & Eat

There is no official camp site in the vicinity but discreet unofficial *camping* is possible

Hristo Botev

The most revered person in Vratsa is unquestionably Hristo Botev (1848–76), a rebellious teacher, poet and newspaper publisher. He later became a leader of an insurgent gang who fought against Ottoman occupation while hiding in the Vrachanska Mountains, near Vratsa. At the age of 28, Botev and several of his men were captured and killed by the Turks. Botev's deeds are commemorated on 2 June each year with a ceremony in the Vrachanska mountains and in the Vratsa town square that bears his name.

anywhere in the hills and picnic areas mentioned in the previous Hiking section and in the Vrachanska Balkan National Park (see that section later in this chapter).

Tourist Hotel (☎ 61 528, ul Leva River) Singles/doubles/triples with bathroom 20/40/60 lv, apartments for 4 people 66 lv. The rooms are clean and comfortable and most have balconies (though some overlook the busy main road). TV costs an extra 5 lv per night and breakfast an extra 3 lv per person for the hotel rooms. TV and breakfast are included in the rates for the apartments. The hotel is along the road to Ledenika Cave, about 300m past the Historical Museum.

Hotel Bolid (☎ 61 649, pl Hristo Botev) Doubles with bathroom 32 lv. The unmissable Bolid faces the main square. It's charmless and not particularly good value for foreigners but is convenient and the friendly staff speak English. The elegant **dining room** (open to the public) lacks the setting and ambience of the cafes along the mall but is reasonably priced (from 3 lv for a main meal).

Restaurant Atlantik (ul Hristo Botev) Salads about 1.50 lv, main meals from 3 lv. This undercover and off-street complex includes a cafe, bar and restaurant that offers tasty food, excellent service and live music most nights. Ignore the prices in Bulgarian on the notice board outside. The prices on the menu in English and German are higher but they're still reasonable (eg, doner kebabs and salad about 3.5 lv and omelettes 1.60 lv). It's at the start of the mall from ploshtad Hristo Botev.

The best places for a drink (and a meal) are the innumerable **cafes** along the mall. Look for the umbrellas.

Getting There & Away

The bus station (☎ 22 558), slightly hidden from the main road about 300m east of the train station, is one of the best organised in Bulgaria. Public and private buses travel between Sofia (5.30 lv, two hours) and Vratsa at least every hour daily (more frequently between 6am and 9am). Also from Vratsa, there are one or two buses daily to Gabrovo, Pleven and Lovech and four to Vidin.

Inside the large train station (☎ 24 415), the Rila Bureau (☎ 20 562) sells tickets for international trains and advanced tickets for domestic services. Each day, three fast trains and one slow passenger train travel in both directions to Sofia and Vidin.

Taxis are plentiful and cheap, and can be chartered to Ledenika Cave (see the Vrachanska Balkan National Park section) and Cherepish Monastery (see that section earlier in this chapter). From the train station, walk 15 minutes up towards the hill, past the market and along the mall, ulitsa Hristo Botev, to the main square.

VRACHANSKA BALKAN NATIONAL PARK
НАЦИОНАЛЕН ПАРК ВРАЧАНСКИ БАЛКАН

An area of 28,845 hectares to the southwest of Vratsa was declared a national park in 1989 to protect more than nine species of birds, 700 types of trees and about 500 caves. Other fragile landscapes such as rocky outcrops are also protected but, paradoxically, they are still enjoyed by rock climbers and hand-gliders. Much of the park's more accessible areas are a sad reflection of its heyday. Most hotels are abandoned and the disused chairlift dangles menacingly above the road.

The **Ledenika Cave** (guided tours 5 lv per person; open daily in summer 8am-6pm) is 15km (about three hours on foot) from the start of the road past the Tourist Hotel in Vratsa – follow the ambiguous dark-blue signs (in Bulgarian). It's mostly covered in ice during winter (*led* means ice), but it's a popular excursion in summer. Entry is only possible on a guided **tour**, for which a minimum of about eight people is needed. The best time to visit is on a sunny weekend. Also, ask your hotel about concerts that are, incredibly, sometimes held inside the cave.

The hourly bus to Zgorigrad from Vratsa should stop near the cave. Locals like to take the bus, drive, hitch a ride or charter a taxi to the *cafes* about 12km up the road from the Tourist Hotel, and then **hike** down the shady road to Vratsa. Alternatively, ask directions at the cafes to the start of the new **Vrachanska Eco-trail**.

Contact the **park headquarters** (☎ 092-33 149, ℮ infocenter@vratsa.net, ul Ivanka Boteva 1, Vratsa) for more information if you're undertaking a major hiking or caving expedition in the park.

MONTANA
МОНТАНА
☎ 096 • pop 54,600

Montana is an unappealing town just off the highway between Vratsa and Vidin. It's a major transport hub so anyone visiting Chiprovtsi or the Lopushanski Monastery, by bus for example, will need to get a connection in Montana. If you get stuck there overnight, stay at the **Montana Hotel** (☎ 26 803, pl Slaveikov). Singles/doubles cost 25/35 lv for reasonable rooms with a bathroom and TV.

The road to Lopushanski Monastery passes the picturesque **Montana Reservoir**. It's popular with locals for swimming and fishing (bring your own gear) but remember to pack your sunscreen because there's no shade. Visitors can walk along the dam wall.

From the Montana bus station (☎ 23 454), there are services almost hourly to Sofia, Vratsa and Vidin, and about four or five daily to Chiprovtsi, Kopilovtsi, Pleven and Belogradchik. The train station (☎ 23 846) is on a spur track from the major line between Sofia and Vidin and is very inconvenient.

LOPUSHANSKI MONASTERY
ЛОПУШАНСКИ МАНАСТИР

Built between 1850 and 1853, this small monastery (*admission free; open daily 8am-* *6pm*) is in a serene setting about 21km west of Montana. It's dedicated to St John the Precursor and contains precious icons created by the renowned brothers Stanislav and Nikolai Dospevski. Like many other monasteries, it was also a hiding place for anti-Turkish rebels.

If the monastery is closed, ask staff at the guesthouse for permission to see inside. The *guesthouse* (☎ 09551-350) is only metres from the monastery and has about 20 rooms available to the public for about 20 lv per person. The older rooms downstairs share a bathroom, but the newer rooms upstairs include a bathroom, fridge and plenty of furniture. The chairs along the veranda outside the rooms are a great place to relax.

The attached *cafe* has outdoor and indoor tables. The service can be poor, and the meals are nothing to get excited about, but the location is delightful. According to the official brochure published by the guesthouse, **mountain bikes** are available for hire, but staff knew nothing about this when we asked. Nevertheless, the surrounding countryside is ideal for cycling.

CHIPROVTSI
ЧИПРОВЦИ
☎ 09554 • pop 3000

This fairly old, but charmless and quiet, village about 30km west of Montana, is famous for its carpets, though precious little is for sale. While Chiprovtsi is worth a visit, especially if you have a private car, avoid coming in winter when the climate can be appalling. Like Belogradchik, Chiprovtsi is a grateful (and needy) beneficiary of the Beautiful Bulgaria Project, which has renovated many crumbling buildings.

Chiprovtsi Monastery
Чипровски Манастир

Also known as the St Ivan Rilski Monastery, this modest structure was probably built in the 15th century as a Catholic church. It was burned down at least five times, mostly by Turks, because it provided sanctuary to rebels in the 17th century. What remains today was rebuilt in the 1830s as an Eastern Orthodox monastery.

Despite indications to the contrary in some tourist literature, accommodation at the monastery is not available. The turn-off to the monastery is 5.8km north-east of Chiprovtsi village and is accessible on any bus between Montana and Chiprovtsi. From the turn off its 400m to the monastery.

History Museum
This museum (*☎ 2194, ul Vitosha 2; admission 2 lv, free Thur; open Mon-Fri 8am-5pm & Sat-Sun 10am-4pm*) offers displays about regional mineral exploration, exhibits about the Turkish occupation of the area and copies of murals from the Chiprovtsi Monastery. (The originals are in the Aleksander Nevski Church in Sofia.) One room is dedicated to traditional costumes from the region and to the type of carpets for which the village is renowned (see Shopping later in this section).

The caretaker, who speaks good English, can provide an entertaining guided **tour** (*3 lv per person, no minimum number required*). The museum is at the top of the concrete steps to the right as you face the Chiprovtsi village square from the main road.

Places to Stay & Eat
The museum has two glorious ***rooms***, which it rents to the public. Singles/doubles are 7/14 lv. The rooms, which share a bathroom, contain lovely antique furniture and are worth booking ahead. There are a few ***cafes*** around the main square; the best are situated along the steps up to the museum.

Shopping
For centuries, Chiprovtsi has been famous for its handmade, woollen **carpets**, but the industry is a small-scale affair these days. There are no workshops where the public can watch artisans ply their trade and no shops in which to buy anything. The museum does sell a few small items, however, such as tiny bags (about 5 lv) and small rugs (15 lv). Larger items can be ordered through the museum but allow at least one month. If you are seriously keen (rather than just curious) about locally made carpets, ask the museum caretaker to introduce you to a local who can show you some samples and take you to a home where carpets are still made.

Getting There & Away
Four or five daily buses travel in both directions between Montana and Chiprovtsi. The road to Chiprovtsi from the Vratsa-Vidin highway (E79) starts about 3km north-west of Montana. From the south, the turn-off is signposted 'Chiprovski Monastery' (sic) in Bulgarian; from the north, it's signposted 'Lopushanski' in English.

BELOGRADCHIK
БЕЛОГРАДЧИК
☎ 0936 • pop 6700
Belogradchik, which translates from the Bulgarian as Small White Town, is nestled among picturesque mountains (particularly photogenic in the early morning). The village seems to have a dual personality: half of it is in the midst of a dramatic reconstruction, courtesy of the Beautiful Bulgaria Project, while the rest appears to have been abandoned, including the two major hotels. The current attraction is the outstanding fortress on the hill but once the renovations around the village are completed (perhaps by mid-2003), Belogradchik will undoubtedly be one of the most picturesque places in northern Bulgaria. But where the expected increased numbers of visitors are likely to stay is anyone's guess.

Orientation & Information
From the main square at the junction of the three major roads, ulitsa 3 Mart leads to the fortress. One street below the village square is the bus station. The First East National Bank, near the abandoned Hotel Belogradchik Skali, will change major currencies in cash only.

Belogradchik Fortress
Also simply known as the citadel, this majestic fortress (*admission 5 lv; open daily 8am-6pm*) is obvious from most places in the village. It was originally built by the Romans in the 1st century BC but several towers, walls and gates were later added

and/or fortified by the Byzantines, among others. Most of what remains today was built by the Turks between about 1805 and 1837. The fortress is a steepish 2km from the main square; follow the signs to the 'fortress'. Naturally, the **views** from the top are outstanding.

Museums
The **History Museum** (☎ 3469, pl 1850 Leto; admission 3.50 lv; open Mon-Fri 8am-noon & 2pm-6pm) is in Panova's House (an alternative name for the museum). As well as numerous coins, jewellery and costumes – and 6000 or so artefacts from the fortress – the museum contains displays about local anti-Turkish rebellions during the mid-19th century.

The **Nature Department** (admission 3.50 lv) is an offshoot of the History Museum. It contains various exhibits about local flora and fauna, but opening hours are irregular so ring the museum beforehand.

The turn-off starts about 600m down the road from the village square and the access road to the Nature Department is 500m long. Even if it's closed, the walk there is lovely.

Belogradchiski Skali
These remarkable rock formations are over 200 million years old. Although spread over 200 hectares, some huge examples are only about 100m down the road from the main square. It's a wonderful place to clamber around, and various **tracks** lead elsewhere around the rocks and into the forest.

Places to Stay & Eat
The two main hotels – the Hotel Belogradchik Skali at the main square, and the Hotel Belogradchik, one street below – have been abandoned and there are no indications of any future renovations. Consequently, there is a dearth of hotel beds in the village.

Hotel-Restaurant Madona (☎ 5546, ul Hristo Botev 26) Singles/doubles with bathroom 30/40 lv, including breakfast. This new hotel is friendly and quiet, but the rooms are really tiny, so if you're built like an NBA basketballer or sumo wrestler go somewhere else. There are only three rooms so book

ahead. It's 600m up ulitsa Vasil Levski, past the old Hotel Belogradchik Skali – look for the signs from the village centre.

Madona Campsite The owners seem to have abandoned this place but two bungalows are still available. It's still better to check with the Hotel-Restaurant Madona before going there. The turn-off is roughly 800m down the road north-east (signposted to Montana) from the village square and the access road is 200m long. Unofficial *camping* is possible at this camping ground, but is far better anywhere near the Nature Department (see Museums earlier in this section).

Hotel Rai (☎ 3735) Singles/doubles, most with shared bathroom, 10/20 lv. This homely place offers a handful of small, cheap and clean attic-style rooms. It's in a central but quiet location one street above the bus station.

Restaurant Eli Meals 2.50-5 lv. About 50m before the Madona, this is one of several nearby cafes with a hill top position, though there are no views directly from the tables and chairs.

Getting There & Away
From the decrepit bus station (☎ 3427), there are three or four daily services to Vidin (4.50 lv, 1½ hours) and four or five to Sofia (5.50 lv, four hours), via Montana and Vratsa. There are also regular buses to the nearest train station at Gara Oreshets, along the line between Vratsa and Vidin.

VIDIN
ВИДИН
☎ 094 • pop 69,400
Vidin is a quiet and compact town, one of few along the Danube to offer any worthwhile riverside views and ambience. Much of Vidin's glory is in the past, though the Beautiful Bulgaria Project has given the town's neglected historic edifices a much-needed makeover. Vidin suffers from high unemployment, no doubt exacerbated by the UN sanctions against nearby Yugoslavia, and the fact that roughly half the population has left the town over the past decade. Vidin boasts several attractions

The Danube

The Danube is the second longest (472km) river in Europe. Called the Dunav by Bulgarians it rises in the Black Forest of south-western Germany and empties into the Black Sea. It travels through four capital cities (Vienna, Budapest, Bratislava and Belgrade) and nine countries (Germany, Austria, the Slovak Republic, Hungary, Yugoslavia, Bulgaria, Romania, Moldava and Ukraine). No other river in the world is shared by so many countries. The average depth of the Danube is about 5m and the water rarely flows more than 3km per hour.

In mid-2000 the International Danube Protection Commission, sponsored by the Romanian and Bulgarian governments, began the first serious environmental study of the river, prompted by two unprecedented ecological disasters. Bridges fell into the river and riverside factories were damaged in and around Belgrade following NATO air strikes against Yugoslavia in 1999. In January 2000 a tailings dam burst at a gold mine in Baia Mare (Romania). About 100,000 cu metres of cyanide-contaminated water spilt into the Tisa and Danube rivers, killing thousands of fish and birds. This spill, described as the worst environmental disaster in Europe since Chornobyl, has so far poisoned river systems in Romania, Hungary, Bulgaria, Ukraine and Yugoslavia. Experts believe the water quality of the Danube will not recover until about 2004 and wildlife habitats will not return to normal before about 2010.

(including a marvellous fortress), and is a worthy alternative to Ruse for travelling to and from Romania, but Vidin's remoteness is a disincentive for some travellers.

History

Some historians believe that the Thracians were the first to settle along this part of the Danube, though there's no evidence to support this. On the site of the 3rd century BC Celtic settlement of Dunonia, the Romans built a fortress they called Bononia to control the Danube crossing. During the Second Bulgarian Empire (1185–1396), Bdin

(as it was known) became an important north-western bastion and trading centre.

The fall of Bdin in 1396 marked the completion of the conquest of Bulgaria by the Ottomans, who renamed the town Vidin (which they believed was easier to say). The Turks built an extensive city wall around Vidin and strengthened the Baba Vida fortress, which remains today. By the 16th century, Vidin was the largest town in Bulgaria and one of the biggest ports along the Danube. In the late 18th century, as Turkish rule weakened, a local *pasha* (high official), Osman Pazvantoglu, declared the district independent of the sultan. In 1878, Vidin was returned to Bulgaria by the Romanian army. Seven years later, an attempt by Serbia to take the area was resisted.

Orientation & Information

The town square, ploshtad Bdintsi, is an eclectic mix of the old and new. The former Communist Party building in the south towers over the ancient Stambul Kapiya Turkish gate to the north. The train station, public bus station and river boat terminal (see Getting There & Away later in this section) are only one block or so apart.

There are foreign-exchange offices along ulitsa Tsar Simeon Veliki and a Bulgarian Post Bank branch facing the main square. The telephone centre, open Monday to Friday from 7am to 6.30pm and Saturday 8am to 1.30pm, is in the Central Post Office between the square and train station. Marc Internet, ulitsa Tsar Aleksandâr II, is reliable and cheap.

Baba Vida Museum-Fortress

At the northern end of the park overlooking the Danube is the magnificent Baba Vida Museum-Fortress (☎ 22 884; admission 1 lv; open daily 8.30am-5pm in summer, 10am-5pm in winter). The Bulgars built the fortress between the 10th and 14th centuries on the ruined walls of the 3rd-century Roman citadel of Bononia. But most of what remains today was rebuilt in the 17th century by the Turks who used it to stockpile weapons. Because it was spared destruction during the Russian-Turkish War (1877–78),

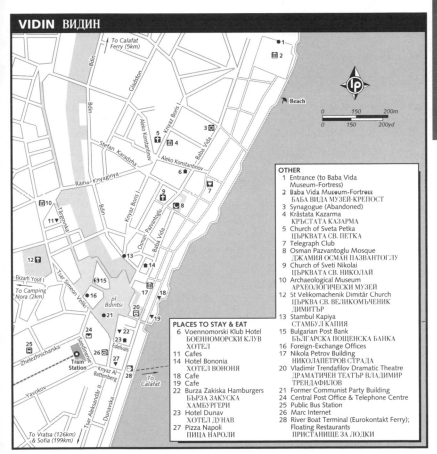

VIDIN ВИДИН

To Calafat Ferry (5km)

Beach

0   150   200m
0   150   200yd

OTHER
1 Entrance (to Baba Vida Museum-Fortress)
2 Baba Vida Museum-Fortress БАБА ВИДА МУЗЕЙ-КРЕПОСТ
3 Synagogue (Abandoned)
4 Krâstata Kazarma КРЪСТАТА КАЗАРМА
5 Church of Sveta Petka ЦЪРКВАТА СВ. ПЕТКА
7 Telegraph Club
8 Osman Pazvantoglu Mosque ДЖАМИЯ ОСМАН ПАЗВАНТОГЛУ
9 Church of Sveti Nikolai ЦЪРКВАТА СВ. НИКОЛАЙ
10 Archaeological Museum АРХЕОЛОГИЧЕСКИ МУЗЕЙ
12 St Velikomachenik Dimitâr Church ЦЪРКВА СВ. ВЕЛИКОМЪЧЕНИК ДИМИТЪР
13 Stambul Kapiya СТАМБУЛ КАПИЯ
15 Bulgarian Post Bank БЪЛГАРСКА ПОЩЕНСКА БАНКА
16 Foreign-Exchange Offices
17 Nikola Petrov Building НИКОЛАПЕТРОВ СТРАДА
20 Vladimir Trendafilov Dramatic Theatre ДРАМАТИЧЕН ТЕАТЪР ВЛАДИМИР ТРЕНДАФИЛОВ
21 Former Communist Party Building
24 Central Post Office & Telephone Centre
25 Public Bus Station
26 Marc Internet
28 River Boat Terminal (Eurokontakt Ferry); Floating Restaurants ПРИСТАНИЩЕ ЗА ЛОДКИ

PLACES TO STAY & EAT
6 Voennomorski Klub Hotel БОЕННОМОРСКИ КЛУБ ХОТЕЛ
11 Cafes
14 Hotel Bononia ХОТЕЛ ВОНОНЯ
18 Cafe
19 Cafe
22 Burza Zakiska Hamburgers БЪРЗА ЗАКУСКА ХАМБУРГЕРИ
23 Hotel Dunav ХОТЕЛ ДУНАВ
27 Pizza Napoli ПИЦА НАРОЛИ

To Calafat

To Vratsa (126km) & Sofia (199km)

Baba Vida is regarded as the best preserved medieval stone fortress in Bulgaria.

Each wall of the fortress is about 70m long, though a few remaining outer walls continue several hundred metres farther down the river towards the town centre. The main structure is surrounded by a deep moat. Notice boards in French explain some of the history and uses of each section. Renovation is continuing with the support of the Bulgarian American Business Centre in Sofia and the US Peace Corps.

Many locals use the upper section for **sunbathing**, and alongside the wall there's a tiny **beach** of pebbles. This is strictly for desperadoes: a quick glance upriver to the factories and tankers, and downriver to the fishermen, will probably deter most people from taking a dip.

Things to See

North-west of the main square is the **Archaeological Museum** (☎ 24 421, ul Tsar Simeon Veliki 12; open Tues-Sat 9am-noon & 2pm-6pm). On show are Thracian and Roman artefacts, including jewellery and statues, as well as exhibits from the Bulgarian national revival period (see History in the Facts about Bulgaria chapter). It's housed in a pagoda-shaped wooden building, which was used in the 19th century as a *konak* (police station) by the Turks.

In the suburbs, between the main square and the fortress, are several interesting buildings such as the 18th-century **Osman Pazvantoglu Mosque** *(ul Osman Pazvantoglu)* and the modern Orthodox **Church of Sveti Nikolai** opposite. Also of note is the **Krâstata Kazarma** *(☎ 23 855, ul Knyaz Boris I)*, which is meant to house the local history museum but seems to be permanently closed, and the 17th-century **Church of Svetka Petka** opposite. The abandoned **synagogue** *(ul Baba Vida)* farther up is worth a look.

Near the entrance to the Hotel Bononia the lovely white **Nikola Petrov Building** houses temporary exhibitions by local artists.

Places to Stay

Camping Nora (☎ 23 830) Bungalows for 2 people 18.50 lv per person. Just beyond the abandoned fairgrounds 2km west of town along ulitsa Ekzarh Yosif I, this well-kept complex includes a swimming pool, bar and *restaurant*.

Voennomorski Klub Hotel (☎ 25 763, ul Baba Vida 15) Rooms with shared bathroom 15 lv per person. The rooms on the top floor of this military club, overlooking the park next to the river, are basic and a little musty, but clean and cheap.

Hotel Dunav (☎/fax 24 448, ul Edelvais 3) Singles/doubles with bathroom 20/40 lv, apartments with bathroom 48 lv. The rooms in this convenient and quiet hotel are simple, but clean and good value. The quality of each room does vary, however. Some have chairs, while the bathrooms in others are unrenovated. The one apartment with TV is excellent value and worth a splurge.

Hotel Bononia (☎ 23 031, ul Baba Vida) Singles/doubles with bathroom 30/60 lv. This hotel is convenient to the town centre, river and park, and is probably the best value in town. Most rooms have sparkling new bathrooms and TVs, but those on the top floors are a little hot in summer. Breakfast is an extra 5 lv per person.

Places to Eat

Burza Zakiska Hamburgers (pl Bdintsi) Burgers about 1.60 lv, soups 1.20 lv. Alongside the lower eastern side of the main square, this informal joint is one of the best of its kind in Bulgaria. The burgers are tasty and fresh and it's always packed with locals.

Pizza Napoli (ul Tsar Aleksandâr II) Salads from 1 lv, most meals from 2.50 lv. This classy place has a snug corner setting and offers some of the tastiest and best-value food in northern Bulgaria. For example, pasta dishes from about 2.5 lv and pizzas from 2.60 to 5 lv.

The best places for a drink are any of the innumerable *cafes* that line the main square and malls. Especially enticing are those near the Archaeological Museum and in the riverside park. Sadly, none of these cafes offer any views of the Danube so try one of the *floating restaurants* near the river boat terminal if you're interested in the view.

Getting There & Away

Most locals seem to catch trains or private buses so there's a distinct lack of activity at the public bus station (☎ 23 179) on ulitsa Zhelezhnicharska. From this station, daily public and private buses to Sofia (10 lv, five hours) leave every 60 to 90 minutes (more frequently between 4am and 7pm). Many private buses also leave from outside ticket counters in front of the train station. Also, there's one daily public bus to Pleven and three or four to Belogradchik (between noon and 2.30pm).

From the train station (☎ 23 184), ulitsa Saedinenie, three fast trains (1st class/2nd class 9.65/6.80 lv, five hours) and one slow train (1st class/2nd class 8.55/5.70 lv, seven hours) travel daily to Sofia, via Vratsa.

To/from Romania From the port, 5km north of Vidin, ferries to Calafat (in Romania) leave about every hour and cost per car/passenger US$12.50/2 (payable in US dollars, euros or leva). The ferry operates 24 hours a day and is accessible on bus No 1 from the train station in Vidin. If you're arriving in Bulgaria, the bus stop for Vidin is about 500m down the road from Customs.

Far more convenient for travellers relying on public transport is the passenger boat (30 minutes) operated by Eurokontact (☎ 23 358). It leaves every day from the river boat terminal in central Vidin at 8am, 10.30am and 6pm, and departs from Calafat at 9.30am, noon and 7.30pm. Tickets cost US$3 (in US dollars, euros or leva).

A bridge, under construction at the time of writing, from Vidin to Calafat is likely to be finished in about 2005.

PLEVEN
ПЛЕВЕН
☎ 064 • pop 138,500

Strategically placed about halfway between Sofia and Ruse, Pleven is an unremarkable city with few attractions but it's a reasonable place to break up a journey. It can also be used as a base for visiting Lovech (see the Central Bulgaria chapter).

Pleven is known for its history. In mid-September 1877, 100,000 Russian and Romanian soldiers under General Totleben attempted (for the third time) to liberate Pleven from the Turks. The Turks eventually tried, but failed, to break the siege in December of that year. This momentous battle, which was the beginning of the end of the Russian-Turkish War (1877–78), is commemorated by a number of war memorials, museums and mausoleums around the city.

Orientation & Information
Along, or just off, the main thoroughfare of ulitsa Vasil Levski is where you'll find most foreign-exchange offices. There is also the United Bulgarian Bank at ulitsa Vasil Levski 1, the Skytech Internet Club opposite the Museum of Liberation and the post office and telephone centre, just off ploshtad Vûzrazhdane. Nadezhda Tours (☎ 26 229) on ulitsa Konstantinov can arrange hotel reservations, regional tours and car rental.

Things to See
The delightful **Church of Sveti Nikolai** (☎ 37 208, pl Sveti Nikolai; admission free; always open) possibly dates back to the 14th century. It was built below street level in the style dictated by the Ottoman rulers at the time. There are famous icons inside and the huge church **bell tower**. A priest may request an obligatory 'donation' of about 2 lv.

In a small, shady park is the **Museum of Liberation of Pleven 1877** (☎ 20 033, ul Vasil Levski 157; admission 2 lv; open Tues-Sat 9am-noon & 1pm-6pm). It honours the battle against the Turks in Pleven (see earlier in this section).

The **Svetlin Rusev Art Gallery** (☎ 38 342, ul Doiran 75; admission 1.50 lv; open Tues-Sat 10.30am-6.30pm) is the large red-and-white brick building on the north-western side of ploshtad Svoboda. It contains various works by artists throughout Bulgaria, including the locally born Rusev.

The unmistakable **Mausoleum** (☎ 30 033) dominates ploshtad Vûzrazhdane. It was built in 1907 as a memorial to the thousands of Russian and Romanian soldiers who died in Pleven in 1877. The building is not open to the public but visitors can see the cannons ominously pointed towards the main square and the eternal flame in front of the mausoleum.

The **Historical Museum** (☎ 22 691, ul Stoyan Zaimov 3; admission 2 lv; open Tues-Sat 9am-noon & 1pm-5pm) is enormous. The 24 halls house over 5000 exhibits about local history, flora and fauna and contain archaeological remains from Nikopolis-ad-Istrum and a nearby Neolithic settlement.

The **Military-Historical Museum** (☎ 22 919; Skobelev Park; admission 2 lv; open Tues-Sat 9am-5pm) was built to commemorate the 100th anniversary of the battle in 1877. Known as the 'Panorama' or 'Epopee (Epic) of Pleven', it's on top of a hill in Skobelev Park. The four halls feature huge, haunting paintings but most locals come for the views and surrounding parklands.

Places to Stay
Miziya-95 (☎ 801 215) on ulitsa Ivan Vazov 5 is a travel agency that doubles as an accommodation agency. Double *rooms* in private homes cost from 15 lv to 22 lv. It's open Monday to Friday from 8am to 5.30pm. The room rates depend on the season and amenities provided.

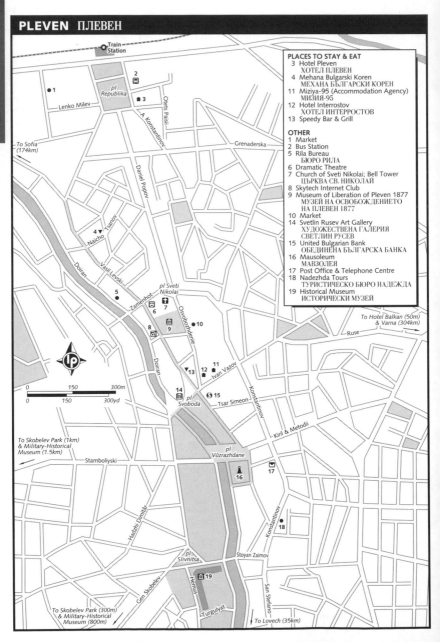

PLEVEN ПЛЕВЕН

PLACES TO STAY & EAT
3 Hotel Pleven
   ХОТЕЛ ПЛЕВЕН
4 Mehana Bulgarski Koren
   МЕХАНА БЪЛГАРСКИ КОРЕН
11 Miziya-95 (Accommodation Agency)
   МИЗИЯ-95
12 Hotel Interrostov
   ХОТЕЛ ИНТЕРРОСТОВ
13 Speedy Bar & Grill

OTHER
1 Market
2 Bus Station
5 Rila Bureau
   БЮРО РИЛА
6 Dramatic Theatre
7 Church of Sveti Nikolai; Bell Tower
   ЦЪРКВА СВ. НИКОЛАЙ
8 Skytech Internet Club
9 Museum of Liberation of Pleven 1877
   МУЗЕЙ НА ОСВОБОЖДЕНИЕТО
   НА ПЛЕВЕН 1877
10 Market
14 Svetlin Rusev Art Gallery
   ХУДОЖЕСТВЕНА ГАЛЕРИЯ
   СВЕТЛИН РУСЕВ
15 United Bulgarian Bank
   ОБЕДИНЕНА БЪЛГАРСКА БАНКА
16 Mausoleum
   МАВЗОЛЕЯ
17 Post Office & Telephone Centre
18 Nadezhda Tours
   ТУРИСТИЧЕСКО БЮРО НАДЕЖДА
19 Historical Museum
   ИСТОРИЧЕСКИ МУЗЕЙ

Hotel Pleven (☎ *30 181, pl Republika*) Singles/doubles with bathroom 33/48 lv. This dreary, two-star hotel is close to the bus and train stations and is, therefore, a little noisy. The rooms are basic but clean, and reductions to 24/40 lv are offered if hot water isn't available (which is often).

Hotel Balkan (☎ *22 215, ul Ruse 85*) Singles/doubles with bathroom 125/176 lv. Although a popular hotel the rooms are charmless and it's inconvenient and overpriced for foreigners. The rooms have TV and the rates include breakfast.

Hotel Interrostov (☎ *801 095, ul Osvobozhdenie 2*) Singles/doubles with bathroom 68/105 lv. Formerly known as the Rostov na Don, this three-star hotel is far better value than Hotel Pleven and more convenient than the Balkan. The rooms are small but have a fan, fridge and TV.

Places to Eat

Speedy Bar & Grill (*ul Vasil Levski*) Salads about 2.50 lv, grills about 5 lv. Similar to the Happy Bar & Grill restaurants found elsewhere, this place offers snappy service, outdoor tables and hearty servings of Western style food at above-average prices.

Mehana Bulgarski Koren (*ul Naicho Tsanov 4*) Main meals 4.50-7 lv. Tucked away along a side street off ulitsa Vasil Levski, this charming tavern boasts one of the nicest courtyard settings in the country. It features live music most nights and is often packed with locals (always a good sign). Service can be slow when it's busy.

Visitors with a sweet tooth may wish to linger longer in Pleven – *cafes* along ulitsa Vasil Levski and ulitsa Daniel Popov offer a superb range of scrumptious cakes, pastries and strudels.

Getting There & Away

From the bus station (☎ 22 961), next to the train station on ploshtad Republika, up to three public buses leave daily for Burgas, Gabrovo, Plovdiv, Ruse, Sliven, Sofia, Stara Zagora, Teteven, Troyan, Varna, Veliko Târnovo, Vidin and Vratsa. Public buses also leave every hour for Lovech (2.50 lv, one hour). Private buses depart hourly for

Sofia (7 lv, 2½ hours) and less frequently to Burgas, Ruse and Varna from ticket offices in front of Hotel Pleven and the train station.

Pleven is along the main northern train line. Every day, three fast trains and one express travel to Varna (1st class/2nd class 15.70/11.40 lv, 4½ hours for the express) and Sofia (1st class/2nd class 10.25/7.50 lv, 3½ hours) from the train station (☎ 24 127) in Pleven. Eleven trains also stop daily at Pleven on the way from Sofia to Gorna Oryahovitsa, from where there are four daily connections to Ruse. The Rila Bureau (☎ 22 390) on ulitsa Doiran 43, sells tickets for international services and advanced tickets for domestic trains.

RUSE (ROUSSE)
РУСЕ
☎ 082 • pop 182,500

Ruse (often erroneously transliterated as Rousse) is the fifth largest city in Bulgaria and the major gateway for most people travelling to or from Romania. It's the nicest city along the Bulgarian side of the Danube River and has several worthwhile attractions, including one of the most magnificent main squares in the country. The city centre, with its striking Austro-Hungarian influenced architecture has been given an extensive facelift thanks to the Beautiful Bulgaria Project. Disappointingly, however, the original town planners thought little of the Danube so most of the riverside is dominated by ugly ports and railway lines. Only the park near the Riga Hotel offers any decent views of the river and incredibly, there isn't one riverside cafe!

History

A Roman fortress, Sexaginta Prista (Port of 60 Ships) was established here in AD 69–70, as part of the Roman's northern defensive line. Although strengthened by Emperor Justinian in the 6th century, the fort was finally obliterated during continual invasions by Slavic tribes soon afterwards. Fed up with these constant raids, most of the populace of Ruse moved to Cherven, 35kms to the south and now part of the Rusenski Lom National Park (see that section later in this chapter).

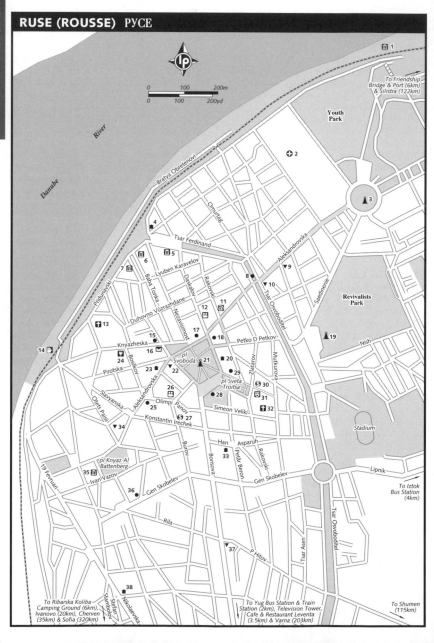

RUSE (ROUSSE) РУСЕ

To Friendship
Bridge & Port (6km)
& Silistra (122km)

Youth
Park

Danube

River

Bratya Obretenovi

Omurtag

Pridunavski

Tsar Ferdinand

Baba Tonka

Lyuben Karavelov

Dastabov

Rakovski

Aleksandrovska

Suedinenie

Revivalists
Park

Duhovno Vùzrazhdane

Neatavolmost

Knyazheska

Borilcov

Pirotska

Petko D Petkov

Tsar Osvoboditel

Mutkurova

pl
Svoboda

Zlatarov

Nish

Stavyanska

Aleksandrovska

Olimpi Panov

Konstantin Irechek

pl Sveta
Troitsa

Simeon Veliki

Otets Pasii

Burov

Borisova

Petàl Beron

Rakovski

Han

Asparuh

Gen Skobelev

Stadium

Lipnik

To Iztok
Bus Station
(4km)

19 Fevruari

pl Knyaz Al
Battenberg

Ivan Vazov

Gen Skobelev

Rila

P Hitov

Tsar Aseen

Tsar Osvoboditel

Stamboliy

Stefan
Nikolaevska

To Ribarska Koliba
Camping Ground (6km),
Ivanovo (20km), Cherven
(35km) & Sofia (320km)

To Yug Bus Station & Train
Station (2km), Television Tower,
Cafe & Restaurant Leventa
(3.5km) & Varna (203km)

To Shumen
(115km)

0   100   200m
0   100   200yd

RUSE (ROUSSE) ПУСЕ

PLACES TO STAY
4   Riga Hotel
    ХОТЕЛ РИГА
20 Danube Plaza Hotel
    ХОТЕЛ ДУНАВ ПЛАЗА
23 Splendid Hotel
    ХОТЕЛ СПЛЕНДИД
33 Bistra & Galina Hotel
    ХОТЕЛ ВИСТРА И ГАЛИНА
38 Hotel Kristal
    ХОТЕЛ КРИСТАЛ

PLACES TO EAT
9   Pauchi Chinese Restaurant
    ПАЙЧИ КИТАЙСКИ
    РЕСТОРАНТ
10 San Benedetto Pizzeria
    ПИЦАРИЯ САН БЕНЕДЕТО
22 Happy Bar & Grill
34 Mehana Chiflika
    МЕХАНА ЧИФЛИКА
37 Restaurant Rila
    РЕСТОРАНТ РИЛА

OTHER
1   Transportation Museum
    (closed)
    МУЗЕЙ НА ТРАНСПОРТА
2   Polyclinic I
3   Soviet Army Monument
    ПАМЕТНИК НА СЪВЕТСКАТА
    АРМИЯ

5   Museum of the Urban
    Lifestyle in Ruse
    МУЗЕЙ НА ГРАДСКИЯ СТИЛ
    НА ЖИВОТ В РУСЕ
6   Baba Tonka Museum
    (closed)
    МУЗЕЙ БАБА ТОНКА
7   House-Museum Zahari
    Stoyanov (closed)
    КЪЩАТА-МУЗЕЙ ЗАХАРИ
    СТОЯНОВ
8   Hali (Supermarket)
    ХАЛИ
11 Ch@t House
12 Cinema Intim
    КИНО ИНТИМ
13 Catholic Church of St Paul
    the Crucified   .
    КАТОЛИЧЕСКА ЦЪРКВА
    СВ. ЛАВЕЛ
14 Maritime Terminal
15 Rila Bureau; Biochim
    Commercial Bank
    БЮРО РИЛА. ТЪРГОВСКА
    БАНКА БИОХИМ
16 Central Post Office &
    Telephone Centre
17 Concert Ticket Bureau
    КОНЦЕРТНО БЮРО
18 Pingvinite Bookshop;
    McDonald's
    КНИЖАРНИЦА ПИНГВИН

19 Pantheon of the National
    Revival
    ПАНТЕОН НА
    НАЦИОНОНАЛНОТО
    ВЪЗРАЖДАНЕ
21 Monument to Freedom
    РАМЕТНИК НА СВОБОДАТА
24 Soundgarden
25 Dunav Tours
    ДУНАВ ТУРС
26 Royal Cinema
    КИНО РОЯЛ
27 United Bulgarian
    Bank
    ОБЕДИНЕНА БЪЛГАРСКА
    БАНКА
28 Muniсipal Building
29 Balkan Air Tour
    БАЛКАН АЕРОТУР
30 Bulbank
    БУЛБАНК
31 Ruse Opera House
    ОПЕРАТА РУСЕ
32 Church of Sveta Troitsa
    ЦЪРКВАТА СВ. ТРОИЦА
35 History Museum (closed)
    ИСТОРИЧЕСКИ МУЗЕЙ
36 Rusenski Lom National
    Park Office
    РУСЕНСКИ ЛОМ
    НАЦИОНАЛЕН ПАРК
    ДИРЕКЦИЯ

During the First (681–1018) and Second (1185–1396) Bulgarian Empires, Ruse remained an insignificant backwater before being destroyed by the Turks in the 14th century. Under the reforming Turkish district governor, Midhat Pasha, Roustchouk (as it became known) was rebuilt and modernised. It became an important economic and cultural centre, especially after the railway from Ruse to Varna (the first in Bulgaria and in the entire Ottoman Empire at the time) was built in 1866 to link the Danube with the Black Sea.

Being so close to Bucharest, headquarters of the Bulgarian Central Revolutionary Committee, Ruse was a stronghold of anti-Turkish rebellion before and during the Russian-Turkish War (1877–78). By the end of the war, Ruse was the largest and most prosperous city in Bulgaria, epitomised by the grand and eclectic architectural style of the city centre.

Orientation

The centre of Ruse is ploshtad Svoboda, one of the most majestic city squares in Bulgaria. Dominated by the massive Monument to Freedom (erected in 1908), the square is always crowded with locals enjoying the shady trees, (working) fountains and (new) seats. Among the 18 streets that join the square is Ruse's main pedestrian mall, ulitsa Aleksandrovska. It heads northeast to the Soviet Army Monument and south-west towards ploshtad Knyaz Al Battenberg. The major landmark in the south is the 206m-high television tower, apparently the highest in the Balkans.

If you're going to be in Ruse for more than a few days, pick up the free *Rousse Info*

City Guide, a highly informative booklet published in English every year and available from the major hotels. All bookstalls sell maps of Ruse, including the excellent one published in Cyrillic by Domino.

Information

Surprisingly, there is no dedicated tourist office in Ruse, though the North Central Regional Development Agency (☎ 225 474, W www.ncrda.bg) can deal with any specific inquiries.

Bulbank on ploshtad Sveta Troitsa, just north of the opera house, changes cash and travellers cheques. The bank's automatic teller machine (ATM) accepts major credit cards, as does the ATM in front of the post office. The Biochim Commercial Bank, ulitsa Knyazheska, near the Rila Bureau, and the United Bulgarian Bank on ulitsa Burov, offer similar services. Dozens of foreign-exchange offices are along ulitsa Aleksandrovska and around ploshtad Svoboda.

The telephone centre (open daily from 7am to 9.45pm) is in the Central Post Office on ploshtad Svoboda. One of the few Internet centres is Ch@t House on ulitsa Aleksandrovska.

Dunav Tours (☎ 224 268, e dtbktu@ dunavtours.bg), ulitsa Olimpi Panov, is open Monday to Friday 9am to noon and 1pm to 5.30pm. It arranges private rooms (see Places to Stay later in this section), organises regional tours and sells tickets for long-distance buses. Airline tickets can be bought at Balkan Air Tour (☎ 224 161) ploshtad Sveta Troitsa. For those wishing to explore, the Rusenski Lom National Park the office (☎ 082-272 397, e n–park@acvilon.com) is on ulitsa Gen Skobelev 7.

Just up from McDonald's, Pingvinite Bookshop, on ulitsa Aleksandrovska, sells a few books in English about Bulgaria and offers one of the best ranges of maps in the country.

Religious Buildings

Behind the opera house is the Russian-style **Church of Sveta Troitsa** (*pl Sveta Troitsa; admission free but donations welcome;open daily 7am-6pm*). Built in 1632 it is the oldest remaining building in Ruse and the church features several large and well-preserved murals and 16th-century crosses and icons. As you walk down the stairs, look up and admire the stained glass windows in the tower. The bell tower in the grounds was added only in the late 19th century, because the Turkish rulers prohibited church bells at the time of original construction.

The **Catholic Church of St Paul the Crucified** (*admission free; open daily 7am-6pm*), just off ulitsa Pridunavski, was built between 1890 and 1892. It still retains its original, and clearly visible, murals and stained-glass windows, chandeliers and icons. It was the first church in Bulgaria to boast an organ and the massive 700-pipe instrument is still played during Sunday services.

Museums

At the time of research, the following museums were closed but may reopen sometime in the future:

Baba Tonka Museum (☎ 32 364) ulitsa Pridunavski 6
History Museum (☎ 236 115) ploshtad Knyaz Al Battenberg
House-Museum Zahari Stoyanov (☎ 222 727) ulitsa Pridunavski
Transportation Museum (☎ 222 012) ulitsa Bratya Obretenovi

At the time of writing the only functioning museum was the **Museum of the Urban Lifestyle in Ruse** (*☎ 227 742, ul Tsar Ferdinand 39; admission 3 lv; open Mon-Fri 9am-noon & 2pm-5pm*). According to legend, the 1866 Kaliopa House (as it's sometimes known) was given by the Turkish governor, Midhat Pasha, to his reputed mistress – the beautiful wife of the Prussian Ambassador. The museum features sumptuous furniture from the early 20th century and crockery, cutlery, porcelain and costumes. It's the mustard-and-brown building opposite the Riga Hotel – ring the bell if no-one is around.

Parks & Monuments

Around the **Revivalists' Park** are the graves of some local revolutionary heroes. The park is dominated by the gold-domed **Pantheon** of the National Revival (☎ 228 913; admission free; open Mon-Fri 9am-noon & 1pm-5pm). Built to commemorate the 100th anniversary of the death of 453 locals who died fighting the Ottomans in 1878, it is of minimal interest to visitors.

North of the Pantheon, and at the end of ulitsa Saedinenie, is the **Soviet Army Monument**, built in 1949. Behind it is the **Youth Park**, a massive area with playgrounds, swimming pools and tennis courts, and one of the few places in Ruse with river views.

Special Events

Cultural events in Ruse include the annual **March Music Days Festival** (last two weeks of March), which features international musicians, and the **Golden Rebeck Folklore Festival** held in early June. The **Days of Ruse** festival, with music, dance and theatre, is in the first half of October and the **Christmas Festival** runs from 15–24 December.

Places to Stay

Dunav Tours (☎ 224 268, Ⓔ dtbktu@ dunavtours.bg) on ulitsa Olimpi Panov, is a friendly and reliable agency that can arrange *rooms* at private homes in central Ruse. In summer it charges 31 lv for singles and 36 lv for doubles. In winter singles are 50 lv and doubles 55 lv. The rates are higher in winter because of extra heating costs.

Camping *Ribarska Koliba* (☎ 224 068) Camping 10 lv per person, bungalows for 2 people with bathroom 25 lv per person. Open May to mid-Oct. This camping ground, 6km south of Ruse on the road to Sofia, is reasonably clean and friendly, but inconvenient. Take a taxi (about 5 lv) or bus Nos 6 and 16 (both are irregular, and stop running at 9pm). Avoid the *restaurant*, which is overpriced for foreigners.

Hotels There is nothing cheap in Ruse. The following hotels all offer rooms with a private bathroom.

Hotel Kristal (☎ 824 333, ul Nikolaevska 1) Singles/doubles 50/70 lv, luxury doubles 80 lv, suites for 2 people 100 lv. This old place has been remodelled and now offers

sparkling new rooms. The downside is that the bathrooms are small, the hotel is on a noisy road and it's overpriced for foreigners, especially considering that breakfast and TV are not included.

Splendid Hotel (☎ 235 951, ul Aleksandrovska, Ⓔ reservations@splendid.rousse .bg) Singles/doubles 60/70 lv. On a quiet, leafy street just off ulitsa Aleksandrovska, metres from the main square, the Splendid is good value. Rates include breakfast, air-cooler and fridge, but rooms are small. Decor is charming but some windows face straight into the back of the opposite building.

Danube Plaza Hotel (☎ 822 929, Ⓔ plazahotel@mbox.digsys.bg, pl Svoboda) Singles/doubles from US$30/40. This very convenient and recently renovated hotel offers quality rooms and (almost) four-star facilities for the same rates offered by other three-star hotels. All rooms have a TV, and rates include breakfast.

Riga Hotel (☎ 22 181, fax 230 362, ul Pridunavski 22) Singles from US$40-55, doubles from US$48-70. This ugly high-rise along the banks of the Danube is the only place in Ruse (and Bulgaria) to offer any views of the river and Romania. Massive renovations at the time of writing should improve the quality of rooms but may also raise the prices. All rooms have a TV and the dearer ones also contain a fan and fridge. Rates include breakfast.

Bistra & Galina Hotel (☎ 823 344, Ⓔ hotel@chamber.rousse.bg, ul Han Asparuh 8) Singles US$30-35, doubles from US$60, suites for 2 people US$110. The B&G is a lovely modern hotel with very clean, comfortable rooms and friendly staff. The singles (which come with fan or air-con and TV) are very small, but perfectly adequate. The doubles and suites have a TV, fridge and air-con. Rates include breakfast.

Places to Eat

Restaurant Rila (ul Borisova 49) Salads about 1.50 lv, mains from 2.50 lv. The Rila is a popular cafeteria-style place with cheap, tasty food. Load up your tray and dig in. It's open Monday to Friday from 8am until 8pm and on Saturday from 10am to 2pm.

Happy Bar & Grill (*pl Svoboda*) Salads about 2.50 lv, grills from 4.50 lv. This nationwide chain spills out onto the square and is ideal for a quick meal of Western food. It offers a menu in English and German.

Mehana Chiflika (*ul Otets Paisii*) Salads 1.50-2 lv, mains 2-3 lv. Far bigger than the outside suggests, the Chiflika has an offbeat decor, quick service and large servings (salad and bread may be enough for a main course). It features live music in the evenings, which is great fun but precludes any conversation. A menu in English is available.

Restaurant Leventa Mains 3.50-7 lv. Next to the television tower (see Orientation earlier in this section), the Leventa offers tasty Bulgarian food and lively traditional music and dance on summer evenings.

San Benedetto Pizzeria (*ul Tsar Osvoboditel*) Pizzas from 2.50-4 lv. The decor and service may be unremarkable but the pizzas are tasty (though a little small) and drinks are cheap.

Pauchi Chinese Restaurant (*ul Aleksandrovska 90*) Meat & rice dishes from 2.50 lv. Popular with locals, this informal Chinese eatery offers delicious oriental food. Meals can be taken away and enjoyed in the nearby parks, or eaten at the few tables inside and outside the restaurant.

About halfway up the television tower a *cafe* (*open daily 10.30am-12.30am*) sells drinks, including cocktails, which are popular with local trendsetters, and offers views of Romania. To get there take a taxi for about 1.50 lv.

Anyone wishing to self-cater should head to the supermarket, *Hali* (*ul Aleksandrovska; open Mon-Sat 8am-6pm*).

Entertainment

Ruse Opera House (*pl Sveta Troitsa*) First opened in about 1890, this is one of the finest buildings in the city. The **concert ticket bureau** (☎ 234 303; *ul Aleksandrovska 61*) is open Monday to Friday from 10am to 1pm and 3pm to 6pm and provides information and sells tickets for events at the opera house and other cultural centres in Ruse.

The Friendship Bridge

This double-decker highway and railway bridge, 6km downstream from Ruse, links the city with Giurgiu on the Romanian side of the Danube. Built between 1949 and 1954, this massive structure – 2.8km long and 30m above the water – is the largest steel bridge in Europe. It has also become one of the busiest, due to increased traffic and delays caused by collapsed bridges across the Danube in Belgrade following NATO bombings in 1999 and the existing sanctions against Yugoslavia.

The bridge's name is fairly ironic as relations between Bulgaria and Romania have been rather unfriendly. This was especially so during the 1980s when a chlorine-and-sodium plant across the river in Romania caused massive air pollution in Ruse and, more recently, following another catastrophic spill in Romania (see the boxed text 'The Danube' earlier in this chapter).

It's important to note that you *cannot* cross this border on foot or by bicycle. You must traverse the bridge by car, motorcycle, train or bus.

Soundgarden (*ul Knyazheska 16*) This venue is a popular hot spot – live bands keep the cellar club rocking most nights until 4am.

Several cinemas, such as **Cinema Intim** (*ul Daskalov*) and **Royal Cinema** (*ul Olimpi Panov*), show recent English-language films.

Getting There & Away

Bus The Yug bus station (☎ 222 974), ulitsa Pristanishtna, about 2.5km south of the city centre, is strangely quiet and disorganised. From this station, public buses depart daily for Shumen (5.40 lv, two hours) at 8.30am and 2pm, Varna (11 lv, four hours) at 6.30am and 4pm, Plovdiv (12 lv, six hours) at 9am and Veliko Târnovo (3.50 lv, two hours) at 8.30am. Also, one or two daily public buses go to Gabrovo and Pleven and four or five to Dobrich. Buses and minibuses leave for Silistra (5 lv, about two hours) every hour or so. Tickets for most public buses and minibuses are only available on the bus or minibus.

Private bus companies offer luxury express coaches every hour to Sofia (10 lv to 12 lv, five hours) from the Yug station.

From the smaller Iztok bus station (☎ 443 836), ulitsa Ivan Vedur 10, about 4km east of the city centre, buses go to regional villages, such as Ivanovo and Cherven in the Rusenski Lom National Park (see that section later in this chapter).

Train – Domestic The restored train station (☎ 222 213) ulitsa Pristanishtna, is adjacent to the Yug bus station. Daily, two fast trains travel directly to Varna (1st class/2nd class 11.95/8.90 lv, four hours), via Shumen, while several others stop at the junction of Kaspichan. Eleven trains head from Ruse to Gorna Oryahovitsa (1st class/2nd class 10.20/6.80 lv, two hours for the fast train) and a few continue to Veliko Târnovo. From Gorna Oryahovitsa, four fast trains connect to Sofia (1st class/ 2nd class 13.80/9.70 lv, five hours), so it's possible to travel between Ruse and Sofia on the same day.

The left-luggage office at the train station is open 24 hours.

Train – International Tickets for international trains, and advanced tickets for domestic services, are available at Rila Bureau (☎ 223 920), ulitsa Knyazheska 33, open Monday to Friday 9am to noon and 12.30pm to 5pm. Tickets can also be bought from the train station (☎ 228 016). See the Getting There & Away chapter for information about international trains that pass through Ruse.

Boat From Ruse port, near the Friendship Bridge, large ferries leave about every three hours (per car/passenger US$25/5) for Giurgiu in Romania. Smaller ferries leave when they are full (per car/passenger US$10/$1). Both operate 24 hours every day and payment can be made in US dollars, euros or leva.

Getting Around
Naturally, there are plenty of available taxis around town.

Eurokontact (☎ 626 241) seems to have the monopoly on local car hire. It charges from US$20 per day and US$0.14 per kilometre, plus insurance and petrol. Contact them by phone and give them plenty of notice because their 'office' is nothing more than a household garage in a remote apartment block. Otherwise contact a travel agency, such as Dunav Tours, or your hotel about renting a car, which is useful for visiting the Rusenski Lom National Park.

RUSENSKI LOM NATIONAL PARK
НАЦИОНАЛЕН ПАРК РУСЕНСКИ ЛОМ
This 3260-hectare national park, established in 1970, hugs the Rusenski-Lom, Beli-Lom and Malki-Lom Rivers not far from Ruse. The park is one of the best places in Bulgaria for **bird-watching**. It protects about 170 species of water birds, as well as endangered Egyptian vultures, lesser kestrels and great eagle owls. It's also home to 67 species of mammals (16 of which are endangered) and 23 types of bats. The park comprises endless valleys and mountains (rare among the Danubian plains), caused by unique geological shifts during the Pleistocene period.

Most visitors come to marvel at the 40 or so rock churches built in and around the 300 caves. The rock monastery at Ivanovo (see that section later in this chapter) is accessible, but only a few other caves are open to tourists. You can visit the second-longest cave in Bulgaria, the **Orlova Chuka Peshtera** (Eagle Peak Cave), between the villages of Tabachka and Pepelina. Also around the park are limited **ruins** of cities built by Thracians and Romans.

Information
A new information centre (☎ 08116-2203) in the *obshtina* (town hall) at Ivanovo should be open by the time you get there. All visitors should pick up the *Naturpark Russenski Lom* map, published by the Green Danube Program. The map is available at bookstalls in Ruse and the national park office (☎ 082-272 397, 📧 n–park@acvilon.com) ulitsa Gen Skobelev 7 in Ruse.

RUSENSKI LOM NATIONAL PARK
НАЦИОНАЛЕН ПАРК РУСЕНСКИ ЛОМ

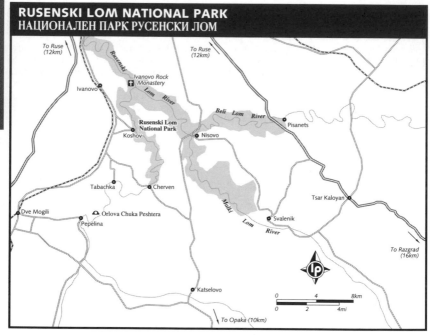

Ivanovo Rock Monastery
Скален Манастир Иваново

Several caves near Ivanovo were used for religious purposes. The most famous was the **St Bogoroditsa** (Holy Virgin's) rock church, the only remaining section of the original St Archangel Mikhail Monastery complex commonly known as the Ivanovo Rock Monastery (☎ *082-231 023; admission 2 lv; open Wed-Mon 8am-noon & 1pm-5pm*). The monastery is built inside a cave that is 16m long, 4m wide and 38m above ground. It is now on Unesco's World Heritage list.

Built during the 13th century under the sponsorship of Tsar Ivan Asen II and Tsar Ivan Aleksandâr, the monastery was linked to the Royal Court and became a regional centre of art, culture and religion. The 14th-century murals inside, which are regarded as some of the finest in Bulgaria, if not Europe, show portraits of various saints and impassioned scenes from the Last Supper. The artists are unknown.

The monastery is signposted along a good road, about 4km east of Ivanovo and 20km south of Ruse.

Cherven
Червен

Cherven was first established in the 6th century AD by people from Ruse who wanted to escape the constant Slavic invasions. The town became an important religious, economic and military centre during the Second Bulgarian Empire (1185–1396). Remains of the 6th-century **citadel** (☎ *082-230 123; admission 3 lv; open Wed-Mon 8am-noon & 1pm-5pm*) are remarkably intact. Recent excavations have also unearthed several streets, towers and churches, now all part of a protected Archaeological Reserve. The ruins are a short walk north of Cherven village, about 15km farther south of Ivanovo.

Places to Stay The park is not particularly well set up for tourism yet, so it's a good idea to check with the national park office in Ruse, or the information centre in Ivanovo, about current accommodation options. There are *rooms* at private homes in Cherven *(no telephone)*, Pisanets *(☎ 08164-280)*, Nisovo *(☎ 098196-343)* and Koshov *(☎ 09819-479)* for about 16 lv per person.

Getting There & Away From the Iztok bus station in Ruse, three buses (6.50am, 2.30pm and 6pm) leave daily only on Monday and Friday. Buses go to Cherven, via Ivanovo and Koshov and an extra bus departs Ruse at 11am on Saturday and Sunday. For Pisanets, take one of the frequent buses towards Razgrad from the Yug bus station in Ruse; and for Nisovo, look for a bus leaving the Iztok station for Opaka.

SILISTRA
СИЛИСТРА
☎ 086 • pop 49,900
Silistra is a likeable town and one of very few along the mighty Danube to offer views and boat trips. Most of the port is a few kilometres away, which makes Silistra more agreeable than Ruse if you're looking for a Danube experience. The town is famous for its apricot brandy, but beware: it can be lethal!

The bus station is 1.5km from the main square, ploshtad Svoboda, around which there are banks and foreign-exchange offices, as well as the post office and telephone centre.

Things to See & Do
Over the centuries, Silistra has been invaded and occupied by Thracians, Romans, Greeks, Russians, Romanians and Turks, all of whom built citadels and fortresses in or near the town. Along the street between the mall and river are obvious **ruins** of the ancient Roman city of Durostorum.

The Turkish **Medzhitabiya Fortress** (built in 1848) is closed but the lovely forested **park** surrounding the fortress is great fun for **hiking**. The fortress is about 5km from town (2 lv by taxi), via the Silistra-Dobrich road, or a 3km-walk up the hill. The TV tower is an adjacent landmark.

The **Art Gallery** *(☎ 26 838, bul Simeon Veliki 120; admission 1.50 lv; open Mon-Fri 8am-noon & 2pm-6pm)* is in a renovated yellow building along the mall opposite the Drama Theatre. The gallery contains hundreds of works by contemporary Bulgarian artists, as well as Japanese engravings.

The **Archaeological Museum** *(☎ 23 894; admission 1.50 lv; open Mon-Fri 8am-noon & 2pm-6pm)* was in the same building as the Art Gallery at the time of writing. It houses artefacts from the Turkish fortress and other ruins in the region, as well as costumes, jewellery and a 3rd-century Thracian chariot. The museum may move in the future, so check the current location at the art gallery.

The MV *Bravo* offers one-hour **boat tours** (5-6 lv per person) along the Danube several days a week. Inquire at the travel agency in the Zlatna Dobroudja Hotel.

Places to Stay & Eat
Zlatna Dobroudja Hotel (☎ 22 861, fax 28 014, ul Dobroudja 2) Singles 40-55 lv, doubles 66-99 lv, all with bathroom . This is the best option in town, because of its central location and reasonable rates. All rooms have air-con and a TV and the price includes breakfast. Several *cafes* and *restaurants* are found in and around the hotel complex, including *Pizzeria Zlatna Dobroudja,* which offers tasty pizzas and pasta dishes from a menu in English.

Orbita Hotel (☎ 25 720) Singles/ doubles/triples with bathroom 30/40/60 lv. In the hill-top park only metres from the Medzhitabiya Fortress and TV tower, Orbita's rooms are clean, comfortable and feature a fridge and balcony. Rates include breakfast.

Getting There & Away
Roughly every hour, buses and minibuses leave the Silistra bus station *(☎ 23 062)* for the Yug bus station in Ruse (5 lv, about two hours). From Silistra, there are also two or three daily buses to Varna, eight to Dobrich, four to Sofia, three to Shumen and one to Veliko Târnovo. There is one daily train to Ruse and three to Samuil.

From Silistra port to Călăraşi (in Romania), a ferry operates every few hours every day (per car/passenger US$15/3). Fares are payable in US dollars, euros or leva. Public transport on the Romanian side is not reliable, however, so the border at Ruse is probably easier.

LAKE SREBÂRNA
ЕЗЕРО СРЕБЪРНА

Lake Srebârna is shallow (1.5m to 5m deep) and connected to the Danube by a narrow, natural canal so it's full of unique types of vegetation and floating islands made of reeds. The lake is home to over 160 species of water **birds**, including colonies of endangered small cormorants, Ferruginous ducks and Dalmatian pelicans. Surrounding the lake is the 8000-hectare **Srebârna Nature Reserve**, established as a World Heritage site by Unesco in 1983.

The **Museum of Natural History** (☎ 086-23 894; admission 1.5 lv; open Mon-Fri 9am-noon & 2pm-4pm) is in Srebârna village. It contains a few exhibits about local birdlife and flora and is the perfect place for serious bird lovers to arrange **bird-watching** trips.

The southern part of the lake extends to within a few hundred metres of the Silistra-Ruse road. Bus Nos 22 and 222 travel several times a day between Silistra and Srebârna village. Otherwise, take the more regular Silistra-Ruse bus or minibus, disembark at the signposted turn-off, and walk (1.5km) into the village.

DOBRICH
ДОБРИЧ

☎ 058 • pop 113,800

For visitors on package tours and those staying at the resorts along the Black Sea coast, Dobrich is a popular day trip. For independent travellers, it's a cheaper and more relaxed base for exploring the coast and Balchik (see the Black Sea coast chapter). First settled in the 15th century, Dobrich has always been renowned for its arts and crafts, and more recently for the quality of agricultural products grown in the surrounding fertile plains.

Around the massive ploshtad Svoboda are the United Bulgarian Bank and the post office and telephone centre. An Internet Cafe on ulitsa Nezavisimost is west of the square.

Stariyat Dobrich Ethnological Museum Complex

Some 37 shops, cafes, bars, restaurants and souvenir stalls form part of this charming complex (☎ 29 068, ul Dr K Stoilov; admission free; open daily 8am-6pm in summer & 8am-5pm in winter). The cobblestone streets are marvellous to wander around and it's possible to poke your head into a shop and watch blacksmiths, potters, weavers and other artisans practice their trade. The shady courtyard is lined with *cafes* and there's a charming hotel (see Places to Stay later in this section).

The complex is hidden behind an ugly modern building – look for the Ethnological Complex sign (in Bulgarian) at the southern entrance. The map (in English) along the main street inside the complex is of some help. The **exhibition hall** (admission 1 lv) at the courtyard contains some antique jewellery but is of minimal interest. Guided tours (in English or French) of the whole complex are available for about 5 lv per person (minimum of five people) if arranged in advance.

Art Gallery

The Art Gallery (☎ 28 215; ul Bulgaria 14; admission 0.50 lv, free Thur; open Mon-Fri 9am-12.30pm & 1.30pm-6pm) houses over 1700 works of art collected over a period of 100 years, including many by 'The Master', Vladimir Dimitrov. The permanent displays have captions in English but the temporary exhibits do not. Guided tours in English are available for 3 lv per person (no minimum required).

Yordan Yovkov Literature Museum

This museum (☎ 24 308; ul Gen Gurko 4; admission 1 lv; open Mon-Fri 9am-6pm & Sat-Sun 9am-4pm) features a range of furniture, costumes, knick-knacks, books and

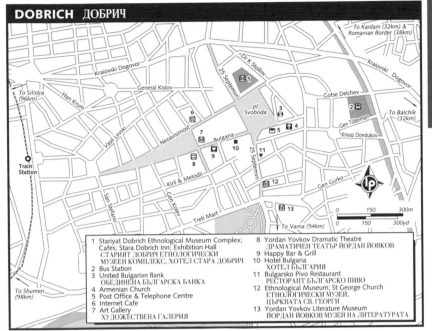

DOBRICH ДОБРИЧ

1 Stariyat Dobrich Ethnological Museum Complex; Cafes; Stara Dobrich Inn; Exhibition Hall
  СТАРИЯТ ДОБРИЧ ЕТНОЛОГИЧЕСКИ МУЗЕЕН КОМПЛЕКС, ХОТЕЛ СТАРА ДОБРИЧ
2 Bus Station
3 United Bulgarian Bank
  ОБЕДИНЕНА БЪЛГАРСКА БАНКА
4 Armenian Church
5 Post Office & Telephone Centre
6 Internet Cafe
7 Art Gallery
  ХУДОЖЕСТВЕНА ГАЛЕРИЯ
8 Yordan Yovkov Dramatic Theatre
  ДРАМАТИЧЕН ТЕАТЪР ЙОРДАН ЙОВКОВ
9 Happy Bar & Grill
10 Hotel Bulgaria
  ХОТЕЛ БЪЛГАРИЯ
11 Bulgarsko Pivo Restaurant
  РЕСТОРАНТ БЪЛГАРСКО ПИВО
12 Ethnological Museum; St George Church
  ЕТНОЛОГИЧЕСКИ МУЗЕЙ.
  ЦЪРКВАТА СВ. ГЕОРГИ
13 Yordan Yovkov Literature Museum
  ЙОРДАН ЙОВКОВ МУЗЕЙ НА ЛИТЕРАТУРАТА

photos relating to Yordan Yovkov. All captions are in Bulgarian but the manager can provide a free informative leaflet in English.

Ethnological Museum
Inside the lovely courtyard of a Bulgarian national revival period home, this museum (*ul 25 Septemvri; admission 1 lv; open Mon-Fri 9am-noon & 2pm-6pm*) offers the usual array of traditional costumes and jewellery. It's adjacent to a **park** with a statue of the ubiquitous Vasil Levski in front of the **St George Church** (*admission free; open daily 8am-6pm*).

Places to Stay
Stara Dobrich Inn (☎ *43 611*) Singles/doubles with bathroom 44/66 lv. This charming guesthouse in the ethnological museum complex offers clean, modern and large rooms with authentic (but not antique) furniture. It's certainly worth considering – if only because it's a pleasant change from

the soulless high-rise hotels found in most other cities. The guesthouse is not signposted – you'll find it behind a wooden door near the prominent clock tower.

Hotel Bulgaria (☎/*fax 25 444*, e *ta@bulgaria.bergon.net, pl Svoboda*) Doubles with bathroom US$45. This massive central hotel has a range of large and comfortable rooms with a fan, TV and fridge. It's good value (less so for singles) and the hotel has a swimming pool, casino and fitness centre. Rates include breakfast.

Places to Eat
Numerous charming ***cafes*** can be found along ulitsa 25 Septemvri, in the shady park to the south and at the ethnological museum complex.

Happy Bar & Grill (*ul Bulgaria*) Main meals from 3.50 lv. Happy Grills will be well known to many travellers for their range of Western style meals at above-average prices.

Bulgarsko Pivo Restaurant (ul 25 Septemvri) Salads 1 lv. grills 3-5 lv. Undoubtedly the best value in town (and possibly anywhere else in northern Bulgaria), the Bulgarsko Pivo offers large serves of tasty food at reasonable prices in a comfortable street-side setting.

Getting There & Away

From the bus station (☎ 22 240), on the eastern edge of town, buses and minibuses leave every 30 to 60 minutes for Albena (3 lv, 45 minutes), Varna (3 lv, 40 minutes), Balchik (2.40 lv, 45 minutes) and Kavarna (3.50 lv, one hour). Four or five buses also go to Ruse (11 lv, three hours) daily. A few buses head directly to Sofia (16 lv to 18 lv, seven to eight hours) but for other major destinations it's probably quicker to get a connection in Varna.

From the train station (☎ 39 078), on the western edge of town, it's possible to get a same-day connection to Sofia (1st class/2nd class 23.40/16.80 lv, 9½ hours), via Kaspichan. Also, three slow passenger trains travel daily to Kardam (1st class/2nd class 3.60/2.90 lv, one hour) on the way to the Romanian border, and two slow trains shuttle along to Varna (1st class/2nd class 5.85/4.50 lv, two hours).

Language

Pronunciation

To a great extent Bulgarian spelling (unlike English) has an almost one-to-one representation between letter and sound. Most Bulgarian sounds occur in English as well – with a little practice you'll have no problem making yourself understood.

The Bulgarian Cyrillic Alphabet

Cyrillic	Roman	Pronunciation
А а	a	as the 'a' in 'father' (but shorter)
Б б	b	as in 'boy'
В в	v	as 'v' in 'vice'
Г г	gh	as the 'g' in 'go'
Д д	d	as in 'door'
Е е	e	as in the 'e' in 'bet'
Ж ж	zh	as in the 's' in 'pleasure'
З з	z	as in 'zoo'
И и	i	as in 'bit'
Й й	y	as the 'y' in 'yes'
К к	k	as in 'king'
Л л	l	as in 'let'
М м	m	as in 'met'
Н н	n	as 'net'
О о	o	as in 'pot'
П п	p	as in 'pen'
Р р	r	as the trilled Scottish 'r'
С с	s	as in 'see'
Т т	t	as in 'tip'
У у	u	as in 'put'
Ф ф	f	as 'foot'
Х х	kh	as the 'ch' in Scottish loch
Ц ц	ts	as in 'lets'
Ч ч	ch	as in 'chip'
Ш ш	sh	as in 'ship'
Щ щ	sht	as the '-shed' in 'pushed'
Ъ ъ	â	a characteristic Bulgarian neutral vowel sound; it roughly resembles the 'a' in 'soda' or 'address'
Ю ю	yu	as the word 'you' but shorter
Я я	ya	as in 'yard' but shorter

Basics

Hello.	zdraveyte	Здравейте.
	zdrasti	Здрасти. (informal)
Goodbye.	dovizhdane	Довиждане. (polite)
Goodbye.	chao	Чао. (informal)
Yes.	da	Да.
No.	ne	Не.
Please.	molya	Моля.

Thank you.
blagodarya Благодаря.
mersi Мерси. (informal)
That's fine/You're welcome.
izvinete me/molya nyama zashto
Извинете ме/Моля, няма защо.
I'm sorry. (forgive me)
sâzhalyava
Съжалявам.
Excuse me.
izvinete me
Извинете ме.
May I/Do you mind?
moga li/imate li neshto protif?
Мога ли/Имате ли нещо против?

What's your name?
kak se kazvate? Как се казвате?
My name's ...
kazvam se ... Казвам се ...
Where are you from?
otkâde ste? Откъде сте?
I'm from ...
as sâm ot ... Аз съм от ...

Language Difficulties

Do you speak English/French/German?
govorite li angliyski/frenski/nemski?
Говорите ли английски/френски/немски?
Does anyone here speak English?
nyakoy govori li angliyski?
Някой говори ли английски?
I understand.
razbiram
Разбирам.

285

I don't understand.
  az ne razbiram
  Аз не разбирам.
Could you speak more slowly, please?
  bikhte li mogli da govorite po bavno molya?
  Бихте ли могли да говорите по бавно, моля?
Could you repeat that?
  bikhte li mogli da poftorite tova?
  Бихте ли могли да повторите това?
How do you say ...?
  kak kazvate ...?
  Как казвате ...?
What does ... mean?
  kakvo oznacha va ...?
  Какво означава ...?

Getting Around

What time does the ... leave/arrive?
  v kolko chasa zaminava/pristiga ...?
  В колко часа заминава/пристига ...?

bus (city)	*gradskiyat avtobus*	градският автобус
bus (intercity)	*mezhdugrad-skiyat avtobus*	междуградският автобус
plane	*samolehtât*	самолетът
train	*vlakât*	влакът
tram	*tramvayat*	трамваят

arrival	*pristigane*	пристигане
departure	*zaminavane*	заминаване
timetable	*razpisanie*	разписание
ticket office	*gisheto za bileti*	кишето за билети

Where is the ...?
  kâde se namira ...?
  Къде се намира ...?

airport	*letishteto*	летището
bus stop	*avtobusnata spirka*	автобусната спирка

left-luggage room	*garderobât*	гардеробът
petrol station	*benzinostantsiya*	бензиностанция
train station	*(zhelezopâtnata) gara*	(железопътната) гара

I'd like ...
  molya daytemi ...
  Моля, дайте ми ...

a one-way ticket	*bilet f edna posoka*	билет в една посока
a return ticket	*bilet za otivane i vrâshtane*	билет за отиване и връщане
two tickets	*dva bileta*	два билета

first class	*pârva klasa*	първа класа
second class	*ftora klasa*	втора класа
carriage	*vagon*	вагон
category (of train)	*kategoriya*	категория
platform	*sector*	сектор
seat	*myasto*	място
train	*vlak*	влак

I want to go to ...
  iskam da otida do ...
  Искам да отида до ...
Please show me (on the map).
  molya pokazhete (mi na kartata)
  Моля покажете (ми на картата).

left	*lyavo*	ляво
right	*dyasno*	дясно
straight ahead	*napravo*	направо
far	*daleche*	далече
near	*blizo*	близо
map	*karta*	карта

north	sever	север
south	yuk	юг
east	iztok	изток
west	zapad	запад

Around Town

I'm looking for a/the ...
    târsya ...   Търся ...

bank	banka	банка
church	tsârkvata	църквата
city centre	tsentâ ra na grada	центъра на града
... embassy	posolstvoto na ...	посолството на ...
exchange office	valutnite a byur	валутните бюра
market	pazara	пазара
museum	muzeya	музея
police	politsiyata	полицията
post office	poshta	поша
public toilet	gradska toaletna	градска тоалетна
telephone centre	telefonnata tsentrala	телефонната централа
tourist office	byuroto za turizâm	бюрото за туризъм

What time does it open/close?
    f kolko chasâ go otvaryat/zatvaryat?
    В колко часа го отварят/затварят?

beach	bryag/plazh	бряг/плаж
castle	zamâk	замък
cathedral	katedrala	катедрала
main square	tsentralen ploshtad	централен площад
monastery	manastir	манастир
old city	stariyat grad	старият град
palace	dvorets/ palat	дворец/ палат

Accommodation

camping ground
    myasto za lageruvane/kâmpinguvane
    място за лагеруване/къмпингуване
guesthouse
    pansion
    пансион
hostel
    obshtezhitie
    общежитие

Signs

Вход	Entrance
Изход	Exit
Информация	Information
Отворено	Open
Затворено	Closed
Забранено	Prohibited
Полицейско Управление	Police Station
Тоалетни	Toilets
Мъже (М)	Men
Жени (Ж)	Women

hotel
    khotel
    хотел
private room
    stoya v chastna kvartira
    стоя в частна квартира
youth hostel
    obshtezhitie
    общежитие

Where's a cheap/good hotel?
    kâde ima eftin/khubaf khotel?
    Къде има евтин/хубав хотел?
What's the address?
    kakâv e adresât?
    Какъв е адресът?
Could you write the address, please?
    bikhte li mogli, da mi napishete adresa?
    бихте ли могли да ми напишете адреса?
Do you have any rooms available?
    imateh li svobodni stai?
    Имате ли свободни стаи?
How much is it?
    kolko struva?
    Колко струва?
Does it include breakfast?
    zakuskata vklyuchena li e?
    Закуската включена ли е?

I'd like ...
    bikh zhelal ...
    бих желал ...
a single room
    staya s edno leglo
    стая с едно легло

a double room
staya s dve legla стая с две легла
a room with a bathroom
staya z banya стая с баня
to share a dorm
leglo v obshta легло в обща
spalnya спалня

How much is it per night/person?
kolko e na vecher/chovek?
Колко е на вечер/човек?
May I see it?
moga li da vidya?
Мога ли да видя?
Are there any others?
ima li drugi?
Има ли други?

Shopping
Where's the nearest ...?
kâde e nây-bliskiyat ...?
Лъде е най-близлият ...?

bookshop
knizharnitsa книжарница
delicatessen
delikatesen деликатесен
market
pazar пазар
newsagency
rep РП
supermarket
supermarket супермаркет

How much is it?
kolko struva? Колко струва?

Health
Where is a/the ...?
kâde se namira ...?
Къде се намира ...?

chemist	apteka	аптека
doctor	lekaryat	лекарят (m)
	lekarkata	лекарката (f)
hospital	bolnitsata	болницата

I'm sick.
bolen/bolna sâm
болен/болна съм. (m/f)

antibiotics
antibiotitsi антибиотици
antiseptic
antiseptichno sredstvo
антисептично средство
aspirin
aspirin аспирин
condoms
prezervativi презервативи
sunscreen
krem protif slânchevo izgaryane
крем против слънчево изгаряне
tampons
tamponi тампони

Time, Days & Numbers
What time is it?
kolko e chasât?
Колко е часът?
It's ... am/pm.
chasât e ... predi obet/slet obed
Часът е ... преди обед/след обед.

today	dnes	днес
tonight	dovechera	довечера
tomorrow	utre	утре
yesterday	vchera	вчера
morning	sutrin	сутрин
evening	vecher	вечер

Monday	ponedelnik	понеделник
Tuesday	vtornik	вторник
Wednesday	sryada	сряда
Thursday	chetvârtâk	четвъртък
Friday	petâk	петък
Saturday	sâbota	събота
Sunday	nedelya	неделя

January	yanuari	януари
February	fevruari	февруари
March	mârt	март
April	april	алрил
May	may	май
June	yuni	юни
July	yuli	юли
August	avgust	август
September	septemvri	септември
October	oktomvri	олтомври
November	noemvri	ноември
December	dekemvri	делември

Emergencies

Help!	pomosh!	Помош!
Call a doctor!	povikayte lekar!	Повикайте лекар!
Call the police!	povikayte politsiya!	Повикайте полиция!
Go away!	mahayte se!	Махайте се!
I'm lost.	zagubih se.	Загубих се.

1	edno	едно
2	dve	две
3	tri	три
4	chetiri	четири
5	pet	пет
6	shest	шест
7	sedem	седем
8	osem	осем
9	devet	девет
10	deset	десет
11	edinadeset	единадесет
12	dvanadeset	дванадесет
13	trinadeset	тринадесет
14	chetirinadeset	четиринадесет
15	petnadeset	петнадесет
16	shestnadeset	шестнадесет
17	sedemnadeset	седемнадесет
18	osemnadeset	осемнадесет
19	devetnadeset	деветнадесет
20	dvadeset	двадесет
21	dvadeset i edno	двадесет и едно
30	triyset	трийсет
40	chetiriyset	четирийсет
50	peddeset	петдесет
60	shezdeset	шестдесет
70	sedemdeset	седемдесет
80	osemdeset	осемдесет
90	deveddeset	девстдесет
100	sto	сто
1000	hilyada	хиляда

one million
edin milion един милион

FOOD & DRINK

I'm a vegetarian.
as sâm vegetarianets/vegetarianka
Аз съм вегетарианец/
вегетарианка. (m/f)

breakfast	zakuska	закуска
lunch	obet	обед
dinner	vecherya	вечеря

Basics

bread	khlyap	хляб
butter	krave maslo	лраве масло
cereal	zârneni khrâni	зърнени храни
cheese	sirene	сирене
chocolate	shokolat	шололад
egg/eggs	yaytse/yaytsa	яйце/яйца
flour	brâshno	брашно
honey	met	мед
margarine	mârgârin	маргарин
milk	mlyako	млядо
olive oil	zekhtin	зехтин
pasta	spâgeti i mâkâroni	спагети и маларони
pepper	piper	пипер
rice	oris	ориз
sugar	zakhâr	захар
table salt	gotvarskâ sol	готварсла сол
yogurt	kiselo mlyako	лисело мляло

Meat & Fish

beef	govezhdo meso	говеждо месо
chicken	pileshko meso	пилешло месо
ham	shunkâ	шунла
hamburger	khamburger	хамбургер
lamb	agneshko meso	агнешло месо
pork	svinsko meso	свинсло месо
sausage	nadenitsâ	наденица

Vegetables

beetroot	tsveklo	цвелло
(green) beans	(zelen) bop	(зелен) боб
cabbage	zele	зеле
capsicum	piper	пипер
red	cheren	червен
green	zelen	зелен
carrot	morkof	морлов
cauliflower	kârfiol	ларфиол
celery	tselinâ	целина

cucumber	*krastâvitsâ*	лраставица
eggplant/ aubergine	*sin domat*	син домат
lettuce	*mârulya*	маруля
mushrooms	*gâbi*	гъби
onions	*kromit*	лромид
peas	*grakh*	грах
potato	*kârtof*	лартоф
tomato	*domat*	домат

Fruit

apple	*yabâlkâ*	ябълла
apricot	*kâysiya*	лайсия
banana	*bânan*	банан
fig	*smokinya*	смолиня
grapes	*grozde*	грозде
lemon	*limon*	лимон
orange	*portokal*	портолал
peach	*praskovâ*	праслова
pear	*krushâ*	лруша
plum	*slivâ*	слива
strawberry	*yagodâ*	ягода

Non-Alcoholic Drinks

buttermilk	*ayryan*	айрян
fruit juice	*plodof sok*	плодов сок
mineral water	*mineralna*	минерална
nectar	*nektar*	нектар
soda water	*gazirana*	газирана вода
soft drink	*limonada*	лимонада

water	*voda*	вода
... tea	*... chay*	... чай
herbal	*bilkov*	билков
fruit	*plodov*	плодов
black	*cheren*	червен
coffee ...	*kafe ...*	кафе ...
espresso	*ekspreso*	експресо
with milk	*s mlyako*	с мляко
with lemon	*s limon*	с лимон
instant coffee	*nes*	нес
Turkish coffee	*tursko*	турско

Alcoholic Drinks

beer	*bira*	бира
bottled	*butilirana*	бутилирана
on tap	*naliyna*	наливна
millet ale	*boza*	боза
brandy	*rakiya*	ракия
fruit brandy	*plodova*	плодова
grape brandy	*grozdova*	гроздова
plum brandy	*slivova*	сливова
... wine	*... vino*	... вино
red	*cherveno*	червено
white	*byalo*	бяло
dry	*sukho*	сухо
sparkling	*shumyashto*	шумящо
bottled wine	*butilirano*	бутилирано
champagne	*shampansko*	шампанско
cognac	*konyak*	коняк
vodka	*votka*	водка
whisky	*uyski*	уйски

Glossary

You may come across some of the following terms or abbreviations while in Bulgaria. For other terms, see the Language chapter.

apteka – chemist or pharmacy
aromatherapy – use of aromatic oils to relieve muscle tension and cure minor ailments
autogara – bus station

Balkans – peninsula in south-eastern Europe between the Adriatic and Aegean seas
Balkantourist – the former government-run tourism organisation
balneology – therapeutic bath of mineral waters, often enjoyed in a balneocentre
banya – bath; often used to describe mineral baths in general
BARET – Bulgarian Association for Rural & Ecological Tourism
bas-relief – a carving or sculpture where a figure protrudes from the background
BBP – Beautiful Bulgaria Project
BDZh – abbreviation for the Bulgarian State Railways
BGN – abbreviation occasionally used to denote *leva*
BSBCP – Bulgarian-Swiss Biodiversity Conservation Programme
BSP – Bulgarian Socialist Party
BSPB – Bulgarian Society for the Protection of Birds
BTC – Bulgarian Telecommunications Company; also abbreviation for Bulgarian Tourist Union
bulevard – main street or boulevard; often shortened to bul
Bulgarian national revival period – era between the mid-18th and mid-19th centuries when a surge in Bulgarian national feeling and economic growth resulted in an unprecedented increase in the quality and quantity of art, music, architecture, theatre and literature
Bulgars – a group of Turkic tribes, originating in Central Asia, who migrated into the

Balkans in the late 7th century AD; also known as Proto-Bulgarians

chairlift – two-person seat suspended above the ground, and pulled by cables

doner kebab – Bulgarian version of the Turkish döner kebap, ie lamb or chicken sliced from a revolving spit and wrapped in pitta bread
draglift – two-person seat pulled up a ski slope by cables (ie, not suspended above the ground like a *chairlift*)
dvorets – palace

ezero (m), ezera (f) – lake

GDP – Gross Domestic Product
gondola – four or six person covered cabin suspended above ground, pulled by cables

haidouks – Bulgarian rebels who fought against the Turks in the 18th and 19th centuries
hali – indoor market
hizha – hut; often refers to a mountain hut
house-museum – a home built in a style typical of the *Bulgarian national revival period* and turned into a museum
hydrotherapy – treatment of diseases and muscle tension by exercising in water

iconostasis, iconostases (pl) – a screen, partition or door in an Eastern Orthodox church that separates the sanctuary from the nave; often richly decorated IMF
IMF – International Monetary Fund
IMRO – Internal Macedonian Revolutionary Organisation
ISIC – International Student Identity Card
ITIC – International Teacher Identity Card
IYTC – International Youth Travel Card
iztok – east

kâshta – house
kavarma – traditional Bulgarian dish of meat and vegetables served in a pot

GLOSSARY

khan – king within a Bulgar tribe, or the subsequent Bulgarian empires; also known as a *tsar*
konak – police station built during Turkish rule
knyaz – prince
krepost – fortress
kurdjali – Turkish gangs that raided several Bulgarian towns during the 18th and 19th centuries

lev (s), leva (pl) – monetary unit of Bulgaria; shortened to lv; equals 100 *stotinki*

Macedonia – historical region in the southern Balkans that encompassed parts of Bulgaria, northern Greece and the Former Yugoslav Republic of Macedonia (FYROM)
manastir – monastery
mehana – tavern
microlight – low-flying, two-person aircraft used for joy rides

NATO – North Atlantic Treaty Organisation
NGO – nongovernmental organisation
NMSII – National Movement Simeon II

obshtina – municipality; also another word for town hall
Orbita – Bulgarian youth travel agency

pasha – high official during Turkish rule
peshtera – cave
ploshtad – town or city square; often shortened to pl
Pomaks – Slavs who converted to Islam during the era of Turkish rule

Rila Bureau – office that sells advanced tickets for domestic train services, and tickets for all international trains
Roma – name by which gypsies refer to themselves

sever – north
spur track – a minor railway track linked to a major train line
stotinki – one-hundredth of a *leva*
sveti (m), sveta (f) – saint

Thracians – an amalgam of tribes who settled in Bulgaria, Greece and Turkey from 6000 BC
TIC – tourist information centre
tsar – see *khan* above

UDF – Union of Democratic Forces
ulitsa – street; often shortened to ul
UNDP – United Nations Development Programme
Unesco – United Nations Educational, Scientific & Cultural Organization
UNHCR – United Nations High Commission for Refugees
Unicef – United Nations International Children's Fund
UtDF – United Democratic Forces

varosha – centre of an old town
VAT – value-added tax
vrâh – mountain peak

yug – south

zapad – west

LONELY PLANET

You already know that Lonely Planet produces more than this one guidebook, but you might not be aware of the other products we have on this region. Here is a selection of titles that you may want to check out as well:

Eastern Europe
ISBN 1 86450 149 9
US$24.99 • UK£14.99

Eastern Europe phrasebook
ISBN 1 86450 227 4
US$8.99 • UK£4.99

Europe on a shoestring
ISBN 1 86450 150 2
US$24.99 • UK£14.99

Read This First: Europe
ISBN 1 86450 136 7
US$14.99 • UK£8.99

Available wherever books are sold

Lonely Planet Guides by Region

L onely Planet is known worldwide for publishing practical, reliable and no-nonsense travel information in our guides and on our Web site. The Lonely Planet list covers just about every accessible part of the world. Currently there are 16 series: Travel guides, Shoestring guides, Condensed guides, Phrasebooks, Read This First, Healthy Travel, Walking guides, Cycling guides, Watching Wildlife guides, Pisces Diving & Snorkeling guides, City Maps, Road Atlases, Out to Eat, World Food, Journeys travel literature and Pictorials.

AFRICA Africa on a shoestring • Botswana • Cairo • Cairo City Map • Cape Town • Cape Town City Map • East Africa • Egypt • Egyptian Arabic phrasebook • Ethiopia, Eritrea & Djibouti • Ethiopian Amharic phrasebook • The Gambia & Senegal • Healthy Travel Africa • Kenya • Malawi • Morocco • Moroccan Arabic phrasebook • Mozambique • Namibia • Read This First: Africa • South Africa, Lesotho & Swaziland • Southern Africa • Southern Africa Road Atlas • Swahili phrasebook • Tanzania, Zanzibar & Pemba • Trekking in East Africa • Tunisia • Watching Wildlife East Africa • Watching Wildlife Southern Africa • West Africa • World Food Morocco • Zambia • Zimbabwe, Botswana & Namibia
Travel Literature: Mali Blues: Traveling to an African Beat • The Rainbird: A Central African Journey • Songs to an African Sunset: A Zimbabwean Story

AUSTRALIA & THE PACIFIC Aboriginal Australia & the Torres Strait Islands •Auckland • Australia • Australian phrasebook • Australia Road Atlas • Cycling Australia • Cycling New Zealand • Fiji • Fijian phrasebook • Healthy Travel Australia, NZ & the Pacific • Islands of Australia's Great Barrier Reef • Melbourne • Melbourne City Map • Micronesia • New Caledonia • New South Wales • New Zealand • Northern Territory • Outback Australia • Out to Eat – Melbourne • Out to Eat – Sydney • Papua New Guinea • Pidgin phrasebook • Queensland • Rarotonga & the Cook Islands • Samoa • Solomon Islands • South Australia • South Pacific • South Pacific phrasebook • Sydney • Sydney City Map • Sydney Condensed • Tahiti & French Polynesia • Tasmania • Tonga • Tramping in New Zealand • Vanuatu • Victoria • Walking in Australia • Watching Wildlife Australia • Western Australia
Travel Literature: Islands in the Clouds: Travels in the Highlands of New Guinea • Kiwi Tracks: A New Zealand Journey • Sean & David's Long Drive

CENTRAL AMERICA & THE CARIBBEAN Bahamas, Turks & Caicos • Baja California • Belize, Guatemala & Yucatán • Bermuda • Central America on a shoestring • Costa Rica • Costa Rica Spanish phrasebook • Cuba • Cycling Cuba • Dominican Republic & Haiti • Eastern Caribbean • Guatemala • Havana • Healthy Travel Central & South America • Jamaica • Mexico • Mexico City • Panama • Puerto Rico • Read This First: Central & South America • Virgin Islands • World Food Caribbean • World Food Mexico • Yucatán
Travel Literature: Green Dreams: Travels in Central America

EUROPE Amsterdam • Amsterdam City Map • Amsterdam Condensed • Andalucía • Athens • Austria • Baltic States phrasebook • Barcelona • Barcelona City Map • Belgium & Luxembourg • Berlin • Berlin City Map • Britain • British phrasebook • Brussels, Bruges & Antwerp • Brussels City Map • Budapest • Budapest City Map • Canary Islands • Catalunya & the Costa Brava • Central Europe • Central Europe phrasebook • Copenhagen • Corfu & the Ionians • Corsica • Crete • Crete Condensed • Croatia • Cycling Britain • Cycling France • Cyprus • Czech & Slovak Republics • Czech phrasebook • Denmark • Dublin • Dublin City Map • Dublin Condensed • Eastern Europe • Eastern Europe phrasebook • Edinburgh • Edinburgh City Map • England • Estonia, Latvia & Lithuania • Europe on a shoestring • Europe phrasebook • Finland • Florence • Florence City Map • France • Frankfurt City Map • Frankfurt Condensed • French phrasebook • Georgia, Armenia & Azerbaijan • Germany • German phrasebook • Greece • Greek Islands • Greek phrasebook • Hungary • Iceland, Greenland & the Faroe Islands • Ireland • Italian phrasebook • Italy • Kraków • Lisbon • The Loire • London • London City Map • London Condensed • Madrid • Madrid City Map • Malta • Mediterranean Europe • Milan, Turin & Genoa • Moscow • Munich • Netherlands • Normandy • Norway • Out to Eat – London • Out to Eat – Paris • Paris • Paris City Map • Paris Condensed • Poland • Polish phrasebook • Portugal • Portuguese phrasebook • Prague • Prague City Map • Provence & the Côte d'Azur • Read This First: Europe • Rhodes & the Dodecanese • Romania & Moldova • Rome • Rome City Map • Rome Condensed • Russia, Ukraine & Belarus • Russian phrasebook • Scandinavian & Baltic Europe • Scandinavian phrasebook • Scotland • Sicily • Slovenia • South-West France • Spain • Spanish phrasebook • Stockholm • St Petersburg • St Petersburg City Map • Sweden • Switzerland • Tuscany • Ukrainian phrasebook • Venice • Vienna • Wales • Walking in Britain • Walking in France • Walking in Ireland • Walking in Italy • Walking in Scotland • Walking in Spain • Walking in Switzerland • Western Europe • World Food France • World Food Greece • World Food Ireland • World Food Italy • World Food Spain **Travel Literature:** After Yugoslavia • Love and War in the Apennines • The Olive Grove: Travels in Greece • On the Shores of the Mediterranean • Round Ireland in Low Gear • A Small Place in Italy

Lonely Planet Mail Order

onely Planet products are distributed worldwide.They are also available by mail order from Lonely Planet, so if you have difficulty finding a title please write to us. North and South American residents should write to 150 Linden St, Oakland, CA 94607, USA; European and African residents should write to 10a Spring Place, London NW5 3BH, UK; and residents of other countries to Locked Bag 1, Footscray, Victoria 3011, Australia.

INDIAN SUBCONTINENT & THE INDIAN OCEAN Bangladesh • Bengali phrasebook • Bhutan • Delhi • Goa • Healthy Travel Asia & India • Hindi & Urdu phrasebook • India • India & Bangladesh City Map • Indian Himalaya • Karakoram Highway • Kathmandu City Map • Kerala • Madagascar • Maldives • Mauritius, Réunion & Seychelles • Mumbai (Bombay) • Nepal • Nepali phrasebook • North India • Pakistan • Rajasthan • Read This First: Asia & India • South India • Sri Lanka • Sri Lanka phrasebook • Tibet • Tibetan phrasebook • Trekking in the Indian Himalaya • Trekking in the Karakoram & Hindukush • Trekking in the Nepal Himalaya • World Food India **Travel Literature:** The Age of Kali: Indian Travels and Encounters • Hello Goodnight: A Life of Goa • In Rajasthan • Maverick in Madagascar • A Season in Heaven: True Tales from the Road to Kathmandu • Shopping for Buddhas • A Short Walk in the Hindu Kush • Slowly Down the Ganges

MIDDLE EAST & CENTRAL ASIA Bahrain, Kuwait & Qatar • Central Asia • Central Asia phrasebook • Dubai • Farsi (Persian) phrasebook • Hebrew phrasebook • Iran • Israel & the Palestinian Territories • Istanbul • Istanbul City Map • Istanbul to Cairo • Istanbul to Kathmandu • Jerusalem • Jerusalem City Map • Jordan • Lebanon • Middle East • Oman & the United Arab Emirates • Syria • Turkey • Turkish phrasebook • World Food Turkey • Yemen **Travel Literature:** Black on Black: Iran Revisited • Breaking Ranks: Turbulent Travels in the Promised Land • The Gates of Damascus • Kingdom of the Film Stars: Journey into Jordan

NORTH AMERICA Alaska • Boston • Boston City Map • Boston Condensed • British Columbia • California & Nevada • California Condensed • Canada • Chicago • Chicago City Map • Chicago Condensed • Florida • Georgia & the Carolinas • Great Lakes • Hawaii • Hiking in Alaska • Hiking in the USA • Honolulu & Oahu City Map • Las Vegas • Los Angeles • Los Angeles City Map • Louisiana & the Deep South • Miami • Miami City Map • Montreal • New England • New Orleans • New Orleans City Map • New York City • New York City City Map • New York City Condensed • New York, New Jersey & Pennsylvania • Oahu • Out to Eat – San Francisco • Pacific Northwest • Rocky Mountains • San Diego & Tijuana • San Francisco • San Francisco City Map • Seattle • Seattle City Map • Southwest • Texas • Toronto • USA • USA phrasebook • Vancouver • Vancouver City Map • Virginia & the Capital Region • Washington, DC • Washington, DC City Map • World Food New Orleans **Travel Literature:** Caught Inside: A Surfer's Year on the California Coast • Drive Thru America

NORTH-EAST ASIA Beijing • Beijing City Map • Cantonese phrasebook • China • Hiking in Japan • Hong Kong & Macau • Hong Kong City Map • Hong Kong Condensed • Japan • Japanese phrasebook • Korea • Korean phrasebook • Kyoto • Mandarin phrasebook • Mongolia • Mongolian phrasebook • Seoul • Shanghai • South-West China • Taiwan • Tokyo • Tokyo Condensed • World Food Hong Kong • World Food Japan **Travel Literature:** In Xanadu: A Quest • Lost Japan

SOUTH AMERICA Argentina, Uruguay & Paraguay • Bolivia • Brazil • Brazilian phrasebook • Buenos Aires • Buenos Aires City Map • Chile & Easter Island • Colombia • Ecuador & the Galapagos Islands • Healthy Travel Central & South America • Latin American Spanish phrasebook • Peru • Quechua phrasebook • Read This First: Central & South America • Rio de Janeiro • Rio de Janeiro City Map • Santiago de Chile • South America on a shoestring • Trekking in the Patagonian Andes • Venezuela **Travel Literature:** Full Circle: A South American Journey

SOUTH-EAST ASIA Bali & Lombok • Bangkok • Bangkok City Map • Burmese phrasebook • Cambodia • Cycling Vietnam, Laos & Cambodia • East Timor phrasebook • Hanoi • Healthy Travel Asia & India • Hill Tribes phrasebook • Ho Chi Minh City (Saigon) • Indonesia • Indonesian phrasebook • Indonesia's Eastern Islands • Java • Lao phrasebook • Laos • Malay phrasebook • Malaysia, Singapore & Brunei • Myanmar (Burma) • Philippines • Pilipino (Tagalog) phrasebook • Read This First: Asia & India • Singapore • Singapore City Map • South-East Asia on a shoestring • South-East Asia phrasebook • Thailand • Thailand's Islands & Beaches • Thailand, Vietnam, Laos & Cambodia Road Atlas • Thai phrasebook • Vietnam • Vietnamese phrasebook • World Food Indonesia • World Food Thailand • World Food Vietnam

ALSO AVAILABLE: Antarctica • The Arctic • The Blue Man: Tales of Travel, Love and Coffee • Brief Encounters: Stories of Love, Sex & Travel • Buddhist Stupas in Asia: The Shape of Perfection • Chasing Rickshaws • The Last Grain Race • Lonely Planet • Lonely Planet ... On the Edge: Adventurous Escapades from Around the World • Lonely Planet Unpacked • Lonely Planet Unpacked Again • Not the Only Planet: Science Fiction Travel Stories • Ports of Call: A Journey by Sea • Sacred India • Travel Photography: A Guide to Taking Better Pictures • Travel with Children • Tuvalu: Portrait of an Island Nation

Index

Text

Boxed Text

MAP LEGEND

CITY ROUTES

Freeway .... Freeway
Highway .... Primary Road
Road .... Secondary Road
Street .... Street
Lane .... Lane
.... On/Off Ramp

⊐⊐⊐⊐ ...... Unsealed Road
.... One Way Street
.... Pedestrian Street
⊏⊏⊏⊏⊏⊏⊏ ...... Stepped Street
⊃)==== .... Tunnel
================ .... Footbridge

REGIONAL ROUTES

.... Tollway, Freeway
.... Primary Road
.... Secondary Road
.... Minor Road

BOUNDARIES

▬·▬··▬ .... International
▬··▬··· .... State
▬ ▬ ▬ .... Disputed
◼▬◼▬ .... Fortified Wall

HYDROGRAPHY

.... River, Creek
.... Canal
.... Lake

⬯ ⬯ .... Dry Lake; Salt Lake
◉ ⤳ .... Spring; Rapids
◐ ⤙ ↞ .... Waterfalls

TRANSPORT ROUTES & STATIONS

◆▬O▬ .... Train
.... Underground Train
▬◍▬ .... Metro
▪▪▪▪▪▪▪▪▪ .... Tramway
⊩⊩⊩⊩⊩⊩ .... Funicular Railway

┅┅┅┅⊡ .... Ferry
┈┈┈┈┈ .... Walking Trail
·········· .... Walking Tour
.... Path
.... Pier or Jetty

AREA FEATURES

.... Building
⊙ .... Park, Gardens

.... Market
.... Sports Ground

.... Beach
+ + + ... Cemetery

.... Campus
.... Plaza

POPULATION SYMBOLS

○ **CAPITAL** .... National Capital
◉ **CAPITAL** .... State Capital

● CITY .... City
● **Town** .... Town

● Village .... Village
.... Urban Area

MAP SYMBOLS

⬛ .... Place to Stay
▼ .... Place to Eat
● .... Point of Interest

⊝	.... Bank	⊡	.... Funicular	✚	.... Police Station	⊠	.... Swimming Pool
⊕	......Border Crossing	✛	.... Hospital	⊟	.... Post Office	⊠	.... Synagogue
⊟	.... Bus Station	⊠	.... Internet Cafe	⊡	............Pub or Bar	⊟	...........Taxi Rank
⊟	............Cathedral	⚐	.... Mounment	⊠	.... Ruins	⊠	............Telephone
⌂	................Cave	◖	.... Mosque	⊠	..... Shopping Centre	⊟	...............Theatre
⊞	.... Church	⊟	.... Mountain Hut	⚲	.... Ski Field	⊡	..................Tomb
⊡	.... Embassy	⊞	.... Museum	⊞	.... Stately Home	❶	.. Tourist Information

Note: not all symbols displayed above appear in this book

LONELY PLANET OFFICES

Australia
Locked Bag 1, Footscray, Victoria 3011
☎ 03 8379 8000 fax 03 8379 8111
email: talk2us@lonelyplanet.com.au

USA
150 Linden St, Oakland, CA 94607
☎ 510 893 8555 TOLL FREE: 800 275 5555
fax 510 893 8572
email: info@lonelyplanet.com

UK
10a Spring Place, London NW5 3BH
☎ 020 7428 4800 fax 020 7428 4828
email: go@lonelyplanet.co.uk

France
1 rue du Dahomey, 75011 Paris
☎ 01 55 25 33 00 fax 01 55 25 33 01
email: bip@lonelyplanet.fr
www.lonelyplanet.fr

World Wide Web: www.lonelyplanet.com or AOL keyword: lp
Lonely Planet Images: lpi@lonelyplanet.com.au